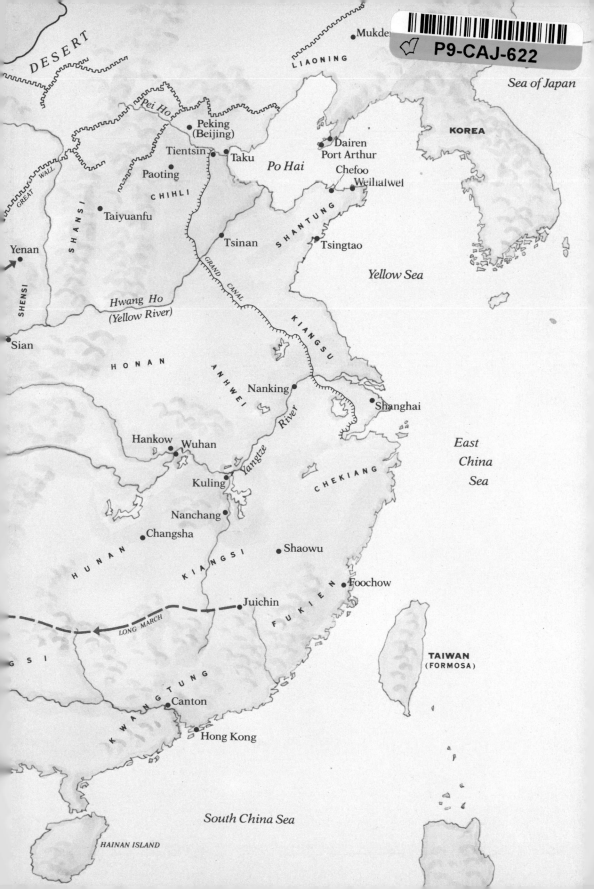

DESERT

Sea of Japan

LIAONING

Mukden

Pei Ho

Peking
(Beijing)

KOREA

Tientsin

Taku

Dairen
Port Arthur

GREAT WALL

Paoting

Po Hai

Chefoo
Weihaiwei

SHANSI

CHIHLI

Taiyuanfu

SHANTUNG

Yenan

Tsinan

Tsingtao

SHENSI

GRAND CANAL

Yellow Sea

Sian

*Hwang Ho
(Yellow River)*

KIANGSU

HONAN

ANHWEI

Nanking

Shanghai

Hankow

Wuhan

Yangtze River

East
China
Sea

Kuling

CHEKIANG

Nanchang

Changsha

KIANGSI

Shaowu

HUNAN

Foochow

Juichin

FUKIEN

LONG MARCH

TAIWAN
(FORMOSA)

GSI

KWANGTUNG

Canton

Hong Kong

South China Sea

HAINAN ISLAND

ALSO BY JOHN HERSEY

THE WALNUT DOOR (1977)

THE PRESIDENT (1975)

MY PETITION FOR MORE SPACE (1974)

THE WRITER'S CRAFT (1974)

THE CONSPIRACY (1972)

LETTER TO THE ALUMNI (1970)

THE ALGIERS MOTEL INCIDENT (1968)

UNDER THE EYE OF THE STORM (1967)

TOO FAR TO WALK (1966)

WHITE LOTUS (1965)

HERE TO STAY (1963)

THE CHILD BUYER (1960)

THE WAR LOVER (1959)

A SINGLE PEBBLE (1956)

THE MARMOT DRIVE (1953)

THE WALL (1950)

HIROSHIMA (1946)

A BELL FOR ADANO (1944)

INTO THE VALLEY (1943)

These are Borzoi Books
published in New York by Alfred A. Knopf.

THE CALL

JOHN HERSEY

THE

⊞

CALL

ALFRED A. KNOPF

NEW YORK 1985

THIS IS A BORZOI BOOK
PUBLISHED BY ALFRED A. KNOPF, INC.

LIBRARY OF CONGRESS CATALOGING IN PUBLICATION DATA
HERSEY, JOHN, [DATE]
THE CALL.
I. TITLE.
PS3515.E7715C3   1985   813'.52   84-48669
ISBN 0-394-54331-9

MANUFACTURED IN THE UNITED STATES OF AMERICA

FIRST TRADE EDITION

A SIGNED FIRST EDITION OF THIS BOOK
HAS BEEN PRIVATELY PRINTED BY
THE FRANKLIN LIBRARY.

CONTENTS

Contents

THE CALL

BOOK ONE

⊞

THE IMPULSE

FIRE IN THE EYE

DAVID TREADUP was born in the incorporated village of Salt Branch, New York, on July 7, 1878, at 4:36 p.m., or 5:17 p.m., or 5:23 p.m.

Discrepancies of this sort, and of deeper kinds, too, matters of linkage of body and soul, were to plague the entire future of this infant. One birthtime is written in a wobbling script on the flyleaf of the Treadup family Bible. The second appears in a ledger kept by Prudence Chin, the assisting midwife. The third is on David's birth certificate, attested to by Pastor Philip Bokase of the Salt Branch Methodist Church, who was hastily called in at the delivery because of the alarming weakness of the mother toward the end of her labor. The inconsistencies evidently arose because no one noticed, in the confusion of an anxious delivery, just what time it was when the newborn David first cried out to greet life. The pull of what John Wesley had called "assurance" —the confidence that with enough faith, alertness, and willpower *anyone* could attain the Kingdom of Heaven—must have been such that each independently felt the need to summon up for God's notice of this small event a speculative minute of the day. It speaks to the profound reserve of these people that they never pooled their guesses.

There is no doubt that the delivery was a dangerous one. In her ledger the midwife, Mrs. Chin, after recording the fee of one dollar and fifty cents for her ministrations, entered in a column headed "Particulars" a laconic note, "A fierce fight." David Treadup wrote in his journal in China, when his mother

3

died six decades later at a great distance from him, "I almost murdered her by the mere act of arrival in this world." Hannah Treadup was a tiny, light-boned woman, and everyone agreed that David weighed at birth a monstrous twelve pounds and two ounces. Further entries in the family Bible show David to have been the fifth and last of Brownson and Hannah Treadup's children, girl boy boy girl boy; perhaps, but for this "fierce fight," there might have been several other births.

As for the baptism, David, wearing a long, lace-trimmed dress that had been handed down through his mother's family for just this single use, was at six weeks touched with water on his forehead and admitted to the religion that would one day make a foreign legionnaire of him.

HE WENT home from his baptism crying and did not stop. It was as if the holy water had scalded him. On and on, all day after day, for weeks, he made a wild, discontented noise. As a student at Syracuse, writing self-consciously in his diary about his own startlingly loud voice in elocution class, David reported having been told that his father, hearing his crying in those weeks, had said he sounded "like Pastor Bokase singing 'Rock of ages, cleft for me.'" Hannah grew frightened. Prudence Chin was called in. She weighed David on her balance; he had lost four pounds. She said it was clear: The baby was starving. Hannah, battered by the delivery, had come up nearly dry and had been too worn and depressed even to realize it.

There followed an anxious period, because Prue Chin said that she had neither served at, nor heard of, any other births in the village for nearly a year: a freakish drought of dragon seed in Blaine County. Finally news came of a sturdy nursing mother in Turcott, twelve miles from the Treadup farm. She was the wife of a blacksmith there, a fat and somewhat slovenly but warmhearted woman, people said; she was willing to suckle the Treadup child, but in exchange for her milk she wanted what the Treadups did not have: cash. Brownson Treadup went to Pastor Bokase, and the preacher arranged for some women of the church to "adopt" the baby, at least to the extent of raising money for the wet nurse. David was taken to Turcott and lived there, in a tight and dark little house, for eight months.

He was soon well; his gigantic little frame became fully fleshed out.

David Treadup believed in later years that he had a distinct and clear memory of being nursed by the Turcott woman. A memory from infancy? He insisted on it. It had come to him one night when he was in college, he claimed, as a kind of sudden bright picture; and it never left him after that. He described it in the manuscript he called "Search," which he wrote many years later—in 1943—in a period when he felt a need to settle his mind about his past.

I see a window's rectangle of light. All around me is a massive welcome of flesh. I can make no distinction between shoulder, arm, breast,

Hannah Treadup. She was, in her terms, though, a loving mother (save for chariness with the material gift of warm life at the breast), and such emanations of hatred as David caught from her were very weak. Indeed, all through life he shed on those around him an intermittent radiance of unsentimental love, which in his huge adult frame often grew very hot.

Hannah Treadup was cursed with a hopeless gentility: hopeless because it was never connected with money. She was pathetically proud of some odd pieces of majolica ware, which she always kept behind glass in a sideboard for fear that use might bring breakage in a family of such turbulent energies as hers had.

SHE PUT David down on paper. "He is a headstrong tyke," she wrote in his Baby Book on his first birthday. Later: "He is much sunnier than the others. He passes off hardships." Then this:

> He will not be denied. Brownie whittled him a tiny little pig—too small. He chewed at it. I took it away. He howled for three days, as if with those old hunger pains. I could not hurt him so, and gave it back, and he was sweet. My land! He swallowed it whole. Now he missed it but did not take on the way he had. I was most anxious. He grew cranky. The second day he took a fever. Brownie did not want to trouble Dr. Fosco all the way from the village. I blamed Brownie severely, but he said a baby's guts are like a goat's, he would pass the little bung. On the third day he did. After I tidied him that baby gave me the same look he had given me when I returned the toy to him. Dearly sweet, but also something of Mama, you are too easy a mark.

Another time: "So big for his age! He has begun to walk. He is like a huge sailor on a pitching deck." "He closes his eyes when I read to him, but I know he is not asleep." "When the others tease him he neither sulks nor laughs. Sometimes I am afraid he will be hard." "In his bath he cares only for the little boat Brownie carved out for him. I think he can say boat." "Fire, fire, fire in David's eye. God have mercy on the poor boy." "A tinkerer. Fits things together. Potlid to pot. Hat to head. Brownson sits for his evening think and behind him comes David with the hat." "His voice is as big as the rest of him. It seems to alarm even himself. He says bird. He says turtle." "He watches the clock. He listens to the ticking." "The other day Brownie took David to see the train come in. Now when the locomotive whistles before the hump, David jumps up and down and that look I fear comes in his eyes." "I am teaching him to pray, Jesus friend of little children. He takes the boat to bed with him at night." "O my big boy do not rush so at life."

*though I always know where the dear bud is. The mass is warm. I am in
a bath of love. My hands mold the source. I have the most exquisite
sense of comfort and well-being.*

When he was about seven, long before this "memory" had come to him,
David was told by Will, the third child and second Treadup son, of his having
been sent away to be nursed. Will put it in a triumphant older brother's way:
"You don't belong to us." David, who never kept in anything that caused him
anger, went straight to his mother, told her what Will had said, and asked if it
was true that he had been shipped away to be fed. Her answer was not
completely forthcoming: "Of course you belong to us." By the time he was
twelve, David had been confided more about the "milker" by his complacent
siblings, and he kept asking his mother who she was. His mother would never
tell him the woman's name. He could never even find out whether his mother
had visited him in Turcott.

When, at eighteen, David went away to board at the Enderbury Institute,
in Turcott, he began keeping a Line-a-Day diary, and one finds frequent
notations: "Looked for the woman." And once: "Looked for the other mother."
What clues could he have followed?

THE REAL MOTHER, Hannah Bledsoe Treadup, was a nimble little rabbit
of a woman who did her share of heavy work on the Treadup farm; yet she
also rigidly reserved certain hours for stillness—for reading, both to herself
and in a murmur to her children. She kept apart an existence in books.
"Words," David wrote after she died, "were her amethysts, beryls, chalcedonies,
and diamonds." She evidently had a need to give these stones their settings,
and she wrote everything down; David's lifelong recording mania must have
come from hers.

Serenity, poise, and sweetness changed guard in her with sudden sallies
of a sharp tongue, fleeting looks of having been grossly cheated, and frowns
implying that a Bledsoe had been intended for something more edifying than
sterilizing the cream separator or hacking at a lump of suet for the obligatory
mince pie of a winter Sunday. In a strong light one could see a tiny glint of
hysteria in the sharp pupils of her dark brown eyes. These impressions come
from David, who once wrote in his journal that his mother pulled at the
kitchen pump as if she had Lucifer by the tail.

She came from old New England stock, and as she stirred things up in
the western New York State village where fate had landed her, she made the
bite of that heritage felt. "Resistance to something," Henry Adams was to
write, "was the law of New England nature. . . . The chief charm of New
England was harshness of contrasts of extremes of sensibility—a cold that
froze the blood, and a heat that boiled it—so that the pleasure of hating—
one's self if no better victim offered—was not its rarest amusement." So with

THE INFANT'S father, Brownson Treadup, was big, wily, resourceful, loud, restless, expansive—and disorganized. He was descended from early trappers in this region near Lake Ontario, and though the frontier had long since swept on westward, he still manifested traits of the huntsman. He hated confinement, and he was triply restrained: by his rundown farm; by the hot eye of his bantam wife; and by his religion, which, though he never quite understood it, was always somehow overhead, day and night—a heaven up there disturbingly unsettled by clouds of doubt.

The farm had belonged to Hannah's father, Stephen Bledsoe, who had had seven daughters and no sons. On marrying Hannah, Brownson Treadup had moved into the Bledsoe farmstead, and when the old man died, Hannah and Brownson inherited the place. Hannah held over him heavy reminders of this delayed dowry, his whole worth. He was always poor. In need, he sold off a third of the original land. He had forever to trot here and trot there to stay one half pace ahead of Winthrop Jall, the mortgage officer of the Salt Branch National Bank—often mentioned in family correspondence.

Thus there were storms and alarms in the Treadup household, but there were also decent measures of civility, aspiration, and thought. At table, David later noted, his father talked not only of the prices corn and oats would fetch, but also of the new rolling stock of the Rome, Watertown, and Ogdensburg Railroad; of the unusual tumbler and fantail pigeons raised by the character down in the village whom people called Irondequoit Pete; of Uncle Don Treadup, the rich spender of the family, who one year bought a hotel, another year a traveling circus; of Mark Twain and Sarah Orne Jewett and even Charles Darwin, with his message—no matter how rude to the Book of Genesis—of hope for the planet, if it was indeed true that all God's creatures could adapt.

The Treadup farm was two miles north of Salt Branch village, on the Clearport road. It comprised fifty-three acres, about half of which were in ill-kept woodlots; there were some five acres of worthless swampland in its back reaches, near stretches of the lower Branch. Brownson Treadup grew feed corn, wheat, oats, barley, and hay; kept a herd of milch cows, usually numbering twelve, and a pen for four or five pigs; had an ox and three horses for draft; tended a kitchen garden; and raised chickens and, in some years, turkeys.

There were never enough hands. As soon as they could toddle, the children were assigned chores, and by the time they were about ten they were drawn into heavy labor of the farm. David's father worked desperately hard, and David's later testimony was that he never heard a word of complaint to a member of the family from his father, never a curseword, never an angry speech to his mother; he reserved his bluster for the livestock and for men in the village.

But Brownson was a hopeless planner. As a missionary, his son David came to be known as almost ferociously meticulous in laying out every undertaking—outlines, lists, schedules to the split minute, gear lined up in neat bundles; this exactness may have been a response to his father's maddening sloppiness. Day after day on the farm brought a critical, yet somehow familiar, surprise. Brownson was always having to send for an emergency hired hand, usually a boy from the village who would not need to be paid much. Once, mown hay lay mildewing in the meadows because Brownson, having three times forgotten to pay his mortgage installments (how easy for debts to drop out of mind!), had to spend two days in the village arguing with Winthrop Jall.

For the children, their father's disorganized ways were deeply confusing. Impressed by his stoic example, by his working to bleak exhaustion for their sakes, they arose each morning docile and willing to do whatever chores they must. But they never knew what to do. Instead of rotating regular assignments, Brownson told each child where to dash off to, and what to do, each morning, as he noticed, as if for the first time in his life, what various jobs needed doing to get the day under way.

From this perhaps unlikely parentage—from a father stamped with a loud and blustering but finally indecisive masculinity, a mother of gentle intellect edged with ferocity and dissatisfaction—stemmed not only the great persistence, the ragelike energy, and the occasional narrow follies of the grown David Treadup, but also his immense reserves of courage, hope, humor, and free-floating love.

"I LIKE crowds," David wrote many years later in China. "I am a school fish."

The small house on the Salt Branch farm contained a preparatory turmoil of children and animals. From the time when David could sleep in a bed, all five children shared one bedroom. They clattered up and down the narrow stairs; they whooped and shrieked in the echoing rooms till their mother put her hands over her ears. There were two dogs, four to seven cats, a series of canaries, off-and-on turtles, and two squirrels for a time which ran and ran forever in squeaky circular wire treadmills, like little Ferris wheels, which the father built within their cage. Here was the Treadup brood when David was, as his mother wrote, "Terrible Mr. Two": Sarah, the oldest, was eight; Paul was seven; Will, five; Grace, four; and then the Terrible Two, already nearly as tall as Will. Besides the seven Treadups in the house, there were often boarders for the sake of a few dollars; hired hands who slept in a shed but ate with the family; visiting relatives who stayed longer than invited; vagrants whom Hannah's charity could not deny; drummers and canvassers and schoolmarms and Pastor Bokase—eaters all. No wonder the Treadups were poor.

Of the older children, only two figured importantly in David's life: Paul and Grace. Sarah was to die at twelve, of diphtheria. Will, who always hated David, went "into business," it was said; in fact, he worked all his life in the mail room of the National Cereal Company, in Niagara Falls. He became a bitter, narrow man, and he and David almost never wrote to each other.

Paul was a tall, sensitive boy whom their father, for some reason, could not help tormenting. Being the oldest male child, Paul always drew the heaviest chores, and he never seemed to get them done to Brownson Treadup's satisfaction. Paul was nevertheless gentle and considerate. "You are the kindest person I ever knew," David wrote him in a letter from China. "I think you are the one, more than anyone else, who caused me to want to help others in life." Paul became David's protector against Will. The two developed a tender fraternal love. It is clear from their correspondence that David was his older brother's most important hero. Paul tried to carry on the farm awhile after their father's death, but he was not strong enough, and he became a much beloved teacher of small children in a public school in Geneseo.

The bond with Grace was quite another matter. She was a mischievous, pigtailed runt—she had her mother's build—and she and David kept up, for many years, a teasing, joking, bantering relationship. They called each other by their names spelled backwards: Ecarg and Divad. They could always find something to laugh about. Often, alas, it was Will, and as the sense of humor grew large with David's frame, one could see firming in him a narrow streak of cruelty—never gross, always witty, but essential in his laughter as it so often is in the wildest of humor. Ecarg and Divad always behaved like a couple of puppies rolling on the floor and nipping at each other. Grace never married. She became a librarian in the town of Cato.

FOREBEARS

WHERE did the missionary impulse come from? David Treadup's heritage was somewhat ambiguous as it bore on his calling. On his mother's side: a line of New England divines, shrewd petty manufacturers, and farmers bitterly dissatisfied with what the glacier had dealt them, their harsh Calvinist temperaments modulating, after their western trek, toward a warmer Methodist optimism. On his father's: the vigor, tough athleticism, self-sufficiency, and forest raptures of the trapper's life, followed by the Indian-threatened farming of newly opened land, and an almost mute religiosity, having to do with the suspected presence of the eye of God in the tops of trees and in the mysterious depths of trout pools in clear country streams. On both sides: strong fiber, ample courage, a constant uneasy dialogue with ancient values, and outcroppings, all along the way, of excess.

THE NAME of William Bledsoe, Hannah Treadup's first American ancestor, is found in the records of New Town, in the Massachusetts Bay Colony, a place later known as Cambridge. The family gift of dissatisfaction promptly cropped up. Along with Thomas Hooker and Samuel Stone and others, William Bledsoe quarreled, two years after they landed, with the narrow-minded and repressive authorities of the colony, over what we do not know, and migrated to establish the Hartford Colony.

David Treadup was proud of his descent from this cantankerous William Bledsoe because Bledsoe was listed as one of the freemen who helped draw up the Hartford Colony's Fundamental Orders, the first coherent frame of an orderly and decent polity on the American continent—a document which influenced the later constitutions of Connecticut and other states, and which embodied the ringing principle that the foundation of authority of a government is the consent of its people. In his early years as a missionary Treadup often urged this simple rule of power on Chinese officials. As time passed, it slowly dawned on him that this idea, which was apt for the Hartford Colony and later as an American ideal, might not work quite so well in a country habituated for thousands of years to "the four obediences"—of subject to prince, son to father, wife to husband, younger brother to older brother.

BLEDSOES appear to have been valued citizens up and down the Connecticut River Valley in subsequent years. We find townspeople of that name, several of the men Congregationalist pastors, in Wethersfield, Windsor, Holyoke, and Greenfield; and Bledsoes held numerous town offices, as fence viewer, haywarden, train-band ensign, sheep-mark recorder, and, in two cases, selectman. Like other colonists of that area and era, the Bledsoes must have been thrifty, self-reliant, and industrious, but also stubborn, suspicious of outsiders, and strong-minded. The farmers among them worked a trashy soil and with their stoic oxen dragged rocks on stone boats year after year to the ragged walls that marked the outermost limits of their strength and patience.

NOAHDIAH SANDERS, a Calvinist forebear of Hannah Treadup, was the Congregationalist minister of Stapleton, Connecticut; one of his two daughters married David's maternal great-great-grandfather Reuben Bledsoe.

"Preacher Sanders's later years," the Stapleton town history tells us, "were clouded by a great tragedy." It seems that when Reverend Sanders was about forty, an orphaned niece was taken by necessity into the Sanders home. This was a young woman of eighteen, "a plain-faced but rounded girl." To his great shame, Reverend Sanders began to feel a lust for this woman which grew more and more relentless. "When she was seated in a forward pew of the meeting house," the history says, "he could not conduct divine service in an orderly or regular manner, and her presence in his home distracted him almost beyond reason." In 1764, he caused to be built in one corner of the room where he wrote his sermons a wooden pen or cage, "to which he used to go voluntarily when he felt that his want of the woman Ruth Cloggs was moving beyond his control, and he would order his wife to lock him in." One day the Cloggs woman, who wonderfully did not know herself to be the cause of this unusual precaution, entered Reverend Sanders's workroom, while the minister was pent up, and began cleaning and dusting. "She was leaning far over," the record tells, "when she heard a most terrible bellowing and then a crash, for Reverend Sanders had burst through the locust saplings of his cage and had escaped his durance. He stood near her for a time, moaning, then ran from the room, crying out, 'Lord God, help me!' " He then had the cage rebuilt with four-inch locust posts, and from then on, with his wife's help, he was safe. "The reading to him by his wife of his own sermons, and the recalling to him of his mother's name and love, would exorcise the evil spirit and restore him to calmness. 'Thank you, my cherished helpmeet,' he would say to his wife, 'you may release me now.' " This practice continued until Reverend Sanders was sixty-one years of age and Ruth Cloggs was thirty-nine; she finally found a nondescript husband, who took her away. Noahdiah Sanders died in his chair eight weeks later.

REUBEN BLEDSOE, whom Reverend Sanders's daughter Rebecca married, was an identical twin. Reuben and Benjamin were called "the two Bens." According to the Stapleton town history, "They were of widespread fame as players on the bagpipes, and the wonder of small boys was how two such little men, who, windbags and all, would hardly weigh as much as a pair of full-grown bullfrogs, could make so much noise."

One day in 1794, tiny Reuben left Stapleton alone on ponyback. He said he was going to Albany to visit a sick cousin. The town history, while not denying that this cousin ever existed, does say that "by this time Reuben Bledsoe had earned a reputation as a swift fox." He had lied about going to Albany. He turned up instead in Schenectady, nosing around the offices of some western-territory land jobbers. Soon he made a compact with a certain Trent, "a weasel."

This was his interest: In the western part of New York, due south from

Sodus through Seneca Lake and on to the Pennsylvania border ran what
was called the Pre-emption Line. The land to the west of this line belonged to
Massachusetts, which had retained its colonial claim to a strip across New
York when yielding its western territory to Congress; New York had sovereignty over the whole region, Massachusetts owned the real estate. That land
was sold in a more or less orderly way. But on the eastern side of the
Pre-emption Line stood the so-called Military Tract, the vast acreage of which
was being sold to pay off the New York veterans of the Revolutionary War;
and because military warrants could be bought and sold, most of the lands
were cornered by jobbers, and trading in them was highly speculative. Weasel
Trent was one of these jobbers, and Fox Bledsoe became his agent in central
Connecticut.

Reuben returned to Stapleton. His cousin in Albany was mended, he
said. Now the fox bought a small letterpress. (His twin Benjamin, a farmer,
had nothing to do with Reuben's ventures.) There soon began to flutter
through all the neighboring valleys a series of vivid broadsides, advertising in
the most alluring terms the Paradise of the West. These circulars touched the
nerves of those who were restless: those with spent land in which the rocks
were breeding; those with many children and few acres; those who had had
scrapes with the law; the disgruntled, the greedy, the aspiring. The broadsides'
most notable feature was a flood of ecstatic letters from early arrivals in the
Military Tract.

Reuben's harvest was bountiful. By 1795 "Genesee fever" had set in.
Soon five hundred wagons a day were moving out on the Mohawk Trail. But
now there began to arrive in Stapleton some disturbing letters from former
residents who had dealt for land with Reuben Bledsoe. Questions hung in
the air. Finally the town selectmen called on Reuben. Had he, in the richness
of his fantasy, himself composed the letters in his broadsides that were
supposed to have come from ecstatic buyers? His answers were evasive.
Further protests, that Bledsoe's prices had been grossly out of line, bombarded
the authorities.

In May 1796, the town constable arrested the man he thought to be
Reuben Bledsoe. Later, at the barn of the town hall, where the lockup was
maintained, the elders charged him with fraud and extortion.

The prisoner loudly protested that they had the wrong twin; he was the
farmer.

The next day the constable went to Benjamin's farm, but Benjamin was
not at home; his wife said he had been away from home overnight: more she
would not say.

Scouting parties went out. Near Hartford they found on horseback the
other twin, who stoutly affirmed that *he* was the farmer, on his way to the
capital to borrow money from the bank.

Both were now locked up, to make sure. The innocent Bledsoe, which-

NOTHING is known, beyond word of his existence as a trapper and fur trader in the region east of Lake Ontario, of David Treadup's paternal great-great-grandfather, Jacob Treadup.

Of his type we know that such fur traders needed much air to breathe. There is a story of a trapper in what was later the Oswego area, a certain William Palliter, who shot one John Fent dead because Fent had intolerably crowded him by building a cabin twelve miles away from his. These trappers were resourceful, and they were trained down to muscle and gristle. They lived on the flesh of the deer, the bear, and the wild turkey, and later on that of the steer, the hog, and the ram; they supped, for trimmings, on bean porridge, mush and milk, toasted bread, and amber cider.

They had to coexist with the Cayugas, Senecas, and Onondagas, and they took on the Indians' ways, borrowing their clothes, their woodcraft, their planting lore, and sometimes their women. It is quite possible that David Treadup had some distant Indian blood; he speculates about this more than once in his diaries, and it is not at all clear that he likes the idea.

Trappers such as Jacob Treadup helped prepare for later settlers by "civilizing" the natives—ironic analogue of the subsequent Western penetration of China—by giving them guns to shoot their enemies, whiskey to inflame their pleasures, knives and knickknacks to swell their greed, technology to raddle their culture, and syphilis to pollute their offspring (though of course it should not be suggested that Jacob Treadup in New York or the missionary army in China traded at all in this last item). As for taking, trappers like Jacob Treadup must have caught from these superior tribes something of their dignity and their irreducible morale.

THE TRAPPERS' volatile relationship with the Indians bore strange fruit in the next generation, in the experience of Jacob Treadup's son Roger. The story of his great-grandfather is one that David Treadup often told to colleagues in China; he seems to have been haunted by it, perhaps because of its elements of exile, hardihood, and primitive survival. In somewhat homesick letters from China to his brother Paul, he sometimes referred to "my hard exile here."

In his middle years Jacob Treadup bought some land for his two sons near the center later called New Haven, New York (where in due course, though the fact has no bearing on this tale, there would be situated a nuclear power plant), and Roger and his older married brother cleared it for rough farming; each son had title to fifty patrimonial acres of hardship. They lived in the same house.

One July day in 1789, Roger Treadup, then twenty-one, took part in a ever he was, was so outraged by this treatment that he connived with his twin. Some days both would say they were Benjamin; some days both were Reuben. The upshot was that after a week, hounded by the scolding Bledsoe wives, the frustrated selectmen dropped the accusation. How could they even know that when the pair was released, the right twin would go to the right home?

The real Reuben Bledsoe quietly let it be known, a month or two later, that his cousin in Albany had passed away.

IN 1793, before the start of this shady real estate game, Reuben Bledsoe's second son, Jonathan, had volunteered for a road-building team on the Mohawk Trail. This was something like military service; young men of good family went off for a few fair-weather months, attracted by adventure in country where Indians were still resisting the advance of the white man. Jonathan worked on a highway that branched away northeastward from the Mohawk Turnpike, headed for Seneca Lake.

Did they call this a highway? The team chopped out small trees and underbrush in a swath averaging twenty feet in width; they sawed off heavier boles eighteen inches from the ground and left the larger trees to stand right in the middle of the thoroughfare. Such was the road. In wet weather it was a quagmire; at best, it was as rough as a sea passage through a typhoon. The team built log bridges over only the smallest streams; rivers had to be crossed by fords or ferries.

Jonathan, never having seen an Indian, returned to Stapleton with a dream of emigration. He married a sturdy, devout woman, and in 1799 his father, to be rid of a son who was nearly two feet taller than he, gave Jonathan two hundred fifty acres, one half of Lot 68, out there in the Military Tract—land that Reuben had bought for one dollar an acre—and soon Jonathan was driving his wagon, no doubt complaining all the way about the condition of the trail he had helped to hack out.

The father also gave Jonathan the means to become "an equipped farmer." It eventually cost Jonathan, to establish his farm, $5 an acre to have the land cleared; $70 for split-rail fencing; $225 for tools and machines; $100 for two oxen and a horse; $35 for a log cabin; and $80 for food until his own first crops came in.

He laid the foundation of his log cabin, thirty feet by eighteen, on November 12, 1799, hoping to be in by the first day of the last year of the century, but three feet of snow fell on the fifteenth of November. He and his wife wintered with a Haverkamp family. He shoveled out the snow in February, built his cabin, and moved in on March 1, 1800.

So it was that the mother's side of David's family found its way to Salt Branch.

cabin raising for a new settler, the communal labor of which was capped by
the serving of a tub of hard cider. Roger drank his share, or more. "Very
inconsiderately, and out of mere wanton sport," the account goes,

> he cut off the tail of a dog belonging to an Indian, who, a stranger and
> entirely unknown, happened to be in the vicinity. The master of the dog,
> though he uttered no complaint, manifested such emotions of ill will and
> revenge that Treadup before they separated deemed it prudent for himself
> to attempt to pacify him. He sought therefore a reconciliation, by pro-
> posing to drink together, and offered, moreover, reparation for the injury.
> But the Indian rejected all overtures and left the ground, evidently in
> a surly and unreconciled mood of mind.

Not long afterward, Roger Treadup and his brother invited their friends
to a corn-husking party in the yard of their house. As they talked after dark,
Roger said he planned to try early the next morning to find his horse, which
was feeding in the forest to the west of the settlement. "This conversation, as
it appears from the sequel, was overheard by Indians, who must have been, at
that time, lurking about the house."

Early the next morning Treadup took a bridle and went into the woods to
look for his horse. As he turned to skirt some boggy ground, three Indians
jumped out from hiding in the underbrush and overpowered him; they tied his
hands behind his back with the throat latch of the bridle and marched him off.

They were Onondagas, and they joined a party that was migrating north
toward Canada. One chilly night Treadup, with his arms pinioned, was laid
beside a fire. "Mischievous ones among the Indian children tickled his tender
bare feet with grass, and in his rage he kicked his tormentors away and
tumbled two of them into the fire. He expected to be killed for this aggression,
but instead the fathers of the burnt children patted him on the shoulders and
said, 'Boon, boon.'" [Was this *"Bon, bon"*?]

In Canada, where the group joined a tribal encampment, Roger was
forced to run naked through a gauntlet, whipped and bludgeoned along the
way. He lost his nerve and bolted from the line into an old squaw's tent. She
gave him sanctuary, at what may have seemed a steep price: "He was," as the
account puts it, "obliged to assume the carnal duties of a husband."

He lived under the squaw's protection for five years. Then one winter
day, pulling her on a sled to a venison feast on the top of a steep hill, he
slipped and fell and, "either by design or unable to hold on," he let go the
harness of the sled, which ran down to the foot of the hill and hit a stump; the
old woman was crippled. Treadup "affected sadness," but he soon arranged,
"through the agency, it is said, of a Papist priest," to have himself sold to a
Frenchman, who allowed him to work as a weaver, on a wage.

In two years he had earned enough to buy his freedom, and he made his
way on foot back to New Haven, where he "appeared as one risen from the

dead." His brother, asserting that after so many years Roger had legally ceased to exist, refused to take him in, and Roger Treadup drifted to Salt Branch. He took work in a lumber mill.

DAVID TREADUP'S two grandfathers: the frugal, slight-bodied, sober-sided Stephen Bledsoe, active in the Methodist church, conservative, a good manager, a gentle and kindly man surrounded by women—his mother, his wife, and seven daughters; and the millworker's son, Samuel Treadup, a hulking, dashing, carefree loner, who bought a rundown farm out on the Turcott road and, in David Treadup's words, "tried the old game of wrestling with a whiskey bottle, with the usual result—to get thrown."

IN THIS missionary's ancestry, religion was a constant presence but by no means an overbearing or crushing presence. The original Puritan colonists, who were mostly drawn from the ranks of English country gentlemen and middle-class entrepreneurs, had other motives besides the desire for religious freedom in emigrating to Massachusetts Bay: theirs was a time of political and economic unrest and change in England, and their discontents were material as well as spiritual; much of their daily concern, and that of their descendants, was worldly. Some of the early Bledsoe ministers undoubtedly preached the brutal Calvinist doctrine of predestination, but John Wesley had intervened in the eighteenth century, and David Treadup's more immediate religious heritage was that of a merciful and confident Methodism, which preached of a loving God who appealed to the free will of all men and women, every one of whom might achieve redemption. And though the Treadup family prayed together daily, and Hannah often read aloud from the Bible, this Methodism was largely a Sabbath matter in Salt Branch, less a constant scourge than a social mode.

Off and on all through his life, David Treadup kept commonplace books, in which he copied prose passages and poems, and noted observations, recollections, scraps for speeches, items of world news—whatever he thought might be useful in his calling. In one entry in 1909 he copied a passage from Jonathan Edwards's famous Enfield sermon, "Sinners in the Hands of an Angry God," and then commented on it:

> "The God that holds you over the pit of hell, much as one holds a spider, or some loathsome insect over the fire, abhors you, and is dreadfully provoked: his wrath towards you burns like fire. . . . Your wickedness makes you as it were heavy as lead, and to tend downwards with great weight and pressure towards hell; and if God should let you go, you would immediately sink and swiftly descend and plunge into the bottomless gulf, and your healthy constitution, and your own care and prudence,

and best contrivance, and all your righteousness, would have no more influence to uphold you and keep you out of hell, than a spider's web would have to hold a fallen rock."

No! no! no! This is not the God I know, not my God of the New Testament. In my family we were not afraid of him, we felt sure of his friendship. [David Treadup never followed the convention of capitalizing pronouns referring to God or to Jesus Christ.] *I remember a story about my great-grandfather Roger Treadup, who learned to play both the fife and the fiddle. He had the habit, after he came home from work at the lumber mill, of taking his fiddle, gathering his children around him on the stoop, and "chasing dull care away." One evening, while he was playing this way, the driver of the Oswego stage, passing by, stopped his horses so the passengers might listen. Having an audience incited Roger to greater effort, and he sawed his sweetest. As he finished the strain, one lady exclaimed, "That is good music, I declare. I hope we shall have as good as that in heaven." Quick as thought, and at the same time drawing his bow, my great-grandfather said, "You will, madam. I shall be there."*

Our folks felt they could even afford to be playful with God. I recall another family story—this one about old Jonathan Bledsoe, who originally cleared our place and put it on a workable footing. One Sunday morning he walked to his dam and was surprised to see a large school of perch. He told his sons about this sight and said it was a shame that it was the Sabbath, which was even stricter then than now, so that the work—or sport—of fishing would have been quite forbidden. When he sat down for dinner a large baked perch was put before him. He began his blessing, "Dear Lord, we thank thee for thy miracles," ate a large portion, and asked no questions.

T R A C E S of Treadups and Bledsoes in the written record, of which we have seen examples here, may have given a somewhat distorted picture of the lineages. Town histories abound with "characters," one-sided personalities, eccentrics, and cranks, mostly male. There must have been among David Treadup's forebears many who would not have appeared in such records— unspectacular people of steady habits, sound and stable and probably often dull men and women. We are to see in this missionary, at any rate, a constant tension between the trembling side and a part of him which is granite. Between the possible saint and the mere healthy man. What is moving in his story, what may in the end be thought to redeem the obvious failure of his mission in China, is his lifelong struggle to subdue the greater but sicker saint in himself and give himself to a more modest state of being: one of balance, sanity, serenity, and realized human love in the face of a shifting and violent and mostly hateful world.

FARM AND VILLAGE: THE SHAPING YEARS

SALT BRANCH, lying in what had been mostly Onondagan hunting grounds, on gently rolling wooded land not far from the eastern end of Lake Ontario, was an ideal missionary seedbed. In one sense it was merely a place of pause. It was a way station of the westward push. Many moved on. "I grew up quite aware of the great American urge to counter the rotation of the earth," Treadup once wrote: New England in one generation, western New York State the next, then the Old Northwest, Ohio, western Pennsylvania, the Mississippi Valley—and on and on, as if American genes were coded with westing; so that the leap David Treadup eventually took, westward even beyond Pacific sunsets, to China, and westward even there, seemed just one tiny inevitable aspect of the endless counterrevolving that had started with religious nonconformity and persecutions in Europe and England.

"BROTHERS PAUL and Will and I worked hard on farm," David wrote as a senior at Syracuse in a memoir, telegraphic in tone, which he entitled "Events of My Early Life." "Father believed boys should work hard and I fear did not give us as much time for play as boys should have. The girls not spared either. We were taught seven days."

A "simple life," one might think. Open country sparsely settled. A pure high sky. Pungent odors—of the creamery, of fresh bread rising, of the hayloft, of the steaming manure heap, of new rain on plowed clods. Mother canning. Father shaping a beam with ax and adze. Cheese press, butter churn. Peepers, catbirds, bullfrogs, cows lowing. The time-stopping quiet of snowbound days.

But life on the Treadup farm was in truth a scrape, a push, a fever. "Father in debt for farm," David wrote in "Events." "He and mother always worked to bone." An agricultural revolution was taking place in mainstream America, but Brownson Treadup was in an eddy of habit and poverty. Farming elsewhere was being mechanized, but the reaper, the thresher, the binder, the baler were far beyond his means. When David, in his sophomore year at Syracuse, turning toward science, took botany and discovered Edmund Ruffin's *Essay on Calcareous Manures,* published seventy years before, he wrote his father an excited letter. In part:

> *This man Ruffin—he could have made things easier for you. He was a Fire-Eater, Dad. He lived in Virginia, but he was a hair-brained* [sic] *states righter and he moved to Charleston and they gave him the honor— imagine, Dad—of firing the first shot at Fort Sumter. A manure man!*

As he learned about these things, David wrote further letters to his father— on the work on wheat rust, of Mark Carlton; on corn strains, of George Hoffer; on hybrids, of Luther Burbank. Yet when David went home during Easter, summer, and Thanksgiving breaks, the notes he wrote in his diaries were the same old ones: "Planted corn in orchard." "Put ashes on corn all day for Father." "Hoed corn." "Helped draw wheat." "Bound wheat all day. Hands sore."

Labor in his childhood years was the habit of life: not a principle, not an aspect of an ethic, simply an unrelenting dark-to-dark fact. Yet so deeply did this habit enter the soul of this young boy that it eventually became a kind of passion, an excruciating joy. In "Events" he writes:

> *I was always very ambitious, often beyond my strength. I used to go to village and pick fruits for Dr. Fosco, and later for C. F. Jonson—weighed 90 lbs. I turned a paring machine for hire, pared 50 bu. a day. I sat next to a large man and tried to keep up with him—used to be very tired.*

And another passage:

> *I shall always remember a record I made in husking corn. It was after my sickness and I was not very strong. I husked 34 bu. and tied my stalks in the forenoon, and Father would not let me continue in afternoon.*

THE BAD NAME missionaries have been given in popular American lore was at least partly earned for all of them by those who were barren-minded, the devotees and bigots, who were often immensely shrewd but were seldom immensely intelligent. "How could a Protestant God have stomached such stupid enthusiasts?" David once burst out in his diary, after a brush with a pair of "narrow" fundamentalists. Whatever David Treadup's other faults may have been, he was not stupid. He was, besides, very lucky in the phases of the training of his mind. The opening stage came in District No. 5 School, of Salt Branch, "located on the Isaiah Chase land on the east side of the Clearport Road next to a buttonball tree." He wrote in "Events":

> *From age six I rode to school on Nellie after she was pretty bad wind-broken. The scholars from outside the village stabled their horses*

*in the barn at the rear. It was understood we were to care for our
animals and clean the stables: a chore, atop of home chores, not
appreciated by this scholar. Some of my teachers were Della Mason, P. C.
Jenkins, Minnie Winters, Lillian Sea, Ed Quennell, Maud Chase. They
gave me the knack of curiosity. I did not go to school regularly after I
was ten or twelve years old but helped on farm in fall and spring and
went to school in winter. I never went two consecutive entire years until
my Soph and Junior years in college. All the same, something caught me
by the ears. We had Curl's Grammar, Robinson's Arithmetic, Steel's
Philosophy. I wanted to know how things worked!*

THE VILLAGE atmosphere of Salt Branch was crucial in the formation
of the missionary. The village was the magnet of his boyhood. There grew
his love of being among people. The farm was remote, isolated, and dully the
same from day to day, while down in the village there were laughter, eccentricity,
preaching and praying, parades, scuffles, tippling, gestures of gentility.

Buggies whirled up dust on unpaved streets lined with maples. Sidewalks were of wooden boards. Late in the day the lamplighter pushed his
wheelbarrow loaded with stuff to trim wicks, replenish oil, and polish chimneys,
and he stood his short ladder against each lamppost to service and light the
lamps. At the center of the main intersection was a bandstand, where once a
week in the summer the village cornet band gave concerts. And at every
turning, it seemed, one's eyes rose to the spearhead of a church spire.

A village historian records that a decade before David Treadup's birth
there were in Salt Branch

> many blacksmith shops, four carriage shops, six grocery and provision
> stores, mills turning out grist, lumber, shingles, woolens, and flax skeins,
> two boot and shoe shops, two milliners, a butcher shop, a tailor, a dress-
> maker, two harness and trunk makers, a hotel proprietor, a livestock
> dealer, an insurance agent, two masons, a number of carpenters and
> builders, a livery stable owner, an undertaker, and a photographer.

By David's time there were also a tannery, a bakery, and a barbershop
with a billiard parlor.

Often, later, David would write about "characters" he had seen around
the village when he lived on the farm: Dr. Semplimus, with his German
accent and bib of a red beard, willing to stop and dispense medicines from his
black satchel right in the middle of the street; Irondequoit Pete, fussing
and muttering pigeon sounds at his dovecote; Win Southly, who grew gin-
seng beyond the pond and mostly sat and whittled—said he could whittle
anything right down to crutches for a mosquito. From China David wrote
brother Paul:

I have encountered many a human oddity out in this field. But after some of those dear friends in Salt Branch I can never fault a person for mere strangeness. I am scornful of fools, enraged by destroyers, but Paul—fixations make the world go round!

Some of the By-Laws of the Incorporated Village suggest that besides eccentrics, there were a few miscreants around:

x. Any person who shall be intoxicated in any street, alley, lane, store, shop, hotel, mill, or other public place in said village, shall forfeit and pay a penalty of ten dollars for each offense. . . .

xiv. Every person who shall keep, maintain, or be an inmate of any house of illfame within the limits of said village shall forfeit and pay a penalty of ten dollars for each offense.

And though the frontier had pushed on westward, it had left a pattern of violence, both accidental and purposeful, that has never since been absent from American life. A few years before David's birth it was recorded that

twenty-one persons have died in this corporation, either by violent or untimely deaths: of which number six were drowned, three were killed with firearms, four were found abroad, dying or dead, one was killed with a pen-knife, two children were burned to death in a charcoal pit, and five were murdered.

AMONG the devout in Salt Branch, Methodists predominated. They had begun to meet in the homes of those of their persuasion as early as 1800, and in 1813 Salt Branch was established as a preaching point of the Sodus Circuit of the Genesee Conference. The first church was of white wood; a more solid fort for the Deity, a brick edifice, had gone up eight years before Treadup was born. Presbyterians formed a church in 1818. Baptists founded one in 1841, but this was destined to fade away until, in 1925, there being more than one way to deal with hell's flames, it became a firehouse. Catholics formed a parish in 1862 but did not have a church until 1875.

The religious life of the village tended to be vivid. Central and western New York seem to have received two sorts of stock from New England, one of them virile, intelligent, and industrious, the other mystical, rather unstable, sometimes fanatical, given to following cults. Salt Branch had weathered the anti-Masonic furor of 1826; the visions and hallucinatory revelations of Joseph Smith, the founder of Mormonism, in the twenties; the end-of-the-world excitement of the Millerites in the early forties; the spiritualistic "Rochester rappings" of the Fox sisters, with trances, sightings, involuntary dancing, in the late forties; and the wild revivalism of preachers like Asabel Nettleton and Charles G. Finney, culminating in the great evangelistic awakening of 1857.

DAVID was nine when something happened to which he often referred in the writings of his adult years as the event that first caused him to believe in God. His fullest account of it is in his "Search" of 1943, written at a time when his belief was beginning to run thin:

> One of my chores was to deliver milk for sale to the creamery in town. Father, Paul, and Will would load the full milk cans in the wagon designed to hold them, while I put the harness on Custer and backed him between the shafts. The ride to the village and back—I must emphasize this, it set my mind for what happened later—put me in a hazy, dreamy mood: the steady rhythm of the great muscles in Custer's glistening haunches, the drumming of his footfalls, the sunshot passage of dusty elderberry and birch and swamp maple leaves—all worked on me to reassure me and sweeten me.
>
> No other child of nine delivered milk. I drew breath deep into my chest, to expand it to the dimensions of a plowman's, as I pulled into the line of wagons waiting their turns. The much older boys and men whom I wished to impress greeted me always as one of them, with unforced courtesy. Some of these farmhands were tough, bitter, violent men, drunks and thieves, but without exception they treated me as a fellow Citizen of the Republic. It was ingrained in them. There hung about the creamery a clean fragrance that reached deep into the darkest places of memory. When my turn came, the creamery attendant, Milo, with much ill-tempered shouting, lowered the hook for me to slip into each milk-can handle, cranked the windlass inside, tipped the milk into the huge weigh tank, then lowered the empty to the wagon. After the lot was weighed and recorded, I would drive the wagon down the ramp to the south side of the creamery and pump out as much whey for the pigs as I had delivered milk that day. Then came the unhurried, meditative ride back out.
>
> It was in the benign, milky, grownup mood of this errand that I stopped off, one morning, at the Paxons' farm, intending merely to say hello to Renny and make some plan with him for the next Sunday. I hitched Custer to the post off the road. Renny did not respond to my hail, and I quickly ran, in order to recharge the chambers of my imagination, to the pile of trash lumber at the back of the Paxons' yard, which Renny and I had transformed, simply by willing the transformation through the urgency of our restlessness, into a clipper ship, on which we had found ourselves able to visit ocean reaches that invested the meager grass plot around us with mad combers, whale spouts, foaming reefs, and, sometimes, unbearable albatrossy calms: Roaring Forties, Cape Horn, Sargasso Sea, the Doldrums.

As I stood there I suddenly heard a high-pitched yet guttural cry, a land cry, nearby, which caused my scalp and buttocks to prickle. I recognized an appeal for help of a sort I knew I could not give. It was repeated. I followed the sound. It led me to a place against the Paxons' milk shed, where their dog Tub, a terrier-hound mix, lay in obvious agony. I could see that she was deathly sick. My approach caused her to cry out more pathetically than ever. She was in a knot of suffering. I crouched down. I thought she had been poisoned. I grew very frightened, because I had never seen Death, and I heard Death rattling in Tub's throat. Then after an immense spasm a horrible, slimy, gray-pink mass plopped out of her rear end. This drove me to my feet in terror. "She has shat her own guts," I thought. Then something even more revolting happened: She turned and began licking this shapeless excrement. Could it be that Death meant that one had to eat oneself bit by bit? Then . . . then . . . the miracle for which I was wholly untutored and unprepared slowly unfolded before my eyes. The vile tumor, as Tub licked away its grease-like coating, began to tremble, then to move. In a short time it took shape. It was a perfect new life. Without eyes to see its way, it dragged itself toward Tub and was soon sucking, with the great instinctual eagerness of the will to live, on one of her dugs. I repeat: I was utterly unprepared. No one had ever breathed to me a word — save the monotonous 'begats' of the Old Testament — of the great circle of sex. Now I saw six pups whelped that way.

Ever since that morning, whenever I have felt fear, I have felt within the fear an incipience of a wonderful surprise, the promise of a great delight and thrill. People have always said I was fearless. No, I have felt fear. But I have always felt that I was taught by nature, that morning, that whatever is terrifying has its superb reason.

Now I have begun to wonder: Reason? — or a mad intelligence behind it all? — or mere randomness? Fear has begun to seem real to me now. Poor Tub. Poor Tub.

IF THE BEGINNING of belief, for David, came with his innocent discovery of "the great circle of sex," the church often seemed, during his adolescent years, to stand for smaller concentric circles within the great circle. As information and misinformation about sex began to trickle his way, first from his friend Renny and later from the toughs who hung around the bakery in the village, there was the troubling matter of Mary, who became Jesus's mother without having performed what was known in the bakery circle as It. Then, perhaps even more unsettling, there was the strange epicene quality of Jesus himself. "It bothered me, haunted me," David wrote in "Search," "when one day Roger Trent down at the bakery asked, 'Where does J.C. come off

being kissed by his chum Judas? Why would a man kiss a man? The gang
made a whole lot of that."

Almost everything to do with the brick church in the village was
pleasurable, because from infancy David's entire social life was centered
there—cradle roll, Sunday school, Christian Endeavor, choir practice, "socials,"
suppers. One gathers between the lines of David's scrawl, whenever the
subject came up, that from the earliest years this social experience was
drenched with sensual hopes and imaginings. Girls—not mere sisters—were
there, tricked out in their best clothes and brightest expectations. The substance of the teenagers' Epworth League meetings was boring, but the hour
was electric with anticipation, for it was followed by the socially sanctioned
two-by-two walk home. The exquisite sensation of the touch of hand to hand!
The slightest advance was a great event. "One church supper in particular I
remember," David wrote Paul in one of his early homesick letters from China:

> Perhaps you will remember it, too. I mean the time when Melville
> Horton brought his automobile to a supper—it was that '94 Haynes—
> remember?—just a buggy without a horse, really—and sold rides for
> 10¢. Those rides raised more money than all the fancy linen and dishes
> and silver and ice cream and cakes the ladies had brought round to a
> dozen suppers. Goodness knows where I got two dimes to rub together,
> but I took Cassie Berns for a ride. When we went over the bumps at 15
> m.p.h. we jounced against each other—it was bully—how I trembled—
> ten dollars worth of thrills.

In "Events" he writes of a perhaps "fast" older woman:

> At fifteen, through choir practice, I fell very much in love with Gertrude
> Jonson, an alto. She was older than I by a year and married a man twice
> her age when she was twenty.

And in "Search":

> The first organ was a foot-pedal reed instrument, later replaced by a
> large organ with some fake pipes for show and a long lever on the side
> for pumping air into the bellows. I got the job! It was in full sight of the
> choir. There I was, during hymns and anthems, working away, and there
> across the choirloft was Gertrude, watching me!

"I WAS both excited and abashed by the violence of the big boys at the
bakery," David wrote in "Search."

The Treadups' one indulgence of David was letting him play in the
concerts of the cornet band. In his youth Brownson Treadup had bought and
half learned to play a battered secondhand B-flat cornet, and, beginning when

David was ten, after much begging, the father allowed the son to take some lessons on it after school in wintertime. Being in the band meant being able in summer to take two evening horseback trips each week to the village, once for rehearsal, once for the concert in the bandstand.

David apparently fudged his departures a bit, arriving in Salt Branch each time a half hour or so early. And each time he would hurry down for a few minutes at the bakery, where the heroes and giants of toughdom hung out, pals of the doughboys who worked there. After the day's baking was done, there would be rounds of the sport of self-defense in the back room, with betting in silver money.

> *They hooted for bloodied noses. They wanted blood. My heart beat very fast. I was afraid of blood, and I think I may have wanted it. Also, being very big for my age, I was terrified they would make me put on the gloves. Yet I went.*

After one of the fights, the very second time David had showed his face in the back room, a bakery worker named Sam, still in his long white apron and white cloth hat like a muffin, and with eyebrows and mustache whitened with flour, came running out of the oven room and called out, "Listen here, you fellows. We're in a pickle. We may lose our Number Two oven 'less we get an oven-stretcher in a hurry."

One of the other doughboys shouted, "Hey! I mind Dr. Appleton has one!"

The first: "Who'll volunteer to fetch it for us?" He turned at once to David, and said, "Here's a strapping fellow. You look strong enough to carry it. Help us out, lad? You know where Doc Appleton lives, don't you?"

"I ran as fast as I could," David tells us,

> *because I wanted to make an impression on the bakery boys. Dr. Appleton had one of the big houses in the village, and I gave the bell pull eight or ten strong yanks. He must have thought there was a hurry-up call for a dying patient. He came to the door putting on his black coat, and he said, "Young Treadup, what's up?" I panted out my report, that there was a crisis at the bakery, they needed an oven-stretcher awful bad. Dr. Appleton had gentle eyes that cured people, I think, more likely than his pills, and he shook his head and put his hands on my shoulders, and he said, "I'm afraid you've been gulled, young Treadup. There's no such animal as an oven-stretcher. Those fellows down at the bakery have had you up for a sucker." I think I may have begun to cry. "It's all right, young man," he said. "You're not the first, and you won't be the last."*

He was not the last. He had the courage to go straight back to the bakery to face the laughter, knowing that he would be branded a skulker if he did not. He was thenceforth accepted as a big boob who had leave to stand around and watch, and in time he was tickled to death to see other raw recruits sent out on later occasions to fetch a rubber crowbar; a left-handed monkey wrench; a bucket of steam from the depot.

IN A LETTER to Paul in 1924, after a train trip from Tientsin to Peitaiho, David wrote:

> *The depot! Remember how we used to go down on Sundays to watch the trains? Remember the waiting-room benches, with the curved, slippery seats? The tapping of the telegraph key in the ticket office? The men lounging on the platform swapping stories? The express!—slowed down enough for the mail clerk to snatch the out-bag off the hook, after he'd flopped the in-bag onto the platform. The section gang riding along, pumping the handle of their handcar. The flag shanty at the crossing. Oh, and the rotary plow going through after a snowstorm! Remember that winter when they had to have a hundred men shovel by hand ahead of the plow?*
>
> *Just about when you and I were down there watching trains, Paul, out here a Chinese thinker named Wang T'ao was writing: "The steamship and the railway are the carriages of the ways of life." What he meant was that those inventions might bring together and unify the nations of the world. We thought something like that, too, didn't we?*

David had had from his earliest years the desire to understand the linkages and couplings of physical phenomena (*potlid to pot, hat to head*) —the fitting together of parts, in literal works and as a metaphor for the possibility of order in the baffling chaos of the universe. Since the Civil War and during his youth a great traffic of new wonders had been coming into public use: railroad trains and steamships; electric lights; telegraph, telephone, cable, wireless; typewriters, adding machines, cash registers, linotype machines. The rate of the world's change was itself exponentially changing. All these new devices thrilled David in their particulars, their clickings and clankings, their push toward speed and power.

And none so much as the railroad train. Beginning when he was minus seven years old, tracks of the Lake Ontario Shore Railroad had been laid down along the old trail from Oswego to Irondequoit. Later absorbed into the Rome, Watertown, and Ogdensburg line, and later still into that of the New York Central, this loop was finally to become, after David's death, part of the Conrail System, its tracks poorly maintained but still able to sustain an occasional slow-moving freight train. The through line was linked up just two years before David was born. The long grade, seventy-five feet per mile, from Silver Station to Salt Branch was locally called "the hump," and it usually took two engines to haul freight over it.

From that early moment, which his mother had recorded, when his father had taken him down as a baby to see the engine watered at the depot, David had almost seemed to want to *be* a locomotive. "I feel I shall burst with joy this morning," he wrote in his journal one day in North China in 1912; and then he added:

> *I seem to see in my mind's eye the engine pulling into the S.B. station. Old 415 has made the hump! The stacks belch, hisses of white plumes below. I can see the glistening contours atop the boiler: the smokestack, then the dome of the sandbox, then the bell, then the throttle valve dome, then the brass whistle, then the safety valve dome, then after all the curves the rectangular roof of the cab. I know it all as I know my own body. The great animal trembles with its strength—and I feel the strength!*

In the sight of this metal creature in the Salt Branch station there had been the incipient dream of motion toward the sunset. Spikes had joined the rails of the Union Pacific and Central Pacific at Promontory Point, Utah, within a decade before David was born, and by the time he was six the Northern Pacific, the Southern Pacific, and the Santa Fe had also reached their long fingers to the far ocean. The Treadup mealtimes rang with tales and legends: Pikes Peak, *Roughing It,* the Black Hills gold rush, the Battle of the Little Big Horn, the massive droving of cattle into the High Plains; and the new statehoods emerging, resonant new names on the distant horizons— Dakotas, Montana, Wyoming, Idaho. In "Search": "I think I heard whispers of the faraway sea in the whooshes of steam escaping from the big steel machine."

ONE NIGHT, in bed, with a stocking cap on, David's Uncle Don Treadup whispered in his wife's ear that he had bought a traveling circus that afternoon. She was used to surprises. Once he had taken her to Chicago and bought a freightcarload of horses. Another time he had disappeared for three weeks and had come home with a tuba, saying he had been taking lessons in Rochester. He was a nonbeliever, but when the brick church was built, he ordered a bell all the way from Philadelphia and dragged it from the station to the church on a stoneboat; it was said that when the bell rang, it intoned, "Come, Don. Come, Don." But Don never came.

All his life he had been a circus buff. He had hung around the wagons, talking to gang bosses, clowns, fat ladies, and roustabouts. He seemed to be able to crack the codes of animal sounds. He now moved a black bear and a lion into the two-story barn behind the house, and he had long talks with them. There were constant conferences with humans, too, during the booking season: advance man and poster man, band director and boss canvasman, as well as the wire-walking "drunk," the Italian head-balancer, the iron-jaw lady who could spin hanging by her teeth, and a certain Hans

Pfefferhalz and his performing animals (elephant, camel, pony, fox terrier).

This was the brief and shining period when Uncle Don Treadup became David's interim deity. The craze lasted three years, after which time Uncle Don sold his cumbersome plaything. In the year of the purchase, David was eleven. Uncle Don had no children, and from David's birth he had been fascinated by his nephew's oversized frame, and now he kept borrowing the big little boy for short stretches, to clean out lion and bear manure, to coil tent ropes, to sell tickets for home stands. Don persuaded Hannah and Brownson to let him take David on one of his road trips. From that magic month of his eleventh year onward, the place where he happened at any moment to be was never again world enough for David Treadup.

AFTER church meeting one Sunday when David was thirteen, Uncle Don suddenly appeared at the farm, shouting, "Where's that roustabout boy?" He said he wanted to take David down to the village to show him something.

The something turned out to be a lapstraked, double-ended rowing wherry with varnished ribs, bronze rowlocks, and a thwart with a cane seat. "It was a corker, and he had bought it just for *me*. After all the dream voyages Renny and I had taken on our lumber-pile ship!"

The rowboat became the center of David's life. He portaged it around the dam of the pond and rowed it down to where the Branch ran past the farm. All summer he would get up at five to have a half hour's row before breakfast, and after supper each night he was off again, skimming all the reaches of the Branch. His mother was deeply angry at David's having been singled out for such a luxury, when the family was so poor, and it took weeks of teasing, begging, whining, and cajoling before David could get permission to row on Sabbath afternoons.

On Sundays, finally, with his mother still calling it a sin, he would go upstream to the pond, where he won great prestige as a generous giver of rides: the passenger would huddle in the stern, making the dink's bow ride high, and David would lean into his strokes "with indescribable pleasure in my chest—it was like being in love." In this role he was evidently in love with himself. It was many years later, in "Search," that David first asked himself whether his generosity and solicitude for others masked a need to establish some sort of power over them.

There were other boats on the pond, sorry articles—except for one— in comparison with *Ecarg* (for David had named his craft for his little sister): squarish, flat-bottomed rowboats used for setting rabbit snares along the banks of the Branch. The exception was a flaring, sharp-prowed dory which belonged to Stanton Jessup, a banker who, it happened, heartily disliked Don Treadup.

One day Olin Tanner, one of the bakery toughs, a sixteen-year-old, announced that Mr. Jessup had offered his dory to anyone who wanted to race it against "that Cleopatra's barge belonging to Mr. D. Treadup." Olin said he would bet David four bits he could thrash him in a race, giving David ten yards' start.

David said he couldn't bet but he'd dearly love to race.

There was a big turnout on the shore of the pond: the whole bakery crowd. David, with strong arms and legs and gut from a month's conditioning, won easily. Then he beat Olin from a scratch start. Then he gave Olin ten yards and beat him. He beat all comers. All summer. Everyone said he won because of the shape of his boat. Perhaps he did. Perhaps he didn't. In any case, the competitive hook was set deep in David Treadup's flesh.

IN WINTER there would be skating parties on the pond, with a bonfire in the cove at the top, hot cocoa, roasted frankfurters and marshmallows, games of snap-the-whip, sail-skating downwind with a burlap bag on a sprit frame for a sail.

Then, when the ice was a foot thick, came the ice harvesting. And at the ice harvesting, in the winter when David was sixteen, he saw something happen that gave him a model of physical courage for the rest of his life. His testimony, at age sixty-five, was that "whenever I was in danger in China, that picture of my father rose before my eyes, challenging me to be as brave as he."

There were no refrigerators in those days; cakes of ice were delivered from house to house on Monday, Wednesday, Friday, and Saturday, at ten cents for a fifty-pound cake, which the average icebox could take. For the harvesting, a communal enterprise, various farmers would supply teams of horses in rotation. First a team would clear away the snow with a six-foot scoop steered by two men. Then the ice field would be marked for cutting by a horse-drawn gauge with metal points that scribed the ice in parallel lines, perpendicular to each other, making a grid of rectangles about eighteen inches by two feet. The ice then had to be sawed by hand, with huge-toothed saws six feet long. The broken-off cakes were scooted or floated toward the mouth of a sloping trough at the ice house, where a man would slip a metal cage over a pair of cakes, and then a team of horses would walk out onto the ice, drawing the cage up into the ice house on block and tackle. The ice was stacked inside the house a foot or so from the outside walls, and the gaps were filled with sawdust, which cost twenty-five cents a wagonload at various sawmills. This insulation, which was also eventually spread on the top layer of ice, would keep the remaining cakes intact right through the following summer.

One day in January 1896 it had come to be Brownson Treadup's turn to supply the team for the afternoon shift of the haul of blocks up the trough. It was three above zero, with an overcast sky and "a wolf-fanged north wind." David managed to keep warm, for he was manning one of the twenty handsaws. The men sang songs to make a rhythm for their strokes; the bodies heaved in a dance of echelons. From time to time there would be ominous deep-throated cracking sounds—dismissed as something the men called "underfreeze."

Then suddenly there was a kind of thunder underfoot that did not stop. David looked up to see a huge floe tipping under Custer and Bonaparte, and the horses slid into the water. The sawing ceased. The men gasped and shouted. David saw that his father was safe on firm ice. He had an impression that the horses' heads, tossing above the water, consisted of nothing but huge eyes and nostrils. Then—no time seemed to have passed—his father was in the water, feeding a rope around Custer's neck; then one around Bonaparte's. Then men were hauling his father up on the ice, and others were pulling at the ropes. For the only way to save the horses, David knew from old lore, was to choke them until, heaving breath in but unable to expel it, they would become bloated and would float high so men could—and they now did—roll them out on the ice.

At sixty-five, recalling this episode, David Treadup had no memory of how his father must have been bundled up and taken off to the nearest house to be restored, or how the horses, which came through unharmed, must have been run and rubbed down. He only remembered the ice forming on his father's beard, and his father's eyes seeking his own eyes, and Paul's, and Will's, with a father's angry defiance, as if to say, "Could you do that?" "Often when I have prayed," David wrote, "I have visualized an utterly dependable God with frost like that in his beard and searching, piercing, furious eyes like those."

"THERE WAS a break in my life at about seventeen," David wrote in "Events,"

> and I became careless and rebelled at the strictness of my home. I started in school and grew careless during the fall until I was severely ill with blood poisoning. I was confined to the house for three months and was left in a weak condition.

So David moved into a period of stress, prefiguring the crisis that led to his conversion in his sophomore year at Syracuse; the same malady recurred just before his late-life crisis in 1943. We know from the later sickness that the disease was not exactly blood poisoning—a term which in those days, like "virus" in a later time, covered many a mystery—but was osteomyelitis: an inflammation of an area of bone and marrow of the humerus of his left arm, about midway between shoulder and elbow.

During his weeks in bed, a door opened in David's mind. He had nothing to do but read—a pastime for which the way had been prepared by his mother's fierce love of books. But it was not his mother who brought this breakthrough. One of his teachers, Maud Chase, who must have been excited by sparks she had seen struck from David's mind in her classroom, took it on herself to be his librarian, and with brother Paul as intermediary, she sent book after book to the young patient.

For David her choices were like a lottery. She managed to establish in him a firm liking for bad poetry. She bombarded him with volumes by Thomas Bailey Aldrich, Bayard Taylor, Henry Richard Stoddard, Richard Watson Gilder. Two slim, poorly edited books of Emily Dickinson's poems had been published by the time of David's sickness, but the ripples they caused had apparently not reached Salt Branch; nor do we find in David's notes any mention of Whitman. Among the appalling false starts in his understanding of China, he noted in his diary after he had gone there, was one put in his way during his illness by Maud Chase: Bret Harte's most popular poem, about the California Chinaman, Ah Sin, cheating at cards, an effusion which Harte himself called "possibly the worst poem anybody ever wrote":

> *. . . for ways that are dark*
> *And for tricks that are vain*
> *The Heathen Chinee is peculiar.*

Understandably missing from the prose works Maud Chase sent David were the novels of Howells and James, which dealt with social worlds far from the humble realities of Salt Branch. But in those months at home David did make two explosive discoveries: *Huckleberry Finn,* with its long dream of floating on waters (how he must have been missing his *Ecarg!*) and, more important, with its powerful message of Huck's love for Jim, a creature of another race; and Francis Parkman's *The Oregon Trail,* with its deep affinities, noted many years later in Treadup's commonplace books, to Melville's *Typee* and Conrad's *Heart of Darkness*—"searches all, in far-away places," he wrote, "into the raw and untamed recesses of the Self as set against an Other"—the Parkman through its unashamed yet distanced staring at naked members of yet another race, the Sioux. These two books fed both David's restlessness and his fascination with whoever might be called a stranger.

In "Events" he wrote:

> *My arm, in which the blood poisoning was, was left in bad shape and I finally after a year had an operation to remove part of the bone. The wound was kept open with a gauze drain in it for several weeks. Then it was sound. I afterward became ambitious to be strong and took better care of myself. I also took a renewed interest in the Christian life. I have sometimes thought it was a providential sickness.*

ABSOLOM CARTER

MAIN STREET, in front of Gavin's Grain and Seed. Yellowish June daylight. Five boys, all about seventeen years old, lounge in swaggering poses against the wall of the store—hips thrust sideways, arms folded, heads tilted back. Treadup's right hand, hidden behind his back, grasps a large hub wrench. He has, as each of them has, a sore place on the tip of the middle finger of his right hand, for they have all recently sworn themselves to secrecy with blood from razor cuts there. The young men are all former gulls of the bakery crowd, but they now call themselves by a better bird's name. They are the Cayuga Eagles.

A farmer drives up in a battered red wagon, hitches his horse, and goes in the store. Young Treadup dimly recognizes him as one who works a place out the Silver Junction road, but does not know his name. When the store's fly-mesh door slams, the boys look at each other. Treadup, the leader, nods. Casually all five sidle out toward the wagon. The other four screen Treadup, who quickly ducks down by the right rear wheel, applies the wrench, and loosens the hub nut to its last couple of threads. He is up again. No one has seen anything. The five ease back to the wall of the store and wait.

Wonderful! The farmer is buying a big load of things—potash in bags, rolls of tar paper, some milk cans. The boys eagerly offer to help him load up. He gratefully accepts their offer. He unhitches. One of the boys takes the horse's bridle and guides it as it backs out. The farmer salutes his thanks. A hundred yards along, the right rear wheel of the wagon begins to gollywobble. The driver seems not to notice. Then—beautiful! The wheel careers off on a course of its own, as if it would rather go to Oswego. Slowly, slowly, the bed of the wagon tilts. The farmer throws up his arms. The milk cans sing as they roll off. The horse rears in twisted shafts. The farmer fights the reins at the peak of his wreck. All the goods are in the dust.

The Eagles run around to the far side of the store to let their laughter free.

ON JUNE 23 the through passenger "up" train, due in Salt Branch just after noon, was delayed five hours. Late that afternoon word went around town that there had been a derailment of a freight car in a "down" train just west of Silver Junction.

In the middle of the night one of the Eagles lost his nerve. The secrecy-cut on his fingertip all too well healed, he confessed to his parents that just after the band concert the previous night, he had gone down to the depot freight siding with David Treadup and the other boys in the gang, and they had borrowed tools from the yard shed, which was never locked, and David had loosened bolts in the undercarriage of one of the freight cars.

At six the next morning the stationmaster sent a flagman out to the Treadup farm to summon David to the depot. By eight o'clock the whole town knew the news. At about eight fifteen, within a few minutes of each other, two adults showed up at the station to look out for the Treadup boy's interest. One was Maud Chase, his teacher; the other was Dr. Ferdinand Fosco.

Of Maud Chase, little is known. During David's sickness she guided his reading, as we have seen, and she now cared enough about him to walk right out of a schoolroom and rush to his defense.

Dr. Fosco, an elderly man with a grand presence, had graduated from the University of Vermont and had emigrated first to Silver Junction, in Cayuga County, and then to Salt Branch. Of the three doctors in the village, he had been the Treadups' choice as family physician because he was active, as they were, in the Methodist Church. As Sunday school superintendent he had pinned attendance badges on David's lapel, and he had put in David's hand, as a prize for memorizing psalms, a Bible which David kept for most of his life, said to have been bound in thin boards of olive wood from the Mount of Olives (David half believed this). On the Sunday school wall hung a large portrait of Dr. Fosco, posed beside a studio tree stump on which sat, as a symbol of the good doctor's wisdom, a stuffed owl. The doctor had often hired David to do odd jobs around his home. No matter how Christian, how kind, Dr. Fosco may have been, there must have been something special about this young boy, there must have been some metallic glitter of mind behind the things he had casually said to his employer, which had impressed a busy physician enough to make him drop his rounds on sudden notice and have a shot at lawyering for a bad boy.

The outcome of the conference in the depot ticket office was a character-istic one for an intimate village like Salt Branch in those days: The station-master entrusted David to whatever correction the teacher and doctor might settle upon.

THE AGREEMENT Maud Chase and Ferdinand Fosco reached must have surprised and chagrined the railroad man. It was that David was made for a bigger world than Salt Branch. He was bad, they decided, because he was bored; he needed the challenge of better schooling than Salt Branch could offer. (Their charitable diagnosis was surely correct; but much later in life Treadup became aware of eruptions of what he called "my badness" — involuntary outbursts of prankishness and destructiveness, which each time signaled the onset of a period of low spirits.)

But sending David away would take money. Dr. Fosco knew from his own dealings with the Brownson Treadups how poor they were. He went to David's Uncle Don, the former circus owner, whose bell summoned the faithful to the doctor's church; doubtless Fosco knew of the childless eccentric's fostering of David. And between them, in due course, these three oddly assorted angels, Maud Chase, Ferdinand Fosco, and Don Treadup, brought the first great swerve in David's life, which rescued him from a poverty-racked farm existence and headed him toward a decent education and, eventually, faraway China.

IN TURCOTT, that very autumn, an imposing brick-and-stone building with the lines, much reduced in scale but not at all in aspiration, of the Hall of Languages at Syracuse University was rising on five acres of high ground that commanded Turcott village. It was to cost an impressive $27,355.86 (carpenters were paid $1.50 a day that year, masons $2.50, and common laborers, $1.25), and its beams, floors, and millwork were to consume forty thousand board feet of Georgia pine lumber. By early November the capstone of the arch over the entrance was raised into place:

ENDERBURY INSTITUTE
18 FREE SCHOOL 96

The weather snapped cold just then, and for the final bricklaying in the next month the men had to mix gasoline into the mortar and then burn it to keep the mortar from freezing. Workmen slated the roof in January, finished plastering in early March, and hung the bell in the tower on March 31.

There were two sorts of secondary education in that region and time. One was the "academic" school, often privately funded, which prepared students for college or business or teaching; such had been the Enderbury Institute, founded in 1856 by Isaac Enderbury, a native of Watertown, Connecticut, who had settled in Turcott a couple of decades earlier, an energetic and public-spirited citizen who had eventually represented the district in the state legislature. The other kind was the free district school, which typically gave its pupils a fair literacy, and ability to figure and reason well enough to get along as farmers or craftsmen or clerks. In Turcott in 1869 the two had been consolidated into a single entity.

Now opportunely just after David's delinquency its new building stood

spanking and ready, and the three angels decided that this would be the ideal
place for him.

D R . F U S C O broached the idea of the Turcott school to the family.

David's parents balked. Brownson said he needed the boy's arms on the
farm; especially he needed his aptitude, much greater than that of the other
sons, with tools and gear. Just when the boys were coming to the age when
they could, at last, give their father's back a rest, were they to be torn away,
one by one?

As soon as Hannah learned that Don Treadup was involved in the plan,
she denounced it as "a conspiracy to kidnap my son." She would never allow
such a crime, she said.

And David, even though he knew he was on probation to Fosco and
Chase, did not want to leave Salt Branch. It would mean deserting his
companion Renny Paxon and the Eagles; he would be cut off from church
social events, choir practice, organ pumping, Gertrude Jonson, Cassie Berns.
And what about his rowboat?

David took refuge in his parents' bristling resistance—until, one day,
Dr. Fosco asked him to come to his house in the village to mow and prune. Dr.
Fosco, with the intuition of a family doctor of those days, refrained from
playing on David's guilt over his gang's dangerous "jokes," and instead
touched the nerve ends of David's ambition, which the illness—perhaps his
reading—had laid bare.

"I went home that day on fire," David wrote in "Search." "I was going to
whip the world."

D A V I D went to see the school, and it was on the day of that visit that he met
a man who was to be one of the two most important models for his future
life as a missionary.

"The first sight I had of Mr. Carter," David wrote in a letter to brother
Paul in 1918 (after the teacher had been killed by a locomotive, when his Ford
stalled at a track crossing),

> was in the science room on the day I inspected the school, or vice versa,
> the school inspected me. He was wearing a green celluloid eyeshade and
> he had rubber sleeveguards holding up his sleeves. He picked up a
> fifty-pound wooden case for beakers and test tubes by one handle as if
> it were a teacup. Said to myself: "David if you come here to school, this
> is a person to whom you will have to be polite." He was 28 or 29, but
> from my perspective then he was middle-aged—at his prime—in mental
> powers, in magnetism, in wisdom. When he began to speak! O he was
> going to be so much more than my match—as I came to know so well in

my terms under his tutelage. He was a polymath. He remembered every
word of every book he had ever read. He had an off eye — a mote, or a
wall eye rather — and sometimes you could not tell whether he was
looking past you or right through you. He did not need to look at the
surface of you because he already knew as much about your innermost
secrets as he did about those of Augustus, Charlemagne, Copernicus,
Shakespeare, the vireo, the snapdragon, sulphur brimstone, and the
fleas on your dog — in other words, of everything. Everything. Everything.
Could I ever know the thousandth part of what he knew?

Absolom Carter had graduated from Cornell, *summa cum laude,* in
1888. He had been captain of football and track, and by a weird coincidence
had been a casual friend of the man who would one day be the second model
for David Treadup: the other big man on the Cornell campus then, the head of
the Christian Association, James B. Todd.

Apart from the flaw in his one eye, Absolom Carter made the perfect
picture of the all-round thinker-athlete — the ideal of young American manhood for decades to come, and certainly what David would want to shape
himself to be. It was not considered at all remarkable that a man of Carter's
brilliance and power should be glad to teach in a small school in a backwater
of upstate New York, for the calling was regarded by all as a dignified one,
and if he could, over the years, multiply himself by ten, by teaching and
example, it would be thought that he had given society a great gift.

David came home from that meeting determined to become a scholar at
Enderbury Institute.

NOW THERE came a new round of a curious habitual series of transactions
between David and his mother. They often struggled this way. Their conflicts
would spin themselves out over several days or even weeks.

He declared his heart's desire — to go to the Turcott school. She refused
permission; he must stay with his father. David teased and whined and
wheedled. While intensifying her disapproval, she showed signs of being
irresistibly drawn to David's wish. She gave in. He then reversed himself and
said he did not want anything she thought wrong. She then avidly urged him
to go, her rage close under the surface of her eagerness. He submitted. She
then held to the permission while savagely denouncing it.

So it had been between them from the very beginning, with the whittled
piglet of his babyhood; so with rowing on the Sabbath; so now with the
question of going out into the big world.

MR. AND MRS. TREADUP, the angels, the school, and David finally struck
a bargain. The first year, David's eighteenth, he would go to Turcott for the
two winter quarters; the second year, for all four.

He would seek lodging in Turcott village. The angels persuaded the parents that though Turcott was only a few miles from Salt Branch, it would be important for David to be absolutely free of home chores and to live close to the school.

Mrs. Treadup's price was that David should not be wholly dependent on Don Treadup's charity. Uncle Don had undertaken to pay the expenses of a scholar from outside the district, eight dollars per term for the classical course, which would include the Latin and Greek that would be essential if David were to go on to college (something not yet even whispered about); and perhaps two or three dollars a week for lodging.

Absolom Carter provided the suggestion that saved face for Hannah Treadup. At one of the stiff conferences in the principal's office on the second floor of the school (with a painting of old Isaac Enderbury, portrayed a bit lumpily by the school's drawing teacher Helen Tackroom, brooding over the embarrassed boy and his angry mother), Mr. Carter pointed at the bell pull hanging down through a hole in one corner of the ceiling and asked Dr. Arthur, the principal, if part of David's tuition each quarter might not be abated by his coming promptly at eight thirty each morning to ring the bell for fifteen minutes to call the children to school. (Mr. Carter did not mention that, up until this time, this had been one of his own duties; David found that out much later.)

Dr. Arthur said yes, two dollars could, each quarter.

ABSOLOM CARTER found a room for David. This was in the home of a Mrs. Farleigh, whose husband had been kicked in the head by a horse and killed two years before. She lived on New Hartford Street, just three blocks from the school.

David's scattered early impressions in his Line-a-Day diary: "So big. Lots of blubber. You have to be careful passing her on the stairs." "Pads around all day in rabbit-fur slippers." "Very fussy about room, troubles me about lint under bed." "Hovers over me like a big pea hen." And once just the single eloquent word, "Faugh."

But as the weeks passed and David began to get his first taste of his lifelong sensation of exile, and as, later, academic difficulties piled up and he plunged into a period of desperate homesickness, the negative comments began to give way to quite a different series of responses. "Big body big heart." "She makes molasses cakes for me." "Good old thing."

In reality not so very old; she seems to have been in her mid-thirties, and it may have been that the constant proximity of David's now splendidly handsome young frame had rather painfully softened her toward him. Finally, as the winter stretched on, we come on this: "She has the rheumatiz. Asks me to rub her upper arm. It soothes her. She reads to me, or quizzes me for school on nominative genitive dative accusative ablative, and I gently rub and rub. And rub." Later: "Her whole shoulder is sore affected. Rub-a-dub-dub. I use camphorated oil."

It is during this period that we begin to see the notations about looking around Turcott for "the other woman." In February, this strange note: "Sometimes I wonder about Mrs. Farleigh." Could it be that he was working it out that *she* might have been the other mother? Mrs. Farleigh was, at any rate, sharply different from his own real mother: chubby, chatty, immensely cheerful, a casual churchgoer, at times bawdy in speech, a lover of juicy foods, a witty lady with "a laugh that rolls like a round rock," even-tempered, overflowing from corsets, pink, fragrant, and "comfortable as a wood stove in Feb."

ABSOLOM CARTER taught anything and everything in the "academic" course at Enderbury, but on David Treadup he made in particular three powerful impressions:

FIRST

Indispensable for a young man who would one day tackle Chinese, Absolom taught David the tricks and joys of learning languages.

The two dealt simultaneously in Latin, Greek, and French—hard for David, like trying to carry three buckets of milk into the shed at once. David indeed had to juggle and struggle, and much later Greek and Latin were to prove heavy going for him. But in these two years Carter made the triple task seem like three delightful games to be won.

He showed David how to set up vocabulary cards; taught him how to mold the shapes of exotic sounds with conscious positioning of the tongue in the mouth and throat; gave the three systems of grammar organic lives, causing them to seem like the bone structure lying under the muscles of meaning; trained David to think from beginning to end in the new languages; and wove around each of them the mythology, the history, the poetry, the temperament of the race of men and women that used the language.

"I would carry my thrills back each evening to Mrs. Farleigh," David wrote in the mourning letter to Paul.

> *I sometimes actually wept, and caused her to weep, at the excitement of discoveries. Mr. C. told me he thought one of the most beautiful words in Greek was ανεμοεντα [anemoenta], "windy." I made the connection to Mrs. Farleigh that night that he had demonstrated an anemometer a few days before—the wind-measuring instrument with little whirling cups. Then I cried. I had remembered my mother's favorite flower—the anemone—always since then, mine, too. The wind-flower!*

SECOND

Like Maud Chase, Absolom kept urging books on the boy, and one day he
put in David's hand a worn leather-bound volume that turned out to be the
most influential book of David's life next to the Bible: Benjamin Franklin's
Autobiography.

Diary scribbles at first tell how David relished Franklin's stories of
his printing apprenticeship to his brother, his frugal trip to Philadelphia,
his start on his own there; and especially of his later inventions, so off-
handedly described. But we encounter an excitement we have never seen
before in David's writing—the hand actually trembles—when he reacts to
Part Two, coming on Franklin's "bold and arduous Project of arriving at moral
Perfection."

Soon the diary reveals that David has copied out the thirteen names of
Franklin's virtues, and their accompanying precepts, and that he has ruled a
little notebook with red ink, making a calendar of thirteen weeks, with lines
for each of the virtues in each of the days of the week, and he has begun to
keep score of his lapses.

Unfortunately the notebook did not survive. But we do know from his
diary that the precept for the thirteenth virtue, Humility, troubled David
so much that he went to Mr. Carter about it, for it adjured: *Imitate Jesus
and Socrates.* How could there be an equivalence between Jesus and anyone else?

Wonderful!—and shocking! The young teacher gave David a translation
of Plato's dialogues, so David could watch the living Socrates. He also told
David about other heathen authors' lists of virtues and ways of enhancing
them, in Xenophon's *Memorabilia* and Aristotle's *Ethics,* among others; and
he had David read translations of some of Plutarch's *Lives,* from which
secular human values could be learned by example.

All this David carefully noted down. But his response to Franklin's
urgings turned out to be of a special and lasting kind. The reason for this was
perhaps to be found in what Dr. Fosco, more clearly than Carter, saw in
David: his ambition. For Franklin's project was less in how to be good than in
how to get ahead by being good. But the agnostic Carter's instinct in giving
David this extracurricular course in ethics was to bear fruit: Something
skeptical, temporal, and sophisticated would stay with David all his life—
and would give him difficulties as a missionary.

THIRD

Absolom made the laws of physics magical. Each day he would shut himself
for half a minute into the classroom closet; then he would burst out in cape,

top hat, and false mustache, and with a wand in hand. He would appoint a scholar as his assistant. Then, as if drawing silk scarves from nowhere, or materializing rabbits, he would flourish through a scientific demonstration — a hardboiled egg sucked through the narrow neck of a milk bottle by the partial vacuum set up inside the bottle by a candle flame; iron filings, randomly scattered on a paper on which two foolish faces had been drawn, suddenly scurrying to form fringes of whiskers on the faces at the approach from beneath of a magnet; a double pendulum, hinged halfway down, hung from the ceiling and set swinging in two directions, so that a tiny pen at its lower end would describe intricate diminishing curves — "harmonics" — on a piece of paper, like the delicate networks of curlicues on printed money.

"Abracadabra!" Mr. Carter would shout at each moment of revelation.

David loved best the wonders Absolom performed with a sparkling little gyroscope, which could dance on a string, or rise from the dead, or quickly stabilize a little vessel rocking in a galvanized tub of a sea.

TWO MAIDEN sisters named Packard taught at the school. One morning Miss Agnes, the school's Preceptress, who presided over the study hall, returned to that room after a brief absence to find her desk strangely aslant. One leg had been propped up on a little wooden box. She summoned the janitor. He and three big boys lifted the desk while another boy removed the box. A natural curiosity led Agnes Packard to lift the lid of the box. A toad jumped out.

ONE MORNING Miss Mary Packard nearly fainted when, in the midst of an algebra lesson, a human skeleton, hanging by the neck from a rope, slowly ascended into the sky outside her classroom window. She sent a boy to summon the janitor and a girl to fetch a bottle of smelling salts from the principal's office. On investigation, the janitor discovered the skeleton (filched from the closet of the science room) sitting on the ground, leaning back against the building. It had been let down by a very trig block and tackle, which had evidently been attached the night before to the mansard up above. It goes without saying that no one was to be found manning the fall of the tackle.

THERE CAME a day, several stunts later, when Absolom Carter learned that Dr. Arthur was on the point of dismissing from the school that unmanageable hulk of a farm boy, David Treadup. He had been caught hot-handed at one of his games. He had cut a rectangle from the cardboard cover of his history textbook and had glued in its place a small mirror and while pretending to study had been flashing reflected sunlight into the faces of girls. After an ordeal of two hours of what Dr. Arthur called "soul search," Treadup had confessed to the whole string of pranks. Once again the boy found himself in the hands of a volunteer defense lawyer.

Mr. Carter respectfully reminded Dr. Arthur, first of all, of the statement in the *Enderbury Institute Handbook,* that the school's discipline would be "strict and impartial yet exercised with kindness, and with a view to incite in the student a noble self-reliance and control."

Next he pleaded that he himself was "partly to blame," if indirectly, for these practical jokes, because Treadup had been applying, one by one, laws of physics and mechanics that Mr. Carter had "taught him too well" in science class: the law of leverage, enabling one person alone to lift Agnes Packard's desk, the technique of overcoming large resistance with small force in the levitation of the skeleton with tackle, and so on.

Mr. Carter argued that "this young ox," accustomed to heavy physical labor at home, simply had not the means in the normal school day of discharging the millions of ergs of his energy. He had heard tell of the young man's rowing wherry. Treadup, he told Dr. Arthur, should be punished by being ordered to fetch the boat from home on a wagon, and being made to row it for two hours every afternoon on Turcott Creek, below the dams.

This Dr. Arthur with a stormy brow commanded David to do.

David obeyed with utter delight. In the great joy of manning his sweeps again, he was able to throw off not only the habit of prankishness but also the homesickness and sadness he had been feeling.

IF THE CRISIS that had led to the osteomyelitis was a species of mild breakdown, his convalescence in his first year at Turcott took all of his inner attention. With his full recovery in his second year, and as Absolom Carter's teaching gave him competence and confidence, he moved into a period of enormous vitality and exuberance.

Despite his later claim that after his illness he "took a renewed interest in the Christian life," his diary notes at the time and his letters home (he was less than twenty miles from the farm, but telephones were not yet available to poor people like the Treadups and Mrs. Farleigh, so he wrote every Saturday to his parents) seem to suggest, as much by omission and indirection as by assertion, that the future missionary was going through a decidedly arid period in his spiritual life.

On the physical side, however, he was vibrantly alive. He was now a splendid pillar of flesh: six feet four inches tall, with a cask of a chest, huge hands, and a face that might have been marred by an oversized jaw and a fullish nose had it not been that his flashing, burning dark eyes gave out such open beams of interest and friendliness.

David soon got his first glimpse of a mysterious magnetic pull on others which his splendid physique and high spirits evidently gave him. This came to him as an astonishment.

IN A BRIGHT flowery week of June, as he approached the age of twenty, David attended his first Epworth League district convention at the lake resort of Silver Bay.

The program of the convention consisted of a mixture of discussion sessions, prayer meetings, outdoor games, campfire parties, and, woven through everything else, a mock parliamentary process that was supposed to lead to a series of "life resolutions" on the final day, as if the conferees were delegates to an international congress of morality.

But David's diary notes seem to have nothing at all to do with Christianity: "Played third base, handled two grounders!" "Hit a triple this aft!" "After hymn sing walked by lake with N.T.!" " 'Jack o' Knaves' Furman has asked me to be his campaign manager in the convention elections!" "N.T.—*la belle dame sans mercy* [sic]!"

A letter to his family announces the great surprise that has come to him:

Wait till I tell you what happened today! After the plates were cleared away from the noon meal we set up the chairs for the Committee of the Whole in the big dining room, and Mr. Clarendon called us to order for the Big Vote for Officers of the Convention. I was backing a fine chap from Sodus name of Jack Furman for Pres. He is a tenor—and can he pitch an outcurve! There were two other nominations. Then an Oswego boy Charlie Dubb got up and—jehosaphat—I couldn't believe my ears— I had no idea!—he said, "I nominate David Treadup the Delegate from Salt Branch." And Mom and Dad he said some things that would have made your ears burn to hear them about your son. Now I thought that's all very well but now we have to count noses so don't go a-counting chicks too soon. But wait! wait! Treadup 43, Furman 8, Cheshire 4, Hendry 3. I swan! To think that so many people respected me! I was so flabbergasted I couldn't speak. I was as red as a beet. Think what this means, Mom and Dad. There is nothing I can't do.

IN FEBRUARY of David's second year at Enderbury, the U.S.S. *Maine* was blown up by a submarine mine in Havana harbor, and what followed, colored for David by Absolom Carter's "great enthusiasm," stirred up in this restless and rudderless young man his first urge to "take up the white man's burden."

Excited scraps in his diary tell us that he suddenly cares about liberty for the Cubans, that Mr. Carter has given him Admiral Mahan's book on sea power, that he thrills to Hoban's attempt to sink the collier *Merrimac* so as to block Santiago harbor. The message gets through to Garcia! "You may fire when ready, Gridley!" "Don't cheer, boys, the poor fellows are dying!" The Rough Riders have left their horses in Florida! McKinley the hesitant cannot decide for a long time which Philippine Islands to annex; then David records that the President has told a delegation of Methodists he has finally decided to "take them all and to educate the Filipinos, and uplift and civilize and Christianize them." The sense of America's inescapable destiny of exporting her blessings to all who might be wanting was in the air David breathed. Puerto Rico annexed.... Hawaii annexed.... Later he records, with approval embedded in the act of copying it out, a protest of McKinley's against the anti-imperialist outcries of Cleveland, Bryan, Gompers, William James, Mark Twain, and others: "No imperial designs lurk in the American mind. They are alien to American sentiment, thought, and purpose.... If we can benefit these remote people, who will object?"

In all of David's reactions at this stage there is a boyish enthusiasm, reflecting Absolom Carter's manly one—a tendency to whoop. Right after his notice of Congress's declaration of war against Spain, he sets down the words of a song that is "all the rage":

> *When you hear dem-a bells go ding, ling, ling,*
> *All join round and sweetly you must sing,*
> *And when the verse am through*
> *In the chorus all join in:*
> *There'll be a hot time in the old town tonight!*

BY THE END of that second year at Enderbury, there were at least three people who shared with David the conviction that there would be nothing he could not do—provided he went on to college. They were Absolom Carter; Dr. Arthur, the Enderbury principal; and Dr. Fosco. Each of them spoke to David, separately, urging him to go on. Syracuse, which was a Methodist institution and was not far away from home, seemed the logical choice, and in the spring of 1899, not long before he was twenty-one, David did apply. Don Treadup, again joining the band of angels, said he would bank the lad for whatever he could not earn on his own. Brownson and Hannah Treadup were apparently baffled and dismayed by the pretension of their farmboy son, but in the American way they could only support and applaud.

ENTRANCE into Syracuse, as into any American university, was no light matter at the turn of the nineteenth into the twentieth century. To get in, David Treadup would have to present evidence of having passed examinations

in Greek (grammar, composition, oral and written sight translation; three
books of the *Anabasis* and either three books of the *Iliad* or four of the
Odyssey); Latin (grammar, comp, and sight reading; the first four books of
Caesar, six of Cicero's *Orations,* six books of the *Aeneid,* ten of Virgil's
Eclogues); English (general knowledge of the authors' lives and subject
matter of certain texts: Scott's *Abbott,* Shakespeare's *Merchant of Venice,*
Irving's *Sketch Book,* Longfellow's *Evangeline,* Macaulay's *Essay on Addison,*
and readings from the *Spectator*); Greek, Roman, and American history;
mathematics (algebra through quadratics, including radicals; plane geometry;
ratio, logarithms, the binomial formula); and science (physics, physical geography, and one of botany, physiology, or zoology).

In setting these requirements, Syracuse was pretty much following
the national pattern. As to science and modern languages, the university
was relatively conservative. At Harvard one could enter with either Greek
or Latin; Columbia, Yale, and some other colleges were beginning to require
French or German. Williams, Stanford, Yale, and Harvard required trigo-
nometry, which Syracuse did not. Shortly before David applied, Chancellor
James Roscoe Day made a statement about a mild revision of the Syracuse
curriculum:

> While holding firmly to the classical course and making it possible to extend
> studies in this direction farther than ever, we have opened out to students
> lines of suited or special aptitudes in philosophy, science, and literature.
> It is our endeavor to fit the courses to the students rather than the stu-
> dents to the courses. We offer one hundred and twenty-five variations thus
> giving . . . the possibility of pursuing a line for which one is evidently
> fitted. . . .

Modifications like these in all American colleges presaged the overwhelming
flood of new scientific and technological knowledge of the coming years,
which would eventually erode the classical learning to the vanishing point.
But Syracuse was so far "holding firmly to the classical course" because it
was thought that American youth should realize that modern Western civilization had admirable ancient roots.

This—with a reverse twist—was indeed to be the significance for the
future missionary of his classical studies: Those studies would have prepared
him to export "modern civilization" to a foreign country without having
revealed to him the fact that that country, too, had a civilization of its own,
with deep roots in its own classical literature. David's ignorance of Chinese
history, culture, and daily life, when he set out for his life's mission, was to be
both appalling and unexceptional. The eventual irony was to be that a band of
Westerners trained in their classics, David Treadup (though rather weakly)
among them, would abet and applaud as China abandoned its civil examination system, abandoned largely the classical Chinese written language, the

wen-li, and opened up to the populace a vulgate language—a process without which China's rush to join the "advanced" nations of the world would probably not have come as soon as it did.

DAVID'S diary note just after he had taken the New York State Regents' examinations at the end of his time at Enderbury said: "I struck the math and physics hard, survived in Eng. lit, barely passed L, think I flunked G." Eventually word came that he had passed even Greek. That he had been able to meet the requirements in Latin and Greek, even barely, after only a year and a half of study was remarkable testimony, not only to the mettlesome capacity for hard work of a youth of that time, but also to the fusion of David's gifts with those of his artful young mentor, Absolom Carter. Much later in Treadup's career there would come, as well, a dramatic fusion of his and Carter's styles and methods.

SYRA–SYRA–SYRA
WAH–HOO–WAH

"THE FALL of '99, I entered Syracuse University, poorly prepared but determined to make something of myself."

Syracuse at the turn of the century was a small denominational school, like so many private American colleges and universities which by mid-twentieth century were to become largely secularized. There were a few more than two hundred students, about two-to-one male to female, in David's class.

The university capped a then bleak hill, its buildings evoking the cultural aspirations of a faraway Europe of a distant past. The centerpiece was the baroque Hall of Languages, built of stones of two colors and partly covered with ivy. Behind it, a bit to the west, stood the gymnasium, as Gothic as a temple of sweat could hope to be, of dark brick, with high windows. Also to the west was the university library, later to become the administration building. Farther still to the west and south, on another rise overlooking the city, was the dark Gothic cathedral-like spire of Crouse College, in which Fine Arts were housed. Wooden walkways, some of them dilapidated, ran between these buildings. There were no trees to speak of. In a muddy depression called the Oval, sports contests were held. To the southeast of the Hall of Languages

were tracts of meadowland, the hay from which was sold each year to support
the university budget.

Syracuse was Methodist. On the top floor of the Hall of Languages, at
the crown of the castle, radiating its influence over the campus, was the
chapel. There every midmorning the students gathered to sing and pray. For
the past five years the university had been presided over with dictatorial
benevolence by a huge-bodied, large-voiced Methodist minister, James Roscoe
Day, previously pastor of Calvary Church in New York City. At his inauguration
he had said that Syracuse

> is to be a Christian university, with a mission emphasized by that fact,
> something superior to the state or secular school in its moral atmosphere
> and equal to it in its curriculum and work. But it is to be a Christian
> university upon the broad foundation of Christ's Christianity, which wel-
> comes men and does not exclude them. It is to be far more Christian than
> denominational. . . . It will be a university Christian enough to make a
> Hebrew as much at home as a Christian; to afford equal facility to Catholic
> and Protestant.* There is no creed in mathematics or in natural science.
> Syracuse University will be a brain manufactory, taking its material from all
> sources of usable brains. It will be Christian not by exclusion, not by
> magnifying a sect, but by magnifying human learning and contributing to
> the same.

The style of this brain manufactory was flamboyantly "collegiate."
Freshmen wore demeaning green caps. Sophomores carried canes. Greek-
letter fraternities and sororities dominated college social life—and occasion-
ally the city newspapers noted with disapproval the forcible entry of male
students into a sorority. Victories in sports called for parades and bonfires.
Hard-fought football games were followed by bitter recriminations and broken-
off relations—from Colgate when David entered, from Cornell two years later.
Each day after chapel students lingered in the corridors of the Hall of
Languages singing class and college anthems and popular songs: "*Quod
Libet,*" "Bingo," "Go Down, Moses," "Ten Little Indians," "Peter Gray." Outdoors there were tugs of war and pranks. The favorite entertainment was a
curious form of party called a "literary," or "lit"—"a strange combination of
the corn-husking, Irish wake, and horning party."

---

*In Syracuse admissions policy up to that time, the phrase "a Hebrew" had been more
accurate than Chancellor Day evidently wanted it to sound; nor had there been much more
"facility" for the Catholic. A few years before David's matriculation, the Syracuse *Annual*
interviewed 132 students and found that of those who declared religious connections, 61
were Methodists, 8 Presbyterians, 8 Congregationalists, 6 Baptists, 5 Episcopalians,
5 Seventh-day Adventists, and 2 Lutherans; and one each of Universalist, Unitarian, Evangelical Lutheran, Jew, and Roman Catholic.

In his first months the hayseed David Treadup threw himself into all these callithumpian doings with a whole heart—and nearly to the point of disaster.

D A V I D ' S first letter home is taken up entirely with the "salt rush," a ritual annual free-for-all that had had its origin in Syracuse's parent institution, Genesee College. The foremost industry of the city of Syracuse in the nineteenth century was its Onondaga salt works, and the custom developed at Genesee of "salting" the new students by sprinkling the first-year benches in chapel, one day early in the year, with salt, the aim being to take the freshness out of the freshmen. Later at Syracuse the technique of the ritual was improved on: Salt was rubbed in the yearlings' hair. Of course the victims fought back, and eventually the exercise became a formalized melee. David wrote:

> I don't know where the word came from—it got round like a snake in the grass—today was Salt Rush day. The entire student body was all a-whisper during chapel. Chancellor Day shouted his prayers and frowned up a storm. The second we were dismissed, all we Frosh and the Sophs—men, I mean—dashed helter-skelter down the stairs of the Hall of Languages, the Juns and Sens and all the women behind us, and ran round back of Crouse College, where the Sophs formed up a ring at the crest of the knoll, and we formed a circle lower down.
>
> Then they began taunting us, making mewling sounds, crybabying, shouting "Nyaaa! Nyaaa!" and calling out in unison a parody of one of our class yells:
>
> > Syra-Syra-Syra
> > Wah-Hoo-Wah
> > Oughty-three, oughty-three,
> > I want my ma!
>
> The upperclassmen were egging us on, too, and the ladies were watching. I'll tell you something, Ma and Da, I felt really small. Remember how I confessed once how the bullies in the bakery at S.B. both frightened me yet I also worshiped them? Up there the Sophs seemed like the bakery boys. They were Syracuse men. We were babes and rubes. I truly hung back.
>
> But some Freshmen I don't know—there's a certain click of cronies who stand out for breaking Frosh rules—they burst into class songs without waiting for the upperclassmen to finish—they carry canes—they smoke pipes on campus—now they gave out a whoop and they charged, and we all felt we had to follow. And when we got up there,

well, those Sophs were just young fellows like us, and I suddenly realized I may be David but I'm Goliath, too. I had some salt thrown at me, but no Soph was going to pickle my scalp I tell you. I had my shirt torn but no bruises. Just as many Sophs as Frosh wound up with shiners and nosebleeds and split cheeks.

It was all over in fifteen minutes, a senior blew a whistle and the Sophs all sang "Orange" and then their spokesman invited us to boxing and wrestling in the gym in the P.M. and a reception at the Y.M.C.A. in the evening. Do you want to know something? I didn't even go to the fisticuffs. Just because I'm big and strong doesn't mean I want to become a bakery boy. But the reception, in fact the whole Salt Rush, made me feel like a Syracuse man.

A few days later Hannah Treadup answered her son's letter:

That you should have waited three long weeks to write us about your new life, and then that you should regale us with nothing but tribal warfare and mob rule came as a painful surprise to your parents. Your father is making a great sacrifice of sinew and sweat for your sake, and you are up there hooliganizing. For shame. It is time to fit your brain to the proportions of your body, son David.

GOLIATH had been noticed. The morning after the salt rush, after chapel, two seniors stopped David on the stairs of the Hall of Languages and solicited his meat for football.

"Declined," David's diary laconically announces.

The decision was not as offhand as that single word would make it seem. David had other plans, no less ambitious—for he held up always before himself the ideal of the thinker-athlete, on the model of Absolom Carter. The first football game of the autumn led to a procession and victory bonfire. "Roman splendors!" David wrote in his diary; but then added: "Still glad I held out for the Navy." In a letter home in the winter David told his family he missed his lovely wherry ("she must be all dried out in the barn"), but it was all right because "there's big talk about a new sport up here."

Early in 1899, Chancellor Day, as much a promoter as a preacher, had convened at the Yates Hotel in the city a meeting which founded the Lake Side Yacht and Boat Club and made plans for building an $18,000 boathouse on the west side of Onondaga Lake. Named as commodore was Lyman Cornelius Smith, proprietor of the L. C. Smith Typewriter Company. A city newspaper next day revealed the chancellor's motive:

Onondaga Lake offers an excellent place for rowing, and there is no reason why Syracuse University shouldn't train a crew on Onondaga Lake as well as Cornell University on Cayuga Lake.

Students cheered and whistled when, four days after the meeting, the chancellor announced in chapel that L. C. Smith was donating an eight-oared shell to the university. At once the students formed what they called the Navy and began discussing tryouts, and whether to adopt the Yale or Cornell style of rowing. Mr. Smith went to Ithaca to interview the great Charles Courtney, who had retired from sculling in 1883 (amateur: 88 wins, 0 defeats; professional: 39 wins, 7 defeats) to train the Cornell rowers and become the preeminent crew coach of his era (eventual record: 146 races, 101 firsts). Courtney stressed, among other things, the need for a rowing machine, to train rowers on dry land before putting them in a shell. Dr. Day soon announced that a university trustee was donating such a machine, and L. C. Smith added two four-oared gigs to his previous gift. And soon afterward the Athletic Board chose as football coach a Cornell graduate, Edwin Sweetland, who had starred at Ithaca in football, baseball, track, and crew — and who, being a Courtney product, would coach the Navy David's first spring at Syracuse.

JUDGING by the exclamation points in David's diary, what caused him the most giddy turmoil in his first weeks at Syracuse was being in the daily presence of a large number of women. Mores, death, taboos, pranks, and God were curiously intermixed in his telegraphic notes about flirtations — God being mentioned at this period mainly as someone who would help choose and soften the right woman.

Syracuse had been coeducational from its founding in 1870. With a liberality rare then in American higher education, Syracuse had laid down the organic law that "admission shall be equal to all persons" — giving notice in the use, a century early, of that word "persons," that it was "the clear and well defined purpose of the trustees," as Dr. Jesse T. Peck said in his inaugural charge to the founding faculty, "that there shall be no invidious discriminations here against women."

There was a strong undercurrent of dissent, however, among Syracuse alumni and male students, often expressed in the campus paper, *The University Herald*: Woman's duty was to her husband and children; her feminine charm was blunted and hardened by campus life; her imperviousness to advanced learning, especially in science, was notorious. Undergraduate men apparently felt inferior to the masculine populations of Yale and Princeton, two rival institutions much on the minds of Syracuse males. And within the university there were distinctions, perhaps best summed up by the fact that of seventy-six women who received undergraduate degrees when David graduated six years later, fifty-one took "certificates" in education, fine arts, and nursing. Except for the important Y.W.C.A., most mainline undergraduate activities were male. Women's sports were somehow not "serious": David saw the ladies' basketball team trot out, like Florodora girls, smothered in yard goods — in bloomers and blouses of white piped in orange, with great orange sashes, and with long capes trimmed in orange which fluttered behind the runners on the court.

But women were all around, and David was huge and handsome, and choices were possible. The goal of flirtation was both forbidden and always there, like the heavy scent of honeysuckle in June. "Andrews told story," David wrote in his diary, in the closest approach to smut ever recorded in it, "about a mother calling downstairs to ask her daughter if her fellow was there yet. Daughter answered, 'He is getting there quite fast.'" David never speaks of "girls" in his diary; they are "ladies," and their surnames, always preceded by "Miss," come and go. Here, for an example — often repeated, with variations of casting — is a triangular drama working itself out:

> OCT. 18 *Miss McNair proposed that she get some music for piano and cornet. I told her she might. She seems to be warm after me!*
>
> 20 *Had sport with Miss Roberts at supper table . . .*
>
> 22 *Finished reading [Emerson's] "Friendship," which Miss Roberts lent me. This loan has doubtless strengthened my friendship with her!*
>
> 23 *Returned Miss Roberts's book had pleasant chat . . .*
>
> 24 *Pleasant chat as usual . . .*
>
> 26 *Thinking about starting in company with Miss R!*
>
> 27 *A junior by name of Knight drowned in Ond Lake. Somewhat troubled in mind about lady affairs. Been with Miss Roberts at game.*
>
> 28 *The body of Mr. Knight was recovered this morning.*
>
> 30 *Bought tickets for Sousa's band. $1.50. Was disappointed in getting the lady I wanted. Engaged Miss McNair for the evening. It was the finest entertainment I ever heard! Arthur Prior played a trombone solo. Miss McNair seemed much pleased to have my company. I put a good joke on Platzer!*
>
> NOV. 3 *Miss Roberts is going to leave our dining circle. This seems sad to me. It is doubtless God's plan.*
>
> 4 *Went to gym in P.M. Saw Miss Roberts from a distance.*
>
> 5 *Not feeling up to snuff.*

A later sequence with another lady suggests stages beyond book lending, though of course the word used in it, "climax," can hardly be expected to bear the weight of the euphemism it later became:

> NOV. 20 *Stayed with Miss Blain [not clear where] until after eleven. At this point in my life I find that I must trust everything to God who will surely open the best way.*

24 *Called on Miss Blain.*

25 *Was with Miss Blain until a quarter of eleven.*

26 *Was with Miss Blain until twelve. The climax was reached. We
found that we were good friends but nothing more. I was
ashamed that I proceeded by desire as I did, but feel that I did
the manly thing.*

IN OCTOBER David achieved university-wide notice, not of the best kind.

Male upperclassmen carried canes; freshmen, who were not regarded as grown men, were not supposed to do so. Each autumn some freshmen would flaunt canes, often silver-headed ones to underline their daring. And each autumn, in yet another symbolic combat in the sophomore-freshman rivalry, a "cane rush" was held, in which the second-year men challenged the fledglings' right to the sticks. This contest, like the salt rush, had become formalized over the years. It had been scheduled ahead of time, and when the opponents, who had discarded hats, coats, and vests, lined up in two facing teams twenty feet apart, their audience included a fair number of alumni, wearing high stiff collars and top hats. The referee, a senior, tossed a single cane between the two lines, and the two classes dashed to fight for it. Soon there were many scattered clusters of writhing combatants, trying to keep their opponent from going to the support of those actually struggling for possession of the cane. As the *Herald* later reported,

> The yearling Treadup, a bull of a fellow, managed to keep his feet and remain unengaged. Perhaps no soph wanted to try muscles with such a Fafnir. At the right moment he put two fingers in his mouth and emitted a whistle to split a rock. At this signal a fellowclassman in the actual cane heap succeeded in flipping the cane out to Treadup, who put his long legs into action, bouncing sophs off as if they were puppy dogs, and he ran with the cane held aloft all the way off campus to University Place. The frosh were judged to have won for the first time in memory.

The congratulations David received from both men and women were redoubled after Chancellor Day in chapel the next morning delivered a sharp little sermon on public roughhousing, which was also reported in the paper:

> We do not wish to threaten. We do not like to be threatened ourself, and hence imagine that others do not like to be threatened. But we do insist that every feature of this barbarous custom of campus warfare, open to the view of the public, shall be strictly forbidden. Any future violation will be disciplined by suspension and probably by expulsion. I trust I shall not

be forced into a contest with the students, for [great emphasis] I will see every seat before me vacant before I will vary a hair's breadth from my position. And in a contest I have a habit of winning. [Laughter.]

IN THE NEXT few days:

 • Wooden sidewalks were found ripped up and leaning against nearby posts.
 • A wagon straddled the peak of the gymnasium roof.
 • A country outhouse stood one morning in front of the Hall of Languages.
 • Benches from Professor Clark's room in the Hall of Languages were arranged in rows on Walnut Street, and the Reverend Dr. Wilbur found Professor Clark's desk on his front lawn.
 • As the chancellor prayed in chapel "for the college, the nation, President McKinley and the Senate, the cause of Christianity and good government throughout the world, and the parents of students who in distant homes are watching with anxious eyes the struggles of their loved ones," there were rustling sounds from near the organ, and a large poster rose slowly behind Dr. Day: a drawing unmistakably of the chancellor's great head atop a tiny body which stood on a prostrate student holding a beer bottle and a corncob pipe in his outstretched hands.

WAS DAVID involved in these pranks? We have no way of knowing; his diary grows unusually discreet in this period. Earlier and later entries divulge that Professor Clark was his least favorite teacher. The lofted wagon does have in it a resonance of Absolom Carter's lecture on overcoming large resistance with small force. At any rate, when the final caper of the series took place—a rather unpleasant nighttime splurge of vandalism in the city, resulting in broken streetcar windows and splashes of orange paint on monuments and buildings—David was one of four students who were caught in the act.

The probationary warning the quartet received next morning from Dr. Day seared itself into David's mind for a lifetime. In his diary there is only one laconic line:

NOV. 5 Believe I must begin to apply myself.

THIS PERIOD of rebelliousness, like that of his seventeenth year, was the forerunner of a winter of low spirits almost as severe as the melancholy that went with his osteomyelitis. Only many years later did David begin to see that episodes of his "badness" signaled major downswings of mood. What proved to be remarkable was that for such a very long time after his conversion there were to be no such downturns; for years on end there would be only rare outcroppings of "badness," and he would remain everlastingly buoyant and radiant. But now the hero of the cane rush fretted and was irritable and anxious.

He became acutely aware of his poverty. This was a time in the country of boom and bluster, of McKinley and gold and the trusts, of Standard Oil and Anaconda and railroad monopolies, of the Rockefeller and Harriman and Carnegie fortunes; and while Syracuse was not as much a seat of privilege as some of the older eastern universities, money-making possibilities seemed dense all around David. "Chancellor Day preached on a text from Luke 12," David writes in his diary.

> *Eat, drink, and be merry: rich toward God. The rightness of getting wealth if our object is to benefit others. Investment in attaining wealth, health, and spiritual growth. Moody's career. The dissatisfaction after attaining worldly goods.*

But David's dissatisfaction, so far, was with *not* having attained them. Scraping along drained his energies. He wore himself out with the striving and frugality of Ben Franklin, only to find himself in meaner and meaner straits.

> *JAN. 12* [1900] *Platzer found a place where I can get a room for attending a furnace. Bought rubbers 80¢.*
> *14 Disgusted with geom. teacher. Afraid I will fail the math exam. Carried out ashes at Leonard's and Smith's. Paid .24 for laundry.*
> *15 Shoveled walks in the morning. . . .*
> *16 Cleaned Dr. L's walk. Cleaned walks at Univ. 2 hrs.*
> *17 Not feeling extra well. . . .*
> *18 3 hrs. work for Curtis. . . .*
> *19 4 hrs. Curtis. Went skating at Lake. 2½ Curtis evening.*
> *20 . . . Had trouble during night.*

There is no mention of the promised support from Uncle Don Treadup. It may be that by that time David had absorbed his mother's stubborn pride about taking money from the quirky relative; or perhaps the mercurial Uncle Don had lost interest in the little giant, little no more. In early February David writes home, significantly appealing to his father through his mother:

> *Would you ask Da to send me twenty dollars as soon as he can spare it so I can finish this term? I had to buy a pair of shoes $2.00, then the apparatus and material I have had to get in botany class raise the amount until it scares me. I have worked harder this term than ever in*

my life. Prof. Curtis gives me chores. I have adopted the habit of getting up in the morning at half past five which helps some. Gloves cost 50¢.

The diary records the begrudging result:

FEB. 10 Classes as usual. Rcd. letter from Father. Grandma was buried last Sunday. Said he sold my cow for $35. Only sent me $15 of it. Andrus tells me he is $300 in debt.

David's blithe autumn trip through the rites of passage into Syracuse manhood was now belatedly collecting its ticket. He was taking advanced algebra, Greek (Lysias, Plato, Demosthenes), Latin (Livy, Juvenal), German, Roman history, elocution, and botany. "The German hard for me. Took C in exam." "The new German book Sappio very hard." "I feel the need of a larger vocabulary to express more accurately my thoughts." "Elocution at 8:30. Miss Richards said I had improved, but not enough in my opinion. I am so loud. A windbag." "Was given a cheesing today in Greek, on third *Philippic*. I was mortally wounded by the mockery." To put on a cheesing, a roomful of students stamped on the floor when a classmate showed signs of being unprepared for a recitation. "Eyes very very tired." Gloom and fear hit him after each examination. After German: "My eyes troubling me. Not feeling at all well. Trust in the Lord and it will come out all right in the end." After algebra: "My eyes very weak. Did not study in P.M. Quite blue."

ALL THROUGH late winter and spring David struggled against his blue mood. He clung to the belief that willpower would give him the lift he needed. "Read a piece on happiness," he wrote in his diary. "I am going to try and stop thinking so much on my ills and failings and take a brighter view of everything."

He started a new commonplace book, with dated entries, into which he copied passages from books of the mind-cure literature that was much in vogue just then—works in an American vein astonishingly similar in intent, though dissimilar in content, to some of the self-help bestsellers of the late twentieth century.

FEB. 2 "Be unselfish; have an ideal outlook, see yourself as you would like to be, healthy, happy, well adjusted to life, helpful, wisely sympathetic, and ever ready with an encouraging word, looking for good, growing strong in wisdom and power, patiently awaiting occasions, yet always sufficiently occupied, so that you will have no time to be annoyed, fearful, restless, or morbid."

The very act of copying in the commonplace book was part of the work of his struggle. Here, in a longer entry in it and a separate note in his diary on the same day, we see the effort he was making to apply the mind-cure homilies:

> *FEB. 12* "*Quicken a man's interest in so-called spiritual things, and you shall find him neglecting his body and the interests of his physical life. . . . Everywhere one finds a want of balance between theory and practice, mind and body, culture and the spirit, the demands of self and the needs of others; between the receiving, accumulating, and developing of property and ideas and the just distribution of that which is rightfully ours only that we may share it. Fragments of men one may find, — good theorists, laborers, and servants. But how far one must search for the well-rounded character, equally sound in mind and body. . . . "*

And the diary:

> *FEB. 12 I have neglected my body. Have rowed a great deal in 'Ecarg' in recent years. Decided to try Navy now. Coach Sweetland says I may compete. Perhaps this will bring a balance.*

TRYING OUT for the crew offered none of the charms of rowing the *Ecarg* on country creeks — none of the dreams of the toy boat in the bathtub of babyhood. David had in fact let himself in for an abysmal spring.

For six weeks he labored indoors on the obstinate and unrewarding rowing machine, getting nowhere, with "Iron Jaw" Sweetland roaring abuse at him. On March 30 the coach sent David and six other freshmen on the squad out in rowboats on the Seneca River to chop away the thin layer of ice that still blocked the outlet to Lake Onondaga. Then David had to wait in the frigid cold while all the upperclassmen in the squad of twenty worked out in turns in one of the four-oared gigs L. C. Smith had donated. David was in the fifth and last seating. He and the others had to wade out through icy water to the gig. With Coach Sweetland shouting instructions on how much to feather the oars and how to be less jerky and stuttering, the freshmen splashed and swashed the half mile to the lake and back, gradually working up to a slow beat of eighteen strokes a minute.

The workouts continued to be nightmarish. The rowers changed clothes in a crude boat shed, open at one end. For baths after workouts they sloshed each other with cold lake water from wooden buckets, screaming as if the water were boiling. With castanet teeth they would dress and run to catch a trolley for the long ride back to the city. The next afternoon they would have to get into still-wet togs.

By early May the Navy men were on the edge of mutiny. After a protest meeting "in a small restaurant sandwiched between a shoe parlor and a saloon," they went to a city reporter to unload their anger. From the Syracuse *Telegram* for May 6:

Not one dollar except the salary of the coach has been spent on the crew this season. The University promised Sweetland that the men would have a training table. The men go out on the water in the early afternoon and do not get back until 8 o'clock at night. It is then too late to get anything more than a lunch at their boardinghouses. In many cases all they can get is a bowl of bread and milk.

Nothing happened. The Athletic Board refused to provide a training table. The last straw for David came in word that after all his slogging work, the Board had scheduled just one race for the Navy for June 15 against the Francis Boat Club of Ithaca, and *freshmen were not to be allowed to compete.* The diary: "Why all the slaving? I feel used and abused."

ON THE MAY MORNING after the last classes and before final exams, the college celebrated Moving Up Day.

This was an occasion of wild joy for the freshmen, who were liberated by it from the oppression of the sophomores, but to David, deeper in the dumps than ever, the cheers and catcalls of his classmates were bewildering and "truly sophomoric," he sarcastically wrote. A ceremony in chapel marked this end forever of classes for seniors, who were virtually alumni now, entitled no longer to pews in chapel. They surrendered their seats to the juniors; the sophomores moved up into the juniors' former seats; the freshmen, hooting and scrambling, took the sophomores' rows; the seniors moved back to the freshman section.

The rest of the day was a holiday, and the freshmen, many dressed and daubed as Indians, paraded to the city, dragging a hearse with a coffin containing their loathed green caps. In the evening they had tugs of war and a bonfire, and someone painted a huge '03 on the grandstand roof in the Oval.

David wrote in his diary:

I tried to join in the general good time. My body was present with the others but my spirit was truant. It all seemed like a huge cheesing to me, and I kept thinking, For David Treadup this is Moving Out Day.

So it proved. David failed both Greek and Latin, and his other grades were barely passing. He was penniless. He was exhausted. He was thoroughly disheartened. On the fourth of June Chancellor Day called him in and, according to the diary,

suggested what he called "a mutual separation." In plain language: dismissal. Remote possibility of re-entry. Who can say now how rotten my life will be?

DROPOUT

THE FLUNKOUT went home from Syracuse. At first his diary entries were masked and heedless, hinting only by their curt brevity at the intensity of his misery. "Plowed all day for Silas Rong." "Helped Mother wash. Helped Father in P.M." "Paul and I went fishing in Clearport. No bites except mosquitoes." "Working for Fred Eastard in wagon shop. Hard."

Suddenly on June 29 there came an abrupt announcement: "Off to N. Bedford." A cousin of Hannah Treadup's named Lloyd Frampton lived in New Bedford, Massachusetts, where he worked as a floorwalker in a dry goods store. David apparently took the initiative for the move, during a visit by Frampton to the Treadups in Salt Branch. Home life, after his dismissal from college, had proved to be tense. Hannah Treadup was sarcastic with a son who had abandoned his parents to overreach at life, and who had then come a cropper—doubtless through malingering and putting on airs. David traveled to Massachusetts with Cousin Lloyd.

June 30, New York City:

We went to the Stock Exchange, crossed the Brooklyn Bridge. I rode on the elevated RR. We took the steamer 'Purallia' at six o'clock for Fall River a sidewheeler very fine in every particular.

For a long time that was all. The diary fell silent.

DAVID TREADUP virtually disappeared from sight. The next two and a quarter years were, he wrote in his "Search," "a black hole in my life. It was as if I had thought I could swim and then found that it took all my strength just to drift and keep my head above water." His ambitious nature could see nothing but failure on the horizon. He could have no way of knowing that this was his dark time of ripening.

His break with his parents was painful for everyone, and letters on both sides were rare, succinct, and bleak. For nearly two years Treadup returned rarely to his diary, and then to record mainly deaths, sexual deprivation, and illness.

One stiff letter home in December 1900—the approach of both Christmas and the new century may have added an attack of homesickness to his other miseries—told his parents that he was working in a bicycle shop. "My boss lauds my work," he wrote, in the requisite stanch tone of Treadup family correspondence (*all's well in a well world*). In view of David's mechanical gifts, the claim was believable. This was, however, small and mean work for a young man who had declared his intention of whipping the world.

"All through that time"—in "Search," again—"I was *in* the world but oblivious to it." For one who was acutely sensitive in later years to the drift of history, this dark period was a time of almost complete indifference to outer movement—a time of abstention. One thing he did record was death:

JAN. *19* [1901] *The Queen of Eng very sick.*
      21 Victoria very low.
      22 Queen still alive in morning. . . . The Queen died at 5:50 P.M.

JAN. *28 A baggage man was killed on William Street just below our shop. I saw him. He was thrown from wagon and struck on curbing. He was taken home dead thirty minutes after he left home.*

SEPT. *7 Stomach knocked out. Eating too rapidly as I have short time for meals. Pres. McKinley was shot by Czolgosz a Pole. He is an anarchist. Pres. very low.*
      8 Went to preaching. President better.
      13 Pres. much worse.
      14 News that the President was dying came at seven. Much excitement during evening. Big crowd at 'Standard' building. Telegram at 1:35 that President might live until 2:00 o'clock. . . . The President passed away at 2:15 this morning.
      15 Went to County St. Church in A.M. Buckley spoke on the Life of McKinley. President's last words: "Nearer my God to thee. Good bye all. Good bye. His will be done."
      17 Dead Pres. taken to Washington. Great crowds all along line.
      19 [This entry is surrounded by ruled lines in black India ink.] Business all closed out of respect to our dead President. Funeral at Canton, O. Robert Raymond delivered the address. He said that McKinley was a man of Fidelity, Kindly Spirit, and a Christian. He was a man who won his way on his merits.

MAY *9* [1902] *Reported that city and 30,000 lives lost in volcanic eruption at island of Martinique West Indies. The city St. Pierre totally destroyed.*
      10 Reports of the Martinique disaster increased to 40,000 lost. . . .

The sexual repression that Calvinism had insisted upon as a rule of being and that Methodism, though more liberal in other ways, rather sternly perpetuated, evidently took its toll on Treadup during that miserable period. In August 1901, after weeks of silence, the diary suddenly burst out in a kind of bewilderment; for the first time Treadup uses the word "girls"—a low species of female, it seems:

> *I am very fond of female company, and admire a 'woman,' but somehow there is but little satisfaction in meeting these N.B. girls.*

Now, from time to time, as he makes sporadic entries, there begins to appear a mysterious small circle opposite certain dates in the diary, even when the lined spaces are left blank. Notes much later make it clear that they were marks of shame. In March 1902, David ends a long silence of the diary with an entry referring to these little circles:

> *I am real well these days. I have not had an ○ for over a month. I am exercising my willpower.*

Before that, all through 1900 and 1901, his reports on his health, suddenly entered in the midst of long empty stretches in the diary were invariably anxious. "Knocked out. Bowels in bad condition." "Did not sleep well last night. Big time in North End. Too much noise for anything. Racket all night. Slept two hours." "Have a cold in my tubes. Applied anti-phlogistic. Am very nearly voiceless." "Not feeling very chirp."

O N E   D E A T H David did *not* record in his diary—it would have meant nothing to him at the time—occurred on June 5, 1900, in Badenweiler, Germany. It was that of a young man of only thirty named Stephen Crane. Many years later, having read *The Red Badge of Courage* during his internment in the Japanese camp, Treadup wrote in one of his notebooks:

> *I wish I'd known something about Crane in that bad time after I flunked out of Syracuse!—he'd come from an even more religious family than mine: father a Methodist minister, mother active in W.C.T.U.—wish I'd known he'd flunked out of Syracuse just like me, just nine years before me. I gather he'd flunked out of Lafayette before that. It would have been a tonic to have known. Because in one way we two were alike: both rebels while we were at Syracuse. But we kicked up our heels in such different ways.—I with my "badness"—breaking things up and throwing things around—whilst he played hooky from the hill and hung around the saloons and brothels down in the city. I wouldn't have dared have that kind of curiosity about the demimonde. But the point is, Crane turned his flunk into success right away—and I didn't have the sand to do that. I just moped. He wrote his 'Maggie' book—how that must have shocked his mother and father—would have shocked me to death. But he did it—and then 'Red Badge' right away when he was only twenty-five! Yes, courage. How dull I was.*

LIKE THAT of a bear regaining its vital signs after a long hibernation, David's big body slowly began in the spring of 1902 to stir out of its long low dormancy. He resumed his diary, at first in snippets and snatches, then finally with its old diurnal pulse. Ambition had apparently started to prick him again. Self-criticism began to be mixed with mind-cure slogans and autosuggestion. "I played cornet at Endeavor. I feel that there is a lack of confidence in my nature." "Cultivate your voice! Use your throat not your nose!" "Hillis in evening. His is a great mind. I shook hands with him. Such lectures make me greatly desire to be a greater man." "Carnegie: 'The rising man must do something exceptional, and beyond the range of his special department. He must attract attention.'" David had saved most of his wages and now even began to spend money. "My new Conn-Queror cornet came! A jim-dandy." "Am having a custom-made suit cut. Paying a good price $17 but believe that will pay."

In April came a letter from his mother that changed everything. In part:

> *A strapping young geezer knocked on the door yesterday. I didn't like the slant way he looked at me. I thought These canvassers are getting to be a nuisance — they'll try to sell you anything — they'll try to sell you your own broom. I was short with him. He said No I ain't selling. He said Does David Treadup live here? I said No. He said Does he live hereabouts? I said What's your business with him? He said I taught him at Enderbury. I said You wasted your time. He said I heard he's throwing his life away, I want him to go back to college.*
>
> *Well at that I couldn't but ask him to stay for dinner. Absolom was his Christian name, I disremember his surname. He thinks there is something 'to' you. He had gone up to Syracuse to ask around about you. He wanted to write to you but I don't believe in giving people people's addresses. I suppose if you wanted you could write him at the school.*

Any letters that Treadup and Carter may have exchanged have been lost, but there is no doubt that David soon was determined to resume his education. "Started in Greek at Kimbal's school. Greatly desire to make up my Greek for college." "Brown University does not require Latin and Greek for entrance to a Phil. course." "Finished reading *David Harum* by Wescott of Syracuse. Commenced *Richard Carvel* by Churchill." Later the reading was more purposeful: Tocqueville's *Democracy in America;* Darwin's *Origin of the Species;* Goethe's *Faust* and *Wilhelm Meister;* Tennyson's *In Memoriam;* Webster's speeches; Renan's *Life of Jesus;* Hegel's *Logic;* Carlyle's *French Revolution* and *Sartor Resartus*. His hankering had its "collegiate" side: "Am hearing about Syracuse ball team through the Boston papers." "I have a good mind to take up the mandolin and try and make the Syracuse club."

A BLINDING LIGHT

ON SEPTEMBER 1, 1902, David Treadup was back on the college hill in conference with Dean Frank Smalley. Treadup's bad time, the long grip of despair, "the black hole in my life," seemed finally to be drawing toward a psychological goal. It had been a hard, dreadful journey into a state of readiness.

THE SESSION with the dean went well. David could be readmitted. Furthermore, he noted in his diary, "Found that by changing my course to science I would not have any 'conditions.'" He could go for a B.S. instead of a B.A. This would mean he could drop the ferocious classical languages. It would also mean that he would come to realize, a decade later in China, that because of his training in science he had something specially valuable to offer as a missionary. He was not sure he ought to take this "easy way." His Methodist conscience and assurance must have told him that with the right will he should be able to master the Greek and Latin. The next day he went to Turcott and asked Absolom Carter for advice. We do not know what David's hero said, but we can guess. David's courses turned out finally to be logic, European history, Spanish (!), solid geometry, chemistry, physics, and drawing.

He ran up the stairs, two at a time, to his first class in the Hall of Languages. "Seems mighty good to be back again." He went to the "Soph Banquet" and not only noted all the toasts but copied the entire menu, down to "macaroons and petit furs." "Ambitious to do the best kind of work. I believe I can take a better place among the men than I could when here before."

But all too soon it began to appear that his high spirits were thin air, that the period of trial was by no means over. The tone of the diary turned darker again, and before long he was in a headlong slide back into melancholy. The first hint, on Sunday, September 21: "Heard Dr. Sims. He spoke on burdens. How they are aids to life." Would it ease the burdens to write that down? His confidence began to ebb. "I find my memory a little slow to retain." "My Math is going to give me more trouble than any other subject." "Up at four A.M. studying. Went to Math. Pesky Math." On Monday, October 6: "I am afraid Monday will be a blue day with me if I do not figure ahead on my work." "Made very near a flunk today." "Math and Chem went sideways."

There is one flash of euphoria in the October notations, but it has to do with an outburst of Treadup's "badness," and we have seen what that signals in his psychic ledger. Although he never tells exactly what happened, there seemed this time to have been a new element in the vandalism: something he encoded as "sentimental excitement." "Went with Miss Bishop to Miss Phillips's room. Private party. Had a hot time in the old town tonight! I broke loose!" But two days later come rue and fear: "It is going to cost me some hard labor to pay for the damage in Miss Phillips's room. If JRD [initials of Chancellor Day] ever found out!" And soon he is writing, "My greatest battles are within." There is a ○ beside this note: "I seem to be sorely tried these days." Is there a new badness? A thought of *cheating?* For he writes: "Chem presented some temptations today."

Altogether: "Am nervous. Wish I could overcome this weakness."

IT WAS at this most unfortunate moment that David fell into a desperate game of hide and seek with a young woman whom David's more experienced classmates would have called "coquettish," or possibly "a kitten." Her name, so far as we know it, was Miss Tenant, and David met her in mid-November.

Even in the weeks of the slide, David had shown signs of delight at the exchange of New Bedford girls for Syracuse women, but he had also suffered a quick letdown, for all his lady friends of freshman year were now seniors, the Misses Roberts, McNair, Blain, and others, and American colleges of those years being as rigidly stratified into classes as was, in another sense, English society, these senior ladies now looked right through the sophomore, even though he was twenty-four years old, older than all of them, and still massive and, because of the imprint of his melancholia on his cheeks and around his eyes, handsomer than ever. So the old transactions of the chase began again: teasing at meals, formal calls, chatting after class, pairings at football games.

The first encounter with Miss Tenant is noted in the diary in a brief sentence garnished with two exclamation points. For almost a month she dominates the entries, and at once we notice that there is none of the joy once associated, for instance, with Miss Roberts. There are no pleasant chats. There are no delicate suggestions made through the loan of books. Instead, there develops a pattern of high hopes followed by sudden letdowns. Miss Tenant is small and fragile, as bewitching and brittle as a Meissen figurine. Between the lines we begin to see that she is physically afraid of the big bear named Treadup, that fear has some kind of aphrodisiac effect on her, and that his presence alternately arouses her and frightens her. She flirts, then disappears; she makes dates, then fails to show up.

On Friday, October 24, after noting that he had "plugged on Conic Sections" during the evening, David writes that he has made an appointment to go up on the hill the next afternoon with Miss T to wait for telegraphic returns on the Syracuse-Yale football game, to be played in New Haven, and he adds: "She is devilish friendly!" The note the following day is painful in its Christian manliness, for his own score equals that of the Syracuse football team:

> *Yale score 24 to 0. Hard luck. Never mind. We will have a chance to redeem ourselves later. No Miss Tenant. Mrs. Barberry said she had left no message.*

She never left a message. David never lost his temper. But a terrible bleakness of a new kind now began to creep into the bulletins on Miss Tenant.

CHRISTMAS vacation at home helped not at all. David's break with his family had never really been healed. His mother ragged him. His father gave him reproachful looks and seldom spoke to him. His dearest friend in the family, older brother Paul, still just a young farmer, stiffened with shame at the sight of David's worldly affectations.

David writes every day in his diary about having written to Miss Tenant but notes no replies. There is a snowfall of O's on the pages of the diary. "Am feeling fagged out. Reading *What a Young Man Ought to Know.*" There are joyless reports of late hours, night after night, in the company of Cassie Berns, with whom he had had such a "bully" time on that twenty-cent church-supper auto ride long before. Compared to Syracuse women, she was a dullard, and it was obvious from his angry jottings that all he wanted of her was a little physical contact, no matter how meaningless—occasional "accidental" bumps and pats.

Back at college in January, Miss Tenant reappears; she "has missed me sore." But again and again she is there, then not there, vanishing like a coin into a magician's assistant's ear. Then David's concupiscence, anxiety, guilt, and sleeplessness quite suddenly collapse into a state of being played out to entropy. Is the mainspring broken? On the last day of January he writes in his diary in capital letters:

> *I NO LONGER CARE.*

DAVID had a friend named Cook. He was a companion of David's freshman year, a senior now. There had been occasional references to "the Christer Cook" in the diary three years back; David had an impression then of a hearty, humorless, googly-eyed young country boy who hero-worshiped big Treadup. Now he was a dandy treasurer of the Young Men's Christian Association, and hero worship of a sort was due *him;* early in the term David had noted, "Cook snoots me." But on February 17 David wrote:

Cook collared me after chapel. Says there is to be a revival starting next week. Wants me to go to the first meeting with him. He says he is praying for me. What bosh!

But three days later there was this cryptic note: "Cook must have noticed." Noticed what? That David was "spiritually parched"—or in other words at the end of his rope? As it turned out, David did not attend the first session of the revival, but the second afternoon Cook

took aholt of the crook of my elbow and steered me into the gym where there were two hundred students and a New York City parson who'd already worked up a preachifying sweat. . . .

OF WHAT happened in the next few days we have four accounts from David. What is fascinating in these documents is not that they confirm each other, but just the opposite: their inconsistencies, their contradictions. David even seems to have been confused as to what person was the actual agent of his conversion, and he attaches the identical image of a sunbeam-induced "halo" to two quite different men.

The first piece is "My Pledge," the story David wrote down at the time for no eyes but his own (unless, in some dim way, considering his ambition, also for posterity's). The second is a letter to his parents written a few days later. The third is a "letter of testimony" he sent during his third year in China to members of the Syracuse Christian Association, who were in large part the financial sponsors of his mission. And the fourth is the passage in "Search," many years later, about this experience.

Parts of the documents follow:

I

MY PLEDGE

. . . I was resistant. The speaker that afternoon was an old Moody-style Bible thumper, Bishop Sutphen of Kentucky. No theology; no hellfire. The one great sin was to hold back from Jesus. The practiced vibrato of the voice and the orotund southern accents were all wrong for me. I was, or thought I was, dead to his appeal. "The moment will come when Jesus will touch your eyelids with his fingertips, and the scales will melt away and you will see, yes, see the good hope that there is for humanity, see the open door and the father's house and the welcome of the prodigal, and the feasting, and see standing over against you the dear son with his thorn-crowned head and nail-pierced hands, and see the rejoicing of the sinners" and so on and so on and so on. It was like that, all of it, tired old pulpit phrases strung together. I went home deeply dejected. . . .

The next afternoon was quite different. We had an electrifying spectacle. The Reverend Dr. Azariah Dudley Morton of Boston was speaking. "You must become God-intoxicated! God yearns for that sort of man today, men inebriated with the Holy Ghost, men that may be called moon-crazed sometimes because of the divine enthusiasm of their zeal and earnestness." At that moment a young man I had never seen before, I do not believe he was a Syracuse student, jumped out into the aisle and shouted, "The trumpet blows for you, sir!" He had a revolver in his hand, which he raised and aimed at the minister. Dr. Morton quickly stepped down off the platform and approached the muzzle of the gun, undoing his gown, his cutaway, his shirt, and even his B.V.D.s to the bare skin. "Here, here, here, here," he said, "is my heart. Take it if you wish. Take it by storm, take it in love. It beats for you, my young friend. The Lord have mercy on you, and on me. We are bound together in danger and in love." The young man first looked overcome with astonishment, then dropped to his knees as the gun clattered on the floor. There were tears on his cheeks. Dr. Morton put his hands on the man's head and began to pray. . . .

I was a bit late for the 4 o'c evangelistic meeting on Wednesday. The talk had already begun. The speaker was one of the handsomest men I have ever seen, the famous All-Scotland rugby scrum half named Jock Terrum. His unruly auburn hair was struck by a beam of the sun through one of the tall windows, and I thought it a kind of halo. His voice was modest and low. He was not one to "work the sheep up to bleating." I was no sooner seated than I heard him speak three quiet sentences which changed my life. "Rejoice, O young man, in thy youth. Remember now thy Creator in the days of thy youth. For many are called, but few are chosen."

The soft tones of these words seemed to pierce my chest. It was almost not their meaning that entered into me but only their sound waves. My heart began to race, but I was not afraid. I felt a delicious coolness of my hands and feet, as if a sweet liquor were running through them. My vision was unusually clear and vivid. Relief! Relief! Relief! All my 'heaviness' was gone, my soreness, my throat was tight with joy. I cannot remember a single further word Jock Terrum spoke. After the meeting Cook tried to accost me, but I brushed him aside and literally ran to my room.

I struggled all night. What had happened to me? Such joy could not be real. I went out walking as soon as it was light. A freezing rain had fallen in the night but now the sky was clear, and as the sun rose the snow glistened under a crust of ice and all the twigs of the trees were made of rainbow-shot glass. I cannot describe my ecstasy. Shallow of heart, I mistrusted it. I cut all my classes. At half past two I cranked up my courage and knocked on the door of the room where Terrum was staying. He sat at a table, quietly reading his Bible. I begged him to tell me what to make of these transports of happiness that he—or Jesus— had let loose in me. He was calm. Do not listen to anyone's dogma, he said. Study the New Testament. Seek a personal intimacy with Christ, who will give you all the guidance you need. . . .

The revival has ticked on: preachings, individuals starting for Christ, Bible classes, a fund drive for foreign missions, social evenings— I soar above them all on wings of gladness. A number of us pray every night with Jock Terrum. . . .

I have just come from Jock, and I wish now in solemn black and white on the page to make this pledge:

'This first day of March, 1903, I, David Treadup, do of my own free will give myself, all that I am and have and will be, entirely unreservedly and unqualifiedly, to him, whom having not seen I love, in whom, though now I see him not, I believe.'

II

*Syracuse University,
10 March 1903*

Loved Ones:

I rejoice within, because I have the most momentous news to give you.

Inspired, as you know, by my teacher Absolom Carter, I first came to Syracuse with an overwhelming desire to "make my mark" in the large arenas of finance or of the legal profession or of academe, but I was not easy in my mind about such worldly hopes, and I was dashed down, you remember, into a wandering and defeatist time.

Beginning in New Bedford and especially since my return to college I have had an ever growing urge to give what talent and vigor I have to the service of the Lamb of God. For weeks I fought off this magnetic attraction. But like a lodestone it pulled and pulled at my heavy iron heart. I was logy. I was numb. Until at last I decided it was time to cut lines and drift toward my desire, even though I could not clearly perceive what that desire really was.

Shortly after the autumn term began I picked up again with a friend from freshman year, Forman Cook by name, who was, so to speak, going my way. He, too, was restless in spirit. We went deep with each other, frankly bared our hearts. We read some sermons aloud to each other, and also the Bible. But I felt on dead center, nothing moved. So then I went straight to God in prayer. Night after night, I played infinite variations upon a prayer of Benjamin Franklin's that particularly appealed to me:

'O powerful goodness! bountiful Father! merciful Guide! Increase in me that wisdom which discovers my truest interests; strengthen my resolution to perform what that wisdom dictates.'

The New Year came and went; God seemed to have turned a deaf ear to me. The month of March arrived; no messages. Last Thursday dawned; I strained to hear, but not one word came to me, and I began to waver. After dinner that noon I went in low spirits to my room to study with Cook.

I must tell you a word about this friend. He is a senior now, of course, but he draws no social lines. He is a fine athlete—a halfback on the varsity. He is one of the handsomest men I have ever seen. As he sat in my room his unruly auburn hair was struck by a beam of light from my window and I thought it a kind of halo. His voice is modest and low. He has the rare faculty of being able both to talk and to listen.

Although I needed all my wits to master the next day's lesson in logic, I found myself looping back with Cook to what had been nagging at us both for so long. We never even cracked our books. We tested each other. We went at each other like bearcats, to tell truth. I had never been keyed up to such a pitch of 'waiting.' It was like putting a fishing line down near the bottom and then watching the bob-float for the slightest tremble of a nibble. Nothing. Finally we resorted to silence. We sat there like dumb animals. Then suddenly we went down on our knees, and I remember crying out loud: "O merciful father! Give me some sign!" And he did. I heard his voice 'within' Cook's soft tones. He, God crouching within Forman Cook, spoke to me, and told me that I must work for the rest of my life not for my interests but in his vineyard.

O dear Mother and Father, what a weight dropped off me then! Everything that had oppressed me for so long was lifted from my shoulders. My vigor, so long lethargic and dim, has returned. My fight ahead is to wash my heart and shore up my imperfections. But I am on a straight course. I know what I am and will be.

Your devoted son,
David

III

Kuling, Central China,
10 April 1908

Dear Association Members:

I have received your letter telling me of your intention to hold a revival at Syracuse and asking for my testimony as to when and how and in what manner the missionary sponsored by Syracuse University first "saw the light," and I am most glad to respond, for it was precisely in a revival at Syracuse that this great joy fell on me. After something more than two years of active work here in close contact with heathenism I am humbly aware of how influences and forces acting through human lives radiate from such revivals to the hearths and school desks of the whole world. I am glad that such a revival destined me to be here and to have a part in God's plan for China.

In the late winter of 1902–1903 a group of us organized a fortnight of revival meetings on the campus. Although I was among the originators and movers of the revival, I had not yet verily been reborn, I had not yet given myself over to Christ. I had had a Christian upraising, of course, and I 'thought' I was a Christian, but a great surprise was in wait for me. The fact is that I was in despair. I could not hide from myself my thoroughgoing sinfulness. Oh my sins were "minor," for I was not a murderer, arsonist, rapist — except I think in the most secret places of my heart. Outwardly my sins were: Lust. A foul mouth. Lying. Ambition. Envy. Desecration of the Sabbath. A reckless and destructive playfulness. A wish to bend others to my will.

Consciousness of these sins had brought me very low in mind. For months I had been trying, trying, trying to open my heart to Jesus, trying by tears, by prayer, by confession. I had failed and thought I was doomed to a lifetime of failure.

Man's extremity is God's opportunity. I was harvested on the third day of the revival.

You all know of the famous incident of the second day, Dr. Morton's saving of the soul of his would-be assassin. The power of his faith shook me to the core. It was wonder at the bullet-proof vest that Jesus wrapped over Dr. Morton's heart which kept me awake all that night. My own heart cried out to me: "I am bare! I am exposed! I am craven! I want such a shield!"

The speaker on the third day was the internationally known rugby player from Glasgow University, Jock Terrum. I wish I could describe the beauty, inner and outer, of this youth. He was truly one of God's fighting angels. Without wishing to blaspheme, I would say that Jesus must have had just such a sweet hurt look about his mouth. I sneaked in late to the meeting, and I had no sooner been seated than I heard a chord struck on my heartstrings by that young athlete's grace and soft-spoken modesty when he uttered three quiet sentences which like three strokes of a bell sent shivers through my body:

"Rejoice, O young man, in thy youth. Remember now thy Creator in the days of thy youth. For many are called, but few are chosen."

At that moment the miracle happened. I 'knew.' I had surrendered myself. I saw a blinding light. My heart pounded with joy. I was

shriven. The tons of my sins were off-loaded from my aching bones.
And from that moment to this I have been verily on top of the world. . . .

In the following days I was never parted from Jock Terrum's side.
After his farewell talk on the Wednesday week after MY DAY OF JOY,
a few of us held a small meeting of silent prayer, to express our thanks.
Do you know the stillness when you drift in a canoe on a glassy calm
lake, the only sound the water dripping off the end of the paddle?
Though our tongues did not move, our souls were on pitch and in
harmony — a noiseless choir of praise. But deeply sad, too. It was very
hard to say good-bye to Mr. Terrum. He seemed, after days, an old
friend. Each of us clasped him to his breast and gave him a loving
go-with-God. I thought my heart might burst, he was so dear to me. He
had saved me. . . .

Faithfully yours,
David Treadup

IV

Excerpts from "Search" (1943)

My readings in Tientsin and in the internment camp in the last two
years have brought me to realize that my conversion was no miracle but
was rather a perfectly natural process of growing up, condensed, in my
case, into a single sudden and rather violent episode. I have talked often
with my missionary colleagues about our conversions; some were sudden,
others were gradual. I have wondered: What made mine sudden?

First of all, be it said that my conversion was no illusion. It was
real. That is to say, a fundamental and long-lasting change took place in
me. My motor had been running badly, and from that moment on it ran
well. I would say there were actual physical changes: a billion neural
synapses seemed suddenly to close and remain closed, so that a sus-
tained neurological and I would say glandular stability ensued. I doubt
whether that is sound physiology but let me say this: Everything in my
body "fell into place."

For the old phrase "I found God" read "I found my adult self." In
other words, the conversion was, in my case, a precipitate realization of
my inner being. In a hundred heartbeats I grew up.

As to the suddenness, I speculate about the following elements:

NEED. I had been unhappy for a very long time. I was puzzled by
my misery and fearful that it would never end. For months I had been
trying by every means to pull myself up from the depths of despondency.
I had just about given up on myself. My soul was a vacuum. I suppose it
was natural that when its seal was broken on that day, what would rush

in would be the kind of love I had been brought up to believe to be both necessary and genuine, without ever having really felt it: Christian love.

HYSTERIA. Crowd psychology and suggestion were surely forces. Those audiences of two hundred or so young men and women in the gymnasium had humming in them — in their silent listening — the tension of an audience in a theater strung up to the nervous limit by dramatic suspense.

HYPNOTISM. The more I have thought about it, the more I am convinced that the Scottish rugby player whose words touched off the palpitation of my heart had a hypnotic power he may not even have known he had. He built the hysteria and then controlled it. The vibrations of his soft voice, his repetitions, everything in threes, above all his strange eyes ranging restlessly above the heads of the crowd — he could have made a cobra dance. And there was the essential element of hypnotic inducement: a concentration on a single focus. In this case, not a staring iris nor a mark on a ceiling, but a faint cameo in the mind's eye of the figure of Jesus Christ. I had grown up from Cradle Roll days to take that image for granted as part of my life — so that at that moment it could serve, like any other spot concentrated upon, as a hypnotic focal point.

FEAR. The pistol episode had brought all our latent fears to the surface in two distilled forms: Fear of death and fear of loss of control. This was a different order of fear from the normal animal fear one feels at real physical danger, or at the sight, let us say, of blood, the sort of fear which, as I have noted earlier in these pages, always seemed to have within it, for me, an expectation of a wonderful surprise. No, this was the elemental fear of the mortality or morbidity of our most precious possession, our thinking brain. This brain-fear was where hypnotism had its perfect opening to bring hysteria to heel. Our revival followed the controlled style of Charles G. Finney's revivals. There were to be no shrieks, no wild outbursts, no fallings and faintings, no frenzies of Bacchantes, howling of dervishes, dancing of Hassids — yet where quiet young hearts like mine were set to racing, and where dim young eyes saw sudden brightness, there was the requisite moment of overwhelming brain-fear and its sudden removal. The absence of frenzies lent great intensity to the fear and to the relief at its abeyance. Sudden faith-producing relief, because the death was not to be of the body and soul, not to be of the mind, but was to be of this brain-fear itself. That was to be the triumph and wonder of my conversion.

TRANSITION

DAVID felt the passionate happiness of the Christian saints. He took long walks in the countryside around Syracuse with a sensation of soaring. When he rowed with the Navy he dipped his oar in clouds. Everything had fallen into place. He began to succeed wherever he had thought he was failing. Study became easy. Answers came to mind. His body thrived. The personal magnetism for both sexes which once had astonished him he now took for granted. Rapidly he gained influence, power, social poise.

His ambition was still fierce, and power was much on his mind, but like everything else these old yearnings were subsumed under a new imperative in his changed state of mind. "O that I may burn brightly for him!" "My soul cries out for a larger life. May it be a controlled life of love and service." "I want to be an 'all round man,' keeping the spiritual foremost." "It is a blessed thing to have influence with others." "I greatly desire not to be selfish in praying for the bestowment of favors." "Am desiring and praying for power with men and with God." "Full of longing to do God's will. I am praying for the power of the Holy Ghost in my life."

Clashing forces must still have been lodged in his psyche, but in his mind the light side in every instance triumphed over the dark. To his renewed perception he was brilliant, good, strong, confident, industrious, happy, and — most remarkable — both pure yet devastatingly attractive to women. He had joined the White Cross Society, pledged to "social cleanliness," which meant something more extreme than mere chastity; yet with a brand new candor he came right out with this in his diary: "My sexual nature is particularly strong these days." Indeed, an altogether new honesty now emerged to deal with the dark sides of the inner oppositions. He wrote sentences he never could have earlier: "Copen's head swelling very rapidly." "Crawford attempted to show off. He gives me a pain."

IN MOST of the Protestant denominational colleges and universities of those days, the Young Men's Christian Association had the prestige and assumed the functions much later taken over by student governments and student unions; it provided some services, in fact, that were later the responsibilities of university bureaus. Along with major team captains and the campus newspaper editor, the president of "the Association," as the Y.M.C.A. was commonly called, was a prominent undergraduate leader, more or less equivalent to a student council president or student union chairman in an American university later in the century. David's new form of ambition—to be useful in God's eyes, "to burn brightly for him"—drew him to the Christian Association. He was soon active in its work.

Founded in London in 1844 and transplanted to Canada and the United States seven years later, the Y.M.C.A. was originally intended to improve the spiritual and physical lot of young urban workers, but there were soon thriving branches on college campuses. In 1877 a convention of the Y.M.C.A. in Louisville formalized a college department and named Luther D. Wishard, who had joined the Association at Hanover College in Indiana before transferring to Princeton, as its secretary. This energetic youth founded scores of college Associations in the East and Middle West, and with what the International Committee of the Y.M.C.A. took to task as excessive zeal he even admitted women to campus branches—thus paving the way for the eventual appearance at many colleges of the adjunct Y.W.C.A. The Syracuse male Association, established in 1880, was later indeed joined by a female Association—which was to prove fateful in Treadup's life. In 1894 both had been given headquarters in the new gymnasium.

It was there, with the din of athletic games and physical education classes in his ears, and the odors of basketball dust and sweat and floor oil in his nostrils, that David Treadup sharpened his organizational skills through the rest of sophomore and all of junior year. Shortly before David joined up, Albert Hurte, '01, an attractive former president of the Association and a prominent undergraduate athlete and journalist, had become Permanent Secretary; it is clear that he liked the big bear Treadup and spent much time training him.

Besides organizing weekday prayer and Bible meetings, and setting up lectures and discussion sessions on missions, the Association also provided essential college services. There being as yet no campus dormitories, students had to live on the town, and the Y served as a clearinghouse for approved boarding facilities. It acted as an employment agency for students earning their way. It provided academic and personal counseling for underclassmen. In the fall it put on orientation sessions for freshmen.

David worked hard. "In office at YM all day. I find heaps that need looking after." "Found things in a mix-up at Assoc office." By the spring of junior year he was having no trouble keeping up in his studies yet also spending much time in the gym office. "I am on the go these days and am out very little. My work keeps me busy more than usual. Feeling good."

Yes, he radiated good feeling—what in the language of cant was called "a spirit of fellowship." He was so cheerful, so giving, so bustling—and these qualities seemed so unforced, so generous—that he began to be first a trusted, then a popular figure on the campus. Yet it is clear that he did not realize how much he was liked. He could not be called self-righteous because he was so unaware of having a self at all. Now and then there would be egregious lapses from this self-denial, and he occasionally performed acts of excessive Christian zeal which, though of high intention, turned out to be mean-spirited. But these would all be part of the transition he was going through, and for the most part he did trim himself to the needs and desires of others. In his junior year (early 1904) we come on these diary entries·

> *FEB.* 28 *I went around to Frat houses to get fellows for fraternity meeting. Thirty representative men were present. All expressed desire to take up Bible study in houses. Called on Hurte in evening. He said he believed I was the man for president next year. This was a gt. surprise.*
>
> 29 *Leap year! I am anxious and determined to see this Bible study scheme go through. Talked Y.M.C.A. election over with Grow. I have had no other thot than to have him run for president.*
>
> *MAR.* 1 *Hurte says they—the Y.M.C.A. people—are going to try to lift me before I graduate. I am thinking they will have a job.*
>
> 11 *The Y.M.C.A. nominating committee met this morning and made out slate. They have nominated me as the only candidate for the presidency. This is still a surprise to me. I am determined by God's help to make the most possible out of this. . . .*
>
> 15 *Annual election of officers in the Y.M.C.A. President D Treadup. Vice-Pres Bob Wood. Treas. — Wear. Secy. — Andrews. This election is gratifying, in that I was the only man mentioned for presidency. Lord help me to meet the need. Higher! HIGHER! HIGHER!*

With these cries, David, without knowing it, had chosen his mountain once and for all. His new success had selected his career for him. His "call" was still a year away, but he was now set on a fixed path from this strength to a far more demanding one.

NOT LONG after his conversion, at a joint Y.M.C.A.-Y.W.C.A. reception for a missionary from Africa named Dr. Hotchkiss, who had spoken at Park Church in the city, Treadup was introduced to a Mrs. Helen Kupfer, the wife of a professor of Roman history; she was an informal adviser to the young volunteers of the Y.W.C.A. "A captivating lady," David wrote.

A few days later he received a written invitation to "drop by the house after services on Sunday. Very informal spread." Professor Kupfer, a Methodist whose foot had slipped, as the saying went, attended neither church nor his wife's very informal spreads. "Aloof and cold," wrote David. But not Mrs. Kupfer, who very soon had become the older woman of David's Syracuse years. He began to call on her every Sunday, and he saw her often at the gym offices.

Outwardly, though large and plump, Mrs. Kupfer was quite unlike Mrs.

Farleigh of Turcott. Mrs. Kupfer wore woolens and was pale. She had eyes, one gathers, of the sort Yeats would have called dream-dimmed. Though sharp and keen in support of her young ladies, she was chary in gesture and deeply reserved. Something in David, however, opened her heart, and vice versa, and they took to confiding secrets to each other; hers apparently had to do with pain in her marriage. "Odd. I feel *pity* for her," David wrote, "yet she has me wound around her little finger." It went without saying that there was never to be, with Mrs. Kupfer, anything so intimate as the massaging of an aching shoulder. And in her case, the goals of the dream of "the other mother," the generous round sources of sustenance, were encased in wool, linen, whalebone, and pallor. And yet: "I have never encountered such large-hearted Christian love as Mrs. K's. It is as sunlight must be on the Caribbees, hot and direct." And how strange this is: "When I pull my Navy oar I think, with each stroke, *Kup, Kup, Kup, Kup,* and with each stroke I gain strength."

COMPLAINTS about studies vanished. "Why, it is as if I had been playing blindman's buff all these years, and now the blindfold has been taken off." The irony was that with his new clarity of vision Treadup doubtless could have seen his way through the classical courses, but for better or worse he was committed to science. The cap of the irony was that in the grip of his new religiosity he was able to learn the "facts" of science by rote without quite being able to pin down (or wipe out) God's role in them. We know he had taken the trouble to read *The Origin of Species,* but there was never any sign that he acknowledged Darwin's assault on the Book of Genesis. Yet he was—or gradually became—aware of the conflict, which was to project itself far into his missionary career. In junior year he took two courses that were centered on it: a course in philosophy, in which the hardest nut to crack was Kant's *Critique of Pure Reason,* and one entitled Theistic Science, an exercise in mental gymnastics, the thrust of which was that one could believe in both science and God. In the latter course, David encountered early inklings of the New Theology, on which the "social gospel" of the liberal wing of the missionary movement was to be based—another future source of conflict in Treadup's life.

NOW CAME one of Treadup's dreadful lapses. It was not to be until "Search," more than forty years later, that he would finally acknowledge his shame over it.

   The spring term of sophomore year was the time of fraternity rushing. Before his conversion, David in his secular ambition had set his cap not only for membership in a Greek-letter fraternity, which would provide the humble farm boy with luxurious room and board in a collegial setting, and would lift him above the forlorn mass of the unchosen "neutrals"; but for membership, furthermore, in one of the more prestigious societies. The fraternities seethed with campus politics; they feuded openly for captaincies, for academic honors, for influence with the chancellor and faculty, for control of the college publications and of the boards of the Y.M.C.A. and other campus organizations. Exclusion from one of these major centers of power simply meant exclusion from power.

The conversion had changed only one element in this picture: Treadup's concept of power. Now power would not be a means to personal aggrandizement but, rather, a means to help others: "power with man and God." At deeper psychological levels, this distinction might be blurred, but it would take decades for David to realize it.

On March 4 a man named Kelly invited Treadup to dinner at the Phi Kappa Psi house. David was impressed. He was given to believe he would get a bid. "They have a good house of fellows." But on the tenth he began to be courted by one Wright, from Chi Alpha Sigma, and on the morning of the twelfth Wright called on David at his lodging house and gave him a formal bid.

Treadup asked what about his close friend and housemate Cook?

Wright said there had been objections to Cook.

Then, said Treadup, he had objections to the bid. According to the diary: "Cook *must* go with me where I go."

That evening Wright returned and offered a bid to Cook. Five days later, "Wright, McClellin, and McLachen came down after meeting and rushed us until late. I am sorry they have rushed me so hard." The next day Kelly, of the other fraternity, talked to Treadup "for nearly an hour" and begged him to wait at least until March 25 before pledging any fraternity.

Treadup's being able to carry Cook with him and the urgency of these rival rushes apparently gave him a sense of a new kind of power—bargaining power—and also got him thinking about something he called "higher necessity." He had a duty to God to join the fraternity where he would have the greatest influence for good. Unfortunately neither of the fraternities that were rushing him were up there in the pecking order with the nationally prominent societies, such as Psi Upsilon, Delta Kappa Epsilon, and Beta Theta Pi.

Then suddenly on April 18 (for he had waited long past March 25) exclamation points reappeared. "Brown was in my room in evening talking Psi Upsilon. This is a new chapter in frat experience!" Three days later:

> Took dinner at Psi U at 101 College Place—colonial mansion, stately pillars, broad roofs, symmetrical turrets! This is oldest frat at Syr. These are the type of men who get things done. After dinner went with the men to the Williams game! Brown is rushing me for all he is worth. He is one of the best fellows I ever knew.

The following day came two terrible sentences:

> I do not fancy the idea of leaving Cook another year, but if Psi U opens to me I think I will go with Brown. I came to college to get and to give.

And on May 12:

Brown and Harry Barber called for me at suppertime and pledged me to Psi U. A higher necessity dictates my choice. May God add his blessing and make me strong.

Cook's name disappeared from the diary, as if he were dead.

INITIATION did not come until the next autumn:

OCT. 6 *Last night I received a command from ΨY to appear at 1140 S. Salina. I am commanded not to speak to any member of the Chapter until I am released from command. A "mum" day. Prayer meeting in evening.*

7 *This initiation makes me laugh. Every member cuts me dead. If such a state of affairs were in earnest, it would be unendurable. As it is, it is amusing.*

8 *At two o'clock Fowler, Cornwall, Perus, and myself reported at the corner of Mad. and Crouse Strs. We were blindfold there until nearly night. We were then taken into the country and 'put thro' cave, hell, ect. The init. was elaborate and splendid. We then were brot to the house, where we singly took an oath of Fidelity, Secrecy, and Brotherly Love. This was extremely solemn. Took the binding oath at the ΨY altar at 8 o'c. The Chapter then went to the Yates where we had a 2 dollar dinner. The initiates were called upon for toasts. I am now a member of Pi of Psi Upsilon fraternity. This is a great privilege and chance. I hope I shall be able to give here as well as get.*

WHAT FORMS did his giving, in the name of the "higher necessity," take? The answer, at first, was dreary: prudishness and censoriousness. These odious traits, common and persistent in many missionaries he would know in China, later disappeared entirely from Treadup's repertory. It was as if the transition period required, among other shifts and changes, a purging of high-minded nastiness, once and for all.

"Three of the brothers did a very shameful act today in getting drunk and then riding up in a loaded car. I have spoken to some of the alumni and they are very much put out about this disgrace." "I had a long talk today with L. Vought. He is drifting. I did not spare him but told him what I thot." "There is trouble in the air about poker playing. This thing *must* be stopped." "Had a talk with Bronson about his life. It is appalling how many of these young fellows lose their heads when they come to college." "There has been more swearing in the house since we returned than ever before. Something must be done." "Attempts at wit at the Pi Lit were near the limit and bordered on vulgarity."

In several cases there is strangely—perhaps coincidentally—a ○ beside Treadup's notations. "It seems that Charleau has been doing considerable harm by not leading a clean life. I was much surprised to learn of it. He has promised me to amend."

ON THE SECOND FLOOR of the Hall of Languages, the Y.W.C.A. had set up a lunch counter where, between ten in the morning and one, students could buy sandwiches, cookies, bread, and milk. There one noonday in the late spring of his sophomore year David Treadup was waited on by a young lady who, he knew, had just been elected president of the Y.W.C.A. for the following year. (David's corresponding election was to be a year later; she was in '04, he in '05, though he was five years older than she.) Her name was Emily Kean, and she made a prompt misspelled debut in Treadup's diary: "I like the appearance of Miss Keen very much."

Later notes specified "dark brown eyes, dark brown hair," "braids coiled in a crown," and he even noticed "amber horn hairpins." "Behind the counter Miss K calm, even at rush hour never gets flustered like some others." Much later David would learn that she was the daughter of a handsome Scot who had immigrated to the United States at the age of nineteen and had eventually established himself as a dairy farmer and dealer in cheddar cheese, near Herkimer, New York. Miss Kean had attended Rome Free Academy, in the town of Rome, a school quite like Enderbury Institute; she was preparing to teach in just such another school—preparing to be a valuable person like Absolom Carter.

There is no sign that Treadup gave Miss Kean any thought over the summer—during which he served as boys' secretary in a Y.M.C.A. in the slums of Little Falls, New York, catering to "genuine toughs," the whole experience "a study in degraded classes." But early in the fall he saw her again and invited "Miss Keen" to go with him to the first Y.M.C.A. reception on Saturday night, September 19. The occasion was "a *great* success!" The following Friday:

> *Played tennis in P.M. I happened to be on the winning side today. I am more and more convinced that I should make the acquaintance of Miss Kean.*

This phrase, "make the acquaintance of," quite often repeated in following weeks, evidently encoded more than its surface meaning. It hinted at a serious intention. A convert was bound to be thinking that a Christian man had a duty to become engaged to be married, for he would need a helpmeet in the service of God.

OCT. 3 *Dissected a frog at lab. Went to a reception for Mr. Ilium at Mrs.
Kupfer's. Had pleasure of seeing Miss Kean home. Made date for
later call.*

15 [Just after the initiation into Psi U.] *Took buggy drive in P.M.
with Miss Kean. Drove down Indian Reservation way. Very pleasant afternoon. Talked to Grow about Miss K. Have decided to
make her acquaintance.*

NOV. 8 *In evening to Park Presbyterian. Miss Kean was my company.
Hope to become better acquainted with her.*

And so through the winter months—always hopeful, always curiously at
a distance. Church services downtown; evening calls, once with a cold which
"made the call unpleasant for me and I fear for her"; fraternity "lits" ("*grand
success,*" "I think the singing made a hit with our friends"); Glee Club
concerts ("I wore Sam's opera hat—well, that was straining a bit"). Mindful
that Miss Kean would be graduating in the spring, he brought God into the
transaction in March: "Believe that I have a big problem to settle during the
next few months. May he direct the whole affair." Code words multiplied. In
April: "I am becoming mightily interested in her. She is the kind of woman
I would like for a friend." Now *he* was elected to a presidency; they made
a natural pair.

Then, suddenly, in early May, an ominous note: "I called on Miss Kean
for a short time in P.M. She seems to be very 'busy' these days."

But a week later the news was somewhat more encouraging, though
tantalizingly indefinite: "Went to Park Ch. in evening with Miss Kean. I tried
to say some kind words and she reciprocated."

The Evangelization of the World in This Generation.
DAVID first heard this astonishingly optimistic slogan in his junior year,
in a weekly mission study group to which he had been solicited by his friend
Grow. Grow was a member of an organization called the Student Volunteer
Movement for Foreign Missions—it was their slogan—and as David Treadup
rapidly became a notable campus figure Grow fastened onto him: this was
just the kind of man the movement wanted. "Believe I shall find it helpful,"
David wrote.

But this was only one of several groups that were courting him just then
(e.g., "Winthrop has asked me to do work on the daily"), and he was halfhearted about the mission meetings. Missions just then represented not much
more than a rather glamorous fantasy to him, idle work of the daydream
world. In the popular culture, missionaries were heroic figures: workers
in exotic vineyards, civilizers of the heathen, and all too often bloodied
martyrs. Treadup actually led the mission discussion one week when Grow

had the grippe, and he offhandedly accepted an invitation to go to the S.V.M.'s conference the next summer at Northfield, Massachusetts: something to do in the summer that sounded like fun, a kind of camp. But compared with other interests, such as rowing, this one was minor.

A more significant, if cruder, stirring of the missionary impulse in David in that transitional year came in what was called "personal work": evangelizing one on one. This suited David's dazed enthusiasm after his conversion, and it brought out a somewhat less offensive side of his prudish carping and judging. "I am in a personal workers' club. Lee is the subject of my prayers at present." "Had a heart talk with Seaforth in evening in office." "I wish that I might lead ten men to Christ this year."

TREADUP'S "Notes on Coach Ten Eyck's Method":

> *Listen carefully for clack-clack of wooden handles of the coxswain's rudder ropes. Clean hard catch of the blade so as to miss no water. Light hands. Long steady drive with the shoulders and back, legs come on, seat slides, smooth finish with oar drawn right home to body. Flick of release. Feather the oar. Light hands. Smooth straight-armed slide forward on the recovery to help urge the travel of the shell between strokes.*

Over and over in the training at Long Branch, David felt the pure joy of the shared labor. It was all so different from freshman year. He was different; the rowing was different.

There was a new coach, James Ten Eyck, a veteran like Cornell's Courtney of the professional sculling wars. Ten Eyck:

> *There is no secret to it nor any mystery. When I consider a man, I consider his sand first, his physique second. There are too many shadows walking around without hearts.*

It took courage to row for Ten Eyck. His was the "get-there stroke." He let each man "do the thing in his own way," keeping his peculiarities; Dempster at Number Five jerked his head at each recovery, Treadup at Four—the meat of the boat at the middling oars—leaned quite far out on the pull. But all had to give everything they had, because Ten Eyck believed that there was "only one way to row, and that is to keep the oar in the water just as much as possible and force it through with just as much power as possible."

In stroke count this translated into Ten Eyck's conviction that no crew, even Cornell's, rowing 28 strokes to the minute with the power properly applied could beat an equally good crew rowing at 34 strokes to the minute. Courtney, the technician of the smooth short stroke and long travel, who trained his crew to concentrate on the single inch of gain with each stroke that would add up to a boat-length victory in four miles, scoffed at Ten Eyck's crude muscular theory and his Syracuse eight that was "simply being yanked along."

Yank or no yank, in the spring of sophomore year, after the conversion, David's pulse sang in response to Ten Eyck's demands. Rowing ecstasy was his again, the exultation of the flying *Ecarg* on the Salt Branch pond. Courage? No, for David it was just a matter of letting go to the very core. He was hardly aware of the element of contest. At the culminating event of the year, the Intercollegiate Rowing Association regatta at Poughkeepsie, Syracuse "dragged considerably." Order of finish: Cornell, Georgetown, Wisconsin, Pennsylvania, Syracuse, Columbia. In his diary Treadup writes only: "I am learning to pace myself. The great thing in life is to know how long four miles is."

All through David's junior year Ten Eyck had his eye on the goal of the next Poughkeepsie regatta, and of beating Courtney; he had some fine sophomores up from the strong freshman crew of the previous year. In the fall and winter he led his men on long hikes up and down all the hills he could find. Going into the spring under Ten Eyck's feverish training, David was beginning to recover something of the competitive spirit of the triumphs in *Ecarg* over the bakery boys.

But there was something else, too, in this pietistic transition period. A letter to brother Paul:

> I am ruled by two verses in the Bible which make me think hard about this big frame God has given me: 1 Cor. 6:19, 20: "What? Know ye not that your body is the temple of the Holy Ghost which is in you, which ye have of God, and ye are not your own? For ye are bought with a price; therefore glorify God in your body, and in your spirit, which are God's." I feel that price keenly, I must make my payment to God every day. I must shore up the temple. I must make my body strong enough to last four times four miles; make it able to endure and pull harder yet — for him.

This lower-case "him" may partly have been, in the back of the mind, the godlike Ten Eyck. And it is surely worth noting that the passage David quotes from Paul's epistle is concerned not at all with rowing, but with fornication.

AS COMMENCEMENT approached for the Class of '04, Treadup faced the parting with Emily Kean with confidence.

> Called on Miss Kean in evening. She is going to be teaching at Chittenango next year, three stations east on Central. Glad she is going to be so near, for it may be I shall see her occas.

But suddenly, on June 4, there is a staggering discovery. "Called on Miss K in P.M. She tells me she has a special friend in Zeedon, '00." In the lexicon of codes "a special friend" stood all too close to the goal of the unmentionable bed—that is to say, to engagement to marry. We have seen the extent of David's hopes all year long; yet apart from his earlier note about how "busy" Miss Kean suddenly seemed, he apparently had no inkling of how important this other relationship of hers was, if he knew of it at all. How carefully one must guard the secrets of desire! A year before, this discovery would have plunged David into caverns of self-pity, but now, in his reborn floating transitional state, he just seemed to move on: the eye was on Poughkeepsie. But in time it will become clear that he has most savingly stored the loss in his heart.

THREE MILES north of the Poughkeepsie railroad bridge the square-bottomed stake boats were anchored fore-and-aft at the starting line.

Lane one: dark blue and gray of Georgetown.

Two: light blue of Columbia.

Three: orange of Syracuse.

Four: red and blue of Penn.

Five: red and white of Cornell.

Six: cardinal of Wisconsin.

Downstream was a bedlam of yachts, river steamers, tugboats, barges, ferryboats, Coast Guard cutters. The race train was ready on the shore. The bookies' betting odds: Cornell, even money; Wisconsin, 3 to 1; Georgetown and Penn, 4 to 1; Columbia, 6 to 1; Syracuse, 25 to 1.

Ten Eyck, gaunt in his following launch as the Syracuse shell moved toward the line: "Spread your strength over four miles. . . . Don't faint. If you do, you're a deadweight. . . . " Last words: "Just row the race you want to—you've got the guts, and I know damn well you'll do it!"

A long wait; Wisconsin was late. The officials' launch arrived. Referee Richard Armstrong of Yale: "Are you ready all?" Five required seconds of pause. The pistol shot—and, to alert the spectator fleet, six colored bombs from the railroad bridge.

Cornell took the lead. Syracuse moved up to 33. At the first half-mile stake boats: Syracuse by three-quarters of a length. At the mile: dead heat. Syracuse 33, 34, 35, a frightful 36. At two miles, Syracuse by open water. To come through under the bridge in front was the test; there, as the boats passed under, more colored bombs went up to show the order: Syracuse by a hair.

Toward the end, Syracuse went up to an astonishing 38, and held it.
Finish: Syracuse by three lengths, Cornell just ahead of Penn, then Columbia,
Georgetown, the Badgers.

"Syracuse," the New York *Herald* reported on its front page the next
morning,

> is the new giant of intercollegiate rowing. . . . If the Syracuse crew at
> Poughkeepsie yesterday had stepped out of their boat on to the water and,
> lifting the shell on their shoulders, had run over the course and crossed the
> finish line first, they would not have surprised the onlooking dumb-with-
> amazement crowd more than they did.

The crew arrived back in Syracuse early the next morning and stumbled
wearily through empty streets to the Onondaga Hotel for breakfast. During
the day, news of the victory spread through the city, and that evening a senior
named Albert Petrie, trailing scores of orange ribbons and holding aloft a
sea-sweeping broom, led a procession of man-hauled carriages with the
oarsmen, Ten Eyck, and Chancellor Day in them, followed by a train of
horn-blowing autos, to downtown Hanover Square, where twenty-five thousand citizens were on hand to cheer the heroes. The huge-bodied and vast-
egoed chancellor shouted: "For the first time in the history of my connection
with the college, I feel as if I amounted to nothing."

David, on the other hand, testified in "Search," decades later, that "the
din of that huge throng is still in my ears." He knew he amounted, and would
always amount, to something.

THE CALL

ON THE THIRD EVENING of the Northfield Conference, the great James B.
Todd stepped forward into the full glare of David Treadup's expectations.

As Todd moved to the podium, David was finely tuned to listen. The
conference, to which he had so casually committed himself in the busy college
springtime, was in a ravishing setting in the hills by the Connecticut River
Valley in soft hot days of early July, and the program, with only one full
meeting each day, left plenty of time for the hundred-odd young men to play
tennis and baseball, to swim in the wide river, or, taking a ferryboat that was
pulled across the river by a cable, to hike to the purple mountains beyond the
valley. David had a fine Old Testament sense of having been chosen: These

young men were the Protestant Israelites, an elite subdivision of God's own band. "Tennis with Tripp of Columbia, Beach of Williams. Each day is better than the day before." The big men of Yale and Princeton acknowledged Treadup as *the* Syracuse man.

And Todd was the super-leader. In his thirties, almost as massive as David himself and handsomer—blond, broad-faced, icy-eyed, and bursting with benign energy and assurance—he began to speak to the mood of these young men who were already, in varying degrees, "ambitious for the Lord." He stirred up in them that most heartwarming of all sins, pride. He spoke of

> your destiny of privilege, for you—chosen as you are—will have the high honor of carrying to the unevangelized nations of this earth the very and only word which can ease the lot of those forgotten and backward nations. It has been given by God to the Republic of the United States and to the Empire of the United Kingdom to spread this word, this uplifting word. We seek for its utterance exactly your sort—not a rabble of enthusiasts, but rather a favored few, the brightest and best of our youth, men of culture and high learning, graduates of our foremost colleges, keen of mind and warm in heart, as you are. The task before you calls for manfulness and brain power and skills of captaincy and courage, no less than evangelical zeal. Because, you see, the Christian task is to train up native Christian leaders, who will not only pass on Christ's word but will themselves be leaders of their nations and will fashion those lands into great new Christian commonwealths.

David was completely carried away. He had that evening found, after Absolom Carter, his second decisive model; and he had heard the first loud trumpet tones of The Call.

> *He is my ideal as far as man can be. I see Jesus Christ in him. I faced the mission question as never before. The need is surely great.*

JAMES B. TODD had been born just six weeks after Lee surrendered at the Appomattox Courthouse. James's father was tough; as a boy he had worked as a logger on the Delaware River, running rafts down through the swift Water Gap; later he drifted to Iowa and became a grain merchant. James's mother was a dreamer of silks and castles; she knew intimately the names and private lives of all the crowned heads of Europe and talked of Queen Victoria as though she lived down the street and belonged to her sewing circle. Todd's flair had in it a peculiar mix of wild romanticism and hardness.

From Poletown, Iowa, where his father had become a successful grain merchant, Todd went first to Upper Iowa University and then to Cornell.

Charming, dynamic, a work machine, he became active in the college Christian Association. When, in 1886, Luther D. Wishard, the young man who had
founded so many college Associations, persuaded the evangelist Dwight L.
Moody to convene the first summer Bible conference held in America for
college men, at the not-quite-completed campus of Moody's newly founded
school for boys at Mount Hermon, Massachusetts, Todd was among those
invited to attend.

Under Moody's spell that conference culminated in the formation of "the
Mount Hermon Hundred," a group of conferees, including Todd, who openly
pledged themselves to become foreign missionaries. They sent recruiting
teams out, and within two years had enlisted more than twenty-two hundred
students. In December 1888, under auspices of the intercollegiate Y.M.C.A.,
the group founded the Student Volunteer Movement for Foreign Missions.

At the first convention of the SVM, Reverend A. T. Pierson spoke in the
military mode that was to permeate the thinking of the entire missionary
phalanx of onward-marching Christian soldiers:

> This is a council of war. In the tent of the Commander we are gathered, and
> the Commander-in-Chief is here. Here are his subordinates, the heads of
> departments, the under captains, and here are the volunteers of the army.
> And the question for consideration is, How can the marching order of this
> invisible Captain be carried out promptly and energetically?

James B. Todd became the aggressive sergeant major of the SVM, and
by the time David Treadup attended the Northfield Conference (which had
succeeded the Mount Hermon meeting as an annual event), the SVM had
penetrated hundreds of campuses and had become the most influential
student movement in the country, analogous, in its feverish growth and
widespread appeal, to the student radical and pacifist movements of the
1930s and to the organizations of the New Left in the 1960s. As Princeton's
Robert Wilder, one of the Mount Hermon Hundred, was to write years later,
"It seemed as if the only thing needed in a college was to strike a match and
the whole college blazed up with enthusiasm for the evangelization of the
world." As it was to turn out, more than half the missionaries sent overseas
into North American Protestant compounds between 1888 and 1919 were
SVM volunteers.

TREADUP of Syracuse managed, before the conference was over, to have
two solo interviews with James B. Todd. "It was like being in to see God."
David's excuse for pressing so hard for Todd's time was that he was to head
up the Syracuse Association, and he wanted, as if by touching a hunchback's
hump, to incorporate some of Todd's magic.

Todd was free with advice, and it was of a kind that thrilled David because it confirmed his own inclinations. For one thing, Todd urged the model of Benjamin Franklin's systematic daily accounting of activities and of moral progress.

> *He told me to write out a Scheme of Development. Sleep — 8 hrs. "Don't waste time in bed thinking. Give yourself over at once to sleep." Exercise — two hours — didn't have to push me on that. Cold water bath every morning right after getting up. Avoid worry. Keep tight leash on emotions. Mental: "Don't try to cook too many loaves in your mental oven at once — they'll come out half baked." "An hour's job deserves an hour's work." "Decide to win." "Choose but few intimates, only of highest caliber." Bible — one half hour per day. Meditation — 15 mins. per day. Attend to business 'at once.'*

Another notation:

> *"You and I are big men. Your physique, Treadup, can be magnetic. It can also be overbearing. Have a care!"*

Another:

> *He talked to me about decisiveness. Said: "Make up your mind and hold firmly to your decision. You will find this gets things done, without a drain on either your time or your nerves." Said he had memorized some lines from 'On Decision of Character' by John Foster and often repeats them to himself. Wrote them down for me:*
>
> *"An essential principle of the character is a total incapability of surrendering to indifference or delay the serious determination of the mind. A strenuous will must accompany the conclusions of thought, and constantly incite the utmost efforts to give them a practical result. The intellect must be invested, if I may so describe it, with a glowing atmosphere of passion, under the influence of which the cold dictates of reason take fire and spring into active powers."*
>
> *This is Todd to a T! I, too, will learn this by heart!*

The conference concluded, for David as for most of the conferees, with a "most solemn act": the signing of a "decision card." This was presented as a kind of betrothal. Bishop William McDowell told the delegates, "God is standing before you waiting for each of you to take yourself and all your powers and your sense of obligation up into unconquerable resolution and cry, for time and for eternity, for weal or woe, 'I will!' "

IT IS MY PURPOSE, IF GOD PERMIT, TO BECOME A FOREIGN MISSIONARY.

(Signed) *David Treadup*

AS EVERY EVANGELIST knew, the signing of a pledge card did not a
martyr make. When David returned to Syracuse in the fall, he had second,
third, fourth, and fifth thoughts.

He was at the top of his game. He thrived in the chair of the Association.
From a letter to brother Paul:

> *I have a staff of thirty men, my officers and noncoms for a regiment of
> 250 members—one fourth of a student body which is influenced as a
> whole, at every turn, by our Association. It takes tact to cut men out for
> the right tasks and keep them grinding. I hold to a fixed regimen, and I
> feel as hearty as I ever did in my life—abed at ten, up at five, cold bath
> at once, every work-minute budgeted, a post meridian hour on the
> rowing machine, thirty minutes of prayer and meditation—and no
> worry, ever. Wesley said, you know: "To fret is just as bad as to curse
> and swear."*

The big man on the campus was beginning to attract offers. The
Y.M.C.A. solicited him for work in an American city of his choice. Chancellor
Day took him aside one day to suggest he put some thought on teaching for
the alma mater—graduate work, first, of course, in engineering. He was
offered a fellowship for a year's study at Oxford. He was invited for interviews
at Union Theological Seminary, which would bend him toward the ministry.
And on three different fund-raising missions to wealthy Syracuse alumni, in
Rochester, Buffalo, and Cleveland, he was offered jobs in business. These last
bids tested a poor man. "Took dinner with Burrow Lewis at their home. They
are rich refined people—he a gentleman farmer. Saw his milking machine
milk." Two days later: "I fear the social unrest of the time has attacked me.
I long to go into business."

AGAIN and again, however, there were reminders of The Call. On January 17
came one that was most explicit:

Farrow R. Blackton of the International Committee of the Y.M.C.A.
visited Syracuse to invite David Treadup to go to China as the university's
missionary, working for the Association.

THE ATTRACTIONS of Blackton's invitation were subtle and complex.
There was much more to them than the slogans and shibboleths with which
David had been bombarded in recent months: "Share the blessings of
Christianity." "Preach the gospel to every living creature." "Evangelize the
world in this generation."

There remained for David, conveyed to him by older preachers he had heard like Azariah Dudley Morton and Monroe V. Trumbull, at least some of the incentive to missions that had drawn the earlier nineteenth-century missionaries into the field. This had started with the Puritan doctrine of "disinterested benevolence" put forward by Jonathan Edwards's disciple Samuel Hopkins. The elect, as this doctrine went, were duty-bound to glorify God through deeds that would add to the world's happiness—to that of "being in general." The doers of these deeds were not to expect rewards for them either in this world or beyond it. The love of God must be disinterested, and Hopkins would not allow the liberal theological line that would have promised paradise to those who served the common good as if for barter. The early missionaries who answered such a call to the disinterested elect bristled with a fiercely confident selflessness. David had by now absorbed some of this giddying strength.

Treadup also had at least a touch of millenarianist fever: Christ was coming to earth again. The early nineteenth-century epidemic of this fever, caught from Edwards and Hopkins, had died out by mid-century, at least partly because of the wild excesses of the Millerites and other Adventists in New York State. But by the later years of the century, American Protestant evangelists, influenced by the Plymouth Brethren and others in England, had begun to preach a "premillenarianist" version of the messiah's return. Signs, they said, pointed to Jesus Christ's return, in preparation for his thousand-year reign ("the millennium") as Prince of Peace, as the New Testament prophesied. It was therefore vital to "preach the gospel to every living creature" in order to pave the way for Christ's reappearance. There was no time to waste.

"The fullness of time has come," David wrote in his commonplace book, quoting from a sermon he had heard at Park Church, "and the end seems at hand, which is also the beginning of the last and greatest age. Now or never! Tomorrow may be too late!" The preacher of that sermon had explained that "evangelization of the world in this generation does not mean total Christianization but only *proclamation* of the gospel to all. *That* is what is urgent."

In the meantime younger leaders like James B. Todd had begun to infuse into the movement something of the humanitarian impulse that had gripped Americans in the last years of the old century and the first years of the new. Jane Addams, founding Hull House to succor poor immigrants on Chicago's West Side; Jacob Riis, crusading for playgrounds for the poor in New York; the beginnings of the Progressive movement, stressing human welfare; and, most loudly, Teddy Roosevelt, busting the trusts and campaigning for "the little man"—all spoke to an American optimism for the future of the oppressed.

And so the SVM speakers urged that it was the duty of each generation of Christian students to take up the task of uplifting non-Christian humanity, and the SVM slogan could be seen to embrace both the hope of clearing the way for the advent of Christ by saving souls and the more "practical" and more widespread American vision of regenerating the backward peoples of the earth by giving them the benefits of Christian institutions.

Beyond all this, and perhaps most seductively of all, Treadup was drawn by the pure romance of the mission field. How could one compare the idea of returning to the cramped little world of Salt Branch and its tiny pond, its cornet-band concerts, its bakery bouts, its church suppers, with that of going out to Dark Lands beyond oceans, described by speaker after speaker on the mission circuit, strange places where one had to have and give all: clear sight, utter love, and, yes, perhaps even the dear gift of wounds and death offered by Christ himself?

MISS KEAN was not at nearby Chittenango after all. Somehow Treadup learned that she was teaching in Madison, New Jersey, for all practical purposes off the edge of the earth. So far as we know, he did not write to her, but she was not out of mind. After going to a "musical," he entered a cryptic note: "Saw Mr. Zeedon. I remember him as a senior when I was a freshman." That was all.

Women in general were very much on his mind. A missionary, more urgently than all other men, it seemed, needed a supporting partner. It would be unthinkable to go to China without a wife. Graduation was coming next June, and he had no prospects at all. The year became a kind of hunt, which grew more and more feverish and frantic.

November 1: "Called on Miss Knapp at Gamma Phi." A fortnight later: "Ed Packard and I made a party call at Phi Nu Epsilon on Misses Taylor and Titus." Three nights later: Miss Knapp. Two weeks later: "Went to a reception at Winchell. I met a Miss Killows, a cousin of Grow (second or third) who impressed me as a fine woman."

Right after Christmas vacation he picked up the search again, and more and more he seemed to have the distant Miss Kean in mind as one who could provide benchmarks of womanhood. January 21: "Called on Miss Knapp in evening. I wish I had more time to call as I need the help that comes from such intercourse"—the social kind, it goes without saying. February 13: a Miss Fellitt. The next night: Emmons. The next night: Knapp. A week later: Emmons.

On March 9: "I refused to dissect a dog in bio. Called on Miss Runnell in evening. She is a charmer but somewhat superficial." Two nights later: Knapp. A week later: a Miss Grant. April Fool's Day: "Have a new suit blue light weight. Called at Delta Gamma on Miss Reynolds. She is a fine Christian woman, not particularly strong face." April 10: "I went to seminar and walked home with Miss Ostrander."

May Day and spring fever: "Called on Miss Emmons last night. These warm days are not conducive to study." Three nights later: a Miss Miller. A week later: Miller again. The very next night: "Took walk with Miss Henderson tonight. She is a good sensible girl. We took a long walk." Two nights later: "Seminar work ended. Took walk with Miss Ostrander after sem. She is a minister's daughter who will never care to live the self-sacrificial life."

Five nights later: a new name, McGregor. Two nights later: another, Foxx. Then another. Ottis. Then: Miller. Then. Graduation, and no one at all.

THE DECISION did not come, like the conversion, in a minute's pounding of the heart; it grew until it was simply there.

In early December he was reading up on Asia from what few books he could find in the university library, and was taking pains to note down a considerable amount of nonsense in his commonplace book: items that tended to argue the need for missionary work. On December 8 he entered this from John Pinkerton's *Modern Geography* (1803):

> *"In visiting the sea ports of China, foreigners have commonly been impressed with the idea of fraud and dishonesty; but it is to be supposed that these qualities are not so apparent when there are few temptations. The indolence of the upper classes, who are even fed by their servants, and the nastiness of the lower, who eat almost every kind of animal, in whatever way it may have died, are also striking defects."*

On December 14, the young man who had marriage (and its unmentionable delights?) so much on his mind, noted:

> *Arthur H. Smith writes that because filial conduct requires that one must propagate, the Chinese have fallen into habits of early marriage, polygamy, and concubinage. Too much sexual activity; too many babies; too many mouths. Much sexual corruption:*
>
> > *Ten Buddhist nuns, and nine are bad;*
> > *The odd one left is doubtless mad.*

Not all that he noted was negative, but even the positive things were rather pitiable. A February entry, also from Smith:

> *"The Chinese have many and conspicuous virtues, among which are their faithfulness to duty, their sobriety, their unfailing industry, their unequaled patience, their inextinguishable cheerfulness, manifesting itself in blooming flowers, in warbling birds, and smiling faces even in the midst of deep poverty, gloomy prospects, and heavy hearts."*

In February there was an SVM rally in the Syracuse gym. "Good crowd and fine address. I thought I might take on strength for service in his cause. Surely the need is great." The speaker, August Childress, to stress that need, suggested that Paul might well have been describing the heathen Chinese when he wrote to the Romans (1:28–31):

> And even as they did not like to retain God in their knowledge, God gave them over to a reprobate mind, to do those things which are not convenient; being filled with all unrighteousness, fornication, wickedness, covetousness, maliciousness; full of envy, murder, debate, deceit, malignity; whisperers, backbiters, haters of God, despiteful, proud, boasters, inventors of evil things, disobedient to parents, without understanding, convenant breakers, without natural affection, implacable, unmerciful.

The backwardness of China, Childress said, was easily explained: Ancestor worship. "They look to the past, not to the future. The Chinaman has eyes on the back of his head."

David was constantly talking with others about his own future. "Grow had prayer meeting. He is a jewel. I think he believes I ought to volunteer." Mrs. Kupfer had suddenly scrapped her earlier views and decided that for the greater good of the world David should go. Hurte of the Association had long thought so. And there came a time when it seemed that David himself had been convinced of it for months.

IN EARLY MARCH he wrote a long, tender letter to both parents, telling them that his mind was settled. He had been invited, he wrote, by Mr. Blackton of the International Committee of the Association to be "the errand-runner for Syracuse" in China, and he had decided that he had a duty to go.

His mother wrote back a tight-lipped letter of resistance: His father, who had sacrificed so much for him, needed, for his declining years, "if not your strong back on the farm, at least some pecuniary support, of the kind a Syracuse education can fetch these days. There is such a thing as obligation in this world."

David at once wrote his father a sensitive and affectionate letter of nine pages, saying at the end, "If you and Mother are not willing and eager for me to give my life to this service, tell me, and I shall curb myself to your wish, and with a whole heart." Then came a short, rather curt letter from his mother, giving permission in grudging words: "We bow our heads to the Divine will."

TWO DAYS after he noted the arrival of that letter and the calm closure of his decision—"I am at ease in my mind"—he was shocked nearly out of his wits by a lecture by a returned lady missionary, Miss Sophia Rook, on the Boxer Uprising. It was as if David Treadup had been forced to realize, for the first time, what he was getting into.

Miss Rook's was a bloody, sadistic tale. She began quietly enough, telling how, in Peking in the 1860s, a remarkable, grasping woman, named Tz'u-hsi,* "gathered power into hands that would one day have fingernails six inches long, protected by jeweled guards — to show that hands of command never had to do manual work." She had been taken into the palace from a poor home as a servant girl at sixteen. Ferociously ambitious, she studied the classics until she knew them as well as the scholar-officials. She became, Miss Rook said, one of the emperor's concubines, then his *kwei fei,* or First Concubine, then the mother of his only son — whereupon she was raised to the position of wife. The emperor died when the son was only three, Tz'u-hsi became Empress Dowager, and the child succeeded to the throne. Then — "for this woman," Miss Rook said, "was like Agrippina, the wily mother of Nero" — to ensure her power she had her sister married to the late emperor's younger brother, and at the death of her son when he reached his majority, she swept aside seven princes who wanted the throne and went to her sister's home to fetch the sister's three-and-a-half-year-old boy, and the next morning, announcing the son-emperor's death, she proclaimed the nephew-emperor's installation, with the title Kuang Hsü, or Brilliant Succession.

As he grew up, the lady lecturer said, this boy became fascinated by Western mechanical toys, which his eunuchs bought for him in the Legation Quarter of Peking. In his teens he installed a miniature railway train in the palace grounds and floated steam launches on Lotus Lake in the capital; he put in palace telephones and electric lights, imported primitive automobiles, and received as gifts from missionaries a phonograph and a "cinematograph." During the boy-emperor's young years, Miss Rook said, a missionary visitor described a palace room teeming with Swiss watches and cuckoo clocks. She read from his account. The room was

> filled with clocks from one end to the other, all ticking a different time. . . .
> I sat down upon a French chair upholstered in red plush, and a music box
> began to play in the seat of the chair. This was attached to an electric fan
> upon the wall which kept me cool on that hot August day. It was the
> Emperor's reading chair, the eunuchs told me.

For the Kuang Hsü Emperor, said Miss Rook, "*was* a reader, with the ticking of the West all around him, and, urged on by famous reformers like K'ang Yu-wei and K'ang's student Liang Ch'i-ch'ao, he began taking up not only Western machinery but also Western ideas." These bore fruit — in the year, David realized, when he was a freshman — in what Miss Rook called "the hundred days of reform." During them the young emperor issued twenty-seven sweeping edicts — wiping out many decrepit governmental institutions and establishing Western-style boards in charge of education, railroads, mines, agriculture, defense, postal service. Some English and American missionaries figured in some of these plans, Miss Rook proudly said, especially plans for

---

*See Index of Chinese Names, pp. 699–701.

new government schools and colleges. But at the crest of the wave of reform the Empress Dowager, long having loathed the near subjugation of China by Western powers, imprisoned her young puppet, who, as she saw it, had got out of hand in his Western craze, and took back control of the government.

Now Miss Rook began to show signs of excitement. For some time, she said, the Empress Dowager had been giving tacit support to an antiforeign secret society called *I Ho Ch'uan* ("righteous harmonious fists"), and after she stifled the Kuang Hsü Emperor's reforms these "Boxers," as they were called in English, began a series of violent attacks on foreigners and Chinese Christians. In a short span, 242 missionaries and other foreigners, and thousands of Chinese Christian converts, were massacred.

Miss Rook's cheeks were now bright red. Her unrelentingly detailed picture of Christian women's breasts being cut off with swords by the Boxers, of castrations of males, of disembowelments and beheadings, not to mention pillage, arson, and desecrations, by the heathens; and her unashamedly gleeful accounts of the revenge taken by zealous defenders of the faith—she particularly praised a Reverend V. R. Prior and a Reverend D. F. Larksbury— who, having persuaded American officers to allow them to lead a squad of cavalry into the countryside near Peking to hunt Boxers, and having found that villagers had fled at their approach and emptied their settlements, thereupon set every house on fire "with a certain conviction in their minds that Boxers had surely been hiding there"—all these things Miss Rook told, David wrote, "with eyes like burning sulphur."

His diary for the next few days was peppered with evidences of pumped-up courage: " 'Though they slay me yet will I trust in him.' " " 'He who would save his life shall lose it, but he who would lose his life *for my sake*, the same shall save it.' "

It was at this time that David, as if he were a soldier about to go into battle writing (in case he did not return alive) a last letter home, sketched out "The Events of My Life."

on april 4, Hurte came to Treadup with astonishing news: He had had a letter from Todd saying that the Treadup candidacy had come too late; the ten men for China had already been named. Blackton's apparently official bid had, it seemed, meant nothing. David's diary on the fifth: "Many who know of Dr. Todd's attitude are extremely unsatisfied."

Now came a terrible struggle. Was this God's will? Must he bow his head to it? He felt hanging over him an unspoken obligation to be a good Christian and accept this painful outcome.

Like a hurt child, he ran to his other mother of that period, Mrs. Kupfer, in puzzlement and for comfort.

Christian or not, she had reacted in rage, he learned, and had written the great James B. Todd a stinging letter.

THE LETTER must indeed have been full of peppercorns, for less than a week later, on April 11, we find a cryptic note in Treadup's diary: "Hurte tells me there is to be a new development on the China question."

The very next night Treadup was in an upper berth on the Empire State Limited, riding to New York, where he arrived at ten o'clock on the morning of the thirteenth. He put up, as Hurte had told him to do, at a cheap hotel, the Breslin, and hurried to the offices of the International Y.M.C.A. at 124 East 28th Street.

There he learned that he was to be seen not by Todd but by Blackton. The latter was over in New Jersey that afternoon, interviewing some other young man. So David, his big body prickling with frustrated curiosity, took a ferry to Bedloe's Island and

> *climbed to the top of the Statue of Liberty—practically ran up. I looked out through the windows of the diadem—I who want with all my heart to be an 'emigrant,' going overseas to "your poor, your tired, your huddled masses."*

Blackton received Treadup early the next morning and said that "Dr. Todd is considering me for Syracuse representative in China." No mention of Mrs. Kupfer's letter. Treadup rather boldly reminded Blackton that Blackton himself, surely with Todd's knowledge, had three months earlier given him a formal bid to go to China for the Association. What was behind the change in signals? Then it came out:

> *Mix-up based on their reluctance to send a bachelor. Once you are out there for life, chance of finding wife slim. I said I would do my best to remedy the situation. Mr. Blackton asked me if I had definite prospects. I hope I was not carried away by my eagerness, I said, "Not definite but I am hopeful."*

Blackton disappeared, presumably to consult with the remote Dr. Todd. He came back after a while with a doctor, who told David to strip to his B.V.D.'s. "He hummed the whole time he examined me." Small wonder; this Gulliver was indecently healthy.

Blackton led Treadup into Todd's office.

> *His first words were, "Ah, yes, I remember this handsome fellow. I think we could find this Lochinvar a bride, don't you, Blackie?" I thanked him and said I would do it for myself. "Well, then, if you will undertake that I think we're ready to announce it, Treadup." The breeze of that man refreshed the most solemn moment of my life. Will probably sail in October.*

BACK AT SYRACUSE on Sunday, the sixteenth, David had the pleasure of hearing the chancellor announce in chapel the International Committee's decision. "Many congratulate me. This development ought to greatly stimulate and arouse the missionary interest here." The next day the city paper, the *Standard,* and the university paper, the *Herald,* both carried long stories about Treadup the missionary-elect. "I believe I am called to a mighty work. The Syracuse constituency greatly pleased."

David got permission to go home to confirm his family's permission.

I took train for home via Weedsport. Father and Mother do not object. It will be hard for them however. Brot home several books on China. My time of prep for this work is short. The Salt Branch 'Clarion' picked up announcement from Syracuse paper, so everyone knows about my going. The different questions are interesting and in some cases amusing. Is it true that the Chinese eat rats? Will I wear a pigtail? Bad question, oft repeated: Am I to go alone? My answers to that are awkward.

The rest of the term sped away. We have already seen how frantic the wife hunt had become. Studies gave him trouble when spring fever struck. He was rowing—and it was at the Long Branch boathouse, in May, that David suffered a sudden outburst of the old "badness."

Coach Ten Eyck had rebuked him for a halfhearted effort in practice, and after the shell had been carried into the boat shed David took his oar outside, whirled it in circles three times over his head, and with a lunge smashed the blade against the trunk of an oak tree.

Ten Eyck threatened to dismiss Treadup from the Navy, but beating Cornell was evidently more important in the end than teaching a lesson about property to the most powerful hulk in his eight; and the penalty was reduced to payment for the oar.

As in the past, a downswing of David's spirits followed the outburst. Notes suggest that he was hard hit by the irrevocability of his commitment—to a lifetime of exile. His wild search for a partner was getting nowhere. And suddenly the sadness and, so far as the hunt was concerned, the finality of graduation was upon him.

Last frat chapter meeting. Farewell speeches. Many regrets. Baccalaureate sermon by Chancellor. We ('05) marched in caps and gowns. I had to preside at Class Day and made a mediocre speech. At Fraternity Alum dinner I responded for chapter. Commencement oration by Dr. Buckley was very good. Obstructive, Destructive, and Constructive Men. Received the sheepskin. Chancellor's reception, I took Miss Miller. It dawns with great force that it is all over. These good-byes are painful. My problem remains unsolved, and I am now to be removed from female company.

THE COURTING

DAVID was by now a huntsman verging on panic. He had heard from Hurte of two cases of desperate bachelor volunteers for overseas, for whom the SVM and the designated missions had simply gone out and *found* deserving brides. He distinctly did not want an arranged marriage. What if James B. Todd, with that Godworthy smile of confidence in what is best for us all, saddled him, "till death do us part," with someone like poor Miss Jenkins at Syracuse: *fine Christian woman, not particularly strong face* — David's euphemism ("and the greatest of these is charity") for *ugly?*

AFTER graduation David was able to steal a couple of days from crew practice to go home. "This is like the olden days, to have the family all together. How we children have changed and separated!" "Paul and I went fishing at night. I speared four. I made some good shoots so have not forgotten how."

The Poughkeepsie race was something of an anticlimax. David did not feel, as he had the year before, the abandoned, ecstatic burst of power of the man possessed by a sport — as if, for a third of an hour, the sport were expressing itself through him rather than the other way around. "I was logy." Syracuse came in second, nineteen lengths behind Cornell. And that was the untriumphant end of being a college man.

DAVID was summoned to a ten-day conference, for the volunteers who were about to go out in the field, at Silver Bay. There they would undergo concentrated instruction for their various missions.

With a fortnight to kill, David decided to hike from Salt Branch across New York State to Lake George, and during those days, easing along the valley of the Mohawk River, stopping now and then to catch a fish on a collapsible rod and to fry it on the banks on a tiny skillet over a fire of sticks, sleeping under the stars, waiting out a day of rain in an old inn in Little Falls, then moving on and on, he was "filled with a piercing melancholy. I strive to make a picture in my mind of a woman by my side in Cathay, but I cannot see her clearly." He was carrying in his pack a copy of a recently published book, *The*

Lore of Cathay, by W. A. P. Martin, the president of the Chinese Imperial University in Peking; he would stop in the afternoons and read for an hour "under these beloved maples and chestnuts and oaks I may never see again, turning the pages and dreaming about a mysterious future shared with a mysterious someone."

When he reached the foot of Lake George, he rented a rowboat and, blissfully at a pair of oars again for his own solitary pleasure in gliding on water, he took three days to row forty miles to the head of the lake and then back to Silver Bay, halfway down the western shore, sleeping nights on fragrant pine needles under conifers. "What will life bring? What will life bring?"

THE PROGRAM at Silver Bay was something like that of the much larger Northfield Conference the previous summer: lectures, discussion groups, prayer meetings, and plenty of time for swimming, tennis, rowing, walking, singing—and thinking: "time to be alone with my master." All too alone. His lack hung over him. Ten of the thirteen men who were headed for China were married, and their wives—some of them attractive ("Ginser made a good choice," "Mrs. Saxe is cheery")—were there in the flesh, in wind-blown bloomers on the tennis court, in knee- and elbow-length woolen swim togs in the cool lake. David was joylessly paired with one of the bachelors. "Adams and I climbed Sunrise Mountain." "Rowed with Adams to Gull Bay, ten miles."

ONE IMPORTANT QUESTION was soon settled. "Todd spoke at 10:30 on the cost of leadership. He was at his best. His addresses always inspire me. Interview with him at 2 P.M. My field is to be Tientsin with Gridley and Harmon." So he knew he was to be in North China, in a city near Peking. At the end of the interview

> *Dr. Todd frightened me. He asked me how my matrimonial plans were progressing. His expression was severe. I had visions of having the post he had just named snatched back from me. Without lying, I made the best of my situation. I said I had given a solemn promise that I would solve that problem, and that I had a habit of keeping my promises. "I knew we could count on you, Treadup," he said. I came away wretched.*

Wretched all day, he doggedly made notes on readings assigned by the convention programmers. One edifying entry, on the heathen Chinese:

> *"This moral mummy [the Chinaman—DT] is embalmed and wrapped in superstition four thousand years old, and more than ten thousand*

layers deep. These superstitions touch every act of life, and every word, and every secret thought. They are victims of luck, fortune-tellers, and necromancy. They live in a world packed to the very stars with powerful spirits, which must not be offended. All ranks and classes, from the emperor down to the poorest coolie, are steeped and boiled and parboiled in superstition. By these superstitions the university men and the priests govern and rob and torment all classes."

Another entry, on the Chinese woman:

"She is not desired at birth, is subject to father, husband, and son, and is denied the privileges of education. To destroy baby girls at birth was formerly exceedingly common, and not regarded as a crime by the majority. Often no name, simply a number, is given to the baby girl, and a father in counting his family members mentions only sons. Girls are simply sold as bondmaids to relieve poverty; and a wife may be legally sold or rented by her husband to another man for a fixed period. The binding of feet is but an outward and visible sign of the crippled lives and energies of one-half of _____ "

IN HIS DIARY for that day, in words obviously written in slapdash haste and agitation, we discover why the note on women was suddenly broken off:

While copying in commonplace notebook just now I was suddenly struck right in the solar plexus by a momentous thought! Why has it held itself back from me all this time? I must write to Emily Kean! [In his excitement he uses her first name, for the first time we have ever seen it in his hand.] *Who can tell how things went with Mr. Zeedon, '00? Perhaps the fact that she did not teach after all, as planned, at Chittenango, near to the city of Syracuse and Mr. Z, can be taken as encouraging. I remember the evening after the Park Church service when I opened my heart to her and it seemed to me she reciprocated. She did like me. I cannot understand why this idea has hidden itself from me!*

It took David two days to get up the courage to shoot his arrow into the sky. "I wrote Emily Kean and am praying for the outcome."

David's letter has not survived. It is likely that if David dared in it to ask Emily Kean whether her hand and heart were after all free, he would also appeal to that side of her which had won her the presidency of the college Y.W.C.A. He would suggest to her the obvious possibilities of "a partnership in service" in the mission field. He might have working for him, besides, though he would never have written it down, the thought that there must be something amiss with an attractive woman not yet married, or perhaps not even engaged, a full year after college. His diary hints that this was one time when David broke the promise he had made himself at Syracuse never to utter self-serving prayers.

AFTER SILVER BAY —no answer had come from Miss Kean—he went to New Bedford, to visit the Framptons, and to see friends from his years there. For the first time in his life he experienced something like a vacation. "Resting. Moonlight sail. . . . Rode to Marion in carriages. . . . To Woods Hole by steamer. . . . To Newport on the trolley. We were exceedingly fortunate in being able to get on the *Missouri* and to see eight of the boats of the north Atlantic gunboat squadron."

"The Russian difficulty darkens," he wrote right after the Newport jaunt, for the sight of the warships must have made vivid in his mind the news of the Russian Revolution of 1905, which had by then reached the stage of naval revolts. The earlier strikes, riots, and assassinations, and public outrage at the government, had been intensified by the destruction of the Russian Pacific fleet at Tsushima by Admiral Togo in May. The war in Manchuria and North Korea seemed (from such a distance) all too close to *his* Tientsin.

On July 15 he received a letter in New Bedford from Mr. Blackton (David must have given correspondents the address there), telling him to attend a gathering of Y.M.C.A. overseas candidates in Bronxville in August, and to go to New York and then Northfield for further interviews and instructions. The letter enclosed money for the trips.

TWO DAYS later he wrote a tightly controlled entry in the diary: "Received a nice letter from Emily Kean."

No more. No exclamation point. But what a head of steam in that careful word, "nice"! Emily had not, at the very least, closed the door in David's face. Perhaps she had cared for him at Syracuse more than he had realized. At once:

> *Wrote again to Emily Kean. I love her! I believe that the greater the sacrifice for Jesus Christ, the greater the peace and satisfaction of life. I spend much time alone with him.*

ON JULY 28 he returned to Salt Branch, and there the laconic diary takes up the story. David's second letter must have pressed a bit too hard, for now Emily's fear of the unknown seems to have been rearoused. She has found an impediment.

JULY 29 Received letter from Emily Kean. She has a duty which calls her to work here at home. Her father has had reverses which made it impossible for him to do for her two younger sisters as he has done for her. Emily must help.

But David nevertheless floats in a nimbus of daydreams. "I am going to do all I can to remove Emily's difficulties," he writes. Two days later: "Wrote letters. One to Emily. Walked in the fields, watched the clouds, and prayed to God." All around him are matings: "Carl Becker has his sweetheart out from New York." "Brother Will came down to stay overnight. He is engaged to Frances Mindorff. I am praying for another worker for China."

His hopes seem to have stirred up delicious fantasies, which must be curbed. "It is a fight for me to stay pure. Fight the good fight with all thy might, Christ is thy strength and Christ thy right." And temptation: "Called on Cassie Berns. She is hurt with me." He is trying to break with the past: is burning papers and selling off belongings, all in a lover's daze. "A most delightful day. Clear and cool. I am feasting on nature, the clouds and sunsets are splendid."

Not waiting for a new answer from Emily, he writes to her again.

ON AUGUST 17 he went by train to Albany, where he visited the capitol and the Association building. Two days later he arrived at the Hotel Grammatan in Bronxville for a meeting with members of the International Committee. There: "Received letter from Emily. Not very encouraging. Dark day."

And the following day: "Rainy, so cannot go out in the hills. Full sessions of reports. I am handicapped in having this problem just now. The time is so short. . . . "

The time had clearly come to talk to Emily face to face. On the twenty-second David went to New York, where he stayed for two days with a young volunteer, a candidate for Canton or Hong Kong, named George Field, at Columbia. Now there comes an explosive entry:

24 Went to Madison, N.J., in P.M. to try to settle the problem which has been long and, in the end, hard. She is the one! Her opening to me was too sacred to write about! God is good to me!

This is all we learn, but it is enough. David is whirled back into a series of indoctrination meetings. "Took train to Northfield, where the foreign comm. met. Todd, Grimes, and Horris lectured. *Happy!*" Two days later: "They are working us hard, giving us last directions. My trunk has been lost several days. HAPPY!" He returned to New York, where he stayed with Robert Service, who was destined for interior China (and to be father of John Service, one of the State Department China hands hounded from office, many years later, by Senator Joseph McCarthy). David notes with some relief that peace has been settled between Japan and Russia. There are more meetings at the Association offices.

Then in three terse entries the story is brought to its swift conclusion:

> SEPT. 2 *Returned to Madison just as Emily received an unfavorable letter from her mother. How I love this woman and how she loves me. Happy!*
>
> 3 *Went to service with my dear. Our love deepens hourly. Telegraphed to Mother Kean to come. We are becoming one in spirit in two bodies.*
>
> 4 *Mother Kean came early this morning. She is splendid and says Emily can go with me. Placed the Psi U pin where it belongs. This winning is the greatest feat of my life.*

BUT THE WINNING was subject to ratification. This "other worker for China" had to be found acceptable to the Association authorities.

David returned to New York for a series of conferences with Blackton, Tinker, Poe, Henry, Irons, Johnson, and a man who was to be one of his colleagues in Tientsin and who was now in the United States on furlough, Thomas Gridley. Ten years older than Treadup, Gridley was a graduate of Princeton, where he had been a football star; people still called him Center Rush Gridley. As big as Treadup, he was jovial, breezy, warm, and bumptious, "with a heart proportional to his build."

David spent two days seeing these men and haunting the New York Central freight offices, trying to trace his trunk. "Things are looking favorable for me to marry before going." He returned to Madison on a Thursday. While Emily taught school on Friday, he read in the public library. "Life is bright even on a rainy day."

On Saturday, David took Emily to New York, where the couple was put through a hideous ordeal. Emily was examined alone by a forbidding panel of male judges, Todd, Blackton, Gridley, and several members of the International Committee; and then from head to foot by a male doctor. David and Emily were kept waiting for an hour while the elders conferred. They were summoned and Blackton delivered the verdict: Miss Kean was acceptable, but it was decided that Mr. Treadup should proceed at once to China, and Miss Kean should devote a year or eighteen months to helping her parents and then follow overseas.

A new and bitter struggle for Christian acceptance which both of them might have had was eased by their being so besotted by love that obstacles seemed like opportunities. Three days later: "After careful consideration we have decided the comm. decision is best. Our love grows."

On September 18, after a last round of conferences, and having found his trunk, David took the Empire State Limited to Syracuse and then went home to Salt Branch. Tersely: "My people are pleased that I am engaged to Emily." He repacked his trunk and crated some belongings, including his large iron bedstead, and with a trusting heart sent everything off ahead to that so far imaginary place, Tientsin, China. On the thirtieth he went to Herkimer, met Emily at the station, and rode with her to her home, a mile and a half outside the village of Newport. The diary:

OCT. 1 *Her father is Supervisor and game protector. This is a superb valley and the color of the trees dazzling. The sun never shone brighter. Her people open themselves to me. Kitty has light and nervous temperament, Jane more like Emily, slower to get close. Mr. Kean a bluff Scotsman. Mrs. Kean feels my taking Emily away very sharply. She gives vent to her feelings.*

A week later David took Emily to Salt Branch. "It seems like a dream to have her in my home. She has a rare spirit." For five days Emily helped David "getting things systematized." She made a scrap album of his past. "These are happy days when we can love and confide. Emily likes the dear ones and they her."

On October 18 David took Emily home to Newport, and the diary notes choke in their tautness in dealing with finalities:

Tore away. Brave sweet woman. She never broke down. Applied for policy with N.Y. Life. Went to S.B. in P.M. . . . Last night at home. Packing all done. . . . Cut home ties with awful wrench. All wept at prayer. I went through it all with dry eyes. . . . Took train at 3 P.M. for Chicago. Changed in Buffalo. I am going to miss Emily oh so much. God bless and keep all my loved ones and give me strength for everything that comes. . . . Bowels off. Wrote to Todd, loved ones, and Emily. . . . Spent morning at Mont. Ward and Co., buying outfit. Wrote E. . . . Awoke aboard Provinces Limited close to the Miss. River and half an hour out of St. Paul. Breakfasted and got shave in barbershop at Minneap. Took Soo Line for Portal. . . . Great wheat fields of the north. Threshing, burning straw. . . . Awoke at Portal two hours late. Two Chinamen were detained. Saw the Customs inspectors go through some trunks. Great expanse of prairies. Men risk everything out here for money. Land away from the Ry. $10 per 640 acres. Wrote E. . . . Entered the Rockies. Train climbs along the ranges, follows crooked streams, shoots through tunnels. Stopped at Glacier. . . . Showed Emily's picture to Mrs. Tower in seat in front. Arrived at Vancouver at one P.M. Am to have stateroom with Dr. Elting older man who goes back out with a mission in West China. . . . Wrote to Grow, Paul, Mrs. Kupfer, Father, Emily, Emily. Went aboard the

'Empress of Japan' and saw staterooms. . . . There will be nine at least in our party. Wrote last letters. Aboard at noon. Many down to see us off. At 3:30 P.M. the gangplank was drawn up, and I was cut off from the continent and from my boyhood and from my dearest dearest Emily. And from changing my mind. The instant when the block and tackle lifted the gangplank's wheels off the dock! Inch of thin air between the wheels and the dock! The rest of my life in that inch.

BOOK TWO

⊞

USE GRAVITY!

TO CHINA

AT DAWN America was out of sight astern. The farm boy vibrated with the largeness of being a world traveler on this white floating city called the *Empress of Japan*. The oval of the carefully varnished rail under his hands had flakes of sea salt on it. All the metal wore an uneven thick skin of white paint. The rolling city creaked, and down in the cabin one heard a constant thumping which Dr. Elting said came from the helical blades of the propeller biting at the miles of the ocean.

Servants in white jackets were always cheerful at your elbow, and they gave one a sinking feeling. Were they Chinese or Japanese? How could one tell? Could a ship called the *Empress of Japan* be manned by Chinamen? Here, in one who had pledged his whole life to the service of the Chinese people, was an ignorance so profound that he dared not ask anyone for the answer.

The puzzle made him dizzy. Or was it the rising and dipping of the horizon? Dr. Elting reserved two deck chairs. The deck steward tucked David into his with a blanket that had an odor of a dampness seven miles deep. Dr. Elting strode round and round the deck, his jaw working as he walked, as if he too were masticating miles. His beard blew like an ample white scarf over his shoulder. David heard roared snatches of the veteran warrior's conversation with fellow pacers as they approached his deck chair on their rounds:

" . . . that great Eleventh of Hebrews with its inspired and inspiring record of Old Testament men and women of faith, and of what God wrought through them . . . "

That day David saw fish that could fly. He saw porpoises in the joy of their breaching and arching. In midafternoon there were shouts on deck, and out on the sea he saw fountains. Whale spouts! Jonah was on David's mind, a man in a dark room in a kind of submarine that was alive—until Dr. Elting shouted in his merciless praying voice, "Thar she blows! Thar she *blows!*" and then playfully started pacing with one leg stiff as if he were clumping along on a peg of whalebone.

THE WIND rose. The waves bared their white teeth. David suddenly felt that he, become Jonah, had swallowed a whale. He threw back the musty blanket and fled on knees of sponge to the cabin, where he disgorged his viscera, his young pluck, and all his hopes of life to come.

He was seasick for three days. Dr. Elting, healthy as a horse in a hay meadow, sloshed and spewed as he shampooed his beard in the morning, and dressing bellowed a hymn that rang in David's perfidious inner ears all day:

> *Jesus, Savior, pilot me*
> *Over life's tempestuous sea;*
> *Unknown waves before me roll,*
> *Hiding rock and treacherous shoal;*
> *Chart and compass come from Thee:*
> *Jesus, Savior, pilot me!*

"Stay on deck!" Dr. Elting shouted. "Fresh air!"

David, in the cocoon of his steamer rug, was able to sip the consommé and nibble on the crisp water biscuits the tactful deck steward offered him; only to have to stagger below again to empty out his emptiness.

Part of his seasickness must have been the effect of a rough voyage of the mind into the unknown. He was a twenty-seven-year-old landsman out on a vast alien tossing sheet of mystery, driven by the unconscious national impulse of westing toward a heathen shore. He heaved his heart out into an enamel basin because he was lovesick and homesick. This was not like the voyages dreamed in the *Ecarg* on the ice pond in Salt Branch. Was the world flat, and would the *Empress of Japan* fall off the edge in the night? He had promised away a whole lifetime. Now he expected the span to be very short. He would die on the crest of the next wave.

BUT HE DOES not die. Instead he rings for the room steward and asks him to fetch the ship's doctor. "Get doctor!" he shouts. "Me want doctor!" In his letter to Emily describing this scene, he tells of his intense shame at falling into childish red-Indian talk in his effort to make himself understood by the Chinese or Japanese servant. The steward nods and grins and goes away. After a while he returns with the assistant purser, a young Englishman. David sheepishly says he was wondering if the ship's doctor could give him something for his stomach. The young Englishman looks at David from the lofty height of a race with sturdy sea legs—this is David's first encounter with the British stare that will burn his eyes for years in China—and says he will see what he can do, sir.

A hundred waves later the doctor comes in. He is English and drunk. He is gallant and jocose. *"Mal de mer,"* he says, "is seated here." He aims a finger like a pistol at his own head. Then he begins to fumble in his black bag. In his condition the motion of the ship throws him about like a rag doll. David, who knows what to think of drinking, does not want to be given the wrong medicine by this sinner, and he is on the point of telling the doctor that he suddenly feels better when the door flies open and Dr. Elting enters singing. The long beard wags for a few moments as the doctor of divinity diagnoses the ailment of the doctor of medicine. Then there is fire in Dr. Elting's eye, and while David wrestles on the bunk with his gorge there is a brief but active exercise of Dr. Elting's gift for the rescue of souls. The physician, who has obviously encountered missionaries before on this run to the Orient, snaps his bag shut with exaggerated dignity, the little finger of the hand at the catch genteelly elevated as if to hold a teacup, and exits with his head high, apparently forgetting that he has not treated his patient.

T H E   A F F A I R of the drunken doctor seemed to tap a deep well of outrage in Dr. Elting. This worthy elder was on his way back to a remote station of the Presbyterians after his first furlough in thirty years. He had told David on the first day that he was a believer in itinerating: the lonely task of wandering in the hinterland with a few Bibles and tracts on one's cart, preaching in the streets of small towns, saving the poor heathen Chinese one by one, "drinking every day," he said, "the sweet nectar of soul-winning." This was the evangelistic romance David had so often heard about and dreamed of. Dr. Elting's wife had died of a quinsy; he had lost a son to a fever as the family fled across the country in rags, disguised as Chinese peasants, during the Boxer time. He prayed angrily to an angry God, and now, dizzied, it seemed, by the fragrance of spirituous liquors hanging on the air of the stateroom after the doctor's door slam, he turned his improving eye on poor David. Seasick David did not need this.

Dr. Elting chose this moment to ask David how much he knew about Confucius.

"Precious little," said a weak voice from the berth.

"He looked at me," David wrote Emily,

as if I were a toad. "Another ignoramus!" he shouted. "Another ignora-
mus for the field!" Then he began to lecture me about "the deceptively
attractive ideas concerning ethics which you will find among the
Confucianists. You must steel yourself, young man, against this most
seductive of the heathen systems that you will encounter. It is almost the
case that with respect to morals a Christian may look in the mirror and
see — with but little distortion — a Confucianist. A looking glass — danger,
my son! — vanity! You will be putting up the true word as it is in Jesus
Christ against a very close semblance of the truth, and you will find that
the native Confucianist is not eager to purchase the wares you offer him.
He stands on the obverse of the reflection, and he sees no great advan-
tage on your side. I advise you in your untutored condition to stay away
from the literati. Your harvest will be among stupid people like yourself.
Even they will argue. Even there, you will need to be armed. I wish we
could tuck into the kitbag of every young recruit like you a concise little
tract with just the nub of the case against all these claims of the
Buddhists and the atheists and the Taoists and the Confucianists and so
forth. You should not go out there with blinders on. Bone up. Get the
main lines of the thing. Don't go out there an ignoramus!" And with
that, Emily, he departed from the stateroom with his head at almost
exactly the same angle as the doctor's when he had left a few minutes
before, and he slammed the door in exactly the same way.

TO DAVID's astonishment, Dr. Elting's wrath acted as a tonic. Instead of
feeling chagrined, he felt much better. He got up and about. The sea was no
flatter than it had been, but David's mind turned to the stability of the little
gyroscope in Absolom Carter's demonstrations at Enderbury Institute. He
paced the decks and scanned the bulletin boards. He played pickup games of
shuffleboard and deck tennis and Ping-Pong, and he noted in his diary:
"About seventy passengers. Businessmen, army officers, pleasure seekers,
sixteen missionaries. Making 350 miles/p/d."

In the library off the main saloon, two days later, he wrote letters on
ship's stationery. To Dr. Todd in New York:

In a day of sports on shipboard, I was fortunate enough to uphold the
reputation of the Association by winning two events. When they learned
that I was an Association Secretary, the officials did not offer me the
prepared prizes — boxes of cigars — but quietly exchanged them for boxes
of candy, thus giving a nice testimonial to the Association.

DURING the night of November 5, the *Empress* crossed the 180th meridian,
the International Date Line, and something happened that quite frightened

David. A day was lost from his life. The ship crossed an invisible line in the ocean, and having retired on Sunday evening, he awoke on Tuesday morning. He felt a yawning gap in his immediate past. What might he have experienced on that lost day? What might he have learned? Feeling a need to make up for the loss, and having heard that there were numerous Chinese passengers down in steerage on this ship—some of them turned back from America by the recent extension of the "yellow-peril" immigration restrictions, others going home discouraged by the hostility they had encountered during their stays—he descended, like Virgil into hell, into the bowels of the *Empress*. What he saw there seared his mind.

Back on the lifeboat deck in fresh air on his chair, he tried to stammer out to Dr. Elting the picture of that pathetic band huddled in unventilated caverns of the holds: students, coolies, businessmen, packed in without regard to person or station, in a miasma of vomitous odors, kept out of sight and mind of the seventy white saloon passengers above.

Dr. Elting, seated stiffly beside him, disdaining a blanket, was unmoved. "Did you preach?" he asked (as David wrote Emily).

"No," David said. He wanted to add: *I fled.*

"You should have preached. You must realize that the Chinese people are dying without God at the rate of a million a month. Look into the hearts of those passengers down there, young man. There is nothing they need so badly as the Gospel of Jesus Christ. The nation they are going back to is rotten to the core. You will not find an honest man in China from the rickashaw puller to the lamentable boy who is called Son of Heaven. Eunuchs rule the roost. Chicanery, rapacity, cheating—there is greed and shame and moral corruption in every transaction. Men sell their daughters into sin. They quarrel and smoke opium. God is truant from their lives. Righteousness is absent from China. Ah, son, those of us who know God see a bleak future for that great empire. The Chinese talk about reform, they dabble in what they call reform, but they must look to their morals and turn them right around toward Jesus Christ, or China as we know it will wither away to oblivion."

"He was putting me on my guard," David wrote Emily, "against a tendency to idealize the conditions of the heathen and the heathen world. Still," he added, "I wish he had gone down there to see for himself."

DAVID was impressed by Dr. Elting. This Moses dressed in black serge was obviously one of the heroes of the penetration of China, and David was moved by things he said. Years later he recalled with embarrassment that one of the old man's outbursts had thrilled him so much he had had gooseflesh all over his body. They were talking about the British officers on the ship. David felt intimidated by them; his way of putting this to Dr. Elting was: "These Brits are starchy, aren't they?"

The big white head swiveled toward David, throwing its white chin-flag around. "Look here," he said. "Mark you the providence of the Lord in opening the door of faith unto the Chinese Gentiles. First he sent the English branch of the Anglo-Saxon race and gave it a hold of the two wrists of the imperial power. God sent the gunboats and God sent the cannons, and God sent these men you call starchy. They planted their standard in Peking, they planted their standard in Tientsin. I am speaking of 1858, 1860. The English power grasped the hands and held them firmly, and then God gave to the other branch of the Anglo-Saxon race, to us, to the Americans, access to the brain and to the heart of the Chinese heathen. He let the English use main strength, to hold the heathen still so he would listen to *us*. He made *us* the prime evangelizers and educators of those people. God had a plan before we ever saw it."

In a letter to brother Paul a decade later, recalling this episode, David tersely commented: "Everything considered, in my preparation for my missionary career there was perilous little left out, of exactly the sort of thing that would most unsuit me for my work."

LACONIC notes from David's diary:

> NOV. 14 *Awoke as the 'Empress' entered the bay before Yokohama. Saw Togo's fleet. Saw Fujiyama at dawn. Rode about town in a jinrickisha.*
> 15 *Arrived Kobe about two today. Found Kobe a town touched everywhere with Western life. Made some small purchases.*
> 16 *On inland sea. The sides of the mountains terraced and cultivated. My vaccination is working lovely.*
> 17 *Arrived Nagasaki at 6 A.M. Nagasaki not as clean as other towns. Saw more of Jap life. Have decided the ship's crew is Chinese.*

So much for Japan. David seemed to be withholding his real excitement for what was to come. The sea south of Japan was as quiet, he wrote Emily, "as a bay. As I near China I am concerned to know what is before me but thankful that I cannot see." What a strange line! Was he savoring his last hours of naiveté and ignorance? Or had fierce old Dr. Elting frightened him? By the time he wrote "Search," years later, he had come to believe that the days of harrowing seasickness on this voyage had marked a turning point in his life. He thought perhaps he had vomited out a great deal of his former priggishness, his self-concern. He was humble. He was ready to try to be kind.

He was out on deck at dawn on the nineteenth, and in the first light of day he saw a strange sea-change. At a definite line, the water turned from blue to yellowish brown. "Silt from Tibet!" Dr. Elting shouted. "That's water from the Yangtze, my boy!"

THE FLEDGLING missionary went ashore at Shanghai at ten o'clock on the morning of November 19, 1905. Three Y.M.C.A. secretaries' wives— Mesdames Keystone, Wolf, and Wood—were on the dock to meet him. As David walked down the gangplank his whole being seemed to be concentrated in the itch of his vaccination. Was this *China*? The river was massed with destroyers, gunboats, and merchant ships flying the flags of European nations. The ladies rode with David in a carriage across the Soochow Creek Bridge and along the Bund—an asphalted path by the river, a lovely strip of tended lawn, a busy thoroughfare. Mrs. Keystone was the tour guide. She waved a white-gloved hand toward the compound of the British consulate. Police Court. Then the first of what she called "the hongs": vast stone office buildings, Fearon's, Dent's, Jardine Matheson. Had there been a terrible mistake? Had he crossed the Atlantic? Was this London? Out on the river—Mrs. Keystone's lips were pursed—were four ugly opium hulks, where the drug, she said, was bonded. The *Yuenfah*, the *Ariel*, the *Corea*, the *Wellington*. "The *Ariel*," she said, "was an American clipper that sailed out of here and was dismasted off the Saddles." The Customs House and receiving shed; then two banks. Kelly and Walsh, a bookstore. The Telegraph Company. The China Merchants Company. David was nothing but a hot arm. He decided in his dismay he had smallpox. *Where* was the quaint Cathay of his heart's yearning? In the wide-lawned public gardens he had seen a gazebo, a bandstand: a grand version of the one back in Salt Branch. Oh, no! The fever was homesickness! He should not have come. Emily! They tricked me! Todd and Blackton sold me a counterfeit country!

The Keystones were gentle, but David woke the next morning with the chills and aches of a cheated man. Mrs. Keystone took him downtown to order an overcoat against the North China winter, and a cutaway and striped trousers that the farm boy would need for formal occasions with Chinese officials. They rode in rickshas past the playgrounds of empire: the race-course, the Swimming Bath, the Shanghai Cricket ground, the Golf Club. The scrupulously tended flower beds beside the pavilions of pleasure were asplash with ravishing chrysanthemums. David saw the November light from these flowers caught glistening in tiny globes of sweat rolling down the neck of his ricksha boy. He wanted to shout: "Stop! Let me down. I'm sorry." The only Chinese he had been near so far were the Number One Boy and the coolie at the Keystones', and this panting human pony. "I'm sorry," he said out loud.

The tailor shop was on Shantung Road. Here in streets in back of the Bund were hints, at least, of a West-facing mercantile China: large Chinese characters on hanging signs over shopfronts adorned with carved dragons and red-tasseled octagonal lamps. Shops of silk, satin, embroideries, curios, purses, pottery, scrolls, cloth shoes, ear guards, tea-root figures, and even, if you had the need, coffins—and David felt he might. The tailor exclaimed in a wild flattery of pidgin English at David's enormous size. The coat would be ready the next afternoon at two.

FARROW BLACKTON, General Secretary of the Y.M.C.A. for all China, was now in the Far East, but he was off in Korea on Association business, and David would have to wait for his return to know exactly what his assignments in Tientsin would be. The next ship north was to leave on the twenty-eighth.

In the meantime he made the acquaintance of the Shanghai secretaries. "Took tiffin with Wolfs." "Dinner with Sinclairs." Keystone took him to some evening classes. He helped measure an athletic field, tracing out racing lanes with lime, for a meet among Chinese athletes the Association was staging; and at the meet he was awed by the presence of six "stewards" who were of "high official rank next to governors," in silks and conical hats with buttons and badges of their haughty grades. With Bulmer Wolf he called on Methodist Bishop James W. Bashford, to be, as it were, blessed out of his shock at this non-China he had reached after so many struggles of the heart. But even the episcopal nods over teacups failed to rescue David from his incredulity and letdown. Near tears, he shopped for some curios to send home to loved ones. He wore his new overcoat everywhere. It was lined with fur. It had cost eight American dollars.

"IT IS WAR"

ON NOVEMBER 28 David started downriver with his colleague F. Albert Wood on a coastwise steamer, the *Hsin Tung*. After the huge white surge of the *Empress*, this tinny black little tremblement of a cargo vessel with room for just six cabin passengers seemed to rock whenever a fish jumped near it in the river. Sure enough, when she reached the open sea, she bucked and rolled and felled poor David. He had recovered from his reaction to his vaccination but not from his reaction to the spurious China he had seen in Shanghai. The ship's captain, a Scotchman named McKinnon, was a soft-spoken Christian, and he dropped by two or three times a day to assure David that the motion would stop as soon as they rounded the Shantung peninsula. That, however, took two and a half days. One of the cabin passengers was a silk-clad Chinese gentryman who had been the Emperor's Minister to Madrid. At the one meal David was able to take at table, this splendid personage ate with chopsticks and made rude slurping sounds; Wood whispered on deck afterward that according to Chinese etiquette these noises praised the cook. David sighed at how much he had to learn.

In midmorning of December 1 the *Hsin Tung* arrived off the bar at Taku, at the mouth of the Pei Ho; a tender took the passengers over the bar and ashore at three, and they caught the Tientsin train an hour later. They rode sixty miles over a flat and dun terrain, every inch tilled but for scattered villages of mud huts, windmills, conical grave mounds, and temples with curved roofs in groves of trees.

Secretaries Henderson and Harmon were on the train platform to meet the new secretary. Behind the warmth of their greeting was a sincerity that came from their knowledge, which David did not yet share, that the neophyte was going to relieve them of horse work so they could do things they had long wanted to do.

It was a damp and foggy evening, and as they stood there David was assaulted by the stink of great China, which came in windborne waves: the smell of night soil spread on fields so that the excrement of the generations would grow food to produce excrement to grow food to produce excrement in the endless cycle of a precarious agronomy; of decomposing human and animal corpses in shallow graves and floating face down in rivers; of decaying vegetation and feces in canals; of burning garbage; of the rotting guts of beasts in shambles; of garlic and sweat and menses and bad teeth and mildewed quilted garments — the hideous compacted smells of the poor. David, standing on the platform of Tientsin East train station, raised his nose to the evening breeze and knew he had arrived at last in some kind of China.

THE HENDERSON family took him in. Happily they lived in a Chinese-style house in the Chinese city — a walled compound containing several buildings on three courtyards. The Chinese-city work of the Association was done in the compound, which was on an alleyway called Ch'ing-tzu Hutung, near where the East Gate of the city wall had been. The Hendersons had two small children. They were warmly hospitable. They gave him a room on the innermost courtyard looking out on an acacia tree. Miraculously some of David's boxes shipped from Salt Branch had already arrived before him; one of the oddities he would soon learn about China was the astonishing combination of delays, false starts, postponements, corrupt deceptions, and lapses in execution, on the one hand, with dazzling efficiencies and expeditious deliveries and prompt and cheerful performances, on the other. Out of a kindness undoubtedly tinged with powerful curiosity, the Hendersons had opened all the boxes. One of them contained his bed frame, and Mrs. Henderson said: "We knew we were to have a grand big man, because the bedstead you'd shipped is seven feet long. I measured it. I said to Henny: 'This new chap must be Og, King of Babylon, whose bedstead was of iron; nine cubits was the length thereof, and four cubits the width of it.' "

Henderson broke some bad news to David that first evening: He knew that "Blackie" wanted David to start immediately teaching English-speaking Chinese students at the Peikai Middle School. This meant David would have to postpone his study of the Chinese language. Henderson had been teaching at the school. David saw at once that he was on the lowest rung of the North China ladder. There went the romantic visions of soul-winning—the young athlete braving famine and plague as a colporteur of tracts and a preacher to the heathen in fluent Mandarin: a great Elting in the making, except more sensitive, more humane. Instead he would grub along "doing" English comp and algebra and geog Monday and Wednesday evenings and Tuesday, Thursday, and Friday afternoons.

In his diary, three burdened words: "Prayed for courage."

THE NEXT MORNING Henny Henderson took David on a ricksha ride through the foreign parts of the city. "Another Shanghai," David dejectedly wrote that night. As they rode along, Henny explained how this strange, polyglot city had come into being. Though many miles upriver from the sea, he said, the Chinese had long used Tientsin as Peking's port. Four times in the nineteenth century, he said, foreign powers had humiliated China: the British, in the Opium War, in 1840; the British and French, in two campaigns in North China, in 1858 and 1860; and the Japanese, in the Sino-Japanese War in 1895. Under the Peking Convention, after the 1860 war, Henderson said, the British and French extracted from the Chinese the right to trade in Tientsin and to lease parcels of land on the city's riverfront. After the Japanese victory, the Germans and Japanese claimed similar concessions, and when the Boxer Rebellion was put down five years later, "the real grab game began," Henderson said. The Russians, the Belgians, the Italians, and the Austrians all carved out miniature countries, a few score acres in area, in the city, and the earlier lessees all enlarged their enclaves.

"This was truly queer," David wrote that night,

> for we traversed Europe—and more—in our rickshas in less than an hour. Without crossing water, we could go through England, France, Germany, and even Japan; Russia and Austria are across the river. Each of the concessions has the national architecture, language, legal system, plumbing, business methods, and costumes and customs of its proprietor.

On Victoria Road we saw Sikh policemen of the British force, with their turbans and beards; on Rue St. Louis we saw the Foreign Legion kepis of Senegalese policemen. Henny pointed out that one eats 'Knackwurst' in the German Concession, takes his shoes off at doors of inns and homes in the Japanese Concession, and plays cricket on the Recreation Ground in the British Concession. There's good living here: parks and racecourse and bathing and boating and golf clubs. The only Chinese I saw were ricksha boys, street cleaners, municipal workmen, and house servants; though Henny told me that some rich Chinese — businessmen and generals and government officials who are out of favor at court and are afraid of having their heads cut off — rent some of the big foreign houses with high walls around them topped with broken glass set in the mortar. What a letdown! In my imagination, I had had such a different picture of the city of my mission.

First impressions in the Chinese city were, besides, depressing. "Human life cheap. Servants dirty. Beggars in streets. Horrible cripples. Saw a leper — nose totally rotted away." He tried to make a home — bought some things: straw matting to cover the brick floor of his room; a screen with lotus blossoms painted on it; a washstand with its basin, pitcher, and slop jar (for there was no such thing here as running water).

IN GREAT TREPIDATION he faced his first class at the school. A bare, brick-walled room. Cold. Thirty students in rows on benches. Blank faces. David spoke slowly so the students would understand. Trying to use primer words, he gave a lecture, improvising as he went, on the republican form of government. The one-way dealings were hard. "Tough English and geog. Teaching going to take lots of time. The difficulties of the situation will call for much sacrifice."

MORE THAN he knew when he wrote those words, for Blackton finally arrived in mid-December and firmly told David that besides teaching at Peikai, he was going to have to take charge of the Settlement Branch of the Y.M.C.A., relieving Harmon for other work. David could hardly believe his ears. He was to take the place of *two* men. And the Settlement Branch! Not even dealing with Chinese but only with the foreigners of the concessions. It had been decided in New York that he was not to marry until the next fall.

David tried hard to be angry. All he could write in his diary was: "I fear these men have put dark glasses on." They could not see how things really stood.

Already, the next day, Christian passivity had set in. The rage David must have felt deep down lurks in his note on his meek acceptance of Blackton's orders:

I knew I must expect hardship and great travail out here. I have given my life to this work. It is war, and I as a general must be ready to face even death. Why not live with a smile and a happy heart?

ON ONE of his first evenings at the Hendersons' David heard a stirring story.

A visitor had come from Peking, an Association man David had met in New York during the trying time when Emily was being examined by the International Committee: "Center Rush" Gridley, the huge, jovial, bustling Princeton man with mustaches like a locomotive's cowcatcher. As they lingered at table after dinner, Gridley said he had heard disturbing news in Peking from a friend at the American Legation.

On October 28 — just three weeks before David stepped off the gangplank in Shanghai — the Presbyterian station at Lienchow had been sacked by a Chinese mob, and five more missionaries had been added to the roster of martyrs. Gridley explained to David that the Chinese had been reacting furiously in recent months against the American extension of the immigration exclusion act the year before — the "yellow peril" act, to keep cheap Chinese labor out of the United States.

"The fellow in charge down there at Lienchow," the big man said, "was a daggoned fool. First he buys a temple and stores the idols in an outhouse. Then, when the villagers build a mat shed for something or other, and one end sticks over onto Presbo land, he calls them in and makes them promise never to trespass again. Of course they do, so he sends out his coolies to steal three ridiculous little cannon the village clan owns to scare off bandits. He gives 'em back when he cools off, but not all the people in the village know he's returned 'em, so they bust into the hospital to look for 'em. While they're rummaging around they find a fetus preserved in alcohol in a big beaker. Well! That's enough! They parade it through the streets to show the people how missionaries murder babies and bottle 'em, so when they're ready they can scoop out the eyes and livers to mix 'em with lead and mercury to make silver. You know all those old stories, Henny. That's when the slaughter began."

David asked what "all those old stories" were.

"Henny and Center Rush told me some of them," David wrote Emily. "Their eyes," he wrote,

became like glass buttons as they talked, and there were red spots on their cheeks; you'd have thought they had a high fever. There were terrible Chinese broadsides and pamphlets that accused missionaries of the most barbarous crimes. They claimed that after the missionaries cut the vital organs out of babies' bodies they boiled the corpses and ate them, or laid them away in pickle barrels to eat in the winter. They said missionaries poisoned lice and spread them among the poor to kill them. And that they carved fetuses out of pregnant Chinese women and used them to make pills that rejuvenated Christians but crippled everyone else.

In this account David must have given Emily the impression that Henderson's and Gridley's feverish look came simply from their having lived so long with danger that it made them hot to tell of it, but from the diary we find another reason. In a hand so cramped and tiny as to be barely legible, David wrote some more things they told him—things he could not possibly have passed on to Emily. We can only imagine David's own pinpoint irises and embered cheeks as he wrote such forbidden words:

Accusations of 'these' sins: That potions, made of "monthlies," sperm, and virgins' ovaries, when rubbed on 'mons veneris' of Chinese women, caused them to be beside themselves with lust for missionaries. That missionaries considered menstrual blood sacred and drank it, and this gave them the famous missionary stink. That Roman Catholic priests inserted tubes in the rectums of young boys to enlarge them for comfort in the doings of Sodom and Gomorrah. That Protestant ministers, who thank heavens even these Chinese haters did not believe went in for such monstrosities, but rather favored the fair sex, initiated each young Chinese bride in the church in holy instruction in coitus. That they baptized nubile girls naked in holy water as a preparation for what the polemicists called "the net of pleasure."

Finally, as David *did* write Emily, the two older men told David of a massacre of foreigners

right here in Tientsin. It was thirty-five years ago, but they said it could happen today. The arrogance of some of the French had driven the city wild. Some French nuns, they were Lazarists, established an orphanage, and in their zeal to win souls for Christ they offered a cash premium for each child brought in to them—and worse than that, they paid to have sick and dying children carried in to them so they could baptize them 'in articulo mortis.' Rumors went around that after going through their mystic rites, the nuns took out the babies' eyes and hearts for purposes of witchery. One day the French consul—very overbearing—touched things off with a temper tantrum, smashing teacups and other things in the office of the imperial commissioner and then firing a pistol into a crowd outside. He was immediately killed and literally torn to pieces by the mob, which went on to set the French cathedral on fire and burn down the French consulate. They brutally killed two French diplomats

—two priests—ten nuns—some tourists who were riding along on horseback—thirty-odd Chinese Catholics. The mob stripped the sisters naked, one by one, and in full sight of the surviving nuns ripped their bodies open, cut their breasts off, gouged their eyes out, impaled them on long spears, hoisted them in the air, and threw them into the burning chapel of the orphanage.

The thrill of danger David must have felt that evening was apparently the first lift he had had since arriving in China. "Poor brave souls," he wrote in his diary, and underlined the phrase three times. Yes, he was possibly in mortal danger. This thought obviously restored his sense of mission, in the face of all that had let him down. Less obvious to us, deeply hidden presumably from him, were his motives in writing as much of this as he did, in such shocking detail, to Emily.

BEGINNINGS

DAVID rides home from his afternoon classes at the Peikai School in a well-kept ricksha, with enameled mudguards decorated with golden dragons and with polished brass lanterns attached to the shafts. He is wearing his fur-lined overcoat and a new fur hat. His ricksha man has his feet bound in burlap against the cold and damp, but David is used to such things now; he no longer apologizes to a puller.

Raw China is in the streets of the native city. David's ample nose cleaves through a fog of pungent smoke at a corner where a chestnut vendor is roasting his wares. Beggars in the most pitiful rags cluster at a gate; David throws them a few copper cash, and there is a hideous scramble in the gutter. Does he feel guilty at his patrician elevation above them? He must know that they, as he is, are professionals. A cluster of Lamaist priests floats along; they are dressed in yellow robes in many layers, so that they seem to bob and bounce like gaudy balloons full of water, and they have yellow hats piped in brown fur topped by crimson silk knobs. They pretend not to see the foreign religionist pass.

Arrived at the Hendersons' house, David steps down and pays the puller the usual sum for the trip he has taken; the puller protests violently (a standard ritual performance); David gives him one more copper; the puller is profuse in his thanks and bows to David's munificence.

The compound gate is open, but one cannot see in, because just inside the gate is the large baffle screen of the sort placed within every Chinese doorway to prevent fox spirits, which are thought to be able to go only in straight lines, from entering. David walks around it and makes his way to the second courtyard, where his room is. As soon as he enters he is greeted by his "boy" Lao San, who seems overjoyed to see him home again. A wood fire is blazing in a stove; David seats himself in front of it in a Morris chair, with its leg rest extended, and begins writing on a yellow pad.

My dear brother Paul:

To save the Hendersons bother, I have set up housekeeping. I eat with them occasionally, but for a week I have been buying pots and kettles, fuel and food, and still my "boy" says I haven't enough. I never before took an interest in this department of the world's industry. Now alas! I must buy brooms, wood, and coal, send the boy after chickens, which he brings home alive, tied together with a string and left to hop about until he wants them. I must put down in my book all these pennies which I so domestically spend. It is not romantic and you do not think of yourself in the light of a hero, when you are counting the sticks of wood which you bought at seven cash (3/4 of a cent) per stick.

When my supper of curry and rice, cocoa, bread and butter, marmalade, prunes, and cake is finished tonight, I will come into this room where I live most of the time, and, stretching myself out in my Morris chair, read the 'Outlook.' Not such a picture of sacrifice and martyrdom, is it? Last night I went out to dinner and wore a cutaway; think of doing such an impious thing! A missionary having good clothes and having the immodesty to wear them out to a dinner, whereat he forgets the seriousness of life and puts away good food! I am afraid you will be ashamed of me. Don't let this get into the printed columns of 'Life and Light for Women,' or that yellow journal, 'The Dayspring,' which we used to pore over Sunday afternoons. But I was about to say that I come home to my bachelor quarters and sit down before the warm stove, feeling very much like one of those young Englishmen you read about in books, Sir Peanut Brittle, R.A., or the Hon. Remington Typewriter, M.P. For my boy came in just now and pulled out my slippers and tried to look intelligent while I put them on, as he had nothing to do at the time, he just wanted to watch me. You should see us communicating! I draw pictures, and he laughs very hard with his hand politely in front of his mouth. And you would laugh to see me eat. I am taking my meals in a little room next to this, whither the boy brings all the food from the kitchen. He is very proud of his culinary skill and is very much delighted when I like the cuisine. But yesterday, the first day in this pilgrimage across the deserts of housekeeping, we had soup. It was a curiosity.

There was milk in it, and tapioca, and what else I know not. This morning, after indulging in an orange, some oatmeal, part of the hen which I bored into and excavated a little yesterday, and some coffee, he pressed me to cap it off with some of his tapioca pudding, but although I come from a state where they are reported to have pie for breakfast, I gently but firmly refused. But the fellow is doing well and is working so hard that today he told me he had no time for his breakfast. . . .

Yes, David, who was very poor by American standards, had a servant. This was most disconcerting. The farm boy was ready to be kind, but despite the apparent ease of his report to Paul, he was not ready for servility. The taste of the imperial made David feel just grand, but quite soon the grandeur began to give him touches of vertigo. The servant, though a grown man, was called "boy." David had the greatest difficulty telling how old Chinese people were, for their skin at any age seemed to have the warm sheen of a most delicate varnish of youth; but he guessed that his boy was five or six years older than he. Henny said that his name, Lao San, meant Old Third—himself a farm boy, third son of a family doubtless so poor they had to send him off to the city to find a rice bowl. He had had some crude training in American missionary homes, and he devoted himself, with the most touching cheerfulness and alacrity, to David's every comfort. David had no way yet of knowing that Lao San's loving deference to him stemmed less from David's own lovableness and superiority than from the deeply ingrained Chinese societal rules of obedience and respect and sweetness in the face of authority that Lao San had grown up with, even in a rural village hovel.

ON ONE of his first days, David set out from the Hendersons' in a ricksha. "I confess," he wrote Emily,

I was a little nervous starting out with a strange ricksha man through the crowded narrow streets of the native city of a million, where foreigners had been massacred, but Henny, who speaks Chinese well, assured me that the ricksha man was reliable, and that he had instructed him exactly where to go and that he knew the temple well. It was like diving into wild and unknown waters, but I plunged. The streets were only ten and twelve feet wide and were thronged with people, but I found they were good-natured, and at the cry, " 'Chieh kuang! Chieh kuang!' "—"lend light" = "open up"—they would always step aside and let us through. I discovered, in fact, that I was exhilarated by the hubbub of the crowds, and since then I have been nowhere so happy as walking in the milling streets.

He safely reached the temple that Henderson had described. A servant met him at its great gate and led him to a hall where Lin Fu-chen—the

Chinese man who was to mean most in David's early life in China—was waiting to receive him for the first time. Lin was the founder of the Peikai Middle School, where David was teaching. His temporary office was in a former Buddhist temple, the grounds of which the school had taken over.

What an impressive figure! You know, we have a wrong idea of the Chinese stature because the Chinese immigrants to the United States are almost all from the single open port of the early days, Canton, and the Cantonese are small. But many North Chinese have a noble frame—and Lin one of the noblest. Shoulders of an ox draped in the gray silk of a long gown with a shadowy pattern. A broad face shining with knowledge and humor. I was astonished to find that he was only about my own age. Oh, I thought, I am going to be a lucky man to be this man's friend.

Mr. Lin greeted David by bowing with his fists pressed together and invited him to sit down on one side of a long table. Mr. Lin sat on the other side. David noticed a large rectangular hole in the brick floor near the table, going down some four feet into bare earth below. A second servant brought a pot of hot jasmine tea and Chinese cups with covers to keep the tea hot. To David's relief Mr. Lin spoke beautiful English, with a slight British accent,

and Em, he dazzled me with his learning. He has mastered the classics; but he is one of the literati who looks to the West, and he put me to shame in my own culture. He quoted Milton and talked about the inventions of Leonardo. He knows the Bible. He has read Darwin. China must modernize, he says, and the key is the education of the young. Now that the examination system has been suspended, it will be schools like his, he said, and teachers like me, he said, who will give China new life.

The tablecloth, David noticed, was a heavy white foreign bedspread, with long tassels hanging down. The high ceiling was supported by handsome fourteen-inch polished wooden pillars, and leaning against one near him, with back to the pillar, was a grinning sitting Buddha, about three feet high. By now Mr. Lin had put his guest at ease, and David risked saying, "What are you going to do with the idols?"

Cupping his hand to the side of his mouth, Mr. Lin leaned over toward David and said very softly, "We're making them part of the general understanding."

Under where we would stand, he meant! He was pointing at the hole in the floor.

AFTER a few weeks of teaching, David was by no means sure it would be he who would give China new life. Unable to speak Chinese, using methods of Enderbury and Syracuse with students who had been brought up shouting rote learning, he became doubtful of his calling as a teacher. He yearned for the romance of evangelizing. Sometimes he thought nothing was getting through; sometimes he thought the students understood everything and liked to poke fun at this *ta-pi-tzu*, this foreign creature with a *very* big nose. "What am I to think, after fourteen days' work," he wrote in his diary, "when I'm told that the name of the Son of God is Satan?"

ON THE THEORY that the most direct access to an awakening China would be through its leaders, the Association secretaries were eager to make as many connections as possible with the literati. Lin Fu-chen generously arranged to have all the Tientsin secretaries invited to the home of the Salt Commissioner of Chihli Province. This was a big fish. Salt being a government monopoly, and graft having been intrinsic to the old system of advancement through examinations and favor at court, this Mr. Wang was very rich. The secretaries all put on their cutaways—their "sugar-scoop suits," as Henny called them, because the coats were shaped like the tin scoops used in country stores back home to measure bulk sugar from open barrels. Again to Emily:

> Henny had a slightly battered top hat, and as we started out from our East Gate compound, he was in the ricksha ahead of me, and I'll never forget the sight of that hat bobbing and swaying up there, glistening in the light of the kerosene street lamps.

Mr. Lin was waiting for the secretaries at the great gate of Mr. Wang's house. The Americans were not allowed to pay for the rickshas; Mr. Lin took care of them—Chinese social manners. He gathered the men around him and said, *sotto voce*, that as they were led across a courtyard porch they would see a big fat man in his undershirt, on the lawn below, cranking the handle of an ice-cream freezer. "Pay no attention to him. That is Mr. Wang himself. He is the only one in his household who knows how to make ice cream, and he is very proud of his new freezer, and he wants you Americans to have ice cream. But you must not look at him."

They passed the big man grinding away. They did not look at him, and he did not look at them. They went into the receiving hall, where several Chinese guests were waiting. Ten minutes after "this sample of Chinese courtesy-play," a magnificent gentleman appeared in the reception hall, dressed in a robe of sea otter fur over a purple silk gown, with two chains around his neck, one of amber beads, the other of coral, and with a Tartar hat topped by a crimson silk knob of his rank—"and I mustn't forget the black satin boots"—a figure straight off a great coromandel screen. It was clearly understood that none of the guests had recently seen this grand person in his underwear—or ever seen him, for that matter.

It seems Mr. Wang was fond of foreign plate glass, for we saw many partitions and sliding doors of heavy plate as we went into the large dining room. On all of them were long strips of paper pasted, with characters that Henny told me afterward said, "Look out for the glass." What a feast! Some of the things I remember we had were bird's-nest soup, Peking duck, salted goose feet and duck gizzards, sea slugs and white fungus, yum!(?)—I don't know what all—thirty dishes, ending with ice cream. The Chinese don't have dessert at the end, as we do, but Mr. Wang served us vanilla ice cream. Very good, too.

After the meal the party went into a kind of parlor, with huge German overstuffed chairs, and everyone was in high spirits. Someone suggested singing. Henderson sang the Indiana song, Treadup did Syracuse, the Americans all knew Cornell's "Cayuga's Waters" and Yale's "Boola-Boola." Then they asked for some Chinese songs. Mr. Wang turned and spoke to a big, handsome young man, and finally,

after a cascade of protests, this fellow put his head back and out came the most remarkable and beautiful sounds—falsetto, high, high, like a woman's voice. I could hear yearning and sadness. It gave me a stab of missing you.

But a secret, Em. I'll whisper: Mr. Wang was a disappointment. Perhaps once a scholar, but a very narrow person. He looks to the West for plate glass. Mr. Lin is ten times the man. There's an Old, and there's a New, I begin to see.

DAVID'S work in the Settlement Branch of the Association, which he carried on at odd times when he was not teaching, had very little to do with China. He might as well have been at Syracuse—except for one thing: his sense of being a foreigner here among foreigners. Americans were distinctly in a minority in Tientsin. There was no American Concession in the city (though a regiment of American regular army troops was barracked there, to protect American business interests, such as they were). The Settlement Branch was in the French Concession, on Rue de Paris, and its clients were an odd mixture of devout Protestant clerks and minor functionaries, enlisted soldiers of several nationalities looking for something to do, and rather declassed businessmen who wanted a place they could think of as their club. The dominant numbers and style were British, and David struggled rather stubbornly against giving in to growing curled-up mustaches, saying "ripping" and "rah*thuh*" and "deah boy," and addressing Chinese, whether servants or not, as if they were donkeys and dogs; and consequently he was rather brutally snubbed even by some of the rather shabby Britishers who patronized the Association.

ONE BRITISH MAN David took to at once was a spry sexagenarian from the London Missionary Society, the Reverend Dr. Rencher Rimmon, who used to drop in at the Branch from time to time to "do a spot of fishing," as he put it—randomly recruiting apple-cheeked young British soldiers and policemen and clerks for Jesus. He was a small man who seemed to whirl about on a powerful engine that ran on a volatile fuel of pure optimism. His was an almost irresistible enthusiasm. He was out of touch with sadness. He never suffered even the slightest dips in mood. It was months later that it occurred to David that there was something pathological about Rev. Rimmon's good cheer; it was as if he had once taken a blow on the head, followed by a permanent amnesia for all that had ever been serious on this earth.

"Treadup, where was tennis played in the Bible?"

"Tennis? I don't know, sir."

"When Joseph served in Pharaoh's court."

Wasn't that excellent? Everything was excellent. Everything good was excellent, and everything bad was excellent.

One reason David was particularly taken with Rev. Rimmon was that he said he often went street preaching in the Chinese city, and he invited David to go along some day. He said he liked to take a party of young white Christians with him, so that the hymns would be loud. All must dress in Chinese clothes that day, he said—so David rather excitedly had a simple straight blue quilted gown made by a tailor Lao San brought to the house for him.

The day came, high-skyed and not too cold. The party assembled at the Branch. Dr. Rimmon had six bellowers besides David—four Cockney soldiers, who cackled and thumped each other when they put on the Chinese gowns Dr. Rimmon lent them; a silent Customs clerk; and a middle-aged L.M.S. colleague. David, who apparently caught that day a touch of Dr. Rimmon's virus of joy, wrote in a report letter to his Syracuse backers:

We got down from our rickshas at the north gate and crowded our way through the streets to the biggest Taoist temple. Inside the temple courts, standing upon a heavy granite railing with grotesque lions crouching before us, we opened our hymn books and began to sing. "A Mighty Fortress" and "Lead, Kindly Light," and—'fortissimo'—"Onward Christian Soldiers." This was last Sunday. In a balcony at one end of the main courtyard there was a native band beating and sawing the life out of brass and other howling instruments. As we sang, on every side hawkers, fakirs, and fortune-tellers plied their own causes, and beyond were long rows of small shops, where, within the sacred enclosure, buying and selling goes on from morn to night, but we were not past the second line of the first hymn before every eye was riveted upon us, and

soon about 400 people were gathered around us in respectful, earnest
attention. After the singing, our Dr. Rimmon announced that there
would be no charge for listening, for in China if you listen to a public
performance the hat is sure to be passed before the show is over. Then in
what sounded to me like perfect Mandarin (he told the rest of us later
exactly what he had said), he announced the purpose of holding the
meeting, and stated that as this was the City Temple, and as they had
canonized all the deities, sages, and divinities from East and West,
North and South, it seemed perfectly proper that we should come to talk
to them about the Great Heavenly Father. Then we sang some more.
Then Rev. Rimmon scrambled up on the back of one of the lions and in
simple reverent tones told the old story of the Great Father's love. When
the service was ended he dismissed the people by proposing to distrib-
ute a leaflet entitled "Happy News," but there was such a surging of the
crowd, and such a squabbling amongst the stronger men to get hold of
the printed statement of the Truth that it was very hard to keep our
foothold—and this in the very heart of the native city of Tientsin! I am
happy to say that before the meeting broke up, a band of globe-trotters
warmed up their cameras on this scene from a distant corner. I was glad
of this, that skeptical tourists could catch on their cameras the true
picture of the deserted booths of the fakirs, fortune-tellers, and seats of
the idols, and of the crowd, almost entirely made up of men, listening
attentively to the Gospel. They came to worship they knew not what, but
they must have gone away with new ideas of What and Who is God.

David was so moved by the illusion of success in God's work that had
been achieved at the City Temple that day by Rencher Rimmon's monkey
climb onto the stone lion's back, and by his dancing eyes and merry voice, that
he, David, wanted to be able to do likewise. The evangelization of the world in
this generation! *This* was what he had dreamed of back at Syracuse. On the
Monday, thinking in somewhat magical terms, he wore his new quilted
Chinese gown to his classes at the Peikai School. As he walked into the classroom, every student suddenly raised a hand to cover his mouth. Like the
baffles at all compound gates, such shielding hands would stop anything
evil—anything discourteous—in irrepressible laughter from reaching its tar-
get. David did not write home about this frightful loss of face, nor did he
record it in his diary. We come on it only years later, in "Search." By that time
he had a different view of Dr. Rimmon's saving of souls.

N o w, early in David's missionary career, came two instances of rebuff by
the home office which shocked him by their arbitrariness, by the sense they
gave him of being a puppet on strings pulled in faraway New York. Back at

Northfield, when James B. Todd had been recruiting him, David had told the great man that he was in debt to Syracuse by about two hundred dollars. With a grand wave of the hand—but not in writing, alas—Todd had given David the distinct impression that this was just a tiny button which the International Committee would tuck away in its big sewing kit. Now, in Tientsin, dutifully worried, David wrote Todd:

> *The problem of paying off my college debt is still unsolved. You will remember we discussed this question in Northfield. I have been thinking that perhaps if this year I did not present any bill for the cultivation of my constituency you would be willing to let the $25, which would be the allowance for this year, apply to my debt....*

David's constituency consisted of his Syracuse backers, who put up most of the money for his support, and they were faithful and needed no "cultivation." Todd's stiff answer:

> *I enter sympathetically into your debt problems but am nonplussed to know what to recommend in the way of relief. I had hoped that the improved financial arrangement which the Committee made last summer might make it possible for you gradually to wear out your debt. The Committee regret that they cannot conscientiously adopt your suggestion of allowing the $25 appropriated to your budget for cultivation purposes to be applied to the payment of your debt. I wish I could think of some way to be of practical help to you.*

The other blow hurt much more. On a visit to Tientsin in December, Blackton told David that there would be a short conference of all Association secretaries in Shanghai in late April, and since that would be Treadup's only chance to get to the port to which ships from America came, it would be a good time for his fiancée to arrive, and for the couple to be married. David sent a euphoric cablegram to Emily, telling her to be ready to leave no later than March 20; and he followed this with a long, careful letter of instructions— what kind of steamer trunk to buy, not to forget long johns for winter, bring a tennis racket.

Two weeks later a peremptory cablegram came from Todd. The agreement had been that the couple were to wait one year. The time for Miss Kean to join him would be at the start of his language study in the autumn. End of message.

BUSY DAILY LIFE wrapped itself closely around David, and even Todd's chilling messages did not long keep his heart from being warm. On New Year's Eve, "Henny and I had a discussion of human progress, provoked by Kidd's *Social Evolution*." One day David went with Mrs. Henderson, Mrs.

Harmon, their children, and Wood for an outing on the solidly frozen river on *p'ai-tzu*s — low, flat sleds with iron runners, on which the passengers, two by two, reclined under fur rugs, while on each sled a coolie, standing at the back, poled the contraption along amazingly fast by pumping an iron-pointed stick backward between his legs. "Smoked out with stove in morning, am getting a new Calorigen stove!" "Enjoy the Hendersons very much." "Excitement! Thieves broke into the Harmons' house [in the Settlement Branch compound]. Called police. Suspect Branch servants. All must go." One day he lectured his students on the whale, and the next day he asked for essays on this creature. One of these themes he sent to sister Grace (commenting, "You may laugh, Ecarg, but I am proud — there's progress here").

THE WALE

The wale is the larger kind of fish and his power is so higher that all the fish live in water are controled by him. But he difference all the fish, for all fish cannot live on land to inspire the air. But the wale can be inspiring the air and drinking the water also for he have no gil but has a large mouse for it is hard when he turns in water and in few very minutes he can appears in the air that he might died. As for his spout can he spit the water almost thirty feet away thus wrecks the smaller vessels and the fishing smacks, the people of the river's bank almost always distressed by him, a king of fish.

David managed, with touches now and then of Rencher Rimmon's blind Panglossian optimism, to turn sad or threatening news into fine signs of the testing of his fiber. On Christmas day he wrote: "Troubles in the south. China for the Chinese becoming ever more assertive." In late February: "Reports of more riots in the south. Six Caths and four Prots killed." Ten days later: "The troubles in the south lead many to believe that the volcano is about to break forth. We are needed!" Word came that the infant child of the Robert Services had died of a fever while the Services were on their way up the Yangtze to a new Association post in inland Chengtu. And much closer at hand, Mrs. Henderson suffered a miscarriage. "How pure," David wrote, "was the enduring heart of Job!"

ONE DAY in March the sky over Tientsin turned weirdly orange, and David felt grit in his teeth. It was a sandstorm — a great weather system of dust from the Gobi Desert lifted by west winds and carried hundreds of miles to China. The dark sky lasted three days. Dust eddied in little drifts under doorways; it settled on pillowcases; it blew into one's eyes. It was a blizzard of Mongolian topsoil. On the second day a cart loomed through the ocher haze at the Ch'ing-tzu Hutung gate with six wooden boxes on which, when Lao San had whisked off the dust, could be seen black stenciled letters:

DAVID TREADUP

Y.M.C.A.

TIENTSIN, CHINA

Here again was a Chinese wonder: With no more address than this, these boxes had come all the way from the village of Newport, New York, U.S.A., to the right house on the right alleyway in the teeming city in China. They were things of Emily's. David hovered over them. He did not know whether he should open them—what if there were "personal" things? That evening he wrote a thoughtful letter to brother Paul:

> *The boxes are over against the wall. I know that my Em will bring a woman's touch to my residence, and I desire that grace in my life. Yet— I wonder often what my boy thinks of the luxuries of my life. I've joined Rotary, and I go to their lunches at the posh Tientsin Club. We are building a tennis court at the Presbyterian compound for the exclusive use of us Y secretaries. Worrying about our high style of living, I spoke about it to my English friend Rencher Rimmon the other day, but he said, "Fiddlesticks, my boy. We must impress these people. We have to keep a proper dignity, don't you know. These Chinamen want us to have a certain refinement, don't you know. Were we to lower ourselves to the level of the masses, it would blow our influence to smithereens—and expose us to innumerable petty annoyances. Oh, no, Treadup, things are first rate the way they are." But I cannot help wondering. I want to be Lao San's brother, as I am yours, Paul. Did Jesus care a fig for his social position? Or his "dignity"?*

IN EARLY MAY David read in the *North China Daily Star* that Dr. Elijah Elting of the China Inland Mission—David's cabinmate on the *Empress*— was to be in Tientsin for a few days for a meeting of a committee of translators of the Bible into common spoken Chinese. He was to be staying at the Astor House Hotel. David found that he yearned to see the frightening old man, his strongest link, besides Dr. Rimmon, with the nostalgic dream of evangelization that had been growing so dim in his urban routines of the Association. He waited two days, then went to call on Dr. Elting at the Astor House—at teatime, when the committee would be sure to be recessed.

The forbidding whitebeard greeted David with a fierce warmth, a fatherly hug, which to David's astonishment brought tears to his own eyes. They sat on the broad veranda of the hotel in white wicker chairs. Dr. Elting asked about David's work. He nodded and waved his immaculate beard. When they had talked awhile David screwed up his courage and asked the old prophet whether he would be doing any itinerating on the northern plains.

Dr. Elting's white eyebrows shot upward and he barked out, "Aha!" Then he was silent for a long time. Finally he said, "I had not been planning . . . Aha! My boy! We'll go on Friday next." The old terror, whom David had thought so insensitive, had seemed with these sudden gasps to have realized the full force of David's hunger.

"You know I can't speak three words of Chinese," David sheepishly said.

"I have tongue enough for two," Dr. Elting said.

Dr. Elting told David he would meet him at the place where the Peking carts gathered at the edge of the farmers' market in the Chinese city, at dawn on Friday. He should of course wear Chinese clothes.

WHEN THE CARTMEN saw the old white man with the white beard accompanied by the boyish white giant, they came in a storm of competition, shouting and haggling for the right to carry them. With unexpected agility, Dr. Elting arbitrarily heaved himself up on the hub of one of the huge wooden wheels, tossed his bedroll and knapsack onto the flat bed of the cart, and climbed aboard, announcing loudly to the cartman that he wanted to go "in the direction of Tsinan." David followed. For some time Chinese travelers gave that cart a wide berth; then a boisterous farmer climbed up, laughing wildly at his own courage. Others then followed in a rush, as if passage on that cart were after all the highest privilege. About fifteen crowded aboard. The breaths of their hilarity were "blowtorch blasts of garlic that could singe one's eyebrows off." All had rolled-up sleeping mats and bundles of various shapes and sizes which they sat upon and among. "The cart on which we traveled," David wrote Emily,

> consisted of two wheels joined by a ponderous axle under a flat bed resting directly upon the hounds without a hint of springs between. The thills were two huge shafts joined at the rear by a heavy crossbeam. This was bound directly to the axle. The whole gearing was without spring or coupling to break the jar. Our company thumped and jounced, our knee joints and hip joints and shoulder joints rattled like a tossed bundle of jackstraws. We were hauled by the largest mule I have ever seen, and the whole cart bed tilted toward the rear.
>
> We were soon out of the city, lurching along on a rutted dirt road so ancient that it had cut itself into a kind of huge gutter two and three feet below the level of the rest of the plain. Some miles into the country, Dr. Elting reached into his gown and fumbled around, as if he were scratching flea bites, and then out came his hand holding a pamphlet of the Acts of

the Apostles, in the vulgar translation his committee was working upon. He began reading this, at first to himself, in a low mumble. Then suddenly he was belling it out in the high falsetto of a scholar reading the classics, in beautiful singing tones almost like those I had heard that night at Salt Commissioner Wang's. You could not have detected from the passengers' faces that this evangelical opera was being sung—tact? —or had they so often passed by the village school and heard such reading that it seemed an ordinary thing?—or heard their landlord, having put aside his abacus for an hour in favor of a beloved classical scroll? Dr. Elting chanted along, as we bounced on the hard wood. When he came to verse thirty-six of the ninth chapter, "Now there was at Joppa a certain disciple named Tabitha, which by interpretation is called Dorcas: this woman was full of good works and alms-deeds which she did," he suddenly stopped hallooing and spoke in a straight voice as if chatting with a friend, talking off the edge of the cart to the open plains, saying that this Dorcas was a simple village woman like any man's wife or mother. Then, as if unaware that anyone might have heard him, he was off with another aria from the holy Book. Then another explanation in normal tones. And so, back and forth, until you can believe me that all the passengers on that crowded cart were raptly following every word. Now for ten miles this white-haired elder, somehow metamorphosed by magic into a passionate minister of the Holy Word, held those common folk in the palm of his hand. To judge by their faces, that must have been a simple, deep, stabbing message of Christ's love and forgiveness. It was a masterly performance! How I wish I had the gifts of that craggy old gentleman!

AT THE LUNCHEON of the Rotary, the following week, David was seated next to a man named Gilbert Olander, a businessman who worked for Standard Oil. In David's diary:

Still excited abt. Dr. Elting's preaching. Told Mr. O. His comment: "I know that old bird. He's been skulking around China for centuries. What an ass. That man is a numskull, a busybody, and an utterly blind creature. He hasn't the dimmest idea what the Chinks are all about."

David wrote no more than that in his diary, but in later years we find numerous references to the Olander remarks, which clearly disturbed him in ways he could not, at the time, decipher. Some of these show up when he is writing home about his joint tours with James B. Todd; they point to growing doubts about the slim harvests and weak holding power in China of old-fashioned campground preaching.

There was one immediate reaction, a small and tentative move in itself but one that was ultimately to have immense consequences in his life. The very next day after the Rotary lunch he wrote to his mother in Salt Branch:

> *I have been somewhat discouraged in my efforts to bring the word of Jesus directly to the classroom. I have been thinking of giving the students some science demonstrations. Mother, would you please send me that little gyroscope of mine? It is in a maplewood box which I believe I put in the old trunk in the attic, in with the few boyhood and college relics I decided to hold onto. If I'm not mistaken, you will find it just under that Psi U wall plaque toward the back of the trunk.*

IN APRIL David went by ship to Shanghai to the conference of Association secretaries. "The days are filled with work—the problems are great—their solutions are beyond us," he wrote. David's future was dictated there by the seniors on the force: He would work in Tientsin through the summer; would go to Paotingfu for language study in October, with time to get settled before his fiancée arrived; he would best be married in Shanghai, probably in November. He would then have two years to master the language.

MORE AND MORE, as the months passed and as his admiration for certain qualities of the Chinese grew and grew, he felt the deadness of his tongue. To get from day to day with Lao San he picked up a smattering of household Chinese, interspersed with pidgin English—a condescending form of communication, used by businessmen with their Chinese compradors, which hurt David's throat. He wanted much more. He wanted to be able to understand these delightful people. His letters to baby sister Grace are full of sketches of little things he saw that enchanted him:

> *Group of boys of about twelve, I judge, on stilts in the street. Some were beating drums, others had gongs. They were jumping, running races, hopping on one stilt with the other one held straight up behind their backs. . . . I often see a fine gentleman in the street airing his thrush. This seems to be his idea of getting some exercise. He just stands there looking off into space and holding the bird, which he has trained to imitate a cat, a dog, a crow, an eagle. Very proud. . . . Street stall where they sell small paper figures, men with wheelbarrows, tiny carts, horsemen—all move around with great alacrity. All harnessed to big black beetles! . . . I love to watch the wonderful controlled agility of the workmen on a new house near here. They are amazingly strong, and they behave like acrobats, shouting and jumping as if before a huge audience. Like this: Man on the ground is mixing mortar. He lifts a*

spade full of it and in one flowing motion throws it, spade, mortar, and all, to a bricklayer on a high scaffolding. The spade flies up in perfect balance and the man above, having pivoted slowly like a dancer at the thrower's cry, stretches out his hands in a pose and the spade handle settles exactly into his palms as if it were light as a feather. Beautiful! . . .

IN OCTOBER a new volunteer came into the field to relieve Treadup for his language study, a young man named Roscoe Hersey. David in his impatience has nothing to say in his diary about Hersey except

He doesn't seem to see the importance of at once getting into the work. . . . At school in morning. Hersey did not connect. . . . Spent time with Hersey. He went with me to school for night class. . . . Took Hersey to school with me so he could get on to work. He is always behind. . . . Helping Hersey get on his feet and packing goods. . . .

EARLY on the morning of October 18, 1906, David had his goods already heaped on the platform at the Tientsin station. In came the train—a tall-stacked engine belching black soft-coal smoke; some open freight cars; then third-class passenger cars, which were just like the freight cars, flat-bedded trucks open to the sky, with lower walls than the freight cars; then second-class coaches, with compartments with wooden benches, one containing the "first-class saloon," which had crimson plush cushions and silk curtains at the windows. Having been advised by his elders on the safest way to travel, David had the platform coolies pile his goods onto one of the open third-class cars; then he carefully counted his boxes and suitcases and made sure his trunk was securely seated; and then he settled down himself there among his things. The car was soon thronged with poor Chinese and their bundles. In this way David could reach Paotingfu and know that none of his things would be stolen. Soot got in his eyes.

BOOK AND RING

HE SAT on a straight wooden chair at a bare deal table. Across from him hovered a round face—"like a paper moon," David later wrote Paul. Very near the center of the great circle of immobile flesh was a tiny cluster of features. The little eyes blinked and the little mouth moved. When the little mouth stopped moving, it snapped into the fixed position of a smile. "I *think* that Wu Hsien-sheng is jolly," David reported. Hsien-sheng meant Teacher. This was their first morning of work. Teacher Wu had bounced vastly into the room half an hour late. Though it was mid-October, he carried a flat straw fan, which fluttered to whoosh away the teacher's loss of face whenever David made a mistake. They had started the session with a prayer, for Wu was a Christian. Their text was Mateer's *Primary Lessons*.

"My messod," Teacher Wu had announced at the beginning of the lesson (in David's transcription to Paul), "is *kwai-kwai-ti, man-man-ti*. Means quick slow. Fust go fast, next go slow."

Accordingly they had gone over the first lesson in the book quickly. David had a pad in front of him. He did not try to copy the characters as Wu pronounced them, but wrote out phonetic equivalents in English letters, and after each romanized word wrote a number to remind him of the proper tone. He repeated the sound of each character after Wu.

Now, nearly two hours later, they were working over the lesson more slowly. Wu asked David to read each character from the book. Then, after what seemed to David an interminable process—"part of the exceedingly *man-man*, the slowest of the slow 'messod,' I'd say"—of ceremoniously wetting his writing brush and ink stone, working up some moist ink on his ink block, transferring some of this to his ink stone, and rolling the tip of the brush and pointing it up with ink, with each motion shooting his wrist out of his long sleeve, poising his brush at the properly artful angle, hesitating, approaching, pulling back, describing little strokes of meaning in thin air— "for to be able to write beautifully in this country, brother Paul, is to feel oneself a prince in a kingdom of letters three thousand years old"—Wu finally wrote down on small slips of paper the characters of the lesson and asked David to recognize and pronounce them from memory.

There came a moment during this slow part of the lesson which the pupil would have reason to remember later on. David, having reached a stage of mental satiety and bewilderment, mispronounced a character for the third time, using a wrong tone. Suddenly the tiny eyes in the huge face were blazing. Wu's voice came whistling out at a high pitch, in a kind of throttled scream. "When teacher *say,* pupil *do.*"

"I was exhausted that day," David wrote weeks later when Wu first threatened to resign.

Our lessons were (and are) five and six hours long, and I had Emily's arrival very much on my mind back then—and this language was presenting problems of cognition of a kind I had never met before. What I have come to realize is how much anger there is in jolly Teacher Wu. I have had to face it that he is a rice Christian. He accepted conversion because he thought it would mean it would make him an insider with foreigners, he would become a comprador and work the Tientsin Bund and make a fortune. But instead he has only managed to become a teacher to these shabby missionaries. Underneath all those layers of good humor and adipose tissue, he is not satisfied with the bargain made with Jesus Christ. I now find it a great strain to look at that tiny frozen smile in the middle of that great pudding of resentment. I have tried to make delicate moves to help him, but I am quickly given to understand that each such move shatters the ritual relationship between teacher and pupil, and is not allowed. His fierce exercise of his dominance over me, which derives from the Confucian teacher's absolute authority over his student, is his revenge on a Jesus who is infuriating precisely because he forgives all.

THE LONG-AWAITED language study marked a paradox — a simultaneous entrance into, and withdrawal from, the real China.

In spite of whatever tension David may have felt in working with Wu, he loved moving at last into the territory of clear meaning. He could leave the terrible imperial desert of pidgin English — that weird code of translated Chinese constructions which was based on the assumption that the whole subservient world had better damn well learn the Anglo-Saxon tongue. He remembered and used all the methods of mastery Absolom Carter had taught him, though the problems here were quite new. Even in Greek with its different alphabet, the learning had been basically phonetic. Chinese was ideographic — a character for every word. David had learned a few such signs in his own language: 9, %, &, $. But here every single meaning had a sign of its own. This made the learning task immensely more difficult. To cross the beautiful moon-bridge from illiteracy to literacy, one must learn at least three thousand of these signs. One could start with characters that were a little like pictures: The sun, originally ⊙, had become 日. A tree was 木 and a forest was two trees put together: 林. A man had two legs: 人. A horse galloped: 馬. The first three numbers were 一 二 三. A mouth was 口, and this sign also stood for mouthlike things: a hole, a harbor. But pictures never could have done all the work of language, and so most Chinese characters had become a marriage of two parts, one carrying a root meaning, and the others telling something about the sound. And so David was plunged into a wilderness of new linguistic technicalities — radicals, enclitics, auxiliaries. And on top of all that there were four tones in the Mandarin that David was studying, those delicate slidings of the voice that made spoken Chinese sound to Western ears a singsong language: a high sustained tone, a falling tone, a rising tone, and a dipping tone, falling then rising. With these he must be most careful, for a wrong tone gave a wrong meaning—and it was their widespread tone deafness that had made some imprudent missionaries a laughingstock among educated Chinese. But David found all these difficulties somehow exciting; overcoming them would give him access to China, as nothing else, not even the most one-sided treaties, could do.

AT THE SAME TIME his life in Paotingfu was a kind of escape from China. The city of Paotingfu had early been chosen by missionaries as a key center for their work. A hundred miles southwest from the capital of the empire, itself the capital of Chihli Province, it was a kind of gateway on the line of travel to more remote provinces, Shensi, Shansi, Shantung, Honan. Unlike Shanghai and Tientsin and other treaty cities, it had no foreign settlement, and the various missions had set themselves up in very large compounds some distance outside the walls of the city. Like other Association men before him, David had been sent to Paotingfu for his language study precisely because of the isolation and tranquillity of life in these compounds.

He had been assigned to the American Board Mission compound in the south suburb of the city. On two connecting plots of flat land of several acres, it was surrounded by high walls made of earthen bricks. Within, all was American in style—brick houses with pitched roofs, turrets, verandas; this might have been a corner of a small town in the Plains states. Brick pathways ran between lawns from home to home. A substantial brick chapel in its own enclosure had Gothic windows, a corrugated tin roof, and a little bell tower that rang out the calls to worship. "I have been here a little over a week," he wrote his parents,

> and I am pretty well settled. I have two rooms in one of the big houses at the east end of the residential compound. I say "I" have two rooms: These are the two rooms my dear Em and I will soon share as our first home. I have received word that she sails from Seattle on the twentieth — the day after tomorrow! I know Em will make these rooms homey, in the meantime I more or less camp out. My bedroom is on the ground floor and faces out under an arbor with a tangle of rosebushes which must be a corking sight in summertime. I have an iron bed which is short for me, I curl my feet around the ironwork of the footboard, oh well. I have a washstand, a screen, a large bureau, a coal stove, a table, and a rocking chair; my "study," which is also my dining room when I eat alone, is quite bare: two wooden chairs and a plain table. There are mats on the floors. I have stocked the study closet with supplies from the States: cans of pineapple, gooseberry jam, apricot jam, pears, peaches, cherries, ect., salmon, cold tongue, coffee, condensed milk, butter, as well as

bottles of pickles, papers of stove polish, cornstarch, soda, tins of baking powder, cocoanut, ect., bags of native meal of different kinds for porridge, sugar, crackers, ect. And of course I have popcorn and a popper.

You see I am in a seven-room house, of which the regular denizens are the Misses Selden and Demestrie. I am their guest, or the waif who has been deposited on their doorstep, depending how you want to look at it. They live upstairs.

David's diary suggests the degree of his withdrawal from China in this period. Apart from brief notations of his work—"Studied 5½ hrs. . . . Studied 6½ hours. . . . "—the notes center around a life that, like the Gothic windows and gooseberry jam, might just as well have been in Nebraska: "Went to the Ta-fang to play baseball. Five men went from this compound. . . . Played two sets of tennis with Mr. Swing. . . . Played cornet at service. . . . Took dinner with Mr. and Mrs. Cowley. They had a turkey roast. . . . "

BUT PAOTINGFU also served as a special reminder of the nature of the missionary calling, for there, in the Presbyterian and American Board and China Inland Mission compounds, just five years earlier, fifteen Protestant foreigners had been martyred in the Boxer uprising. The missionaries had had ample warning that they might be killed, but they had chosen to stay in order to try to defend their native converts, who were also threatened. Very soon after David arrived, he heard the tales of "the crowning day": of thirty-two-year-old May Simcox going out on the porch of her house to plead with the mob to spare the infant daughter in her arms—but in vain; the house set on fire with the Simcoxes and Hodges in it; the two older Simcox children rushing out of the burning house, caught, cut down, and thrown in the cistern. Horace Pitkin, thirty-one-year-old Yale graduate, who had sent telegrams in Latin asking for help from Peking, holding the Boxers at bay from the porch of his house, to defend the native converts inside it, armed with nothing but a pistol—beheaded after his few rounds of ammunition had been spent. Annie Gould, marched off with others toward the city, fainting, then, hands and feet tied, slung from a pole as the Chinese carry pigs—later beheaded, with others. David, writing to Paul about these stories:

Hearing all this, I have been forced to realize two things: how literally frenzying it must have been to the Chinese to have been so humiliated in the last fifty years by outlanders whom they consider inferior to themselves; and also that under the universal sweetness and good humor and natural grace of manner of the Chinese, there lurks, at least in some of them, a strain of unthinkable ferocity—imagine the savagery of a man who could run a spear through a little girl like Gladys Bagnall! How I honor the compassion in the face of death of Dr. Taylor, who showed the

Boxers his pistol and said he disdained to take human lives and threw the
pistol into the flames of the Lowrie house, in which flames he then died!

THOSE DAYS of work were days of waiting. His bride was coming. David
had reason to be anxious. He had fallen in love with Emily Kean, to be sure,
but he hardly knew her. It is virtually certain that apart from having held her
hand a few times, and probably having stolen a few sweet kisses, he had no
way of guessing at what marriage would bring in the privacy of nights at
home. He had given signs of past guilt over urges and acts marked ! and O.
They were nothings. Here in the mission compound, cut off from the world by
a high wall—"Isn't it bracing," a Mrs. Elliott said to him, "to be away from all
the filth and dirt?"—he must have been cut off from fantasy, even. How could
a pure man imagine the abandoned wrestling of naked bodies on this too-
short iron bed, which creaked and clanked like a rolling metal drum full of
rocks when he merely heaved a sigh in the night?

David did what he had done before. He encoded his sexual yearnings
and ignorance and fears and offered them, in a sweetened form of dependency,
to an older woman. This time it was to Miss Letitia Selden, the more dynamic
of the two upstairs ladies. In this context we must approach the nickname of
this strong-jawed woman somewhat warily. She was called by all her friends,
without the least embarrassment, Miss Titty. This was understood by all as a
purely phonetic diminutive of her first name. Letitia Selden was a native of
Maine, and in her spare strong speech one heard the pounding of the sea on
coastal rocks. She and the younger Miss Demestrie ("true yokefellows," as
everyone said) were in charge of a school for girls run by the mission. Miss
Selden, who had served in the field since 1894, had been spared the Boxer
horror because she had been in the United States during it, on furlough; Miss
Demestrie had arrived after it, in 1903. Miss Titty pictured herself to David as
an only child who had grown up in a playground of printed words. She had
lived her entire childhood indoors, inhabiting the magazines then considered
"instructive"—*St. Nicholas, Our Young Folks, The Youth's Companion*—and
she said she had practically memorized all the books in Godwin's "Juvenile
Library," especially Charles Lamb's *Tales from Shakespear* and *Adventures
of Ulysses*. Stories of sorrows and suffering had always especially moved her;
Enoch Arden had almost broken her heart. And so, just as under this lady's
whalebone-ribbed corset there was a warm and pulsing amplitude, so under
the Down East shell of personality there was a boundless romantic softness.
Perhaps to humble this dangerous flesh and even more dangerous sensibility,
she drove herself without mercy. Miss Demestrie told David that Miss Titty
had been valedictorian at Mt. Holyoke not because of any easy brilliance but
because she had worked so hard that her eyes often gave out and she had to
get her lessons by having someone read aloud to her.

"Miss Selden said to me today, 'When a bachelor is about to be delivered up for the slaughter, he needs a mother near him to pat his cheek.' " The diary begins to punctuate this lady's sympathies, which take the form of a voracious curiosity about Emily, with an abundance of exclamation points. "She says: 'Tell me about her! Tell me! What color are her eyes?' 'Hazel.' 'Hazel! How sweet! I shall call her Hazy!' " . . . "She asks: 'Is she slim? Tell me about her posture!' 'Well, what should I say? Straight and lithe.' 'Straight and—did you say lithe! How lovely she must be!' " The younger yokefellow was apparently slightly miffed by the mothering, or at least by this interrogatory form of it. "Miss Demestrie walks back and forth. She seems an unhappy person."

ON THE SIXTH OF NOVEMBER David received a telegram from Wolf in Shanghai saying that the *Doric* with its precious cargo would arrive there on the fifteenth. "Miss Titty actually did pat me on the cheek when I read the telegram to her! She is very dear to me. She seems almost as excited to see Em as I am!" Hectic, David packed his cutaway and a few other things and took the ten fifty train the next morning for Tientsin. There he "engaged passage on the coastwise bucket *Tung Tien*," which was to leave in two days. He stayed with the Hendersons—and found that in his excitement he had forgotten to pack his shaving brush, his straight razor, and his stropping strap. "Hate to buy new ones," he wrote in his diary. The second evening he went to a meeting of a temperance society for foreign soldiers and sailors, then, feeling all too sober himself, he went aboard the "bucket" at midnight. It cast off from the Bund at two in the morning. The ship anchored outside the Taku bar to take its cargo from lighters. "Not many congenial passengers. Captain Jewar is a tough." The voyage, except for one "dirty" night, was tolerably smooth. The *Tung Tien* tied up in Shanghai at one thirty on the twelfth. "Found everyone getting ready for *the event*."

DAVID got up at five in morning on the fifteenth. His friends had secured him a place on a launch that would take him twelve miles downriver and across the bar into the shallows of the sea where the *Doric* would be anchored with other ships waiting for high tide before going up the Whangpoo to the city. Thus he would gain a few hours on the long wait to see Emily. We can guess he had swallowed hard when this plan had been proudly announced to him. What if it was rough out there? What if Emily's first sight of *him*, at long last, should be of her stalwart fiancé decorating the carpet of Tibetan silt with his breakfast? But the launch turned out to be much larger than he had imagined it would be, and the sea was calm, and he climbed a gangway on the flank of the ship, and there she was. She stood in a crowd on the promenade deck, her face aglow with the light of her surprised pleasure.

That night he wrote: "She is far more beautiful than I had remembered."

They reached the Bund soon after noon. Several Association people were on hand to greet Emily. In the carriage on the way to the Wolfs' house she frightened David with a sudden groan. She had seen, for the first time, a Chinese woman tottering on tiny bound feet.

It seemed as if there was not a minute to wait. They rehearsed the ceremony that afternoon, then went to Nanking Road to see the three pieces of furniture the Association secretaries were having made for their wedding gift. They had dinner with the Blacktons, where they met two unmarried young women who had just arrived in China, pale as a pair of White Leghorns, named Miss Paddock and Miss Coppock.

The next morning the wedding couple were kept apart. Just after twelve o'clock Emily Kean, luminous in her slightly yellowy lace wedding dress (which had been her grandmother's and her mother's), took sedate steps with little pauses, timed by Mendelssohn on a Victrola, into the Wolfs' living room, where David stood waiting in his sugar-scoop suit. She had trustingly packed the dress in her steamer trunk back in Herkimer County, New York, before setting out on an incredibly brave voyage to the opposite side of the earth down there, where people walked around upside down. Here she was, in creamy lace, right side up. She stood like a willow by her groom. In the hush of the twenty guests during the first of the vows, the ring bearer, a golden-haired boy of five—David in his haze had no idea whose child it was—with a little satin pillow balanced like a tray in his hands, suddenly began to howl, and the ring slid off the pillow and rolled under a chair. Alarmed at the thought of an omen, David looked anxiously at Emily's face behind her veil. She was laughing. David's diary: "I knew then that my Em would be all right in China, and I with her."

IT GOES without saying that no written record of the consummation survives—except by indirection. One reason there had been such a hurry to get the wedding over with, quite beyond the young couple's having waited for it so long, was that the *Koon Hsing*, on which a cabin was being saved for a Mr. and Mrs. D. Treadup, was to sail for the north that very afternoon. "Our good friends came to the boat to start us off. Rice and red paper hearts were in evidence." By suppertime the lovebirds were vomiting. The next day David was able to write only one line in his diary: "I was never this sick in my life." And the next day: "We lay in our berths all day. Rather hard lines for a honeymoon." On Sunday the ship made only four knots through mountainous seas. Captain Anderson said he had never seen such a gale. Early Tuesday morning the *Koon Hsing* dropped anchor off the Taku bar, and it was finally calm. While the cargo was offloaded onto lighters, all the passengers except the Treadups went ashore. And here came the cryptic announcement in the diary: "We greatly enjoyed the ship to ourselves." At last the honeymooners were in luck: the next morning the ship tried to cross the bar and went aground. Again the other passengers went ashore. This time the author of the diary loses all reserve. "Sunshine after clouds, sweet after bitter." On the crest of the tide the next morning the ship drove free and entered the river. David, too, had crossed over the bar that for so long had lurked under the surface of his mind. From here forward he floated free. Years later, in "Search," he was able to express his gratitude to Emily for the "naturalness" she had shown him in those days at the rivermouth, for she had, as it were, taken him gently by the hand and led him away from the idea of one sort of sin.

OBJECTIVELY we now see a huge leap in his growth as a person. He has zest for his work. He begins to see Teacher Wu's anger, and he devises ways of teaching himself. Each day he memorizes six verses from the translated Gospel of St. Mark. He carries his character cards everywhere. A tennis partner laughs at him one day for pulling the cards out of his pocket between points. He and Emily take long walks—along the railroad tracks, to the south suburb, into the countryside. He has begun to call her Hazy. Nothing daunts him. He visits the hospital to watch operations. Two weeks later a Miss Perkins falls under a moving train at the railroad station; both legs have to be amputated below the knee; David stands in as anesthetist, dripping ether onto a cone over the wrecked lady's nose. Teacher Wu threatens to resign, then does. "I am relieved. He is not a man of strong character." In the evenings David laughs loudly with Miss Titty, who adores Emily and fusses over her. Emily is strong; her accepting the fussing, as she might accept the buzzing of a fly around her head, is like a precious gift to Miss Selden. "Hazy has a quick ear for the language." On the seventeenth of December a new teacher arrives. "He is off in pronunciation but may answer all right if I apply myself." David and his friends play hundreds of sets of tennis, right through the winter. One day he notes: "Played four sets. Snow on the ground but court had been cleaned." "Popped corn last night." He and Emily read Arthur H. Smith's *Village Life in China* aloud to each other. On Christmas day, "Hazy gave me many remembrances. Handsome cloisonné napkin rings." "Emily is a jewel of a wife." "We are very happy these days."

He makes extraordinary progress in the language. His second teacher, whom David has called "not a learned man," quits in late February. David does not consider that two personal teachers' having resigned could be attributed to his being hard to get along with; he is inclined to be sorry for two limited men.

He thinks he will not ask to be assigned another teacher for now, for he has learned that he is to go soon to Shanghai. There he will first assist at some evangelistic meetings with harangues by the awesome James B. Todd, who is on a world tour; then he will attend a great conference, also in Shanghai, of most of the Protestant missionaries in China, to celebrate the hundredth anniversary of Protestant missionary work in China. After that, he is to stay in Shanghai a while longer and then spend the hot months studying the language at the missionaries' summer resort of Kuling, in the mountains up the Yangtze.

So he will bide the time now with self-teaching. He is cocky. In late February he asks to be allowed to go to the college at T'ungchow to be examined "for a year's work," though he has studied only five months. Wolf in Shanghai is doubtful. Treadup presses. Wolf demurs. Treadup gets testimony on his progress from Cowley and Swing at Paotingfu. Wolf grudgingly gives permission.

T'ungchow, March 5, 1907.

Dear Brother Wolf:

I take pleasure in reporting to you that in accordance with your request I have examined Mr. D. Treadup in his study of the Chinese language. He has made amazing progress, the likes of which I have not previously met with. He has fully completed one year's work in less than half that time. He was excellently prepared on sixty lessons in Mateer, twenty in 'Kuan Hua Chih Nan,' the Gospel of Mark, ten selected hymns, writing three hundred characters, free conversation, and memorizing ten Chinese proverbs and the Ten Commandments.

I was impressed by the thoroughness of Mr. Treadup's work in these various lines of study. His pronunciation and tones were accurate, and his use of Chinese natural and easy. I usually have marked examinations on the basis of 100 for perfect work, but will not do so on this occasion because this man's accomplishment throws the standards I have applied to others all out of kilter.

I congratulate you on having a younger associate following in your tracks who will overhaul you some of these days if you do not keep face to the front!

Very cordially yours,
(signed) E. Y. Sterling.

SEVENTY SHEAVES

DAVID sat in the back of the big room. It was already packed with an all-male audience an hour before the scheduled time of the meeting. David could hear an angry buzzing in the anteroom. Many who had been invited had come too late and were being turned away.

The largest available auditorium in Shanghai was the decidedly unfinished Martyrs' Memorial Hall in the new Y.M.C.A. building. The hall was months away from completion; but the Todd meetings were deemed so important that the Association had taken down the plasterers' scaffoldings from the interior walls, covered the empty windows with straw matting and flags, hidden the lathing of the walls with bamboo fronds, and rented chairs and lights and a speaker's podium.

This was the third of three Todd meetings. To the first had come native pastors and leading Chinese Christian laymen, for a discussion of struggles of the native church; at the second Todd had talked to a hundred and fifty Christian leaders of the Association and native churches about efficient ways to attract and organize and manage their flocks. Tonight's was to be the main event. Tickets had been issued to four hundred members of the Association and of its Bible classes; six hundred students in Christian schools and colleges; two hundred graduates of those institutions; and two hundred "inquirers" from the native churches—men who had heard a little about Christianity and wanted to know more.

David, with no sense whatsoever, apparently, of the cultural incongruities in what he was describing, wrote his Syracuse "constituency" the next day:

> *Special hymn books had been prepared so that every man could sing—and sing they did. Twelve hundred Chinese men singing might have been bedlam but not these men. The choir of one hundred fifty voices from the Christian schools was lost, not in a heathen howl but in the strains of "All Hail the Power of Jesus' Name" from the voices of twelve hundred men who in the mission schools and churches and the Association had learned to sing. It was more like the Silver Bay or Northfield conventions than anything I've heard on this side of the earth.*

Then James B. Todd spoke, and David, forgetful of Todd's faraway brutal rebuff of his request for help on his college debt, and of Todd's faraway heartless insistence on the full year's probation before David could be married, was now wholly carried away by the vibrating woodwind voice of the confident, handsome, straight-backed, blond-haired man. Of the artistry of Z. T. Tao, Todd's interpreter, David could only grasp the amazing external translations— the gestures, the swoops of bassoon tones turned clarinetish, the sudden crescendos, the solemn pauses, the piercing stares from a face thrust forward, the great Todd rendered into a Chinese personality with a slightly skewed mimicry which to outside eyes might have looked both witty and wicked, but which seemed to mesmerize this audience.

David, so moved that the metaphors began to scramble in his mind like the squirrels in the treadmill in the cage back home in Salt Branch, wrote his Syracuse friends:

> The blood of the martyrs, the memory of which is to be kept green by this hall, is doing its work, and it was fitting that this first meeting in the hall should have its harvest of seventy sheaves, of seventy men who had not previously declared themselves for Jesus. Among the Todd Seventy, who may yet be sent out "two and two into the villages and towns," there was the silk merchant who was a charter member of the Association, the military director of the leading Government college of this port, seven students from one college and a dozen men who had been studying in our Association enquirers' classes.

What we must note for the future about this experience of David's is not simply that it stirred up once again his romantic daydreams of itinerations and street preaching, of playing his own dashing role in the evangelization of the world in his generation; but rather that his awe of James B. Todd was almost too much for him. He felt somewhat as he had as a freshman at the foot of the hill at Syracuse on the day of the salt rush—"really small." He wrote in his diary: "He made me into a cipher sitting there at the back of the Martyrs' Hall." There was some deeply puzzling ingredient in the great Todd's magnetism. We will see, a few years later, some unraveling of the puzzle when David goes on tour through China as a fellow lecturer with Todd and a remarkable shift takes place in the balance of power between these two vigorous creatures.

IN THE DAYS of waiting for the Centenary Conference to begin, David was given the task of following up with some of the "Todd Seventy" who were known to speak English. The very first man he called on, to enroll him in an Association Bible class, lived in a fine house deep in the Chinese city. A strange confession in David's diary: "Even though I knew I was on a sacred mission, I must admit I felt like one of those house-to-house 'canvassers' Mother used to hate so much. Sellers of pans brooms mousetraps ect." The young man was a student at St. John's College.

He had a long face. "My family is nobody Christians," says Chen, "I
have no friends in Christian church. I want so much Jesus Christ, but
my mother . . . " He stopped short there and wouldn't say another word
more, he had lost face, but it wasn't hard to finish the sentence. I am
praying hard for him.

In the agonizing of "Search" David recalls this Todd evening and his
own rather discouraging follow-ups as having hung in his mind back then,
contributing to a later skepticism about the old ways of evangelizing:

Only seventy declarers for the mighty Todd out of an audience of
twelve hundred—a motheaten six tenths of one per cent! Motheaten
because how many of them had parents who refused permission—or
wriggled out for other "practical" reasons? I myself could not say I had
confirmed for future cultivation a single declarer among the famous
"Todd Seventy."

THE TREADUPS were staying in a third-floor room in the Keystone house.
On the ship down from Tientsin, Emily had developed a sore throat, and now,
in damp March, as David had to go off for a few days at a time, first to
Soochow for a get-together of Association secretaries, then north with the
Todd party, she felt worse and worse. A Dr. Marshall came to see her during
one of David's absences, and he off-handedly said she had a quinsy. Her
diary: "It was as if he had stabbed me with an icicle." For David had told
Emily about the travails of old Dr. Elting, about how, for one thing, his wife
had *died* of a quinsy. Her fear—and perhaps her sense of dependency on
powerful David, and her helplessness without him (though he might have
said that *he* was already hopelessly dependent on *her*)—seemed to hone the
pain. She refused food because she could not swallow without the most
cutting anguish; and she began to imagine that she would starve to death.
Finally one day Dr. Marshall lanced the abscess. The next day David was back
in Shanghai, and she suddenly was able to sit up and to eat some custard.
Within a week she was herself. This was the first of many, many times when
the silently arching Milky-Way calm of Emily's married life would be torn out
of her sky by one of David's sudden departures.

THE CENTENARY CONFERENCE

IN MID-APRIL the scattered herd began to assemble. One could see strid-
ing in the streets of Shanghai, their heels crashing on the pavements as if with
strokes of the hammers of history, all the famous missionary stalwarts of the
late nineteenth century. Arthur H. Smith, Timothy Richard, Joshua Bagnall,
C. W. Mateer, W. A. P. Martin, Young J. Allen, the brothers Moule—legends
were walking around. They had terrifying faces, these giants, ravaged by a
fixated, unyielding love of humanity. The huge frosty bushes hanging from the
chinbones of most of them proclaimed their fierce seniority. If the Christians
had gone in for idolatry, these figures must surely have vied for the honor of
modeling for the One and Only Godhead.

Under the watchful eyes of men like these, this conference to celebrate
one hundred years of mission work in China had been well prepared. For a
decade committees had been sitting to grind and sift the grist of resolutions
on which there might be the astounding possibility that all the sects of
Protestantism and all their eccentric devotees and mystics and down-to-
earthers might *agree*. The Chinese church and ministry, methods of educational and evangelistic and medical work, women's work, translation of the
Bible and the preparation of tracts, the dream of comity and federation of the
sects for united work in the field, and the difficult question of what part
missionaries should play in public questions in China—these and other
subjects had been endlessly thrashed over, and resolutions had been prepared
to be presented to the conference for discussion and, it was hoped, passage.

HUGE DAVID TREADUP was an usher. He was wearing a stiff wing
collar with a gray foulard tie, and a blue serge suit newly cut for him by
the tailor on Nanking Road who had made his fur-lined coat. Emily (who
was to sit in the balcony with most other wives) had said on the way to the
hall that he was the handsomest creature on earth, but as he walked down
the center aisle of the Municipal Council's Town Hall on that first evening,
April 26, now and then by the side of one of the fierce old male giants of the
spirit, he felt shrunken, misfitted, and awkward. He realized he was lucky to
be there at all. Here were to be assembled some seven hundred of the more
prominent of the thirty-five hundred Protestant missionaries then in the China

field. The conference would set the tone of life for missionaries in China for at least the next decade. But David felt raw, new. He knew only five hundred Chinese characters; he had experienced only enough of China so far to have recognized that the mission romance he had swallowed at Syracuse had been a delusion. He was, besides, distracted. He burned with something very much like lust for Emily. He was ambitious, and it cut him to have good Dr. Mateer look right through him as he directed the old man to a front-row seat. Perhaps hoping to be heard if not seen, he had offered to the arrangements committee to play the cornet at some meeting, but they had brushed him off. The point of David's rather boyish discomfort and distraction was that he was in no position to take in the real meaning of what was going on around him from moment to moment. He just lolled by the door to the hall and listened to the words.

THE OPENING ADDRESS, that evening, was a review of the first century of Protestant China missions in China by the redoubtable Arthur H. Smith, author of quirky and opinionated but generally quite fair books, *Village Life in China* and *Chinese Characteristics,* among others. He had been in the field for almost half the century. Men like Dr. Smith had grown up listening to, and later delivering, sermons two hours long, and his speech this night did not stint the teeming past.

The brethren were gathered, Mr. Smith roared out in his pulpit voice, to celebrate the arrival in Canton, one hundred years ago, of the first Protestant missionary in the China field, a young Scot named Robert Morrison.

Why had he come to Canton? Ah, Mr. Smith could sniffingly tell that part, and with a somewhat malicious relish—for it had to do, as he saw it, with a blunder and failure on the part of "our esteemed Catholic friends." The Ch'ing Dynasty of Manchus had come to power in the seventeenth century. Already by that early time Arabs, then Portuguese, then Dutch and British traders had been sailing to China to buy her famous silks; and in that century came an incursion of Jesuit missionaries, with their astrolabes and cross-staffs and spring-wound clocks. Mr. Smith could grant that the Chinese— particularly the so-called literati, the scholar-gentry class, who regarded their country, the Central Kingdom, as the hub of all civilization—tolerated Jesuits decked out in Chinese clothing and graced with Chinese manners. But they were contemptuous of the crude and uncultivated Western traders with their grayish skin and their body odor of sheep fat. How well the present brethren knew that the Chinese had come to call all pale-skinned interlopers, over the centuries, "foreign devils" (*yang kwei-tzu*), "hairy men" (*mao-tzu*), "big-noses" (*ta-pi-tzu*), and other worse names. But the too clever Jesuits let themselves be divided over the so-called Rites Controversy—the slippery issue of how far to accommodate to Christianity the Chinese practice of ancestor worship— and the Chinese court became increasingly hostile to the foreign religion and indeed to all foreigners, and in the eighteenth century imperial edicts forbade Christian worship and restricted foreign trade to the one southern port of Canton.

So that was where Morrison had come. He worked there for twenty-seven years and managed in that time to translate the Bible into Chinese (rather poorly) and to convert exactly ten Chinese. He was early joined by others, including one William Milne, whose study of the Chinese language led him to assert that mastering that tongue was a task for persons "with bodies of brass, lungs of steel, heads of oak, hands of spring-steel, eyes of eagles, memories of angels, and lives of Methuselah." The first American Protestants to arrive, in 1830, were Elijah C. Bridgman and David Abeel of the American Board of Commissioners for Foreign Missions, who were followed by the first medical missionary to open a hospital in China, Dr. Peter Parker.

What prodigies of courage and prickliness, Mr. Smith said, some of those pioneers had been! There was Karl Friedrich Gutzlaff, a Pomeranian, who had "an intolerable assumption of omniscience," and who got around the restriction to Canton by working as an interpreter on Jardine Matheson opium ships, toting his tracts and Bibles with him; he also invented the practice, much imitated later, of hiring Chinese to act as colporteurs to sell Bibles and preach where foreigners could not go. (Some of them, then and later, it was said, sold the Bibles for their paper, which was made into clothbound soles of Chinese shoes.) Another early hero was Dr. James Legge, who arrived in Canton in 1843 and who spent his life translating the Chinese classics into English, to the extent of sixty-six volumes, in order to "open the door to the mind of the Chinese."

For the bearers of the Word, as for the bearers of mercantile goods, Smith said, Canton was not enough of a market. Guns opened up the rest of China to the message of the Prince of Peace. During the Tientsin negotiations after the British-French campaign of 1858, Rev. Samuel Wells Williams, author ten years earlier of *The Middle Kingdom,* an explanation of China to Westerners, remarked that "nothing short of the Society for the Diffusion of Cannon Balls" could be understood by the Chinese. "They are the most craven of people, cruel and selfish as heathenism can make men, so we must be backed by force if we wish them to listen to reason." Williams managed insertion into the treaty of clauses on religious toleration. These were elaborated in the Treaty of Peking two years later, Article 29 of which provided that

> the principles of the Christian religion as professed by the Protestant and Roman Catholic churches are recognized as teaching men to do good and do to others as they would have others do to them. Hereafter, those who quietly teach and profess these doctrines shall not be harassed on account of their faith.

These provisions opened China's interior to missionaries, as other provisions did to traders and diplomats. The treaties gave missionaries the shield of "extraterritoriality." They were exempt from Chinese laws and taxes; they were subject to the legal jurisdictions of their own governments only. What was more, they now had a social status most of them had never dreamed of at home, for they were to enjoy most of the perquisites of Chinese officialdom; they were a protected elite, like the learned gentry.

As it turned out, foreign merchants managed their business adequately, by and large, in the coastal ports, and it was the missionaries, Mr. Smith said, who made the most of the right to penetrate to the very heart of China.

Mr. Smith's lungs were tireless. The speech went on and on. Before long David's restless mind ran off like a dog on its rounds in the dark.

BETWEEN SESSIONS he was with Emily, and there was much socializing—formal calls, tiffins, chafing-dish suppers. David enjoyed getting together with the younger men, who tended to be, unlike him, thinnish, with taut neck muscles and often with pince-nez spectacles. With them he could recapture some of the Northfield elation of being among the chosen. "Have met Goudy Beach of Wesleyan," David noted, "Huntington of Yale, Nichols of Trinity, Clements of Chicago, Young of New York, Marshman—all Psi U." But in the presence of the China veterans, who seemed like so many direful prophets, Elijahs, Amoses, Ezras, Isaiahs, the shrunken sense of callowness would hit him again. It came to him, during a morning session, that his state of confusion was a product of his ignorance. He desperately wanted to be clear about what was being transacted.

ACUTELY CONSCIOUS of Emily sitting above him in the balcony, David perked up on the day devoted to the topic of Woman's Work. The speakers that morning were of two sorts, who looked interchangeable to David: elderly spinsters and wives of the giants. They had eyes of angels; their mouths could chew nails.

The first to speak was a Miss Benham of the London Missionary Society, who started out by pointedly saying, "We are met today on behalf of the women of China. For two short hours this conference"—which was to last two weeks—"will consider their special needs, and how to meet them." Miss Benham presented some resolutions. Based on the aim of "the development of the whole woman, physical, mental, and spiritual," they were largely devoted to the Chinese woman's right to, and need for, education—an idea outlandish to the Confucians. Elsewhere in its documents, the conference would deplore the debased condition, indeed the utter worthlessness, of Chinese women in the eyes of traditional Confucians: "One man has, besides his wife, several concubines. . . . Husbands are wicked enough to sell their wives, and other people are wicked enough to buy them. Mothers drown their daughters or sell them to be slaves or prostitutes. . . . "

During the debate, Mrs. Arthur H. Smith, speaking on the evangelization of women with a brevity her husband could well have aped, struck at ways in which missionaries had perpetuated that worthlessness: "Let us use our influence against building any more chapels which place [the Chinese woman] in a separate room, or behind a high screen. Try it yourself one Sunday and see how much less you get if sitting out of sight of the speaker. Make the most of these neglected mothers if you wish to make sure of the children. . . . "

Later in the morning the delegates reached Resolution VI:

> That the influence of Christian schools should be against the adoption of foreign dress and customs, and especially that a stand be taken against masculine dress and manners; that the ideal woman to be held before girls and young women in schools is the wife and mother in the home. . . .

In the discussion that followed, the elderly ladies who had sponsored the resolution explained that the reason it was so conservative was that Chinese custom was so very much *more* conservative that any attempt to move faster would discredit all other efforts, especially those in education.

Up popped old Dr. W. A. P. Martin, who had been in China since 1849, had long been president of the Imperial University in Peking, and was the author of *The Lore of Cathay*, the book David had read stretched out on carpets of pine needles beside brooks during his hike across New York State to Silver Bay two years before. The venerable warrior moved that "the first part of the resolution, as to dress and customs," should be struck out.

A MISS NEWTON Dr. Martin, the ladies know a little better than men the effect of foreign dress.

DR. MARTIN I leave the question of *taste* in dress to the ladies. The question of dress, however, is not of taste but a lesson of politics. I refer to the Dowager Empress of China adorning herself in a foreign dress from Paris, and when she asked her Chief Eunuch how she looked, he replied if she continued to wear such a "barbarous" costume, he would dash his brains out on the floor. Whereupon, Her Majesty discarded her Parisian robes. Are the ladies here to put themselves on a line with the eunuchs, and object to Chinese women wearing civilized dress?

Dr. Martin's amendment was voted down by an overwhelming show of hands, and the whole of Resolution VI was adopted.

THAT EVENING David sought out Goudy Beach, who had had two years in Soochow and who had struck David as the brightest of the young men he had met. Could Beach help him to get all these resolutions straight in his mind?

"Don't you see what's going on, Treadup?" Beach said.

"Well, I hear the votes, but —"

"Ah, man, there's been a struggle going on. Don't you see, the elders — the fogies, I call 'em — they've always thought that the only proper work of God's shepherds in the field is the saving of souls. Oh, for them, it's urgent — the judgment day is near, and there's so much to be done before it. It's ironic, they're a lot like the old Confucianist heathens, they put all their stress on morals. Right morals will make a right world. These old boys believe this. But there's this new generation — the majority right here at the conference — you've seen them — their beards aren't white yet — some of them shave their chins. They're turning things around. Didn't you read the Dennis book?"

"Dennis?"

"Look here, Treadup, *Christian Missions and Social Progress*. I'm surprised at you. Dennis? — a chap in Syria. It's what the new people here have taken up. They're fighting for a new idea — that missions can help bring about the *social* regeneration of the world. Western nations are superior because of Christianity. We don't say the Christian nations are free from all evils, not yet, but at least we have a spirit of protest against all those things that degrade human personality. Among the heathen nations, corruption, thievery, licentiousness, cruelty to the weak — all taken for granted. Our Christian missions have a duty to instill in these nations a new conscience, that will rid them of both moral laxity and social injustice."

In "Search," David wrote:

> Beach made me see some of the ways the new people in the missions had been making themselves felt. Since the Boxer Rebellion, he told me, the more forward-looking American missionaries had been much more sensitive to the Chinese than the United States government, much less inclined than their elders to view acts of imperialism as acts of God. They were embarrassed by bristling gunboats. They were opposed to the harsh Boxer indemnities. They had tried hard to get the United States government not to extend the exclusion of Chinese immigrants. And in the follow-up of the Lienchow massacre — which Gridley and Henderson made so vivid to me just after I arrived out here — these people argued against heavy reparations, for which the State Department had been pressing; they said that excessive claims created a painful impression in China and harmed the missionary cause.

THE CONVERSATION with Beach helped David to make sense of the two final documents that came out of the conference. The first, entitled "Letter to the Chinese Church," struck him as a triumph of the white-beards. It spelled out for the missionaries' Chinese colleagues how Christians should strive to live. The Christian message was not one of judgment and punishment, but rather a call for repentance of sins and a promise of salvation through righteous living—right morals. The catalog of sins in this letter was presented as if they were universal on earth, but in fact the list was cut to patterns of ills the missionaries saw as typically Chinese.

> Men do not love God or love their neighbors. They quarrel and they cheat one another. They lie and are insolent to one another. They are passionate, and they fight as if they were dogs instead of men. They gamble and smoke opium. They get drunk and injure one another. The strong trample on the weak. They love money more than they love goodness, and are more anxious to see their children rich than to see them good. The customs of society are depraved. Men worship idols and not God; they burn incense, light candles, bow and prostrate themselves, but do not repent of sin. . . . Under the influence of temper, or out of revenge, men and women take their own lives. . . .

The importance of this "Letter" for David's future was that it provided a checklist of the Chinese social ills that missionaries were authorized, so to speak, to fight against. It set limits. Any missionary who took it upon himself to go farther or deeper would do so without the sanction of this impressive ecumenical body.

THE OTHER final paper, David could see, was at least a partial victory for the younger missionaries. It was called a "Memorial to the Chinese Government." Its purpose was to present a petition to their Imperial Majesties the Empress Dowager and the Emperor, asking for complete religious liberty to all classes of Chinese Christians. One of the important arguments in favor of granting this, the Memorial said, was "the non-political character of Christianity."

> Some Christian countries have been absolute monarchies like Russia, some have been limited monarchies like Great Britain and Germany, some have been republics like America and France. Christ said nothing about forms of government. The Scriptures say, "The powers that be, are ordained of God." We are bidden to pray for kings and all in authority. In all Chinese churches prayer is regularly offered for the Rulers of China. We ourselves constantly exhort Chinese Christians to be loyal subjects, to honor the Rulers of their land, to love their country and pay their taxes regularly. We entirely discourage among them all connexion with political and secret societies.

The very next passage, however, spoke subtly for the kind of social change missionaries could and would support—reform:

Our great desire for China is that it may prosper and take a leading part among the nations of the earth, and we believe that the slow, gradual, steady influence of our missions is in the direction of bringing in that national prosperity which is based not on military power, but on justice, mercy, and truth.

It would take David many years to begin to see how political "the non-political character of Christianity" really might be. In the meantime he would become more and more involved, if only by the indirection of his remarkable work, in the "slow, gradual, steady" politics of reform.

BEACH had opened David's mind to some comprehension of the quiet revolution that had been taking place in the missionary movement, yet David felt himself still drawn to the elders. "I need advice," he confided to Emily, "from one of these wise old heads." As he watched and listened to the elders during the weeks, he found himself more and more attracted to Joshua Bagnall. Like the other old men, Bagnall was dour and cranky, but somehow everything that that old bird said resonated in some inner cavern of David's sympathy—a place in him that had nothing to do with comprehension. Perhaps, David later thought, it was that Bagnall seemed more aware than most of the other elders did of the whereabouts of the center of gravity of the Chinese soul.

The talk wore on and on. "Tired of attending meetings," David petulantly wrote in his diary. On May 8, at the last session of the conference, he received a medal "for ushering ect." And that evening he entered a fascinating decision in his diary: "Think I'll grow a mustache." Were "the wise old heads" particularly hairy? He must by this time have heard the Chinese term of scorn, *mao-tzu,* hairy ones. Did he think there might be awe tucked in the scorn? We see a photograph of David at Kuling two months later. He is holding a tennis racket, and he is wearing a white pith helmet. His teeth, which glisten in the grin of a winner, are overhung with a glorious dark brown drapery. He looks like a cross between Center Rush Gridley and Teddy Roosevelt.

Just before the last session, David approached Joshua Bagnall, who was sitting in an aisle seat at the very front of the hall. "Put a mental squeeze on my liver, till I was full of gall, and asked him for a conference. He obliged. Curt nod. 'Hotel Astor, teatime,' he says. 'Don't be late, Mr. Treadup.' Knew my name! How? How? Why, I walked back down that aisle on air!" So, casually, was arranged what turned out to be one of the most important conversations of David's whole life.

A TALK WITH
JOSHUA BAGNALL

DAVID TREADUP left a sheaf of notes in longhand, entitled "Minute of D. T.'s Conference with Rev. Dr. J. B., 8 May 07," written on sheets of letter paper of the Astor Hotel, The Bund, Shanghai—suggesting that he must have sat down at a writing desk in the public rooms on the ground floor immediately after the conversation to write out his record of it while it was fresh in his mind. Attached to the memorandum are a number of pages of the same letter paper, covered with almost illegible scribbles; Joshua Bagnall must have allowed him to write bits down as they talked, reminders which became the basis of these more extended notes. David's document does not set the scene, so we must imagine it:

A large high-ceilinged room. Wooden-bladed fans slowly stir the air. Potted bamboos and palms are interspersed with stone pillars around the sides of the room. There is a discreet murmur of conversation, punctuated by the tinkling of spoons. Chinese "boys" in starched white jackets and black trousers and shoes move silently among the tables serving tea and watercress sandwiches and Fortnum and Mason biscuits; they bow to a guest after each filling of a riceware cup from a silver teapot. Dr. Bagnall [as we can judge from photographs taken at the Centenary Conference] *is rather small of stature, though stocky. He has a beard of a sort usually painted on a head of Moses holding the slates. He is pompous, but often his face fires up and is merry. Having come here straight from the Town Hall, he is wearing a frock coat of an elegant light material lined with figured black silk.*

David's document dispenses with preliminaries:

D.T. *Are you happy, sir, with what we have seen these two weeks?*

J.B. *Immensely.*

D.T. *Forgive me, Dr. Bagnall, if I say I feel bewildered.*

J.B. *You're a big bronco, Mr. Treadup. You need to be run round and round on a bridle. I wouldn't like to see your spirit broken, but you'll have to accept a saddle sooner or later.*

D.T. *What do you mean?*

J.B. *When I first came out here, and there was a drought, I used to pray publicly for rain. Sometimes it rained. More often it did not.*

D.T. *Are you saying I have a lot to learn? I know that.*

J.B. *Look here, my boy. Protestant missionaries are harvesting converts in China at a rate of fifteen thousand per annum. Not bad, eh? But babies are born in this country faster than adults die, by 'three million every year.'* [Great emphasis.] *What I mean is, we Protestants have to find some new stunts. Your generation. Up to you. We have to bring 'em in by the million or give up the idea of converting China at all. Consider one of these new Shanghai industrial plants. One modern man can do the work of two hundred ancients. You, young man, will have to do the work of two hundred of me.*

D.T. *How can I do that? You know so much. I—*

J.B. *Look sharp! Keep your eyes open! In 1882 they sent me out to a famine. It was in Shansi. I saw carts loaded with women and children who'd been sold so the men could have something to eat. You had to carry a knife, because some of those people would kill you. Slice you up and put you in a cauldron. There were fat wolves scouting the villages. Crows and magpies ate the cadavers. I got famine fever. Almost died. When you've seen a famine in this country, you're left with a scar on your brain. That scar burns if you forget for a single moment the word 'education.' Education, Treadup! These people have to be lifted up.*

D.T. *I have been teaching, sir. It goes so slowly.*

J.B. *You know that water runs downhill, don't you?*

D.T. *Yes, sir.*

J.B. *Well then.*

D.T. *Excuse me . . .*

J.B. *Think, man! Education has to run downhill, too. Use gravity! Start at the top. We have to enlighten the literati first. The government men, the scholars. Those street chapels are all bosh. If your water's at the bottom, you have to use pumps to get it uphill.*

D.T. *How do I start?*

J.B. *That is easy, Mr. Treadup. Do what the Bible says.*

D.T. *—the Bible?*

J.B. *It says, "Seek ye the most virtuous."*

D.T. *"Most virtuous" . . . in Tientsin? As far as I know, they are all Confucianists, Buddhists, Taoists, Mohammedans.*

J.B. *I see no mention in the Bible of your Confucianists, Buddhists, Taoists, or Mohammedans. It says "most virtuous." There are some "most virtuous" in Tientsin. In every city in China there are men who are upright and incorruptible, men of probity, with good hearts. Go back to Tientsin and hunt out those men. Tell them you want to help the young men of the city. You will find them interested. They will cooperate with you.*

D.T. *But I thought the Confucianists were the most heathen of the heathen. Aren't they the most resistant of all?*

J.B. *If you let them know you're trying to help the younger men build nobler characters, they won't hesitate to cooperate with you just because you're a Christian. I have repeatedly proved this in my own experience.*

D.T. *Forgive me, sir. That sounds like something the Jesuits —*

J.B. *Mr. Treadup, I was the first foreigner and the first Christian the reformers trusted. Those people were Confucianists. K'ang Yu-wei invited me into the 'Ch'iang hsueh hui'—the Society for the Study of National Strengthening, they called it. We got ten thousand Confucianist students to sign a memorial to the throne, begging for reform on the lines suggested by our Society. The leading mandarins were on our side. For three years the whole empire was ablaze with reforms of all kinds, intellectual, material, spiritual. The Mandarins and students everywhere became most friendly with all the missionaries. Even Hunan, the most antiforeign province in the empire, asked us missionaries to supply them with teachers. I was drawn very far into things. On the very day appointed for my first interview with the Emperor in my new capacity as one of his advisers, the Empress Dowager wrested the reins of government away from him. Well now, you've seen how things have come round since then. Examinations abolished. They are riper than ever for reform. The opportunities are dazzling. Your generation this time, Mr. Treadup!*

D.T. *Dr. Bagnall, I started out by saying I'm bewildered, and now I'm more so than ever. Why didn't the conference talk about these things?*

J.B. *Well, we did, only you never got the wax out of your ears. You whippersnapper, you had the nerve just now to call me a Jesuit —*

D.T. *Oh no, sir! I only meant —*

J.B. *— but look here! We faced the issue of ancestor worship in a way the Jesuits never did. It broke 'em. Were you at the conference? Did you read the resolution? Very nice. We just danced around it, but didn't fudge an inch. Said we should be careful not to destroy in our Christian converts the feeling of reverence for the dead. What's wrong with preaching filial piety? We believe in it. What's wrong with preaching to the Chinese that they have a duty of reverence to their parents?*

D.T. *I didn't mean to call you —*

J.B. *We made strides! The spirit of union in these two weeks has been something phenomenal. Do you have any idea what it has been like, working in this mission field? Talk about your tower of Babel!*

Protestants! Look 'em up! It's like the Montgomery Ward catalog. Take the Lutherans alone — twenty flavors at least. Your German Lutherans, your Swiss, your all-kinds-of Scandinavian, your separatist each of those, then your American immigrant groups corresponding to every one of those. Heaven knows. And look at us Americans: Methodists, Congregationalists, Presbyterians, Episcopalians, Baptist Hard and Soft, Adventists, Universalists, Moravians, Friends, whatnots. Barely speak to each other. All those sects, and more, from England, Scotland, Canada, Australia. Well, we have one voice now — or something more like it than we've ever had before.

D.T.   *When I go back to Tientsin —*

J.B.   *And the resolutions on women's education! This is a radical thing in China — the idea that a woman should be allowed to know as much as a man. Why, that's radical with some of our own flock. I may look old to you, Mr. Treadup, but I tell you, some of my colleagues were born old. No, there's a new mood, Mr. Treadup, and I'm young enough in spirit to want to be part of it. I'm a Modernist. My theology is based on the simple idea of God's incarnation in man through Jesus Christ. If God is what we think he is, then that indwelling of God has to mean to me that man is more good than bad. Maybe it's a close thing; I've seen some powerfully bad men in my time; but let's say the balance is on the good side by a hair. If it is, then the prospects for human society are a hair more hopeful than not. And if we really believe in an indwelling God, he must be everywhere. He doesn't appear in Americans and Englishmen and not in Chinese. He doesn't play favorites. So if you believe that, Mr. Treadup, you must accept it that we Americans are not innately better than the Chinese. Our own society has evils in it that are just as great as those of China. If Western evils are allowed to persist, the credibility of Christians to the Chinese will be strained. But we have to go on with our work in the missions, both because the Gospels are true and because it would be bad of us to allow all these Western merchants and gunboats to ride roughshod over the Chinese untempered by Christian influences. So I think of myself as a planter. I'll plow and put the seed in. Nothing to do after that but let things grow. I am working to make myself superfluous. With the help of the indwelling God, the Chinese can take care of themselves. I just want to try to make them aware of their possibilities, if I can. And then get out.*

D.T.   *When I finish my language study, they're sending me back to Tientsin. What do you think I should do? How do you think I should start?*

J.B. *You went to college?*

D.T. *Yes, sir.*

J.B. *A degree?*

D.T. *B.S., Syracuse, oughty-five.*

J.B. *B.S.! Capital! Capital! Let me tell you something. In 1879 I settled in Taiyuanfu, in Shansi. I took my new wife there with me. Are you married, Mr. Treadup?*

D.T. *Oh yes, sir!*

J.B. *Good. One needs an intelligent wife. I had one such. I spoke a moment ago about follies of the West. My wife Mary took no time at all to point out that if the footbinding of Chinese women was bad, so was the waistbinding of British and American women. Squashing the stomach and pancreas and gizzard with torture machines made of sailcloth and whalebone! Ladies fainting right and left. . . . Ahem. Where was I? Ah! Bachelor of Science! Do you know what I did there in Taiyuan? Do you think I started one of your hymn-whining Bible-pounding street chapels that your literati just howled with laughter at? No no no. No, no, Mr. Treadup. I had very few pence to my name, but I bought a microscope. I bought a telescope. Spectroscope. Wimhurst machine, know what that is? Induction coils. Galvanometer. Geissler tubes. Pocket sextant aneroids. A magic lantern worked by oxy-hydrogen, to show slides on how to grow coffee and cocoa. Mary had a sewing machine, to show how one could do the work of many. The literati came flocking, believe me, Mr. Treadup. They were hungry for my lectures. Miracle of Light as Seen in the Magic Lantern and Photography. Astronomical Miracle as Discovered by Copernicus. You see, I told them God had stored up all these forces for our benefit, and we should thank him by obeying his spiritual laws. I don't know. It was not easy. It was not easy to lead them from the study of Nature up to Nature's God. You are a Bachelor of Science, young man. That is more than I was. Think about it!*

D.T. *Yes, sir, I will.*

[Here, for the first and only time in the notes, David enters a comment:]

At this juncture Dr. B. stood up. I thought he was dismissing me, but he began to talk in a somewhat louder voice, and I confess I was much embarrassed, because people who were having tea in the salon turned their heads. It was suddenly as if he were preaching a sermon. As if he had said it before and would say it again. I was so abashed. The depth of his feeling shook me. He was an old man angry perhaps because of the very great difficulty of passing his power along to a young person. I must have stood there with my mouth open, looking no doubt very stupid. Here is what he said:

J.B. *But there is one side of the literati you must not forget. They are rich. They are privileged. You are to remember that you have made a deliberate choice of using gravity so that what is learned flows downward. Downward to the people at large. The year of Jubilee is coming, Mr. Treadup, in this unhappy China, when the hereditary rights of the poor, as well as of the rich, will be restored, and when the accursed land laws, which permit the poor to be oppressed at will, shall be changed, and when the wicked monopoly granted to landowners in town and country shall be withdrawn, and the poor laborers who have largely made the cities prosper shall have their due share of the profits of their labor. The landlords only raise and raise and raise again the rents without limit and do nothing in return for rack rents, but on the contrary spend it on extravagant living. One orders a special railroad train for four hundred dollars to go a short distance to his grouse shooting. Another gives dinners which cost six hundred dollars per head. Countless numbers spend all their time in sport and gambling away fortunes, while numberless poor widows and orphans die of slow starvation in the same city. What wonder is it that people are driven to anarchy? God has provided a salvation for all. It is our duty to see that this is preached till the poor and needy get their year of Jubilee. Don't ever forget that, Mr. Treadup.*

KULING

BY THE END of May the lowlands steamed. With a party of ten, the Treadups boarded the *Ta Li* on the Whangpoo. The paddlewheeler started up the Yangtze. In the night there was a frightful hullabaloo of screaming. David was told the next morning that when the newly hired ship's cook had learned that these *yang kwei-tzu*, these foreign devils, were going to dig at his food with metal machinery in their hairy hands instead of using civilized bamboo chopsticks, he had gone berserk, and had thrown all the ship's knives, forks, and spoons into the river. Thereafter most of the missionaries, informed by a

Miss Evelyn Gurney that there were often microbes on chopsticks, ate with their fingers.

After three days on a river as slick as a streak of grease on a flat hot griddle of a terrain, the *Ta Li* reached Kiukiang. The party set off at once across the plain for the mountains. Emily was launched in a sedan chair with four bearers. David's huge bulk caused prolonged dickering among the chair coolies. They walked around and around him, examining his thighs, his buttocks, his shoulders, arguing at the tops of their voices. Finally, eight men agreed to carry him, four and four, but they were extremely sullen. He rode out of the city. The weather was oppressively muggy. When he saw how wide the plain was, he halted the men. "Decided to hoof it," he wrote in his diary. "Couldn't stand their groans." As soon as he dismounted, the eight bearers, who were suddenly the most fortunate of men, to be paid for carrying thin air, began to joke and prance. Now and then they would cut suspicious looks at David, apparently believing that he would change his mind and ride after all. Then they would resume their celebratory giggling and chatter. It was a long walk in terrible humidity, even to the foothills, but the men made David stubborn.

Now the caravan of bearers, moving with their rapid, rhythmic tread, wound through rice fields and bamboo groves into rolling hills. The air was still heavy and depressing, but as the climb grew steeper, here and there winding on steps cut in rock, breaths of sweet cool air began to kiss David's cheeks. By midafternoon they were in a tumbled garden of rocky gorges down which curtains of silvery water plunged to deep green pools, and where strange nameless flowers crowded the path: great white cornets of the lily family, spotted rolled-back red tigerish flowers that seemed made of enameled papier-mâché, vines that had thrown great veils of white stars over whole trees, and long intricate quills of ferns on banks of velveteen moss under dark pines. High in a pass on the mountain the procession stopped, the bearers let down their cargoes, and then, merry as boys at a game, and touchingly eager to please—and David's light-limbed men most eager of all—they cupped their hands at their mouths and shouted, many in falsetto tones, at cliffs across the way; and soon there came back a shower of echoes, in which David thought he heard a weird effect: "The rock faces over there had torn away the pretense from the shouts and gave back something angry, mocking. I don't know. It may have been my own weariness. I was tuckered out. I couldn't help thinking what it would have been like to have carried a person all the way we'd come."

Then they had one more short climb to arrive at the cool bowl of Kuling. A cup of a valley at the very top. A resort exclusively for foreigners. Little cottages of white stone, with even whiter seams of mortar, dotting the slopes. A small stone church. Playing fields and swimming pools. Slanting light filtered through soft clouds. Crisp evening air. . . . A hiding place from China.

FIVE PEOPLE and three nonpeople shared a house. David and Emily had two rooms overlooking a tennis court and a swimming pool; a couple named Colt were across a hallway; and Miss Evelyn Gurney had an airy room beyond. The three who lived in a single windowless room next to the kitchen off a cramped back courtyard dug into the hillside were, of course, Chinese servants, all male. Li, Lao Erh, Ho. Cook, boy, coolie.

Charles Colt was outraged by the luxury of the foreigners at the resort. He had come to Kuling (under orders) for language study from quarters he had chosen in the most squalid part of the Chinese city in Canton. Mr. Colt was a scarecrow. Bones stuck out all over him. He would not swim in the swimming pool but threw buckets of cold water over himself at six in the morning. He ate only raw vegetables; Miss Gurney begged him to pour boiling water over them to kill the germs, but he refused. He moved all the furniture out of one of the couple's rooms and slept on the bare floor. Miss Gurney, who was a South Carolinian, planted a garden full of "American" flowers — bachelor's buttons, hollyhocks, wallflowers, Virginia creeper, morning glory; but Charles Colt was never seen to approach his nose to a blossom. He never drove away a fly. He never rested. When dinner was late he thanked God. His theology was pessimistic; he saw life as a prolonged penance for sins he had no intention of committing. He took a dislike to Emily; his nostrils flared when he was near her, as if he could smell something vaguely sensual about her. He prayed on his knees on the floor at the dining table. He only drank water when he was not thirsty. When he saw David and others playing tennis he snorted as loud as a horse snuffling. Li, Lao Erh, and Ho presented themselves one evening after supper to quit, because Mr. Colt had chosen to humble himself by defecating in their outhouse. David calmed them down. As for Mrs. Colt, she sighed and sighed; her rib cage was a bellows of resignation.

Miss Gurney was a different case. She was germ-crazy. She had Ho, the coolie, sprinkle down all the brick floors of the house every morning with boiled water and pine disinfectant. Twice a day she ordered a cauldron of boiling water from the kitchen, which she poured into a huge galvanized tub in her room, and when it had cooled enough, she bathed with naphtha soap; then she dabbed herself with boracic acid solution. The Treadups knew this because she advised them to do the same. When she went to the kitchen courtyard she tied a nurse's gauze filter over her nose and mouth, and she spoke explosive pidgin English with little muffled puffs of the gauze. She swatted the flies Mr. Colt loved, and she festooned the house with helical strips of sweet-smelling flypaper, to which flies adhered in gooey death struggles. With her garden sprinkling can she daily watered the porch and paths and a fair stretch of the dirt road outside; she said there were "spores galore" in dust. Li, Lao Erh, and Ho presented themselves one evening after supper in another effort to resign, because Miss Gurney had taken to asking for boiling water before each meal to pour over the "family silver," as she called the tinware knives, forks, and spoons that had come with the house.

" 'Ain't it nice?' Emily whispered to me in our room," Divad wrote in a letter to Ecarg describing their housemates. " 'Everybody in this world is "teched" but me and thee.' "

BULMER WOLF was in charge of the summer language school the Association had planned. The daily schedule called for five hours of classes divided into half hour periods. For three of the periods, the whole group of sixteen (which included spouses) met together; the rest of the time they worked alone with Chinese teachers. Four of the sixteen were studying Cantonese; two, the Shanghai dialect; the rest, Mandarin. Bulmer Wolf taught a group character-writing class. Each afternoon there was a lecture on Chinese culture by Professor Orville R. Strand of Yale; he had, some time before, spent six years in China, and now, on his second trip around the globe, he had agreed to pause in Kuling to speak to the language students on Confucianism, Taoism, and Buddhism, and on what archaeologists and scholars had learned about early Chinese writing: about oracle bones, about myriad books of printed characters six centuries before Europe had paper or movable type. There were also lectures on Chinese etiquette—rituals of courtesy so all-pervasive and so subtle that the position of one's hands tucked in one's sleeves or the handling of one's fan could with a tiny movement be turned from respectful to insulting.

David was in a somewhat special position. Bulmer Wolf, doubtless remembering that Dr. Sterling had warned him that this young man, who had learned so much in such a short time, might "overhaul" him one of these days if he did not "keep his face to the front," tested David in the first week and found that David could write five hundred forty-three characters straight out from memory. Mr. Wolf excused David from the group classes and assigned him full time to the best teacher, Chuan Hsien-sheng.

TEACHER CHUAN opened David's eyes. For here, it appeared, was exactly the living figure that Joshua Bagnall had urged David to cultivate: the literatus. The cut of his pale gray silk gown on the first day they met, his sweet manner, his flawless Mandarin—he was obviously a man of style and culture. "This is the first *real* Chinese teacher I have had," David wrote. On that first day, Chuan told David that besides the standard missionary texts they would study certain great Chinese works; they would start on a humble plane, with the *Sacred Edict*. Using nothing but simplified Chinese, all of which David clearly understood, he said that in 1670 (giving the Western

date, he used the Latin Christian phrase *anno domini*), the Emperor K'ang
Hsi had written sixteen maxims in the highest literary style; later these were
enlarged upon, with an exposition in colloquial language that could be easily
understood by the common people. Here a kindly monarch talked intimately
with his subjects on the concerns of their lives: on human relationships,
courtesy, thrift, learning, and even farming and the culture of mulberry trees
for the feeding of silkworms. The work had had an enormous influence on
the public; from time to time it had been read aloud by criers in every city
and town.

As Teacher Chuan talked in his gentle, respectful voice, David had a
peculiar reaction, as he later wrote:

> *I felt as if Salt Branch, the 'Ecarg,' Absolom Carter, Mrs. Farleigh, the
> Salt Rush, the victory over Cornell—everything and everyone I had
> cared about and considered important in my life at home in the States—
> all were being wrenched out from under me. I guess what I really felt
> was a sense of inferiority. I was shallow and uncultured. Across the
> table from me was the experience of three thousand years. My legs were
> cut off at the knees! Yet how generous Chuan Hsien-sheng was! Six
> hours of work, and I suddenly have an entirely new picture of China,
> and of all that lies before me!*

David repeated the words from the *Sacred Edict* after Teacher Chuan:

> *"Duty to parents is an obvious rule of nature, and the root of virtuous
> conduct in man. . . . When you were an infant, were you hungry? You
> could not feed yourself. Cold? You could not clothe yourself. Your parents
> gazed at your face, listened to your voice. If you laughed, they were
> pleased. If you cried, they were sad. When you toddled, step by step they
> followed you. If you had the slightest illness they were so upset they could
> not eat. . . . Think of this: You were born a small naked being and did not
> bring a stitch of silk or cotton with you. Till you grew up you had food
> and clothing through your parents' kindness. Can you ever repay them?"*

David wrote his mother and father a long, sentimental letter that
evening, in which he repeated these words—and wrote them, for the amusement of all Salt Branch, in Chinese characters.

FOR DAVID and Emily together, Kuling was a playground in the sky.
Soft rain came every second or third day; they inhabited the clouds. In
early mornings when it was clear, under a heaven that was sunlit though the
sun itself still hid behind the hilltops so that a vast pale blue parasol seemed
to cover their cupped world, they played tennis. Emily would shout, "Yours!
Yours!" leaving seven-eighths of the court to David. They walked to the

Dragon Temple and held hands in awe of a sight Buddhists had discovered centuries before. Goddess of Mercy Bridge, Emerald Pool, Big Cedars—alone in such trysting places they were lovers who did not feel the need to stint their demonstrations. There at four thousand feet of altitude, reality, like the air around them, was thin, rare, and bracing, and caused a slight shortness of breath.

BULMER WOLF subscribed to *Scientific American,* and in a copy that David had borrowed from Wolf, he came across in July an article by the French mathematician Jules Poincaré. David wrote in a commonplace notebook:

> *" 'Poincaré says, "On having a problem presented to me, I gave it rather hasty and casual attention, gathering perhaps a little data and thinking of it somewhat and then putting it aside for a time, then picking it up again later, surveying the field over more carefully, gathering more precise data and perhaps making some investigation but again putting the material aside. And then, one day under most unexpected circumstances and environment, as, for instance, being at military maneuvers at the time of my forced service, and suddenly between the time when my foot left the ground and landed on the step of an automobile into which I was getting (in this short space of time), I found the answer in my mind.' "*

In an article he wrote in 1925 for the magazine *The Chinese Recorder,* entitled "Using One's Mind to Master a Language," David told how his reading, back then, of Poincaré's account of his mental processes had started him thinking that since mastery of Chinese was largely a matter of rote learning, he should let his subconscious mind help him with the work, between lessons, as Poincaré's subconscious mind had helped him solve his problem when he was away from his desk. He had backed up this conclusion with some tricks he had learned from Absolom Carter, and with Teacher Chuan's enthusiastic cooperation, he had devised a routine for memorizing three hundred Chinese proverbs from a collection Arthur H. Smith had put together.

He inscribed proverbs in lots of twenty-five on file cards, with the Chinese on one side and, on the other, both a completely literal translation and one in colloquial English. He made tab cards, marked "Memorized," "Partly Memorized," and "Unmemorized." He would hold up the first card of one batch between himself and the teacher, looking at the English; as the teacher read the proverb, he would watch the teacher's lips, then repeat aloud; then he would turn the card around and look carefully at the Chinese characters as the process was repeated. "In carrying out this exercise," he wrote,

> *avoid any worry, concern, great effort, or expenditure of much time. Make it a rapid but careful exercise. . . . If the writer's experience is not*

misleading, you will, about the second or third day, when you look at the
English of the proverbs, find that there are several that you can repeat.
Put these aside under the heading "Partly Memorized," testing yourself
on them again the next day, and if you find you can satisfactorily repeat
them, then put them in the third group as "Memorized." It may be that
you will not even have to wait until you come to the exercise with your
teacher, but as you are walking along the street thinking of nothing in
particular one of the proverbs will suddenly pop into your mind and you
will find yourself repeating it automatically.

If, on any succeeding day, you find that you are not able to repeat
those that you have put under the heading "Partly Memorized" on the
day before, put them right back into the "Unmemorized" group and
repeat the process.

Teacher Chuan's pleasure in David's method, and in his rapid progress
using it, no doubt stemmed from its similarity to the time-honored Chinese
method of rote learning—the great difference, of course, being David's
involvement of the eye as well as the ear. David simply gobbled the language.
After the proverbs, he quickly memorized the Chinese primer, *The Three-*
Character Classic. "Much impressed by the amount of learning and system
in its compilation," David wrote.

One day in late August Teacher Chuan and David, "I with a fast-beating
heart," began copying out on his memory cards the first lines of the *Lun Yu,*
the *Analects* of Confucius. "Now I have to climb a new mountain—from the
flat plain of spoken Chinese, the colloquial, where I have roamed so far without
exhaustion, to the heights of the *wen-li,* the exquisite, formal, and subtle classical language. *If I am to make my mark with the Literati, as Dr. Bagnall*
challenged me to do, then I MUST REACH THESE HEIGHTS."

EARLY in the summer David had been named chairman of the Athletic
Committee of the resort, and he had made several new friends on the tennis
courts. Two he particularly liked were a young graduate of Yale, Penn
Landsdown, who was helping to establish a school in Changsha that would
come to be called Yale-in-China; and Charles Tunney, a teacher at St. John's
College in Shanghai, son of the Buffalo doctor who had tried to save President
McKinley's life.

On July 29 Landsdown, Tunney, Treadup, and two other men, named
Herr and Sage, set off on a hike down the mountain to visit the White Deer
College, a scholars' retreat which had been founded in the ninth century, in the
T'ang Dynasty, and was famous as the workplace in the twelfth century, in the
Sung Dynasty, of the sage Chu Hsi, author of commentaries on the classics. A
few days later David wrote the Landsdown family an account of what
happened:

We started out just before dawn. There had been torrents of rain all through the night, but the clouds were breaking as we set out, and by the time we reached Nankang Pass the sky was clear. A big ball of fire came up over the horizon at Poyang Lake. On the way down the mountain we saw vistas that took our breath away—they made one understand the ancient urge to paint on scrolls.

Thus we were in an impressionable mood by the time we reached the College—a scholars' retreat nested among trees in the hills, cupped by the "Five Old Peaks." Herr was the only one of us who could make out the old inscriptions in the various courts—the Writers' Hall, with only the characters of the eight virtues—the Hall of Memories, with figures of Confucius, Mencius, and their disciples—and, most beautiful of all, the cave used by Chu Hsi, graced by a Ming Dynasty stone figure of a white deer.

We ate our picnic in this serene setting. It had grown hot. As we started back up, Penn said he couldn't wait to take a plunge in our pool; he was a devoted swimmer. Sage said there was a beautiful natural basin with a gravel bottom in a stream by the road we'd come down; it was perfectly safe; he had swum there before. This news put spring in our pace. All the way, Penn regaled us with stories of his boyhood in Keene; he could be very funny, and that afternoon he sparkled—cheered us all. We reached the spot at about two o'clock.

Here a huge slab of sandstone slanted slightly off to one side; on its upper reach it carried the track we were following and then dipped to offer a stream a fast passage to its lip, whence the water fell some twenty feet into a deep kettle below. Sage said the basin where we would swim was one of a series of pools descending from there on.

Sage and Tunney and I started down to look for it. The night's heavy rain had given the stream a deep voice, and, as we slipped and slid down the steep canyon bank, the mist of splashed spray from the waterfall rose like a sea fog around us. Sage said, "It's high. We'd better be sure it's safe." Just then we heard an alarmed shout from above.

I said I'd climb up and see what the matter was. I was hot and weak and scratched by underbrush by the time I reached the big slab. There Herr wildly told me he'd started down, then had gone back to see why Landsdown wasn't following. He had barely emerged at the slab when he saw Penn, who had taken off his shoes and trousers, evidently getting ready just to wet himself in the stream there above the falls. Perhaps he was shy about being naked among comrades. As Penn started to pull off his coat, he lost his footing in some slime, crashed to a sitting position, and, caught by the fast stream, shot over the edge.

Both of us dashed down the slope. We shouted ahead that Penn had gone over the falls. At that Tunney plunged into one of the lower pools and started to fight his way upstream. I slid head over heels into

the water after him, hurting myself on the rocks. The current was fierce.
I got through two pools and reached the chute into the pool at the foot of
the falls just in time to see Tunney strike out into it. He was swept at
once around under the waterfall. I saw him dive. I waited and waited.
He never came up.

I tried once to make it through that uppermost funnel; I was
dashed back. As I started to try a second time, I suddenly stopped.
Rightly or wrongly, I made a conscious decision not to follow the others
to a certain death by drowning. No one, not even the men with ropes in
the rescue party the next day, ever got over that chute into the pothole.
I don't know how brave Tunney did it.

After two hours we gave up. There was a temple by the path a few
hundred yards above, and Herr and I took shelter there while Sage
climbed up to Kuling. He got there about six, and a party of three men
and ten coolies, with ropes and lanterns, started down. They reached the
temple about midnight. The next morning a large party came down with
grappling irons and ladders. We found Tunney's body in the second pool
and, an hour later, Penn's, in the basin in which we had planned to
swim. Penn had on his running pants, his shirt, and his pongee jacket.

Coolies carried the two up the mountain on slings. They were
buried together the next morning in the lovely Kuling graveyard, after
a service in God's open air, attended by a host of Penn's admirers. The
rites were conducted by Rev. John Thompson of Boone College, and by
Penn's dear college friend, Rev. George Love, of the Presbyterian Mission
in Siangtan.

We find a significant entry in David's diary on the thirty-first: "I remember Father plunging into the water off the ice to save the horses." That is all.
These two losses, besides, made a deep impression on David. "Landsdown
first to break family circle," he wrote, as if Penn had been a brother. During
his time of low spirits in the New Bedford period, the "black hole" in his
young years, death had obsessed him in a morbid way; now that he was
strong and vibrantly happy, these deaths close at hand made him, he wrote a
few days later, "strangely hungry. I mean that literally. My appetite is wild.
I want to eat all the time."

IN AUGUST David had what seemed to him an alarming call from F. G.
Harmon, who said that Blackton was considering transferring David to
Shanghai. It seemed that Center Rush Gridley was trying to get his Princeton
constituency, which supported his work in Peking, to take on full support of
Tientsin, as well; this would mean that Tientsin should be handled by secretaries who had graduated from Princeton. The Y.M.C.A. was considering
opening a branch in Paotingfu, but that would be in some distant future,

and the present need for someone as active and promising as Treadup was in Shanghai.

David did not respond to this feeler with Christian passivity. "I laid before Treadup," Harmon wrote to Blackton,

> *the reasons which led us to feel that he would fit into the Shanghai picture. He expressed himself so strongly regarding the bearing such a move would have on his language that after some prayer and thought I am asking myself whether we should not search out other possible solutions. He feels that he is making rather unusually good progress in Mandarin, and that to switch at this point to the Shanghai dialect would, as he put it, "seriously cripple me." He also said, "If I move to Shanghai, I will be giving up my life purpose, to work for the Chinese in Chinese." I told him I thought the consequences of a move to Shanghai might not be so drastic as he imagined, but he was vigorous in holding his position. From what others tell me, it is true that his progress in Mandarin, both spoken and written, has been quite brilliant. It would be too bad if, by forcing the issue of his transfer, we were to sour in any degree the ultimate fruit of that brilliance.*

David consulted with the two Shanghai secretaries, Keystone and Sinclair, who were then also in Kuling, and went back to Harmon with redoubled arguments against the shift. He won his point, and wrote in his diary:

> *August 14. A comet is visible in the night sky now at four in the morning. Emily and I have come to a decision on the Shanghai bid—against it. We believe it our duty for the present to prepare in the language.*

So the threat blew over. A revealing note in the diary a few days later suggests an indirect reason for David's vehemence on the transfer: "They almost took Chuan Hsien-sheng away from me."

BUT THEY did not, and the work went on. In mid-September, Teacher Chuan gave David, as a reward for his progress in memorizing the *Analects*, an exquisite tiny jade carving of a horse, set in a little box covered and lined with black silk, in turn enclosed in a red plush box (color of happiness, used for brides' dresses, brides' sedan chairs, New Year's gifts), that in turn enclosed in a carved teakwood box, and the whole fitted into a simple box of pine. "Never before has a teacher so touched my heart," David wrote —not even, apparently, Absolom Carter. The next day David wrote Blackton asking that Teacher Chuan be assigned to Paotingfu, to which Treadup was now to return, so that the two might continue "our partnership in God's work of plowing." No decision had come when the summer school ended. Preparing to leave for Paoting, David bought an L. C. Smith typewriter from Wolf for "sixty dollars Mex"—the silver dollars circulated in China worth about fifty U.S. cents apiece. "The machine will help in setting up my memorizing cards."

On September 30 Emily rode and David walked down the mountain.

THE DECISION

DAVID'S decision about how to bring his mission to life came to him in a moment. It was almost like a sudden conversion. Many threads both from the past and from his new daily life in North China spun themselves into his readiness for it.

THE MISSES SELDEN and Demestrie were on the platform at Paotingfu to greet the Treadups on their return. Miss Titty hugged Emily so hard that her rib cage hurt for three days. "I have missed you till I thought my heart would break!" Miss Titty cried, and she kissed Emily on both cheeks and then on the lips. Miss Demestrie sulked. "Miss Selden reached up and love-tapped the top of my head as if I were a bad little urchin who'd run away from home and then had got scared and come back," David wrote.

After the heights of Kuling, all summer, with their rhythms of enchanted mists and reality's dry skies; after the daydream of meandering down the glassy Yangtze on a river steamer to Hankow; after a sightseeing outing "with Fehren a globe-trotter" to Wuchang and Han Yang, which, along with Hankow, made up the incipient industrial triangle and future revolutionary capital that the Chinese called Wuhan; and after a train trip northward which revealed the two Chinas, the rolling ricelands of the south giving way to the remorselessly brown and dusty plains of the northern granary—after so much printed on his imagination, familiar Paotingfu seemed to David, and was, flat, gray, and changeless. The compound was new to Emily, of course, but even for her the expected thrill of setting up housekeeping with their wedding-gift furniture was something of an anticlimax after the lovely quarters at Kuling.

David entered a period of stagnation. His request to be allowed to go on with Teacher Chuan had apparently been ignored. He was assigned a man named Hua, who refused to have anything to do with David's system of file cards; nor would he allow any departure from the standard missionary syllabus. Love thy teacher as thyself: very hard. He took his woes to Miss Titty, who like an angry mother poured her energy, as if it were kerosene, on his dissatisfactions, and set fire to them. David, aroused, shot off a series of urgent telegrams to Blackton, Wolf, and Harmon, at his own expense, begging for Teacher Chuan.

Dark words in the diary: "Mrs. Henderson is sick with dysentery." "Wentworth has typhoid." "Wolf is not fit for work for some time." "Talk of war between America and Japan goes on." "Sad news of the death of Mr. Bole of Kobe, Japan, the first man to die among the secretaries." "Cold. Had fire built in stove. Coolie green as July grass."

Then, on November 8, the sun suddenly breaks through the clouds: "Harmon writes that T'ungchow has decided to let me have Teacher Chuan!"

HE WAS back. He sat across from David on the opposite side of the study desk. Had he changed in some subtle way, or was the light of Paotingfu different from the light of Kuling? David had learned in the etiquette classes at Kuling to put out a pot of tea and two cups whenever a Chinese guest arrived. From time to time during the lessons Chuan Hsien-sheng would pick up the teapot and take a swig from the spout. Had he done this crude thing at Kuling? David couldn't remember. Had the whites of Chuan's eyes been yellowish there? Had his hands delicately trembled?

No matter. Teacher Chuan was back, and the delights of the language were back. He gave David *A Dream of Red Mansions* to read. The novel, he said, would instruct David in the private, inner life of a Chinese family of the highest type. "Instruct indeed!" David writes. "The more I read, the more shocked I am!" We can imagine that that great masterpiece, with its brightly rendered scenes of wild carnal pleasures, told David something that may not yet have crossed his mind: the Chinese people enjoyed sex. To David, who had evidently wandered as if by chance into a guiltless Eden of sensuality with Emily, the sweet enthusiasm of desire and the total absence of shame in *A Dream* must have given instruction in something far deeper and more personal than Chinese sociology.

But his eye, all along, was glued to the surveyor's transit, laying out the road to the future. "Continuing with *Analects*," he wrote. "Plan to commit 100 Bible verses to memory and to do considerable reading of newspapers for current events and current terms."

HE WAS unsure where the road would lead. He had so much to think about. Joshua Bagnall's words were often on his mind. He moved from day to day. He had heart-to-heart talks with Letitia Selden, who like another mother gave him to suckle freely the milk of praise. He played the cornet at services, triple-tonguing his religious joy. He sprained his ankle slipping on a streak of snow on the tennis court. He and Emily read aloud to each other W. A. P. Martin's *The Awakening of China*. One evening at a gathering at the Cowleys' they heard a demonstration of the new Victor phonograph by a friend who was touring the Far East to advertise the machine. "Excellent. We had Caruso, singing '*Ridi pagliaccio*' as if he were right there in the room." On Christmas afternoon they were invited to the Lattimores', who had decorated a Christmas tree; he and Emily took Chinese tops as gifts to the two little boys (who were to grow up to be Owen Lattimore, a Sinologist, an expert on Mongolia, an adviser to the State Department, finally a mauled victim of Senator Joseph McCarthy; and Richmond Lattimore, a distinguished classical scholar and translator of Homer). Every day with Emily brought discoveries. She was serene, yet she could be thrilled—one afternoon by the sight of the servants climbing trees to fasten meat there to attract the crows of good luck. She received a grade of 95½ on her six months' exam in Chinese. The farm boy was alive in David. "Walked with Emily beyond the R.R. Saw wild pigeons which made me yearn for a gun." Every day there was a notation of hours of study: 6½, 6, 7. He now knew more than four thousand characters, and he could read with enjoyment.

ONE DAY in January 1908, Chuan brought to David's study a book that was to have an enormous influence on David's thinking about China's future, and about how his own future might impinge on that other, larger future. The book was printed on elegant linen paper. It was entitled *K'ung-tzu kai-shih k'ao* (*A Study of Confucius as a Reformer*), and it was by K'ang Yu-wei, the thinker behind the failed "hundred days of reform" a decade earlier.

As he handed David the book, Chuan was intensely agitated. "I want you to read this," he said in Chinese. "My country is weak," he said with great emotion. Suddenly he was weeping. "I have never told you this. You have been looking at me with eyes that pierced me, since I came here to Paotingfu. You have been wondering what was wrong with me." David was embarrassed, both by Chuan's tears and by Chuan's having seen through what he thought he had successfully hidden. "I never thought I would tell you this. I fight against opium," Chuan blurted out. "Every day I fight. I am no good. Can you help me? Will you pray for me?" David stood up on his side of the desk; he wanted to step around and put his hand on Chuan's shoulder, to pass warmth through his hand into the shaking shoulder. But Chuan also stood, with tears running down his face. "No, no!" he said, "I want to talk to you about that book."

"It was one of the strangest conversations I have ever had," David wrote his brother Paul that evening:

Two men standing up. Right away he stammered out that he had failed the Imperial examinations three times. He was referring, you know, Paul, to the ancient system of exams in the classics to qualify for officialdom, for posts in the Imperial Court and bureaucracy. The exams were installed during the T'ang Dynasty, way back in the seventh century, and that system of competitive winnowing had been a remarkably shrewd—and, it had proved, durable—way of enlisting in the government men of ability who were thoroughly indoctrinated in the official orthodoxy. But a thousand years had passed, and the world had changed, and China had been taking it on the chin, and that old orthodoxy was no longer worth its salt; and I don't know whether you know it or not, but the year I came out here, they abolished the whole rigmarole. But that didn't help Chuan's sense of failure. He asked me if I could imagine what it was like to be locked in a cell among three thousand cells in rows and rows all containing young scholars, trying to write what he called "eight-legged essays," the rigidly formal disquisitions, with theses and antitheses and balances and counterbalances, like Chinese boxes within boxes carved in ivory, that the examiners had come to require as the test of those who wished to rise in the world. He flunked three times. Think of the years of work! Hoping to relieve his pain and loss of face in making this confession, I said the foolish examinations had been done away with. But this only made him angry with me. "You are my pupil," he shrilly said, reminding me of my first teacher here, about whom I wrote you, Paul, fat Teacher Wu. "You have no right to interrupt!"

This outburst calmed him, and, still standing, he began to explain to David the weakness of his beloved China. It came indeed from the incompetence and corruption of the ruling scholars, the literati—of whom, Chuan had just so frankly admitted, he was not one. "You missionaries," Chuan said, "blame Confucius." But this was wrong. The official state Confucianism which had so oppressed generations of scholars and bureaucrats was, Chuan said, "a lie to make us obedient."

He stood there, Paul, with the paths of the tears glistening on his cheeks, lecturing me. I was deeply touched, because I felt that he was staking his entire authority as my teacher on this conversation. The little jade horse he gave me in Kuling was on the desk between us. He had noticed it. Whatever his weakness, his addiction, his failure as a scholar, he obviously did care about getting something important about China across to me. I was really touched. He made me feel important. "This is what I believe," Chuan said. "Take your pencil. You have a habit of remembering by putting things on little cards. Take your pencil." So I did.

"At about the time of your Jesus Christ," Chuan said, one Liu Hsin, in order to support the reactionary and backward-looking usurper Wang Mang, claimed to have rediscovered a set of the classics written in an archaic script; these came to be called the Old Text. In the Sung dynasty, about a thousand years ago, scholars wrote commentaries on this "Old Text" which the Ming emperors, five hundred years later, decreed as official state doctrine because of their emphasis on authority and their assertions that China was the center and apex of the universe. But late in the eighteenth century and early in the nineteenth, scholars developed the theory that the classics in the Old Text which Liu Hsin had promoted two thousand years ago were forgeries, and the Confucius in them a distortion. They worked to rediscover what they believed to have been the true Confucius in the works of the New Text — particularly in Tung Chung-shu's *Spring and Autumn Annals.* That real Confucius, they argued, was not a pedant or a formalist who cared only about ceremonials and submission to authority, but a warmhearted and progressive religious leader and man of action — a political reformer. His philosophy pointed toward reform of the instruments of government, concern for the economic welfare of the people, a recognition of the rights of ordinary people, and need for knowledge of foreign countries. K'ang Yu-wei, the author of the book Chuan had just handed to David, gathered these studies together in several books which, Chuan said, "have swept the spider webs out of my country's house. They have taken away the Confucius who said you must obey the authorities and have given me a Confucius who used the events of the past to show that you could change things and make life better for everyone. K'ang has helped me to see that China does not have to stand still while the rest of the world moves."

"It will take me a long time," David wrote Paul,

> to sort out the complicated emotions stirred up in my heart by Chuan's confessions and assertions. I do know one thing. It is as if he had given me a magnifying glass with which to read the 'Analects.' Jesus has real competition! In his way, old Dr. Elting tried to alert me to this. I wrote you about his grim warnings on Confucius on the ship coming out. Only now Chuan has taken the grimness away. And something else: Chuan gave me a glimpse of an eagerness in China, a desperate desperate wish for better ways of doing things, which I suppose I had heard about, but which I had not seen in the quivering flesh before. In his case it is all the more poignant because of his sense of his personal failure and weakness. O I hope I can help — and not just Chuan!

TUCKED AMONG notations in David's diary of tennis matches with Swing and walks with Emily was a terse sentence on January 20: "Had letter asking me to go to famine relief district."

It took two days for him to be able to write: "Have offered to go to the famine area."

TREADUP spent three weeks in February in the great famine district as the Y.M.C.A. representative in famine relief. David wrote Todd:

> The extent of country involved and the population affected has been given in the press, but the misery and suffering no pen can describe.
>
> In truth, according to others, I was spared the worst sights, because by the time I arrived the missionaries had done a remarkable job of organizing the relief. But it was bad enough, Dr. Todd. I will give you just one picture. For a week I was assigned to "write villages"—that is to say, work with a team assessing the need and writing food tickets. In one village, T'a kou, a man approached us carrying two baskets hanging from the ends of a carrying pole. Each basket contained a baby. He begged us to buy the babies. He said it would save both their lives and his—no mention of the mother. No matter what we said he would not leave us, but followed us, tugging at our clothing and finally shrieking curses at us.

A large part of the central plain of North China was liable to famines because of alternating droughts and floods. Across the flat land the rivers silted up and, not being protected by strong dikes, easily overflowed. During nearly the entire spring and summer of the previous year there had been heavy rains, and the country over an area of thirty thousand square miles had been covered with water. The region was densely populated and every inch of the land cultivated. An immense garden supporting nearly ten million industrious farmers became a deadly marsh. The houses, built of sun-dried mud bricks, simply dissolved. The people were obliged to emigrate—for hundreds of miles in every direction. But all the space into which they fled was already full, and the sudden crowding in of such great numbers caused frightful distress everywhere.

Chinese officials had eventually established refugee camps, so that the homeless might be under some sort of supervision. Treadup visited one camp near Yang Ts'un, in which there were five hundred thousand refugees.

Early the previous fall, missionaries and other foreigners had begun to plan relief. Several committees were formed and urgent appeals were sent everywhere. Soon funds began to pour in, especially from America in response to appeals from *The Christian Herald*. With these funds five main distributing centers had been opened, each having from three to fifteen outstations. These were all manned by missionaries, at no small sacrifice to their regular work.

"It is very difficult," Treadup wrote Todd,

for a Chinese to understand why the foreigner loves him, but when the truth does dawn upon him — after he has some food in his stomach — he becomes most devoted to the missionary and even perhaps to what he has to say. But food must come first. I have the following reason to know that:

In the second week of my work of writing villages, Dr. Merriam Joachim, the famous Lutheran from Georgia, whom you have doubtless met, joined our team. As you may know, Dr. Joachim is a very decisive old gentleman, and it was his decision to preach first and feed after. Both John Sewall and I tried quietly to urge the reverse, but NO! Up he stood. He started a service. Unfortunately his dialect was wrong, so he had to use an interpreter. There were several thousand famished people gathered around us. He has a voice to make your hair stand on end, and when the starving people heard his shouting, they began to get on their knees and kowtow to him. He had never seen so many people on their knees in one place before, and he thought he was making a wonderful impression. But they were begging for bread, not talk. He bent down and took out of a portmanteau a large packet of hymns printed in Chinese, which he began to hand out, hoping to get this crowd with horrible stomach cramps to sing! Sewall and I could not believe our eyes. But as soon as the hymn leaflets appeared, the mob thought they were food tickets, and they rushed on the old man from every side, and I think they would have torn him to pieces in their primal craving. Sewall and I shouted. Even he saw the danger, and in panic he threw the hymns up into the air as far as he could, so the wind caught them — literally "casting Gospel seed broadcast" — and all three of us ran for our lives.

At first the Chinese officials had been very much opposed to famine relief by foreigners. They said, according to David, "The famine came as the Decree of Fate, there were too many people, it was the Will of Heaven that they die." They were especially opposed to distribution of food through construction of public works. But the missionaries went ahead, in spite of the officials' resistance, and, David wrote Todd, "Now in the providence of God a most wonderful change has come over the officials." They had begun assisting with money and influence and were urging the missionaries on with public works. David wrote that he found it a most inspiring sight at Yang Ts'un to see the delegations from the gentry and officials come to the missionaries' headquarters with maps and estimates, begging the missionaries to open new public works and save the starving people.

So now the missionaries were building dikes, opening drainage ditches, constructing roads, and digging canals all over that territory. This, they all felt, was the most practical form of relief. The gentry and officials took responsibility for securing rights of way, for dividing the families into working sections, and for seeing that the work was done. Teams set up by the missionaries laid out the work and oversaw it, and if it proved satisfactory, the missionaries paid each head man in rations of food.

From Treadup's letter to Todd:

This relief work has given our people a great opportunity to teach the Chinese honest administration. Every bag of food stuff is checked over some 6 times before it reaches its destination, and is then given directly to the hungry. In a land of universal "squeeze" where 'calamities' are most often 'opportunities' for corrupt gentry and bureaucrats, this may have been the greatest good to come out of the suffering.

David took delight in reporting one by-product of the famine relief. The flour the teams distributed mostly had come from America in cloth sacks. The weather was cold, and more and more he saw the poor people wearing "imported clothes, because in large red letters you could read XXX ROLLER PATENT *Made in U.S.A.* or, in blue, STAR ROLLER MILLS *Made in U.S.A."*

David described to Todd the opening of one of the relief works:

The officials had asked the committee to rebuild the great roads out from the east and west gates of Yang Ts'un. Dr. Burns, who is in charge, replied that we would do both if only famine refugees were employed. This was agreed to, and I was asked to open the work. I went out with the officials, looked the old roads over carefully, planned for the width, amount of excavation or filling needed, bridges to be built, etc., for the first mile. In 2 days word came that everything was ready to begin. I went out and saw a most interesting sight. For nearly a mile the roadsides were lined with famine refugee huts, built in those two days. These were made of reed matting hung on bamboo framing and were smaller than the top of a Western "prairie schooner." Each was the home of an entire family, possibly 8 to 12 persons. Standing in front of each hut was the head of the family, in many cases women, the husbands having starved to death, in several cases little boys 10 or 12 yrs. old, both parents having died. The head of each family had been provided with a Chinese spade, the rest had earth-carrying baskets, all were standing around in the most eager anticipation of the missionary to come and review them. We divided them into companies of 100 families each, and each company had a certain section of road to repair.

Imagine this double line of little huts along the road for a mile, thousands of human beings, sick and haggard, having lived on bark of trees, roots and herbs or mud from the bottom of the river, possibly for months, and now the longed-for help has come. The intense eagerness, the inexpressible longing pictured on their faces — these were most painful to see.

But even with all their feverish anxiety to begin work to get food for their famished bodies, the work must be opened auspiciously. The head man brought a table and placed it on the exact spot where the road was to start. On this he placed incense, candles, images, etc. Next he spread a mat on the ground, and all the heads of families took turns in worshiping the spirits of heaven and earth. Then the required number of strings of firecrackers was set off, to drive off evil spirits, and when the smoke cleared away, all the shovels went into the ground at once, and the work was, from a Chinese point of view, most favorably begun. Was this a bit heathenish? Perhaps, but I felt that refusing to let them do according to custom in beginning a work of this kind would have done no good and would only have prejudiced them against foreigners. You are a great preacher, Dr. Todd, but I feel I have to work, perhaps more slowly, by teaching and example.

I shall never forget the work of the past 3 weeks. I only wish I could have stayed longer.

TWO THINGS in this letter, one having to do with David's development, the other with China's, should perhaps be pointed up.

The first is David's bold assertion, challenge almost, to Todd—that though Todd was a great preacher, David preferred what he presumed to be the deeper penetration of teaching. Thus David intuitively drew the line that would define the nature of the strange struggle, of which they would hardly be aware themselves, between these two strong men in their later collaborations.

The second interesting point in the letter is the description of the system of public works, with its built-in insurance against corruption—a pattern the world would see imitated and expanded upon in the great public-works projects of the Communists, involving vast numbers of citizens with spades and earth-carrying baskets, especially in the huge flood-control campaigns on northern rivers. The Chinese had for centuries used this form of labor in family and clan units and for slave labor, but what was new here was the idea of carefully organized works *pro bono publico*, through which no prince or gentry or middleman would benefit. This would prove to be one of the many innovations of the missionaries which the Communists would later take up and magnify in their transformation of China.

DAVID'S letter, written immediately after his return, did not give any real sense of the state of shock and prostration into which the brief famine-relief stint threw him. At first he was just glad to be in a place he could call home. "Great joy to get back with Emily. She is happy to have me back, and I am that to be back."

But a few days later David, knowing that he had been spared the grimmest sights of a famine—sights he would have to face in another famine years later—nevertheless wrote in his diary: "Joshua Bagnall was right. There *is* a scar on the brain."

His shock registered on his body. In April, there is a brief note: "My left arm is giving me some trouble." A few days later: "Dr. Malley operated on Mrs. Malley, removing a tumor from the anterior of the uterus. I helped with anesthetic." On May 11: "Have discovered a swelling on my neck. Dr. Malley is treating it." Four days later: "Mrs. Malley's fever up." The next day: "Gave chloroform to Mrs. Malley while Dr. Malley opened wound." On May 21: "Swelling on my neck seems tumorlike and is growing." The swelling worsened. By the second of June, Mrs. Malley was sitting up in bed, but on that day Dr. Malley advised David to have the growth removed from his neck. He went to Peking and saw three doctors: Teale advised rest; Hull, an operation; Atkins, operation. He returned to Paoting, and the next day wrote: "Helped Dr. Malley get sponges ready for operation." On the sixth, with Dr. Hull down from Peking to assist, Dr. Malley excised the growth. "Took long time nearly 3 hours." June 7: "In bed. Life seemed scarcely worth living."

It turned out that what had been removed was not the cancer he had become convinced was there, but a harmlessly infected gland.

THE WOUND on his neck itched with its mending; the one in his mind still burned. It was during this period of a tenderness of David's sensibility— with its mixture of relief and bitter memory—that Teacher Chuan interrupted a lesson suddenly one morning to ask David whether he knew about the Taiping Rebellion.

David, not wishing to seem stupid, covered his ignorance by saying he had heard of it.

"You must think what you are doing when you make Christians of us," Chuan said. Then he told the following story (as David noted it right away in the commonplace book he was keeping at the time):

Back in the 1840s, a missionary gave a thrice-failed scholar in South China named Hung Hsiu-ch'uan a Christian tract. Hung had a vision— a sage appeared to him, commanding him to down demons and save humanity. He decided the Christian pamphlet gave him the means to obey the sage. Became an itinerant preacher. Organized a sect, "God Worshipers' Society." Two months with a Protestant missionary in Canton—he is by now a moonstruck fanatic. His preachings begin to have an anti-Manchu ring. Some of his converts start a military organization. The Christian nations have armies—why not Chinese Christians? By 1851 the movement has a dynastic name, "Heavenly

*Kingdom of Great Peace" ('Tai-p'ing t'ien-kuo')—this is the Taiping
Rebellion of which I'd heard. Two years later Hung has an army of half a
million soldiers. He announces that he is the younger brother of Jesus
Christ. He sets up in Nanking a rival government to the Manchus. He
and its other leaders become more and more corrupt and brutal. They
copy the old dynasties: found a nobility, a bureaucracy. They play at
empire but can't govern the countryside and never gain the support of
the scholars and gentry. In 1864 they are beaten by the "Ever-Victorious
Army" loyal to Peking, led by famous Charles G. ("Chinese") Gordon—
martyr of Khartoum, later on.*

This little history lesson of Chuan's stayed with David. In "Search" he
wrote that the warning implicit in it—a caution about the risks in old-
fashioned evangelizing—"helped open the way for the leap my mind was soon
to make."

O N E D A Y late in June a small wooden box arrived from Salt Branch. Prying it
open, David found his little gyroscope. He had completely forgotten having asked
for it. He put it on his desk beside the tiny jade horse Chuan had given him.

A C H A N C E remark by old Dr. Cowley (whom David had characterized in
his diary as "the most conservative *strong* man with whom I have ever been in
touch") started David reading up on Jesuit missionaries who had come to
China in the seventeenth century.

In "Search" David wrote about some thinking the Jesuits made him do:

*The first of them, Matteo Ricci, dazzled the Chinese with his brains, his
goodness, and his tact. One entry in his diary speaks of his even having
trained himself to blush in the accepted way when a high official
complimented him! Before he died, he persuaded Rome that the only
hope of converting the Chinese to Christianity lay in convincing the
literati of the superiority of Western minds. The Jesuits learned, among
other things, that the Chinese were terrified of eclipses—they thought
the sky dragon was eating the sun or the moon. So the order sent out
men specially trained in astronomy. One of them, Adam Schall, made
patient preparations for twelve years, from 1623 through 1635; the Court
gave him an observatory on a terrace against the Peking city wall. An
eclipse of the moon was due on January 22, 1636. There were three
Chinese schools of astronomers competing for ascendancy, and Schall's
men got permission to pit themselves against them. The Jesuits were
afraid that this eclipse might be obscured by local clouds, so they
prepared exact predictions not only for Peking but also for Szechuan,*

Honan, and Shansi, and asked the government to set up stations in each of those places to record the time and length of the eclipse. When it was over, all stations reported that the Jesuit predictions were accurate to the minute, while those of the three Chinese schools were way off. The Jesuits were "in," and a few years later the emperor made official a new Chinese calendar that the Jesuits had drawn up. It is used to this day.

What struck me with great force, reading these things, was that the thing the Chinese needed most, to catch up with the modern world, was the idea of rigor—exactitude. Over and over I had heard my teachers use the phrase 'ch'a pu to.' "How long is it?" "As long as my arm, 'ch'a pu to.'" "How much does it weigh?" "Five catties, 'ch'a pu to.'" The phrase means "more or less."

That allowance always had to be made. But you simply couldn't measure tolerance in machines 'ch'a pu to.' You couldn't measure delicate chemical ingredients 'ch'a pu to.' You couldn't modernize a huge country 'ch'a pu to.'

An even more important lesson was borne in on David by this reading. We find the following note, dated July 17, 1908, in his commonplace book:

'Science can convert' (much better than street preaching?). Ricci's saintliness and accuracy converted many scholars, e.g., Hsu Kuang-ch'i (d. 1632), who wrote this: "Buddhism has been in China 1800 years; but the morals and customs of the nation have continued to deteriorate, and the Buddhist faith has not been able to produce men of good character. I am convinced that the Christian religion will be able to transform every man into a good and virtuous character, to elevate society to the high level of the best ages of classical antiquity, and to place the government and state upon the solid foundation of everlasting peace and order."

THEN ONE EVENING it came in a flash. We are able to piece out an account of the moment of decision from David's diary and from letters he wrote to his parents, to whom he always dutifully reported important new plans, and to brother Paul and Absolom Carter.

He was sitting at his desk. He had just closed the book in which he had been reading about Ricci and Schall. He leaned back in a kind of daydream. Pictures of the desperately eager heads of families, holding spades at the ready over the road in the famine district, loomed before him; he thought of Joshua Bagnall's scientific instruments, his galvanometer, Geissler tubes, "Wimhurst machine, know what that is?"; he saw Chuan's tearstained face as he talked so passionately about the New Texts of Confucius; the word so often used about Ricci, "saintly," reverberated in him. His mind was "like a finely tuned harp string waiting to be plucked." As he absentmindedly moved the book on the desk his eye fell on the little jade horse and the gyroscope.

"I felt something like a sudden blow," he wrote his mother and father.

I stood up. It was as if something that had been there all along, but had been hidden from me, was suddenly visible. The gyroscope! Absolom Carter's demonstrations! I could use demonstrations like those to teach thousands and thousands of Chinese! Not just a tiny classroom at Peikai—no, I could go everywhere, like a Wesley or a Finney or a Todd, preaching scientific exactitude to the multitudes. It would be a way of teaching the complexity and precision—and the wonder—of God's plan. It would be the best way to use my skills to help Chuan and my erudite friend Lin Fu-chen in Tientsin and those fiercely yearning people in the famine district. I was so excited! I picked up the gyroscope and held it level with my eyes. It gleamed in the dark, like a grail!

DAVID slept restlessly that night. The next morning he was still fired with his idea, but he felt he had to test its validity somehow. Perhaps it was too ambitious, too grandiose; perhaps he would never be able to generate a magic like Absolom Carter's.

At the end of the fifth hour with Teacher Chuan, David said he would like to show Chuan Hsien-sheng something. He took up the little gyroscope, and, speaking in Chinese, sometimes improvising equivalents or simple metaphors for technical terms, he went through all that he could remember of Absolom Carter's delightful act with the instrument. Chuan's response was almost more than David could have desired; his eyes were liquid joy, his face was pinked with pleasure and interest, and at times, when the gyroscope did what seemed impossible, he bounced in his seat and threw up his hands as if to protect himself from such marvels.

When the session was over David felt "as if I had on a beautiful new suit of clothes." He thought he had at last found a way of thinking about his future that was large enough to contain and fit exactly his vitality, his passion for life, and his love for his fellow creatures.

Here began a new relationship between Treadup and Chuan—one of equality and reciprocal friendship, in which each taught the other. Knowing now of David's science side, Chuan, in order to give David a vocabulary to match his enthusiasm, began to bring him books in Chinese on science and technology which an immensely talented Englishman, John Fryer, working in the last three decades of the nineteenth century with Tseng Kuo-fan and the Self-Strengtheners, had translated, inventing new technical terms as they were needed. Beyond that, Chuan began to bring to David's attention new sorts of words that were coming into use in China, expressive of new hopes and expectations. There was, for example, the word for "ideal," which David found moving, for it literally meant, "the thing you have your eye on." Speaking of a man's purpose in life, one said "his magnetic needle points in such-and-such a direction." There was a cluster of meanings loaded with intention and not yet worn flat like old coins: *society, public good, constitutional government, protection of life, taking the initiative, removing obstructions, volunteering services.*

THE MONTHS wore away with work. The autumn came on, and David had to face the end of his two years of language study; he would have to go back to Tientsin; he would have to find out whether the elaborate plans he had begun to make in his mind—and on paper—for science lectures would make sense in the "real world" from which he had been so long sheltered.

Two announcements brightened David's last days in Paotingfu: Chuan told him he had not smoked opium once since the day David had first shown him the gyroscope dancing on the string; and Emily told him she was long overdue on a menstrual period.

LIN FU-CHEN AND EM

DAVID TREADUP now entered a rehearsal room of his life in which he was obliged to pursue, with dogged stubbornness, the patience of a Jesuit. To do credit to the reach of his ambition, he would have to spend years (Schall had spent twelve!) preparing himself to prove to the Chinese the worth of his new dream.

He could never have got through this trying time without the help of two people: his Emily, and the head of the Middle School at Peikai where he taught, Lin Fu-chen. Except for Emily, Mr. Lin (as David always called him) was to be the most important person in David's life for some time to come. The two had become dimly acquainted, of course, during David's earlier stint as a teacher at Peikai, but now David knew Mr. Lin's language, just as Mr. Lin knew his, and the two men, each in his way brimming with emotions that sensitized him to the other's hopes and needs, became partners in the work of helping China to transform itself, and became loving friends as well.

LIN FU-CHEN was an intellectual of a new type in China. His father had started him on the road of classical learning that would normally have led to the Imperial examinations and a government post, but the parent became caught up in the wave of outrage at the pillage of territorial concessions from China by foreign nations. Besides the grabbing of small concessions in port cities like Tientsin, the imperial powers were carving out other, larger spheres of influence. Russia leased all of Port Arthur and was extending the trans-Siberian railway to the Gulf of Peichihli. Germany took over Tsingtao on the hip of the Shantung peninsula. Japan claimed Fukien Province as its baili-wick. Britain increased by two hundred square miles an earlier lease at Hong Kong. And France took the southern port of Kwang-chow-wan, near her imperial holdings in Indo-China. As these humiliations followed one after another, a conservative scholar-soldier named Tseng Kuo-fan started some-thing called the Self-Strengthening Movement. While clinging to the Confucian principles of social order, Tseng persuaded the court of China's need to catch up with these Western aggressors in material ways, and he and his followers set up arsenals to produce modern weapons, built gunboats, and supported the translation of Western works on science.

Excited by this movement, Lin's father entered Fu-chen at thirteen in the Pei Yang Naval School. Here Fu-chen studied Western science, and par-ticularly Western naval technology and strategy. Fu-chen graduated at eighteen, first in his class. He had expected further training on a naval vessel at sea — but the Chinese navy had been destroyed earlier that year in the Sino-Japanese War. A year later he became a cadet officer on a new gunboat called the *Tungchi*. In 1898, this vessel was sent to supervise the return of the naval base at Weihaiwei from the Japanese, and its transfer the following day to Britain. "I was there," Lin later wrote,

> and saw the flags over Weihaiwei change color twice in two days. I saw the Dragon Flag replace the Rising Sun; and on the very next day I saw the Dragon replaced by the Union Jack. Sorrow and indignation set me to thinking. I arrived at the firm conviction that our national survival in this modern world could depend only upon a new kind of education which would produce a new generation of men. And I resolved to dedicate my own life to this task of national salvation through education.

Later that year a retired Chinese official in Tientsin invited Lin, then twenty-two, to become tutor to his five children; he did so well with those first pupils that three years later a literatus of great distinction, named Yen Hsiu, asked Lin to take on his six children as well. Yen Hsiu was commonly addressed as Yen Han-lin; the Han-lin meant that he held the highest of all scholarly ranks, as Member of the Imperial Academy. He was vice-president and acting head of the Board of Education of the Peking court—a man who could be, and as it turned out would be, very important to both Lin Fu-chen and David Treadup. Yen set aside a courtyard in his vast house for Lin's First Private Middle School. It grew so fast that Yen Han-lin soon bought an old Buddhist temple in the Tientsin suburb of Peikai, and the school moved there as the Peikai Middle School; it was at that temple, in the time of its being changed over for the school, with a hole being dug in the floor to bury the Buddha, that David had first met Mr. Lin. The school was to grow from eleven pupils in 1901 to over a thousand in 1917; in 1919 Lin would open Peikai University, which would become one of the most important educational centers in the country, with colleges of liberal arts, science, commerce, and mining, and graduate institutes of economics and chemistry.

What Lin brought to his work was a wonderful intensity; by David's account he literally trembled—"you could see his hands shake and the tears often welled up in his eyes"—in his fierce yearning for a younger Chinese generation that could bring his country out of the Middle Ages into the twentieth century. David's own emotions were powerful just then, too. He was charged with excitement about his lecturing idea; his wife was five months pregnant and he was beginning to be able to feel the reality of a new generation vigorously kicking in her belly—and in his mind; and he was finding teaching, now that he spoke and wrote Chinese, a thrilling craft. And so these men were like two fine-tempered tuning forks, close together, and when one was struck by an idea, strong sympathetic vibrations would be set up in the other.

MR. LIN stood in the back of the room. The students were torpid. David suddenly began to swing his arms in wide movements and to exclaim certain magic formulas—imitating a Chinese street juggler he had seen one day doing slow-moving balancing acts and keeping whirling dishes poised in level gyrations at the tops of light bamboo sticks. The students sat up, laughing. With mysterious flourishes ("I tried to *be* both Absolom Carter and that street juggler in rags working his head off for a few coins") he lifted the little gyroscope from its box, its copper flywheel and brass outer ring glistening in his hand. And soon he was bringing to life before a gasping and guffawing class the dynamics of rotating bodies, telling the story of the sun and of the rolling through space of the earth and of the moon, and of how the principle of this instrument could be used to help steer a vessel or make it possible for a train to travel on one, not two, tracks!—or, for that matter, make a revolving dish hover on a horizontal plane, held up by nothing but the tip of a slender stick. Above all he kept showing how the little wheel could defy the laws of falling that every Chinese youth had taken for granted since the tumbles of babyhood. After class the students crowded around the desk, wanting to examine the magical machine, wanting to touch it to confirm its reality. "In my imagination," David wrote,

> *they became an audience of a thousand. I had them enthralled! But what encouraged me most was Mr. Lin's reaction. When the students had finally left, he took both my hands in both of his, and he thanked me over and over again, as if I had given him a beautiful vase or a painted scroll. What a lecture I can make of this!*

EXCITED by this response, David decided to share with Lin Fu-chen his vision of itinerant demonstration lectures on science which would bring to the consciousness of thousands and thousands of the literati and of the official class all over the country China's need to move out of the zone of indifference defined by the phrase *ch'a pu to,* "more or less — that's about it — give or take a little."

That very afternoon, in the room where the Buddha lay buried under the floor, Mr. Treadup told his dream to Mr. Lin — and once again the reward was greater than David could have hoped it would be. Mr. Lin rose to his feet and spread his arms like wings. There were tears in his eyes. "We must go at once to Yen Han-lin," he said.

It took a few days to arrange an audience. Mr. Lin had time to coach David in the proper behavior. No matter how far away the realization of David's plan for the lectures might be, he said, it would be essential to get the active support of the Imperial Board of Education. With it, all doors would be open; without it, the lecture program would be regarded as subversive. Mr. Treadup must not introduce the subject of the lectures during at least the first two visits, which must be purely times of gaining Yen Han-lin's confidence "by being brilliant."

"How can I do that?" David asked, abashed.

Mr. Lin said, "By saying very little and being attentive."

THE SPIRIT SCREEN at the main gate was of marble, with fruits and vines carved on it. Beyond it, one entered a fairyland. This tranquil estate — in the heart of teeming Tientsin — was called, Mr. Lin said, *Yu-ts'un lu,* The Wanderer's Lodge. There were, within the compound, a large main house of several courtyards, three other smaller houses, and some outbuildings and mat sheds, all for relatives, disciples, guests, and servants. Mr. Lin's school had originally been in one of the houses. One could wander under pine trees, past fishponds, up little artificial hills to kiosks and gazebos with fragile curving roofs. Going around another, larger marble screen, Mr. Lin and Mr. Treadup entered a wide courtyard, onto which faced the main hall of the big house, with carved beams and crimson pillars. A servant led them to a moon terrace beyond that hall—the receiving place. They waited, standing, a long time. Then came a slender man in a red coat embroidered with butterflies and flowers, wearing a purple hat studded with precious stones; a piece of carved jade hung from a multicolored silk cord around his neck. A crimson silk ribbon decorated the end of his braided queue. Black mustaches curved down around his mouth, and he had a slender beard of a few hairs. His hands were tucked in his sleeves.

He led his two guests to his writing room. Mr. Lin had told David that among his many other abilities, Yen Han-lin was a famous calligrapher; this room was where he practiced his art. On one wall was a painting of the Han scholar Liu Hsiang, at a moment of enlightenment; on either side hung twin scrolls: *To know through and through the ways of the world is Real Knowledge* and *To conform in every way to the customs of society is True Accomplishment.* From the beams were suspended ornate cages with thrushes, siskins, and finches, which had been trained to sing softly when the master was present. In a bowl at one side was a grotesquely beautiful goldfish, with a very long double tail falling away in a graceful mass of multicolored drapery which, at the approach to bowlside of David's huge nose, the fish suddenly threw forward, veiling its whole body. All three men laughed, the two Chinese with their hands screening their mouths.

David tactfully remarked on the fragrance of books in the room and asked Yen Han-lin what he was reading just then. David glanced quickly at Mr. Lin to see whether that had been the right thing to say, and Mr. Lin nodded ever so slightly.

More answer came forth than David expected; he did his best in his diary to record the speech:

> *"I divide the day into two parts," Yen said. "As the sun moves upward, I turn my back on the dust and sweat of the material world; as the sun declines, I open myself to the future.*
>
> *"In the early morning I come here and, using a heavy brush, I write as beautifully as I can words of the sages—the true meaning of which I come, by this act, to possess within me. I long ago ceased writing stilted eight-legged essays. I read about the past. Just now I am rereading the 'Pei Wei shu'* [history of the northern Wei], *the 'Sung shu'* [history of Sung], *the 'Ch'i shu'* [history of Ch'i], *and 'Liang shu'* [history of Liang], *and also miscellaneous narratives, biographies, exegeses on the classics, and the works of the Sung philosophers, especially the 'Cheng-i-t'ang chi'* [complete works of the Cheng-i Hall] *and the 'Chu-tzu ch'uan chi'* [complete works of Chu Hsi].
>
> *"In the late morning, I stroll in my gardens, imagining that there are ten thousand trees in it, a wilderness, temples on the crags. I whistle like a finch, I sing softly to myself the songs of warriors from operas— sometimes women's songs. I may stand for a long time, watching the*

carp under water, motionless but for the gentle movement of their fins. In winter I marvel at the snow clinging to the new shoots of bamboo.

"Then in the afternoons I break away from all that and study practical things —just now, electricity, chemistry, optics, acoustics, mechanics. I needn't tell you the names of the books — you know those subjects. I am not afraid of machines; man has made them in order to have more time to be himself.

"When I have had my dinner, I go in to my mother's courtyard, and we talk and laugh together. I revel in the joys of family life; I growl playfully at her little dog; I reverently observe customs. In the evening I stand on the bridge and watch the moon rise over the wall; it puts down its silver path on the pond. I walk to my own chambers and light the lamp."

When the scholar said, "You know all those subjects," David could hardly restrain himself from pouncing on that line to bring up his lecture scheme, but Mr. Lin quickly changed the flow of talk.

From a letter to brother Paul:

On the way home from the audience, I was thinking: So this was a literatus! The real thing. My poor dear Teacher Chuan was but a poor counterfeit. Mr. Lin said, "You made a good impression." I did not think I had. I had been out of patience, and with me that always shows. Yen Han-lin had struck me as being so pretentious, so arrogant! I did not want to offend Mr. Lin, so I merely said, "Isn't he rather stiff?" "Ai-ah, my friend," Mr. Lin said. "The past is like the bamboo that he spoke of. Do you know how bamboo is engineered by Nature? A tube, with bulkheads closing off compartments of time! A perfect design to resist bending! But bamboo puts out new shoots. You heard what he studies by lamplight in the secrecy of his bedroom. Western science." "Yes," I said, "When I heard that I very nearly stopped being brilliant."

THAT WINTER David and Emily lived in the house in the compound of the Settlement Branch of the Association, at 23 Rue de Paris. "In September last we came into this house," Emily wrote home,

which doesn't remind one of an American house, having been built by a German, after Alsatian models, in the French Concession. It's a mountain chalet on flat ground. The first floor is made up of storerooms, kitchen, laundry, and coal room. Above are our living rooms, dining room, sitting room, two bedrooms, bathroom, and a big enclosed porch, which we have partitioned off into three sections, using one for a study, one for an out-of-doors sleeping apartment for Mr. Treadup, and leaving the third unused, unheated. It did not gladden the heart of this Ameri-

can housewife to find that the house contained not one clothes closet or dish closet. Chinese carpenters do very well, and after one had made a wardrobe and a dish closet we felt more comfortable. Imagine a house without a single shelf or cupboard!

We hope to use our home for the Chinese as much as possible. We have already entertained several times.

That Emily is so laconic about these entertainments suggests that they did not exactly thrill her. In one of their talks, Mr. Lin had deplored to David the lack of a "wholesome" social life that would bring together progressive Chinese and sympathetic foreigners in Tientsin. They consulted with others, and the upshot was the formation, early in 1909, of something they called the Alpha Social Club. Its thirty met once every two weeks in the homes of members, alternately Chinese and foreign. The first meeting was in the Treadup house, and two sufficient reasons for Emily's not enjoying the occasion were her by-then extreme greatness with child and the fact that the club was entirely male; she excused herself to the bedroom as soon as all the guests had arrived. From behind a closed door she heard much excited talk and a great deal of the peculiar laughter that comes from surprises over differences in culture and manners.

Out in the living room the gents played games and music. The game that caused the greatest hilarity had been Emily's idea. The names of famous men of all nationalities were pinned on the backs of all the guests, and each one tried to find out "his" name by asking the others questions that could be answered only yes or no. Emily came out at eight o'clock to serve hot coffee. The coffee made most of the Chinese tea-drinkers giddy, and they howled as they played Western children's games, pin-the-tail-on-the-donkey, Jenkins-up, and Crokinole. David played the cornet, and a Mr. Shih played a Chinese instrument called the *p'i-pa*. At nine o'clock small prizes were given to the winners of games, as well as humorous booby prizes to those who came in last; the latter, through which face was not so much lost as stolen, caused gales of extremely vexed cross-cultural laughter from the Chinese. At nine thirty Emily emerged again and served sandwiches, ice cream, and cake.

MR. TREADUP and Mr. Lin began to have heart-to-heart talks. In the late winter David wrote Todd in New York:

I have been discussing with Lin Fu-chen such books as Hyde's 'Practical Idealism' and King's 'Rational Living' and Waggett's 'The Scientific Temper in Religion.' To me this seems almost the most important work I am doing, for he is the key to the finest body of young men I know of in Tientsin. His school goes on improving rapidly and will I think become a college in a short time.

Both men were teachers. We can guess that not all of what David Treadup taught Lin Fu-chen was any more productive for either the evangelization of the world or the modernization of China than were the meetings of the Alpha Social Club. For one thing, David records that he read to his friend some of the poetry his teacher Maud Chase had sent his way during his boyhood illness: the Hoosierisms of James Whitcomb Riley, "The Rubaiyat of Omar Khayyam," the rub-a-dub of Kipling.

David, on the other hand, did learn at least two very important things from his friend.

First, he learned that the Chinese people were never going to be really interested in what he, as a good Christian, understood as "the religious life." The Chinese, Lin made clear to him, were not so religious as the Hindus, nor even as the Japanese. The Chinese word for religion was *chiao*, which meant teaching or a system of teaching. Teaching people to believe in a deity was a *chiao;* but teaching them how to behave toward other human beings was also a *chiao*. Teaching a moral life was what mattered. China's first great philosopher, Lao-tze, had been a naturalist, who taught that heaven and earth were unkind, for they treated all beings like dogs and grass. The second, Confucius, was a humanist, an agnostic, and a supreme realist. "Worship," he advised in the *Analects*, "*as if* something were present; worship a god *as if* he were present." The struggle for existence on China's share of the earth had always been so hard that the people had never had time to develop a belief in a benevolent heaven; they believed in the spirits and powers of natural forces and in the importance of perpetuating the family line—or, in other words, of surviving from generation to generation.

The other thing David took in from the talks with Mr. Lin was a sense that the Westernization of China was not going to be a simple matter. Mr. Lin pointed out that from ancient times Western philosophy had been centered on science; the Greek philosophers had been interested in plants and animals, and in the nature of matter. Chinese philosophers had been concerned with something quite remote from science: ethical and political theories, the practical, day-to-day arrangements of human life. When the Chinese did develop something like a scientific spirit in the seventeenth century under scholars named Ku Yen-wu and Yen Jo-chu, the work was directed to the study of the products of the human mind, the study of words and texts; while in the West the scientific spirit had gone on dealing with corporeal and physical things and had produced Kepler, Harvey, Galileo, Torricelli, Boyle, Newton, Darwin. Mr. Lin made it clear that the Chinese were acutely aware of this difference, and had a great desire to approach science in the Western way, but he warned David that he must try to understand the nature of the resistance he would surely encounter.

ON THE CHINESE NEW YEAR, toward the end of January 1909, David and Mr. Lin went on a round of courtesy calls on Chinese friends. One visit was to Yen Han-lin. David kept looking for an opening to bring up his lecture scheme. As they were talking, Yen Han-lin mentioned a recent scandal involving one of the Viceroy's generals, and he then spoke with scorn of military people as a class. David, realizing that Yen must have known of Lin Fu-chen's naval background, was acutely embarrassed for his friend, and he felt a sharpness rising in him. "Perhaps China would be stronger," he said, "if her people did not despise soldiers so much. It might be better if more of her best men, like my friend here, had gone to her defense. We in America honor our soldiers. Our first president, George Washington, led our troops in our Revolution. Our president who has just gone out of office, Mr. Roosevelt, was a famous soldier when he was younger."

Yen Han-lin smiled. "Yes," he said. "A thousand years ago we Chinese had just such feelings, but I am glad to say we got over them. You revere the sword; we honor the brush with which we write. We have a saying: 'No good steel will be made into a nail; no good son will make a soldier.' Westernize? We want the skills of your civilization in the West, but we shudder at the barbarism of the West."

David decided to wait until another day to speak about his lectures.

ON APRIL 14, 1909, Emily and David Treadup begat Philip Kean Treadup, an eight-pound ten-ounce son, named for Emily's beloved father. Emily's labor began at four in the morning. David sent a servant to fetch Drs. King and Stevenson. Emily's fortitude was no surprise to David. He prayed to God to hasten a bit the fall to earth of this little sparrow. But God must have been busy elsewhere that day; perhaps he was on the other side of the world, worrying about the excessive layers of fat on the body of a new president of a country there. The infant was not born until early afternoon (no one noticed exactly what time). David was relieved to find that it had ten fingers and ten toes. An experienced amah had been engaged in advance to take care of both mother and baby, but she was late, and the servants who were repeatedly sent out to summon her could not find her anywhere. David was left in charge for the first night. Emily, exhausted from her hard work, was drowsy. David was tired, too. He got a long piece of string. He tied one end to Emily's right big toe, and he told her that if she needed anything during the night, she should give a kick with that leg. He ran the string out through a window to the sleeping porch, got in bed, and tied the string to his own big toe. Only once in the night was he yanked up out of sleep by the foot.

The amah came the next day. The first thing she did was to bathe the baby in water in which she had boiled an acacia bough, to give the infant vigor and make it disease-resistant.

IN HONOR of the newborn, the Chinese members of the Alpha Social Club called at the Treadup house on the Rue de Paris one afternoon in a body, bringing with them a large red silk banner with appliqué gilt characters on it, congratulating the dear American friends on their acquisition of a precious stone.

In a letter home about this salute to Baby Philip, Emily wrote:

It is a Chinese custom that one gift calls for a return, so we gave a foreign "feast" to the Club after receiving the banner. I wonder what the banner would have said if our precious stone had been a girl. Condolences for having acquired a brick?

In another letter to her mother, Emily wrote:

The greatest shock for me out here has been the way these sweet men treat their women. David has great respect for Confucius, but to me "the sage" is the one who laid down the three laws of subservience: When a woman is young, she obeys her father and older brother; when married, her husband; and when he dies, her son. I have given my life to David and to his cause, but I thank God he thinks of me as a partner, not a servant. (I'm lucky that way. You'd be surprised, Mother, some of the older fogies in the missions are just as imperious with their wives as the Chinese.) It's immemorial custom out here that when a man gets tired of his wife, she "gives him" a concubine. Imagine! (Ooh la! I take it back. None of the fogies' wives do that!—at least, not that I know of!) We hear all this talk about ancestor worship. But a woman is not allowed to worship ancestors. She has none. As soon as she marries she becomes part of her husband's family and cuts every tie to her own. Her parents become dead to her. Oh, Mother, I weep for this woman—and for myself, that I can do so little for her. Some other Tientsin ladies and I are forming an anti-footbinding society. Maybe that will help at least a little.

Emily was able to face truths, no matter how unpleasant. David gives an account of how she happened to become a founder of the Tientsin Anti-Footbinding League. Once when Lin Fu-chen was visiting with David in their house, she asked Mr. Lin if some day he would take her to see a professional binder work on a young girl's feet. He said he would; it would take some arranging. A couple of weeks later Mr. Lin took both Emily and David to a modest house in the Chinese city. A binder had come on her monthly visit to wash and rebind the feet of a little girl of about eight, who was sitting on the edge of a *k'ang,* or brick bed. Mr. Lin did all the talking. He asked how long the binder had been working on this girl's feet. Two years. The binder unwound wide bandages and finally the "golden lilies" were uncovered. David gasped; Emily was deathly pale but remained silent. The toes had been relentlessly curled back under the soles. They were darkened and crusty. David thought they were like the misshapen feet of some small earth animal—a baby badger or groundhog. The binder washed the feet, sloughing away flakes of deadened skin. Then she rewound the same bandages, tighter than before, because each month's binding must turn the little petals farther back. Yes, sometimes bones were broken, but they mended while bound. How long did the whole process take? Four years. The little girl had been given to believe that she was a person of great importance, to be inspected in this way. She never whimpered, but when the work was done, she sat holding her feet in her hands, and she rocked and rocked on the *k'ang.* When she was fully grown, the binder said, her feet would be very beautiful: this long—measuring a span of not more than four inches. And she would walk like a willow, the binder said, with seductive mincing steps, swaying back here—the binder placed her hands on her buttocks—so as to cause great excitement among all the young men!

"Hoofs!" Emily burst out when they had left. "They are giving that poor child hoofs!" Emily said she had decided while she was pregnant that she wanted to volunteer to work against this criminal practice, but she had wanted to know what she would be talking about. Now she was almost sorry she did know. It was too much to bear.

Mr. Lin quietly said, "One of the things that made me want to grow up to be a reformer was something I heard when I was in naval school. I was fourteen or fifteen. I heard that the reformer K'ang Yu-wei had refused to permit the binding of the feet of his daughter T'ung-wei. His kinsmen laughed at him and said she would be nothing but a servant or a concubine. No one with money would marry a girl with flapping feet. K'ang had to go on a trip to Peking, and while he was gone the elders of his family almost succeeded in binding T'ung-wei's feet, but K'ang's wife, whose feet were bound, honorably prevented it. That story excited me so much! You must know, Mrs. Treadup, that we Chinese have been thinking about this ourselves. When I was nineteen, K'ang Yu-wei started an Anti-Footbinding Association in Kwangtung and then Shanghai, with his student Liang Ch'i-ch'ao in charge. I admit they may have got the idea from missionaries. Many of K'ang's ideas came from missionaries—this is one of the reasons I chose you as a friend, David. I follow his example. I can learn from you. I hope you can learn from me. And I know that you know that *I* am the one whose country is at stake."

ONE DAY in March 1909, the students of the Peikai Middle School saw a bizarre sight. T'ao Tu Hsien-sheng—as they called Professor Treadup, T'ao Tu

being the closest approximation of Treadup they had been able to find from
accepted Chinese names, and Hsien-sheng meaning Teacher—was seen in
the main courtyard of the school in his shirt sleeves turning cartwheels and
letting out astonishing whoops. They had never seen a foreigner behave that
way, and they were afraid he had lost his mind, but when he stood up again
they saw a look of great joy on his face. During the previous class period some
of them had seen a man some of them knew to be a Treadup servant,
breathless from having run all the way from the French Concession, burst into
T'ao Tu Hsien-sheng's classroom and hand him a piece of paper, and when
their teacher had finished his astonishing cavorting, they gathered around
him, asking what had brought on this display. He handed around the piece of
paper. It was a cablegram:

> REMEMBERING YOUR POUGHKEEPSIE SUCCESSES HAVE PLEASURE
> INFORMING YOU SYRACUSE SUPPORTERS TODAY SHIPPING YOU
> SINGLES SCULL WISH YOU STRONG ARMS AND BACK FOR
> YOUR CHRISTIAN LABORS
>   CHANCELLOR JAMES ROSCOE DAY

The word "Poughkeepsie" stumped every student, so David conducted a
geography class right on the spot: Poughkeepsie, Mississippi, Appalachia,
Tuscaloosa. American heritage of the Indians. He startled the students with
an exultant Onondagan war shout that he had learned as a boy in Salt
Branch. When they had recovered, he warmed to a definition of "singles
scull." He was so happy!

David had by no means forgotten, either for himself or for his students,
the corner of the Y.M.C.A. triangle that stood for BODY. Missing the daily
tennis of Paotingfu, he had taken to coaching a Peikai track team—and racing
with the students himself. On rainy days he was out there spreading sawdust
on the muddy track to make it negotiable. In his "Fourth Annual Report to the
International Committee" in New York, later in this year, he would write:

> One feature of the year has been the inauguration of a campaign with
> the slogan, "When will China win a place at the Olympic Games?" This
> is followed by, "When will China be able to send a winning team?" And
> then, "When will China be able to invite the Olympic Games to come to
> China?" The Association has introduced numerous sports. Basketball
> and Ping-Pong are great favorites.

In late April David's great day came. A long, narrow crate was off-loaded
from the *Koon Hsing* (David's lucky ship, in one of whose cabins, we have
deduced, he had learned from Emily the secrets of "naturalness") onto the
Tientsin Bund.

On a beautiful afternoon two days later Principal Lin Fu-chen and
almost the entire Peikai student body lined the Bund as David, dressed in

shorts, knee socks, and an undershirt to which Emily had sewn a crimson P, christened his glistening cedar racing shell the *Ecarg II* and launched it in the swirling brown water of the Pei Ho. He pulled out with slow strokes into the current and eased downstream. It was to his "little sister" that he wrote an account of what happened next:

> *I was too excited for words. So apparently was everyone else. I turned "you" around. I gave a good look upstream, and the way was absolutely clear. I thought I'd try a little sprint, just to see how she went — a fast hundred strokes. I had reached seventy-three in my count when there was a terrible crunching sound and I was lurched into the water. They told me later that some boat people in a sampan had panicked, thinking me some sort of evil spirit let loose on the waters, and had cut right across my path trying to get as fast as they could to the protection of a small shrine on the Russian Concession side. I had the presence of mind to stay with the shell, and eventually a Customs launch towed me to the Bund. This may be the greatest loss of face our dear Lord Jesus Christ has had in North China since the Boxer Uprising!*

The bow of *Ecarg II* was badly smashed, but Lin Fu-chen found some master carpenters who were able to do an exquisite job of repairs, and two weeks later David was on the river again. He had attached two good-sized rearview mirrors to the iron riggers that stood out from the shell on either side to hold the oar swivels, and anyway the boat people became accustomed to him and left the channel clear when he was out. David wrote Grace that he could see their hands lifted in front of their mouths to hide laughter, but "I don't care. I work up a sweat, and the blood courses through my veins, and I can lick the world, little sister!"

MID-MAY 1909. Something was wrong with Lin Fu-chen. He seemed nervous and forgetful. His eyes were bloodshot. David felt some estrangement; taking cues from an ancient etiquette in which gestures spoke as loudly as words, David felt, in the way Mr. Lin crossed his arms when they conversed and tightly hugged himself, that his friend was holding himself at a distance, aloof. As they talked, Mr. Lin would often put his hand to his face, his first two fingers up against his cheek, the other fingers curled in front of his mouth, as if he were afraid that beetles or roaches might jump out from his lips. He seemed tired all the time, yet he kept running through the days like a poor ricksha puller.

After talking it over with Emily, David decided he must behave in the Western way, go directly to Mr. Lin and ask him what the matter was. They were sitting in Mr. Lin's reception room at the school. David sipped tea. Mr. Lin looked at him guardedly. "My dear Mr. Lin," David finally said. "Your friendship is more important to me than anything in this world except my wife's love. Are you offended with me about something? Something I've done? What have I done to anger you?"

Mr. Lin turned pale. He was silent. David was afraid that his direct American approach had been a disastrous mistake.

Then suddenly Mr. Lin put his hands to his face, and his shoulders began to shake. Unsure what to do, David did nothing.

At last Mr. Lin lifted an anguished face and, suddenly speaking himself as directly as an American, he said in English: "You have done nothing wrong, Mr. Treadup. I can't sleep. I am so defeated."

David asked if he could say what the trouble was.

"My father is very sick and has terrible pain. I am greatly puzzled about human suffering."

David asked if there was anything he could do to help.

"One suggestion has been made," Mr. Lin said, "that no more children should be born into the world, so human suffering could come to an end."

David said that was a cure worse than the disease. He said he was sure that was not really Mr. Lin's answer.

"It is the suggestion of one of our Buddhist teachers."

David asked if Mr. Lin had ever read "the great Hebrew classic on the mystery of human suffering—the Book of Job."

Mr. Lin said he had not read it. "But it is not just my father's pain—" He paused. "It is my own."

David gathered, from what Mr. Lin now began to pour out, that he was ill with anger and sorrow over the decay of his miserable country. He began talking about the broken promises and failed reforms of Peking. "Last November the Kuang Hsü Emperor died, remember? And *the very next* day the Empress Dowager died! Wasn't that a strange coincidence? After that I had a smell of carrion in my nostrils for a month. Not that either of *them* was going to save China! Then the Empress Dowager's valedictory edict gives us P'u-yi, a three-year-old boy, as the next emperor—and his father, Prince Ch'un, as regent—a weakling, an ignorant, proud fool. Who do you suppose wrote *that* edict? I don't trust Yuan Shih-k'ai [the viceroy of Chihli Province, the "strong man" of North China]. Everyone knows he wants the power. There has never been so much bribery. The throne is taking influential posts away from Chinese and giving them to Manchus. What a proclamation that was last year!—full constitutional government after a period of preparation of *nine years!* Now they promise us provincial assemblies. When? When?"

We have the details of this scene from an account David wrote in August of that year entitled, "An Incident in the Regeneration of China." "The things he began to say," David wrote then, "made me feel I might soon be able to speak to him about Jesus." Mr. Lin began denouncing "the old outlook." "Stupid superstitions, *feng-shui* [the rules of geomancy having to do with the relations of wind, water, and spirits], fortune-telling, magic, 'luck,' placation of demons! What a backward people we are! Educated men believe in these things. And not just Taoism: Confucius holds us in a trance—the authorities will take care of everything. 'The way' of Buddhism—this 'way' leads us nowhere except to no more births." The one man he had counted on, the great reformer K'ang Yu-wei, had fled the country. "He writes from overseas long messages to his followers—tells us the Ch'ing government has no intention of giving us a real constitutional government. We *know* that!" Finally he turned to David and cried out for help. "Mr. Treadup! Mr. Treadup! Where can I turn?"

ONE FINAL TIME Mr. Lin took David to call on Yen Han-lin, and this time David more or less forced the moment of proposal. With due regard for Chinese formulas of modesty, he described his plan.

The great Yen sat as immobile as an unthinking block of wood. He let the silence stretch out until it was a kind of horizon, beyond which nothing but a wide sky of doubt was visible.

Finally he spoke. "Our scholars—our literati and gentry—whom you say you want to reach, would not be receptive to you. You must realize that it was only thanks to an army gathered by these same scholars that we were able to turn back the Taiping Rebellion; our scholars remember what those Christians did—devastating every Buddhist, Taoist, and Confucian temple in their path, tearing down ancestral shrines, and trying to dig out all the roots of our old civilization. Those fanatics had been poisoned by missionaries. Our scholars remember that. They do want to learn about modern science, but they want to learn on their own terms—not from poisoners. Have you been told about the Chinese Christian professor at Wuchang who was beaten with bamboo rods in court until he fainted, and then beaten again, for refusing to admit that the Salvation Army was a revolutionary force? Do you see the connection? The Taipings had burned Wuchang! The magistrate had not forgotten!"

On the way back to Peikai, Lin Fu-chen kept shaking his head. "What have we come to? The head of our educational system looks back fifty years for his opinions! The Taipings! And he is supposed to be a progressive!"

"Never mind," David said, "I'll find a way."

Lin was silent for a long time. Then he said in a low voice, "I think I should kill myself as a protest. Would anyone notice?"

David's diary: "I was chilled to the bone by the conviction in his voice. I really think he might harm himself."

A SOUL SAVED

TIENTSIN in the summer was a brick-lined oven. In order that Emily and the baby might not suffer from the heat, David arranged to rent half of a two-family house—so Emily would not be alone when he was not there— at the seashore health resort of Peitaiho, on the coast of the Gulf of Peichihli, a hundred and fifty miles from Tientsin. David took them there by train early in June.

Here was another Elysium on Chinese soil. Here—figuratively, at least— the foreigners gave their famous, if apocryphal, notice: No Dogs or Chinese Allowed. No Chinese, of course, except servants; the Treadups had brought three. This was a lovely stretch of hilly shoreline, with clean sandy bays for swimming. Neat stone cottages with cool verandas under corrugated tin roofs. Unpaved roads, on which the only means of transportation was astride cloth-saddled donkeys, tended by grooms who would come competitively galloping for a fare at a halloo from any porch. From its hills, views of the wide sea to the south and of bluish toothy mountains in the distance to west and north beyond plains green with sorghum and millet. All was most tidy. There were an American beach, an English beach, a French beach—ladies of all nationalities well covered in knitted wool. Tennis courts; white flannels, white shirts, white sun hats. The Treadup half-house was on Rocky Point, which was not a point at all, but was a hill entirely owned by the American Methodist Episcopal Mission, which leased houses in perpetuity to approved clients. A medical missionary from Peking named Dr. Tulley, whom the Treadups did not know, had rented the other half of the house; Treadups peeked, but no Tulleys were yet to be seen.

DAVID returned to Tientsin, leaving Emily and Philip with the three ser-vants. The term at Peikai was over, and David was given chores to do at the City Branch of the Association, where Roscoe Hersey was now General Secretary, a serious, gentle, good-hearted young man, somewhat literal-minded but devoted to the work and meticulously tactful with the Chinese. David now had some time for language study; in spite of Yen Han-lin's thumbs-down, he daydreamed about his lectures to the literati on science; he rowed on the river, even on the hottest days; and he spent anxious hours with his downhearted friend Mr. Lin. He was sweaty and lonely. Through the spring we had seen surprisingly few references to the baby in his diary, but now in his letters he is all father.

Emily's letters from the shore are the castings of a cheerful mind. She has an eye for the absurd. The Americans at Peitaiho, she reports, play baseball. Yankee businessmen get into "rhubarbs" with missionary umps and use shocking words, but to no avail, for "we must face it, Mr. Treadup, there is a higher morality in third strikes called by men of God which all the blustering power of Standard Oil can never shake." The British play a most amazing kind of polo on donkeys instead of horses—amazing because "sometimes all six mounts will stand stock still for minutes on end, reverencing their mulish parentage in a stubborn refusal to run here and there after a small white ball; and if one starts to hump along very slowly at last, the others queue up behind it, in a row, pack fashion. But the Brits don't care, they have their pith helmets on, and white riding breeches, and boots that have been polished deep into the night by Number One Boy."

Five Tulleys have arrived. Dr. Tulley is a surgeon. "I believe he loves to cut," Emily writes.

Be careful when you come, dearest, don't mention any aches or pains, the next thing you know, he'll be under your skin. He does pushups on the rocks in front of the house. On the Fourth of July he was very angry with me for not hanging out the Stars and Stripes. He told me, "Christianity has allied itself to the more virile races. Our flag 'means' something, my dear. Vigor! Citizenship of the United States carries some responsibilities. You have to be able to hike all day with sixty pounds in your pack—no whining! Mark my words, as America goes, so will go the world!" You'd think the mate of such a scalpel-rattler would be a little country mouse—but wait till you see Madam Tulley. She has a chin like the Rock of Gibraltar. She is in command of the Anti-Prostitution League in Peking. I pity the poor little flowers of the night! It is the Tulley children who are mice. Three rickety pale boys who wear shorts that hang down below their knees. They haven't been out in the sun once since they've been here. They play Parcheesi on the veranda, quarreling over every roll of the dice. Come soon, my dearest husband! I need you!

DAVID'S vacation began on July 24. His six weeks in Peitaiho were among the happiest of his life. He had a great appetite for joy. He adored his son, and his "active sexual nature" again had its guiltless scope. He and Dr. Tulley rather surprisingly became companions on indefatigable hikes—to the nearby

Lotus Hills; to the strange desert of sand dunes beyond Eagle Rock; to Shanhaikuan, where the Great Wall reached the sea; to the hot springs at T'ang Ch'uan Szu; to the temple at the crest of a sheer cliff at Pei Niu Ting. They fished for trout in the mountains and shot snipe at the ponds in the dunes. Muscular Dr. Tulley turned out to have total recall for the names of the most delicate flowers, and David took home, for Emily to press in a book, miniature violets, tiny English daisies, pale blue harebells, yellow blooms of loose-strife, blossoms of bloom-grape and hawkweed and bellflower, and the showy little mouths of yellow-and-orange toadflax, which David "recognized with a burst of homesickness as the dear old weed we called 'butter-and-eggs' in Salt Branch."

IN THE MIDDLE of the month David received a letter from Lin Fu-chen. Mr. Lin said that because the Chinese fishing industry had been made a monopoly, the income from which was used to support government educa-tion, he had been appointed to go to Washington as a representative of the Chinese government at an international conference on fisheries. He was also to travel afterward in America, France, England, and Germany, studying educational methods. But he doubted, he said, that he had the strength for such a trip. The letter turned dark, almost threatening. It seemed to David a choked cry for help. He took a train for Tientsin the very next morning and went at once to Peikai. He persuaded Mr. Lin to go back with him to Peitaiho, "to stay for a few days with an understanding friend." All the way on the train, Mr. Lin stared out the window like a sitting bronze.

Treadup wrote about the train trip, years later, in "Search":

We had stopped in the station at Ch'angli, and I suddenly realized that the dreary brown hills there nearby were the very ones we loved so much, seen against the western skyline from our house at Peitaiho—so purple from that distance, so magical, so verdant in our imagination: East Heaven, West Heaven, Buddha's Tooth! Here now was Buddha's Tooth itself, just by Ch'angli, a barren sandstone cone. Disillusioning, seen in the immediate foreground.

I pointed this out to Mr. Lin.

"Don't sit so close to me," he said.

I understood what he meant. I was to look at him from a sparing distance. At that moment I was overwhelmed by his sadness and pain, his barrenness, close to, and I felt a thrust of great tenderness. I was not brought to tears: I felt a wonderful warmth. I believe my feeling was almost what Paul meant by "charity" in First Corinthians. Not the charity of those who condescend to give gifts—Paul makes the distinction—and though I bestow all my goods to feed the poor and have not charity, it profiteth me nothing—no, this was one moment in which I think I really did experience Christian love. Rare moment. I'm not sure I can think, right now, of any other, in all my years in China, quite so uncontaminated.

THE FOLLOWING AFTERNOON, Dr. Tulley knocked on the door of the Treadups' half of the house. He asked David to take a short walk with him; there was something he wanted to discuss. When they were some distance from the house, the doctor cleared his throat with the sounds of a motorcyclist revving his engine. Some of the people in the Rocky Point Association, he said, had been wondering if it was wise to carry on Tientsin work with Chinese colleagues in a health resort like Peitaiho.

"Are you saying," David asked, "that it is bad form to have a Chinese guest in Peitaiho?"

"Well," Dr. Tulley said, "many people feel that it is important for our health and well-being to get *away* for a short time."

David now spoke in a very low voice ("I menaced him," David wrote, "with the glower of a murderer"), saying, "Mr. Lin is a dear friend of mine who is in deep trouble. Your half of our house is *away* from our half. I will thank you to stay *away* from our half from now on. Perhaps you will want to stay *away* from your own servants' quarters, too."

The motorcycle in the doctor's neck roared, sputtered, and stalled.

THERE NOW began at the shore a series of intense conversations. On the first day, David produced the Moulton translation of the Old Testament, and he and Dr. Lin read aloud to each other, in Chinese, the Book of Job.

The next day Mr. Lin asked, in English (as David later recorded the words), "What is the secret of the enthusiasm and constant cheerfulness of the Association secretaries at Tientsin? I often wonder about it. You, Mr. Henderson, Mr. Wood, Mr. Hersey. Mr. Gridley was the same way, too. Now that I am so miserable I envy and covet that solid happiness and optimism—covet it both for myself and for China's leaders. We need that strength, to get things done. But then I grow suspicious of that cheerfulness. Is it real? Might it be just as morbid, in its way, as Job's misery? And even if it is genuine, I suppose it isn't possible for us Chinese to have it, considering the conditions under which we live and the inheritance that has been given us by our past."

"I said," David wrote in a later account of these talks,

"What you have remarked interests me greatly, for you have mentioned two of the great factors that condition and determine life, but you have

not mentioned a third, one that is perhaps an even more important practical working factor." Mr. Lin asked, "What have I said and what have I left unsaid?" I then said: "You've mentioned the conditions under which you live—i.e., 'environment;' and what your ancestors have given you—i.e., 'heredity.' Now the third great factor that is yours to use and that is so significant is the 'will'—your power of deciding for and persisting in and following out the deepest convictions of your soul."

The talks went on; David pounded at the wall of Mr. Lin's bleakness. On August 21, the third day of the conversations, there is a most interesting entry in David's diary: "Realized today for the first time that I am in the act of saving a soul." It appears that Lin Fu-chen was soliciting his own conversion. In David's busyness with planning his science lectures, his dream of evangelizing the world in this generation had apparently been tucked away in long-term storage in the back rooms of his mind. He was not just cheering up a gloomy friend! Nowhere does David record having made a connection between Lin's low spirits and his own depression before his conversion. After what was really happening dawned on David, he began more actively to "prepare" Mr. Lin.

Late one afternoon Mr. Lin asked, "What is it really to be a Christian? I ask because I have seen so many people who call themselves Christians but who do not seem very Christian to me." David did not write down his answer, but laconically noted: "After a short discussion of that question we knelt in prayer and he came to his great decision." But Mr. Lin did not tell David just then. That evening, when a number of Association men and their wives were gathered on the Treadup veranda—Gridleys, Hendersons, Herseys—Mr. Lin suddenly stood up and with great emotion announced that the terrible coolie burden of his grief had been lifted from his shoulders.

I T   W A S no small thing for a person of Lin Fu-chen's brilliance and promise, a noticed man, a favorite of the chief of the Imperial Board of Education, to convert to Christianity. The Association secretaries certainly knew the significance of this catch. Wood later wrote Todd: "One prominent Chinese said that in [Lin's] conversion Christianity in Tientsin had made a greater conquest than in all of the rest of its forty years' work put together." Hersey wrote Todd: "Without doubt the reaching of this young educator is the most significant event in the history of our movement in Tientsin."

For Lin himself the implications, as he must have known, were staggering. The morning after his announcement he told David that he had been unable to sleep because of his happiness, and he handed him a written note:

I will try to do the great good instead of the little good that I have been trying to do for years. I pray God through Christ to take me and use me as a sacrifice for the benefit of my country.

He returned at once to Tientsin and announced his decision to his mother, father, and brother. He gathered the school together, pupils and teachers, and told them. The storm began to break. That evening his second-in-command at the school, a man named Hua, told him that his parents had said they would not let him stay at the school if Lin remained as its head; whereas he, Hua, did not want to stay at the school if Lin did *not* remain. The next day Lin took a train for Peking to announce his conversion to Yen Han-lin, who was in the capital just then for meetings of the Imperial Board of Education. On the train he met three men he knew, the president of Pei Yang University, the director of the Provincial Normal School, and a prominent member of the Tientsin gentry. He told them. They were appalled. The president of Pei Yang said he must have had heat stroke at Peitaiho. The director of the Normal School said he knew a weak-minded fellow who had become a Christian, but "for a man of your education and strength—very strange!"

Lin offered Yen Han-lin his resignation as principal of Peikai and as delegate to the Washington fisheries conference. Yen refused both offers. He said Lin had been running the school on an annual grant of five thousand taels (then about U.S.$3,250), but that the government would not be able to maintain Peikai's high standards on twice that sum; and said it was too late to find a substitute for the fisheries conference—and besides, since his conversion was creating such a sensation, it would be just as well for him to be out of the country awhile, till the disturbance died down.

A week later Lin Fu-chen left for Washington.

A WELL-WROUGHT
CAMPAIGN

DAVID was naturally pleased but also embarrassed by the congratulations he got from all sides for having "landed" Lin Fu-chen. Only he could know that he had more or less stumbled onto the success. In his diary he wrote: "To me the important thing is that Mr. Lin is no longer in pain."

Important as the conversion may have been, the entire episode seems not even to have cracked the hard shell of David Treadup's single-mindedness. He was obsessed with the lecture project. He still carried language flash cards in one trouser pocket; in the other he had begun to carry cards on which, while walking to the beach or between innings at a baseball game, he would jot down notes on cards marked "Gyroscope," "Wireless Telegraphy," "Magnetism," "Electricity," and so on. The diary: "Emily says I will *never* learn that what is supposed to be vacated during a vacation is the head."

He was delighted to get back to Tientsin in early September. He cleared a storeroom on the ground floor of the Rue de Paris house and set up a laboratory in which, with materials he scrounged from various, mostly British, machinists and technicians and ship's engineers and from the repair shops of the Tientsin Municipal Council, he assembled a magneto and a wireless set and a magic lantern, and he built a portable cabinet in which he could transport demonstration materials for scores of simple physics experiments from place to place. He rehearsed his outlined lectures on his Peikai classes. He entranced those who had not heard it before with his lecture on the gyroscope. He took his students to the Tientsin power plant and then lectured them on the magneto. He thrilled them by sending telegraph messages across the campus.

In October he mounted a more ambitious public lecture. He invited all the educators of Tientsin to Peikai for an evening on electricity. "Not a true 'demonstration,'" he wrote,

> because my equipment was not suitable for a large hall. But I was much encouraged. I had prepared some eighty lantern slides. I had my magneto and various circuits mounted on boards, with colored lights, buzzers, bells, magnets, ect., ect. Our Peikai science teacher ran the lantern, I gave the lecture, and Mr. Hua presided. I felt sure this would make a strong lecture but I was not prepared for the power of the message for these eager educators. It was in fact an electric evening.

ONE DAY Yen Han-lin summoned David to his Tientsin house. David had somewhat changed his hostile view of Yen because of Yen's having refused to let Lin Fu-chen doubly resign just because he was a Christian. Still, he felt on the defensive, especially since he did not this time have Mr. Lin's comforting company during the audience. Yen led David into his writing room. David tested the veil-tailed goldfish by approaching his nose to the bowl; the fish obliged with a sweeping modesty, hiding in its own delicately striped draperies. Yen laughed; David laughed.

Yen said, "I was walking beside the river early one morning last week, to watch the mists come off the water. I believe I saw you rowing a boat."

"Yes. I often go out early in the morning—the air is so fine then."

"May I ask you a question?"

"Of course."

"Why do you lower yourself by doing such labor? Why don't you hire a coolie to row for you?"

David, writing his sister Grace:

I burst out laughing. Then I realized that was a mistake. Mr. Yen had been serious. He was trying to tell me that there are two kinds of people in an ordered world: those who labor with their bodies, and those who labor with their minds. I was causing him to lose face—and being a stupid barbarian, to boot. But I hardly cared. Had he summoned me all the way from Peikai to give me this incredible advice? Imagine hiring a Chinese coolie to row that lovely racing shell! Then, out of Chinese politeness, Mr. Yen was laughing too. He stood up then and came toward me. "T'ao Tu Hsien-sheng," he said, "you have been very kind to my protégé Lin Fu-chen. I want to tell you that the Board of Education is prepared to support your lectures—not with money, you understand. But we will authorize meetings in all cities, we will notify the viceroys, we will give you authority from the court." Little Ecarg, believe me, I let out an Onondagan war whoop, and do you know something? I turned two cartwheels right in the main courtyard as Mr. Yen was showing me out. How he threw up his hands at the antics of this barbarian!

ONE GREAT DOOR opened the very next day, as if by magic. A courier from the yamen of Viceroy Yuan Shih-k'ai came to Peikai looking for David with a message written on a scroll in the most elegant *wen-li*, or classical Chinese. Its flowers yielded a heady fragrance, the drift of which was that T'ao Tu Hsien-sheng had been warmly recommended to the Viceroy by Yen Han-lin, and that he would be welcome to borrow, for use in his famous lectures, anything at all he wished from the Viceroy's unworthy (though in fact it was remarkably good) museum of modern science. David hurried around that very afternoon to the yamen, to bow in the approved way to the Viceroy—and thus he made the acquaintance of a man who in a few years was to have a large and malign influence on China's destiny; and, perhaps more important, began to make the acquaintance of the circle of brilliant "returned students" from American colleges who were in the Viceroy's entourage. And from the Viceroy's yamen that afternoon he literally ran to the museum, which was housed in an abandoned Taoist monastery. How pleased he was with what he found! He began at once to ransack its eccentric gadgetry to use in his beloved lectures.

Tientsin, China,
October 20, 1909.

Dear Mr. Todd:

I now want to propose to the International Committee a carefully wrought out campaign to reach the modern literati of China through demonstrated lectures on science. You will doubtless have heard that we have been carrying on extremely successful experiments with lectures of this type in Tientsin. It is now time to extend this service, which the Chinese themselves are eager to receive and which the interests of the Celestial Kingdom imperatively demand, to other cities of the country.

The method of procedure is as follows: When we receive or devise some particularly attractive science demonstrating apparatus in Tientsin, we invite the officials and educators of the city for a special lecture. After it, they are given an opportunity to set dates when they can bring student bodies or fellow provincials to follow-up lectures. In this way we are able by a series of lectures to present a great idea to the strategic classes of the city.

We need now to be able to shift such a series of lectures successively to the important cities of the empire. . . .

David's letter went on for nine single-spaced pages. The farther he went in the letter, the grander the program became, and on the last page he set out, in his innocence, what he called "a tentative budget."

For equipping demonstration apparatus	*$ 75,000*
Administration & maintenance of above	
@ $5,000 per year for 5 years	*25,000*
10 workers @ $2,500 per year for 5 years	*125,000*
5 American scholarships for Chinese workers,	
2 years each, $1,000 per year for 5 years	*50,000*
Total for 5-year campaign	*$275,000*

IT DID NOT take James B. Todd long to answer. Nor did it take him nine single-spaced pages to say what he wanted to say: No! and again No! The International Committee couldn't possibly take on such an exorbitantly expensive new program. It was hard-pressed enough to carry on its already-in-place operations.

BUT DAVID had learned with the Syracuse crew "how long four miles are." He went to work. He persuaded Blackton, Gridley, Wood, Harmon, and

Hersey to write letters to Todd telling how effective his lectures had been. He himself wrote a series of letters, not waiting for answers, reducing his "tentative budget" letter by letter, and coming around gradually to a suggestion, first stated on November 3, that he be allowed to return to the States and raise the money and solicit contributions of equipment for the program himself. On December 18, his resistance finally worn down, Todd wrote approving David Treadup's return to the States with his wife and child for a period of "some months," to raise money for a "Literati Program in the China Field." It went without saying that Treadup would have to forgo the normal sabbatical furlough of one year that would have been coming to him in 1912, after seven years in the field. David, hot for his brainchild, blithely agreed to that, and on January 22, 1910, the three Treadups boarded the *Empress of Japan* in Shanghai.

FURLOUGH

TREADUP knew exactly what he wanted, besides money, from his furlough. He wanted the big apparatus — mechanical devices, working displays, the newest gadgetry — that would loom for all to see during scientific demonstrations to large audiences in large halls, in forms that could be taken apart, if necessary, and packed in small boxes suitable to be carried by river steamer, by train, by cart, by wheelbarrow, by donkeyback, or by coolie carrying-pole into every corner of a China whose town-to-town communications ranged from shiny new rails to ancient muddy tracks for the bare feet of peasants walking single file. He wanted clarity in the lecture hall and reach on the landscape. And money, of course, to back it all up.

AMERICA was a blur to Treadup. He hardly even noticed that he was "back home." He had the energy of the obsessed, and he seemed to be at the heart of a "dust devil" — one of the sudden miniature summer whirlwinds that would dance a sinuous cone of dry powdered topsoil across a field of his childhood in Salt Branch. His trip must remain a blur to us, too, because he was moving so fast and working so hard that his usual recording mania seemed to lapse, and except for two or three episodes that he described in letters to Emily, whom he had deposited with Philip at her home in Newport, New York, we have to depend on his summaries and rough notes to piece together what he had been up to. His furlough lasted eight months, and in that time he visited "the following centers," listing them in columns in a later annual report to the International Committee:

Brooklyn	Oil City	Trenton	Omaha
New York City	Pittsburgh	Princeton	Chicago
Buffalo	Sewickley	Detroit	Dayton, O.
Albany	Wilmerding	Denver	Salt Lake City
West Point	Harrisburg	Portland	Vancouver, B.C.
San Francisco	Coatesville	Lafayette, Ind.	Nashville, Tenn.
Berkeley	Ridgway	Tacoma, Wash.	Chattanooga
San Jose	Worcester, Mass.	Seattle	Waterloo, Iowa
Fresno	Kansas City, Mo.	Everett	Marshalltown
Los Angeles	St. Joseph	Walla Walla	Cedar Rapids
Philadelphia	St. Louis	Spokane	Charlotte, N.C.

His typical regimen in these "centers" could only be described as a frantic skid from one sort of breathless effort and interest to another and another and another. A day might go like this:

Breakfast with the owner of a ball-bearing factory, possible donor of apparatus. A session to examine an ingenious exhibit of the Palmer Penmanship System — possible aid to teaching Chinese to write English. A midmorning presentation to a large Y.M.C.A. audience on the need for Christian workers who wished for "the renovation of the great Empire of China" to penetrate "the neglected upper classes" of that country and educate them in science and technology. A siege in the office of a manufacturer of microscopes. Inspection of a U.S. government display entitled "Telling the History of Typhoid Mary." A luncheon speech to business barons at the Downtown Club. A dash to a cornfield outside town to inspect a barnstorming airplane. A call on the executive secretary of the Scientific Temperance Foundation for ideas on antisaloon propaganda that might be converted for antiopium displays. Tea with a difficult rich lady known to have a large heart but a tight purse. A rush to a cannery to see whether a lecture on the canning industry would make sense. A dinner speech to a church group. A brief after-dinner call on a university professor of mechanical engineering. Attendance at a lecture on Race Betterment at a Scottish Rite Temple. A half hour of writing letters to others and notes to himself before going to bed.

Bashful he was not. He always went right to the top. Sometimes he arranged appointments ahead of time, sometimes he would simply present himself at the office of the president of a company and refuse to leave until the man saw him. He moved at such a pace that he must have grown haggard, and we can be sure that the police were occasionally summoned to relieve a terrified secretary of an obvious madman. But if he was a lunatic, his was the lunacy of that absolute integrity and faithfulness to a single idea which is sometimes understood to be the valuable raving of genius. Besides, he was both crafty and charming in honor of his obsession. And so he had great successes—more, to be sure, in the line of wheedling mechanical objects than in raising cash; but he got some of that, too.

The very first person he approached was Elmer Ambrose Sperry, founder of the Sperry Gyroscope Company and inventor of the gyrocompass and the gyroscopic automatic steersman. David's enthusiasm and obvious love for the gyroscope apparently touched Sperry, and he donated several wonderful devices which we will have occasion to see in action on Chinese platforms later. He called on Charles F. Kettering, who contributed exhibits of the Delco ignition and lighting systems. (We can guess that businessmen who showered their products on this mendicant did so partly out of Christian charity and partly out of a conviction that Treadup's demonstrations might help sell their goods to the Chinese government.) He visited Henry Ford, got nothing. Adolf Lewisohn gave him a small amount of money. He called on Mr. and Mrs. Thomas A. Edison; Mrs. Edison did most of the talking until Mr. Edison began demonstrating a "cinematograph"—a motion picture projector—at which point Mr. Edison supplied the narration for the slightly jerky scenes before their eyes: "Now we shall see the monkey jump out of the box. . . . " No contributions, but "I know I will never forget the sharp foxy eyes of that white-haired gentleman."

FROM the very beginning James B. Todd had been skeptical of young Treadup's ambitious plans for a "Literati Campaign." Todd's letters could not douse the blue flame of David's obsession, but they were annoying, and David responded irritably and not quite tactfully. From Pittsburgh:

> *I was somewhat disappointed when I received your letter responding to mine from Chicago about securing the fund for the Literati in China.*
>
> *I have felt that this campaign was not given a place in proportion to its importance to our work in China. It is essential that we reach the upper classes who are in such a marked degree leaders in that marvelous reform movement in the midst of which we find ourselves in China. As I sought in my mind for an explanation for your indifference, there have come two answers. Either, first: the demands on the available staff of our ever extending Foreign Work have been so great that it has been impossible to entertain any new suggestions; or second: that you were not convinced of the significance of this method of approach. I would greatly appreciate a frank statement of your views on either or both of these points.*

David got what he had asked for—a "frank statement," which in its controlled politeness expressed a stinging Christian rage. The tone of this response penetrated even David's single-mindedness, and he decided he must find an ally to work on Todd. Fortunately Blackton was also on furlough from China, and David began writing appeals to him.

WE DO have a full account of one of David's solicitations, in a letter he wrote Emily from Waterloo, Iowa. This had taken place in Chicago.

David was invited by a devout man named John Lummer to give a presentation at the Union League Club to a dozen of the rich and influential members of the Club's board of control, including men like Henry P. Winkler, president of Puritan Oats, and John B. Masters, president of the Chicago and Southwestern Railroad. These gentlemen decided Mr. Treadup was worthy of introductions to Judge Marriott J. Sutter, who had just been appointed by President Taft to be the new Minister to China, and to Mrs. Brutus M. Miller, widow of the inventor of farm machinery who had founded the National Reaper and Binder Company.

The latter would be especially important to David. Nettie Miller, who had so far survived her husband by a quarter of a century, was one of those moneyed American women who grow quite at home with power. She had confidently moved in and run her late husband's vast company with a jaw of iron ever since his death. More important for David, she was famous for making a fuss over handsome young missionaries, and for being openhanded, too. Often wildly generous charity checks would flutter before the grateful eyes of those fine young men. David must have known that she had recently been especially munificent with the Y.M.C.A.'s stunningly good-looking James B. Todd.

A tight schedule was arranged for the following evening. David would call on Madam Miller at six; would make two separate speeches at the Central Branch of the Chicago Y.M.C.A.; and then would spend the later hours with Judge Sutter, who was most anxious to be informed about China by someone who had recently been there.

David presented himself at precisely six at Madam Miller's house at 217 Rush Street. A butler, dressed in a sugar-scoop suit exactly like the one David had left in China, ushered him to the library on the second floor, and soon his hostess materialized. David was impressed. "I use that word 'materialized' advisedly," he wrote, "because in her long chiffon gown she seemed to move forward from darkness into light like a figure solidifying in a dream." She had a long tube in one hand.

When David first spoke, he was astonished to see the gracious lady lift the long tube to her right ear and aim it across the room straight at his mouth. He had no trouble hearing her, because, evidently being quite deaf, she shouted, giving certain words a sudden, startling emphasis. David peeled out some photographs he had brought to show her. She loved the story of the conversion of Lin Fu-chen. She bade him sit beside her on a divan, and she looked at the snapshots: "I adore it! . . . Heavenly! . . . Goodness me, how lovely!" After a while she said, "Judge Sutter—he's going to China, you know—lives just around the corner from me. I would be glad to introduce you to him. He would be greatly interested to see the pictures. Why could I not put on my bonnet and step around to his house with you?"

David explained that he already had an appointment to spend from eight thirty to ten with Judge Sutter.

Rather tartly, Madam Miller said she was delighted that that had been settled.

Then she brightened and said that there was a statement President Taft had made that had been printed on the cover of the Association's publication *Foreign Mail,* she had it upstairs, she wanted David to take it to show Judge Sutter. She disappeared to run upstairs for it; soon she reappeared with it in the hand that did not hold the tube. She also had in that hand a checkbook.

"Now," she cried, "I want you to show your lovely photographs to my son Brutus Junior." Brutus was in the parlor, reading and sipping a toddy. He grunted at each of David's pictures. "Isn't he charming?" his mother said, tapping David with the tube to show whom she meant. Madam Miller sat down at a desk and began writing a check. She said she wanted to support the wonderful lectures Mr. Treadup had described, but she also wanted to alleviate some of his personal expenses. The check she gave him was for a hundred dollars. "This is not for your work! This is for you!"

She asked what time he would get through with Judge Sutter. David said ten o'clock. She insisted he must then come back to her house. She had another son. She wanted *him* to see the pictures. She wanted *him* to hear about the work Mr. Treadup planned to do in China. "I tried to be excused from this," David wrote; not having received the main check, he was obliged, however, to be as tactful as possible.

"Nonsense!" she said. "You must spend the night with us."

"But I have a room at the University Club."

That had to be repeated. It was hard to be tactful at the top of one's voice. She insisted that he cancel his reservation. He must save for the future. He did not think it worthwhile to announce through the tube that the room was costing him nothing.

"Just in time," he wrote,

> I managed to get away and went to the Central Branch and having finished my two addresses cabbed to Judge Sutter's house and had a most delightful evening with him and Mrs. Sutter. At his request I am preparing a list of books on China and also a short Who's Who of the people he should meet outside of diplomatic circles.

When David returned to Rush Street at ten o'clock he found Madam Miller disappointed that her other son had not yet come home, and she insisted that Mr. Borman, her secretary, should accompany Mr. Treadup to the La Salle Hotel, to see if the prodigal could be found there. He could not. Mr. Borman then took David to the University Club, where David packed his bag and returned for the night to Rush Street. Next morning he packed again and shuttled back to the University Club, still without the second check. But later that day the following letter arrived:

217 Rush Street,
December 18, 1910.

Dear Mr. Treadup
    I have been lighter hearted for having known you and having heard all you have unfolded to me of your interesting work in China. I will contribute $500 toward your great plans for China. The little sum I handed you, I meant to be entirely personal for your own private use, and not to go thru Mr. Todd's books. My wishes are that you get an overcoat out of that sum. Can you go to Field's store and ask Mr. Anderson to show you some coats? Mr. Anderson is floor manager. He has already upon my telephone request sent nice underclothing to you at the University Club. I directed it to be of the best. My heart and interest are enlisted and will follow you ever.

Very cordially yours,
N. P. Miller

DAVID, Emily, and Philip had a week in Salt Branch. The whole Treadup family, except brother Will, who had always disliked David, had reassembled to greet the travelers. David's parents doted on their grandson. Little sister Grace was sweet, brother Paul quiet and loving. But for some reason David felt hemmed in and stifled in the old haunts. The fact was, he missed China. The porcelain sky at Kuling; the spume on the American beach at Peitaiho; the moon bridge over the carp pool in the house called Wanderer's Lodge in Tientsin—he now could recall a deep-draft, wide-beamed world that moved like a great ship through the universe; and Salt Branch was what it was, provincial, tight, gossipy, glad of its smallness. David's childhood seemed in ruins. He cast a sad eye on *Ecarg* the First; the wherry lay neglected behind the barn, cracked, peeled, and hogged down at bow and stern. David burned with shame at his sense that his mother and father were narrow and dull; he had moved out into a heady world of vivid people, of Lin Fu-chen and Yen Han-lin and Joshua Bagnall, Nettie Miller and Henry Ford and Thomas Edison. In his diary: "I am praying for humility."

    Emily was pregnant.

NEGOTIATIONS with Blackton and Todd culminated in a conference in Lake Forest, Illinois, in November, the understandings of which David summarized in a letter to Todd on the letterhead of Reba Armour, Public Stenographer, Cedar Rapids, Iowa:

First, we may count upon an appropriation of $15,000 during the next four years for the national lecture campaign. Second, this is exclusive of what money I may raise for the purpose. Third, I may count upon $2,000 of this fund being available for the purchase of equipment before returning to China. Fourth, my return to China will take place just as soon as the assembling of apparatus and formulating of lectures and other indispensable parts of this enterprise permit.

Fifteen thousand dollars! What a comedown from the "tentative budget" David had first urged on Todd, of $275,000 for five years! With what a thud David must have landed on the hard ground of reality during that talk! But now something new came up, which the three seem not to have discussed at Lake Forest:

One of the results of my experience in searching for ideas and equipment for these lectures has been my learning the following things: first, motion picture films will have to be secured largely in England and France, and science apparatus in Germany; second, it will be necessary to have someone in each of these countries in whose judgment we have confidence to cooperate with us in the securing of new apparatus from time to time, as it is invented and as we need it; third, for the purpose of making such arrangements, for the securing of the initial equipment, to take advantage of the very much lower prices for both new and second-hand apparatus in Europe, and to complete preparation for most important lectures on aviation, the telegraphone, kinemacolor projection, gyroscope, and wireless telephone, it seems necessary for me to return to China by way of Europe.

Blackton persuaded Todd to swallow that, but then David got this terse letter from the godhead:

The International Committee recommend that if you deem it essential that you go to Europe, your family go in company with one of the parties traveling to China via the Pacific, and that you yourself proceed alone to Europe and from it to China via the Siberian route. Another plan would be for you to attempt through some of the best-trusted sources to secure the materials you want from Europe by correspondence and then go with your family via the Pacific. The Committee are absolutely opposed to your taking your family via the Siberian route, as we cannot consent to run the physical risks involved where a child is in the party. We are very clear on this point. Kindly let me know which of the plans you favor.

David favored neither. He went back to Blackton, and a memo for Todd of their next conversation included this sentence:

D Treadup feels that the state of Mrs. Treadup's health demands that he should travel to the field with her. He proposes their return to the Orient from Europe by ship.

There was a bulldog beneath David's skin. It held on. He got his way. One other issue was settled in these triangular dealings. It was that after his return to China, David's headquarters would no longer be in Tientsin but would be in Shanghai. Apparently the resistance he had felt in Kuling against moving to Shanghai had been overcome; he was persuaded that travel to remote parts of China could be more easily arranged from that great nerve center.

DAVID'S trip to China by way of Europe, so long fought over, turns out to be a complete blank to us. Not a shred of record remains. His diary is empty. He apparently wrote no letters to Todd or to his family. It is not even certain that he went to Germany at all, though he does later show up with some Telefunken radio equipment in China. We learn from a letter that Gridley wrote Todd from Peking in December 1910, that

Treadup is supposed to be reaching Shanghai about the middle of this month. We understand from his brief notes that he is barely touching the high spots of the earth's crust such as Chicago, New York, London, Paris, Geneva, Rome, Calcutta, Hong Kong, Shanghai, at which latter point he is to "assemble" his famous gyroscopes and various apparatus with which he is to undertake the "National Lecture Campaign." It will be good to see him back in China, and he will do his part (a generous one at that) in the "renovation of the people" of this great Empire.

BOOK THREE

⊞

THE TEST

BEAUTIFUL LAWS OF NATURE

ALL IS READY. This may be the most exciting hour of David Treadup's life. The demonstration apparatus is arrayed on an impromptu stage in the great hall of the Admiralty Building in Canton. David's enthusiastic engineer, A Ch'u, his eyes flashing, hovers like a magnetic force field over one mechanism after another, revving each one up to see that it is working right. We are about to hear the first lecture in the great Literati Campaign: "The Gyroscope and Its Applications."

Mr. Treadup stands at one side of the stage, impenetrably calm. His bulk is as solidly affixed to the planet as that of a stone statue. The only tiny motion we can make out is of rehearsal thoughts, which we detect hurrying like thin cloud shadows across his face. The huge man cuts a rather official figure in his new lecturing outfit — a Western costume that in its somber way will do reciprocal honor to the glistening embroideries of the Mandarin gowns that will soon fill this hall. He is in a long double-breasted frock coat, with silk facing on the lapels and with silk-covered buttons; under it is a double-breasted vest, similarly garnished. The trousers are diplomatically striped.

The frock coat shows delicate wrinkles from having been packed a little damp in Mr. Treadup's trunk on the steamer voyage southward from Shanghai. At his throat is a very high stiff collar with rounded points. His hair is parted near the middle. His mustaches have been brushed into a rage of nut-brown drapery, itself silken. There is nothing wrong with his eyes, yet for authority's sake he is wearing rimless clear-glass pince-nez spectacles attached to a black ribbon that runs to a lapel buttonhole. This is in truth an impressive statue of Occidental Learning, implanted here on a wooden platform in a grand hall in the city where Protestantism got its first foothold in China a century earlier.

Everything in order, A Ch'u? Then—turning to the officials at the back of the hall—open the doors!

M O N T H S —no, years!—of work had gone into that moment. The more recent months had been intense ones. David had put so much on the line—with his colleagues, with Todd, with Emily, above all with himself. He had to bring his wager through, no matter what the odds against him might be.

In Shanghai's damp winter he had set up his laboratory. He had rented a small building at 22 North Szechuan Road, and in it he had established his office, a machine shop, a blacksmith's shop, a carpenter's shop, a tool room, and a laboratory for assembling and testing the apparatus for his lectures. Boxes began arriving from all over the world. Boxes, boxes, boxes! Beautiful disassembled scraps of technology! The boxes had to be opened; the mechanisms had to be fitted together and put in working order; then perfect small felt-lined cases had to be fashioned, into which the broken-down components of demonstration materials could be packed for any sort of transport, from vast ship's hold to weary human back.

David found and hired—all Chinese—a coolie, a blacksmith, two carpenters, a brass smith, two machinists, an electrician, two office assistants, and wonderful A Ch'u: an engineer trained in the machine shops of the Shanghai Municipal Council, a man as enthusiastic as David himself, who immediately caught with his whole cheerful being David's vision of a China waking up from a long sleep into a world that would tick and whir and hum, for everyone's plenty and ease. Jesus Christ did not figure in the calculations of A Ch'u; he was as tiny as David was huge; he was East and David was West—yet in a very short time this brilliant uneducated man became a remarkable alter ego to the Lecturer, able to leap into the big foreigner's thoughts almost before he had them.

Partly because David adored the subject, and partly because he had found in the United States, with the help of the inventor Elmer Sperry, the impedimenta he would need to deal with it, David had decided to devote the first lecture to what had thrilled him so long ago in the classroom of Absolom Carter at the Enderbury Institute: the gyroscope. But he had also long since begun working up, both in his mind and in the shop, future lectures on wire-less telegraphy, aeronautics, astronomy, electricity, sound, light, and chemical phenomena. With the help of the staff, he was designing, building, and assembling the devices and models he would use to bring the subjects to life in Chinese eyes.

His only annoyances in this productive period were caused by recalci-trances in faraway New York. David was convinced that the great Dr. Todd thought little of his lecture program. The office was $500 short in the $2,000 advance against the budget he had been promised. When he asked New York to buy from Underwood and Underwood, at a cost of two dollars, a small box with grooved sides to hold lantern slides, which he wanted as a model for many such boxes to be made in his Shanghai workshop, New York held up the order, questioning its need. David went, in a state that was a Protestant substitute for seething, "prayerfully," to Blackton, who wrote New York a rebuking letter.

David and his family, which was very shortly to be increased, were living in a modest Association house on Yates Road, not far from Chang Su Ho's Gardens, where David delighted to walk on Sunday afternoons with little Philip on his shoulders, watching the cyclists wheeling around the track and the little boats skidding down the water chute. Emily, sailing through the late months of her pregnancy like a full-sailed sloop, accommodated herself with grace and ease to a new home in a new city. She joined a reading circle called the Stanley Club, in which some thirty American and English women kept each other informed about the newest flowers and weeds of their respective cultures. David had his shell shipped down from Tientsin, and quite unself-consciously he joined the Shanghai Rowing Club; he rose at six every morning, took a ricksha to the club's boathouse, launched his shell, rowed half an hour, put up the boat, took a ricksha home, bathed, breakfasted, and studied Chinese for an hour before going to his lab. He had decided not to convert to the Shanghai dialect, but to stay with Mandarin, which would serve best for his lectures; he would pick up enough of the Shanghai dialect from day to day to get along in the streets.

On February 7 David and A Ch'u boarded the S.S. *Kwang Ta* for Hong Kong. All the way the two men "put the finishing touches on the apparatus," as David wrote in his diary. On the fifteenth they arrived in Canton, to find the Association people in no state to help David organize his lectures; they were just launching a campaign to raise funds for a Y.M.C.A. building. David began nosing around on his own. He wangled from the American consul a letter of introduction to one of the most influential men in the city, a certain Admiral Li. David put on his frock coat and called on the Admiral, who in his uniform "looked (no disrespect intended) like a cross between Napoleon Bonaparte and Madame Pompadour"—"I used all the wiles Mr. Lin had taught me to use on Yen Han-lin!"—and the upshot was an invitation to David to present his first lecture in the Admiralty Building to exactly the audience he would have wanted, the city's leading officials and scholars, most agreeably invited by the Admiral.

THE DOORS swing wide. The grandees enter. David is thrilled to see that they have worn their best—great winged gowns overlaid with embroideries of herons in flight, flirting butterflies, lotus blossoms pearled with dew; naval uniforms evidently designed to overpower an enemy by sheer dazzle, without resort to cannon; scholarly gowns of subtly patterned silks bespeaking calm minds. All have queues; many keep the shaved fronts of their crowns hidden, even indoors, by hats of velvet and satin.

There is a great deal of murmuring. Strange articles on the stage! On the left, protruding out of the top of a copious trunk, is a large metal derricklike contraption, reaching some six feet above the floor. Two little national flags— the dragon and the stars and stripes—hang left and right from the square frame at the top of the derrick. Various large wheels, with weights attached, lie here and there. At the right is an easel with a blackboard on it, and table, on which there are several odd devices. Farther to the right is a stepladder, as high as the derrick. Behind the table stands a huge hairy one, indeed a big-nose; the brute is dressed, however, with a sense of courtesy, in such style as to compliment his guests. Beside him stands a tiny Chinese man in a gray gown. Behind the derrick is another small Chinese in the short blue coat and trousers of a workman.

The big-nose stands like a stone man, waiting for the buzzing to stop. At last it does. He steps around the table to the front of the stage. He bows low from the waist. Ah, he has some manners after all! He speaks in Chinese. "Ten thousand apologies," he says, "that I speak in Mandarin; I have been in your esteemed city only three days and I have not had time to learn your honorable dialect!" He waits for the man in the gray gown to translate into the Cantonese dialect. Very delicate! He speaks the Peking dialect well, though on account of his huge nose the words seem to come out of a dark cave situated on a distant continent. He chooses his words well. The American consul who has been here six years cannot speak any sort of Chinese at all.

But suddenly he is very blunt, very American. He extends his right hand; the Chinese man behind the derrick darts forward and hangs a sturdy circular chain over the hand. "I have here a steel chain," the big man says. He waits for the interpreter. The links hang limp from his fingers. "Can this chain stand up and walk? Can this chain run across the room? Tell me, Admiral Li, can this chain climb that ladder over there?"

Admiral Li stands up in the center of the front row. He is confused. It is not his fault that he is ladylike. He waves his hands about in mute agitation.

The big man repeats the three questions, addressing them through the interpreter to the distinguished officer as if he were a cadet at naval school. Others in the audience come to Admiral Li's assistance. "No!" they call out. "No! It cannot!"

"Are you sure?" The big man shakes the chain, but it resumes its limpness.

Now there are shouts all over the hall. "No! No! It cannot!" Admiral Li, emboldened by all the support, joins the outcry.

Now the big man hands the chain to his helper, who takes it to a metal wheel, about two spans of a hand in diameter, that stands up from the trunk on a strut near the base of the derrick. He fastens the closed circle of the chain to the perimeter of the wheel, nods to the big man. The big man signals, dropping his hand sharply. The helper begins to turn a crank on the side of the derrick. It is geared to the wheel, which is soon whirling at great speed.

In a big voice the big man addresses Admiral Li, who has remained standing. "Are you ready to be surprised?" The interpreter echoes the sharp question.

Admiral Li's response is ambiguous: lips silent, he sits down.

The big man whips his hand upward this time.

The helper bends toward the whirling wheel. He flips a lever. The chain is forced sidewise off the wheel. Whirling now free of the wheel, it keeps its perfectly circular shape, jumps to the floor of the stage, rolls at astonishing speed across the room, jumps off the stage, and keeps running until it crashes into the side wall and falls limp to the floor.

The crowd gasps, then chatters. The helper jumps down and retrieves the chain. He hangs it again from the big man's hand. "*Now* would you like to see it climb the ladder?"

The Nos have changed to clamoring Yeses.

The big man moves the ladder forward on the stage. The helper spins up the chain on the wheel again. The big man's hand flicks. The helper trips the lever. The chain jumps down, dashes across the stage, hits the bottom step of the ladder, blubs a bit out of its circular shape but jumps upward, strikes the second step, jumps in the same way, then faster and faster climbs the remaining steps, leaps off the top of the ladder, blubs again when it lands on the stage but recovers and keeps running on until it hits the wall.

The whole crowd is standing now, exclaiming, gesticulating, and laughing.

"I KNEW I had them then!" David wrote Emily that night.

I wish I could describe to you the lift in my heart! I knew at that moment that my lecture campaign is going to be a great success. O, wait till the news gets to James B. Todd! Emily, a marriage of two of the simple, beautiful laws of nature won the day for me! A marriage made in heaven!—of the Law of Centrifugal Force with Sir Isaac Newton's First Law of Motion.   1) A rotating body is acted upon by a force which makes it fly off at a tangent from its definite path around the center. 2) A body remains in a state of rest or of uniform motion in a straight line unless compelled by some external force acting upon it to change that state. Forgive me, I don't mean to be didactic with you, my dearest, but I am so excited! God's laws are so simple, yet how they can surprise! But Emily, the best was yet to come! . . .

THE HIGH POINT of the lecture came, as David had guessed it would, with the device he had come to think of as the Wrestling Gyroscope. He introduced it just before the final passage of the lecture, the unraveling of the puzzle—the explanation, at last, of the principles that made the gyroscope behave in the strange and almost magical ways the audience had gasped again and again to see.

There had been other wonders along the way. David had devised a gyroscope that could be seen by an audience of a thousand in a large auditorium; it was a bicycle wheel, weighted at the rim, its hub placed at the midpoint of a long axle which was hung by wires at the ends from a bar. A Ch'u clamped the bar to the square frame at the top of the derrick. At David's command, with the wheel at rest, he detached the wire from one end of the axle. The wheel at once flopped down sidewise. Then A Ch'u reattached the axle and spun the wheel up. At another command, A Ch'u again detached the wire from the one end. Now the swiftly revolving wheel did not fall! The axle remained horizontal even though supported by only one end! David hung a derby hat over the open end of the axle to show that there was nothing holding it up but the spinning of the wheel!

To demonstrate the principle of a gyrocompass, David had A Ch'u remove the bar from the derrick and suspend it by the middle from a wire. Then A Ch'u spun the wheel up. Using a magnetic compass to find true north, David placed the plane of the wheel in a north–south direction. A Ch'u held the wheel aloft by the wire, so the whole apparatus was free to turn as it wished. He then went down in the audience and walked around the hall, turning in circles here and there in a kind of dance of mystification (which A Ch'u greatly enjoyed)—but no matter where A Ch'u faced, the wheel never veered from its faithful north-pointing plane!

The monorail! Between hooks attached to the side walls of the hall beforehand, A Ch'u quickly set up a tight wire, waist high at the stage. David held up to the wire a flat car, with single grooved wheels at each end and a battery-operated electric gyroscope in its middle. He feigned reluctance to let go. It would surely fall and be ruined! He switched on the motor and floated

his hands away as if they had suddenly become weightless. A Ch'u gave the
car a push along the wire. Then he added cubical weights on top of the car at
each end. Placed a board on top of the weights, making a bridge over the
gyroscope. More weights on the board. Soon a tower of heavy blocks nearly
five feet high loomed on top of the car, which ran back and forth on the wire
with absolute sobriety and constancy!

By now the men in the audience—these dignified Mandarins, proud
practitioners of the ancient art of calligraphy, officers and officials to whom
that appearance of mastery known as face was everything—had lost all
decorum. They were gaping and exclaiming like unruly boys at every wonder
they saw. But David was sure that they would surpass themselves in excitement when they saw the Wrestling Gyroscope at work.

SEVERAL YEARS later, when his lecture techniques had been brought to
their highest pitch of skill, David Treadup tried to articulate just what he was
trying to do through his demonstrations. To get a full sense of the almost
overwhelming stab of joy he reported having felt during that Canton lecture,
at the moment when the Wrestling Gyroscope was publicly put to the test for
the first time, we can do no better than to jump ahead to those later words
of his:

> *I seek to come to the city as the guest of the city, but at the same time to
> be in a way a host to the multitudes of the city, and in the name of
> Western culture and Christianity to extend a series of courtesies that
> people have long desired, but which they have never yet had a chance to
> enjoy and which they will never forget.*
>
> *What I want is to make a deep, attractive, inspiring, unforgettable
> impression upon a number of individuals, as well as an impact in a
> collective sense on the life of the city itself.*
>
> *I have the clearest feeling of the need for a hesitant caution with
> the individuals of the audience, of the need of going slowly and of feeling
> the way, arresting attention, focusing interest, and not only putting out
> energy and ideas and impressions, but receiving them as well. You can't
> run away with the audience; you must lead them, contribute enthusi-
> asm and understanding. You must wait.*
>
> *There is for me in science a marvelous beauty, a great exultation,
> an inexpressible enthusiasm that makes these experiences seem priceless,
> and I have a great yearning that each of my friends in the audience shall
> also experience the thrilled yet calm certainty that this beauty makes me
> feel. I want to fill them with a sense of power, a sense of victory, and a
> sense of potentiality. This emotional and dramatic experience that they
> go through with me makes a deep and abiding impression upon them.*

They can carry it away and can go on remembering and thinking about it, and acting on it, both consciously and unconsciously, long afterward. This is of great moment for the future of China.

There are dangers. The demonstrations are so remarkable that many tend to regard them as magical. This must be dealt with frankly and vigorously, so that the audience becomes secure in its reverence for truth.

Also, I must bring the audience to recognize that science in its present definitions and limitations is quite inadequate to the task of improving our lives. It is only part and on the whole secondary. Intellectually stated, science gives us materials, forces, powers, and principles — tools — but it carries the limitation of indifference to moral issues. It is a limitation that scientific men wisely put on science. Science can be used for good and for evil, and it is entirely indifferent to how it is used. The bigger issue is: 'How shall these tools be used?'

I never preach. I try to let the beautiful laws of nature and my own enthusiasm and courtesy give the message. The audience knows I come to them from the Young Men's Christian Association. If I measure up, that is enough. I do have a great yearning that each member of the audience shall become a "more God-like man." By this I mean he shall acquire some of the characteristics which we formerly ascribed to God alone. I seek for each individual an elevation of ideals; an increase of powers and capacities; an enhancement of personality; a control over self, nature, and destiny; and the attaining of a new poise and peace. That is the direction of the "God-like man."

HE DEPRECATES the magic but uses it. With a wave of a hand the magician bids his assistant come forward with the next innocent device. See! There is no false bottom in this hat! Only here it is not a hat but a wheel, another familiar bicycle wheel. One can say quite openly: See! It is more heavily weighted at the rim than the gyroscope wheel! In place of a tire there is soft lead pipe bound in with spring brass wire. What a clumsy, useless object! And here is the wooden shell we use to cover it with — cleverly carved by a Chinese artisan to look, when assembled over the bicycle wheel, quite like the tire and solid hub of the wheel of an automobile. We hide nothing! The weighted bicycle wheel can turn on its ball-bearing axle within the shell.

The magician waves his hand again. The assistant dashes forward, assembles the shell over the wheel, and with the obligatory flourishes of a magician's assistant's arms, rolls it forward to the magician. The latter balances the wheel upright and says: Look! I can push it over with my little finger! And he does so, with the little finger of his right hand. The ungainly object falls to the floor.

"Admiral Li! Please come up on the stage. I want the audience to be quite satisfied that there was no trick to my pushing the wheel over in that way."

With mincing steps the pudgy Admiral climbs to the stage. The assistant lifts the wheel from the floor and balances it. The magician bids the Admiral push it over with his little finger. With a despairing look at the audience, the Admiral bends over and applies a fat pinky to the wheel. It falls over! The audience shouts its approval and claps delightedly in the Western style. The magician nods, permitting the Admiral to return to his seat.

Now the magician waves once more. The assistant attaches the wheel to a strut from the derrick, raises it off the floor, cranks up the protruding hub of the bicycle wheel within until it is revolving at a very high speed, lowers it to the floor, and detaches it from the strut. Now the wheel stands alone, at a queer, slight list to one side; it turns very slowly on its tilted axis.

"Admiral Li, please tell me, who is the strongest man in the audience?"

Admiral Li stands up, turns, surveys the audience. From various quarters there are shouts of candidacies—men nominating their friends, men proposing themselves. Near the back a giant is standing, waving his arms. Admiral Li appoints him strongest. The magician invites him to the stage. The magician bows to the strong man, then shakes his hand in the Western fashion but holds on to the hand. He announces to the audience that he is examining the strong man's little finger, to see if it is truly powerful. It is! Please! Push the wheel over with your little finger!

The strong man steps confidently forward, applies the certified little finger, meets resistance, the finger bends, the face is puzzled.

The magician bids the strong man use his whole hand. He does so. Far from falling over, the wheel restively pushes back at the pushing hand.

The magician waves. The assistant runs forward with a stout bamboo pole about five feet long, one end of which is padded with a solid rubber ball. The magician hands the pole to the strong man. Push it over! Get your body behind it!

The strong man places the padded end of the pole against the wheel and leans his body into his effort to push it over. The wheel, momentarily very slightly tilted, reacts as if in anger and resumes its former position, forcing the strong man to retreat.

"Admiral Li! We need another strong man."

Two men push together, but *within the shell the bicycle wheel is revolving with the tremendous energy of a flywheel, and the strange laws of a gyroscope's stability and precession govern, so that any attack on it above the hub develops a powerful and instantaneous counterreaction.*

But the vigor of the wheel's reaction is nothing to the vigor of the reaction of the audience. Throughout the wrestling of the strong men with the gyroscope, there has been absolute silence in the hall, broken only by the strong men's baffled grunts. But when they give up, dismay on their faces, there is an explosive outcry which, David is later to write, gives him "the joy of a small boy whooping at the marvelousness of life as he leaps into the hay from a high beam of the barn." The roar and the buzz go on and on. Amazement, puzzlement, delight in the sheer drama of enigmatic powers the magician has unfolded, a sense of wonder at forces that must always have been *there*, all through eternity, but have never been seen or even imagined before, wild pleasure at the discomfiture of boastful strong men, a response to the strange look of both yearning and exultation in the eyes of the magician, a more open sympathy with the look of pride on the face of the Chinese assistant, a vague thought of the possible taming of these mysteries, an inkling perhaps of future power, Chinese power, an incipient sense of victory even in the moment of defeat of strong Chinese men, a sense above all that this entire lecture has given of *potentiality*—there is so much to applaud!

OCCASIONALLY pausing to write characters for certain technical terms on the blackboard, Mr. Treadup explicated the simple, pure, God-made laws of the gyroscope which had governed all the marvels those in the hall had just seen. This took only a few minutes. It gave the audience the great relief of understanding. Then it was over.

THE SLUMBER OF SUCCESS

THE STIR in the hall afterward was Treadup's reward.

Within half an hour arrangements were made for ten subsequent lectures in Canton—which were given on the following days, sometimes three in one day, to gatherings of Chinese Christians, businessmen, teachers, officials; and to student bodies of several Chinese and mission schools and colleges.

In Hong Kong the audiences were even larger and more varied; they included the student bodies of the Chinese Engineering Institute and the Seamen's Engineering Institute. His Excellency Governor General Lugard presided at one lecture. After another an immensely wealthy Chinese man named Ho K'ai, who had never before been persuaded to attend any Y.M.C.A. affair, pledged a contribution to the Association's campaign for the purchase of a building site.

In Foochow, an ebulliently immodest Treadup later reported, "the lectures were a key factor in one of the most striking victories of our movement in

China—the raising of $48,000 (Mexican) for the Association building campaign under what person after person assured us were impossible conditions.

"In Shanghai," he wrote, "the Martyrs' Memorial Hall was filled day after day with audiences of whatever class we chose."

"Treadup's lectures," Blackton wrote New York,

are more than meeting with our highest expectations. He has traveled with only one so far, namely on the gyroscope. It is opening doors and winning friends for us. Here in Shanghai he is being invited right into government institutions where the prejudice against anything foreign, not to speak of Christian, has been very great. We must lay ourselves out for him.

And so David Treadup moved, as the months passed, from strength to greater strength.

NOW MUCH PRAISED, and confident of a long-range success, Treadup worked in his Shanghai laboratory in the spring of 1911 with an athlete's striving energy. He was wonderfully inventive. He was sure of the steps he took; the list of his good qualities was prominently posted in his mind. Not that he had grown vain, or conceited—though he might well have, for he had become, almost overnight, the sensation of the missionary enterprise in the China field; so many people, both Chinese and foreign, had begun trooping in to see his laboratory that he had recently had to establish strict visitors' days. No, Treadup knew his strength, but there seemed to be a total blank in his makeup in that place where, in normal people, a trait of egotism is implanted. He seemed unaware that the people trooping through his shop were watching him, or that in the bright light of his notoriety he appeared to others to be hopelessly obsessed by his science lectures. He was locked so tightly into their preparation that he evidently did not hear some signals that the real world seemed to be trying to send him.

ONE DAY, as he was supervising the construction of a model airplane by A Ch'u and one of the carpenters, at the crucial moment of bonding in a delicate gluing of frame members, Wei, the family's "boy," came running into the laboratory and cried out breathlessly, in the pidgin English that the Treadups' servants used because David's Shanghai dialect was still flawed, "Missy wantchee Mastuh walkee homeside chop chop."

David waited until the glued joint was fast and then took a ricksha to Yates Road. Suddenly in a hurry, he urged the ricksha boy to run for his money. He found Emily well advanced in labor. She had sent for the doctor some time since. She damped her pain with her usual serenity. She had begun to dilate. The doctor did not come. David ordered a hot charcoal brazier on a tripod brought to the bedroom, with a kettle of water to boil, and a basin besides of hot water to wash his hands in. He sterilized a knife. The crown of the infant was visible. David, with clean hands, received the little head, pulled gently at the shoulders and chest, and took the child into the world. He cut the cord and tied it. He held the body up by the heels and spanked it, and Emily, hearing the first squalls of a new life, weakly smiled. Her lips moved. She was trying to say something. David leaned down to make out her whisper.

"Don't leave me alone."

For answer he put his hand on her shoulder. Apparently reassured by that touch, she closed her eyes. He bathed her child.

One by one the four servants appeared, to offer their condolences, for they had learned that the mistress had, worst luck, produced a daughter.

Was David impatient to get back to his model airplane? He recorded Emily's whisper in his diary that evening, but we will have reason to wonder whether he had the slightest inkling what she had really meant.

A CH'U was a bird fancier. Each day he would bring to the laboratory a different pet bird. The cages were marvelously varied works of art, and David, missing entirely at first the tenderness of A Ch'u's relationship with each living pet, rebuked in his diary the impractical patience of a Chinese workmanship that could devote so much care to a useless artifact like a birdcage. But gradually David began to understand that there was another kind of patience here, for A Ch'u, using a teaching method exclusively of rewards, was training each bird to do stunts. It might take years to produce a single trick: on command, a siskin turns a somersault.

Then one day A Ch'u began to tell David about the way the flesh of birds was used in Chinese medicine. He said the meat of the crested mynah—that chatty creature—was given to cure stuttering. Oriole meat was fed to women to cure jealousy, because of the obvious domestic felicity of pairs of orioles. The breast of the restless cuckoo was a remedy for drowsiness. The charred and powdered flesh of woodpeckers was applied to dental cavities. A tincture made from the head of the hawklike kite, which soars at great heights, was given as a cure for vertigo.

David wrote these prescriptions down as amusing. But the very next day there are two significant notes in his diary. The first served his obsession:

We need a series of lectures on medicine. There are reports of pneumonic plague in Manchuria and North China. Heretofore plague has always threatened us from the south—the bubonic—but now three very dear friends in the north Doctors Menzies, Seto, and Wu have succumbed as they were directing the fight against the epidemic. And TB! When I returned to Shanghai from Europe I found three of our Association secretaries (nearly one-fourth of the force) in initial stages of tuberculosis — and my neck gland that had to be removed may have been tubercular — made me realize the fearfulness of this scourge in China.

The second note bespoke David's sense that a lecturer on science must try to *become* a scientist through and through; but it inaugurated a new activity which, like his rowing, his study of Chinese, his constant rehearsals of lectures out loud in the parlor at home, was solitary, exclusive — left Emily alone:

Have set up feeding stations within the walled yard at Szechuan Road. One in mulberry tree; one in bamboo; one in umbrella tree. Intend to record Shanghai birds according to seasons.

In a separate notebook:

MAY: lark (bedraggled), bunting, shrike, pipit, wagtail, ousel, crake, stint.

JUNE: Java sparrow, bulbul, cuckoo, swallow, blackbird, dove.

JULY: crow, magpie, turtle dove, mynah, oriole, hawfinch, water-hen. . . .

IN THE HOTTEST part of the summer, David and A Ch'u took a river steamer up the Yangtze to Hankow. On the way David developed dysentery. In Hankow he delivered five gyroscope lectures, his head buzzing and his gut cramped; yet the demonstrations were the most successful he had given. All the gear was taken down and put in its boxes, and the two men went with a flotilla of little bumboats across the way to Wuchang. David by now had a high fever and was seriously dehydrated. But news of the lectures had traveled ahead, halls had been reserved, expectations were high; he was unwilling to disappoint his audiences. Too weak to stand, he arranged to have himself carried onto the stage on a litter, and he gave the first of three horizontal lectures. These were nothing short of sensational in their effect. At the end of the third, an army officer in the audience stepped up on the stage, introduced himself as Colonel Li ("The armed forces of China seem to be entirely populated by men named Li," David wrote in his diary, evidently thinking of his friend the Admiral in Canton), and made a graceful speech of thanks. David, oblivious to everything but his mission, had no feel for the powerful influences that were stirring at that very moment in Wuchang and Hankow, and that would very shortly make this Colonel Li the first vice-president of the Republic of China.

I T I S true that David records in his diary the currency of "rumors that something is going to happen soon." But he seems to have no curiosity about this "something." Terrible floods in the Yangtze Valley had just recently subsided; in Hankow itself, water had stood two to three feet deep in the streets, and on the river steamer on the way up, the crew had said the Yangtze had in places on the plain lately been fifty miles wide. Would the "something" be merely the pestilence and famine and unrest that always followed Chinese floods? David does not even ask this question.

EVEN STRANGER were the complacency and lack of curiosity with which David watched a bizarre—and, to any other eye, obviously significant—event in Shanghai, not long after his return from the Yangtze trip.

In September we find in the diary: "A Ch'u told me today he is thinking of having his queue cut off. I told him it would improve his looks."

What an inadequate response! The declaration must have meant a great deal to A Ch'u. For more than two and a half centuries the alien Manchus of the Ch'ing Dynasty had enforced their decree that non-Manchus—the real Chinese—must wear the plait of hair foreigners called the pigtail, as a sign of their submission to their Manchu rulers. In the single-mindedness of his lecturing mission, David had apparently not even noticed that there had been a growing campaign, backed by young men of the upper class, and especially by students who had returned from abroad, to get rid of this humiliating imposition by the Manchus; and it is obvious that it had not dawned on David that getting rid of the queue was a metaphor for getting rid of the Manchus themselves. In this sense, queue-cutting was a revolutionary act, and one that took courage. Older Chinese were largely against it, for with the passing generations the wearing of the queue had become a custom and, as with all customs in China, a thing to be cherished. But the young upper-class radicals were now stressing the shame, the inconvenience, the discomfort, the dirtiness of the queue, and were clamoring for its extermination. It was indeed quite remarkable that a working-class man like A Ch'u would dare to follow the lead of the elite radicals; his association with David Treadup must have been exposing him to the influence of some of the returned students who worked with the Association. We must imagine the pounding of A Ch'u's heart as he made his quiet announcement to T'ao Tu Hsien-sheng. But the great lecturer said only, "Good. It will improve your looks."

With all due Chinese courtesy, A Ch'u insisted on Mr. Treadup's attention. He believed he would have this thing done at the public queue-cutting that was to take place at Chang Su Ho's Gardens, right near the Treadup house, the next afternoon. He would like to invite T'ao Tu Hsien-sheng to witness it.

What? And lose an entire afternoon in the laboratory? Out of the question!

In that case, A Ch'u said in a barely audible voice, he would have to resign.

Nonsense! He could no more resign than fly! He should stop acting foolish and get back to work.

A Ch'u did in fact resume his work—that day. But the next morning, the engineer did not show up at the laboratory.

To David's credit, he realized, months later, when the revolution had opened his eyes, how foolishly *he* had behaved over all this, and we have a rueful account of it in a letter he wrote then to brother Paul:

At first I did not even make the connection—I thought A Ch'u must have come down with something. He had been so faithful to me! I was the most important person in his life. How he had pampered me! When we would go aboard a ship, to Hong Kong that time, for instance, or to Hankow, there he would be on the deck, assuring me that all the boxes had been counted, wanting to make sure I knew the way to my cabin. He could not possibly resign from me!

When I went home to Yates Road for tiffin that day, I was amazed by the traffic moving toward the gate of Chang Su Ho's Gardens—the park near us where I often take Philip on Sundays. Only then did I remember. A Ch'u! The public queue-cutting! I ate a hasty meal, then went myself on foot to the park, where I found a teeming spectacle. Hundreds of people were already unable to get into the large teahouse. They were milling among the numerous carriages, automobiles, and rickshas in which the more well-to-do had been conveyed. It took some real American go-get-'em for me to push my way into the hall—my size always helps me in a Chinese crowd. The place had been cleared of tea tables for the occasion. I found two chairs near each other, at the very back, each with an unoccupied corner, and I climbed up, planting one foot on each chair, and I stood there like a Colossus of Rhodes and observed the proceedings.

I would say that two thousand people were packed and jammed on the floor and in the galleries. Every pair of eyes was focused on a platform at one end of the building, on which were gathered the "elect," those who had already been separated from their queues. One glance and one could see that they were young men of the better classes: modestly but very well dressed. They were exhorting the horde—how I was reminded of a popular revival back home!—and one by one, young men in the crowd would screw up their courage and make their way to the platform. With each, a wave of applause would sweep over the tense crowd. The possessor of the queue would yank it out at full length with a vicious jerk or lift it gingerly up with a grimace of contempt, and then one of the elect would hold the end while another with a huge pair of shears would perform the amputation. Two or three snips, and off would come the long, heavy braid, the possession of which would have filled many an American woman's heart with pride. Then that which is "the glory of woman" but the shame of man was handed its late wearer, who would wave the despised object before the audience, always with great drama — for every Chinese, down to the humblest coolie, is a born actor.

I confess that I was quite blind to the meaning of all this. I had no interest in the world except to get A Ch'u back to work in my lab. What would I do without him? He knew every nuance, every pause, every beautifully timed gesture of the teamwork of our gyroscope lecture!

Finally there he was! Sure enough. He had meant it. The men on the platform made a great fuss over him — this baffled and confused me — and angered me, I must say. They were trying to lure him away from me! Only now have I come to realize it was because he was a rarity for them, a man wearing not the tasteful long gray silk gown of a son of privilege but rather the short blue coat and trousers bound at the ankles of a workman. They were making much of him as an exemplar.

I got down from my chairs and tried without success to make my way forward. I then remembered one of the men on the platform announcing that thirty barbers were busy in other parts of the building, giving the shorn men proper short haircuts free of charge, for the cause. So I made my way around to the platform end of the building, made some inquiries, and finally found a room where barbers were at work — and there indeed, found A Ch'u, pale and small-looking.

"You came," he said, when he saw me.

"Hurry up, A Ch'u," I said. "We've wasted two hours."

N A N C Y, the baby, had chronic colic. She was fretful because of her sickliness, and Philip was fretful because of her existence, and Emily was fretful, too, because of what? — for Emily's unrest was expressed in code — a code of behavior that David, in his state of otherworldly concentration, was unable even to try to decipher until much later.

She became an active woman. She was out of the house almost as much as he was, and often when he was in it, in the evenings. Her busyness was not just the Stanley Club and ladies' socials, now. She was at the work of a Christian missionary in her own right. Her energy — for with all her charging about she did not shirk the duties of a mother of two — was so superb that we are led to suspect it was fueled by a deep anger, which, if she recognized it in herself at all, she would have been much too proud to show in any open way.

Emily Kean Treadup joined some English ladies in agitating against the shame of the four opium hulks in the Whangpoo River, right there off the Bund. It was Emily's idea—not enthusiastically received by the English ladies—to get up a petition to the throne, to be signed by all the leading Chinese women of Shanghai, urging an imperial decree that would forbid any further importation of opium to China. A few years earlier, such an appeal would have been an example of pure waste motion of a kind all too often undertaken by well-meaning missionaries. But in this year of 1911, the petition would be one of a torrent of demands and requests that were pouring into Peking, and that were helping to overload the throne with a burden of popular hatred and resentment—a burden too heavy, finally, for it to bear.

Excited by her idea, Emily had the nerve to call by herself on one of the prominent Chinese ladies of the city, about whom she had heard a great deal, a Mrs. Soong. This woman was the wife of Soong Yao-ju, called by Shanghai foreigners Charlie Soong; he had graduated from Vanderbilt University and had returned to China first as a Methodist missionary, but had then become a merchant and had made a huge fortune. She was also the mother of four children who were to have, in differing ways, astonishing impacts on the destiny of China: Ai-ling, then twenty-three (recently back from Georgia Wesleyan), who would be the wife of H. H. Kung (Oberlin and Yale), briefly a Y.M.C.A. secretary, eventually finance minister of Kuomintang China; Ching-ling, twenty-one (also Georgia Wesleyan), who would be Sun Yat-sen's wife; Tse-vung, seventeen, known to foreigners as T. V. Soong (about to go to Harvard), who would become premier of Kuomintang China; and Mei-ling, fifteen (Wellesley in due course), who would be Chiang Kai-shek's wife. Mrs. Soong took a great fancy both to Emily and to her idea, and she undertook to be the hostess of a mass meeting to get the petition started.

The meeting was held in the Martyrs' Memorial Hall. Eight hundred Chinese women came, most of them wives and daughters of officials or rich businessmen. Antiopium songs had been written to kindergarten tunes, which a choir of schoolchildren sang. Mrs. Soong made an emotional address, with tears finally streaming down her cheeks, on the ravages of opium. While Christian girls from St. John's College sang songs and played selections on the piano, sheets of paper on small boards were circulated, and the ladies of the audience were asked to sign their names. In a side room, Chinese refreshments were served.

This meeting got the petition off to a fine start, and within six weeks it had 3,512 signatures.

"Then came the most touching part," Emily later wrote home.

*After the demimondes had heard of the movement, they wrote an appeal,
asking that their names be sent—not on the same list—they could not
ask for that, but in a separate list, saying that most of them had been
sold into their life of shame by opium-smoking fathers or brothers or
husbands, saying also: "We are on a shoreless sea. There is no way to help
us, but it may save others from a similar fate. There are those who think
we are flippant and enjoy this life. They do not know how often we must
smile upon guests we despise. We beat our breasts and cry aloud, but
there is no help for us. We feared to write this lest it would soil your eyes."*

Thirty-three prostitutes' names were on this list, one of whom, Emily
reported, was the daughter of a man who had been educated in the United
States.

ONE EVENING in September, David told Emily that he would be leaving
shortly for a lecture trip in North China—to Taiyuanfu, Peking, and Tientsin.
Little Nancy was still not well, and he hated to be away while she was still
weak, but, alas, arrangements had been made some time since.

We might have expected Emily to repeat her appeal of the day when
Nancy was born, "Don't leave me alone." Her response was quite different.
She said, "Get your hat."

What? At nine o'clock at night?

"There are some things I want you to see."

"There was a brilliance in her eyes, he wrote later in "Search,"

*a sort of glitter, that I had never noticed before. I had neither the impulse
nor the penetration, then or for months to come, to delve and find out
what that look signified. My dullness, in my total absorption in my
lectures, was part of what I think of as my slumber of that period.*

Emily sent the "boy" out for rickshas. She gave the ricksha men an
address on Nanking Road. Arrived there, she handed some money to an
attendant at the door, who led them up some stairs. They found themselves in
a large, elegant room, decorated with coromandel screens and paintings on
scrolls; some thirty padded divans were scattered around. On some, men were
cooking little pellets on lamps on standing braziers; others were inhaling
smoke from heavy pipes; some were conversing with animation; some were at
tables playing mah-jongg; some were eating snacks ordered from nearby
restaurants; some were lost in dreams.

In his account of this in "Search," David writes that his eyes swept from
divan to divan, and that only later did he realize that he was looking for, dimly
hoping *not* to find there, his dear teacher Chuan. Was *this* the life Chuan had
fought so hard to escape?

"They look very pleased with themselves, do they not?"
They do.
"They don't look like one's idea of 'dope fiends,' do they?"
They do not.
"Come."
Where now?
"We can walk."

Emily led David to Foochow Road, close by, a narrow street with many
people strolling in and out of buildings lit up with paper lanterns. They
climbed again to a second floor, into a room richly furnished with carved
blackwood from the south. Men were sitting at the tables, sipping tea and
talking. To one side, Chinese musicians were playing. Emily pointed. In and
out among the tables were moving three different little processions of girls,
each led by an older woman. The girls were very pretty and very young.
Dressed in bright silks and satins, glistening with jewelry, their faces whitened
with powder, they would pause from time to time while the woman in charge
of them ingratiatingly called to the attention of a tableful of men their various
charms. Once in a while one would be chosen, and would sit down with the
men, or leave the room with one.

"Those little whores," Emily said, using a word that almost seemed
to stick in her throat, "are the daughters of those men we saw over on
Nanking Road."

In "Search":

*I could not make out what she was driving at. Did she mean this
literally? Did she want me to put together a lecture on the relationship
between opium smoking and prostitution? I could not see it. She took
me to a counter at one side of the teahouse, and there she pointed out the
aphrodisiacs for sale. I could hardly believe the words I heard pass her
lips: "Powdered boar's testicles permit many repeated ejaculations in
one night. Minced dog, donkey, and stag penises, mixed, give hardness,
strength, and length to erections. That is what they say. Yes, I have
learned a few things. David! Those girls are fourteen and fifteen years
old!" Was I dreaming? Was this the pure and sweet-minded woman I
had married?*

In the single-mindedness into which he was locked during those months,
David could no more imagine anger in Emily than A Ch'u's quitting his
side (or than the Emperor of China's being toppled from his throne), and the
high color of Emily's cheeks, the charming little girls being led off to back
rooms, those powders of male potency on the counter, the blatant taboos
on Emily's shameless moist lips—all those things seemed only to carry
David back to the edge of adolescent worries about himself: about unmen-
tionably sinful imaginings. Or was it possible—though David could never

have conceived such a thing as this, either—that his wife's encoded anger roused in him new cause for guilty thoughts?

HE WENT north. (*Don't leave me alone.*) In Taiyuanfu, the capital of Shansi Province, David had more difficulty than ever before in getting started. He was baffled by the reasons, though they stared him in the face: the Governor of the province had been impeached on charges of disloyalty to Peking and had "fallen ill"; the students of the Imperial University were in an uproar of protests and meetings; the citizens were on edge from rumors of troubles in the south; the country teetered on the brink of a great change. But to David in his "slumber" the only thing that mattered for the entire future of China was his lecturing, and he doggedly worked at arrangements.

At last he succeeded in getting permission to use the great hall of the Imperial University for his first presentation. He and A Ch'u had brought north with them three new lectures, besides the trusty "Gyroscope and Its Applications": "Electricity and Magnetism," "Aeronautics," and "Wireless Telegraphy." By the third lecture, the atmosphere had magically changed, and, as David later reported to Todd, "from that time on, all the leading institutions suspended work and came in appointed order to the Association for the lectures."

At the end of the week the "ill" Governor invited David to come to his palace, and to bring his assistant and his equipment for the talk on men flying in the sky. The Governor sent his personal carriage, and David rode in gilt-and-rosewood splendor through the gate where, in the Boxer time, fifty missionaries had been massacred in cold blood.

THE VISIT to Peking is a mystery to us. David left not a word about the week spent there early in October. His silence suggests that it was a bad time for him. Was the city in such a state of confusion that he was unable to stage any lectures at all? Had he, in his closed world, had dreams of setting his gyroscopes whirling before the eyes of the young Emperor and the Prince Regent—and been somehow rudely wakened from the dream? He undoubtedly saw his old friend Center Rush Gridley, but he does not mention him. His last day in Peking was the fateful date of "the double ten"—tenth day of the tenth month of 1911—long to live in Chinese history.

Our first sight of David in Peking is as he goes to the railroad station, just outside the vast city wall, to take the train to Tientsin, on the eleventh. Here we pick up the record:

I found on the great station platform an excited, gesticulating mob, hustling baggage and all sorts of possessions—furniture, goats, a porce-

*lain bathtub, believe it or not!—in indescribable confusion onto the
train, jamming every possible space, to the chagrin and envy of crowds
left behind, who could not find room to get away. At Tientsin, we saw
trains going through loaded with troops of the Imperial army. The
Tientsin East platform was just like that at Peking. People didn't seem to
care which direction trains were going in, if only they could get away.
From what? From what? We were in the full cry of a Chinese panic. We
could get no coherent news. Only—war! In Tientsin, all day and all
night, carts, drays, and jinrikishas groaned under their burdens of
household gear, as country people rushed into the city and city people
rushed out of it. Rumors were scurrying about as wildly as the people.
The trouble seemed to be in Hankow. Many of the panic-stricken Chinese
had heard that the Manchus were going to massacre all Chinese; then
came a "definite report" that the Manchus were going to kill all foreigners.
I rode out toward Peikai in the new electric streetcar. What a welcome
sight, my bosom friend, Lin Fu-chen. Yet a strange sight, too, for he was
wearing a Western felt hat! No panic in him. His face was radiant. His
first words were, "It has begun."*

REVOLUTION

THE REVOLUTION had begun. On "double ten" some of the Imperial
troops at Wuchang, on the Yangtze, had mutinied, and by the next day the
city was in the hands of the revolutionaries. Two days later a republic was
proclaimed and a military government was set up in Wuchang, and Li
Yuan-hung (he who had thanked David Treadup for his lying-down lectures—
though David would not be able to make this connection) was named military
governor. China now had two governments. On the fourteenth, Yuan Shih-k'ai
(the northern strong man, he who had put the Tientsin museum at David
Treadup's disposal—this David *did* remember) was appointed to suppress the
rebellion; he was in command of the troops that David had seen moving south
through the Tientsin station.

Civil war. On the eighteenth, Imperial troops entered Hankow, hard by
Wuchang. But Peking's army was shaky. On the twenty-ninth, the Imperial
troops stationed at Lanchow, near Tientsin, refused to obey orders unless the
throne assented to three memorials that had been submitted to the National
Assembly, demanding the granting of constitutional government; immediate

appointment of a responsible cabinet which would exclude members of the Imperial family; and amnesty to all political offenders, including those of the reform movement of 1898. The next day the Prince Regent issued a Renunciation Edict, granting these demands. On November 2, the National Assembly adopted the nineteen articles of a new constitution which rendered the Emperor virtually powerless.

As the war raged on, one province of China after another declared its independence of the Peking government.

THE SCALES had fallen from David's eyes. He had been jolted out of his slumber. He was back in Shanghai, at work in his laboratory, and the look of everything around him had suddenly changed. His great surprise, his chagrin, was that his absorbed mind had been so cut off from the obvious reality of recent months—the impending collapse of a civilization. Vivid in his memory was the expression of ravishing happiness on the face of his dear Christian friend Lin Fu-chen, under his Western hat, up in Tientsin, with his news that "it has begun," and gradually David felt himself suffused with a corresponding excitement. A new time was coming! Here at last was a real opening for a New China—a China that he could have a hand in helping to fashion! There would be more need than ever for all that the Y.M.C.A. strove for! There would be more need than ever for David Treadup's lectures!

Thus, in the very moment when he was freed from his obsession, he dived straight back into it. He wrote Todd:

> Many people have been saying, "I suppose your work is quite suspended." "Oh! No!" we were able to say. "Only changed in direction." The revolution enabled us to turn attention to work in the laboratory and shop, where answers to persistent calls for work in the field had left us much behind. We are farther along than we would have been without the revolution. This is a great encouragement.

AT THE SAME TIME, the quickening of all his feelings opened his eyes at home. He was sensitized to the hurt and anger in Emily, and he felt a renewed tenderness toward her. It dawned on him that her whisper after the birth of Nancy meant much more than a wish not to be left alone on that very day. Yet he knew he was going to have to carry on his lecture work; there would be times when he would *have* to be away from home. It is quite unlikely that David, in what we can guess to have been the renewed gentleness of his glad and guiltless embraces of Emily, ever realized in his conscious mind the nature of the "solution" he found for keeping her anger in a latent state. He got her pregnant again. Not at all against her will. No, it was almost as if her restlessness had driven her to want fecundity along with other successes. In time her body's work calmed, or at least covered, her restlessness.

David could now join with her in a vigil at the bedside of little Nancy, who was constantly ill with colic and an alarming croup.

And he could now admire with a whole heart Emily's compassion that was so hot with energy. "The agony of this war," he wrote Todd

> is acutest not as we see it in the large, but as it touches us close at home. There is Mrs. Treadup walking to the gate with the wife of one of our brightest Christian men, a graduate of Yale, who went to the front a while ago. She has come to Emily partly to know if we can give her news, and partly for a chance to weep on the shoulder of one who loves her.

And in a letter to brother Paul:

> Yesterday the wife of Z. T. Tao, the treasurer of the Shanghai Association, came to Emily in great distress. She and her husband have a son, a bright youngster of fourteen. On the day before my arrival back from Tientsin, the boy was missing. His father looked for him everywhere, and finally at ten o'clock at night found him on board a steamer about to leave for Wuchang to enlist as a soldier in the revolutionary army. His father of course took him home, telling him that he was glad the martial spirit still lived on in the family of Tao (Mr. Tao's father studied at a Baptist university in the South at the time of the Civil War and fought in the Confederate Army!), but that he was too young to be of any use as a soldier, and that the most patriotic thing he could do would be to continue his studies and prepare to serve his country in the future. The boy was very unwilling to give up his purpose, saying that if he did not serve his country now he might never have another chance, for if the revolution failed China might cease to exist as a nation. He so worked up his mother that she finally said to her husband, "Since he is too young, why don't you go to Wuchang and take his place?" It was in her distress at having, in this way, figuratively threatened her husband's life that Mrs. Tao had come weeping in need of Emily's wise comforting. Mr. Tao finally promised his son that if he stayed in school now, he would send him to America in a few years and let him study for either the army or the navy, if he wished.

David was much moved at seeing what he considered the best of young China rushing off to the war—students of the missionary colleges, students who had returned from abroad, Christian converts, intelligent educated boys and men. And the reports from the front told an amazing story about these young people. "This revolution," David wrote his Syracuse constituency, *and the qualities that the Chinese have shown in carrying it on have come as a surprise even to old China hands. The ignorant slander that the Chinese are a cowardly race has been splendidly given the lie times without number. It comes as a sharp surprise to old residents in China to see a people's army spring up in such a little time and make such a gallant and desperate fight. There is much food for thought on the military future of China in the events of the past few weeks.*

ANOTHER YOUNG MAN who joined the revolutionary army at this time was an eighteen-year-old student of peasant stock named Mao Tse-tung. He resigned after six months, thinking the revolution was over.

WITH THE UNFOLDING NEWS, David became more and more euphoric. On December 18, peace negotiations between representatives of the Imperial and Revolutionary governments began in Shanghai. On the twenty-ninth a convention in Nanking, with delegates from fifteen provinces, proclaimed the Republic of China and named Dr. Sun Yat-sen its Provisional President. Li Yuan-hung was made Vice-President.

Sun Yat-sen was the revolutionary leader who seemed to epitomize all that the missionary enterprise was trying to accomplish. He was a Christian. Born in South China, near Canton, where the Western influence had been longest at work, Sun had been educated in mission schools in Hawaii and Hong Kong, and he had been strongly influenced as a youth by Western ideas. In 1884 he was baptized a Christian by an American Congregationalist missionary, Dr. Charles R. Hager. Sun took training as a medical doctor, but he became involved in politics, and in 1905, the year of David's arrival in China, he was chosen, in exile in Japan, as leader of the T'ung Meng Hui (Revolutionary Alliance), which was dedicated to the overthrow of the Manchu Dynasty and the setting up of a republican government. He would later marry the American-educated daughter of the American-educated Christian Charlie Soong. He had made several visits to the United States, and frequently praised American ideas and institutions; he was in the United States, raising money and recruiting overseas Chinese students for the T'ung Meng Hui, when the revolution broke out in central China. He had now rushed back and had emerged as the spiritual leader of the republican revolution.

A military stalemate at once set in. Neither regime, neither the republicans under Sun Yat-sen at Nanking nor the Manchu government dominated by Yuan Shih-k'ai at Peking, could impose its will on the other. The wily Yuan Shih-k'ai, bargaining adroitly with both the revolutionaries and the Manchus, maneuvered Sun Yat-sen into stepping gracefully aside in return for the abdication of the Emperor so that a permanent republican government could be established—with, yes, Yuan at its head. On February 12, 1912, the Peking palace issued its last Imperial edicts, through which the infant Emperor abdicated his throne and empowered Yuan Shih-k'ai to form a republic— bringing to an end a political institution that had lasted for 2,133 years. Sun promptly resigned as Provisional President and recommended that Yuan be named to succeed him; the Nanking parliament complied.

To David this was the best of all possible outcomes in the best of all possible worlds. Yuan, the formal leader, seemed to be the only man in China strong enough to pull things together after such a cataclysmic change; and he had already recognized the importance of the work David Treadup was doing! Sun, the spiritual leader, was a Christian, and as the weeks passed it became evident that nearly half of the principal officeholders in the new government were Christians, mostly Western-trained; other returned students were emerging as presidents and faculty members of government colleges, as editors of papers and authors of books.

In the past the principal obstacle to missionary work had been the fear of religious persecution on the part of national and provincial authorities. The very first proclamation of the revolutionaries at Hankow had granted religious liberty. This had been reaffirmed by President Sun at Nanking; was again assured by President Yuan's personal representative speaking before the Christians of Peking; and was implemented by the new National Education Association, which abolished the worship of Confucius in the schools and placed all religions on an equal footing. "Never before," David Treadup wrote to Todd, "have the gates been thrown so wide open to us!"

WE GET a signal in March, however, that though Treadup was willing to be delighted that the Chinese revolutionaries were open to Christianity, his own Christianity was not as yet reciprocally open to revolutionary ideas. In his diary he notes: "Disturbing article in *The Chinese Recorder.*" The *Recorder* was a magazine published in English in Shanghai, by and for Protestant missionaries in the China field, and the article that had given David pause was signed by a Rev. H. K. Wright, and was entitled, "The Social Message and Christian Missions." An obvious response to what had been happening in Nanking and Peking, it was an overt call to missionaries to push for social change and even further revolution in China. It was a trumpet blast for the "social gospel" which had first shown its timid hand at the Centenary Conference, and which was to dominate missionary work in China for the next decades. There was no contradiction, Wright wrote, between the idea of individual salvation and that of social salvation. He drew on the Bible for authorizations of missionary work for social and economic betterment. Missionaries in China, he wrote, had acquiesced in a social system that tolerated coolies, "beings beside whose position that of the American slaves was enviable." If missionaries even noticed such miserable souls, all they were inclined to say to them was, " 'Be ye warmed and fed with the Gospel,' not stopping to consider that Christianity is for beings in their position a simply impossible thing." China must change, Wright argued, and missionaries must support that change—they would do well to examine the proposals of Christian Socialists.

David had long been thinking about, and working for, "the regeneration of China," but he had thought, so far, only in terms of helping China to become Christian and to "Westernize," and by the latter he meant—in the heat of his obsession—only helping China to learn about Western technology. Of course he approved the "Westernizing" represented by the adoption of a republican form of government. But should a "social gospel" go so far as socialism? It is obvious that what he found disturbing in the article was its lines about coolies.

> I do feel compassion for the coolie, for the very poor. How I am still haunted by the faces of those people with their shovels at the ready in the famine district! Yet I am not sure. Is it my proper work to try to remedy all the wrongs of this society? What does bringing Christianity to China really mean? I had thought Dr. Bagnall was right in what he said in that talk we had in Shanghai—that we should work from the top down—influence the influential, the literati, the educated, the "better classes"—with a hope of seeing the message of Jesus' love run down the slopes of society to all of China. If that message of love were to be fully realized, cooliedom must surely disappear. I had thought I was succeeding in my efforts. But Dr. Wright troubles me. Am I doing enough? Am I doing the right work?

Thus, in David's uneasiness, we see the seeds planted of a minor psychological crisis he will go through in the next few weeks, but also, much deeper, seeds of the profound changes that are to come in future years in his entire concept of his calling.

VIEW FROM THE INTERIOR

TREADUP was drawn as if by a centripetal force to the center of things. He wanted to see with his own eyes—and influence with his own voice— the new men of the revolution. He packed up the gear of two new lectures and went upriver to visit the base of their power, at Hankow, Wuchang, and Nanking.

He and A Ch'u were supervising the unloading of the lecture boxes on the Bund at Hankow, early in the morning of their arrival, when the purser of their river steamer came to them with a wireless message for Mr. Treadup. It was an unexpected summons to a command delivery of the first lecture, that very afternoon, before General Li Yuan-hung at the vice-presidential palace at Wuchang. David was astonished. How had Vice-President Li known of his existence, to say nothing of his arrival?

There was no time to waste. A Ch'u ran off at once to arrange a squadron of bumboats to take the apparatus by water across to Wuchang.

When the bedraggled little fleet pulled in to the Wuchang waterfront, a military band struck up a very odd martial tune, a hybrid of a bumpy Sousa march with whining Chinese theatrical music, to greet the visitors; a military escort accompanied Mr. Treadup to the palace, on a hill on the edge of the city.

At the reception hall, a man in uniform, whom David took to be an orderly or bodyguard deputized to greet the guest during a ritual wait for the Vice-President, came forward and in the new style of Westernized manners shook David Treadup warmly by the hand. The greeter was a stocky man in a uniform without insignia or decorations of any kind; he had ferocious black warrior mustaches which ran down aslant on either side of his mouth to his jowls.

He took David aback by saying, "Do you remember our first meeting?"

David said he was afraid he did not.

"Do you remember that lecture you gave here reclining on a steamer chair after the coolies carried you into the auditorium?"

Indeed he did.

"Do you recall at the end a certain Colonel Li stood up and expressed thanks for the audience?"

Quite well. David felt the hot rush of blood into his cheeks. (In his diary: "I thought of the Jesuit Ricci having learned to blush at the right diplomatic moment. This time I needed no practice!")

For Vice-President Li then said, "I was that man."

David was afraid that after such a start his performance would get a chilly hearing. But the big man seemed not to consider that he had lost face at all. He introduced David to the leading military officers of the revolutionary wing of the Republic, whom he had assembled to hear the lecture.

THERE EXISTS in the Treadup files in the Y.M.C.A. Historical Library in Rosemont, Illinois, a charmingly odd account of what followed. It is an awkward translation into English of a report in the Wuchang Chinese newspaper for April 21, 1912:

A meeting of the military authorities in connection with Aviation was held yesterday in the afternoon at one o'clock.

The American aviator named T'ao [Treadup] *(his initials we did not learn, nor whether he was an Englishman) has come by the Butterfield & Squire's steamer to Hupei Province going to visit the Vice-President Li Yuan-hung.*

First they had a short conversation with refreshments. The Vice-President gave a most cordial and urgent invitation to demonstrate the subject, wishing to examine carefully into it.

All the electric lights in the reception room were lighted. Mr. T'ao first took certain models and demonstrated and explained, taking things in order and discussing one by one.

He had brought with him a leather case in which were parts of two flying machines which in about thirty minutes were put together. One model was a very excellent reproduction of an aeroplane and was somewhat more than ten feet long. Another model [a dirigible], *about three feet long, had within many things, such as steel wire, steel sheets, rubber, a gas bag, a metal wheel, and electric battery.*

When these models had been thus assembled in detail, Mr. T'ao spoke in order of the principles. The important use of the flying machine is to be able to see clearly over the surface of the earth and when the machine gets in motion many wonderful things may be observed. In history Mr. T'ao explained that man first arose in an aeroplane off the earth exactly nine years ago.

General Li especially appointed three interpreters, one named Hu, another named Hu, and another named Jung. All these pains were taken that there might be no mistake in General Li's understanding of the subject.

One of the models was put in motion and set in flight about the room, going east, south, west, and north; and while in motion the yellow lamps inside were lighted, making a very beautiful spectacle.

At the end the applause was like thunder and General Li arose shaking hands and saluting Mr. T'ao. He asked one of the two Mr. Hus to express his very great appreciation.

When the noise of the applause had died away, the guests were taken to a banquet where they enjoyed a fine social time until the sun was sinking in the west.

AFTER the lecture, General Li said that there were two tasks of a pressing nature for Mr. Treadup. One was to go to Nanking and meet Dr. Sun Yat-sen, who, though he had just relinquished his duties as Provisional President of the Republic, remained the first man in the heart of every Chinese revolutionist; General Li wanted Mr. Treadup to deliver a lecture in his presence, so that Dr. Sun would see the importance of this sort of education for all of China. The other mission was to go immediately up the Yangtze River, inland, into Szechuan Province, one of the strongholds of the revolution, where the message of modernization was especially needed. The Vice-President would alert the governor of the province.

The Vice-President also amazed David by quite casually pulling from a pocket and placing in David's hands a fat roll of paper money, which turned out to be no less than $1,000 (Mex).

David was thrilled by this encouragement and the opportunities General Li had given him. But that evening he had the uneasy work of composing a telegram to Emily, telling her that he would be some four or five weeks longer on the waterways than he had expected.

A B O U T his first meeting with Sun Yat-sen David later wrote Todd:

> *What impressed me beyond expression was the fact that this great revolutionist was alone when I called on him — not a retainer, not a soldier, not an official of any kind, only a servant to open the door. It certainly represented republican simplicity. Gone were the brocaded gowns and jade necklaces of officialdom; he wore a simple gray semimilitary jacket and trousers — not even the fancy knee boots Vice-President Li had affected. Outside the gate under the old regime were carriages, rickshas, and sedan chairs by the score, and the audience room itself was often filled with men who had no other seeming function than to make a show for the "big man." Interviews were more like receptions than private conferences. But in this interview there were no panoply, no peacock feathers — only Dr. Sun himself. A second unusual feature was that the interview was in the English language. No interpretation, no struggle for the proper term with which to address the great man. Furthermore, no bowings and kowtows, merely a handshake and greeting as in our own land. Can your imagination take in what a wonderful change this signifies in a land of Oriental ceremony such as China has been up to the present?*

Here we see a tinge, in David Treadup's choice of the phrase "as in our own land," of what came much later to be called cultural imperialism — an obviously unconscious assumption that what was done in the American style was clearly superior to what was done in the "Oriental" style. Because of Dr. Sun's pro-American bias of that time (it was later to give way to a pro-Russian preference), and because of the emerging role in the Chinese Republic of young men who had returned from study in the United States, Treadup saw this moment in history as peculiarly favorable to the missionary cause. No country, he perceived, was held in higher esteem than the United States, and he evidently could not help hoping for a China that would both be Christian and be an aspiring replica of his homeland in its customs and institutions.

None of this, however, detracts from the admirable modesty and simplicity of the revolutionary style of Sun Yat-sen that David noticed—qualities attractively adopted at first, much later, by the leaders of the Communist revolution, but then finally and ironically elevated by them to a new condition of pomp and pride—the magnificent showiness of the humility of power.

SUN YAT-SEN has gathered the most distinguished audience David Treadup has yet faced—numerous officials, many of them visiting Nanking from outlying provinces; officers of the revolutionary army; members of the revolutionary parliament. Before these worthies, Treadup gives his new lecture, "Wireless Telegraphy":

"This"—*moving to one of the numerous mechanisms arranged in orderly fashion about the platform*—"is part of a small demonstrating set of the Marconi type. The all-important electricity comes"—*he hovers over a four-cell, eight-volt storage battery*—"from this source, following these wires to the Leyden jars, which store up an accumulating charge of electricity, as if in an electrical savings bank, until there is enough to travel"—*as his index finger does*—"along these wires to the governing key, where the Rhumkopf coil induces by its inner coil an intense current in an outer coil and"—*he presses the key*—"see! a bright spark jumps across the adjacent terminals. . . ."

All this, rendered in Chinese, thoroughly baffles the listeners. But he moves across the platform to another apparatus: the receiving station. He explains how waves from the sender can activate a switch in the receiver that can ring a bell—*here!*—or light a lamp—*here!* He returns to the sending set, presses the key. The bell across the way rings. Presses the key. The lamp lights. Presses the key. Wonderful! A miniature cannon, which A Ch'u has been setting up while no one noticed, goes *BANG!*

NOW FOLLOWED the strange, unsettling experience of David's inland trip. He made the voyage upriver on a small flat-bottomed river steamer, designed to be able to negotiate the rapids of the famous Yangtze gorges.

It was the overwhelming grandeur of those gorges that produced in David the first feelings of disorientation of this trip into, it seemed, another era of time. Time! Eons! Something so soft as water had cut its narrow way down the ages right through stone mountains; the sheen of this delicate abrasive river lay now between towering walls of rock. And on those walls were the marks of a Chinese patience that seemed almost to match that of the river: pagodas on high crags; characters, somehow painted on inaccessible cliffs, celebrating the bright hills and dark waters; paths cut in the walls of the gorge above flood level for the paths of trackers who with heartbreaking stubborn labor pulled junks upstream on long towlines; and—there!—a wooden coffin wedged in a cleft in the sheer rock four hundred feet up—how in the world had it been raised to such a height and lodged there? David was flooded by such a sense of a long Chinese past, of an acceptance of endless tasks of survival, of a willingness to wait and work and wait and work and wait, that his own abrasive eagerness to help China change began to seem no more effective than water against stone.

And when he reached the city of Chengtu, it seemed as if he had truly entered another time, a forgotten time. The Association man there, Robert B. Chalmers, was a valiant modernist; but all around were missionary types David had somehow lost sight of in his narrow world of the lectures. Chalmers wanted this Association secretary from Shanghai to see some of what he, Chalmers, was up against in the interior, and he took Treadup here and there in the city. And in the days of setting up his lectures David began to encounter the inland evangelists:

• Here was the Rev. Dr. Samuel Manfill, who, it was famously known, liked to preach from hilltops. He took great pains and used the most devious methods to lure his flocks to summits.

• Here was Mrs. Dorothea Wells, a portly lady of great resolve, who was obviously not a distinguished linguist, and who was light-years from being a scholar, but who had mastered what David described in his diary as "a dreadful system of romanization known as the Chinese Phonetic Script." David came on her, in her house, as he called with Chalmers on her husband. She was teaching a wrinkled and squinting old illiterate Chinese woman the words of *The Gospel Primer* in C.P.S.; though evidently a slow learner, the old Chinese woman was dotty with the pleasure of the attention she was getting and with the conviction Mrs. Wells had long since given her that her soul was assured of a climb up the great golden ladder.

• Here were Thomas Orton, known as Tommy-O, and John Owens, known as Johnny-O, English athletic instructors both keenly desirous of making known the physical strength of Jesus's love. They were just passing through Chengtu, with a Chinese wheelbarrow full of tennis rackets and soccer balls. Their best work, they said, was in smaller towns. It was their habit to call on the principal of a local government school to discuss with him the need of his pupils for healthy outdoor sports, and to offer instruction in how to play some strength-giving games. Such offers, they told David, were always accepted, and (David's diary) "a couple of hours' vigorous running around would ensue." They would usually be asked to stay for a couple of days; in the stayover evenings they would "lecture" to ranks of pupils racked with charley horses. The next day they would move on.

• Here on a narrow alley was an old shop converted into a street chapel, and before it Rev. Jeremy Lothrop was preaching to a ragged gathering of some thirty poor people; from time to time his wife Christine played a hymn on a melodeon—a small movable reed organ through which she pumped air by working a treadle, like that of a Singer sewing machine, with her feet. The preaching—the Chinese of which David could understand because the Szechuanese dialect was quite close to Mandarin—had a haunting, melancholy poetic quality, which the Chinese listeners obviously found just as entertaining, and just as deeply baffling, as the itinerant native puppet shows and shadow shows they often saw in these same streets, which told of ancient warriors and dragons and spirits of the hills. After the service, the Lothrops invited David into their humble chapel. There were two small rooms, which the Lothrops shared with three bachelors, Nyquist, Greenhedge, and Blunt, who spent their days itinerating in the countryside. There was a tiny hole of a kitchen off the back room, from which charcoal fumes poured. "We sleep on the *k'ang* in the chapel," Mrs. Lothrop said, "and the boys are in the back— Blunt sleeps on the table, he's the shortest, Nyquist under the table, and Greenhedge on that bamboo settee. We have a cook, a kettle, and a saucepan. We fare very well, really! No tinned goods, I can tell you. For butter we use rendered pork fat!" What pride there was in this frugality! Dr. Lothrop, a Baptist from South Carolina, who obviously measured this Treadup person as one of those false missionaries from the big cities, began to warm up on the subject of saving souls. As his praise of the work intensified, his speech soon fell into the pulsing cadences of tidewater poetry, tongued with the resonance of a John C. Calhoun, of a sort that might never find a way to come to pause: "The street chapel is the missionary's fort, where he throws hot shot and shell into the enemy's camp; the citadel, where he defends the truth; the hill of Zion, where he sings sweet songs . . . "

DAVID TREADUP drew six hundred listeners to his third lecture in Chengtu. It was a shouting success. He had decided, probably because of the mighty persuasiveness of the Wrestling Gyroscope, to give his original and favorite lecture in this inland city. He confesses in his diary that he was beginning to grow a little vainglorious, "contrasting in my mind this cheering crowd with the dazed-looking handful of idlers listening the other day to Rev. Lothrop's street preaching." Something white flashed near the back of the hall. It was Dr. Elting's beard! How pleasing! He had gone along with Dr. Elting on an itineration from Tientsin on the wheelbarrow that time; now the good doctor was witnessing *his* itineration. He must have come in to Chengtu from his outlying station just to hear his young cabinmate speak.

The moment the lecture was over, David jumped down from the platform and made his way toward the back of the hall, to see his old shipmate. Dr. Elting, too, was coming forward. Then David saw his face. What a dark look! "Terrifying Isaiah must have looked like that, when he cried out, 'Woe to thee that spoilest!' " He did not even greet David, but began by shouting, "Not a word about our Lord!" Which was more heathen, the Chinese student in the audience or the lecturer on the platform? Science—anathema! Not to preach! It was a shame and a disgrace to the calling. The old man wheeled and strode away, his receding, stiff, black-coated back itself a fierce reproach.

The following day, in a meeting of the English Baptist Mission station, a Mr. Roper announced that at the next provincial council of the Szechuan Mission he intended to bring in a resolution stating that the Young Men's Christian Association, in introducing secular lectures of the sort he had just had the humiliation of hearing, was injurious to the missionary work of the province, and should be asked to retire from the field; all connection of the English Baptist Mission with the Association should be withdrawn throughout China.

The diary:

And so I left Chengtu under a cloud. They told me Roper had lost his wife during the Boxer trouble, and that he seems to have lost his mind. He spends the greater portion of his time at his wife's grave. All the same, I felt rudely shocked. Dr. Elting, then Mr. Roper. What I kept seeing in my mind's eye, as we traveled downstream on a small river junk, were the faces of those Chengtu people—Lothrop, Mrs. Wells, Dr. Manfill, even mindless Tommy-O and Johnny-O—underneath the narrow folly (as I saw it), some sort of purity of motive, a deep kindness, a final disinterestedness—not wanting anything for themselves—that made me search my own heart very closely. My vainglory was punctured.

IT WAS still early. A mist was on the river. There was a loud report. A gunshot. Brigands! the crewmen said. By keeping the small junk well out in the middle of the broad stream and by rowing hard, the crew, seven men in all, got the boat past the danger. But at eleven o'clock another shot came from the left bank. They were in a narrow stretch easily commanded from the shores. "I was not afraid," David wrote. "I kept thinking, as the crew strained at the oars, of the struggle against Cornell on the Hudson River in '04." The crewmen rowed with splashing courage—until two sampans carrying armed brigands put out farther down the river to cut them off.

Now there could be no escape. Reluctantly Treadup's junkmen rowed into a small cove where the brigands had a beachhead. As they pulled in, David stood in all his imposing height on the prow of the little junk, and, confronting the brigand leader who was impatient to come on board, he asked in a tone of surprise and quiet indignation the meaning of this intrusion. The Chinese crewmen, knowing the meaning all too well, were profuse in their welcome, greeting their captors with pipes, tea, and some fried bean curd and rice the crew's cook had just been preparing. The brigand chief carried no arms; he was finely dressed as a Chinese gentleman. But guarding him were two ugly toughs who carried—not in their belts, but in their hands, aimed at the huge white man—wicked-looking Mauser pistols; while a third, a pirate right out of the picture books, with his rifle evidently still warm from the shots aimed at the junk, began rummaging in the boat's cargo. The chief demanded opium; the huge white man threw up his hands to ridicule this order. Then he asked for silver; the huge white man guffawed and said he was too poor to have silver. The chief became abusive; the hands holding the pistols were raised higher for a more careful aim. "I was no longer thinking of Poughkeepsie! I did not know then that a well-known missionary in west China had recently been murdered by bandits like these. No, I was terrified not for myself but that they would steal—or worse, destroy—some of my beautiful apparatus. Then that very anxiety gave me an inspiration!"

He said to the chieftain: "Please wait. I have something to show you." He told A Ch'u to unpack the Wrestling Gyroscope. He beckoned to the chief to come to the flat deck abaft the junk's mast; the chief suspiciously approached with a thug at each elbow. David set the wheel up on edge. Look! He could push it over with his little finger! He nodded to A Ch'u. A Ch'u attached the outer crank and spun it up. David asked the chief, "Which is your strongest man?" Then . . .

We know the outcome without David's needing to tell us. First one thug, then two, grunting, unable to overset the wheel. Then panic. The brigands scrambling ashore. The junkmen back at the oars. The open river. David and A Ch'u convulsed with laughter.

BUT WHEN David reached Chungking, people told him it had been no laughing matter. He might well have lost his life. In the quiet of his guest room at the Methodist mission at the top of the hilly city he thought of the death he might have had long before he had brought his labor to its proper fruit—still with the faces of Dr. Manfill, Mrs. Wells, Rev. Lothrop, and Tommy-O and Johnny-O somehow rebuking him—and he prayed, not to be spared to do his work, but to be given, for the love of Jesus, a sense of proportion. It was at this most vulnerable moment, as he came down from his room to join others for supper, that he was handed a telegram:

> MAY 14 1912 TREADUP YMCA CHUNGKING BABY NANCY EXPIRED
> STOP SUFFOCATED DURING CROUP ATTACK STOP EMILY
> PROSTRATED STOP ADVISE IMMEDIATE RETURN STOP KEYSTONE

IT TOOK a week to reach Shanghai—"the longest week of my life." Baby Nancy was in the cold ground when he got there. Emily was in bed, in danger of miscarrying her new burden. David felt as if she had built a brick wall around the bed. He took his guilt and confusion to the laboratory and converted them into a rage of work. His diary: "I feel as if I must start again at the very beginning. In the evenings I am restudying the Bible."

IT WAS apparently at this time of irreplaceable loss that Emily started a secret practice about which she did not tell David until many years later. She began to slip one Chinese silver dollar each month into a black silk bag, which she kept in the one sanctuary she knew was sacred: David's eyes would never pry there—her underwear drawer. This habit she faithfully continued for more than a decade.

WE CAN imagine the agonies of contrition, pain, and self-doubt David Treadup must have been going through in this period, and the delicate efforts he must have been making to right himself with Emily. Yet in his Bible study—so far as he gives us any clues in writing—he was most concerned, after the shocks he had suffered, with the nature of his calling. We come across this in the diary:

> What has struck me first of all is the task of 'understanding' I have! I've now learned enough to be able to see the huge gap between my nurture and that, say, of Teacher Chuan or of my dear friend A Ch'u. I was brought up on this Book of Books, but what can those men make of it? So many things utterly meaningless to them. Mrs. Wells teaching that poor old woman up in Chengtu! So much about shepherds! I have yet to see a single sheep in China, and I'm told that where they do have them, in the far northwest, sheep are considered the vilest of animals, taken care of by negligible men. And customs in the Bible like the washing of feet! The holy kiss! So many Chinese customs are opposite to ours: In the 'credo' Jesus rises from the dead and sits on the right hand of God—but in China the seat of honor is on the left! Chinese mourners wear white. We think of the serpent, the dragon, as Satan—St. George slays the dragon! But to the Chinese the dragon is the symbol of power, wisdom, and benevolence. It was on the emperor's banner! At the heart of it all, the biblical message of 'sin'—utterly, utterly foreign to the Chinese. I've been talking with Brock about all the efforts to translate the Bible into Chinese: the Marshman version, the Morrison, Medhurst, Gutzlaff, Bridgman, the Delegates' version, Bridgman & Culbertson, I've probably left some out, versions in high classical 'wen-li,' in easy 'wen-li,' in colloquial dialects—and yet all this time we missionaries haven't even been able to agree on what word should be used in Chinese for "God"! Oh, what a task I have!

But it is in "Search," written many years later, that we see the real importance of this new Bible study in David Treadup's development:

One night as I was studying the Gospel according to St. John, I had a vivid memory of a particular evening in the period of struggle before my conversion. That night, I was in Cook's room. We played a kind of game, in our desperate (and always inadequate) effort to be "real" in our Christianity. Each of us in turn would choose a biblical character and — impersonating him, as in a charade — would make an effort so completely to identify with that figure as to 'experience' him. Cook roamed on the terrain of Jesus's preaching, playing the parts of disciples, or beneficiaries of miracles, or sometimes even daring to be Jesus. I found myself attracted, as I had been since childhood, to the prophets of the Old Testament — so craggy, so ferocious in their scourging of the Israelites for whoring after other gods. I felt that mimicking those powerful figures might give me enough 'enthusiasm' to be born again. On the night I was thinking of, I had chosen to be Elijah, denouncing Jezebel and the priests of the Baal of Tyre. I poured my scorn on Ahab for marrying the Tyrian Jezebel and opening the way to the false gods the Canaanites called the Baal. And, perhaps with the glamor of missions in the back of my mind, I began speaking of the Canaanites as heathen Chinese. I worked up quite a sweat — but at the end of the evening, I had, yet again, a feeling of failure: something was terribly wrong with my charade.

So now, in my new studies, recalling that night and trying to puzzle out what had been so wrong, I turned from St. John back to the Book of Elijah, and read and thought — and suddenly I was struck by a dizzying idea: Here in China, I am, to the Chinese, not an Elijah but 'a priest of Baal.' For Elijah was a native, fighting against the incursion, not only of foreign rites and graven images, but of foreign political intrigue and power. In his religious zeal, he was also a patriot. And I, in China, am a priest of a foreign god, and I have at my back (and on my conscience) foreign gunboats, opium, plunder, extraterritoriality.

This was a shocking and humiliating idea. My inland trip, so tragically ill-timed as it had turned out to be, had brought home to me that the real China would not change overnight with a change of administrations in faraway capitals. The old forces for order and obedience in the Confucian scheme, and the ancient pride that was the Chinese substitute for patriotism — these would by no means be wiped out by a Nanking decree proclaiming religious liberty, opening the way to me.

I was working harder than ever in those days after my return — at home, with Emily, with Philip, as well as at the shop — to try to square with the whole world my feeling of having abandoned Emily when she most needed me — of not having been with her to tender a farewell to our

dear little wraith of a Nancy. And now this sudden apparent loss of the
Elijah in me forced me deep into myself, there to face haunting questions:
Was I doing the right work? In the right way?

THE BUREAU

SIX MONTHS later. Treadup is in top form. Mrs. Treadup has given birth
to a second son, Absolom Carter Treadup. Emily is effective in good works in
the Settlement. The diaries of both partners are quite cheerful. Young Philip
blossoms. He is already teaching himself to read! The parents congratulate
him and themselves. Baby Absolom is plump. This healthy son does not, of
course, eclipse the pale moon of poor Nancy in the night sky of the bereaved
mother and father; but the loss of the sickly child has somehow come to bind
the Treadups together.

What has heartened David and Emily Treadup?

AFTER the Yangtze trip and the death of Nancy, David, feeling that his
rudder needed repair, sought the counsel of wise Farrow Blackton, the organizing genius of the National Committee of the Y.M.C.A. in China. He and
Blackie talked often together. They prayed together. One day Blackie said he
had been visited from time to time by bright young returned students,
Christians, who said they had heard one Treadup lecture or another. Treadup
had set them on fire, and they had come to think that they themselves might
be able to give their fellow countrymen valuable lectures in the Treadup mode
on subjects other than science. It was the policy of the Y.M.C.A. — preeminently
in the mission field — to develop Chinese leadership and to surrender to it the
moment it was ready to take charge.

Yes! Yes! Farrow Blackton's quiet voice touched off a chain of understanding in David's mind. Blackie's returned students were the young Elijahs!
David had long been afflicted, he suddenly realized, with the arrogance of a
priest of Baal. He had been going to save China by opening its eyes to the
science of the outside world. He single-handed. This hubris must have made
him seem detached, must have been at least part of what had caused Emily to
shudder with the feeling of being alone on a dangerous cold sea. And this,
really, must have been under the surface of Dr. Elting's shock and anger — no
matter how "narrow" Dr. Elting might be — after the Chengtu lecture, and it

must have been what had made him, David, feel so unaccountably queasy as he remembered the faces of inland "fools," Manfill, Mrs. Wells, the Lothrops, the English athletes. It was not easy to face it that, with all his apparent success, he had been quite likely no less a fool, perhaps a fool of a different sort, than they. In this sudden shame of realization he did not lose sight of his strengths; Blackie had said he had lit a fire in those young men. But perhaps his prayer for a sense of proportion was beginning to be answered. He was grateful to Blackton, for he felt relieved of a baffling weight on his heart.

In high summer he went back to the river and rowed his singles scull with the devoted concentration on smooth strokes that always seemed to mean he was working something out that had nothing to do with rowing. And in the city, soon, he went to work in a new way.

BLACKTON introduced David Treadup to David Y. S. Liu. Blackton had first met Liu some years before at a Y.M.C.A. conference for Chinese students at Kuling. Liu's father, a Confucian literatus who had been converted to Christianity and had become an Episcopal minister, insisted that his son both master the Chinese classics and secure a Western education. The young Liu had graduated from Wuchang College and from St. John's University in Shanghai, and then had gone to the States and had taken a master's degree *cum laude* in education at Harvard, where he had also won a $500 prize for excellence in scholarship. (While at St. John's he had taken on an "American" given name; and while at Harvard he bought American clothes, which he henceforth wore in China.) On his return Li Yuan-hung had made him head of the Department of Foreign Affairs in the transitional reform government right after the revolution; despite his youth — for many of the new leaders were very young — he might well have gone on to be foreign minister in the Republican government. But David Treadup saw his stunning gifts, and he saw that David Liu would be able to lecture on modern education to Chinese educators who were still at heart Confucian scholars with a conviction and power no Westerner could match. Together that summer the two Davids worked up a lecture, "The Challenge to Chinese Education." In the fall Liu took it on the road; Treadup went along to help with arrangements.

The tour was strenuous. In Peking, Liu repeated his lecture seven times in two and a half days. The president of Pei Yang University was present on the first afternoon. David Liu used two telling demonstrations. On a table was mounted a device with five spools of ribbon, three inches wide, of various colors. To demonstrate the amount of illiteracy in each of Japan, Great Britain, Germany, the United States, and China, the lecturer's assistant, on command, pressed one button after another, and out came various lengths of ribbon. For Britain, less then a foot; for the United States, somewhat more; for Japan, less than two feet; for Germany, about a foot. Then the China button. The ribbon ran and ran, forming a heap on the floor of the platform. Liu asked his assistant to take it down and stretch it out over the audience. It ran for thirty feet.

Then the lecturer's assistant moved to a table of cubes of various sizes, and of colors corresponding to those of the national ribbons of illiteracy. Liu asked him to place at the base the British cube of educated citizens, which could easily support the tiny cube of the illiterate. So with all the other countries, save China — whose huge cube of the uneducated toppled from the tiny base of the literati.

Pei Yang's president came again the next morning; his students made up the audience. When David Liu came to the ribbon demonstration, the president stood up and begged Liu not to show it. He said that fourteen years earlier, in the Emperor's Hundred Days of Reform, wonderful promises had been made for Chinese education. "Our hearts were broken then. Now you want to show how bad things still are, and we have no second heart to be broken."

Watching this from the back of the hall, as David later wrote,

> I could not help wondering what I would have done in response to that plea, and I decided that I would have answered with as much tact as I could but would have gone ahead with that demonstration, because it provided the most vivid and agonizing moment of the whole lecture. But David Liu was more delicate — he was Chinese — he complied. He asked Wen [his assistant] to go to the table of cubes. Dr. Fu stood up again, and again begged David not to shame China with those cubes, either. But the magistrate who was presiding stood up and, with a bow of apology to Dr. Fu, told David to proceed. Dr. Fu then turned to the audience, and I saw his face for the first time. Tears were streaming down it. He told his students to take a good look at what they were about to see, and to remember it, and to do something about it. There had never been such a moving moment in any of my lectures.

The following morning the magistrate sent a messenger to David Treadup ("assuming, I suppose — and I regret — that the foreigner was behind all this"), requesting that the lecture be presented one extra unscheduled time that afternoon. Meanwhile he had sent out sixteen men to gather the head men of all the towns and villages within a radius of twenty li to hear the special lecture. More than four hundred showed up. At the close of the lecture, the magistrate made an appeal for the establishment of elementary schools in all the towns the next year, and he assured them he would remove every obstacle and personally supervise the work; he urged them to cooperate by spreading word of what they had just heard, and by sending their own children and the children of their clans to the schools. He then asked the District Inspector of Education to explain in a few words what a kindergarten, an

elementary school, a middle school, and a normal school were. The president
of the university spoke passionately in support of the magistrate's plea.

(There are no records to show that the schools were ever established.)

IN HANKOW, where the previous year floodwater had stood two and three
feet deep in city streets, Y. Y. Han (Ph.D. in forestry, Yale University) gave his
first lecture on the Conservation of Natural Resources. He and Treadup had
designed, in the Shanghai laboratory, the most elaborate device yet for a
demonstration:

Here on the platform is a model of a village seated at the edge of a
sloping plain at the foot of a mountain. A stream runs down the mountain in a
narrow gorge. Below the village are fields of rice and beans, and a grove of
mulberry trees, the leaves of which furnish food for silkworms. The temple,
the hall of ancestors, the tile-covered roofs of the landowners and the thatched
roofs of the poor—it is a charming and credible picture. Dr. Han gives a brief
description of the tranquillity of village life; but then he calls attention to the
mountain above the village. The ancient trees that stood there for centuries
have been cut down, one by one, for beams, for charcoal, to make carts and
sampans. The mountain is denuded.

Suddenly the audience is startled by a flash of lightning! A clap of
thunder! A cloudburst of rain!

The water pours off the naked heights, fills the gorge, dashes down on
the village and washes it away, and floods the fields below, leaving there,
finally, the miserable death and debris of China's sorrow. It is all so real,
so familiar.

THERE CAME to David another young man—this time, an American—
who had heard, and been excited by, one of the Treadup lectures: the gyroscope. This was a medical missionary, a graduate of Rush Medical College
who had just recently come to China with the missions of the Evangelical
Association, named J. R. Charles. He thought that there was a need for
demonstration lectures on health, and that he might be just the person to give
them, once he had mastered Chinese. David had long felt the desperate want
of such lectures. On almost every other Chinese face you saw the pits left
by the "divine black flowers" of smallpox; rotting lepers lay in the streets;
legs of the poor were fouled by volcanic ulcerous sores; scalps were hideous
with white fungus and red ringworm. And the native remedies! Powdered
deer horn for stomach pain; ground tiger ligaments for weakness; bear's paws
for coughing; and frightful brews for whatnot—"concoctions," as one account puts it, "that contained frogs' bellies, red-marble filings, calves' blad-
ders, plum kernels, snakes' necks, rabbits' pellets." David found Dr. Charles

articulate and "a dynamic person," and he went at once to Blackton to suggest their taking Charles on; Blackton would have to arrange, through Todd in New York, for Charles to be released by the Evangelical Association for the lecture work.

It would be at least two years before Dr. Charles could begin to lecture, for he would have to study the language first. But he and David began at once to spend long hours together in the lab planning the first health lecture, "Sanitation."

IN THE VERY WEEK in which approval of Charles's release came from the States, the Shanghai papers carried alarming stories of an epidemic of cholera in the port city of Foochow, in Fukien Province, south of Shanghai. There was a call for doctors. Dr. Charles would have to go; but Treadup said *he* was going, too—because, he said, it would be absolutely futile for Dr. Charles to spend all his time treating one patient after another, when a hundred thousand might be sick. What had to be attacked was the epidemic itself. Right here, in the lecture that they had been preparing, were the means for mounting that attack. They had been designing a display on cholera, to make the point that the cholera germ was spread by flies—*there* was the whole secret! Flies surely swarmed in the great marketplaces of Foochow; they would speckle the fresh fruit, some of it cut open, in the countless small shops of the market districts. If the Foochowans could eliminate the flies, they could stop the cholera. But the city had a million people; probably less than five hundred knew that cholera germs were carried by flies. What Treadup and Charles must do was to lecture to an entire city. They must teach two simple sentences in ten days to a million people: *Filth attracts flies. Flies cause cholera.*

They boarded the first ship south, taking with them seven workers from the laboratory. In Foochow, David's experience in the advance work before lectures was invaluable. They went first to the Governor of Fukien Province. In a panic of helplessness—he had spent $10,000 (Mex) on a great procession of idols through the streets to drive away the spirits of cholera, only to have the epidemic redoubled—he welcomed the two young men with joy. Soon they were in touch with other officials, with faculties, with the Chamber of Commerce, and with ministers and priests, and within days they had formed a committee of cooperation with 2,500 members. They put up posters everywhere. They trained professors and students in government and mission schools to give brief addresses to the people on the two sentences all through the city. Every theater in the city, every church, every temple courtyard, every auditorium in every college and school—every single available public space was requisitioned for lectures. Soon tens of thousands of people a day were being taught the vital sentences.

Finally they organized a huge parade, in which 50,000 people marched. At the head of the procession were floats bearing enormous flies, five feet high, as fearful as tigers, quickly built with extraordinary lifelikeness out of papier-mâché by the laboratory staff. The climax of the parade was a series of floats: On the first, huge pieces of (papier-mâché) watermelon with big flies on them; on the next, a paper man eating the paper melon; on the third, the man writhing in the agonies of cholera; on the fourth, starkly, a real coffin.

The committee calculated it had reached 350,000 people in two weeks' work. Back in Shanghai Treadup and Charles were told that shopkeepers had begun putting mosquito netting up over their displays; some had even installed glass. Teams throughout the city were cleaning up piles of rubbish. The work of teaching the two simple sentences was continuing. There was some resistance, some suspicion of the foreigners who were behind all this — perfectly expressed in the remark of a Chinese bystander at the big parade: "Ay! If the Americans have flies that big, no wonder they want to exterminate them!"

But on the whole, the results were encouraging. Reports were that the epidemic was abating — perhaps faster, doctors thought, than it would have if it had simply been running its course.

ON JANUARY 1, 1913, the Lecture Bureau of the (Chinese) National Committee of Young Men's Christian Associations was formally inaugurated. It had been sanctioned in December by the sixth National Convention of the Associations in China. David Liu was named Executive Secretary. David Treadup was now just one of its lecturers, in science. Dr. Charles would lecture on health. Other notable Chinese in the Bureau, besides Liu and Han, were Dr. John Y. Hu, a graduate of the University of Chicago in physics, where he had worked under brilliant men, one of whom had won, and the other of whom would later win, the Nobel Prize — with Dr. Albert A. Michelson in research in optics and with Dr. Robert A. Millikan on the isolation of the electron — now to be head of the laboratory where demonstration materials were to be built; and C. T. Wang, a Yale graduate who would one day become premier of China, to lecture on government. There were soon to be a dozen lecturers and twenty-two Chinese mechanics in the laboratory. A particular joy to David Treadup, in due course, was that with some assiduous letter writing he was able to track down his language teacher, good Chuan; he learned that Chuan was still free of opium; and he brought him into the Bureau, first as an assistant, later as an additional full-fledged lecturer on education.

What is remarkable in retrospect about this Y.M.C.A. Bureau is that in so many ways, ranging from its basic demonstration methods to such various things as its cries for reforestation and flood control, its vividly practical science lessons, its teachings about cholera and plague and tuberculosis, its use of processions with floats for mass education, its development of simple slogans, and even its down-to-earth admonition to kill flies—and in many, many other respects, too, soon and late—its work foreshadowed techniques and ideas that were used all over China during and after the ultimate Chinese upheaval, that of the Communist revolution.

AS FOR David Treadup, this outcome was in every way a boon. He was now free to concentrate on what he really enjoyed, the lecturing itself. The immense load of supervising the laboratory and at the same time developing and delivering a multiplicity of lectures was off his lonely hands—though he would still have much work in keeping funds and equipment coming from the United States and Europe, and in helping to develop fresh ideas and new gadgetry in Shanghai. The greatest satisfaction, touching on his sense of his mission in life, was in having turned over much of the leadership and initiative to Chinese co-workers. And such workers! What a tonic it was just to be in the company of such bright, idealistic, and energetic young men! All this meant that his obsession was gradually being eased, and despite the fact that he was still away from home from time to time, he was now able to be much more openhearted with Emily, and was beginning to try to be to Philip and Absolom the kind of father his own work-ridden father had never been to him. For her part, Emily responded with relief and warmth to the return home, so to speak, of her husband. Besides, she was pregnant again.

THE GREAT TODD

THE HOME TARRY was all too brief.

In January 1913 Blackton told Treadup that James B. Todd was coming to China for a revival tour of thirteen cities. The great Todd—a founder of the Student Volunteer Movement, one of the coiners of the slogan "Evangelization of the World in This Generation." When David had first seen him at the Northfield Conference, he had thought that this blond, handsome, dynamic, reed-throated man incarnated his own college-boyish picture of the ideal male creature; but since then, over the years, in Todd's function as Y.M.C.A. wire-puller in faraway New York, he had seemed cold and negative: God's great bureaucrat. He had never appeared to David to believe in the lecture program. He had been chary with funds and a niggard with what would have been worth more than money, praise. But he was the great Todd, and he was going to do in three months what the sluggish Protestant missions had not accomplished in their work since 1807 — win China! So, at least, many people seemed to think.

And many people *did* think, according to Blackton, that the best way to lure audiences to Todd's addresses would be for him, Treadup, to stage a series of his science lectures in each city just before Todd came on.

David's diary: "I guess the carnival tent needs a barker!" But in the diary's next sentence, Treadup quickly rues his sarcasm: "I'll try to do all I can."

What he did, as it was to turn out, astonished even him and complicated, rather than answered, his questions about his calling.

He packed up the three lectures — on the gyroscope, wireless, aeroplane — and took a ship to Hong Kong, where the evangelistic tour was to begin.

TODD was due to arrive on Wednesday, January 29. The Hong Kong Association people had rented a brand new Chinese theater, called Kau U Fong, which seated fourteen hundred, for four nights, from January 30 through February 2, for $200 (Mex). They had been able to strike this extraordinary bargain — less than $25 in U.S. money each night — because the Chinese New Year was coming on February 6, and during the great holidays before it everything public would be shut down. Blackton had gone to Singapore to meet Todd and bring him on to China, and he had cabled: all well, our man hale and hearty, going aboard Japanese steamer, will be there on dot.

Treadup, the shill, gave the first of his preparatory lectures, on the wireless, in the Association building on the twenty-fourth. He repeated the lecture nine times in five days. The first two audiences were students from Queens College; then students came from three other government schools and three mission schools; then a large crowd from Hong Kong University. The students were thrilled by the little tapped words winging out the windows of the hall to warships of His Majesty King George V out in the harbor, and the peppery British ripostes flying right back through thin air into the crowded room. As for the Association people, they were ecstatic. At the end of each demonstration, they handed out far more tickets for each night of the Todd meetings than there were seats in Kau U Fong. One wrote New York:

> The great value of the lectures from a moral and spiritual viewpoint lies in the way Dr. Treadup makes the audience feel the reality of the unseen.

Professor C. A. Templeton Jones, dean of the Faculty of Engineering at
Hong Kong University, a Britisher, wrote a letter of thanks to the Hong Kong
Association:

*I have listened to lectures on wireless telegraphy by Mr. Marconi and Sir
Oliver Lodge. I am bound to say that I consider Mr. Treadup excels those
great scientists in capturing the attention and continually interesting
an audience. I would like to hear that fifty men like Mr. Treadup were
at work in China, carrying the same message and doing it in the same
able manner.*

The appointed Wednesday came, but not the ship. Thursday, no ship.
Three thousand tickets sold for fourteen hundred seats, no Todd.

There was nothing to do but put Treadup on, with the gyroscope. The
male choir from the Wesleyan Church, directed by Mr. W. Leung, opened the
meeting by singing songs in English. "The Glory Song" was such a hit that it
had to be flung forth twice. The words of the new Chinese national anthem, to
the tune of "America" (or of "God Save the King"), were flashed on a screen
and learned and roared by the audience. Everyone was in great heart. The
wrestling gyroscope almost caused a riot. When Mr. J. M. Kung, president of
the Hong Kong Association, proposed a prayer for Mr. Todd's safe arrival—
there had been reports, he said, of a typhoon—the young men in the audience
broke into wild and inappropriate cheers. Were they cheering Todd's chances,
or the typhoon that might drown him?

Friday, no ship.

Friday night, Treadup, with aviation. After the beautiful ten-foot aeroplane flew east, south, west, and north near the ceiling (attached to a wire),
President Kung announced, without conviction, that Mr. Todd would surely
be there on Saturday.

As it turned out, he was. The ship, battered by the typhoon, limped in.
Big blond Todd stepped ashore with the aplomb of a moose coming out of a
swamp. Bully voyage! Waves like Alps! Hadn't been seasick for an instant!

Was David Treadup disappointed? Had he begun to enjoy his repeated
successes a bit more than he realized? We can only judge aslant, by the
laconism in his diary entry for that day: "Taller than I had remembered him."

Todd went on that evening, with "Patriotism," interpreted by Ho Lei-
son, chairman of the Association's Religious Work Committee, "a man," the
report to New York said, "of great moral power." On Sunday Todd with his
irrepressible vigor spoke three times to three full houses, on "Spiritual Atrophy,"
"Temptation," and "Religion a Matter of the Will." After these meetings,
832 students signed inquirers' cards, promising to "study the four Gospels,
pray to God daily for light and guidance, and accept Christ if I find him true."

Treadup's diary critique, when the Hong Kong series ended, was
generous:

He has honey on his tongue. Each address lasts an hour and a half, to the minute. No text, no notes. There seems to be no appeal to the emotions; doesn't resort to stories or anecdotes to salt the meat. Severely logical, straightforward. What makes it dramatic is the fire of his conviction. Very slight trembling of his deep voice: intensity.

But how revealing the last line of the entry is! "Attendance at science lectures: 8,274. Attendance at evangelistic addresses: 7,700. Of course I had the benefit of two extra nights."
First round on the Todd-Treadup scorecard.

NANKING. Science Lectures: 12,600. Evangelistic Addresses: 8,600.
F. E. Mason, the Association's advance man, who went ahead from city to city alerting officials and hiring halls, reported that Todd had been "impressive" in Nanking, but then added:

As in Hong Kong and Canton, Mr. Treadup had prepared the way by a series of science lectures, reaching an immense number of students from government schools and colleges. Indeed, he has gained a larger hearing among the recently inaccessible classes of China than any Westerner during the entire missionary history of the country. The value of the scientific lecture department as a direct contributory agency to the evangelistic campaign has been incalculably great.

Inquirers: 409.

TRIUMPHS in Hankow, Wuchang, Anking. In Tsinanfu, capital of Shantung, the Governor, dizzied with pleasure by whirling gyroscopes, let Todd use the Provincial Assembly hall for the call to Jesus.

IN HIS OLD language-study haunts, in Paotingfu ("24 hours crowded with glorious opportunity in this city made sacred by the blood of the martyrs"—Mason), David basked in an evening of praise from his "other mother" of those days, Miss Letitia Selden. "My lands! How my little boy has grown up!"

IN TIENTSIN, David was able to have two hours with his dear Christian friend Lin Fu-chen, who after listening to the wireless lecture said, "Do you remember when Yen Han-lin's goldfish covered itself in alarm when it saw your *ta-pi-tzu* [big nose] that first time? All the goldfish love your nose now!"

BY THE TIME the team arrived in Peking, an obvious shift had taken place in the balance of power between these two dynamic men. Todd no longer condescended. And Treadup, secure in a sense of his value to the enterprise, now could afford to be modest. "What a drummer I must have seemed to James"—aha! first name!—"when I started pushing the literati program. I blush when I think of that first budget I sent him." But the blush could resolve itself into a glow of recognition: not he, but his lecture program—worth every cent New York had spent on him. Somewhere under the surface of David's optimism, the scorecard was doing its curious work; the social message was proving to be more powerful than the gospel message. For David, this must have been both bracing and disturbing. Was it the intrinsic message that was more attractive to the Chinese at this moment? Or was it a matter of personality—spellbinder versus magician? Either way, David must have felt strong, for Todd was a formidable and wonderfully attractive seducer of souls. To outdraw Todd was to be a big man; to open doors to Todd that would otherwise have been closed was to wield power in the missionary movement.

THERE WAS one crucially important gate, in particular, that Treadup was able to open. He introduced Todd to President Yuan Shih-k'ai, who a few years before as viceroy in Tientsin had put the equipment of the city museum at the young American lecturer's disposal. David noted in his diary that Yuan received them "in a style much less retiring than that with which Sun Yat-sen received me in Nanking. We had to wait half an hour in an anteroom. Many attendants and soldiers scurrying about. The word I would use for him is 'bristling.' " He was most cordial. He said he had a good habit of contributing "well-spent" money to the Y.M.C.A. each year.

He had an hour ago, he said, given orders to the Minister of the Interior to build for the Treadup and Todd meetings a large pavilion of bamboo poles and straw matting in the Forbidden City—the sacred inner sanctum of Peking, the walled grounds of the former Imperial palaces. Yuan said he had ordered the Minister of War to provide two hundred tents to spread on the roof to make the pavilion rainproof. What was more, he was proclaiming a day of public prayer for the Republic in the Christian churches of China.

The volatile energy of China's strong man could not but appeal to such a vibrant personality as Todd's. In a letter to New York, Todd wrote of Yuan:

With a clear black-eyed gaze which comes at you like an auger, a large head topped by a brush of hair in a military cut, a thinker's forehead, bold mustaches, and short, muscular, bounding figure, he somewhat

resembles Theodore Roosevelt in personal appearance. Keeps constant
touch with Western advisers like Dr. Goodnow of Johns Hopkins and Dr.
Morrison of the London 'Times.'

—as if to say, in the mode of the unconscious cultural imperialist, that any
Chinese leader who was like and consulted Anglo-Saxons could not be all bad.

Bad? Neither Todd nor Treadup had seen any signs of anything bad.
Neither had had any way of knowing of Yuan's increasingly high-handed
governance, of his disregard for the provisional constitution, which set limits
on his authority, or of the growing friction between him and Sun Yat-sen.
Neither happened to have heard that just two days before their meeting with
Yuan, an odious political assassination had been pulled off. Sung Chiao-jen
was a brilliant young Hunanese revolutionary who the previous year had
amalgamated the T'ung Meng Hui, the anti-Manchu subversive group to
which Sun Yat-sen had belonged, with several minor societies into a new
political party, the Kuomintang. In recent elections for the national Parliament,
the Kuomintang had gained a majority of seats. This posed a hostile threat to
Yuan's growing domination of the government—and the murder of Sung was
immediately and widely attributed to Yuan. But this was beyond the ken of
the two buoyant messengers from the Western world.

Todd could hardly wait to get back to their hotel after the interview with
Yuan, to dash off a cable to his good and devout friend who had just been
inaugurated President of the United States, Woodrow Wilson, urging that
the United States should hesitate no longer to recognize the government of
the Republic of China. Wilson's predecessor, William Howard Taft, though
beseeched first by missionaries and later by business interests to recognize
the new Chinese government, had dragged his feet and failed to act. Todd's
long cable stressed China's

RIGHT TO RECOGNITION BY PROGRESS ACHIEVED IN MOST
DIFFICULT YEAR. . . . WOULD ENORMOUSLY ENHANCE OUR
PRESTIGE IN THE EAST.

THE FORBIDDEN CITY! Never in numberless years of China's dynasties
had the spokesmen of an alien religion been allowed to make a public stand
within those sealed innermost walls of the Emperor's palaces. A handsome
rectangular temporary building of bamboo and straw matting, able to seat
more than a thousand, arose as if by magic in two short days—surprisingly
and pleasingly placed right next to a sacred altar where for centuries, Todd
wrote home, "the Emperor himself worshiped once a year."

The day the great shed was finished, Todd and Treadup climbed the Coal
Hill, from the summit of which, standing under an ancient pine tree, they
could look down on the golden roofs of the Forbidden City and see the

shimmering materialized beauty of the long history of the Imperial sway. David Treadup must have realized, quite beyond any issue of personal vanity, the importance to China and to Christendom of the visit the two men were entering upon. Indeed, the next few days could be taken, at least symbolically, as the highest point yet — and, perhaps it was to prove, ever — in the missionary movement in China. For the new China of that moment hungered for what these two seemed to offer: the possibility of the moral and physical regeneration of an awakening country.

But many years later, in "Search," Treadup was to record some strange undercurrents in that potential moment:

> Todd brimmed over, that afternoon on the peak of the high artificial hill, with energy and Christian love — a great deal of the latter aimed at himself. People who are deeply loved usually have confidence in themselves. Todd was so deeply loved — by himself — that he almost burst open with assurance every minute of the day.
>
> "Ah Treadup!" he shouted at me. "I am going to reap such a harvest down there!"
>
> "Yes," I quietly said, "we will get good crowds."
>
> Noticing the change of pronoun, Todd darted a look at me that was as dangerous as a bowie knife. He was just as aware as I was of the scorecard of attendance at my lectures and his: right there in the Forbidden City, in the following days, I was to draw nearly twice as many auditors as he.
>
> "David," he said — matching the change of pronoun by a change in his address to me, closing in on me, so to speak, with a first name — "I wish you would include some devotions in your lectures. You are too dry. God made the physical world, you know."
>
> Was it Em's love that gave me confidence? — or did I, too, have the benefit of some self-love? I had, anyway, the benefit of the scorecard, and I said, "James, I don't trespass on your ground. Leave mine to me."
>
> Normally he would have pressed his argument, for he was used to overbearing all opposition. But he could see that I was very angry. He remained silent for a long time, then he said, for he surely saw himself as a true Christian, "We will have a fine harvest, Treadup."
>
> Only now can I see what venom there was in that charitable surrender. He never forgave me. And I never got over — though I would have denied the notion till the cows came home — never got over hating him.

FOR THREE DAYS David Treadup cast his nets.

Then, on the Day of Prayer which had been proclaimed by President Yuan, Todd gave his first addresses. There were welcoming speeches by Chinese officials, and Yuan's proclamation was read. Treadup afterward wrote, in a letter to brother Paul:

> *This audience was unlike any I have seen. It did not just sit there intently, as student crowds so often do. Such a clamor! They put on organized cheers like those at a sports contest at home. Ten thousand years to the Republic! Ten thousand years to President Yuan! Ten thousand years to the church of Christ! There was an active hunger on the faces of those hundreds of young men which made me rejoice for them—my goodness, to think—think back—the centuries—Emperor after Emperor, and now suddenly there is a Republic, and these youths so open to our message. It makes one glad to be alive.*

WHEN the two men return to the hotel after the first day of Todd's addresses in the Forbidden City pavilion, a cablegram is waiting for Todd. It remains in its sealed envelope in Todd's hand—his motor is still running at high speed, he is too busy talking to be bothered to open it. . . .

The message has a background:

Considering Woodrow Wilson's strong religious bent, it is not surprising that much of what he learned about China while he was president of Princeton had come from missionary friends. After his inauguration, he and his Secretary of State, William Jennings Bryan, strongly agreed that the diplomat chosen to represent them in China must be a man known as a sterling Christian leader. In February 1913 Wilson wrote Bryan:

> *The Christian influence, direct or indirect, is very prominently at the front, and I need not say, ought to be kept there. Mr. James B. Todd, whom I know very well and who has as many of the qualities of a statesman as any man of my acquaintance, is very familiar with the situation in China, not only that, but he enjoys the confidence of men of the finest influence all over the Christian world.*

The Todd cable on recognition quite likely confirmed Wilson's inclination to choose Todd for the China post, and yes, this cablegram in the evangelist's hand, finally torn open as friends David and James climb the stairs to their rooms, is an invitation to Todd to accept appointment as United States Minister to the Republic of China. Wonderful! Without a moment's hesitation, Todd turns right around on the stairs, goes down to the concierge's desk, and writes out in his bold hand a cablegram refusing the appointment.

Treadup (the scorecard, continuing in his favor, makes it possible for him to rise above the animosity he scarcely realizes he feels, and be unaffectedly generous) later writes his Syracuse supporters:

In my opinion no American Minister to China in his entire term has done more for China than has Dr. Todd in the ten weeks he has been here this year. This might go a long way to explain why he declined.

PART OF DAVID'S success in his science lectures was that he delivered them in excellent, if cavernously nasal, Mandarin.

Part of Todd's success—and part of the symbolic significance of this Peking visit—lay in the fact that his interpreter was a fiery young Christian, C. L. Nieh, whose revolutionary courage in the face of his distinguished conservative heritage had made him a hero with young Chinese. His father had been the Imperial governor of four provinces. His uncle, Marquis Tseng, had been the Imperial Minister to England, France, Germany, and Russia. And his grandfather had been the scholar-general Tseng Kuo-fan, the most influential Chinese statesman of the nineteenth century, suppressor of the Taiping rebels and leader of that first failed effort to give China a new life, the Self-Strengthening Movement.

"One might well ask," Blackton wrote later, in a commentary on the revival tour,

> *why not put Nieh himself on, rather than the alien Todd? To these young men, Nieh was a hero of the revolution with a special value—that of a familial reach back to nineteenth-century roots of all these new aspirations for China. He was, besides, a devoted Christian with a vibrant delivery. Why have Todd at all? One answer, I suppose, is that you couldn't have kept James B. off any stage! But there is, of course, a deeper and better reason. These two together were more than a sum of their separate dynamic selves. They made a symbol of something for which the younger Chinese yearn at this moment—a bridge between Orient and Occident, a world kinship that can bring China, at last, out of its ancient isolation into the modern era.*

AFTER the meetings in the Forbidden City, Treadup and Todd appeared at the Imperial University, the Law College, and several other government institutions, "into which," Mason wrote, "no Christian speaker has ever before secured an entrance." This was thanks to David Treadup's science lectures. They also spoke at Tsing Hua Academy, "the keystone of the educational system," Mason again, "where are gathered the flower of the student body of China preparing for matriculation into American universities and subsequent official leadership in China." The principal of the Academy, Tong Kai-son, was a Christian, and so were eighteen of his professors.

THE TEAM was asked to address the government's military garrison in the capital. Present at Todd's address at the Peking Methodist church was a young major named Feng Yu-hsiang, a tall and heavy-framed Northerner, who with one of his lieutenants had for some time been trying to set examples of Confucian virtue to their men, in the hope of discouraging them from drinking, gambling, and whoring. One image Todd used hit Feng hard. Todd said a man was like a tree. Outside, the wood of the tree looked fine. But if inside it was eaten out by worms, any wind could blow it down. . . . After the address, Feng went forward and introduced himself both to Treadup (who would see him more than once again) and to Todd. "In that moment," David wrote later, "we three, all happening to be very large men, defined a triangular space in which considerable energy was trapped." David interpreted for the other two. Todd gave Feng a book he had written (in English) and told him to attend Bible classes. This Feng did, in the home of the C. T. Wang whom David had recently taken into the Lecture Bureau and who was long afterward to be premier of China. And in due course this young officer became the legendary Chinese "Christian General"—but that is a later story.

ANOTHER sealed envelope is torn open:

> FEEL THAT MY DUTY TO THE PUBLIC INTEREST OBLIGES
> ME TO URGE RECONSIDERATION ON YOUR PART. THE
> INTERESTS OF CHINA AND OF THE CHRISTIAN WORLD
> ARE SO INTIMATELY INVOLVED.
>
>   WILSON

Todd knows his mind. He again declines.

ONE MORE EVENT of the Peking campaign needs recording. It only took a few moments, long enough for three handshakes, but it was of enormous symbolic consequence.

David Treadup had just finished his lecture on aviation in what was still being called the Imperial University. He joined Todd and Nieh off the platform. A man of about forty came forward dressed, not, as so many of the revolutionaries were, in Western clothes, but in the fine silks of an old-style man. Nieh recognized him at once, and introduced him to the two huge Americans. His name was Liang Ch'i-ch'ao.

Probably Todd had no idea of Liang's importance. Indeed, it is questionable whether Treadup did, either; what he notes in his diary is discolored by vanity:

> Nieh introduced us to Mr. Liang, a member of the Peking Y.M.C.A. Board of Directors. He thanked me for my lecture, said he wished China had more vigorous men like T'a Hsien-sheng (Todd's Chinese moniker) and T'ao Hsien-sheng (me, of course!).

Liang Ch'i-ch'ao's membership on the Association board, though it was what gave symbolic importance to the handshakes with Nieh, "T'a," and "T'ao," was the least of his distinctions. Liang had been one of the students of the great reformer K'ang Yu-wei, and like K'ang he had fled for his life after the collapse of the reforms of 1898; he had lived in exile in Japan for fourteen years, and had returned to China only with the abdication of the Manchus. During the years of his exile he had through his writings become the most important Chinese voice, next to that of Sun Yat-sen, in calling for a modernized China. Liang's essential message was that more than new armies, technology, industry, universities, or laws, China needed a new kind of Chinese, with a new set of values—a "new citizen" (hsin-min). The term was taken from the classic Great Learning, but Liang gave it a new meaning, applicable to the humblest of people. The Chinese, he wrote, needed a new system of values. Each person must trust his own thoughts and not depend on the authority of the sages or of the past; he must not be "the slave of custom," "the slave of his environment," or "the slave of his passions and desires." He must have a "consciousness of rights"—must not wait to have his rights bestowed on him by a benevolent ruler; he must actively seek them for himself. He must, moreover, cultivate the civic virtues of the citizens of modern nations—a sense of responsibility, self-respect, and self-discipline. Liang was calling, in other words, for much more than the overthrow of the Manchus; he was calling for a great moral revolution.

In this call—all of it new at the time of its utterance—Liang shaped many of the basic assumptions of twentieth-century Chinese thought. They were assumptions shared by conservatives and radicals alike. Years later Mao Tse-tung told Edgar Snow that as a youth he had "worshiped K'ang Yu-wei and Liang Ch'i-ch'ao," that he had "read and reread" Liang's writings in the Hsin-min ts'ung-pao (The New Citizen) until "he knew them by heart." Liang was popularly known as Jen-kung, and for a time Mao adopted the alias Tzu-jen, or "follower of Liang."

In the period of highest hopes after the fall of the Manchus and his return to Peking, Liang had seen in the Y.M.C.A. a group which, though originally foreign, was turning its leadership over to the Chinese, and which was working in its way for the moral regeneration he had so long urged. Liang remained a Confucian, but he joined the Association's Board of Directors, and now, in this moment charged with meaning, he touched hands with Nieh, Todd, and Treadup. It was a symbolic climax of a week that had brought together, in a gossamer web of associations, the highest hopes of a rollcall of remarkable Chinese names: the grandfather Tseng Kuo-fan, the Self-Strengthener; the teacher-reformer K'ang Yu-wei; Liang Ch'i-ch'ao of *The New Citizen;* Yuan Shih-k'ai, who bridged the empire and the Republic; the future "Christian General," Feng Yu-hsiang; the murdered Sung Chiao-jen, founder of the Kuomintang, the party of Sun Yat-sen and Chiang Kai-shek; and the still potential Mao Tse-tung.

The configuration of hopes personified on the American side by David Treadup and James B. Todd (and Woodrow Wilson) would somehow, for baffling reasons, come open at the seams; and indeed the Chinese hopes would lose their cohesion, as Yuan turned out to be a powermonger, Liang a conservative, Feng finally not a Christian but a Communist sympathizer, Sun a disappointment, Chiang a reactionary, and Mao a Marxist emperor. But all that was to be a long, sad story for the unfolding future, and at the moment of the handshakes after the Treadup lecture on flying machines, wonderful things — great marvels in China! — seemed altogether possible.

score of the Peking lectures: Treadup, 15,900; Todd, 8,000.

THE LAST STOP of the tour was Foochow, where cholera had vanished in the cold weather along with flies. On the night before the Foochow meetings were to begin, Todd, Treadup, and Nieh went to pray together in a quiet cemetery where Foochow's missionary and Chinese Christian martyrs lay buried — "eleven mounds — eleven modest headstones," Todd wrote later,

> *of men and women who had died most gruesomely, as if wolves and buzzards had ripped them open. The angry Chinese mob had seen the missionaries as "foreign devils," but I feel that we would never have been able to address the vast and receptive crowds of the next few days, had it not been for the groundwork laid down years ago by those brave souls before they offered their bodies up in Christ-like sacrifice.*

The meetings were indeed huge. The Provincial Parliament adjourned and invited Treadup and Todd to speak before it; the Confucian presidents of thirteen government colleges postponed examinations for a week so their students could attend; and in a remarkable innovation, the team held one meeting for women only — two thousand strong.

The Foochow score: Treadup, 15,300; Todd, 13,000.

W H E N I T W A S all over and David had returned to Shanghai, to Emily and Philip and Absolom and the laboratory, he was, as never before, sure of his mission. In a glowing letter to his Syracuse constituents, he modestly referred to the science lectures as merely "the entering wedge" for the Todd campaign, but about that he wrote: "I know of nothing in the Christianizing history of China from the arrival of the Nestorians till now that surpasses the work of these few weeks." Behind the modesty lay his knowledge, which the scorecard had given him, that his words had been much more than a wedge. He was more highly valued by Chinese listeners than the man who had been asked by Woodrow Wilson to be Minister to China. The numbers suggested that nothing in Christianizing history in China since those Nestorians in the fifth century A.D. had surpassed *his* work. A few days after his return to Shanghai, news came, on May 2, of the recognition of the Republic of China by the United States of America, and David could think that by having introduced Todd to Yuan he had played at least a small part in that outcome.

At the same time, the echoes in his mind of the applause of the huge crowds on the tour were troubled now by insistent murmurs of doubt. One other number the scorecard yielded was the sum of all the inquirers from thirteen cities: 7,057. Seven thousand out of four hundred million! David vividly remembered the emphasis with which Joshua Bagnall, in that conversation in the tearoom of the Astor Hotel after the Centenary Conference, had said that "the annual increase in population is *three million.* . . . We have to bring 'em in by the million or give up the idea of converting China at all. . . . " How many of the 7,057 who were inquiring would eventually become Christians? Blackton showed Treadup a disquieting letter from Hong Kong about the follow-ups by "personal workers" in that city:

> *Time after time has the report been given of the worker going to visit the men and being unable to find them. In some cases wrong addresses have been given. In others the "inquirer" was afraid to see the visitor fearing that he had some money-making scheme in mind. Unspeakable difficulties have been put in the way.*

"**W E H A V E** again become familiar with the sights and sounds of war," David wrote New York on July 17. For the Chinese news had suddenly turned sour. In June Yuan had dismissed three Kuomintang provincial military governors, and on July 12 one of them declared war on Yuan, beginning what came to be called the Second Revolution. From the outset, this uprising, in which Sun Yat-sen participated, was an unmitigated disaster for those who challenged Yuan's power. Americans were against it and gave it no chance of success. As the fighting had begun in Shanghai, Consul General Amos P. Wilder (father of Thornton Wilder) predicted it would fail because the grievances against Yuan were not sufficient to get the populace behind it. David's New York letter:

> *For four nights the booming of cannon has had the constant underroar of rifle fire interspersed with the ripping buzz of machine guns. The government troops are holding out in the Arsenal. We have no personal concern of danger here in the foreign Settlement. All boundary lines between the Settlement and the Chinese city are barricaded, with regulars from the navies and volunteers from the Settlement manning the guns. Yesterday the Settlement's officers took action, expelling the revolutionary leaders, and also causing the evacuation of the rebel general's headquarters behind the Settlement.*
>
> *There is no excuse or basis for a successful counterrevolution. China is tired of it. Commercial men are against it. The menace from without is serious. President Yuan has done better than anyone else could have hoped to do, and is now in a strong position. The row is due to malcontent politicians and, I believe, cannot succeed. Sun Yat-sen's part in it is bad for us. We were once proud of his Christianity, but now it may prove to be an embarrassment. I came back from the tour with Todd on the crest of a wave, but now I fear a reaction against us in Peking because Sun and several of his people are Christians. In the meantime, there is lots of work right here—for the refugees, houses and food; for the wounded, hospitals and doctors and nurses; for the dead, a rough coffin with a red cross on the end of it. Pray that that sign may come to its full significance in our needy field. China is in peril. Pray for her.*

Whether or not as a result of prayers, the Second Revolution was quickly suppressed, and Sun Yat-sen once more fled into exile.

THE REACTION David feared came all too soon. In August he noted in his diary:

> *Blackie showed me a letter from C. T. Wang which says there is a movement on foot in Peking to make Confucianism a state religion. Wang says that if this turns out to be a success, it will be embodied into the Permanent Constitution, and that would greatly curb the growing influence of Christianity.*

Behind this movement was the revered reformer K'ang Yu-wei, who was joined by many literati; they, like K'ang, clung to Chinese values of the past.

C. T. Wang, as it turned out, formed a committee of seven influential Christians, and they were able to quash the move. The flurry, however, dramatized the fragility of the gains of the great Todd-Treadup tour.

DAVID was still aglow from the successes of the tour and, no doubt, from the numbers on the scorecard. On September 16, Emily presented him with his third son, whom the Treadups named Paul in honor both of David's beloved brother and of Christ's greatest missionary. David was busy in the lab, designing new lectures: "High and Low Temperatures," "Wonders of Light," "Sound and Some Recent Advances," "High and Low Pressure Electrical Phenomena," "Scientific Measurements," and "Marvels in Astronomy." He knew now that he was a confirmed success as a missionary. Everyone told him so. Yet as he happily worked he kept worrying, he wrote in his diary, about that fragility, about the two troublesome numbers—seven thousand and four hundred million.

Then one day, while he was building some gear for the sound lecture, he was struck by an idea. The diary that night:

> I have it! A test! We'll send out half a dozen teams, on the Todd-Treadup model, and see how far we can get with evangelizing an entire province. Then if that works—

The entry breaks off, with the lingering eloquence of incompletion.

THE TEST

IN WHAT he wrote about it at the time, "The Great Test," as David came to call the provincial experiment, seems to have been nothing more than an adventurer's probe into a native heartland. He presents much of the trip as an outdoorsman's camping junket with two dear Chinese friends. The farm boy responded to the bare essentials of life on a backcountry river. He was ever afterward nostalgic about the trip, as if it had been his last sweet voyage before the loss of innocence. At the time he seemed to be hiding the real meaning of the trip from himself. He gave very few words to the actual campaign, to its science lectures and evangelistic meetings, and least of all to the significance of the test itself: to the reckoning whether, in the phrase of Joshua Bagnall, missionaries might have to "give up the idea of converting

China at all." One of his companions on the trip wrote when it was over, in a cryptic expression of the doubts all three travelers must have felt, "Who can tell the results of the Fukien Evangelistic Campaign? Or of the whole great Christian missionary enterprise in China? We will not know until we all gather around the throne of God on high." David himself was forced, in due course, to draw some conclusions from it that were more down-to-earth.

THE BUREAU chose Fukien Province. Foochow, its capital, a city then of about a million, at the mouth of the important Min River, on the coast opposite the northern tip of Taiwan, was where Dr. Charles and Treadup had earned great credit with their anticholera campaign. From that city missionaries had long since penetrated much of Fukien Province, with as great success as in any part of China. It seemed a likely place for the test.

The Lecture Bureau decided to use five teams in Fukien, composed of a science lecturer and an evangelistic speaker each. The teams assembled at Foochow on August 1, 1914 (the day, as it happened, on which Germany declared war against Russia; two days later came the German declaration of war against France and the invasion of Luxembourg and Belgium—but Treadup and the others knew nothing of that for weeks). All the lecturers but Treadup were Chinese; one of them, to his joy, was Teacher Chuan. The two Davids would comprise Team I, Treadup as the science lecturer and Liu as the evangelist; they would be joined by Y. Y. Han, of the Bureau's Conservation Section, who wanted to tour Fukien because it was one of the best-forested provinces in a China that over the centuries had devastated so much of its woodlands. Team I, equipped with the wireless lecture, would ascend the Min River to Yenping, then go overland to Kienning, then to Kienyang, and from there three days by land to the strong mission station at Shaowu, on the headwaters of the Min. Teams II, III, IV, and V would fan out elsewhere through the province.

The first task was to equip and train those other teams. Liu and Treadup had brought down from Shanghai every bit of demonstration apparatus they could assemble; they supplemented it with scientific equipment borrowed from Foochow University. For backcountry traveling all the apparatus had to be packed to be carried by bearers using shoulder poles, and Liu and Treadup had bamboo baskets made in Foochow, some round, some squarish, some long and narrow, to fit the instruments.

Early in September they were ready to set out. The journey of Team I to their first lecture city would have to be made in three stages: First, on a small junk with sleeping quarters, hauled upstream by night by trackers on the riverbank to a landing stage. Second, on a steam launch, towing a barge, departing at dawn for a daylong run to the river port of Chui Kou. And third, three days by small houseboat to Yenping.

AT THE BEGINNING of the trip, David Treadup is in a zestful state of mind. He must still be buoyed by the sense of worth that the Treadup-Todd scorecard has given him. He is at the top of his hill. Each crisis is an entertainment. He reports dangers as if they were moves in a game. He is fascinated most of all by the primitive but sound mechanics the boatmen use to push and pull a wooden mass through a resisting flow of water. The first night:

David is sleeping soundly on his folding cot under the arching mat roof of the junk's cabin. Suddenly there are shouts forward. He scrambles out on deck. He can make out that the trackers and crewmen are trying to maneuver the junk between the stone piers of a bridge at a place where there are rapids in the river. Double towlines have been rigged, one to straining coolies up on the bridge, one through the span of bridge and far beyond to trackers on the right bank. Crewmen are fending the vessel off the stone piers with poles. David can make out wild whitish froth on wave tops of the dashing water. The precious wireless apparatus is heaped under a covering of jute sacks amidships. The junk yaws and falls back with a sudden jerk; men cry out in panic. The lines hold. The junk inches forward. With a lurch like that of an exhausted frightened creature heaving itself into a safe lair, it climbs the upper lip of the rapids and shoots forward onto smooth water. The boatmen are sullen. David crawls back onto his bedroll. Later in his diary:

> *The law of the parallelogram of forces! Towlines, fending poles, current, rudder—the resultant of vector quantities represented in magnitude, direction, and sense by two sides of a parallelogram ect. ect. Beautiful!!*

Again, he makes notes on an ingenious mechanical device: The towline is attached to the top of a flexible five-foot post set in a hole in the deck near the bow. "Magnificent! The post bends a little with the tug of each unison stride that the trackers take, and that bending, together with the elasticity of the sag of the line, distributes and makes constant the strain on the men's shoulders!"

DAWN. They have been up for an hour, supervising the loading of the gear onto the barge. David and his friends are summoned to board the launch. On the simple principle, much honored in China, that guarded goods do not evaporate into thin air, the three decide to ride on the barge, along with their gear and a mountain of bags of grain thrown aboard every which way. Scores of copper fish—poor river people who have paid a few coppers for passage upriver—share with these gentry crowded perches atop the grain bags. The river sights of morning are lovely; by noon David feels drugged by beauty and by memories of a shouty night. He spots a boxlike cabin amidships, almost buried by grain bags, with access from its roof through a trap door. He gets David Liu to shout to the Lao Ta ("the Old Big," the captain) on the launch for permission for the three to nap in that box. They let themselves down into it. There is headroom for Liu and Han but not for the hairy one. The box seems too narrow for the three to lie down side by side. David reasons: Men are wedge-shaped. He lies down with his feet to starboard; Liu and Han on either side of him with their feet to port. The ill-assorted triplets dream in the womb of the barge.

AT CHUI KOU the local Chinese pastor, alerted beforehand, was down to meet them and had three boats already hired for the trip to Yenping. The vessels were clean and trim, with a boatworthy varnish finish. They were long narrow craft like huge canoes, with about a foot's width of walkway along each side deck, and a living space amidships just wide enough for a couple of folding cots, and a second cabin aft for the boatmen. Treadup embarked on the first boat with his cot and baggage; Liu and Han on the second; and on the third, A Ch'u and the team's cook, with all the bamboo baskets of lecture equipment and the party's baskets of food and utensils. David was worried about A Ch'u; he was having stomach pains.

The team slept on the boats that night. At dawn the boatmen started off poling in the shallow river. In David's meticulous notes on the mechanics of poling, there appears for the first time a hint of what is to become one of the central themes of David's self-doubt in the next few months: the thought that in endlessly repeating the same lectures he is stagnating, that he is not growing in power for God, that he is "Treadup on a treadmill."

> At the extreme bow two crewmen, one on either side, set their poles slantwise on the bottom and facing aft walk along the narrow deck with their shoulders braced against the upper ends of the poles. At the stern each gives a final stiff push-pull, for momentum and to free the pole from the bottom, and then walks the pole forward for another fore-and-aft propulsive walk. How terrible! Over and over again. They walk the full distance of the voyage, but always the same few paces on the same wooden path, back and forth, like caged animals.

ONE ENTRY, which starts out as a celebration of friendship, turns out to be the deflation of a romantic ideal. "Evenings are best," David wrote. At sunset the rivermen ran the boats up on a sand bar or sandy beach and drove a sharpened pole down hard into the ground through a hole in the bow of each boat, as anchor. The cook had been busy on the third boat, and he served a steaming supper to the men sitting on the sand. "I greatly enjoyed these suppers," David wrote later, *and the chats we had. We got very near to one another on this trip, and David Liu told us some intimate stories — especially about the outbreak of the Great Revolution, October 10, 1911, just three years back. I began praising the courage of the Leader [Li Yuan-hung?], whom I had met in Wuchang. "Not so brave," he said. Then he told what had happened. (I have never before or since heard this story.) David was one of a band of young college men who were with this Leader, and they were urging him to step out and start the revolution, which all China was waiting for. But the Leader refused and finally mounted his horse and was going to gallop off. The young men surrounded him, one aimed a pistol at his head and forced him to get off his horse and lead them in the stroke that was to sweep victoriously over all China. So started the great revolution that changed an Empire of 400,000,000 to a Republic!*

A SOMEWHAT COMICAL (cultural imperialism, reverse twist department) proof that the friendship between Treadup, Liu, and Han was real and tender — yet fragile — is found in one playful note in the diary:

Back in Shanghai I consulted David and Y. Y. on what they would want to eat on the long journey. They both said, "Oh, we'll live off the country. We'll buy rice and whatever we need as we go, in villages and cities; but you take along anything you as a foreigner eat that we wouldn't be able to buy upcountry." I said, "I like rice and eggs and all that, so I won't take much of anything. There's really only one thing extra I want. Jam. Shall I put some in for you, too?" "Oh, no, " they said. "We're Chinese, we'll live off the country as the people do." So I carefully estimated how much jam I would like each day, multiplied it by the number of days, and put in that exact stock divided between plum, apricot, and strawberry. The first day out, at breakfast on the boat, I opened a can of strawberry jam. I didn't like to be discourteous in eating it all alone, so I said to David and Y. Y., "Won't you have some?" David hesitated a second and said, "Well, I'll take just a taste." And Y. Y. would have "just a taste," too. Next meal it was the same, and the next, and the next. Naturally by Yenping, all my beloved stock was gone. Fortunately, Mrs. Bankhart, a kindly missionary lady at Yenping, came to my rescue and sold me all I wanted out of her large stock; she then ordered again from Foochow. I had to snicker! My friends were Chinese patriots but oh, that foreign jam which they had learned to love at Yale and Harvard!

THE DIARY notes one casual exchange which planted a new and probably disturbing idea in David Treadup's mind: that instead of trying to convert all of China, perhaps the best way to work would be within a microcosm —to provide a compelling local example for the country at large to follow. This idea took a decade to come to fruition in David's life.

One evening David Liu pulled from a pocket a telegram that had been delivered to him as they were loading the barge at Chui Kou. "This is a typical Chinese trick," he said, laughing. The telegram:

AS OF THIS DATE YOU ARE APPOINTED GENERAL MANAGER OF TIENTSIN–PUKOW RAILROAD.

He explained he had several times been urged to accept this position, but he had steadfastly refused to leave the Y.M.C.A. His friends, he said, had taken this way of trying to make him take it.

David asked him what he would really like most to do.

"I would like," Liu said, "to be made magistrate of a *hsien* [district with a seat in a second-class walled city] and be given a free hand to see what I could do with it."

ANOTHER AFTERNOON the boats were hauled up for the night earlier than usual, and the three went for a walk ahead along the towpath. When they returned Han noticed that his prized foreign steamer rug was missing. At the first town on the shore the next morning Han and Liu went to the magistrate's yamen, explained who they were, said they would be known all up the river, and pointed out that it would give his district a bad name when everyone learned that these important visitors had been robbed there.

When the team reached Yenping, the rug was waiting for them. David's diary: "Cops and robbers know each other in China!"

"THE CHINESE," David wrote with blind foresight in another entry, "may be selfish at times, but when they are up against it, they have an instinct for socialism." As the little fleet had approached Yenping, he had seen ahead, "gleaming in the sunlight," an abrupt short stretch of rapids, almost as steep as a low dam, and he wondered how they were going to get up it. He found that the Chinese had worked out a way "hundreds of years ago." They waited until enough upstream boats had gathered. Then all the boatmen, as many as a hundred, joined each other on a long bamboo towline and "by brute communal strength" hauled, one by one, their and each other's boats up the rushing slope.

AT YENPING, David Treadup lectured for two days on the wireless, then David Liu for two days on "Jesus Christ, the Hope of China." This is all David records, except: "Worried about A Ch'u."

From Yenping the team walked along a cow path all day, for twenty miles, to Kienning. Here again David's notes are offhand. He writes only that in the meetings held in a Confucian temple, David Liu, delivering his evangelical message with some politics thrown in, ran into the old-fashioned local authority system. As he spoke of the evils of graft and injustice among government officials, the most revered local elder, obviously a rich literatus, thumped his cane on the floor in approval of Liu's criticisms; only after that signal was it safe for others in the audience to applaud. After one meeting Liu received a tribute in the form of a letter from a young man inviting him to join a secret society planning revolution against Yuan Shih-k'ai.

IN KIENYANG, the next stop, Treadup, looking for the best large space in which to set up the Telefunken sending apparatus, persuaded the district's Buddhist abbot to let the team use the main temple for their lectures. The abbot led him into a hall where a man was kneeling on a mat praying to an eight-foot image of Buddha. Treadup drew back and closed the door to the hall, and said, "We mustn't disturb him at his devotions." The abbot pushed the door open and said, "He can come any time." The man got up and left. Treadup said, "What about him?"—pointing at the Buddha. "Will he be disturbed?" The abbot said, "Look at his smile." So "with approval of man and god," as David wrote in his diary, he set up his science demonstration right in front of the benign fat idol. And in that same spot, two days later, David Liu urged one flock after another to sign for Jesus.

NEXT CAME a three-day journey to Shaowu. The members of the team were tired, so they decided to go by sedan chair. A Ch'u, being of the working class, would normally have had to walk, but David insisted that he be carried in a chair. Much of the trip was on a level plain. "We figured," David wrote, "that if there had been a good hard-surfaced road, the journey that was taking us three days could have been made in a good automobile in one hour!" The second day was cold and rainy; it often poured. "We started out in the sedan chairs, but soon compassion for the coolies (my weight 195) got the best of me, and I got down and walked; so did Liu and Han. Loyal A Ch'u wanted to, but I wouldn't let him." The travelers were like muddied wet sparrows when they staggered into a village inn at Ma Sze. They put down three coppers each for a "bed"—a wide wooden board. They were blue from cold and wet. Here at last came the reward for foresight Treadup had had in Shanghai before they had set out:

I had had our mechanics in the lab make up a 5-gallon Standard Oil tin into a portable stove, 2½" × 5" damper hole in bottom with sliding door, hole with replaceable cover in top to insert fuel, corner round hole to insert chimney pipe. Then! Best feature! Lengths of pipe just long enough to stow within the can, with fitted ends, capable of being assembled into a long chimney out of that corner hole. All the way upcountry David and Y. Y. had been teasing me about this piece of "unnecessary" baggage — but not after Ma Sze! We set the gadget up on a base of bricks, fitted the chimney pipes together and put the end out through a hole in the paper pane of the window, and soon had a fire of sticks going merrily. Oh boy! No anthracite stove or blazing wood fireplace fire had ever felt so good in all my life!

THE NEXT AFTERNOON they reached Shaowu. The city magistrate authorized their use of the Confucian temple and provided benches for indoor and outdoor seating for two thousand. Before the first lecture David went with a missionary host to make sure everything was in order. On the pathway to the hall they saw a pigtail on the ground, then another and another. The missionary was startled, because in some nearby cities *heads* of revolutionaries had been coming off. They hurried to the gateway to question the guards. Just as they got there, a young landowner still wearing a backcountry queue entered the gate. A uniformed guard with a huge pair of shears stepped from behind the great door, stopped the man, cut off his pigtail, and handed it to him. The shorn man took a few steps looking at the queue, did not know what to do with it, and finally threw it down in disgust. The guard said the magistrate had told them, "This is a modern, scientific lecture, and everybody who attends it must have a modern haircut."

IN SHAOWU David sought out a medical missionary to examine A Ch'u. The man he found was named Dr. Ezra Finn. Dr. Finn, David wrote, was "like the Ancient Mariner — has a long gray beard and glittering eye." He said that A Ch'u's complaint was definitely not appendicitis; the best thing would be to get him back to Shanghai as soon as possible, where he could be X-rayed and tested in the hospital. "Sure enough," David wrote, "after the last meeting, the Ancient Mariner stoppeth one of three — me — holds me with his skinny hand, and says, 'I have things to show you.'" He wanted David to see the health conditions in the back alleyways of the city. They took a tour by sedan chair. "That morning, to Dr. Finn's delight," David wrote, "I saw every known form of decaying and suppurating and crudding and scaling human flesh. And the flowers of smallpox! Every little child, it seemed, with the red pimples of recovery. How many dead out of sight?" Dr. Finn made his point: Lectures on wireless telegraphy? Why not on smallpox? Why not on child care? He said he had recently been in the home of a fellow missionary who was entertaining some Chinese friends, among them one of the brightest young Chinese teachers in a mission school. The teacher noticed the hostess diluting milk for a formula for her infant child. He asked in surprise: "Do you have to dilute milk for your children?" The mother said it would be extremely dangerous to give a baby whole milk. Then in dismay the teacher asked: "Do you also have to dilute the condensed milk you foreigners have?" Of course. It needed *much* more dilution. "That," the man said, "must be the cause of the death of my little girl. Two weeks ago we were given some tins of it, and my wife and I thought it must be a wonderful nourishment."

F R O M   S H A O W U, the last stop for Team I, A Ch'u went alone by the fastest route down the Min River to Foochow, and then by ship to Shanghai; he insisted on taking charge of his beloved Wireless lecture apparatus. Treadup, Liu, and Han took a one-day trip by chair northwest over hills to a branch of the Tien River, which led to Nanchang, capital of Kiangsi Province. At the Tien tributary they hired a large houseboat. Treadup foresight was again rewarded: he had brought a double-barreled field shotgun, for he had heard that there were two kinds of population pressure in central China: of humankind and waterfowl. After sundown their houseboat floated on glowing sheets of dusk. Soon the water was black with birds; from inwheeling flights of geese and ducks Treadup bagged many good meals.

At Nanchang they rode on wheelbarrows to the city gate. There an armed guard allowed Treadup, a foreigner, to pass but took Liu and Han to the command post with their baggage for inspection. On the way, David Liu realized with alarm that he had carelessly left right near the top of his suitcase the letter from the young revolutionary in Kienning, inviting him to join a conspiracy against Yuan Shih-k'ai. He had reason to be alarmed. China may have become a republic, but its petty officials had not yet broken long-standing habits of impulsive decapitation. David's diary:

> BUT—who do you suppose this commander was? David's classmate at the missionary college in Shanghai, St. John's! They were delighted to see each other, fell into each other's arms—and all was hunky-dory! Such is China in these days of the great revolution!

From Nanchang they took a steamboat across Poyang Lake to Kiukiang, and there they caught a Yangtze River steamer down the river to Shanghai, and home.

Y E S, they had kept a scorecard. The columns on it encoded much that David may have been trying to hide from himself. In the Fukien campaign, in round figures, 2,800 men had signed cards of inquiry. Out of four hundred million Chinese. David, noting these raw numbers long before he was able to think through the results of the Great Test, entered in his diary two bleak words: "I wonder."

IN ''S E A R C H'':

We had just arrived. We were unloading the gear at 29 Quinsan Gardens. I met Teacher Chuan in the hall outside the Lecture Bureau lab. It was obvious to all of us that the campaign had been a failure; the Treadup-Todd pattern would not Evangelize the World in a Million Years. I remember with utmost pain the look in Teacher Chuan's eyes there in the hall. He had been so important to me. He had given me the gift of the Chinese language; introduced me to the Chinese classics; responded, with thrilling excitement, to my first inspiration for the science lectures; confessed to me his addiction; conquered it in my honor; and accepted my recruiting him to the Lecture Bureau without the slightest resentment of my assuming power over him.

It was an X-ray look he gave me. Right through me, casting shadows of my inner self against the far wall. That look asked terrible questions. Is it all over? What are you going to do with me now? Do you remember our days in Kuling; in Paoting? Do you remember my tears? Are you a Christian? What are your true thoughts now about China's future?

I am not proud of the answering look I gave him. It did not answer any of his questions. I was down about our "test." My look must have said, "Chuan, am I my brother's keeper?" I went into the lab and closed the door behind me. I can hear, now, the click of the door latch. I will never forget passing Chuan in the hall, walking out of his life and closing the door.

From then on, I saw less and less of him. He was kept on by the Lecture Bureau, but I think David Liu thought of him as one of Treadup's mistakes.

MISGIVINGS

THE EQUIPMENT from the Fukien trip was at the lab, still packed in its baskets. A Ch'u was not there, and none of the lab workmen had seen him. He had left no message. He was not at the hospital. David went to his hovel of a home, off an alley in the Chinese city, and found him there, comatose on a brick *k'ang*.

David rushed frantically around town until he found Dr. Charles and the two men hurried to A Ch'u's house. A Ch'u had recovered consciousness and was fairly lucid. The two men had just got his consent to their hospitalizing him when the Chinese doctor who had been treating him arrived, an old-style gentleman in slightly threadbare silks, with the black beard of fifty hairs of a wise man waving from his chin tip. Here was a sensitive moment of contesting authorities, in which A Ch'u's devotion to the magician of Western science was put on the scales with his traditional Chinese pride, delicacy, and courtesy. A Ch'u said he had been having acupuncture treatments for four days; he would like one more. The Chinese doctor "took a needle several inches long from a case and stabbed it four times full length into A Ch'u's abdomen." Soon Dr. Charles said he could not stand by and watch any more of this. Unsterilized! He pointed out to Treadup the angry inflammation around the puncture holes of previous treatments. Peritonitis was certain. The Chinese doctor suffered a massive loss of face. The patient passed out. Dr. Charles hurried off to the hospital to set up an exploratory operation. Treadup went out for a conveyance; he thought a mule cart with a bedroll on it would be the quickest thing to find and get ready. He returned to A Ch'u's in fifteen minutes and found him dead.

DAVID TREADUP'S mourning for his assistant grew in a complex way into something much bigger than itself. At first he was full of A Ch'u's loyalty, alertness, ingenuity, and skill:

> *If in Shanghai we were out on a search for some hard-to-find piece of apparatus, he would look out to see that I was not run down by streetcars, automobiles, and the like. He was always thinking ahead and saying, "Now if we don't look out it will be 'lai pu chi' ('come not around')."*

Six months before, A Ch'u had "decided for the Christian life," and two days after he died the Lecture Department staff and other friends gathered in the tiny house for a short Christian funeral service. David

> *helped carry the coffin across the fields to the Christian burying grounds on the outskirts of Shanghai. There, by an awful coincidence, I noticed that one of the gravediggers who helped let the coffin down was blind in one eye, the other fast losing its sight. We asked, and we learned that when he had had some disease in one eye, a Chinese doctor had punctured it and then, with the same needle, the other, causing it to become infected. The constant wholesale ruin of lives by ignorance and*

malpractice in China puts iron in one's blood to be doing something about it.

For a long time there had been no anger in David, but in the next few days, he wrote, "I reached in my quiver of arrows and pulled out one with a poisoned tip that I could only call a shaft of resentment." He testified that he felt the "bitter unfairness" of the red pimples of smallpox on the faces of the children in Fukien, the "appalling waste" of the cholera in Foochow. News had just come of a cruel outbreak of pneumonic plague in North China. David thought of the anguish of the teacher in Shaowu, understanding that the foreign condensed milk in which he had had such faith had killed his baby daughter. Suddenly David virtually collapsed; for two days, off and on, he sobbed in Emily's patient arms. "I realized, with great shame, that I was crying out against Jehovah at last, at last, for taking away our little Nancy."

Then one night he was jolted out of a deep sleep and sitting up in bed was terrified by the sight of a finger pointing at him. It seemed real — slightly gnarled by arthritis and stiff with rebuke. He could not sleep the rest of the night. In the morning, while he was shaving, he deciphered the vision — a memory, he realized, not a dream: Dr. Ezra Finn's accusing finger looming in his face in the Shaowu street. *Lectures on wireless telegraphy, when there is all this suffering around us?*

DAVID rose at dawn, dressed in his rowing togs, and took a ricksha to the Rowing Club. He rowed hard on the river. Afterward he carried his shell back into the boathouse and set it up in its place on the layered racks. He was about to turn away to leave, when — as he reported for the first time many years later, in "Search" — he felt himself in the grip of an old familiar impulse. "I don't think I knew what I was doing," he wrote. He reached up and grasped the rigger of the singles shell just above *Ecarg II* on the racks and pulled, wrenching the craft off its supports and letting it crash sideways to the boathouse floor.

> *I did not even bother to check and see whether its landing on the end of its rigger damaged the scull. The worst of it was that I felt so happy as I did it. It was if I were setting myself free in some mysterious way. I still cannot understand it.*

We have no way of knowing whether David ever acknowledged what he had done; whether he might have explained it away as an accident; or whether, if the shell was damaged, he made amends, either openly or anonymously. All we see in the diary at the time are these brief notes: "Feeling at sixes and sevens." And, a few days later: "Turned things upside down at the lab."

We can deduce from subsequent reports what the latter note meant. Some time in those next few days David apparently persuaded his colleagues to uproot all the work that was being done on his own most beloved subjects — "Wonders of Light," "Marvels in Astronomy," "High and Low Pressure Electrical Phenomena" — and to concentrate on developing lectures on public health. By this time Dr. Charles had completed his two years of language study, and he and David together now began to assemble the demonstration materials for several lectures: "Sanitation in a Chinese City," "Prevention of TB," "Flies Kill People," "Cholera," "Bubonic Plague," "First Aid." David seems to have thrown himself into this work with all his usual energy and outward enthusiasm, but we can tell from what surfaced in the next few weeks that he must have been struggling to keep his footing against a powerful psychic undertow.

• For the tuberculosis lecture Treadup and Charles designed, and the Chinese workmen built, a vivid exhibit of the death rate from the disease: a Chinese man walks out of his house and falls into his coffin — one every thirty-seven seconds.

• To dramatize the value of social cooperation in mass public-health campaigns, they constructed two panoramas, operated by electrical motors. On one, many men turn small wheels in different directions and at different speeds; on the other, their combined and coordinated efforts at small wheels make a huge central wheel go round.

• The laboratory workmen crafted with startling realism two large heads: the clear and benign face of a clean-living man, a paradigm of glowing health; and the ravaged, wrinkled, burnt-out, scabrous, soul-stung, and unrepentant face of a man who has ignored all the laws of hygiene.

• The hookworm exhibit had no mercy on the squeamish: a glass case containing arms and legs with sores; a life-sized boy showing the symptoms of an extreme case — sores, emaciation, pallor, a pot belly, the face of an old man.

WITHIN A FEW WEEKS J. R. Charles was on the road, in Hunan Province, and he began sending back ebullient messages:

> The race is on, the horse's tail is in the air, the driver's hat is far behind in the dust — no time to mention details.

> The crowds on the second night were so great the streets were blocked, the police helpless, and we finally had to shut down the lantern-slide lectures. We were not prepared for such crowds. We almost had a riot, the people were fighting to get in.

Here [in Changsha] *600 students, headed by two brass bands, bearing flags and banners with antituberculosis slogans ("Don't spit on the floor!"), marched through the streets. As crowds emerged from side streets and alleys, the students handed out thousands of leaflets, giving simple facts in simple language. At the principal street corners, student speakers with charts addressed the gathered masses. Now! Note this! Immediately behind the antituberculosis parade came a procession of sixteen condemned criminals being marched to the execution grounds. Each had a long spear tied upright behind his back, marking him as a man about to have his head amputated. The contrast between the old and the new could not have been lost even on the poorest and least educated citizens.*

We have established seven plague inoculation centers. The chief of police is raising a fund to help him buy dead rats and to give further inoculation to 10,000 people. We have already sent to India for $500-worth of serum to start with.

O N E   D A Y a party of students from the Institute for the Chinese Blind visited the Shanghai Lecture Bureau laboratory. Five of the staff each took a small group and guided their hands over the different pieces of apparatus. What David wrote of this experience reveals the unsteady movement of his state of mind during this period—in its swings from sensitivity and generosity to bleakness, self-doubt, and impatience:

How eagerly they felt things! How intent the expression of their faces, even the posture of their heads, as they took in the wonderful new conceptions!—the big alternating-current electromagnet: the flying machine: the gyroscope: the wireless telegraph. The flickering of amazements in their facial muscles as we began to get these different pieces into operation— with the big gyro sweeping around in a five-foot circle, to hold out their fingertips to feel it as it went by and to realize how it swung through space without any apparent means of support—and then the start of the aeroplane in a wide circle around the room, the group huddled in the center, swiveling their heads as they followed its path by the sound of the propeller—then the cocking of their ears to the buzzing messages of the wireless as we listened to the signals of the battleships up and down the ten miles of river between here and the sea! How open they were to new sensations and new ideas! They thrilled me and disturbed me. I shivered with envy. What was it that they were seeing behind those shut windows of theirs that I had never been able to see? Was it a dimension of time? The immanence of a deity within these wonders—no matter whether Christian or not—an ordering intelligence of some kind? Whatever it was, I felt dull to it. The hands I guided to feel the apparatus trembled; mine did not. Who in that room was truly blind—they or I?

THE OUTWARD MOTIONS of David's normal life went on. He had been
booked for another tour in northern and central China, with the three dependable mainstays: gyroscope, aeroplane, wireless — to Mukden, Tientsin, Paoting
(under the Republic, the city's name had been shortened), Peking, Wuchang,
Changsha. David's existence had been so headlong and so exciting that he
had never felt the slightest need of vacations, and he and his family had not
had a summer break in Kuling or Peitaiho for more than four years; this time,
by way of compensation, Blackton approved his taking Emily and the children
with him on tour. Their company made the trip seem — at least at first —
festive, a vacation in itself even though he was lecturing. The start was
impressive. In Mukden he gave an outdoor lecture on the wireless which was
attended by the biggest single crowd he had ever had, ten thousand boys and
men, standing on their feet to listen. "The police used a clever scheme," he
wrote, "to keep the crowd from surging too close to the apparatus: they got
several rows of boys in front to sit down on the ground."

In Peking, however, two things happened which were followed by a sharp
downturn in Treadup's spirits. While setting up the wireless apparatus before
a lecture, his new assistant, a man named Ching, who had been showing
promising aptitudes in the Shanghai laboratory, dropped the receiver to the
floor; the glass tube of the coherer broke; Treadup had a spare, but the lecture
was delayed nearly an hour, with a hall full of Peking luminaries — "the most
important audience since the lecture before Sun Yat-sen in Nanking," David
bitterly commented. The diary: "What bothered me most was that I was so
bothered. I imagined I saw *the finger* while I was lecturing."

Two days later he heard the conservation demonstration by his friend
Y. Y. Han, with material from the Fukien trip worked into it. He wrote in his
diary that he did not like it. "Shallow." In the next sentence he rushed in with
Christian charity: "Not that Y. Y. was shallow. It struck me that the method is.
The method is mine, not his."

We gather from later correspondence that during the Paoting stopover
Treadup had at least one long talk with Letitia Selden, in which he evidently
poured out some of the doubts that had been building in his mind ever since
the death of A Ch'u. On the surface, however, the Paoting visit was a most
happy one, especially for Emily, seeing old friends and having them coo
over her children. Even Miss Titty's young yokefellow, Miss Demestrie, was
less jealous and gloomy than usual. David and Emily took some of the familiar
walks together. But underneath Treadup's dogged cheerfulness, a gnawing
was going on. "Prayed for the souls of the martyrs," David wrote. Somewhere at the root of his unease the old romantic fantasy of Syracuse days —
of selflessly giving much more than he had so far been able to give, giving
one's *all*, even one's very life, as Jesus did, for love of others — must have
been at work.

Changsha, November 5, 1914.

My beloved Miss Titty:

 We approached Changsha from the river, rather dismal in the rain, the city straggling up over a hill to the left. The stone flagging of the streets is coated at this season with black mud. But they are broad streets, and the people in them seem to me better looking, healthier, and happier than those in the cities where more foreigners have penetrated. (I've seen Sage, by the way, of the Yale school here — friend from my Kuling language-school days.) There's more self-respect and indepen-dence among the Chinese here, you find neither that groveling servility nor ill-concealed dislike that is so common in the "settlements." Fewer beggars. The faces of some of the commonest laborers seem robust and luminous.

 Or do I imagine all that solidity and strength? I wish for it in myself. You were so good to let me unburden myself. I value the afterglow of the touch of your hand on my cheek! Will you bear with me if I tell you — it is easier to be truthful at this remove — that I don't think I told you the half of my concern?

 You see, I think I was trying to make myself seem worthy in your eyes. I am unworthy. I must stand naked before you. Where can I begin? My lectures? It is easy to dazzle, and I enjoy it too much. I am addicted to applause, to excited laughter, to the total silence of amazement fol-lowed by murmuring in the audience. I need more and more. I have begun to wonder about the real effect of the lectures. I told you about Han's conservation lecture, my sense of the shallowness of what I had spawned. It is my shallowness. Han's show depends on mechanical tricks I invented — the flood! Oh, things like that thrill the audience, but I'm afraid that in the end all we are left with is entertainment. The audience is more interested in the devices behind the magic — the tank from which the deluge pours and the collecting tank under the table that receives it — than they are in taking home a determination to reforest China. I fear for our holding power with the social message — is it really any better than that of street preaching or that of our old fanatical itinerators, with their message of salvation? What then of the gospel message that is supposed to lie behind my social message?

 I told you of the amazing results Dr. Charles is having. They rankle with me. He is having a bigger success than mine. I think I am envious of Charles's happiness and high spirits — isn't that awful? I feel that my pocket has been picked. They are taking my idea away from me. (I realize that I freely gave it to them, yet I have this awful feeling of having been robbed.) I feel a petty anger at being copied and absorbed into the very Bureau I invented. I devised the whole enterprise, yet now I am just one of its lecturers.

Forgive my trying to be honest with you. You were always so understanding. Your loving hand calmed me. I am so ashamed. The worst of my shame lies in my secret feelings about my Chinese colleagues. Our whole purpose is to plant seed and then leave and let it grow in native soil. When Ching dropped the receiver and the coherer was broken I spoke to him in an undertone (lest others hear) as if he were an idiot. He was spoiling 'my' show. A Ch'u would never have dropped it, I might have, but the real point is that I know that I would never have spoken to an American, to Blackie or Bert Wood or anyone, no matter what clumsy thing they did, in the tone I used with Ching.

The hostility of Chinese toward me fills me with agony. There is a school principal in Shanghai with whom I have been trying to do personal work. But he finally asked me not to try to convert him. He said, "It is like asking me to identify with everything I hate," and I realized that when you think about it, it is me he hates, not some faraway Jesus.

Help me, Miss Titty. Write to me. I don't want to be a small person. My foot is slipping.

With needful love,
David

WE MAY wonder at David's entrusting these deep misgivings to Letitia Selden. Was he unable, or unwilling, to discuss them with Emily?

Emily seems to have made her peace with her husband's periodic absences; with being "alone." Almost as remarkably — or improbably — as if she were a wife accepting a husband's philanderings, she had accepted his wanderings. "His legs itch when he sits still," she writes as if with a shrug in a letter to her family. In one diary entry David himself recalls the trip he took with Uncle Don Treadup's circus when he was eleven: "From that time on I've needed the open road." Emily's remarkably serene nature has helped her adjust to this physical restlessness of David's; she has kept active, apparently without the edge of anger, in good works in Shanghai, and the three children delight her, even though they cause anxieties. From Emily's letters to her sisters, spanning several months:

The flies and mosquitoes are pestiferous, even as late as this. Paulie got so badly chewed last night that I could have spent today weeping over him and my own criminal qualities. I had seen that his net was tight when I tucked him in, but somehow the mattress got wriggled loose and the mosquitoes just flocked in. The swellings are down tonight, so the bites look more like measles than smallpox.

Paul has been gaining weight fast. He's going to be big as his dad one day — healthily round and solid as a pumpkin. He's the happiest one we've had, grins at anything or nothing. Maybe he's an imbecile — but just try to prove it to us!

We had a scare about possible scarlet fever with Abbo last week, but his fever has gone down.

The best goat is sick with a goat disease that affects her hind legs with a sort of paralysis, and no one here knows how to cure her. The other gives only about a quart a day, and as soon as she is bred will dry up, I suppose, so we shall have to buy milk all winter. I'm about ready to adopt Klim and evaporated milk and let the goat business fade into oblivion.

But in the late fall, David hardly notices the children; at times he is brusquely impatient with them. He is suffering an emotional restlessness which cannot be relieved by mere motion, mere travel. So far as we can tell, however, this unease of his, while Emily notices its toll on the children, seems not to have harmed the life she shares with him, seems not to have shaken either the prevailing surface calm of the marriage or the underlying power of its carnal side. Among the rather somber notations in David's diary, we still come across exclamations like these: "What a ruby I have!" "Em is my better self!" "Lucky husband!"

Yet there is something strange in his apparently not sharing his deep and painful soul-searching with Emily. On her part there seems to be more at work than Christian acceptance, or than a conditioned accommodation to "woman's place," in her unvarying quietude of spirit. Whatever it is, the serenity it produces is both wonderfully attractive and perhaps, to a restless man, both forbidding and confining. On his side, there is a powerful need to be calmed by his "better self," as he calls Emily; and a powerful if puzzling need, too, to get away from it, or her, from time to time.

AT DAWN of the winter solstice, December 23, 1913, President Yuan Shih-k'ai had driven from his Peking palace in an armored car, over streets entirely covered with yellow sand and lined three-deep with soldiers who had been stationed along the route the night before, to the exquisite round Altar of Heaven, on the southern edge of the city. Each year, for centuries before the republican revolution, the Emperor had been the only human being privileged to pray to heaven in that magic circle. When the President's cortege arrived at the gate south of the Altar, he transferred to a horse-drawn vermilion coach, which took him to the Altar. He rode in a sedan chair up into the temple. Two generals helped him change from his field marshal's uniform into a robe of royal purple with twelve round dragon designs, and a headgear of ancient Imperial design. Then he prayed; "I, Yuan Shih-k'ai, representing the Republic of China . . . "

There had been many portents like this that Yuan aspired to be more than a mere President. He had outlawed the Kuomintang Party, dissolved the National Assembly, replaced the republican Provisional Constitution with a Constitutional Compact which gave him dictatorial powers. Obviously dreaming of paths of golden sand and the nine strings of beads on the hat of an emperor, he faced the realities of 1914, saw that the European powers were taken up with the war in Europe and that to be installed and secure as emperor he would need the support of Japan.

That country had rank ambitions of its own. After the outbreak of the war, it had seized the German protectorate in Shantung Province and during the fall began to enlarge it. On January 18, 1915, the Japanese Minister Hioki handed Yuan a paper watermarked with dreadnoughts and machine guns on which were written twenty-one demands on China. In effect, these would reduce China to a satellite of Japan; would put Shantung Province, southern Manchuria, and eastern Inner Mongolia under Japanese control, and would greatly encroach on British interests in the Yangtze Valley. Minister Hioki was remarkably frank with American Minister Paul S. Reinsch: "When there is a fire in a jeweler's shop, the neighbors cannot be expected to refrain from helping themselves."

Several months of what passed for negotiation followed. In May, Yuan accepted the substance and the humiliation of all but the most devastating handful of the Twenty-one Demands. The Chinese people reacted with an unprecedented fury. Mass rallies in the big cities called on the government to resist Japan. Ricksha pullers, coolies, students, small shopkeepers donated money to finance an army of resistance. Nineteen of Yuan's own generals declared they were ready to fight to defend China. Instead of encouraging these signs of an awakening nationalism, Yuan suppressed them. And on December 12, 1915, he "accepted," as if it had been thrust upon him, the throne of an emperor of China.

Many of Yuan's most influential advisers and generals suddenly fell ill and found it necessary to retire from public life. A general named Ts'ai O, who was famously in love with a prostitute, persuaded Yuan that he had caught a venereal disease and got his permission to go to Japan for treatment. Instead he went secretly to Shanghai, where he consulted with others who opposed the monarchy, including Liang Ch'i-ch'ao—the onetime reformer and voice of *The New Citizen,* and Y.M.C.A. board member, whose hand Treadup had shaken during the Todd tour. Liang's powerful pen helped to rally an army under Ts'ai O, and on March 22, 1916, Yuan Shih-k'ai, having lost decisive battles, abdicated the throne. On June 6 the overreaching "strong man" died, as the old stories would have it, of a broken heart.

All this left China's government in disarray, and there followed a decade in which provincial warlords fought each other for national and local power.

In these events Treadup saw the crumbling of the wonderful high hopes for the missionary enterprise, and for his own role in the evangelization and modernization of China, that the 1912 revolution had brought. And with them, his personal misgivings were confirmed and deepened. But his was a remarkably vigorous temperament; his confessions to Letitia Selden had seemed to purge and refresh him; and soon he was entering in his diary blurted expressions of his will to carry on in the face of all his doubts.

A few months after Yuan's death a warlord enticed him into an experience which started him thinking about his mission in an entirely new way.

THE CHRISTIAN GENERAL

EAST TIENTSIN railroad station platform, April 1917. Chaos. Some kind of troop movement is under way. The discipline of the uniformed men is unusually good, but the coolies who are loading equipment run here and there shouting at the tops of their lungs, trainmen are hysterical, and a bee swarm of ordinary passengers who have been put off the train to make way for the soldiers is buzzing its protests and trying to push its way back aboard.

Treadup, Ching, and three workmen from the Shanghai lab are trying to shepherd the lecture gear onto one of the third-class passenger carriages of the type that is simply a freight gondola car with slightly lowered side walls, open to the sky.

Treadup, on yet another swing north with his lectures, is distracted and tired. Among the parcels of apparatus, now, are outfits for "Wonders of Light" and "Marvels in Astronomy," but even with these new topics he has been feeling the dead weight of repetition; the phrase "Treadup on a treadmill" has recently appeared in his diary for the first time. Besides, deeply unsettling word came a few days ago that on April 6 the United States entered the conflict in Europe, so that this bustling of soldiery reaches subliminally into some obscure region of patriotic outrage and anger in David; he blurts in his diary later this very day: " 'Thou shalt not kill'—but I don't like being so safe when my brothers . . . " The sentence breaks off.

He hurries ahead to one of the open third-class gondola cars, and begins to dicker with an officer for space enough for the lecture goods. He senses that being a foreigner and being a huge man are, for once, of no help. The officer firmly denies him the space. He pulls his wallet from his pocket and slips some bills half out, but the officer shakes his head. Treadup is astonished—a Chinese soldier who won't take a cash push! Ching has now joined him; other officers ring the man Treadup has been talking with. It is obvious that a high hand will not be effective. Ching politely asks who the officer's commander is.

The officer says it is General Feng Yu-hsiang.

Treadup and Ching both shout with pleasure. They recognize this as the name of "the Christian General," about whom they have heard so much. Ching hastily tells the officer that Treadup is with the Young Men's Christian Association. The officer softens at once, bows, apologizes for his rudeness, and turns to command his men to make room in the car for the boxes of apparatus.

Treadup asks where the General can be found. The officer says that he is in his "private car." It is four cars forward. Treadup looks for a velvet-curtained first-class carriage but finds instead that General Feng's "private car" is just one more open gondola. And there—not having made the connection before—he sees the huge soldier who came forward at the Todd lecture in Peking four years ago. He is dressed in a plain cotton uniform like those of his common soldiers; he sits among piles of duffel with a group of enlisted men. He instantly recognizes Treadup, recalling the day of "Mr. Todd's teachings," and he invites Treadup to ride with him. He and his men are going to the military camp at Langfang, between Tientsin and Peking.

During their ride through the countryside, Feng asks Treadup about his work. As Treadup describes it, Feng in all his hugeness cuts at the air with his hands, stretches his face this way and that, groans with pleasure at what he is hearing. He insists that Treadup must come and lecture to his troops. They are mostly poor farmers, he says—but eager to learn about the world of machines. Treadup says he grew up on a farm. Feng roars, claps his hands, and asks his men if they heard what the *ta mu-shih*, this big missionary, has said. A farmer! Delighted laughter all around.

IT IS doubtful whether David Treadup had any sense yet of the real nature of the nascent warlord system of which General Feng was to be such a vivid and mercurial representative in the next decade. Treadup was naturally excited to encounter the already famous Christian General. "My thrill that day in the railroad car," Treadup wrote from the safe distance of "Search,"

> was, I guess, understandable, but it was also, in some unfortunate way, undiscriminating. I realize now how strongly attracted I was to any Chinese leader who was touched, no matter how lightly, with the Christian brush, and who gave hopes, no matter how real, of gaining power enough to change China.

So had it been, indeed, in Treadup's almost fawning attitude, at first, toward Li Yuan-hung, who had favored religious freedom and had been so hospitable to the missionary Treadup; toward Sun Yat-sen, himself a Christian, converted in his youth; toward Yuan Shih-k'ai, who had early declared to the Christian community his support of freedom of religion, and who even earlier had directly helped Treadup; and now with this boomingly cordial man, the Christian General. And would be, one day, at least for a while, with Chiang Kai-shek, married to a Christian woman and himself eventually converted.

The warlord system, a product of the breakdown after Yuan's death of any true national authority, was an almost animal arrangement of regional hegemonies. The warlords were like bull sea lions or great buffaloes or bighorn rams establishing and fighting to defend the territories where they would be supreme. They gave off heat waves of vigor, grandeur, and greed. Years later Pearl Buck would write:

> Without exception the warlords I have known have been men of unusual native ability, gifted with peculiar personal charm, with imagination and strength, and often with a rude poetic quality. Above all, they carry about with them, in them, a sense of high drama. The warlord sees himself great—and great in the traditional manner of heroes of ancient fiction and history who are so inextricably mingled in the old Chinese novels. He is, in effect, an actor by nature, as Napoleon was. The warlord is a creature of emotion; cruel or merciful, as the whim is; dangerous and unstable as friend or enemy; licentious and usually fond of luxury.

Big warlords came to control areas as large as Germany or France; at the other extreme some petty warlords controlled no more than a few villages and might be pocketed within the territories of grander ones. The only difference between most warlords and bandits was that warlords controlled territory while bandits hit and ran. There was a circular logic in warlordism: A warlord needed an army to control a territory that would support an army. It was easy to recruit soldiers: poverty-ridden farmers, younger brothers, hungry jobless youths, glad to be clothed, fed, sometimes even paid, or at least given chances to loot. Since greed for power and money was the commanders' driving motive, battles were often dances, or discreet surrenders, or "victories" in which the only bullets fired were silver. "We shall undoubtedly win," said an officer of one conflict in which Feng was to be engaged. "It is simply a matter of waiting for treason." "China's wars," a Chinese admiral said, "are always civil."

Not always, in fact. Some, where relatively great power was at stake, were earnest and bloody, with bitter fighting and many casualties. The treachery was often cruel. One way of capturing an army was to invite its commander to a banquet, stuff him, seize him, and shoot him. Many units were superbly trained; Feng's were. Most of the arms came from foreigners. This caused great resentment: In all the wars, one intellectual wrote, the rifles and field guns come from abroad. The bullets and shells come from abroad. Bombs and powder and hardware all come from abroad. The money comes from abroad. . . . Only the blood and flesh of our dead countrymen who kill one another on the battlefields are Chinese.

A deep, voiceless, and futile resentment against the warlords would come eventually from the Chinese people, who were tragically oppressed by the greed that was built into the system. In the hands of the warlords, the land tax became a tool of frightful exploitation. Taxes were sometimes collected for years in advance. Ingenuity galloped on greed's back, and here and there we find a pig-rearing tax, firecracker tax, opium-smoking lamp tax, marrying off one's daughter tax, narcissus bulb tax, superstition tax (on candles, paper money for funerals, etc.), lower-class prostitute singing tax, and, terrible thought, night-soil tax, so that one couldn't even defecate without paying. The people suffered horribly in other ways. Carts and donkeys and boats and wheelbarrows were seized; men were conscripted and torn from their homes as cartmen, porters, or boatmen. Disorderly troops robbed, looted, beat, raped, and burned. Masses of the population were in constant flight from place to place. During plague, flood, and famine, the warlords indifferently taxed and taxed. This next decade of their ravaging wars was to prepare the way, among the bitterly harassed common people, for China's larger revolution to come.

BACK IN SHANGHAI, David wrote his brother Paul about the train ride with General Feng:

I have every intention of visiting his encampment and lecturing to his men. It will be a great challenge: to speak to Chinese farmers and working men who live in a Christian setting. I will have to remember that I am not addressing the literati; I must pitch my discourse to simple hearts. There will be a great tension in it, between clarity and God's truth. By that I mean: To make the laws of physics that govern the gyroscope clear to raw, untutored minds, I must take short-cuts, simplify, use rather crude mind-pictures, and tell much less than the whole truth, which would only confuse. Yet what I want to teach the Chinese, above all, is a love of exactitude. I know that in the Christian General's camp I will have to teach exactitude inexactly. That will be painful.

But necessary! This man may well come to power, and if he does, think what a boost it will be for our cause! In his way he is a missionary. He sat there in the train on a bedroll, with his legs crossed — he is huge — big gestures — elastic face — and he talked to me about the stages of his coming to Christ.

He said he was the son of a poor soldier, and he joined the army when he was a small boy. The first stage was rank superstition. Soon after his enlistment, an epidemic broke out in Paotingfu, where he was stationed—smallpox, probably, or plague—and his unit was ordered to go through the streets shooting rifles just to make a noise to put to flight the evil spirits that were thought to be causing the disease. He told me he vividly remembers having fired at a sign in front of a Christian church. Foreign devils!

Next stage, puckishness. He went to that same church out of idle curiosity, listened to some sermons. The preacher talked about turning the other cheek—"If someone takes your outer clothing, give him your inner clothing, too." Feng and some friends carried a table out of the church rooms. The minister stopped them with roars of outrage. In mimicked pulpit tones they said he should be offering them the chairs that went with it! But Christ's message apparently didn't reach that far, and he made them return the table.

But next, gratitude. He was sick, and after failing to get help from Chinese doctors, he received it free on two occasions from missionary doctors, and when he tried to thank them they told him to thank God.

Then, he said, he became impressed by Chinese Christians, who never smoked opium, were industrious, always educated their children even if they were poor, and did not bind their daughters' feet. He said he admired those simple things and thought that if all China could follow such rules, the nation might "find a way."

And finally he began reading Christian literature and attending church. A particular sermon he heard in Manchuria moved him to the soles of his feet—and then James B. Todd in Peking! I wrote you about meeting him that day. Tears glistened in his eyes when he talked about Todd's message.

He is such a feeling man. Emotions seem to rise from deep in him and burst on the surface, like big bubbles of air from the depths of a lake. While we were talking about recent events, he told me that when Yuan Shih-k'ai declared himself emperor, he wanted so badly to go and fight Yuan that he cried until his head ached—and even as he said this, he began to weep! He embraced me, Paul, when he detrained at Langfang, just as you, my dear brother, might have done. . . .

There is a great deal of evidence, especially from Feng's later history, that he was a shrewd and devious man, and many in China came to think that he may have cynically put Christianity on, as if it were a new fashion of clothing, in order to ingratiate himself with powerful foreigners, and in order to bewitch his troops with a ritualistic mystique like that of the Taipings. Years later, when his allegiances had begun to swerve with opportunity, he gave a mixed picture of his motives:

During the last years of the Manchu dynasty, revolutionaries were being arrested right and left. Therefore many of us became Christians in order to avoid difficulties. Moreover, that faith had its good points. It proposed universal love, sacrifice, no smoking or drinking, no gambling or chasing after women . . .

It is obvious from Treadup's letters and diary that he had no inkling of Feng's calculating side. The actor in Feng took him in. The ripples and bounces of strong emotion on the Christian General's "elastic" face must especially have appealed to David in his time of misgivings; he needed the reassurance of the sincerity of salt tears brimming in eyes of power.

DURING HIS SUMMER in Shanghai, Treadup learned that a so-called Chinese Labor Corps had been formed and sent to France to dig trenches and offload ships and supply human backs, arms, and legs for the supply lines of the Allies; and that there was some talk on the British end of asking the Y.M.C.A. to furnish canteens and other services to help ease the growing unrest of the Chinese coolies, who had found their life in a hostile alien setting brutally harsh and dangerous. Treadup took note of this news briefly in his diary, without comment.

IT WAS mid-September before Treadup could travel north again. General Feng sent an "honor guard" to Tientsin to accompany him to Langfang. Its commanding officer told Treadup that this might not prove to be the best time for a visit, because there were said to be floods to the southwest of Tientsin; the waters were still rising, and General Feng might move his whole force out to give help to the refugees.

Treadup arrived at the camp of the 16th Mixed Brigade at suppertime. The General greeted him warmly: bear hugged bear. Feng said he would not be moving to the flood area for at least a few days. "No lamps," David wrote in his diary. "A bugler put the troops to barracks not long after dark. Impressive discipline of silence thereafter."

There was sufficient reason for early quiet: reveille came at four the next morning.

The day that then began in the darkness of the North China plain was "my most thrilling in China," David wrote. There was so much to stir him — first of all, an air of male exuberance, men shouting and singing, always on the run, willing and cheerful under pressure of fierce and sometimes nasty competition: the Chinese gift for laughter given free play by high morale. All day, the movement of faith: prayer, hymn singing, Bible reading — images of the evangelization of the whole world in one generation! And a martial spirit with no signs of real blood. From the beginnings of David Treadup's recruit-

ment by the Student Volunteer Movement there had been the idea of evangelization as a struggle of Christian soldiers against heathenism. "It is war,"
David had written on his first arrival in Tientsin, "and I as a general must be
willing to face even death." Now there was a subtle undercurrent of another
attraction of militarism: David Treadup's feelings of guilt toward his "brothers"
under arms in France. David's blood brothers, like himself, were by now too
old to enlist as soldiers (David was thirty-nine); his guilt reached out to a
larger and more figurative, but no less poignant, fraternity. It now extended to
this "brother General in Christ," Feng, and to these "brothers in the arms of
God," his officers and men—as the diary would have it after this ecstatic day.
From a report to Todd in New York:

> *The first order of the day after dressing was a bit of spiritual drill. The*
> *brigade assembled by companies in the open air in the quiet of first light.*
> *They sang! Oh, the singing all day! At dawn; at noon; the last thing at*
> *night. Before meals, at meals, as they march. The faces of the men show*
> *the heartiness of the singing as unmistakably as the continuous full-*
> *voiced shout. (The power of the 'pianissimo' to move the listener has not*
> *been discovered as yet by the Christian soldiers of the Sixteenth.) Their*
> *favorite song, needless to say, is "Onward Christian Soldiers." They roar*
> *out—in Chinese, of course—"Stand Up, Stand Up for Jesus! Ye Soldiers*
> *of the Cross," "Room for Thee," "All People that on Earth Do Dwell," and*
> *"O Happy Day." And the good General has written some words of his*
> *own to hymn music: There's a patriotic song of his called "The Nation's*
> *Shame," and then there's "We Must Not Gamble or Visit Whores."*

General Feng in person took Treadup around the encampment to show
him "how to keep an army busy." "He made it seem as if it were all being
staged just for me." During an inspection of one unit, David was impressed by
the General's courtesy to his men. He knew the names of an astonishing
number of enlisted men. He pointed out to David a notice posted outside a
headquarters tent: "Eight No-Hitting Rules," placing strict restraints on officers'
rights to beat soldiers, the most important being that they must use bare
hands, must never use sticks or rifles or shovels.

"Feng is like Coach Ten Eyck: 'You can't win if you aren't strong.' " On
the exercise ground some men were jumping, vaulting on a gym horse, and
doing bar exercises "with quite an amount of freak displays." David watched
obstacle races: "a long jump over a ditch; a run along a narrow baulks bridge
across a pit; the swarming of first a brick wall, then a higher wooden barrier,
and ending in a final run up a steep mound." Pairs of officers competed
against pairs of men and nearly always defeated them, but "there was rarely
more than a second or two between the first to reach the goal and the fourth."
One unit went off in the countryside on the double under full pack. "The
General said they would run twenty-five li"—nearly ten miles.

On another field Feng's elite company, the *Ta-tao-tui,* the Big Sword Unit, in which each man carried a pistol, a rifle, and a large curving sword, was running through a dazzling series of dancelike exercises, their blades flashing in the sunlight. General Feng called one of the men over and showed Treadup the patch on his uniform that read:

> When we fight, we first use bullets; when the bullets are gone, we use bayonets; when the bayonets are dull, we use the rifle barrel; when this is broken, we use our fists; when our fists are broken, we bite.

"But what moved me most, almost to tears like those that actually stood in the General's eyes when we entered the building and saw the men bending over their work," David wrote, "was the *school!*" The General wanted his men to learn a trade while they were in his army, so they would have a means of support when they went home. "As you pass through one room after another you see the young men busily engaged in making shoes and clothes, knitting stockings, weaving rugs, boiling soap, and making chairs and other articles of furniture." But the reading classes! The General himself had written a lesson book of eight hundred basic characters, and "here were illiterate farm and coolie youths chanting their excitement at their march into the sacred ancient region of literacy. What optimism! What a dream for all of China!" And: "He told me missionaries had inspired much of this. He has a school for the children of his officers in the Methodist mission in Peking."

At twelve o'clock a gun was fired. Ten minutes later the men gathered by companies outside their quarters for half an hour of Bible reading and prayer. They formed circles of about ten each. First they sang a hymn, then officers or noncoms would read a chapter in the New Testament "verse about, often with brief explanations, followed by a number of earnest petitions from the men."

THE AFTERNOON was set aside for the *ta mu-shih.* At the edge of the parade ground was an earthen platform about six feet high from which Feng's speeches and foreign missionaries' and Chinese ministers' sermons were customarily delivered. Treadup told the General that he needed more space for the apparatus of his gyroscope demonstration than that platform gave. Fine! They would enlarge the platform. They would make a game of it. The General ordered two companies to compete in digging and carrying earth to add two wings to the existing mound, widening it until it would be large enough; the companies would race to see which could complete its side first. "How zestful the men were! They dug earth from an area where a road is being widened, outside the camp, and carried it in baskets to the mound—running, shouting, laughing. If only human beings could be like that all the time!"

By about two o'clock, the stage was all made, the earth tamped down hard. With the help of Ching and the lab men, Treadup set up his gear. Feng assembled the troops. "My heart was pounding. Could I rouse in these uneducated men anything like the *life force* I had seen on their faces when they were running obstacle races or building my stage—or singing to the glory of God?"

Treadup got his answer with the very first demonstration: the chain loop that could run and climb a ladder. "There was a kind of rumble," he wrote,

> as if intelligence could cause earthquakes, and then an explosion of violent laughter—a laughter, it seemed, of utter relief, as if a great danger had passed, a danger that they might never have had a chance to see such a magical event. Their response was so much more visceral than that of the literati, intense as that had been in its way. There was an earth-moving energy in it of groundlings catching just a glimpse of the possibility of a better life. I felt relief, too, but I was shaken. I felt that I was losing my grip on an idea that I had clung to ever since my talk with Joshua Bagnall—that my duty as a missionary was to teach from the top down. Here was a hunger as sharp as that of the famine victims at Yang Ts'un. It shook me, in much the way those famished faces there at Yang Ts'un had shaken me.

General Feng was declared to be the strongest man in the army, and it was *he* whom the men chose to pit against the Wrestling Gyroscope. And then that the great and beloved hero of the brigade should be defeated and rendered impotent by the physical laws of God—after all the time in which his prayers for victory in the field had *brought* victory, and all the time in which his wishes had been the wishes of his lowliest private!

> There was complete silence. I could hear crows cawing in the distance. An eerie, eerie, eerie moment. I believe that that long hush has transformed me. I have a different sort of work to do than I had thought.

FLOOD

A CHANCE EXPERIENCE of the next two weeks hastened the outcome of what Treadup had thought of as his transformation.

He wanted to see his dear friend Lin Fu-chen in Tientsin, and he asked the Tientsin Association secretary, Roscoe Hersey, if he could stop over with him for two nights. The Herseys, with three children, nine, seven, and three years old, now lived in one of a pair of handsome brick-and-stucco houses the Association had built, on Recreation Road in the British Concession. While the family was at supper with their guest on the first evening of his visit, a messenger came to tell them that the floods to the southwest of the city were spreading, and that the river that ran through Tientsin, the Pei Ho, was dangerously high; it was expected to crest and overflow its banks the next day.

The Hersey house was surrounded by a brick wall, which would dam out floodwaters, but it had two wooden gates, which would not. Hersey fetched some burlap bags from the attic of the house and had the three servants dig up earth from the yard to fill the bags, which Hersey and Treadup then set firmly in the gateways. Everyone went to bed feeling secure. "We promptly got a demonstration," David wrote,

> of the not-to-be-denied power of "China's sorrow." I was sleeping on the Herseys' sleeping porch, and just as it was getting light I was awakened by a weird swishing and bubbling sound. I got up and looked out. There was water in the street. The walls and gates had held, all right, but now the water was simply bubbling up from beneath, all through the yard.

By ten o'clock the water was hip deep in the street and slightly shallower in the yard. Hersey, learning that trains were still running, decided to send his family off without delay, before it would be too late, to the hills of Peitaiho by the sea. A sampan picked them up shortly after noon.

TREADUP was caught. Every hand would now be needed. The city authorities, knowing from experience that the flood of water would be followed at once by a human flood, a cresting wave of homeless, penniless, sick, and starving refugees, quickly organized a relief committee, of which it was to be Hersey's lot, this time, to be chairman. Within a week the peaked waters had slowly drained off toward the sea. In order to make a reconnaissance of the worst-flooded area, the committee chartered a large native houseboat and stocked it with emergency supplies, food, money, and medicines. Because of Treadup's intimidating build—there would be great danger from bandits—Hersey asked him to go along. Hersey, three doctors, four armed and uniformed British volunteers, and Treadup made up the foreign party; several Chinese were also aboard. Treadup sent a wireless message to his new friend General Feng, telling him of the rescue vessel's first destination, a stop on the Grand Canal, and asking for a guard unit from the 16th Mixed Brigade.

From a letter to Emily, in which David seemed to be groping toward telling her that some great change, which he himself could not yet clearly picture, was impending in their lives:

We spent the day ashore. The high water simply dissolved many of these houses made of mud and straw. Much of the population has fled, but some, loath to leave their few belongings, stayed. How many were cut off and drowned, refusing to be taken away from all they had in the world? We entered standing houses — wretchedness everywhere, a muddy 'k'ang,' two or three poor pieces of furniture, huddled people sick from the dampness breathed forth from walls and floors, others out begging. We went from place to place, handing out chits for ten, fifteen, twenty-five, and fifty cents (gold), which the people could take to the houseboat and exchange for food or Chinese money.

We returned to our boat about sundown. Feng's guard had not showed up. All day I had been thinking that these ruins were what was left of the hovels and families of men just like those to whom I'd lectured a few days ago: Think of the absurdity, here, of that essence of the whirling weighted wheel that I'd rhapsodized about, God's stabilizing force in nature! The boat was too packed for us to eat inside, so we had the table placed out on deck. There we pretended to partake of our dinner, but we had no appetite for it. As soon as possible we stretched ourselves out on the roof of the deckhouse, among long oars and boat hooks.

Small junks and sampans were crowding around us. We were soon surrounded by them and found it useless to ask them to move farther on. We had treasures aboard — survival stuffs. In greater and greater numbers they came, until the anchorage was choked with them. There was sullen self-constraint in the air, and a change was feared. I knew there was no use going below, so for some hours I lay under the stars and tried to keep calm.

A boat carrying Chinese musicians was moving about. One player beat rhythmically on a resonant strip of bamboo, another sawed on a one-stringed violin, a third sang shrilly in a high falsetto. Another boat moved about with refreshments — imagine it, profiteers in this zone of empty guts! — cold jelly, peanuts, and — no foreigner would want to think what else.

The vendor calls out his wares in a monotone or hits a little bell at regular intervals. A watchman ashore moves from one quarter to another, sounding his conch shell from unexpected directions. There is a quarrel among some of the boatmen. Every man in any way interested joins in and they all shout and curse at once. Are they arguing about boarding us? No one can hear what anyone else is saying, and the trouble comes to a natural ending, with exhaustion. I know it is after midnight. I lie sleeplessly. Low voices sounding here and there across the still water prove that mine is not the only wakeful mind.

Suddenly there is a noise, so loud, so startling, that I spring up. It is a hoarse yell from many throats. "Thief! Thief!" It seems that the boatmen are always ready for this threat, and when a tiny sampan stealthily sculls alongside, or a suspicious figure creeps along the shore, one sailor cries out, and the cry instantly travels up and down all the boats.

The cry subsides. I am left in a turmoil of bleak thoughts. I realize what a shock I received in General Feng's camp—a shock of the discovery, after all these years of misdirected labor, of the audience I now think I should have been trying to reach. An audience far too large for one man, or one Association, to reach—the audience of "the poor and needy" whose "year of Jubilee," in Joshua Bagnall's phrase, was so long overdue. "Don't ever forget that, Mr. Treadup." But Bagnall was wrong: Knowledge did not run downhill with the natural ease of gravity from the literati to poor people like Feng's soldiers and the victims of this flood.

And then, to confuse me, this: This fear of thievery. I lay on the roof of the deckhouse afraid that the mob of boatmen in the anchorage would swarm onto our privileged vessel to ransack it; while on each boat the water people lay in fear that the starving victims of the flood would steal from them; and on shore the poor villagers had risked life, and lost it, some of them, rather than lose what paltry nothings they owned.

Ignorance, poverty, suspicion, envy, brigandage—yet the soldiers at Langfang, sons of these boatmen and these villagers, were so cheerful, so exuberant! Something in the heritage of having lived crowded and suffering lives for 3000 years had given the Chinese this mysterious range of responses to life. Could my sharing my knowledge of God's laws of the forces of rotating bodies ever touch and change those versatile ancient responses? I have to believe that it will. It is my life's work. I have nothing left otherwise.

It was quiet again. Then new sounds stirred. On every boat there was scurrying, for rain was coming. Sails were covered, doors were closed, hatch boards were slid into place. We crowded into the deckhouse. We were shut in without a breath of air. The rain drummed—rain on top of flood rain on top of the flat land—China's deep and seemingly endless grief. I wondered, Emily: Would my life be long enough?

AT THE END of the second week it was Lin Fu-chen—a member of Hersey's relief committee—who took Treadup to see one of the consequences of the flood. For it was in the Peikai district on the north rim of Tientsin, near Lin's new university, that the huddled masses of flood victims had set up their terrifying encampment: thousands of improvised huts, some made of straw matting, others of the ubiquitous rectangular Standard Oil petroleum tins, cut open and beaten flat and hung like fish scales to make crude shelters, their cheerfully flashing reflections of the sun blinding one to the squalor beneath. The thousands driven here by water had had no water to drink. They had scooped it from drainage ditches and from shallow holes dug near their huts; and now the camp raged with dysentery. Lin had loaned the committee rooms at the college for a Camp Office, a dispensary, a clothing depot.

Standing with Treadup at the heart of the camp, surrounded by supplicating faceless crowds, Lin asked with an irony that, though it was almost drowned in the sadness of his Christian eyes, hit with startling accuracy the bull's-eye of David's discomfort at that very moment: "Would you like to give these people one of your lectures? Perhaps you have worked up a lecture on 'The Wonders of Hydraulic Power'?"

"Felt so angry," David wrote in his diary.

Angry that I did not know what to be angry at? At — can I write it? — at the riddle in God's plan? Could not shake from my mind a bewildering connection between the picture of these hollow-eyed ghost-faces and the memory of the faces of Feng's soldiers (sons of these people?) building my stage, running, shouting — such high spirits!

A FEW DAYS after Treadup arrived back in Shanghai, we know from a spare note in his diary, a general call went out from the National Committee of the Y.M.C.A. for secretaries — American and Chinese — to volunteer to go to France to work with the Chinese Labor Corps there. For one who was so prone to set down on paper the struggles of his heart, David was remarkably silent about what followed. We have almost no clues to the discussions of great consequence he must have had with Emily. Only such notes as: "Tuckered out from talking all night." "She is granite." What did he mean by "granite"? That she was dependable, or immovable? Perhaps his conflicts were such that he could not, just then, face their implications. The decision he reached in a very few days, to go to France, certainly did not resolve them. It evidently stemmed from the "transformation" he felt had taken place in him on his last trip north; but it must have seemed an expensive choice, for it would mean being separated from his family for an indefinite period, and it would mean breaking away from his beloved lecture program and leaving in midair the question of what the proper audience for it really should be; leaving in midair, therefore, the much larger question of how his mission in China, to which he had given so much of himself, should really be defined.

There was a disturbing note of haste, almost of flight — flight perhaps from just those awful questions. David volunteered; Blackton approved. The

Treadups decided it would be best for Emily and the children to travel home to America with David, who would go on from there to the war. The Treadups boarded a Butterfield & Swire steamer on November 3, 1917, and sailed north along the China coast for Tsingtao, the port of embarkation in Shantung Province for the Chinese Labor Corps.

FRANCE

EXACTLY THREE WEEKS later, near the head of a procession consisting of a British commanding officer, two missionary doctors, eight British and American officers, eight Chinese interpreters, and four thousand deloused Chinese coolies chattering with excitement and bewilderment in their strange new gray Western coats and trousers, Mr. and Mrs. Treadup and their three children filed through a gauntlet of hundreds of pitiably whining flood-refugee beggars in the Tsingtao streets to the waterfront, where they climbed the gangplank of a British transport, H.M.T. *Tyndareus*.

In earlier phases of the transfer to France of the Chinese Labor Corps, ships had sailed to Marseilles by way of the Suez Canal, but recent German depredations in the Indian Ocean and the Mediterranean had made the trip by way of Canada and two oceans seem safer. Indeed, this very transport, the *Tyndareus*, had just come back into service after repair of damage caused by a mine off Africa. Before the war she had been a freighter of eleven thousand tons; now she had in her holds wooden bunks in high tiers with only enough inches between layers to allow men barely to turn over, and with the narrowest of aisles between the stacks of bodies.

For their first ten days at sea, the Pacific was not pacific. The coolies were too sick and terrified to venture on deck. David was not as seasick as he had been on his first voyage across this ocean, but to hold his own he had to stay in the open air. Emily and all three children, on the other hand, flourished wherever they were.

MRS. TREADUP was the only woman on a ship with more than four thousand men. She mothered them all. She spent much of the day in the stinking holds, putting her cool hand on the foreheads of poor ignorant adult males who thought they were about to die, mopping up vomit that the crewmen would not go near, fetching a doctor for men who were feverish, and, most preciously healing of all, explaining to the coolies in her fairly good Mandarin some things no one had bothered to be precise about before: exactly where they were going and how long it might take to get there, and about the nature of the vast war in France, and about the kinds of work they would be doing, and even about wind and waves on a wide water—for they were North Chinese, men bound to the soil who had never seen the sea, and who in the dark holds with no portholes had no conception whatever of the reason why they had dizzying sensations of falling and why they had to hold the stanchions of their bunks to keep from rolling out; all they could guess was that evil fox spirits had taken over this huge iron prison and that nothing was being done by the foreign devils to exorcise them. When some of the Chinese began to get their sea legs, she served four hours each day behind the counter of a canteen, selling peanuts, rock candy, and, among other things, for any who might have forty coppers, one-stringed Chinese fiddles, which a few men bought and took below to console themselves and their fellows with haunting melodic reminders of the greatness of the folk. David in his diary resorted to the exclamation points of a renewed closeness to Emily as the sea grew calmer: "I first saw her behind a counter like that in the Y.W. shop in the Hall of Languages! Angel! Even more beautiful than she was then!" She was now a woman of thirty-four, her brown eyes more knowing, more canny than they had been back then, the look deepened and darkened by the death of her Nancy, delicate lines incised beside her mouth by the always active scalpel of concern about the restlessness of her husband; a beauty above all of a serenity that included but transcended Christian acceptance of a woman's lot. Her sexual success with David, her "naturalness," which, judging by clues in the diaries of both partners, seemed to weather whatever pain and loneliness she suffered at his hand, must have suffused her body with a sweet and subtle scent of wisdom. We get the impression that in her mid-thirties she had a beauty of bearing that could satisfy the dreams of four thousand men on a ship: of a mysteriously integrated mix of submissiveness with a self-confident energy which was matriarchal in its distant promise. At meals at the captain's table, light-years away from the vomit of the holds, British laughter swirled around her, until one could wonder who really was in command of His Majesty's Transport *Tyndareus*.

PHILIP, Absolom, and Paul had the run of the ship. They were given, by everyone aboard, the impression that their little triangular constellation was at the exact center of the universe. That place seemed to them to define heaven. Their laughter was music of fifes and flutes. The ship's officers rigged a deck tennis net for them. One day all three took turns steering the ship. They were given a table alone in the officers' mess, where they were waited on by lascars as if they were admirals. At table serious Philip, eight and a half, wiped the chin of four-year-old Paul and whispered instructions on how to behave like a man. They sang adorably faulty rounds, "Three Blind Mice" and "Row, Row, Row Your Boat," to entertain the Chinese in one hold after another, and the devotion and courtesy of Chinese toward children formed shields around them, seeming to ward off from them the below-decks stink. Philip, his shoulders squared to bear the weight of his seniority, took it as a matter of course that he should be his mother's helper in mopping up Chinese puke. Absolom, who was five, the mischief maker and clown of the family, tagged around after the Labor Corps officers, tugging at their coattails, putting salt in their coffee, untying their shoelaces. Paul, the youngest, who had inherited his father's big build and was already taller than older Absolom, had to be advised by Philip not to swagger so much. All three were innocent. They did not share in imperialist guilt over the use of Chinese slave labor in a war in which China had no real stake. No, this was the world, and everything was quite natural in the world. Anyway, it was time for elevenses! — beef broth and salt crackers! — hurry!

ON DECEMBER 13, the Chinese laborers and their escorting officers were offloaded at Vancouver Island, where they would camp for some weeks before being sent on by train to the Atlantic. Here the Treadups left them. They traveled east by the Canadian Pacific Railroad. To the children, habituated to the flat parts of China, the Canadian Rockies loomed like fables, and four-year-old Paul asked, "Why are there so many foreigners in Canada?" — a foreigner, of course, being anyone who was not Chinese. In a week they were in New York. The International Committee assigned Mrs. Treadup and the children to a small and rather bleak rented house in Montclair, New Jersey. With orders to rejoin the labor contingent at their port of embarkation, Halifax, in mid-January, David Treadup said good-bye to his wife and children on the front porch of the Montclair house. His diary: "Heavy parting. Going to a war is different from going on a lecture tour."

IN HALIFAX HARBOR David found a convoy of camouflaged ships riding at anchor. He was now in an officer's uniform, sans insignia: high-collared tunic, riding breeches, leather puttees. With his oarsman's frame and his piratical mustaches he cut a fine false figure of the romance of war. His orders took him by lighter to a troopship, *F-8261,* the *Justicia,* a magnificent four-funneled vessel of 32,000 tons, intended when it was built to be a luxury liner. Already aboard was the Chinese labor contingent he had left at Vancouver; the coolies had camped three weeks on Vancouver Island and then taken twelve days in primitive Canadian Pacific coaches to span the continent.

The Atlantic crossing was fairly calm and, apart from one torpedo alarm and the unsolved disappearance of 350 of the ship's soup spoons, uneventful. The coolies drilled on deck each day. Many complained of terrible headaches — migraines of the unknown. A Scottish ship's doctor, running low on aspirin, tried something new: A coolie came into ship's bay with one of these splitting headaches. The doctor applied a small square of adhesive tape, a substance no Chinese coolie had ever seen, to the temple on the side that hurt most. Within minutes the patient felt no more pain. Others stormed the dispensary for the treatment. It worked nearly every time.

The laborers landed at Liverpool and traveled by train to Folkestone, and by ferry to Boulogne, and then, "packed like tinned meat," as David wrote, in cattle cars, to the central control camp of the Chinese Labor Corps at Noyelles.

THE LABOR CORPS had been formed, after China had entered the war, at the instigation of the British and French, who by shipping coolies from China would be able to free able-bodied white men from work behind the lines to go to the trenches, to replace the dead and be slaughtered themselves. In February 1917 the British had opened collection camps at Weihaiwei and Tsingtao, and by the time Treadup arrived in France, some 140,000 Chinese coolies had been imported. Ninety thousand were working in the British zone, unloading ships in the base area from Le Havre to Dunkirk, building and repairing roads and railways on the approaches to the front, and handling ammunition and digging trenches on the battlefields from Cambrai to Ypres. The French had 40,000, doing the same sorts of work as those for the British, in ports from Brest to Marseilles, inland from Rouen to Creusot, and on the front from Arras to Verdun; the French also had some working in munitions factories. The Americans had about 10,000, borrowed from the French. Noyelles was the nerve center. New recruits arrived there, to be assigned in time to one work center or another. It was a vast camp; it had, to give its measure, the largest hospital exclusively for Chinese patients anywhere in the world.

IT IS not surprising that historians of the Allied cause in the First World War have played down, to the point of disappearance, the suggestion that the Allies used slave labor to relieve the manpower shortage which followed the gruesome carnage of young men in the first years of that conflict.

The phrase "slave labor" is, of course, not strictly accurate. The Chinese coolies were paid for their work. In the British zone they were paid one franc for each ten-hour day, or at a rate of two American cents an hour; the French paid all of five cents an hour. In most cases these rates of pay were probably as high as, or higher than, what the coolies could have earned in cruel China.

But in a deeper sense, theirs *was* slave labor. The Chinese government's motive for entering the European conflict was to ensure that the flow of loans to China from the British and French would not be cut off. China was not threatened in any direct way. Germany had taken its bite from the China coast, but so had other nations. Most Chinese citizens hadn't the faintest idea who the Kaiser was, or even what or where Germany and France and England were. Nothing but memories of endless suffering — hunger pains, animal squalor, the rhythmic and murderous wash of swollen rivers — could have persuaded coolies to offer their bodies for a voyage into the zone of the unknown, where their work would be to help strangers kill each other.

AT NOYELLES, it took a whole week of importunity before Treadup could even get his orders cut.

At last they were: Given the assimilated rank of first lieutenant in the American Expeditionary Forces, he was ordered to report to the C.O., Chinese Labor Corps, British Area, Le Havre.

Within a few days he had amended all that, in his diary, to: "Commanding Hornet, Chinese Hornet Corps, British Hornets' Nest, Le Hornet, France."

Items from those first few days, from various letters and diary entries:

• "Reported on arrival to H.Q. Boss is Colonel Urquhelmsy, which as nearly as I can tell is pronounced whimsy. Retired from Indian service. Nose seems to wobble from side to side, as though a pint of what? — port wine? — is sloshing around in it. Eyebrows and mustaches could be traded without slightest change in appearance. Never been near China. Calls the laborers 'these blaahsted Chinks.' First words to me: 'Name of Christ, sir, who sent humph *you* here? Enough trouble keeping humph discipline, now they send me bleeding Young Men's Christian Association.' He does everything he can to keep me away from the laborers."

• "Uproar in the barracks this morning. The Colonel called me in and said: 'Raddup' — never gets my name right — 'you talky-talk their bally palaver, don't you? Go in there and humph find out what the bloody fuss is.' So I went in one of the huts. Bedlam. When they found out I could speak Mandarin — these are Northerners, you know — they gradually quieted and let a noncom explain things. One of the Brit officers here was a Leftenant Brend, who'd once done a tour in Peking, spoke a few words of Chinese, and was very considerate, and the Chinese adored him. He was shipped out by the C.O., who probably thought he was soft at the core. He was to leave this morning. The Chinese decided they'd all muster out at dawn and give him an honor march — *all* of them! — to La Gare Centrale. So they got themselves up an hour before reveille and formed ranks on the parade ground. Someone reported their being out there to Whimsy. He flew into a rage and without any idea what it was about, he ordered them to quarters. They deeply resented the rudeness with which the order was given, and they sent word to the C.O. that they were going on strike. Enter yours truly. I suggested they should stay in the barracks all day, take their mess as usual in the evening, go to bed as usual, get up in the morning as usual, and go to work as usual. I assured them if they would do this, I would explain to the C.O. their good intentions and they could know that nothing more would be said. The old boy, it turned out, was relieved to have things come out that way."

• "Another frightful ruckus. A real riot mob was marching from the waterfront to attack headquarters. They were armed with nasty staves and box hooks and poles, and I tell you, they had murder on the agenda. Raddup into the breach! I met them in the camp street. Got them to stop shouting and explain. It was so simple. These men belonged to three new Labor Corps companies that had just come in. They had finished unloading one ship and were to march to another. Apparently there was some delay, and the British noncom in charge, I finally figured out, shouted impatiently, 'Let's go! Let's go!' He gave the word *go* an exasperated dipping inflection that made it precisely the word meaning 'dog' in Chinese. No possible greater insult. I said to them, 'This is not the way we do in China when we have important matters to discuss. We do not settle them by shouting in the middle of the road. We do it with more dignity by taking a cup of tea together.' They liked my saying that. They calmed down."

• "Supreme habit of Chinese life: frequent sipping of tea or hot water. No one had taken the trouble to learn this. Terrible gastric consequences. Rage. I persuaded Whimsy that a ten-minute recess for tea in midafternoon would increase late-in-the-day productivity by 20 percent. Grumbling in his whiskers he allowed it. I was proved wrong. The improvement was 100 percent."

• "Boche air raid. We ran for our dugout. Found that a coolie had hanged himself in the entrance. I learned he had done this to show his countrymen's displeasure at the unbearableness of this life *and* at Whimsy's bad manners. At next morning's muster on the parade ground, Whimsy said to the interpreter: 'Tell the blighters that if any more of them must hang themselves by the neck, be so good as to humph do it in their own dugouts. We don't like such a mess in ours.'"

• "Two plagues, spread by boredom: gambling, opium. It seems that within a couple of days of each payday, most of the money in the camp of three thousand men winds up in the hands of five or six sharks. Enough left over, however, for many to buy a pipe's worth of the poppy from despicable French parasites—one-legged or one-armed army dischargees—who skulk about."

• "They flock to me with their woes. Misunderstandings about hours and wages. A Paris bank has undertaken to deliver money to families in China, and many coolies, never having heard from home about what had been sent, are wildly suspicious of French swindles. Befuddled interpreters. Constant loss of face because of haughty manner of British and French and American officers. Innocent, accidental, or purposeful violations of incomprehensible Western military regulations, resulting in rude reprimands, fines, extra hours of labor, and even imprisonment in stockade. Untreated diseases—especially trachoma, every other pair of eyes, it seems. Chinese army officers who have been shipped to France against their will. Petty thievery. Two murders; firing-squad executions of the killers. Desertions. For the Chinese, in this ambience of peculiar customs and bone-grinding work, *everything* is topsy-turvy."

• "The first question every coolie asks me: 'When do we go back to China?' "

"I **NOW SEE**," Treadup wrote in "Search," many years later,

> *that my real function, the real reason why scores of Y secretaries like me had been recruited for France, was to keep the Chinese slave laborers docile and hardworking. We were gangers, whip men, in benign disguise. At the time all I understood was that these were miserable human creatures wrenched from their habitat and desperately in need of the warmth of Christian love.*

But even then, he added, he dimly perceived "something having to do with the colonial system"—namely, that the coolies in the Le Havre camp needed a more comprehensible love than that of Britons whose experience in dealing with "natives" had been acquired in nineteenth-century Poona and Hong Kong. In 1917, before the American entry into the war, the British Y.M.C.A., with the reluctant permission of the British military authorities, had begun establishing "red-triangle huts" at the Labor Corps camps; and there was one such at Le Havre. The hut had a "tuck shop," where coolies could buy Huntley and Palmer biscuits, Players "smokes," and hard candies and caramels. There were pictures on the walls of King George, of Crystal Palace, and of a race horse named Baracloo. Four soccer balls were available for sign-out, but they seemed not to have been used for a long time and were partially deflated. Classes in English were offered, but there were no takers, and Treadup learned that a rumor had run around the camp that any coolies who learned English would have to stay five or six more years. A British noncom was assigned to the hut to lead dawn calisthenics—"nip-ups," he called them—for men exhausted by an endless succession of ten-hour days of physical labor. In Treadup's first week a stereopticon lecture, "Western Civilization and Its Christian Safeguards," was offered to a hutful of dispirited men who came to see the funny pictures.

COLONEL URQUHELMSY, for all his opacity, quickly saw Treadup's "way with the Chinks" and its sudden effect on camp morale, and he began to give him tether to do pretty much what he wanted with the hut. Treadup went to work with his oarsman's energy and with a craft which, he wrote Emily, he had "learned from Chinese tradesmen."

His first huge success was that he "chivvied from a Brit officers' club two idle badminton sets." He did not string up the nets and he never took the racquets out of their cases. What he did do was to take out the shuttlecocks and announce a Chinese battledore contest on the camp parade ground. Nearly two thousand coolies showed up. They already knew which dozen men were most expert in the graceful, dancelike game of bouncing a shuttlecock off one foot, with dazzling moves, knee bent, foot swung backward, *pock!*, then left, *pock!*, then right, *pock!*, back proudly arched and head canted to watch the flying feathers, then hunched over and, having instinctively judged the arch of the bird, taking the next bounce blind! — beautiful! — then a fast series of little six-inch bounces, then *whoosh!* into the sky—always the flying foot right there, perfectly in balance, never touching the ground, ever ready to receive the shuttlecock, each movement of the whole body smooth as a poem, now chatter-rapid, then suddenly with a brief slow flowing motion as if doing *t'ai ch'i.* What roars from the crowd! What a stir in the camp that night! They had had something of *home!*

Soon, other Chinese pastimes appeared. Treadup set up a woodworking and mechanics shop in a corner of the hut, and artisans among the coolies built elaborate Chinese-style kites: flying insects, birds, and even fabled tigers and dragons, all of which soon rode the evening skies. Others made singing diabolo tops, which could be kept spinning on a loop of string attached to the ends of a pair of batons. One man built "stone locks"—round stones with metal handles affixed to them, for a game of strength and grace in which the locks were thrown from man to man with elegant formal fluid swinging gestures that made great strains appear to be delicate handling of featherweights.

But David Treadup knew the ultimate secret: The Chinese temperament, even that of the most abject coolie, preferred mental diversion to games. A stereopticon with slides of no matter what subject drew evening crowds. The men flocked to brief reports he gave on news from China and news of the war. Somehow he wangled a movie projector and a half dozen Charlie Chaplin shorts, and the laborers fought for seats for the privilege of grasping, with laughter and tears, the international language of those who are put upon.

All the time he was doing mysterious work in the hut shop. He was taking a bicycle apart, doing strange things with the wheels; making a kind of cover for one of them; building a queer, derricklike frame; attaching a crank to a kind of flywheel which held a circular chain. . . . And then one day he announced at morning muster that he would entertain anyone who was interested that evening with a talk on "The Magic of Whirling Wheels."

It was, of course, the dear old gyroscope lecture, couched in the simple language he had used at Langfang with the Christian General's soldiers. Nearly six hundred men showed up. Treadup basked in the heat of their appreciation. When the lecture was over, the men just sat there. *"Wan-lao,"* he said. "It's finished." They did not move. Finally he asked, "What are you waiting for?" One of the men stood and asked him to start again at the beginning. He was obliged to repeat the whole lecture then and there.

N E W S of Treadup's successes spread, and in the summer of 1918 he was put in charge of all the Y.M.C.A. huts for the entire Chinese Labor Corps throughout France. This meant moving to Paris. "I am amazed," he wrote Emily,

> at discovering how 'European' our Chinese treaty-port cities really are. Here in Passy where we have our little office I could be in the French Concession in Tientsin or in the International Settlement in Shanghai— except that Passy's a bit hilly.

In his new responsibilities, in honor of which he was promoted to the assimilated rank of major, he was technically in command of about thirty British and American Y.M.C.A. secretaries, many of whom had served in China, and about the same number of educated young Chinese men, most of whom had come to France straight from American universities, where they had been preparing themselves for leadership in China. This latter constituted a brilliant cadre, which included such men as T. F. Tsiang, who many years later would be Nationalist China's ambassador to the Soviet Union and representative at the United Nations; and Franklin Ho, who would become a distinguished economist, eventually a professor at Columbia University. At the same time, another stunning group of Chinese youths—beyond Treadup's reach—had come to study in Paris during wartime and were taking a more radical direction. Among them were Ch'en Tu-hsiu, who would found the Chinese Communist Party; Chou En-lai (Zhou Enlai), who would be second only to Mao in the Communist revolution; and Teng Hsiao-p'ing (Deng Xiaoping), who would be the country's most powerful leader after Mao's death.

Treadup's first task was to tour the huts in all the camps and make the acquaintance of "his" men. One visit on this tour was to have a decisive effect on the rest of his life.

A U G U S T   1 9 1 8 : the Boulogne encampment. Treadup had just sat down to chat with a recent Yale graduate, Wu Ch'u-sun, who quickly let it be known that he was called "Johnny" Wu. There was a sudden burst of what sounded like angry shouting inside a nearby barracks.

TREADUP "What's all that noise?"

WU "That's not 'noise.' That's my evening class, studying Chinese. Come and see."

They entered the hut. There Treadup saw about forty coolies, seated on benches. A teacher—another recent graduate from America, named Ma Kuo-fan, called Peter Ma—was writing characters on a blackboard, and the pupils, grown men, were shouting just like upper-class Chinese schoolboys, potential literati, in an old-fashioned Chinese primary school. Except, as Treadup could see at once, the words were not from *The Three-Character Classic* or *The Sacred Edict,* but were simple sentences of the sort that belonged in letters home to China. Treadup couldn't believe his eyes and ears. He interrupted the recital and asked one pupil after another to go to the blackboard and write a character or two. Seeing the alacrity and élan with which they showed off, he suddenly burst into tears.

"I wept," he wrote Emily,

> to see these lowly men writing the sacred characters! Think of it! For three thousand years the Chinese intelligentsia had taken it for granted that the Chinese peasant could never learn to read and write: he was stupid, lazy, his value was locked into his arms and back. But look! One man wrote the characters from which "coolie" comes: 'k'u li.' "Bitter strength." O Emily, I still get shivers up my back remembering his hand holding the chalk—decisive strokes!

JOHNNY WU had grown up in Szechuan, in the heart of China. His father, a classical scholar, having taught Chinese to some missionaries, thought his son should get a taste of Western learning and sent him off at the age of seven to a missionary boarding school. Eventually, impressed by the boy's gifts, the head of the school, a man named John Winthrop, said young Wu should not let himself be buried in provincial China, and he himself took the boy, when he was fifteen, to Hong Kong—a forty-day trip overland—and got him admitted to St. Stephen's College, which could prepare him for Oxford or Cambridge. After one year, Wu took the university matriculation exams and placed first in the Colony. But he and two Chinese friends decided to go not to England but to the United States. They chose a college of which they had heard vague good things, Oberlin. On the ship Wu met an American graduate of Yale who was returning to the States after having taught for two years at Yale-in-China, and Wu liked the sound of Yale. So he presented himself at New Haven, and was accepted. He waited on table in Commons and was thrilled to study under William Howard Taft, an ex-President of the United States. Out of gratitude to John Winthrop, he took the name John for his own. He made Phi

Beta Kappa. In the spring of his senior year he was recruited, along with other Chinese Christians studying in America, to go to France to work with the Y.M.C.A. in support of the Chinese Labor Corps, and he sailed a week after he graduated.

THE COOLIES at the huge Boulogne camp were heartbreakingly homesick. Wu reverberated to their pain, for he would never forget having had to stifle his sobs in his pillow as a seven-year-old at the missionary boarding school. One night soon after his arrival at Boulogne, four coolies came to the hut and asked him to write letters home for them. He did. The next night thirty men appeared, wanting letters home. Soon, night after night, as many as two hundred would come and stand in line. Not many nights had passed before Wu had had enough.

At morning muster, with five thousand coolies assembled in open air, Wu called out, "I have been writing letters home for many of you. Beginning today, no more." Laughter in the Chinese style of disbelief. "I mean it. Those of you who want to learn to do it for yourselves, raise your hands." No hands, louder laughter. This was shockingly "foreign," alien to the ancient proprieties. Farmers daring wholesale to be scholars? "I mean it." Very loud laughter. Wu simply waited, silent, for a long time. Then: "How many?" Forty bold souls put hands up. "You are my students. At night you come to my hut."

So far (Wu told Treadup) the "school" had been a harrowing, pathetic, thrilling experience. Wu and Ma were teaching the men just enough characters to be able to write letters home and to read rudimentary news bulletins. Some evenings men would arrive late, out of breath; their work squad had returned to camp late, they had been afraid they would miss the class, they had skipped supper to get there. Wu had begun posting a daily news sheet on the outside of the hut. His students would read them in loud, authoritative criers' voices to crowds of envious coolies.

Wu invited Treadup to come back to Boulogne for the "graduation" of the first class in about a month.

WHAT JOHNNY WU was doing at Boulogne was to become, in its distant consequences, a significant offshoot of the movement known as the Chinese Renaissance—a movement in which we see a dramatic intersection of the lines of history of the missionary movement and of the Chinese Communist revolution.

On the first day of the year 1917, a brilliant student at Cornell named Hu Shih—who had come to the United States on a Boxer Indemnity Scholarship—had published simultaneously in the *Quarterly,* a magazine of the Chinese students in America, in English, and in *New Youth,* a magazine edited in Peking by Ch'en Tu-hsiu, who was later to be a founder of the Chinese Communist Party, in Chinese, an article entitled, "Some Tentative Suggestions for the Reform of Chinese Literature." Hu argued that the classical language so long revered by Chinese scholars, the *wen-li,* was long dead. "No dead language," he wrote, "can produce a living literature."

"The only possible medium of the future literature of China," Hu later wrote, summarizing that first call for reform,

> was the 'pai-hua,' the vulgar tongue of the vast majority of the population, the language which, in the last 500 years, had produced the numerous novels read and loved by the people, though despised by men of letters. I wanted this much-despised vulgar tongue of the people and the novels to be elevated to the position of the national language of China, to the position enjoyed by all the modern national languages of Europe.

Ch'en then published other essays by Hu arguing for "a constructive revolution in Chinese literature." The essays stirred up a great deal of discussion, and by the summer of 1917, when Hu returned to China (and when Wu and others went to France), the swing toward a Chinese literature based on common speech was well under way, and before long the New Literature, as some called it, had become a powerful instrument in social reform. Peking University, where Ch'en was dean of the College of Letters, became the center of the movement, and for a time the streams of Christian reformism and Chinese radicalism converged. Ch'en himself was to write in *New Youth* in 1920, the year before he founded the Chinese Communist Party, that students should study Christianity seriously and "knock at [Jesus's] door and ask that his lofty and magnificent character and his warm sympathetic spirit be united with us." The scholar Wu Lei-ch'uan pictured Christ as a social reformer, just as K'ang Yu-wei had earlier pictured Confucius. In the fiercely felt need to revivify the culture, every force for change, including the social gospel spread by the foreign missionaries, was enlisted — for a time.

The Christian Johnny Wu's search at Boulogne for a frugal vocabulary to serve the needs of previously uneducated peasants and laborers was a humble by-product of this literary renaissance. It was destined to feed back significantly into China's drive for change, for it would bear fruit several years later in an inventory of basic characters, chosen by Wu and others, which would be used in a mass-education movement, led by Wu himself. And this movement would have an enormous influence on all subsequent education in China — including, in particular, Communist mass education.

FROM A LETTER to Emily:

> *General Burton-Kemp, the C.O. of the entire Labor Corps, was on hand.*
> *We stood behind some tables on the parade ground. You'd have thought*
> *Colonel James Fort, the Boulogne camp commandant, had thought the*

whole thing up. He pranced around as if we were handing out the King's Honors List. All 5,000 coolies were in ranks. Johnny Wu had given his forty scholars two tests: of the ability to write a simple letter home and to read a simple news sheet. Thirty-five had passed. Wu called these forward one by one, and the General handed each a diploma which "Professor" Wu had written with a scholar's calligraphy on the red paper of joy, and which had then been framed so as to hang proudly on hut walls. Each one said:

SO-AND-SO

IS HEREBY CERTIFIED AS A LITERATE

CITIZEN OF THE REPUBLIC OF CHINA

The 5,000 coolies had learned well the Western custom of clapping, and they roared, too, for each "graduate." I tell you, Em, that ceremony stirred up the whole crowd, and now Johnny has more than two thousand applicants on his hands for the second "term"!

IN NOVEMBER came the Armistice. For the Chinese Labor Corps this was the end of nothing but actual physical danger, for those who had been in the way of it, from shelling or aerial bombardments. Their boon of victory was more and worse work. Their greatest and most depressing task remained: cleaning up the battlefields; filling trenches; deconstructing dugouts; clearing away barbed wire; filling shell holes—cosmetic cover-up of the gruesome absurdity of the Western nations' ritual of trench slaughter. The coolies loaded British soldiers onto ships for home; saw the French walk out into mufti. But they could find no hope of their own release from bondage. Morale dived.

Practically the only bright spot was Boulogne, where the spreading epidemic of literacy gave the coolies a dim hope of a future in China that might be different from their past, and where the constant posting of news sheets had seemed to the men to have brought them already into a relatively lighted space. David Treadup could not help seeing this, and he summoned Johnny Wu to Paris and told him he wanted to appoint him head of education for the entire Labor Corps, which now numbered more than two hundred thousand. Wu declined; it was too tall an order for him, he said. Treadup said, "Let me remind you of something. You're a lieutenant, I'm a major." "You mean it's an order, tall or not?" "Exactly." Wu said he would accept on one condition—that Treadup would have all the Chinese student volunteers (from Harvard and Yale and Cornell and elsewhere; there were now sixty-seven of them with the Labor Corps) go to Boulogne for ten days to watch what was going on: Chinese coolies teaching Chinese coolies to read and write. For Wu had divided his mass of pupils into squads of ten and had trained some of his brightest "graduates" to instruct the squads part of the time.

DAVID TREADUP itched. The war was won. Brightened Paris was bewildering. Emily was far away. "I was not cut out for administration, I am building another bureau, I am a 'crat,' " he wrote in his diary. It did not ease his restlessness to drive in a towering Citroën from camp to camp, on his supervisory tours. "Once in a while I give the gyro lecture to blow off steam." But he wrote that the lecture "is just a substitute for Charlie Chaplin as *The Waiter.* It's an evening's amusement, but it isn't *real* teaching—Wu's the one who is doing the *real* teaching." As he had once been haunted by the faces of the men, women, and children holding shovels and baskets in the famine district at Yang Ts'un, he was now haunted by the faces of the men coming forward at Boulogne to receive their "degrees" as LITERATE CITIZENS OF THE REPUBLIC OF CHINA. His diary:

> *An irony in my life: The notion we got at Student Volunteer Movement meetings was that we as social-gospel missionaries would show the Chinese a new way to live and love, but now, for me, the reverse has come about. A Chinese person has turned me right around. True, Wu gives credit to the missionaries who got him started—told me one night about one of those nineteenth-century English eccentrics, William Aldis, who went into the wilderness of Szechuan, wore Chinese clothes, shaved the front of his head, grew a pigtail behind, and taught a homesick seven-year-old boy, by example, some aspects of Christian love that the grown-up man will never forget. But that same night Wu taught me lines from the classics that he had learned from his father when he was five:*

>> *'Min hui pang pen.*
>> *Pen ku pang min.'*

>> ["People are the foundation of the nation.
>> Strong foundation—tranquil nation."]

> *People—these coolies—a chance to be able to read and write—a strong foundation. I have a great deal to think about.*

AS A RAW, incipient literacy spread from camp to camp, the newly created need for reading matter became pressing, and in the spring of 1919 Treadup moved Wu to Paris to edit a newspaper, *Chinese Laborers' Weekly.* There was no Chinese movable type in Paris. Wu acquired large sheets of cardboard, marked them off in rectangles, and with his own hand wrote in news from

China, European news, and even editorials; then he had the paper printed, in editions of scores of thousands, by lithography.

Treadup took Wu into his modest apartment. "I've lost my privacy," he wrote Emily,

> but I've gained a companion who is the strangest combination: he is a brother and a teacher. I am learning lessons of courtesy and civility such as I've never known. I don't suppose there is any such thing as a typical Chinese—certainly Johnny must be a-typical in his enthusiasm, which is excessive and would be too much in a citizen of any country—it is exhausting—I have rowed four miles after every conversation with him—but his in-built kindness (civility is the only word for it) is something we've seen in almost all our Chinese friends. I think of Chuan, David Liu—so many with this wonderful insistence on consideration for others. Some of it is ceremonial, a matter of manners: the hot cup of tea set out for a visitor, no matter how hot the day. But opaque manners—those you can't easily see through—are formal exercises of the self-control without which there could be no such thing as love in an overpopulated country. Such sweet forms relieve crowdedness; Johnny makes my tiny apartment seem roomy. And that's what makes the company of my new brother so unstrained.

CROWDEDNESS soon became a lively actuality in Paris. On December 13, Woodrow Wilson arrived for the peace conference with a delegation of thirteen hundred Americans. Within a few days ten thousand delegates of assorted nations and five hundred journalists of the tongues of Babel had poured into the capital. Among the invaders was a small delegation from China, led by Wu T'ing-hsiang, determined to make one point, above all: that the contributions to the Allies of a Labor Corps of 240,000 men—equivalent in manpower to five American divisions—entitled China to be relieved of the burdens of concessions and trade disadvantages in the treaty ports, imposed under the "unequal treaties" of the mid-nineteenth century.

The frustrations of the Chinese mission in the next few weeks led to consequences for David Treadup that he never lived down in his own mind. When it began to be obvious that in the great squabbles over European settlements and in the drama of the losing battle of Wilson's idealistic Fourteen Points against the hard-nosed territorial demands of Clemenceau and Lloyd George, China was going to be ignored, Johnny Wu reported it with some bitterness in the *Laborers' Weekly.*

When much worse news leaked out—that Britain, France, Russia, Italy, and Japan had entered into secret treaties in 1915, long before the United States had joined the Allies, and that under them Japan was to be awarded virtual hegemony over Shantung Province—Johnny Wu reported it with even greater bitterness. This was the same old imperialist carving up of China. He wrote sharp editorials about the unequal treaties. He brought home to those who had been given the job of cleaning up the leavings of the greed of the major powers the true meaning of *k'u li:* they were indeed slave laborers.

One day in late February 1919, Treadup was called in by General Burton-Kemp, the British commander of the Labor Corps. The General had translations of the *Laborers' Weekly* spread out on his desk, and he was in a rage. He ordered Treadup to shut down the paper and sack its editor—"send the bugger back to China."

There must have been a sudden struggle of contradictory forces in Treadup's heart: Christian acceptance, respect for the canons of military discipline, good sportsmanship and good form, loyalty to a dear friend, an understanding of Chinese sensibilities, an athlete's combative spirit, and the smarting of a slapped cheek. "With as much courtesy as I could summon up on short notice," he wrote his brother Paul,

> *I reminded His Nibs of the graduation ceremony at Boulogne. And of the fact that Johnny's news sheets were just about the only thing that kept the coolies slogging along. He finally swallowed the idea of getting Johnny to tone things down.*

That, in the end, was what Treadup could never square with himself. "I had compromised," he wrote in "Search,"

> *and I had to go back to Johnny Wu and censor him. How angry he was—and how helpless! What a humiliating lesson for me, in how one could let himself go along with the workings of the colonial system! And yet it's strange: My greatest anger at the time was at Woodrow Wilson, for having raised my hopes—Johnny's hopes—China's hopes—with high-sounding principles which then, in the outcome, he was allowing to be blown away like feathery dandelion seeds to broadcast the weeds of "reality."*

Within a week David had written New York for permission to return to China—by way, of course, of Montclair, New Jersey. On March 10, 1919, he started on his way.

STATESIDE

HE WENT straight to Montclair. Emily shocked him. She was thin. Her eyes seemed to look out at him from dark woods. Her three middle fingers drummed a message of nerves on the table as he and she talked. He thought of her wild whisper when she had delivered herself of her first child: "Don't leave me alone!"

That first child, Philip, she said, who had always been so self-contained, had, at ten, in his father's absence, appointed himself head of the family and had begun to expect Emily to love, honor, and obey him. "I can't do anything with him," she said. He had picked up curses at school that would scald your soul, and he wouldn't keep the Sabbath because "they" all played baseball on Sunday, and gambled with marbles.

Absolom's mischievousness had taken an ugly turn: His teachers said he was constantly involved in pranks on his classmates, some of them cruel. There seemed to be something wrong with his hearing.

Paul was an outsized angel most of the time, but he was not doing well in his studies.

"They were better in China," Emily said. "All the children here are so . . . so *immigrant!* Every day is a game they have to win."

She had had a fearfully close time with money. Shame on the Y's allowances! There had been periods when she had thought the children were seriously undernourished. They had all had measles at once. "Acres of rash," she said.

She was able at last to smile. The tight muscles of her face and neck gave way. "Ah, David," she said. "You're back with us."

BUT HE WAS NOT. Within three days he had slipped off to New York, to report to James B. Todd—and that, as it turned out, was the beginning of new wanderings.

The interview with the great Todd was exceedingly painful. Gone was the easy familiarity David had won as Todd's shill on the evangelical tour. Todd seemed distracted; seemed scarcely to know at first who Treadup was.

"Tried to present him," David wrote in his diary,

my excitement about Johnny Wu's methods with the coolies, and about Johnny's dreams for a new kind of education in China. The Y should be in its vanguard! James B. was very stern with me. "Stick to your last, cobbler," says he. "You have drawn us very heavily into your famous lecture program. Blackton and others endorse it. I myself have seen its pulling power. You owe it to us to keep it vital." When James B. uses words like "power" and "vital," his eyebrows shoot up and his eyes snap. It is as if he hugs you with the enthusiasm of his disagreement, and you are smothered into acceptance. So: I'm off on a cultivation tour for the good old lectures!

Much of what Treadup had been mulling over with growing eagerness since he had left France was, in that hour, rudely rebuffed, but even in troubled times his own temperament had so much stubborn enthusiasm in it that after a few nights in Montclair he seems to have swallowed his disappointment and recovered his bounce. Being with Emily obviously helped; perhaps prayer did, too. At any rate, he soon went out on the road "newly inspired," as he wrote, to drum up support for the Lecture Department of the Young Men's Christian Associations of China.

HE STARTED in New York City. With some businessmen he had met on his previous fund-raising furlough, he set up a series of meetings at which he could not help proposing the lectures in China as a model for a new sort of education in the United States.

Treadup made haste then to visit once again his "old friend" E. A. Sperry, the inventor of the gyrocompass, in Brooklyn—"a man of strong Christian character whose Sperry Gyroscope Company and whose interest in the Lecture Bureau have both grown in a pleasing way since last we met." Treadup's infectious enthusiasm reached right into Mr. Sperry's pocketbook, and the inventor donated $5,000 gold, for the equipping of a special building in Shanghai for the Bureau, and $5,000 in cash for general uses. Not only that; he also gave Treadup "a remarkable and unique set of gyroscopic equipment, including a gyroscope that Mr. Sperry has been using for his own lecturing purposes, the only one of its design in existence."

The next thing we know, Treadup has dashed off to Syracuse, then to the Middle West. His Syracuse contingency says it will "do its best to raise five thousand dollars a year." In Dayton, Ohio, we get a glimpse of him, in the company of "such men as C. F. Kettering and A. E. Deeds," lecturing on lecturing to the Dayton Engineers' Club. Together these men pledge $10,000 a year for five years for Treadup's work. In Chicago, he collides again with the munificent Madam Miller, and presto!—the National Reaper and Binder Company donates "thirty lecture outfits, consisting of large charts, exhibit stands, lantern slides, and films," as well as money to ship them to Shanghai. Another wealthy lady whom Treadup cultivated on his previous furlough, a Mrs. Percival B. Campbell, pledges $5,000 a year for "as long as she can afford it." He also visits, in Chicago, the Academy of Science, the University of Chicago, the University Extension Association, and the Y.M.C.A., and, he reports,

> *a good deal of fine lecture work of a popular sort is being done here, but in comparison with the methods and plans that we have in China, a very great advance is still possible for the city of Chicago.*

Treadup next reports that "the Ford Motor Company has donated $2,480 in apparatus for demonstrations," and that "Dr. E. Howitt and Mr. R. Q. Malt of the Western Electric Company are designing and assembling for us a wireless outfit which involves a number of the latest inventions and discoveries and is much in advance of the material that can now be purchased on the market."

WHEN TREADUP finally impressed on the New York office that upon his return from France he had found Mrs. Treadup in some danger of a nervous collapse, a medical examination was arranged; the doctor ordered "a complete rest in a quiet country setting." So it was that David Treadup went home to Salt Branch, with his family of four in tow.

Home? What had happened to his little principality of memories? Where had his childhood gone? He had known that the farm had been sold, but he had hardly taken in that his parents—tremor of the hands, milky films forming on the irises—should be living with sister Grace in a miserable block of "railroad flats" over a Woolworth's five-and-ten, in the village. Automobiles everywhere; dust, fumes, explosions of motors. The old farm, sold as a ruination for a mere half pint of dollars, was now fat land in other hands, with a *tobacco* cash crop! Vast enterprises wherever you turned: Grange Silo and the Mott Lumber Company both building silos for the relatively new green storage of crops. A huge apple evaporator near the pond, where dried apples were processed. The creamery, where he had used to deliver the milk, now a big cheese factory, with a sideline of casein, which was sent off in multitudes of identical bags to a button factory in Rochester.

And his childhood friends! Renny Paxon—Renny of the watery dreams of the back-lot lumber pile!—had turned out to be a vulgar, profane, ill-educated, and prosperous dealer in auto tires. Cassie Berns—Cassie of the church-picnic ecstasies!—was a paunchy slattern who had survived two husbands and was well on her noisy way to wearing out a third, an alcoholic surveyor.

But it was the lot of dear little sister Grace, the bouncy, playful Ecarg, that brought home to David an America he had not dreamed of—an America of thin times and mean work. Now a dry spinster in her early forties, a bit hunched, wearing glasses, Grace had lost both her sense of humor and her job in the Cato Public Library. She was working at the Salt Branch Canning Company. He went one day to see what she did there. "It might have been in Shanghai!" he wrote in his diary. Long tables with sixteen or twenty women on each side of a broad moving belt, along which apples came to them from paring and coring machines; they would trim off remaining peel and quarter the apples and put them in large buckets. Men collected the buckets as they were filled and punched tally tickets on the backs of the women's chairs. Grace earned ten cents for each bucket she filled, and if there were not too many spoiled apples, she could eke out altogether ninety cents or a dollar in a ten-hour day.

DEAR BROTHER PAUL came to Salt Branch for a few days to be with David, and this gave David a chance to talk to a pair of hearing ears about what was so much on his mind: the exact nature and purpose of his sacred calling. Paul had grown up to be a mild and shy man, who knew his modest worth as a teacher of small children; he was the perfect listener for David, for he loved and idolized his younger and much bigger brother, and he himself was fairly at peace with life.

David was distinctly not. "Talked to bro P this eve," he wrote,

> about the wakening giant that is China. So much to be done! Confessed to him that the approach to the literati, about which I used to write to him with such high hopes, was way off the mark. It is the common people who need lifting up. Johnny Wu may have the key to the lock. But the task is so overwhelmingly vast. Paul has eighteen children in his classroom. There must be three hundred million illiterate Chinese!

The next day's entry:

> Paul gave me a hard turn. Asked me: "Do you still believe that Jesus Christ is the answer for the Chinese people?" I said very sharply: "Of course I do." "But for two days," he said, "you have been talking about illiteracy, flood control, cholera and the pox, gunboats, bad treaties, and what did you call those English business sheds? Godowns? Not a word about the Sermon on the Mount. Any loaves and fishes out in the field? And by the way"—his face grew dark—"you were complaining about the wringer they're putting sister Grace through down there at the cannery. Is that the Golden West you want the wakening giant to copy?" I very much regret my response. I was angry at my dear brother. I quite shouted, "I believe in what I am doing!" Paul calls himself "a shallow

*Christian," but in his charity he put me to shame. "Davy! Davy!" he
very softly said. "Of course you do."*

A few days later, after Paul had left:

*I am past forty. Dr. Prinfell fitted me for my first glasses yesterday. I can
see everything more clearly with them on—everything but the future.
Em seems herself again. She is the most remarkably realistic person I
know on this earth. She is my gyro-stabilizer. She says I look more like a
real missionary with my glasses on: I remember I used to wear clear-
glass pince-nez for my early lectures, thinking, I suppose, that they did
make me look "real." It was so good to talk with my beloved Paulie. My
mind is unsettled about what a "real" missionary, specs or no specs,
should best do for great China, but I feel able now to face going back,
even into the thicket of my uncertainties. I will go on with the lectures;
I will keep my eyes, behind their glasses, alertly open. I will keep in
touch with Johnny. And pray for understanding, and for proportions.*

BACK IN MONTCLAIR, Treadup learned that Johnny Wu had decided to
go for a doctorate at Princeton. Whatever might come of keeping in touch with
him would have to wait, perhaps for two or three years.

JUST BEFORE the Treadup family was to leave for Vancouver and thence
for China, David pulled off a little coup, of which he was to be very proud.
He persuaded the New York City committee in charge of Victory Day, the
city's celebration of the successful end of the war, to donate to the Lecture
Bureau the up-to-the-minute vacuum-tube radio transmitter and receiver that
was used to send congratulatory messages all over the world on that day. He
shot off a triumphant note to Todd about this acquisition:

*James, this will be the first radio-telephone station in history to be
mounted on a Chinese wheelbarrow! It has power, sending, receiving,
and amplifying units. I will pack them all in a strong trunk to go on the
road pick-a-back on a wheelbarrow, ready to travel into the deepest
reaches of Chinese understanding!*

ON MAY 10, 1919, the family left for the Far East—which was far, far
to the west of Montclair, New Jersey.

On the train station platform Emily, now a handsome woman of thirty-
six, wearing a pink veil touched with black polka dots tied back over her
velvet-trimmed hat, fluttered over her brood, wildly happy to be leaving the

scene of her gruesome ordeal of loneliness. Philip, ten, who had been sulking at his displacement as head of the family, petulantly brushed aside her hand when she tried, with a saliva-moistened handkerchief, to wipe away a dirty spot on his cheek. (The lost child Nancy, always in moments of emotion present in Emily's mind, was a sprightly ghost of eight, dressed on this hot day in a pretty pinafore.) Absolom, six, was pale, bewildered, passive. Big little Paul, at five taller than Absolom, kept a firm grip on a handful of cloth—his father's trouser leg. The father stood huge and hale against the sky, flipping through tickets tucked into a fat billfold. He would have his forty-first birthday in two months. His face was slightly flushed. Emily, recording the scene in a letter to David's father and mother, wrote:

> I could tell from the way his big hands moved—I can see the jump in the muscles of his thumbs when he's excited!—that he is thrilled—as if he were about to row again for the Orange!—to be going back to his dear China. But it is not easy for him. This is a new beginning—the outset of a new career, almost. I think starting out this time is harder than it was the first time. How blithe he could be in his ignorance that other time! Now he has begun to know the immensity, the sadness, the difficulties. One of the vivid phrases the Chinese have is 'chih k'u'—"eat bitterness." David knows now that he will have to eat bitterness, in the sense that—well, the job is too big. He has talked with me and prayed with me about this. I think he is very brave.

BOOK FOUR

⊞

GOD-INTOXICATED

THIS NOBLE FEELING

ROBERT KEYSTONE stood at the foot of the gangplank. He looked, as Treadup wrote that night, "as if a fox were gnawing at his liver and lights. Pale as paper."

The Treadups debarked. Wordless, Keystone greeted David with a hug, Emily with a frugal handshake, and Philip, the eldest boy, with a distant pat on the top of the head. He was tongue-tied; he looked as if he needed a hard thump on the shoulder blades to start the words coming past his lips.

Treadup bluffly said, "Robbie old man!" and gave him one.

The force of the blow did seem to cause Keystone to cough out a few hesitant words. He was embarrassed, he said, to have to tell the Treadups that David Liu, who was now General Secretary for all of China and kept "a blacksmith's grip" on every detail, had some time ago assigned the Treadups' old home on Yates Road to the family of a new secretary, Henry Burrell. For now the Treadups would be in a smaller house, nearer the Racecourse. Perhaps in time there would be a better house.

"So that's what had you looking so bleak!" David said. "I thought for a moment you had something important on your mind."

Oh, but he did. He did, he said. Later. He'd talk about it later.

AS THE FAMILY'S procession of rickshas crossed the Soochow Creek Bridge, Treadup, "having thought all across the ocean that I was a blessed lucky man to be making a fresh start in my calling,"

> felt the first rush of doubt. It was like a moment of losing my balance and being in risk of a dangerous fall. My senses were assaulted by a lowdown China. At the dock I had thought, Yes, we're back home, now it starts! But here in my foreign nose: this foul ebbtide stench of the Creek. I saw the many jostling sampans of those tattered boat people. What a din, as we flew over the bridge! Quarrels down there. Bitter laughter. Children crying. Gamblers shaking up jumping sticks in bamboo cups. Vendors ringing their bells and whirling their hand-drums in restless syncopations — the very poor battening on the most poor. Boatmen chunking their sculling oars against tholepins and crying out for clear water ahead, with no hope of it. What did I think I was going to do for this China?

THE HOUSE they were to live in was, indeed, smaller than the Yates Road house. Much smaller. The three boys were going to have to sleep in the same room; they were reaching ages at which cheek did not rest easy by jowl. Emily was dismayed by the cramped servants' quarters. David saw that for the first time since their earliest Tientsin house — save for a brief stretch in Paoting — he would not have a study at home. He realized that on the wharf he must have been swept into his so very blithe and casual, so very Christian, acceptance of Keystone's announcement about the house (accepting, too, without their consent, for Emily and the children) by his bewitched illusion, just at that moment, of having reached the landing stage of a new chance in life, on what seemed a home shore. Now he felt the heaviness of his feet on hard ground. The most painful reality of all: He had been away; an absent man is a zero.

THE KEYSTONES, having servants, kindly took the Treadups in for supper that first night. The meal was awkward. The Keystones' children were older than the Treadups'; Philip, Absolom, and Paul were tired and cranky. "So was I," Treadup wrote later, "without realizing it."

In the parlor after dinner Treadup reminded Keystone that he had promised to tell him something important later. What was it?

A very bad letter had been published in the *North China Daily News* just the day before, Keystone said, accusing the Association of having taken an active part in the boycott. "We have been frightfully compromised," he said.

"The boycott? Whoa! Back up, old Robbie! We've been at sea!"

A STORY came out—in blurts, false starts, and stammered rushes—that made David realize he had come back to a different China from the one he had left nineteen months before.

News had reached the Far East, a few weeks ago, that at the Paris Peace Conference the Western Powers had completely ignored China's contribution of the Labor Corps to the Allied cause ("You know all about that, Treadup, you were in the thick of it") and had awarded Germany's former possessions in Shantung Province outright to Japan. A wildfire of protest had swept across China, and on May 4 some five thousand students from Peking University had held a demonstration at the T'ien-an men, the gate to the palace. They set fire to the house of a pro-Japanese Minister and found and beat almost to death the Chinese Minister to Japan. ("Violence against the established authorities, Treadup. It won't do!") The government arrested some of the students, but the whole nation seemed suddenly to be on the side of the students and against the government—such as it was. Real power, here and there, was in the hands of various warlords, and the shaky Peking government kept appeasing a Japan that was greedy for a larger share of the foreign nations' grip on the wealth of China. Student rallies against this appeasement spread to all the major cities, and soon merchants closed their shops as a protest against the Paris awards. A boycott of Japanese goods began. The Chinese delegation at Paris was deluged with messages warning it not to sign the treaty; it obeyed. Just a few days back, the Peking government had capitulated to the wave of national feelings: it had released the imprisoned students and dismissed three particularly pro-Japanese ministers. The worst of the fracas was over, but the boycott continued. By now, Keystone said, the protesters were speaking of momentum and were calling their illicit activities "the May Fourth Movement."

There was confusion in the room. The Keystone adolescents were bored and noisy; the Treadup children had begun to quarrel with each other. Treadup felt "irritably elated," as he wrote later, to hear that at last, at last, a flame of something like real patriotism seemed to have sprung up in Chinese minds, where before there had been only that passive complacency which held China to be the center of the universe, even when trampled by all comers. "Wonderful! Wonderful!" David said. "Our dear Chinese are coming to life!"

"Oh? Wonderful?" Keystone said. "Read this."

He handed Treadup a sheet of the previous day's paper, folded back around a letter from a reader.

To the Editor:

SIR,—In the windows of many shops in the Settlement a small notice in Chinese appears stating that the shop is taking part in the boycott. These have been issued by the Y.M.C.A. and bear its stamp with the well-known inverted triangle. It was to be expected that such an organization as the Y.M.C.A. would range itself upon the side of the authorities in this time of anxiety, instead of helping on such an illegal attempt.

Hitherto the Y.M.C.A. has been considered a religious and missionary organization, is it not a great fall from the original purpose of its founders that it should now in the International Settlement take such a prominent part in this despicable political maneuver? During the war the Inverted Triangle has won a magnificent place in the esteem of men of all nations, is it not dragging that worldwide symbol in the mud by the present actions of the local Association? If it prefers to be political ought it not to drop the word "Christian" from its title? Then we should know where we are.

I would suggest that the authorities of the Settlement, who are responsible for law and order under the treaties, should take the matter up, and send particulars of these activities of the local Association to the International Committee in New York.

I am, etc.,
A MISSIONARY.

IN "SEARCH," years later:

My heart sank as I read the letter—not because of its substance, but because it seemed to hit me, personally, a blow below the belt. The experience with Wu in France had pumped up my sense of possibilities, and I had built a fantastic castle of hopes for this new start of mine in China. To come back and find such a petty issue looming so large—were my hopes built on sand?

David looked up from the folded paper. "Here, Em," he said, handing it to her.

"Devastating for us," Keystone said.

"Why devastating? I say, *good* for the Association!"

David would never forget the expression on Robert Keystone's face at hearing what he had said. It was as if Keystone had caught him stealing money from a till. "I'm shocked at you," Keystone said. "We didn't sponsor any boycott. You know we couldn't do that!" He said there must surely have been some kind of mischief involved—somebody using the Y's symbol to give respectability to the boycott. It was being investigated. The Association had never been political. "You know that as well as I do, Brother Treadup."

Brother Treadup, now! Keystone had for years addressed David with the simple, manly, familiar last name. The pastoral "Brother Treadup" amounted to a sharp slap, and David felt, he later wrote, "the heat going up my neck." "Look here!" he said. He hoped the investigation would find that there *had* been Y sponsorship of those handbills—"sponsorship by our Chinese members. The Y is theirs!"

David wrote in his diary:

Went on and on. Pointless and futile argument. It came to me finally as a Christian that I was being unfair to Robbie. He had been in the middle of things. In the middle of the passions out here. He is almost sick with worry. I'd been on a serene ocean liner on a calm blue sea, just sitting on a deck chair thinking—and this, I suppose, was what had put the burrs in my shoes to make me so pesky—thinking about all the deep things that had been worrying me ever since France. The things that rolled over with a bump inside me when we were crossing the Soochow Creek Bridge this afternoon. Robbie was paler than ever after we talked. Em, poor thing, had nodded off to sleep even in the hullabaloo the children were making. When I rose to wake her and come back to this awful house, Robbie kept his distance, more or less holding his breath, as if I had a communicable disease.

H E W E N T next morning to the Lecture Bureau offices and workshops in the Quinsan Gardens headquarters of the Association. John Y. Hu, the physics Ph.D. who had worked with the Nobel laureate at the University of Chicago, and whom David had recruited, was now in charge of the Bureau, and briskly so. "Told me he'd scheduled me for a lecture tour to Hupei and Hunan starting *next week!*"

Hu was very cool to Treadup's triumphant report of all the funds he had raised for the Lecture Bureau, and he was particularly critical of Mr. Sperry's gift of cash for a new building for the Bureau. The workshops, Hu said, were entirely satisfactory where they were. The Association paid for the overhead, which it might not, with a separate building. Why move? In a long confessional letter to Paul, in which David reminded his older brother of "that deep soul talk we had when I was home, about my mission out here":

Mr. Hu took me around the shops. It was wonderful to see his assurance. His chest was pouted out. Gave orders like a ship captain. I would never say this directly to him, but it was obvious to me, from a hundred tiny clues, that standards have slipped. I must get to work "behind the screen." I cannot bear to watch my old show fall on sloppy times. Good old Chinese 'ch'a pu to'—more or less, not off by much! But I can see that I have the most delicate problem of tact on my hands. More than tact: the burden of the kinds of things I told you I've been wrestling with since France. Just as much as Hu, I suffer from the sin of pride. I was astonished how hurt I felt this afternoon by the feeling that I was a mere hired hand. "Devolution"—handing the torch on to the native Christians —in our heart of hearts do we really mean it?

IN THE MAIN OFFICES there was nothing in the air but the letter in the *North China Daily News*. Keystone, Wood, Charles, Wolf, and the new man, Burrell, were all, says the diary, "in a state of hysteria. Keystone eyeing me like a stranger, so kept my mouth shut. Their 'investigation' has it all worked out that some students in the Y.M.C.A. middle school organized a branch of the Shanghai Student Union, and *they* issued the circulars inscribed 'Chinese Student Union, Y.M.C.A. Academy Branch.' " Treadup gathered that some of the secretaries, including Keystone, had been present at meetings held by these students in the Y.M.C.A. restaurant, and far from having tried to suppress the students' activities, they had applauded "the moderation and constructive character of what was said." David Liu did ask them to stop using the emblem of the inverted red triangle—well before the letter in the paper. Now the feeling seemed to be that the Association should write the chairman of the Shanghai Municipal Council a cautious letter disclaiming any responsibility for the use of the logo; and that a similar letter should be written to Todd in New York before the International Committee got wind of the business from anyone else.

David went home seething and sat down and wrote a letter (which he later thought "somewhat incoherent, I really did not know the true facts, but I was so mad") to the editor of the paper. It appeared three days later, on June 23.

To the Editor:

SIR,—"Missionary" was a bit hasty in his letter about the Y.M.C.A. and the recent strikes and boycott.

The triangle's support of the recent movement in no wise drags it in the mud. It is difficult to gather what "Missionary" means. Does he wish to imply that the recent political upheaval was bad, or that it was nothing more than "a political maneuver"? Does he further maintain that Christian institutions must have nothing to do with politics? If he entertains these views both his Christianity and politics are thoroughly bad and unenlightened.

The Y.M.C.A. is a national institution for China. Its membership is mostly Chinese. New China looks up to it. It is well the Chinese have some center of inspiration in these disastrous times. We believe the Y.M.C.A. is an instrument for the training of manhood. China needs such an institution. Being so, it would be strange if the recent movements left the Y.M.C.A. wholly untouched. Patriotism is a precious thing. I venture to think that it is the inherent right of even students who happen to be connected with the Y.M.C.A. to give expression to this noble feeling. That the students who live in Shanghai may not give an expression to lawful sentiment is a fantastic idea, as is the idea of reporting to Headquarters.

> I am, etc.,
> ALSO A MISSIONARY.

ON THE MORNING this letter appeared, Treadup was at the Quinsan Gardens building, mostly in the Lecture Bureau shops, but also in and out of the main offices, getting set up for his Central China tour. The letter seemed to go through the Association headquarters like one of those lightning bolts in the form of a rolling ball of fire that sometimes tears through a house doing very little structural damage but leaving black scars of its heat. The place smoked with suspicion. Robert Keystone walked from door to door with the clipping in his hand, stating his conclusion that "Also A Missionary" was an Association secretary. He cited "internal evidence" in the letter, especially the sentence, "We believe the Y.M.C.A. is an instrument . . . " Everyone began looking aslant at everyone else. Which of them could it have been? Surely not one of the Chinese secretaries, for a letter writer had to give his real name to the editor, and the paper would never have run a letter of that kind authored by a Chinese. That left not many suspects.

A long time afterwards, Treadup was deeply ashamed of his behavior that morning. In "Search," from a distance:

> I was Mr. Mouse. Discretion itself. I felt a peculiar tightness of the set of my lips when Keystone or Wood, or especially new young Mr. Burrell, who sucked at his curved pipe with the supercilious inquisitive hawk-eye of Sherlock Holmes, looked keenly at me. Robbie Keystone must have been sure I was the culprit, after what I'd said to him that other night. I kept wondering if that funny knot in my lips was going to give me away. I was like a bad schoolboy. Why didn't I take credit for the letter? Couldn't I stand up for my opinions? Why did I slink around with my tail between my legs?

VACILLATION

ON A JAPANESE river steamer, with a ton of lecture equipment aboard, Treadup and two assistants crossed Tung Ting Lake, "the bull's-eye of China," as the diary puts it. Then, after an all-day run up the Hsiang River, which was "like a misty, fluent dream," they arrived at Changsha, the capital of the province of Hunan.

"Feeling rather shabby and dim," Treadup wrote,

> because my lecturing along the way has been so lifeless — my heart-beat isn't in the spiel. Doing Radio-Telephone, and of course I have my spiffy new Victory Day equipment along, but I feel as if I had a blockage in my throat. The wrong words keep coming out. Don't want to talk about E-tubes. Want to be talking about literacy, Johnny Wu, the coolies in France — a future for coolies — a future for those miserable humunculi who bothered me so much in Soochow Creek the day we landed.

So far he had lectured in Nanking, Hankow, Wuchang, and Han Yang. Treadup hoped that Changsha would "pep me up" — this place where, he had observed on a previous trip, the people seemed more robust, cheerful, and warmly responsive than those in the Yangtze and coastal cities.

Here in Changsha, he was immediately informed by local missionaries, the May Fourth Movement was vigorously alive. The missionaries deplored the incessant demonstrations — near riots, they said. Hunan Province had been a seedbed of revolution. There is no clue whether Treadup learned on this trip that a young Hunanese radical named Mao Tse-tung had just started in the city an anti-imperialist, anti-warlord journal called *Hsiang Chiang;* probably not one of the missionaries was even aware of it.

In the milling about before the Changsha lecture, the magnetic figure was Governor Chao Hung-ti, who, David wrote in a letter to Paul, was "unreservedly gracious. He was a huge chunk of high living covered with medals. Permanent smile as wide as a slice of cantaloupe. All the little people jumped like jiminy crickets at every word he uttered." The lecture was to be graced by His Excellency in the presiding chair, and was to be before an audience of officials and gentry — the old familiar atmosphere of the failed literati.

Treadup and his assistants had to hustle to get their radio-telephone stations up and working in time for the evening meeting. "Lecture not bad. It was an appreciative audience," Treadup later wrote, "who were delighted when we effected a fine exchange of messages with the American Navy gunboat *Villalobos*"—one of Admiral Dewey's prizes from the Battle of Manila Bay, now anchored in the river off the city. Treadup's radio reached through to the ship strongly, and the answering voice signals were amplified by the receiving set on the stage "loud enough for an audience much larger than the one we had."

After the meeting ended, Treadup took the Governor for a look at an auxiliary radiophone in a closed room on the other side of the compound. This done, the Governor took his leave. David, following the formula of Chinese courtesy in seeing off a guest, escorted the Governor to the outer gate of the compound. Governor Chao was soon seated in his sedan chair. David stepped just over the high stone sill of the gate, to wave and bow. Bearers raised the chair, which was thickly surrounded by armed bodyguards.

Suddenly there was "a deep-voiced thump—like rock being split in a quarry."

Treadup saw the chair careen through smoke. Rushing forward, he found several people wounded and moaning on the flagging, gashed by fragments of a bomb which must have been thrown from somewhere in the dark. Soldiers grabbed the shafts and got away with the Governor unharmed. David counted seventeen who had been injured. One of the chair coolies soon died. Treadup helped lift the wounded onto litters.

From his later account:

How harrowing an experience this was I did not realize until, after having helped remove the maimed to the Red Cross Hospital, I washed off the blood and grime and turned in late at night. It never even occurred to me until I was stretched out on my cot that I may have missed being killed by just a few feet—my life saved by some brief unthinking hesitation back there by the gate, as I was pushing forward for one last farewell near the sedan chair. I prayed in the dark for understanding. I saw the dawn before I slept.

TREADUP arrived back in Shanghai disturbed and confused.

In later years he spoke of the night of the bomb as "the first time I died." His own narrow escape from death receded in his consciousness, and the figure of the dead sedan bearer lying on the pavestones loomed larger and larger. "Everyone agrees—the Communists agree—that the bomb was thrown by a Communist. But look! It is a worker who lies there dead, not a Governor." Later: "I feel that that bearer was my other self. Only an instant stood between him and me." "I would gladly have changed places with him. Then I might have lived out the meaning of my mission in China for Immanuel"— Immanuel meaning, in Hebrew, "God with us," a term used for the name of Jesus Christ by some who thought the name itself too holy to utter; used here by Treadup, it seems, in the stress of his relief. Immediately following, in the diary, were these hymnal lines:

> *There is a fountain filled with blood*
> *Drawn from Immanuel's veins,*
> *And sinners plunged beneath that flood*
> *Lose all their guilty stains.*

EMILY'S DIARY:

> *He is gray. I am tired. I try to help him. It is as if I have to carry him to*
> *work on my back every morning. He has the gift of generalization; that*
> *bomb enlarges in his mind.*

He kept going to the Bureau lab and offices, and in spite of his fretfulness a perverse, puzzling, and radiant energy kept burning in him. He became involved in a fierce intrigue which he later described as "an outbreak of my badness." It was, however, unlike anything he had called by that name ever before.

Through several weeks he sat down in long conferences with the General Secretary, David Y. S. Liu, with the chief of the Lecture Bureau, John Y. Hu, and with Dr. Charles, Bert Wood, Y. Y. Han, and all the other lecturers, and somehow—with patience, stubbornness, sweetness, ferocity, and reason, all tooled by a wily craftiness which seemed to well straight up out of the deep disturbance of his mind—he persuaded everyone, he even persuaded the recalcitrant Hu, to accept a wildly ambitious five-year plan for the Bureau. It provided for separate sections on science, education, health, sociology, religion, and something called "efficiency"—conservation had disappeared. Each section was to have a Chinese and an American lecturer, and each to have elaborate new demonstration materials built in a new laboratory housed in a new building. Treadup talked everyone into sending on to New York a budget proposal that was as preposterous as the very first one he had sent Todd so long ago. He surely knew how extravagant it was. He had raised $5,000 from Sperry for the new lab building; the budget for the building was now $64,000. The total request was for $416,420 in U.S. dollars over five years. What made this crazy figure malignly spendthrift, as David realized as he wrote "Search," was that he had, in the larger part of his mind, lost interest in the idea of the lectures. Expensive lectures would not bring the sedan bearer—his "other self," his secret sharer — back to life. Nor would they reach fast enough into the lot of the sedan bearers who survived — China's coolies — China's peasants — China's poor — those in China who had to get along on their "bitter strength."

IN THE MONTHS that followed the Changsha bombing and the Lecture Bureau budget campaign, Treadup fell into a quite desperate period of groping and vacillation. In younger years his episodes of "badness" had always foreshadowed periods of melancholy, and he was often gloomy now. He was especially discouraged by all that he saw going on in the upper levels of Chinese society:

> The intellectuals at Peking University call this the Chinese Renaissance. Yes, it has many of the features of life in Europe at the end of the Middle Ages: wandering bands of licentious soldiery, turbulent robber barons, the rapacious dictatorship of local lords, widespread public restlessness, impatience with the greed of those in control, resentment against worn-out religious and political shibboleths — and at the same time, the one saving hope, a consuming intellectual curiosity. The trouble is, the students are like those in the German and Italian universities of the Middle Ages, they won't take time to study any one field thoroughly but with the vulgar tongue at last available to them they rush breakneck from subject to subject, tasting everything, mastering nothing. The motto of this Chinese Renaissance is wonderful: "Save the country by science and democracy." But the science is (in my view) 'ch'a pu to' and the democracy is (in practice) warlordism. While the warlords battle each other, Sun Yat-sen has surfaced again in the south. I have a feeling he is less a man than an idea. Will he stand by his Christianity any better than the Taipings did?

THE RESPONSE from New York to the request for the huge Bureau budget could easily have been foreseen. It had no doubt been the essence of David's "badness" that he had foreseen it. Todd sent a sizzling cablegram to Liu and Hu, accusing them (not Treadup at all) of being megalomaniacs.

TREADUP'S way of dealing with his confusion was to turn his back on it, to deny it, by throwing himself with a blind and frenzied energy onto the old familiar treadmill of the science lectures. Through late 1920 and early 1921 he forced himself to care about the lectures. "It was no matter to me," he wrote brother Paul, reminiscing about this period in a letter three years later, "that my famous *enthusiasm* on the lecture platform was at that time mostly bluster, just like the sound of Father's shouting at the farm animals when we were small — remember?" What deeply bothered him in bed at night, he told Paul — "this was the awful part" — was that the lectures were just as big a hit as they had been when his enthusiasm "rang as true as a silver dollar."

In July 1921, he sent to all those Americans who had contributed money to the Lecture Bureau a mimeographed brochure entitled "A Vision of Science." It described a dogged year. He had traveled ten thousand miles, visited twenty-two cities, and lectured, he wrote, to 167,724 Chinese, including two national ex-presidents, twelve provincial governors, and two dozen current or former cabinet members. His journeys had taken him into four main regions of China. "In one were bandits, in another famine, in the third pirates, and in the fourth mutinous and looting soldiers."

> So pleased was the Governor of the last province we visited that he presented me with a beautiful case of specially inscribed and burnt porcelain cups from the famous pottery at Ching-te-chen, of which Longfellow wrote, in "Keramos":

> > And bird-like, poise on balanced wing
> > Above the town of King-te ching,
> > A burning town, or seeming so, —
> > Three thousand furnaces that glow
> > Incessantly, and fill the air
> > With smoke uprising, gyre on gyre,
> > And painted by the lurid glare
> > Of jets and flashes of red fire.

E M I L Y wrote her sister Jane that she felt "needed on the home front as never before." The boys — now aged twelve, nine, and eight — were

> like three dynamo-electric machines. If they could just be connected up, their energy would provide enough volts to light up all Shanghai. I get tired just from hearing them thump around in their room in the mornings before school.

They were in a phase, Emily wrote, of needing a father "to do battle with," but David on his lecture trips kept winging in and out of Shanghai, alighting for only a few days at a time, and on those occasions spending most of his time at Quinsan Gardens "doing battle with his Chinese spiritual sons in the lab."

> So I have to be ma and pa, with a darning egg in one hand (you can't imagine how fast their toes poke holes in their socks) and with a monkey wrench in the other (bless me, they're all tinkerers — this house is like one big Meccano set). The trouble is, when he is home, David needs me

even more than they do. I have never seen him quite like this. He's like an elevator, up, down, up, down. Dark as doom one day, then wildly excited and glad about something he sees as the greatest thing since creation. I never know how to approach him. He's not right, Janey. You know how a bluebottle darts in one direction and then suddenly in another and another? Sometimes I'm frightened. He was in the famine district a while ago, and he came home looking as if he hadn't eaten for a month — burned out hollow by a rage such as I'd never seen in him. On the other hand, he heard Bertrand Russell lecture at Peking University, you know, the British freethinker, and he was all perked up, invigorated — by that atheist! socialist! free-lover! I don't know whether you know it but this so-called philosopher has brought with him to China a woman — not his wife. Both of them advocate free love. The woman lectures for it. He has a wife in England and admits it. I think this creature must have made eyes at David. He said the other day, "My gracious, Em, the man's human."

HE HAD traveled by cart for two days near Taiyuan, in Shansi.

Once again the famine-scar on my brain burns. I have seen skeletons covered with skin staggering by the roadside. The balloon bellies of children. A woman dying before my eyes. Stinking shallow exposed graves, no coffins. A man with delirium in his glance clutching at my sleeve and with a breath foul with the rot of the nil in his stomach cursing at me for being so 'fat.' He screamed it: 'P'ang! P'ang! P'ang!' Fat! Fat! Fat! I have never thought I was fat.

In a later entry, the sentences appeared to shrivel and the handwriting looked like that of an old man with the shakes:

The infamy of it! Sorghum and millet — large sacks — contributed by International Famine Relief Society — shipped in by train under the hiding of tarpaulins. By night!! The sacks find their way into godowns belonging to the magistrate, the district boss. This monster sells the bags at highway-robber prices to local landlords. They either hoard or resell the grain to speculators — at even higher prices. In one village word got out — some landlord must have used starving coolies to carry his treasure and they told on him. Huge famished crowd stormed the landlord's gates. Had his servants fire on them — automatic weapons! I heard that the magistrate called him on the mat — he said the rabble would have died of hunger anyway — they laughed together — young Winthrop, who's writing up village relief tickets, told me that.

The last line of the entry: *"This is the Chinese Renaissance for you!"*

IN THE AUTUMN of 1920 Treadup learned that Peking University had in the previous year invited John Dewey as a visiting professor and that Bertrand Russell had followed and was teaching in the current year. Treadup wrote brother Paul a troubled letter on these two visits:

> I am jealous. I am the inventor of a lecturing technique which I believe has served China's needs well. But here come these two interlopers and apparently make more impression on the Chinese educational system in two short seasons than I have in more than a decade. They say Dewey's lectures were dry as dinosaur bones; one chap who heard him said that if this educator should be announced to speak in the average American university, it is doubtful if fifty noses could be counted when the head of the department of education arose to announce the distinguished speaker. Not so with Chinese students. Dewey lectured in many provincial capitals. In one place there were a thousand middle-school students who did not have tickets to hear a lecture. They marched in a body to the hall, broke past the armed policemen at the door, and jammed in against the walls of an already filled hall. We might imagine a thousand American college students tramping over a squad of policemen to get out of a hall in which a two-hour lecture by this educational theorist was about to begin. I have my own heady knowledge about this eagerness of the young Chinese. They have mobbed me, too. But Dewey's message "took"—I'm not sure mine ever did. He was very simple and down-to-earth—advocated that all education should have its 'use;' that courses of study should equip a student in after life to be useful as a citizen. Above all he was practical. Students should learn by going out to life and 'doing things'—learn from the doing. This made a great dent on the Chinese mind, which for centuries has been shaped by classical scholarship—exquisite reflections "about" life, yes, but from a discreet distance—life as if seen in a vista from a scholar's study, set in a templelike retreat in a pine grove on a lonely mountain. Dewey put them out in the streets.
>
> Now Bertrand Russell must be placed in a pigeonhole with a little different wording on the label. The English philosopher is much more disturbing. I heard him the other day. His philosophy contains social dynamite. He is a most attractive Anti. He is a pacifist. He served time in England during the war because he opposed it. He champions free love. He turns up his nose at the Church and Christianity—if Dewey was an agnostic, he is a roaring atheist. He is not violent but he is outspoken in his belief that religion is a part of the order which will pass when his superior ideas are in force as laws. Above all he is a confirmed

socialist and revolts against the order of things in our Western civilization. What an appeal this has to the Chinese, who feel they have been robbed and contaminated by the West! This man's socialism has had a great hearing from Chinese students.

Now for the moral. Into China come the missionaries, broad-gauge ones and narrow-gauge ones; the morally sound materialistic educational theorist; the scintillating, humorous, sarcastic socialist philosopher with his female affinity by his side; me, with my harmless science lectures; then also the Christian businessman (there are many more than there used to be); and the crooked businessman who, given the chance to choose jail or China, takes the latter; as well as the British opium dealer and the American Tobacco Company gent, who wish to fasten their respective habits on Chinese men, women, and children; and foreign government officials (the present Minister to Peking represents the best of what we like to call American); and American globe-trotters, who are by turns good, bad, and indifferent. These are the "modern" Western personalities that are influencing China today. Is it any wonder that China is confused — or that I am, brother Paul?

YET THIS confused David Treadup is at this very time playful, frivolous, and vain. Back from the Northwest, he devises for the foreign community of Shanghai a delightfully entertaining lecture on Einstein's theory of relativity. Martyrs' Memorial Hall is packed to the very top of the gallery. Treadup, delighting in the flashes of surprise of the sorts Absolom Carter used to deal out, displays at the outset a gigantic chart:

SOME DIAMETERS (Centimeters)	
An Electron	.000,000,000,000,07
An Atom	.000,000,004
The Earth	106,000,000.
The Solar System	74,800,000,000,000.

Then he begins to rattle the listeners' minds with all sorts of dizzying oddities: the planet Mercury's perihelion, the gravitation of light and gravitational elipses, the phenomenon of interference fringes in soap bubbles, and only Dr. Albert Einstein could know what all else. He tries to get his audience to believe that objects affected by forces of drift in the universe have, as the force directions vary, different lengths at different times. When at long last he announces that there will be a second lecture the next week, there is a loud groan, and then prolonged laughter and applause. What a good time he is having!

OBLIQUE NOTES in the diary on dreams and thoughts of those days tell us that the assassination attempt on Governor Chao still reared up often in his mind, especially in bed at night. This memory fixed in him a deep hatred of violence, which in the next few years would color his attitude toward powerful Chinese men—toward his friend Feng, the more or less "Christian General"; toward Chiang Kai-shek, who would eventually convert to Christianity; and toward Mao and other Communists, who would take over from the Christian missionaries some of their methods while driving them out of the country.

Treadup was by now deeply convinced of China's need for an upheaval of change. On this, at least, he agreed with Dewey and Russell. He wanted what seemed impossible in China—radical change without violence. The kingpost of his house of belief was the New Testament rule that made violence unthinkable: "As ye would that men should do to you, do ye also to them likewise." Christ may not have intended it so, but there was great potential political power in the commonsense bargain of that rule, the canny generosity of which frequently invaded the promises, then cruelly slipped away from the practice, of Christians like Sun and Feng and Chiang—and, for quite different but no less dynamic reasons, of Communists like Mao, as well; and Treadup's hatred of the violence to which they all eventually resorted would leave him, in the end, with no power center to turn to. So finally he and his Golden Rule became in China utterly without influence and futile.

DANGER ZONE

INTO HIS OFFICE at the laboratory one morning walked a bizarre procession. First, a very tall, gaunt Chinese, in peasant dress, with "eyes that burned like charcoal embers fanned by some wild fixation." Behind him came four quite small men who looked like wharf rats, carrying between them two huge covered baskets.

The big man's speech told that he was a Northerner, and indeed he said he was a farmer from a village not far from Tientsin. His name was Wang Tun. He had come to Shanghai, he said, on purpose to see T'ao Tu Hsien-sheng (Mr. Treadup). Mr. Treadup would not remember him, but he remembered Mr. Treadup.

How had he come to know Mr. Treadup? After the flood that had ruined large parts of Chihli and Shantung provinces in 1917, he, Wang, had been left without land or any resources to feed a large family. The British were calling for Chinese to go to France as coolies, and Wang, not knowing what this meant, had volunteered. He had many months of drudgery, ten hours each day, at the camp at Abencourt—he was obviously bright, he gave this name a quite good French pronunciation—and while there he had learned to read and write, and Mr. Treadup, he said, had been a famous man to those coolies who, like himself, had each week devoured the *Laborers' Weekly*. At last the Armistice had come, but it had meant no relief for the Chinese. Wang's company continued for a year rolling up the barbed wire, picking up shells and wreckage, and filling in dugouts and trenches.

During that time, Wang told Treadup, he thought and thought. China was weak and France was strong. Could he do something about that imbalance when he got back home? He was disgusted by many of his fellow returnees who were farmers, he said. They were satisfied to use their savings to buy a few mou of land and go back to the old ways. Some of his friends who had gone to Tientsin and Tsinan and Paoting, he said, were better. They had "eaten bitterness" because it was hard to get work, but those who had finally found jobs had joined the new labor unions and were insisting on some of what they had seen in a "strong" country—better working conditions, shorter hours, easier work, higher pay.

But Wang, Treadup wrote,

> wanted to make life better in his own village. In France, he said, a Y.M.C.A. secretary named Larch had taught him some mechanics, and after his repatriation he had gone on with his studies at T'ungchow. "At that time," he said, with his hands hovering over his two big baskets as if they were where all truth was hidden, "I practiced meditation, and one day I saw the sky open and there in the crack in the sky was an issue of the 'Laborers' Weekly!' It said: 'Do not waste time by hurrying.' I had to think about that. At last I realized that that warning meant that my village should not be in a hurry for big iron machinery, it was not ready for big iron machinery. Perhaps here a very small motor, there a very small pump. At that time," he said, his hands moving down toward the covers of the baskets, "I started my work."

Wang took off the first lid. "I cannot do justice to the simple elegance of the objects he gingerly began lifting out of the baskets," Treadup wrote. They were models of labor-saving devices: A wooden threshing machine to be run by wind power on windy days, by donkey power on still days. A boat for shallows to be run by a small engine which in time of drought might be converted into a pump for supplying water from rivers to fields, or which, Wang said, might be used to generate power to run a moving picture machine.

A hydraulic flour mill, operated by a wooden waterwheel. A water-powered wooden machine with metal feet to crush stone . . . And dozens of others.

> *These beauties were put together from cardboard cut from British-American Tobacco Company cigarette boxes, sorghum stalks, heavy Chinese paper, pins, and rice paste! All the wheels and handles and rollers and belts and brakes and spokes and pistons were there in miniature! What's more, they worked. Tiny gears turned "big" arms. Wang answered every engineering question I could ask. Every machine, it seemed, could be turned to alternate or numerous uses.*
>
> *What thoughts this man Wang opened up in my mind! A transitional modernization of the farms of China! Wind, water, wood, a few small motors and pumps. What a vision!*

FOR SOME TIME this vision bedazzled Treadup. He had several further talks with Inventor Wang, and before Wang set off for home David had him write down the name of his village and give a full description of its exact location. He wrote an excited and somewhat grandiose letter to Johnny Wu at Princeton telling him all about the wonderful devices Wang had put together and suggesting that one day Johnny and he could find a way to give a real and widespread life to the "transitional modernization" of the countryside of China.

BUT SOON this vacillating Treadup had dashed off in quite another direction.

One day not long after Wang had departed, the four "wharf rats" who had carried Wang's baskets showed up at David's office. David discovered first that these ragged creatures were, like Inventor Wang, literate and articulate men; their native dialect was Shanghainese but one of them, named Fu, spoke fair Mandarin. Then David learned that they, again like Wang, were returned laborers from France. Inventor Wang had found them by asking at the Shanghai resettlement camp for returnees. They, too, had learned to read and write in Y huts in cantonments in the British sector. But unlike Wang, they had been repatriated only a few months ago.

With all due Chinese good manners, they invited T'ao Tu Hsien-sheng to visit their "unworthy residence." It was in the Whangpoo industrial quarter, they said. "The shining future" about which they had read in the *Laborers' Weekly* in France, they said, had arrived. It was now. Could he come the next day to see it with his own eyes? Since they were, as they put it, their own masters—in other words, unemployed—they could come for him at any time he chose.

When Treadup followed the four downstairs from his office the next morning, he discovered that all of them were wheelbarrowmen. Fu insisted that the Hsien-sheng ride on his flat-bedded barrow; the other three pushed their empties along behind.

In twenty minutes they had arrived at their destination. This, Fu said, was Little France.

A vast area, apparently an old marketplace for country produce, abandoned when the surrounding district had been taken over by silk filatures and other factories, had been turned into "the most squalid sinkhole of humanity I have ever seen," as David later wrote Todd. Fu said the entire shipload of returnees in which the four had been lucklessly included had simply been dumped into this area to fend for themselves. Some had been able to return to their previous homes, but most had been younger sons or brothers without futures in their native villages. The most princely houses in Little France were huts made from flattened ten-gallon tin oil cans; the majority were of reeds and mud; some were mere lean-tos made from stolen boards and scraps of tar paper and reed matting. The passages were deep with slime. There was a stink of whatever human beings could void; excrement was kept in neat piles before the huts, to be carried on barrows many miles to the country and sold to farmers as night soil. Fu said many men had brought their families here, but there were no women or children in sight because, he said, they were all there—and he waved toward the mills between the encampment and the river. His own wife and two daughters were there.

Had T'ao Tu Hsien-sheng ever been in one of those silk mills?

THEY ENTERED the long reeling room. Treadup felt the sweat leap in hot terror from his forehead, cheeks, and neck, because he thought for a moment that without dying he had arrived in hell. He was relieved, looking at his host, to see that Mr. Hsieh, too, suddenly had pearls on his round face. The room was unbearably overheated. Steam rose from myriad pipe ends. Mr. Hsieh, the owner of the filature, was a Christian and a member of the Y.M.C.A. Board of Directors, so it had been easy to arrange to visit the mill. Mr. Hsieh stood beside the huge missionary and, with delicate courtesy disregarding the foreigner's awful ignorance, explained all.

Down the long room ran four double rows, facing each other, of copper basins, into which boiling water was run from time to time out of the ranks of steam pipes. Along one side of each row little girls, who looked to be from six to twelve years old, stood at their basins swashing cocoons in the steaming water with small reed brushes, to soften them. When the threads on a girl's cocoons were loosened enough, she would scoop a batch through a small gate in a wire-screen divider to the basin of a woman reeler beyond, who also had in front of her a shallower copper basin full of boiling water. The woman would dexterously pick up a filament from each of five or six cocoons and, working a treadle, would spin them together into a silk thread, which would eventually pass on pulleys over her shoulder onto a reel behind.

The children's faces were pallid and pinched. Many were excited by the arrival of a huge big-nose, and they looked up in inattention from their basins. Women overseers, passing constantly up and down the lines, were quick to get them back to work, by the expedient of pushing their small fingers down into the boiling water before them. Almost fainting from shock and distress, the big strong missionary walked down one of the aisles, and he saw that though the girls and women were amazingly skillful at keeping their hands clear of the water, nevertheless their fingers were wrinkled and parboiled, like poached pig's knuckles. On rags on the floor by some of the women's stations lay nursing babies. None of the infants cried; they seemed to know by instinct that they must not.

Treadup searched the faces above the steaming basins, wondering which two girls and which woman were the members of the family of the man named Fu, who had learned in France to read and write and dream of a new dawn in his homeland.

August 31, 1921.

Dear Todd:

I desire to write now concerning the terrible industrial need of this nation. I have found, after visiting many mills and factories here in Shanghai, there are thousands of girls and boys from six to twelve years of age working in the cotton and silk mills twelve hours a day, seven days a week. In the native weaving mills and other industries, children are working up to fourteen hours a day, often standing on their feet all that time, for wages varying from three to seven cents a day. Many of these children receive no pay whatever, but only food worth six cents a day during several years of apprenticeship. I have never seen such conditions in my life.

The Young Men's Christian Association has the unique opportunity to help change these conditions. Our social gospel impels us, does it not, to work for nothing less in the long run than the complete abolition of all wretchedness and poverty?

I have made contact with returned coolies from the Labor Corps in France. When I was in New York I told you how their horizons had been widened there. Many have come home to disillusionment and vile living conditions. Chinese life is being completely turned on its head by what is happening to industrial workers in the cities. Countrymen come here and are "emancipated" from the Confucian restraints. They gamble, find prostitutes, consume foreign wines and drugs, not only opium. They are indifferent to religion. Their customs of participating in country home duties, festivities, and simple daily pleasures such as kite flying or bird training are exchanged for the craze of more and more rapid excitement. The lurid, breathless cinema. The quickly consumed cigarette. Materialism is rampant, filial piety is forgotten, younger brothers become less poor than older brothers and snap their fingers at them. It is each man for himself.

The Y.M.C.A. has no man in all China with industrial training. I have been talking with David Liu, with all our foreign secretaries, and with church leaders here, and they all join me in urging you to send out a National Industrial Secretary to grapple with this situation. I would like to do it myself, but I lack the training. . . .

Ever yours,
David Treadup

A NEW bamboo-framed mat shed goes up in Little France. It is to be a Y hut, just like those in France. Treadup rushes around, supervising Y.M.C.A. students who are doing the actual work. On his own initiative and without clearing it with the National Committee, Treadup has raised the money for this project from one man, Mr. Hsieh, the silk filature owner, a Christian.

DAVID LIU stood in the doorway of Treadup's office. "He had that certain look of geniality which I instantly recognized as a signal of trouble." Liu asked Treadup to take a walk with him. Treadup knew this meant Liu wanted to get away from all ears.

They walked on the Bund. As always they talked in English. Liu said he had had a confidential letter from Todd in New York which was extremely disturbing. It was not easy to speak of its contents. The two men walked as far as the Customs House without further words. Treadup observed the ceremonial silence of Chinese courtesy. Finally Liu said, "You have been my good friend." (Treadup's translation: "This is going to be very unpleasant.") Liu said, "I know you, and there is nothing to worry about." (Translation: "I am worried sick. I have begun to lose my trust in you.")

Here Treadup could wait no longer, and the blunt American in him spoke out: "Come to the point, friend David. What did Todd write?"

Liu said that the International Committee was considering the question of sending out an industrial secretary. The cost would be heavy. They had some other questions. . . .

"David! David! What did he really write?"

Moratorium. Pacing. Then:

Todd had written that since David Treadup's return to China, three different missionary groups had asked the International Committee to withdraw him from the field.

The most importunate had been that new organization, the China Bible Union, which had written—and here David Liu reeled off complaints he seemed long since to have memorized in pain—that Brother Treadup was a Godless modernist who through his lectures on secular science called in question every one of the saving truths of the Holy Word, such as and even including the deity of our Lord and Savior Jesus Christ, His virgin birth, His atoning sacrifice for sin, and His bodily resurrection from the dead, as well as the miracles both of the Old and New Testament, the personality and work of the Holy Spirit, and above all the necessity of the new birth of the individual as a prerequisite to Christian social service—"and so on and so on and so on," Liu said. Oh, and the creation of the universe, and of man in the image of God from the dust of the ground, and of woman from a rib of the man.

"Makes me out to be mighty eloquent," David said, "to wipe all that out"—then realized that sarcasm was in the circumstances his worst possible resort. Liu walked on, very pale.

Liu finally said the second complaint had been in his opinion much more serious. It had come from members of Shanghai's British mission community and clergy, which had written a round-robin letter signed by, among others, an Anglican bishop. This letter had suggested that the said Treadup was associating with Communists among the laborers returned from France and among the returned students posing as returned laborers. It was not thought that the said Treadup was necessarily conspiring in political activities with these people; only that he had been duped by them. But the extent of Treadup's agitation of the industrial issue was beginning to be an embarrassment to a religious establishment cautiously constructed brick by brick in this field since the year 1807. "The wisdom of this world," their letter had said, quoting St. Paul, "is foolishness with God." The diary:

> This horrified me. I doubted myself. Could it be—the simple wheel-barrowman Fu? Was it after all strange that Inventor Wang, a country-man from the north, and the four Shanghainese wheelbarrowmen had come in a delegation, then the four came back, and Fu and the others had pointed my way first toward silk, then cotton, then weaving, then the other factories, and more or less suggested the hut, and—oh, I was stung, stung, by that word "duped"!

Liu turned as if to go back to Quinsan Gardens.

Treadup: "You said there were three."

It took much more time to get this one out. At last: It seemed that "two of our fraternal secretaries"—the euphemism for the Americans in the Y.M.C.A., now that the Chinese secretaries were in charge—had found out—it was rather irregular, there had been a breach of confidentiality—from the editors of the *North China Daily News* the authorship of a letter which purported to speak for the role of the Y.M.C.A. in the anti-Japanese boycott that had been taking place. They said the opinions of the author, spread out that way to the world as if they were the Y.M.C.A. position, had not been tested with the rest of the Association staff. They mentioned "other dubious activities" without specifying what they were.

Treadup was suddenly "blazing angry." "David! You have to tell me who the two were."

No! No! No! Liu fluttered his hands. "Enough confidentiality has been broken already," he said. "I had no right to tell you any of this. James B. Todd's letter was marked 'For Liu Only.' "

"But can't you see that I now have to go around guessing—and we will *all* begin to mistrust each other?"

"I started by saying you are my friend." (Translation: "Now this has become too difficult for me. Please, David Treadup.")

But now Treadup felt an even deeper anger, which condensed itself into three sharp words: "What about China?"

"China?"

"Are we to do nothing?"

"Ah!" Liu said. "Ah."

A FEW DAYS LATER, in Treadup's office at the lab:

FU "You said last week you would be coming to the hut to give a lecture on sanitation."

TREADUP "I have been given another assignment."

FU "What does that mean?"

TREADUP "It means . . . I will not be able to come."

THE "ASSIGNMENT" was in David Treadup's head. He was in igno-minious (or "Christian") retreat. He was not exactly frightened. It was rather that he was driven, by all that he had always lived by, to "try to do the right thing." His reaction was very much as it had been at Syracuse when Chancel-lor Day had severely dressed him down for his pranks of vandalism: "I feel I must buckle down and apply myself." He had decided he must repair his relationships with the other "fraternal secretaries," and with the missionary community at large. At least for the time being he would cut off the visits to the (Communist?) returnees; he would stop pressing for industrial work; notwithstanding the attack of the China Bible Union, he would again busy himself with, and restrict himself to, his well-established and "respectable" science lectures. "My rationalization at the time," David wrote in "Search,"

> was that I had to maintain the usefulness of my mission. I had invested my life for Christ in China. I saw that in my sincere desire to discover, among all of China's urgencies, the one to which I could most fruitfully give myself, I had unwittingly crossed boundaries into certain danger zones, marked out by my elders in the missions. I must get back inside the fences, at least for a while, or I might even be "withdrawn from the field." I know now I was too controlled — or, in other words, too careful. I remember I felt, some nights, as if I would burst. I suppose there must have been a terrible righteous anger down underneath, mostly at myself for not fighting back. Worse, I had frightful dreams of little girls with their hands and feet in boiling water. Inventor Wang's hot fixated eyes burned holes in my field of vision.

THEN ALL PROPORTIONS changed, because on August 24, 1921, Johnny Wu arrived in Shanghai aboard R.M.S. *Empress of Russia*. David Treadup was with David Y. S. Liu on the Whangpoo wharf to meet him.

A SWEEPING GAZE

"IN VOLUME and weight of raw meat," Treadup wrote, "he is about one half of me. But he is ten times me in directed will."

Johnny Wu was five feet five inches tall, to David Treadup's six four. Wu cut his black hair in the Western style and parted it on the left side. Like almost all students returned from the States, he wore clothes he had bought in America: blue serge in cool weather, cream-colored "palm beach" in hot. His forehead was broad and as flat as a plank; there appeared to be a big box of brains behind it. He had flashing eyes, sharp speech, and no sense of humor, though he managed a most agreeable and forgiving smile at the humor of others. He constantly quoted humble sayings from the Chinese classics. His

English, with an eastern American accent, was grammatically perfect. He took Christ seriously, but he was not "a Christer," in the sense students had used the term at his colleges, Yale and Princeton, to describe a holier-than-thou prude and meddler. He was, in fact, quite naturally warmhearted and kind and, with his nervy energy and enthusiasm, utterly charming. But he also burned to a fever of ambition that made his eyes glitter, sometimes, with a prophet's searing, out-of-focus beams.

"In ten short days," David's diary recorded, "he has lifted me out of my doldrums. He makes me feel as if I were his age!"

Johnny Wu was twenty-six; David Treadup had had his forty-third birthday two months before.

EMILY, who was thirty-eight, had for some months been going through one of the most trying periods of her life. Her husband, when he was not off on one of his lecture trips, had been in that charmed protean state of his. This, that, and the other job of good works had suddenly been "just the thing I've been looking for," then in a few days it would not be heard of again. Before she and David had left the States, she had written David's parents that it was as if he was starting all over again, at the "outset of a new career." But he had not seemed able to settle on the nature of that career, and he had been living out the ragged ends of the old one. One evening, not long before Johnny Wu arrived, he had sat down to read a pamphlet that Roscoe Hersey in Tientsin had written, called "Social Service." This work set forth fifty different avenues of effort for missionaries in China. Half an hour into the booklet David threw it against a wall of the room, shouting, "Too much! Too much!" The worst of it for Emily was that all through this shaky period he had always been outwardly cheerful with her and the children—patient, forbearing, polite, loving; but if you were to rap your knuckles on his demeanor, there would come the sound of hollow wood.

Johnny Wu's arrival seemed, at first, to change all that. Wu's fierce single-mindedness was just the stimulus this waverer needed. Here, it must have seemed to David, was the match to set fire to all the tinder that had been accumulating in his restless soul ever since France.

Wu had scarcely stepped off the gangplank when he began to talk, without the slightest concession to modesty, about the grandiose task he had chosen for himself—nothing less than the utter transformation of vast China through literacy. His passion was irresistible. He conferred often with the two Davids, Liu and Treadup, both of whom were soon caught up in Wu's fanatical excitement. David Liu, realizing what prestige the Y.M.C.A. might gain from the triumphs this driven young man was sure to have, persuaded Wu to work through the Association and gave him the title of Education Secretary for the National Committee.

"What thrills me most about little Johnny Wu," David wrote brother Paul,

is the grand scope of his imagination. It is as if he looks at the world through binoculars, sweeping his gaze all along the far horizon. The beauty part of it is that he sees so clearly what needs to be done to make a genuine democracy of China.

He is more than ever convinced that the only way to build a base for democracy in China is through an attempt to educate and Christianize the masses. It certainly is true that China's government can never become truly representative if the great masses of her people are illiterate and ignorant. The country can't expect to put a stop or check to the present prevailing corrupt and unscrupulous officialdom if there is not a public opinion formed to battle against it.

"WHAT A BIG new broom we will need!" David wrote his brother Paul.

The task would indeed be a daunting one. The so-called Republic was a shambles. David explained to Paul that its founders, a few of whom had studied in the United States and had come to admire the American system, had replaced the ancient Empire with "a hastily glued-together papier-mâché model of a Western democracy." But the founders were either idealists or academics, who had "no hardheaded administrative experience at all." They had overlooked the fact that the American Constitution was the product of a long, slow evolution of European ideas that suited the Occidental mind. The Chinese mind, so long habituated to authority, was far from ready for " 'democracy,' registered with the U.S. patent office."

The true oligarchs, the men who really dominated China, were the warlords. The great powers just then were Chang Tso-lin in Manchuria, Wu P'ei-fu and Ts'ao Kun and Feng Yu-hsiang in North China, and an assortment of smaller warlords and tuchuns in the Southwest and West. Each was out to fatten himself. Sun Yat-sen, the hero of the revolution, was in Shanghai, and that "Christian," Treadup had heard, had cooled toward America and had just made an agreement with Lenin's representative which encouraged members of the Chinese Communist Party to join the Kuomintang.

The political outlook was bleak. But here came Johnny Wu, with his infectious confidence; and Treadup, excited by him, felt all alight with possibilities.

HE WAS going to have to bank his fires. It turned out, as weeks passed, that Wu had a great deal of concrete thinking yet to do about how to carry out his vaultingly ambitious work. "It's obvious that Johnny will have to spend the better part of a year plowing and harrowing," David wrote in his diary when the heavy sense of postponement began to crowd in on him.

The situation Wu faced in China was quite different from that in France, where impressive success had seemed so easy. There the fairly homogeneous corps of coolies had had fixed hours of work, had been under military discipline, and had had no pressing worries about livelihood or family, so finding time to study had never been a problem. The very fact of being in a foreign setting, with an advanced technology so visible, had given the coolies incentive to learn. In sprawling, chaotic China the job would be much harder. Just getting the attention of the adult illiterate in the first place would be hard. Even those poor Chinese who might want to learn to read and write would find scant time or strength to spare for study from the endless hours of labor needed to keep from starving. Conditions in the cities were quite different from those in the countryside. And what was to be done about women?

Johnny talked at first of starting a pilot project in his native province of Szechuan, in central China, far up the Yangtze, where, he argued, the need was even greater than in coastal China. And where, too, he could live with his mother, then over seventy years old, whom he had not seen for eight years. But the others ("not entirely unselfishly, I must admit" — Treadup) persuaded Wu it would be a better strategy to start in the east, with headquarters in Shanghai. Moving from there into the principal cities, he would have the well-developed resources of the city Associations on which to build.

It was decided that Johnny Wu would spend several months traveling to Tsinan, Tientsin, Peking, Nanking, and other centers of education to study what was being done and what could be done; then he'd go home to Szechuan to visit his mother; and think; and then go to work.

"He is crestfallen that he cannot spend more time with his elderly mother," David wrote, "but he is philosophical. He quotes the old Chinese proverb, 'It is not easy to be a filial son and a good citizen at the same time.' "

THE SURFACE of Treadup's life during the next few months seemed unchanged. After the excitement of Wu's arrival, waiting was hard. He wrote that he was "dull as a donkey." He traveled with his repertory of set pieces, performing, as he wrote, "like a robot"; he dutifully helped the staff in Shanghai devise new lectures; he tried with all tact but without much success to restore the standards of the Bureau lab. But the number and insistency of the references to Wu in his diary and letters suggest that his abstractedness was really impatience.

Many of the notes on Wu were brief: "Letter from Johnny, Tsinan." "Johnny, quotation from classics: 'The mechanic who wishes to work well must first sharpen his tools.' " "Wu writes penetrating criticism of my lecture program: lack of follow-up. People are excited for a few hours, then what? Johnny says: 'Can't find any gyroscopes in use in the schools I visit.' Ouch." "Johnny, letter: Will Dr. Charles and I teach him how to go into a city and organize a campaign? You bet!"

There were numerous notes about the sharpening of Wu's tools. The thousand characters that Wu and Peter Ma had chosen in France had not been scientifically selected; they were simply the words that they thought the coolies would most likely need in writing letters home and reading sketchy news of China and the war in the *Laborers' Weekly*. One note tells that Wu is excited about having found two returned students at Nanking National Southeastern University, C. H. Chu (Harvard) and Wellington Ts'ao (Columbia), who were already embarked on a scientific reduction of a basic vocabulary. Gradually over the months, as Wu revisited Nanking from time to time, their work evolved a vocabulary that was a compromise between Wu's "practical" thousand characters from France and the one thousand characters scientifically found to be most frequently used in *pai-hua*, the vulgar language shaped by the scholars of the Chinese Renaissance. And the end product was a textbook, the *People's One Thousand Character Lessons*. It was divided into four volumes of twenty-four lessons each, introducing ten or eleven characters in each lesson. Each lesson had three parts: a drawing that showed what was to be learned in the lesson, a simple brief text using the new words, and the new words standing alone. At a lesson a day on weekdays, the course could be completed in four months.

FOR EMILY the waiting period was especially difficult. Her home was cramped. "The house," she wrote her sister Jane, "is a tasteless small stucco affair of the sort that I suppose would be found in a poorish London suburb, with an aspiring address like 31 Favenham Crescent." A cavernous two-story hallway lined with dark-stained wood took up more room than the whole family had to sleep in. The servants' quarters were so bad that even three Chinese countrymen, of the sort who could usually be counted on to be grateful for the luxury of Western squalor, complained: "Missy, one-piece loom no can do."

"One-piece room" wasn't enough for the three boys, either. Philip, now twelve, was at the foot of the cliff of manhood, and he abused his mother, whom he adored, and was like a lamb with his father, whom, just then, he loathed. One doctor after another peered into the shells of nine-year-old Absolom's ears and then shook their heads; the boy heard less than half of what the rest of the world heard—and that was just as well in the boys' room, where Philip and huge little Paul carried on shouting matches. Half-deaf Absolom's mind was brilliant, and he failed most of his schoolwork. Paul, who at eight inhabited a promising copy of his father's physique, was by turns charming and a terror of unconsumed energy.

At Treadup's insistence, all three boys were attending the Shanghai American School. This put a severe strain on the family's finances, which had never been easy, for David Treadup, though he was much impressed by Chinese silks and forty-course banquets, never seemed to be aware of the threadbare sheets and worn upholstery in his own home. Emily managed household money. She gave the cook a monthly allowance to buy food at the market, on the understanding that whatever he could save each month, after taking tiptop care of the family, was his, in accordance with ancient rituals of "squeeze." But the weakness of the Peking government had caused a sharp drop in the rate of exchange, and though the Y.M.C.A. had in theory guaranteed that secretaries' salaries would be kept at an exchange rate of $2.25 (Mex) to a U.S. gold dollar, the actual disbursements had been closer to the old two-to-one. Many evenings Emily pored over her ledgers.

These new trials brought out the best in Emily—her Christian serenity, which was somehow sensuous and seductive. Her friends among missionary wives praised the glow of her skin and the perfection of the whites of her eyes, using phrases that stopped just short of suggesting that anyone so blooming must feel guilty about something. And though David might flounder in the world of work, his diary carried its small home signals: "Em—jasmine!" "Lucky man I am." "Thank Good Lord for Emily Kean Treadup."

EMILY felt that those absurd complaints about David to the International Committee had not really seemed to upset him; he appeared to have gone calmly about the work of reparation. And especially after Johnny Wu had come, he seemed to have shaken off all worries about New York. He had showed her a quite tough letter he had written to James B. Todd, forthrightly facing New York down in the most subtle way, without ever revealing that David Liu had told him about the accusations. But in the letter he was also frank about his frustrations—and in that frankness he may have embedded, quite shrewdly, a subtle preparation of Todd's mind for changes to come. After a stoutly defiant review of the strengths of the lecture program, he added:

> And yet in spite of all this, I am acutely concerned as to whether I am best following the vision of The Christ and doing the most I can for the Kingdom of God.
>   You know something of the dream I have had of a company of Christian lecturers working to mold the public opinion of China in the direction of a Christian civilization. With the present trend of the Y.M.C.A. in N.Y.C. and Shanghai I see no prospect of that dream being realized. When one comes to an issue like surrendering a life's dream, it is a fair question whether one should not consider a new sleep— a new dream.

I understand that you will be in China in the spring for the conference of the World Student Christian Federation. Please reserve an afternoon, so we can sit and talk and pray together about what I have written here.

RUNNING DOG

THE HALL was packed. Treadup stepped out on the stage and sensed at once "a kind of hum, like that of an electric motor working against unusual resistance."

It was March 25, 1922—seven months into the doldrums after Johnny Wu's return. Once again his role was that of the carnival barker. James B. Todd had cabled him from the *President McKinley,* en route to China, asking him to set up with urgent speed a series of lectures in Peking as a warm-up for the huge conference in April of the World Student Christian Federation. Youthful Christians would be coming to the Chinese capital from all over the world, and Todd had cabled:

> MUST MAKE MOST OF OPPORTUNITY FOR GREAT HARVEST
> BEST FRUITS YOUNG CHINA.

Treadup had chosen for his first lecture the hardest nut to crack—Peking University—in order to make the greatest possible impact. And he had decided to risk his densest and most "mental" new lecture—Einstein's Relativity, adapted in Mandarin for this keen young Chinese audience. "My heart pounded as if I were on the sliding seat of a shell, leaning forward to the ready oar, at the stakeboat, just before the start."

The first few minutes seemed to him to go well. "There was not exactly a silence—too intense—more like radio reception between messages, occasional light crackles of static." He had just asked his assistant to uncover the big chart of "Some Diameters," when there came a startlingly shrill shout from the back of the hall. Treadup saw a student standing in one of the rear rows, who was shouting over and over: "Down with this running dog of imperialism!"

"I could not imagine what to make of it. I had never faced such an outburst. I did not know what to do. Finally I raised my hands in stopping motions, commanding silence." Treadup was not at all surprised that the gestures worked. The shouter sat down. Treadup went on. But when he asked for guesses of the speed of the swinging ball, three students stood and began shouting in unison: "Down with the Y.M.C.A.! Down with the Y.M.C.A.!" Soon others were on their feet, shouting "Down with Christianity!," "Down with Capitalism!," "Down with spies!," "Down with churches!"

Now the professor who had been Treadup's introducer was on his feet, wearing the agonized look of a Chinese who has lost face, and he called out in a high, cracking voice for silence. Treadup heard sharp cries from other students, calling for quiet. But more and more voices had joined the heckling. Soon most of the audience was on its feet, shouting either at Treadup or at each other.

It was Babel. For a moment my heart leaped for joy, as the only thing I could think was that we were getting back to apostolic days. But there seemed to be signs that some of the students were going to rush the stage, and I became alarmed for my apparatus. I called out to Ching, and we made haste to pack things up. . . .

Order could not be restored, and as Treadup and his assistant and the professor began carrying the demonstration materials backstage, a triumphant cheer went up.

THAT EVENING when Treadup returned to his room at the Hotel Wagons-Lits, having had no appetite for a dinner alone with his assistant, Ching, he found nailed to the door of his room this broadside, typed in English:

The Non-Christian Student Federation opposes the World's Student Christian Federation which is about to meet on conference in Peking.

Of all religions, Christianity is the most detestable.

Who was Jesus Christ? Like all other religious leaders, he was not mentally sound. The fact that he sometimes called himself "son of God" and sometimes "son of man" shows he had the trouble of "double personality." The fact that he saw the devil three times within a period of a little over a month clearly shows serious disorder of his senses. The fact that he suddenly sat down on the ground which by no means was the ceremony of the ancient Jews, and set his fingers to write on dust, leads us to doubt if that was not a kind of "automatic writing."

Who are missionaries? The majority of them are, as far as our observation goes, below the level of intelligence of the average adults of their own countries. They would not have had the same positions and enjoyed the same material life as they are now holding and enjoying in this country.

What sort of doctrine have they been preaching? Extremely negative morals, so extreme that we would take as vices. The love of the enemy as taught in the Sermon on the Mount is an instance. Our object is to study everything in a scientific spirit, so we are naturally opposed to religion, which is unscientific and superstitious.

What kind of organization is the Y.M.C.A.? Had it not the magnificent buildings for advertisement, hotel plants for receptions, there would never have been so many members, all businessmen and tuchuns and exploiters.

The sin of Christianity which particularly makes our hair rise on end is its help to militarism and capitalism. As capitalism is fast dying out in the West, European and American capitalists are rushing into China to carry out their plan of exploitation so have been using missionaries as their vanguard for the conquest of China. On one hand, missionaries and especially Y.M.C.A. are misleading the Chinese people, and on the other, serving as spies for the capitalists.

Now they see that their last day is drawing near, so they gather together in Peking for reinforcement, preparing for the last and decisive fight. Well, we will give it to them, without any regard of nationality, sex, or race.

Treadup tore the broadside off the nail and stood in the doorway of his room, "my hands shaking so hard that I could barely read." What hurt and angered him most was the assertion, "Our object is to study everything in a scientific spirit." Why, this was exactly what he had spent the best years of his life trying to inculcate in the minds of Chinese students! He was sharing a room with Ching, who could not read English and who asked, with real concern, What was so upsetting to T'ao Tu Hsien-sheng? David said, "I am thinking of the work we have to do tonight and tomorrow."

AT SIX the next morning, Treadup and Ching could be seen on the campus of Peking University, tacking up placards which read:

MEMBERS OF THE CHINESE ANTI-CHRISTIAN STUDENT FEDERATION!

You declare that your object is to study everything in a scientific spirit. If this is true, you will be able to learn about the latest scientific thinking on the shape and inner workings of the universe in a lecture by T'ao Tu, the famous American lecturer on scientific matters, to take place at Yenching University this evening at 8 p.m. Come early because the hall will be crowded to capacity.

HE GAVE the same lecture. It was a great hit. It was true that at Yenching, the church-supported university, he was on hospitable ground. It was also true that the anti-Christian students had shrewdly decided to boycott the lecture. Almost a thousand of them picketed outside the hall, chanting the phrases some of them had shouted the day before. But David Treadup's voice was strong, and he quite easily made himself heard in the big hall.

But he wrote in his diary that night: "I have entered a part of the forest I have never seen before. I may meet tigers."

THE NEXT TWO LECTURES —good old gyroscope and good old aviation —went off without incident, in theaters in the city. He was both heckled and picketed at a fifth lecture at the Y.M.C.A., on temperatures. He began to feel that the opposition, distressing as it was, quickened the appreciation of the sympathetic students. It also spiked his own enthusiasm with anger. But under the anger lay the heavy weight of his own doubts, which had been growing ever since France, and which, though he did not like to think it, were fed by these incoherent new attacks.

He felt a need to air those doubts with a trusted Chinese friend. He sent off two telegrams to Tientsin—to the Roscoe Herseys, to ask if he could spend a night with them, and to Mr. Lin, his wisest Chinese friend, to ask if he could spend a day talking with him. His carnival-barking lectures were over; Todd was about to launch into a series of evangelical talks—the "harvest" of which, it would turn out, would be the smallest he had ever had in China. Picking up his room key at the Wagons-Lits one night, Treadup had found an excited letter from Johnny Wu, saying that his plans had moved faster than he had thought possible—"come to me, David!" Treadup wanted to talk with Mr. Lin not only about his misgivings but also about a possible relief from them in "a new sleep, a new dream."

LIN FU-CHEN met him at the East Tientsin station. David was surprised to find him in a long Chinese gown, because for years he had been wearing Western clothes. He looked haggard—almost as distraught as he had looked on that sad train ride to Peitaiho the summer of his conversion. And quickly David found that Mr. Lin needed to talk perhaps even more than he himself did.

The supposedly Christian students at his own Peikai University had begun attacking Mr. Lin for being a Christian! Each morning huge characters were posted on the spirit-screen of Lin's house: *pan-fan* ("half foreign"), *yang-nu* ("foreign slave"), *erh-mao-tzu* ("hairy one's younger brother"). The students charged that Lin was trying to denationalize them. They mocked his foreign clothes until, trying to see their side of things, he courteously changed to Chinese dress. This appeasement roused them to new furies. They accused him of training them not to love their country. Of forgetting that China was a nation!

Mr. Lin said he had not had an hour of sleep for a week.

Now David Treadup's anger "moved through my tongue," as he put it. What did these youngsters know? They were being used! Perhaps it was true that the Y.M.C.A. had made ties with Chinese businessmen: it needed money to do its work. No one in the Y.M.C.A. had ever wanted money—"come and see how I live in Shanghai!" No Y secretary wanted power—how ridiculous! At every step of the way missionaries had fought the British and American "imperialists," if that's what the merchants were—on extraterritoriality; on reparations for the Boxer Rebellion or any other violence against missionaries; on opium; on gunboats; on recognition. . . . The Y had been one of the few barriers between the greed of foreign businessmen and the imbecile corruption of Chinese bureaucrats.

Suddenly David realized he was railing at his own dear friend—and that what he had just said might have been insulting to a tender Chinese sensibility. He put his hand on Mr. Lin's arm, and said, "Forgive me, old friend. I forget myself."

Mr. Lin said, "You're right. Partly right."

"Surely the Bolsheviks are behind all this," Treadup said. "If you analyze the language . . . "

Mr. Lin raised his hand—and in his diary David tried to report word for word what Mr. Lin said next, because the reproach reached to the very heart of his own uneasiness.

> *"No! Don't make the mistake of writing off the anti-Christian movement because you think it was stirred up by 'outside agents.' We Christians can't by any means wash our hands of these criticisms and so feel smug. I tell you, David, we need a contrite heart. These young people may not phrase their accusations too well, but there's a lot in what they say that should make us search our minds. 'This' is why I've lost sleep. It's true that we Christians have failed to lift our voices high enough in protest against the injustices of this poor country. In our eagerness to 'save men,' we've been guilty of the sin of pride. In order to exalt Christianity—"*

—"and here," David interrupts his report to note, "he looked me straight in the eye, because he was obviously not talking about Chinese Christians but about those of us who really are 'outside agents' "—

> —*"Christians have often failed to appreciate other peoples' civilizations and cultures. They've also failed to appreciate the personality of others. Why is it that a man like Ch'en Tu-hsiu* [the co-founder of the Chinese Communist Party who a few years before had urged Chinese to study the admirable spirit of Jesus Christ] *has become without any hesitation a bitter enemy to present-day Christianity and the Christian church? The*

keen appreciation he once showed of Christ's spirit of internationalism should put many of us to shame. Have we not consciously or unconsciously 'crucified' Jesus again?"

On the train back to Peking, Treadup noted, "I thought to myself: I converted Mr. Lin, but I have a terrible feeling we may lose him."

ALL THE TIME he was able to get, back in Peking, for "a soul-to-soul talk" with the great James B. Todd, in the hurly-burly of a conference which was constantly harassed by anti-Christian students, was a meager half hour, and that in one corner of a room in which two noisy committee meetings were simultaneously taking place. It was most unsatisfactory. Thinking that after all these years he understood Todd's personality, David decided to spend the time on "Godworthy plans," even though he felt his tone of confident manliness was forced. He talked about Johnny Wu's great hopes. Through thick and thin Todd had always believed above all in "saving men," spiritually rather than materially. As to the literacy program, he was noncommittal.

A PICNIC FOR EVERYONE

TREADUP, angry and discouraged, returned to Shanghai. There he found Johnny Wu, drunk on his own edgy keenness, impatiently waiting for David's return. For Wu, racing ahead of the schedule he had set for himself when he had returned to China, was ready to start his first campaign, and he wanted David's help.

The experiment was to be in Changsha, which Treadup had not revisited since the assassination attempt on Governor Chao. All day and far into the night, for three days, Johnny and David, and sometimes Dr. Charles, and sometimes David Liu and others of the staff, and most of the time all the workmen of the lab, made plans and prepared posters and proclamations and dodgers and even, at David's suggestion, four sandwich boards with appropriate texts.

They loaded everything onto a river steamer and started off.

D A V I D felt a surge of his old energy. He was staying at the Yale-in-China cam-pus. He could not wait to get out of bed each morning. As soon as he did, he let himself down into a cold bath with a roar which made servants run here and there in great alarm. Doing something worthwhile again! And so much to do!

The first task was to raise the consciousness of the Changshanese. Here Wu and his team used methods that dated all the way back to the cholera campaign in Foochow ten years earlier:

• They formed a large committee of leading citizens.

• They put up fifteen hundred posters, picturing a blind man holding a letter and begging for someone to read it to him.

• They persuaded Governor Chao's successor, Governor Huang, to issue an official proclamation urging all citizens who had illiterate children or apprentices to avail themselves of the chance to make them literate, and they put up five hundred copies of it.

• They held a meeting of shop masters, chiefly from the manual trades, to urge them to send their apprentices to school.

• The Governor presided at a mass meeting, which was covered by the city's newspapers.

• The climax came in a huge parade of college and middle-school students, who carried banners and lanterns with slogans: "An illiterate man is a blind man." "A blind nation is a weak nation."

NOW THEY DIVIDED the city up into sixty districts. They organized, trained, and sent off into those districts sixty teams of students, who canvassed, block by block and building by building, the homes, stores, workshops, and factories in each district, signing up illiterate men and boys on registration cards. This recruiting had to be called off after two-thirds of the districts had been covered, because in three afternoons nearly fourteen hundred prospec-tive students, far more than Johnny Wu had thought he would be able to handle, had signed up.

In the meantime Wu enlisted eighty teachers from the staffs of govern-ment, mission, and private schools. Each teacher was to keep on with regular schoolwork during the day and would teach one and a half hours each evening. All had agreed to do this for no pay, except for four dollars a month for ricksha fare. David helped Wu train these teachers in the special methods—including singing and game playing—they would need to use in the thousand-character course.

Wu's team secured rooms in buildings all over the city for the classes, so that working people would not have to go too far for their study. The team got commitments from primary schools, churches, guild halls, temples, clubhouses, private homes, police stations, and of course the Y.M.C.A.

David to Emily:

I don't know when in my life I have worked so hard with so little sense of effort. We are at it twenty hours a day, yet I am not tired. I feel as if I am swimming, breast stroke, in calm and very deep waters, toward a lakeside beach where there will be a picnic, with tablecloths spread on the grass, and cucumber sandwiches, and deviled eggs, and watermelon pickles, and sponge cake, and grape juice—a picnic for everyone.

Submerged in Treadup's benign, dreamlike image of the swim toward a picnic, one senses something darker, which Treadup himself did not recognize until much later. There are no other swimmers in the picture. He is alone. The water is "very deep." In a letter to Emily during a later campaign, in Kashing, Treadup writes:

In that first hurly-burly in Changsha, everything went so fast, everything was so improvised and jerry-built, that I felt as if I were floating along without having the faintest idea where I was or what I was doing. Part of it, I see now, was that I was not in control. My lectures had been mine. This was my first experience of being a follower. It put me in a kind of daze. I realize now that I was happy but I was also not happy.

IN APRIL the term began. What a student body! The pupils ranged in age from six to forty-two, though most of them were between ten and twenty. Nearly three hundred of them were coolies; nearly two hundred were apprentices in various small trades. There were, besides, adult tailors, ricksha pullers, cobblers, silversmiths, scavengers, policemen, mortar mixers, varnishers, bamboo workers, coinsmiths, herbalists, barbers, firecracker makers, pig buyers, professional beggars. . . .

DAVID could not justify, either to the Lecture Bureau or to Emily, staying in Changsha through the entire four months of the course, but he did manage to get back to the city again for the promotion ceremonies at the end of the first month, when the first quarter of the course was completed. Wu had invited, to applaud the students, their families, their shop masters, and their friends, and to whoever passed the first examinations he awarded the first of a series of badges keyed to the colors of the Chinese national flag. The proud wearing of these badges in the city helped spread the word about

Johnny Wu's bold aim, which began to appear on posters in the city: ALL CHANGSHA ABLE TO READ!

One thing Treadup learned in that June visit was that even though Johnny Wu's literacy program was openly advertised as a project of the Y.M.C.A., there was not a single disruption of any of its sessions by anti-Christian students. Indeed, in later years evidence was found that a young man of twenty-nine named Mao Tse-tung, by then already a member of the Chinese Communist Party in Changsha's Hunan Province, had himself been one of the volunteer teachers in that campaign. It was reported that one of Mao's associates had rewritten the textbooks for his students.

ON AUGUST 20 David Treadup managed to get himself to Changsha again, this time for the commencement exercises of the first course. The staying power of the program had been amazing. Of the 1,370 impoverished workers who had matriculated at the beginning, more than twelve hundred stayed through to the end, and of those, 967 passed their finals. On that triumphant afternoon, Governor Huang handed them certificates as Literate Citizens of the Republic of China.

The city decided to continue the courses on its own, and in September over fifteen hundred new illiterates were enrolled for the second term.

TUCKED AWAY in a letter to Emily, written from Changsha on the day of the commencement ceremonies:

"I think I've finally found a rock on which to stand."

A THRILLING IDEA

IT IS May Day, 1923. Treadup is in Paoting, where, last evening, he delivered his lecture on aeronautics. He is up early, taking a long walk before breakfast. He stayed overnight with Letitia Selden and Helen Demestrie, and on the old rattling bed memories flurried in his mind in the dark. He feels a need to sift them in the heady air of first light.

He strikes out on a rutted earthen road to the southward. The air is misty and fragrant with the odor of damp soil. In less than a mile he comes to the first village; in the habit of such country roads, this one bypasses the village. Smoke is rising in a thin blue ribbon from a fire in the village; some way up, the ribbon seems to burst into renewed flame as the rays of the sun, poised on the distant lip of the day, strike it. There is a fork. Drawn by the sunrise, he turns to the east.

He comes to the bank of the river. He stands still for a long time on the tow path. Later he will write:

> I had a distinct memory of having walked to this very spot, once, on one of my country strolls with Emily. Now, as I stood there, in the intensity of my remembering, I had the strangest mental experience: there was something puzzling and extremely attractive at the edge of my mind, but I couldn't bring it into focus. Was it a kind of expectation? Straining to call it to the foreground, I thought over the recent days, guessing it might be something I had meant to do, which had slipped my mind.

"HAVE BEEN leading a double life," he had written in his diary a few days before. "Juggled between Hu and Wu." He was still a lecturer for the Bureau, being scheduled for engagements here and there by John Y. Hu, the man in charge of the Lecture Bureau. But the more active and eager part of his mind was committed to Johnny Wu's ambitious new venture.

Early in April, Johnny had invited him to help prepare a new literacy campaign in the treaty port of Chefoo, in the north. As it happened, John Hu had already posted him for lectures in the northeast in late April and early May. He could manage both, but to make sure there would be no confusion, Treadup had cleared his going to Chefoo with the General Secretary, David Liu, and Liu had given him permission with an alacrity which surprised him. "But on reflection"—Treadup in his diary—

> I know that David Liu has invested his heart in Johnny's wild dream for China, and he knows that the showmanship we've developed in our lectures can help make that dream come true.

The prospect of the Chefoo campaign was particularly exciting. This was not just because Chefoo, on the upper coast of Shantung, the northern province jutting out into the China Sea like the head of a camel, had long been a fruitful center of missionary activity. Numerous schools and colleges were located in and near the city, and nearby stood, among other wonders, a villa which had been the home of the Presbyterian missionary Henry W. Luce, whose son Henry R. Luce, back in the States, was in that very year fresh out of Yale, raising money to start a weekly news magazine. Nor was the Chefoo prospect so promising just because the team now had some experience behind it—though this gave it confidence and saved it the energy of waste motions.

No, this campaign would be special because they were going to try something new and most radical: This time females were to be given a chance to learn to read and write.

THE WHOLE TOWN had backed the literacy campaign. Shops and schools throughout the city had closed down on the day of the opening mass rally. So many people turned out that it was necessary to hold simultaneous meetings in the largest guild hall and the largest theater in town. Right after the meetings fifteen thousand businessmen, students, gentry, scholars, and artisans marched in a parade. Student recruiters scattered into fifty-two districts, and in two days 1,466 boys and men and 633 girls and women were enrolled.

WITH THE CHEFOO CAMPAIGN well launched, Treadup had swung off to lecture at Tsingtao (Electricity), Tsinan (Radio), and Paoting (Aeronautics). There had been sporadic heckling at all three lectures by students involved in the May Fourth Movement, but at all three cities he had blunted the disturbances by talking about the Changsha and Chefoo literacy campaigns, in which Movement people had been taking part.

Standing there on the towpath in that mental state, I racked my brains. Whatever it was, off there in the mist, was so desirable. As in a child's game, when, blindfolded, you're hunting an object and the other players call out "You're cold," "Getting warmer," "No, no, cold again," I groped for this elusive something. Chefoo? No, that felt cold—except—perhaps there was a—what was it—that I had seen on the city streets? The lectures? The angry young students shouting about imperialism and capitalism? Cold. I veered off in completely different directions—earlier times in Paoting? Miss Titty's hand on my cheek? The martyrs of Paoting—Annie Gould slung like a pig on a pole before they killed her? Then better thoughts—Emily! Emily! Then: The light in Teacher Chuan's eyes, responding to the little show with the gyroscope Mama had sent me? Cool. Then suddenly a clear view again of the sun on the tower of smoke rising from the village—warm, somehow warm. . . . But I could not find whatever it was, and I turned away from the river and started back.

An hour later, sitting over coffee cups at the dining table, "I snapped out of it. It came to me in a flash." Two images—a country beggar in filthy rags on a paved sidewalk in Chefoo, and the sunlit ribbon of smoke—came together, as he wrote, like the *yin* and the *yang*, and "I had it. What a thrilling idea!"

But that is all he wrote in the diary—"a thrilling idea." He did not share the idea even with the diary. Was he afraid that someone—who could it be but Emily?—would peek? On his return to Shanghai he apparently did not tell Emily, for a long time, what had hit him.

IN MAY, the wise old man of the Association in the China field, Farrow R. Blackton, was in town. He was now based in New York, as Associate General Secretary of the International Committee, but he had come to China on an inspection tour. He had cabled ahead asking if he could stay with the Treadups. In David's absence Emily had had to suffer the chagrin of cabling Blackton on his ship to say that they did not have a guest room. Blackton stayed then with the Keystones. After his return David had several warm, confidential talks with Blackie. David was full of two topics: the delicate issue of the slippage of standards in the Lecture Bureau lab under Chinese management; and Johnny Wu's mass education campaign. "I was emphatic in saying I thought this was the best thing the Y had ever done. I wanted him to get the message to Todd and the others in New York." Unless this last passage was a hint, there was nothing to be found either in his diary notes for those days or his later exchanges of letters with Blackton to suggest that he had divulged in these talks his thrilling Paoting idea.

One day Farrow Blackton said, "Of course you know Johnny Wu is in Shanghai."

This took David by surprise. He had assumed that Johnny was still in Chefoo. How could Wu possibly have come to Shanghai without being in touch with him?

Blackton said he had heard he was having a series of meetings with some of the big men of "the Renaissance"—notably the great Dr. Hu Shih, and W. T. Tao, Huang Yen-pei, Yuan Hsi-tao, and some others. And a rich and powerful elderly lady, Madame Shen Hsi-ling, widow of an ex-premier, was constantly with Wu, Blackton said.

The diary:

Asked around. All staying in a private mansion. Did not dare run Johnny down. He evidently didn't want to be in touch with me, and if I had pursued him, we both would have lost face. What is this about? Hurt.

A FEW DAYS later the hurt was healed. Treadup received an excited and affectionate letter from Johnny Wu, postmarked Chefoo. It said that he had decided to put on a literacy campaign in a smaller city, and had chosen Kashing, in Chekiang Province, not far southwest of Shanghai. Would David take a major role in getting it started?

Treadup at once wrote back:

I have been wrestling with the desperate realization that there are some 300 million illiterates in China. We must hurry! One way of hurrying is to make it possible for each teacher to handle, let us say, 250 students in one room, rather than 12 or 15. May I try an experiment in Kashing? Stereopticon! With a magic lantern we can project enormously magnified characters onto a screen. One teacher can easily preside over recitals by a large class. . . .

Two days later a telegram came:

GO AHEAD YOU ARE GENIUS.

Was *this* the brilliant idea? We find out later that it was not, but for the moment it was enough to engage fully the trait David Treadup rightly valued most in himself—his wholeheartedness. Here he was no one's assistant; he was in control. His keenness vibrates in his report of the Kashing experiment, written at the end of the term for Johnny Wu, James B. Todd, and the whole world to see:

A very expert teacher is assigned a class of 250 in one room. Lights go out! The stereopticon flashes a brilliantly colored picture on the screen. It is a picture of a man. Following a discussion—who is this man? is he like the students themselves?—the character for "man" is thrown on the screen in gigantic size. The pupils see the written character for the spoken word and are called on to repeat the word, "man." Two hundred fifty voices shout "man" as loudly as possible. You can't imagine the noise they make. Hundreds of voices pour the sound in upon the eardrums, and the hands draw the character first in the air, then in chalk on slates.

Do you think they will ever forget it? Never! A powerful subconscious action is induced by means of the repeated crossover of the senses: Eyes see the graphic material, throat repeats, the hand writes in air, mind grasps the meaning, the hand writes on cold slate, and 250 other voices pound on the eardrums in unison.

The results: amazing! Students eat, sleep, and dream Chinese characters. They come through rain, flood, and mud, and will not be denied.

At the end of the term we are forced to the conclusion that not only can large numbers, 200 to 400, be handled by one teacher, but that the work can be carried forward on this quantity basis with greater speed and with higher-grade learning results than in the individual small classes.

This method is soon to be adopted widely through the country. A great light begins to shine in Asia. I believe it will reach in beneficent and healing rays around a dark and needy world.

AN INTERLUDE in Shanghai. Treadup feels that he is, at last, God-intoxicated. He has almost too much energy. He systematically resumes rowing. He is at the boathouse as dawn begins to break. He streaks in his shell through the new light, his oars leaving pairs of circles of ripples on the metal-smooth water. He comes home and eats a lion's breakfast. Emily, with a delicate gray veil over her velvet-piped brown hat, and pulling on immaculate white gloves, is ready to go out to the mills. The boys, in white shorts and shirts at the breakfast table, will have a morning of tennis and swimming at the Shanghai American Club. They chaff each other without malice. Their father is calm, benign.

He chooses not to ride a ricksha to Quinsan Gardens; he walks at a brisk pace.

David Liu, who sets all the staff an example of industriousness, is already at his desk. He is a short, wiry man with gold-rimmed spectacles, in a Western suit with a fresh stiff collar on his shirt. He is tightly wound up. The cords of his neck are like the strained ropes of a working block and tackle, as his brain struggles to lift from his torso the weight of all his responsibilities.

Treadup asks if he may close the door. Liu nods. Treadup has never been more charming. Liu, who knows all the craft and the ceremony of the sages, has guessed that Treadup wants something. The balance of forces between these two men is most delicate: Treadup hired Liu as his assistant in the early days of the Lecture Bureau; now Liu has risen to be General Secretary of all China; Treadup is an underling and a supplicant. The resonant fact is that this conversation is taking place in China; one man is native, one foreign. Treadup pulls back, postpones. Liu is suddenly quite American: "What is it, David?"

Treadup rhapsodizes about the Kashing stereopticon experiment.

Liu's dark eyes give a glistening reflection of Treadup's animation.

Then Treadup blurts it out: He wants to be transferred from the Lecture Bureau to work full time for Johnny Wu's mass education program.

The Paotingfu idea? Almost but not quite, we infer, for that evening's diary entry laconically says: "Didn't spill all the beans." For the moment, there is such a look of relief on David Liu's face that David Treadup wonders if something is wrong with his request.

Liu beams. "Certainly. When?"

Treadup has a puzzled feeling that it has been too easy. Had he been such a nuisance to the Lecture people, bucking up their standards, that they wanted to get rid of him *that* much?

AS DAVID recovered his bounce, Emily flagged. There was not room in that poky Shanghai house for a cheerful man.

To get back her strength, she strayed out of the house and into the city to "contribute." The advanced concerns among female missionaries just then were child labor and the factory life of women, and these became Emily's. Though it would have been hard for the missionaries to admit it, there could be no doubt that the increasing agitation of the Communists in the Yangtsepoo Road factory district was what had finally opened their eyes to the appalling conditions of work in the mills. Emily headed for the district.

First she toured the plants owned by members of the Y.M.C.A. Board of Directors and by large contributors to the Y. David had given her a vivid description of the little girls dipping their hands in simmering water in the cocoon tubs at the filature he had visited; but still, she was deeply, deeply shocked. She wept a good part of each day at what she saw, and, empathy proving therapeutic, came home in rather good spirits.

After she had canvassed the mills for a couple of weeks, she called on certain owners and treated them to some forthright American speech. These elegant Chinese gentlemen were not used to having women of any nationality speak sharply to them. Nor could they have imagined that a missionary lady would be strongly inclined to blackmail them—to the extent, that is, of threatening exposure through articles in the foreign press if they would not take certain steps.

The gentlemen fanned themselves, as if it were hot, or tucked their hands in the sleeves of their gowns, as if it were cold.

Far from responding to such signs of loss of face with delicacy, Emily pounced on the men with new onslaughts of frankness. She asked the men for promises. If she got none, she returned again and again. Any small promise she got from one mill owner she used against another—until there came to be a regular trade war of promises.

Soon: lunch hour a few minutes longer in one filature; a quarter-hour shorter day at another; better ventilation at a third. One very small gain after another. Each announced with warm praise in the foreign press. The changes were by no means fundamental; they were minor palliations. But they made news in the Settlement. There was never mention of Mrs. David Treadup's name, of course; leave it to Philistines to parade their piety on street corners, for all to see.

And soon the norm was restored. Emily became as usual more cheerful even than David. The cramped little house became cozy.

AT JOHNNY WU'S invitation, Treadup attended, on August 1, the Chefoo graduation exercises. Here Treadup met and talked with Johnny Wu's friend and patroness Madame Shen—a woman who was to be a decisive figure, later, in David's life. She was a great lady of the New China. She wore silks with in-woven patterns as subtle as watermarks in delicate paper. She had bound feet. But she was "modern": she cropped her fingernails and wore makeup. She was a dowager whose money power clung to her like a sensuous fragrance. She had given her endorsement—and some of her wealth—to "causes": first to the safe Red Cross, then to schools for the trades, then more daringly to the Women's League, and now to this campaign in which, for the first time, females were being relieved of the blindness of illiteracy.

Madame Shen was the principal speaker at the commencement exercises. The Chefoo Police Department Band and the American Fleet Band furnished music. Evidently moved deeply by her own generosity, Madame Shen wept as she said, "I have never seen barefoot scholars before." She placed certificates of Literate Citizenship in the hands of 372 girls and women and 775 boys and men.

Then she made an announcement which, David wrote, "shook me, because I was so astonished that Johnny Wu had not told me about it beforehand." On August 20, she said, there would be held at Tsinghua College in Peking a National Convention on People's Education. Delegates had been invited from twenty provinces, including far northern Chahar and Heilungkiang.

Treadup assumed that Johnny Wu had been so busy that he had simply forgotten to invite him. Surely he would.

WHILE TREADUP was in Chefoo, John Y. Hu, the chief of the Bureau, wrote to Blackton, now back in New York:

> I am not sure if word has come to you regarding the condition of our friend David Liu.
>
> You probably know that when David returned from his trip to Manchuria, where he was put into a very heavy schedule, he complained several times that he was unable to get sufficient air in his lungs. Recently he had a series of uncomfortable feelings and pains in his heart. He was confined to the hospital for about a week to undergo a thorough examination. The doctors now insist that he must have at least three months absolute rest. He returned a few days ago and is now living comfortably in his home, where Mrs. Liu is guarding him most carefully.
>
> Two nights ago the National Executive Committee in granting David a three months' sick leave from the General Secretaryship for all China, asked me at the same time to act in his place during the interim. I shall need the friendly advice of all of you as well as your prayers that the work of the National Committee may not suffer until such time as David can resume his work.

Returning to Shanghai and finding Hu in charge and David Liu absolutely cut off for three months from all decision making, David was in a quandary. Liu had approved his request to be transferred full time to the literacy work, but had he communicated the approval to anyone else? David decided to go directly to Hu and ask again for permission. If David Liu's so very enthusiastic acquiescence had meant that the Bureau people wanted to get rid of him, Hu would make no difficulty. David felt that he needed a decision right away, before Johnny Wu's invitation to the imminent National Convention in Peking would come, so he would be free there to tell Johnny of his enlistment full time in the mass-education work.

Again, the same careful approach: the closed door, the charm, the holding back, and finally the question.

Hu in a dead flat voice: "David. We need you in the Lecture Bureau. Now that I've been taken away from it, we especially need you . . . to keep our people toeing the line. . . . You said it yourself—exactness in every measurement."

David sensed that Hu would not like his saying that David Liu had approved the idea. He decided to let it ripen a few days.

HE POUNCED on the mail every morning, but no invitation to Peking arrived. David felt a chill. It came to him, one morning while he was rowing, that Johnny Wu's meetings in Shanghai with the Renaissance people must have been to *plan* the National Conference! His not having been told anything then, and his not being invited now—there could be no doubt, he was being deliberately excluded.

ON AUGUST 20, the day of the opening of the Convention, this letter came:

> My dearest friend:
>
> The insane busyness of my life in recent weeks has led me to an oversight which lies very heavy on my heart. I should long since have sat down, looking straight into your brown eyes, to unburden myself to you.
>
> I know you know about the Conference that is to begin in Peking in a few days. David, we have come to a crossroads. Look here, we have become too big for the Y.M.C.A. More than 50,000 students have now graduated from our schools, nearly a quarter of a million more are enrolled or are about to be. Over 1,400 teachers have offered their services for no money. A hundred thousand people have taken part in our campaigns to wake up the illiterates. Governor Chou of Fukien has issued a proclamation that after a certain date anyone who does not

know the one thousand characters will have to pay an Ignorance Tax!

So at this Conference we are going to form an autonomous National People's Education Association. I know that you, dear David, with your keen sensitivity to what is right for our poor benighted country, will understand one aspect of what we are doing which is essential. Namely, this must be an all-Chinese undertaking.

You must not, my beloved friend, feel cut away from me and my work. Feel instead that you have been successful! You have tutored me in the ways of Christian love, I hope I have learned well from you. Furthermore, I need you as much as ever. Your fecund ideas — the stereopticon! — the sandwich boards! — the parades! I need your thinking, I need the way you sometimes turn cartwheels, I need your heart which must be huge and warm in your generous body.

Think what we can do for China! There is no limit!

> *Your devoted friend,*
> *Johnny Wu*

THE DIARY:

Emily heard me blowing nose after I had read the letter. She: "Is my baby boy boo-hooing again?" I: "This is no teasing matter." She rushed to me, swift in contrition. At once I told her the idea I had had at Paoting. It is somewhat changed, now that Johnny is cutting himself off from the Association, but in a way it is more valid than ever. Despite the enormous wrench it will entail, she is in complete accord. Em, my sapphire!

DAVID decided to "make haste slowly." Blackton had written that he was coming out again in the autumn on another tour of assessment, and Emily agreed with David that since David Liu might be back at work by then, it would be best to hold the proposal until Blackie arrived.

In the meantime, he wrote, the prospect of living out his "Paoting idea" gave him "that endless irrepressible playful energy we see in the rhesus monkey — always jumping about like a gymnast, playing pranks, picking fleas off friends, grinning and making faces, swinging and leaping and running here and there."

With John Y. Hu's approval, he began an intensive series of what he called "raids" on the Bureau lab, driving the technicians to take each measurement three times, never to be satisfied with rough tolerances, to "back the Germans off the map in fine precision."

His correspondence with Johnny Wu was exuberant and full of suggestions. Why not the slogan: "The Educating of China's Millions in This Generation"? Johnny Wu had long recognized the need for intensive follow-up work—in "People's Continuation Schools," with four more months of classwork, and David had many suggestions for ways of getting things to stick in the students' minds. How about encouraging reading circles? And perhaps "Question Stations," places to which people could go at odd hours to ask about characters or borrow texts?

He carried on with his lectures. "On the platform," he wrote,

> *my zest almost bursts the buttons of my jacket! I feel a great freedom, because I know that one day soon I will step off the treadmill. I want each lecture to be the best I have ever given!*

He managed on one trip to get to Peking. There he found Johnny Wu's great national organization holed up in a tiny courtyard of two rooms in Madame Shen's palatial compound. "Our talk was like badminton. How we hit the feathercock back and forth across the net!"

Finally Treadup asked about plans. Wu said it would not be possible to put on any campaigns in the north, for the time being, because of constant disruptions by the warlords. In recent weeks the disintegration of the country had been disastrous. Johnny had heard that the province of Kwangtung alone had twenty-seven different governments! Wu said he was planning campaigns for the fall far away from the most dangerous battles—those in the north between Wu P'ei-fu, the biggest warlord of the area around Peking, and the Manchurian warlord, Chang Tso-lin. The literacy campaigns would be in central China, at Nanking and Wuhan. Would David come and "keep us on our toes"?

AT RISK

"THE TIME has come," Treadup wrote in his diary, "to roll the dice."

Wise Farrow Blackton had arrived back from the States in October, and he had now called a meeting of the senior people in Shanghai, for what he later characterized in his report to the International Committee in New York as

> *a penetrating and sobering review on the part of the staff here of the most difficult question in the entire history of the Association out here in China—the balance of power between the Chinese secretary and the*

American secretary. Or, to put the question more deeply and more bluntly: If the foreign missionary pulls out, leaving things to his Chinese brother, will Christianity survive in China? David Treadup was after me when I was here last spring to air this fearful question, and he pressed for the discussion this time. David Liu was well enough to take part. Those present: Liu, Wood, Keystone, Hu, Treadup, and myself.

It was true that Treadup had urged Farrow to have this discussion, but we can deduce from the way things turned out that his real motive in pushing for the meeting was quite different: He wanted to put at risk his Paoting idea.

SUMMARY MINUTES OF INDIVIDUAL POINTS OF VIEW,
Staff Conference, October 12–13, 1923.

F. ALBERT WOOD "We American secretaries cannot do the job. The Chinese must do it in their own way. In training work, however, I see the big place for the foreigner — creating leaders — not doing the job. Leadership in China is created often by our getting out, not by our feeling so terribly important. Of course the golden mean is needed here. And we are apt to err in being too conscientious about our divine call."

DAVID Y. S. LIU "Be careful! The Association in China is yet a very tender plant and the work, by a false move, could be put back for twenty years. The Chinese staff is still young, inexperienced — quite unable to stand alone. So far our Chinese Associations have not been able to secure many men of outstanding strength and possibilities to serve as local secretaries. The Boards of Directors are on the whole not yet men of the kind of vision of Association work that is so essential, and they're not themselves of high enough standing in the community to make it easy to get the best type of men for the secretaryships. We are working on the problem, but I do not see how we can maintain even the present work with any considerable withdrawal of foreign secretaries."

ROBERT H. KEYSTONE "I agree. We must fight for all we are worth to get the American Brotherhood *not* to turn loose the work that has so far been accomplished. The Chinese Movement has avoided most of the serious mistakes which held back the American Movement during its first fifty years. It hasn't entered any city of importance in which the Association has died, or in which it has made such blunders that the name of the Association has become anathema. There is no city in which the Association has incurred great debts. None in which it has bought property and lost it. None in which the Association has had to be abandoned. None in which it has fallen permanently into bad hands. None in which the program has been prostituted onto wrong lines. I marvel when I consider that the Association has had to be developed in China in the midst of great political disturbances, and that the Christian Church has been weak in every city where the Association has gone to work, and that the Y has had to make its way against non-Christian traditions, prejudices, and agitation. The magnitude of the achievement is amazing."

JOHN Y. HU "You speak of making way 'against' non-Christian traditions. There's the rub! Hu Shih—and, as you know, there is no more profound scholar in the country than he—has written somewhere that in a hundred years of work in China the Christian religion has made no appreciable impression on the life of the people. Its chief contribution has been in education. On the whole Christian work, he said, has 'been worthy neither of praise nor of condemnation,' and he predicted that if the Christians kept going as they had been, they would be 'eliminated' in the natural course of things. I put it to you that we know through our own life experience that Christianity is very much a superimposed growth in China and that it hasn't really taken root. The only way to fight for its survival is to take it into the innermost recesses of the Chinese mind and spirit. To do this, we need men with the ability and devotion to find the preparation for Christ in the classical literature of China, and to find the consummation of the Chinese sages in the teachings of the Bible. No man can do this who is not a thorough Chinese scholar and a great spiritual Christian. *This* is the real Chinese leadership we need in Christian work."

DAVID TREADUP "I somewhat disagree. What you suggest, John, looks too much to the past, if you will forgive my saying so. And China in the past has cut itself off from the advances that science has brought to the rest of the world. On the other hand, perhaps we missionaries have not stopped to study carefully enough how those advances might best be adapted to enter, as you say, all the way into the Chinese mind and spirit. Introducing American cotton seed to China, missionary agriculturists have found that the scientifically refined American seed does not grow in Kiangsu soil as it did in Georgia. One way to remedy the situation might have been to try to transport Georgia soil, Georgia climate, and Georgia workers to Kiangsu, but of course that couldn't be done. The other way was to orient the seed to China, cross it with the Chinese staple and adapt it to Chinese soil, Chinese climate, and Chinese farmers. Working along this line the past few years the results have been remarkable. Should the agriculturalists have insisted on growing American cotton by American methods in Chinese soil by Chinese farming methods, they would have failed utterly, and Chinese Doubting Thomases would have said, 'I told you so.' Would that we Americans who work with ideas and minds in China could have learned to be as 'practical' as those who work with seeds and soil!"

AN HOUR LATER. The moment was perfect. The mood was just right. Blackton and the staff sat in overstuffed chairs, covered with white muslin, in the boardroom. Teapots and half-emptied cups were on the tables before them. The topic had more or less run its course. Nothing had been solved, but there was a feeling that new insights might be possible in the near future and that—equally heartwarming—further funds would be forthcoming from the International Committee for tillers of the field who wanted so badly to be right-minded. The Americans had to some extent humbled themselves; the Chinese had made face.

Treadup began talking, rather casually at first, about Johnny Wu's "people's education campaign." Here was a Chinese Christian doing something totally new, something that was obviously "practical," something that got important results with amazing speed, something that challenged the old ways of Chinese thinking but that was manifestly needed if China was to become a modern nation. A vast undertaking, to make all China literate!

So far, Treadup said, now choosing his words with caution, Wu had been working in the centers of population where the need seemed most urgent and the techniques he had developed seemed most productive—in the cities.

"Recently, while visiting Paoting, I was struck by a great parallel need in the countryside. The peasants have been just as 'blind' as the urban workers. And they are, after all, four-fifths of China."

He paused, allowing a long silence in which the others could think about what he had said. Then, looking from face to face:

"Johnny has left us. But I have worked closely with him. We love each other as brothers. I would like the permission of the National Committee and of the International Committee to go and live in Paoting to tackle this rural need on an experimental basis in the countryside there that I know so well. Working for the Y.M.C.A. and with Johnny."

Treadup made the case that the lecture program had been, and still was, an important contribution to an awakening China; the Bureau was now flourishing in strong Chinese hands. His own role as founder of the program, and innovator in it, had long since been phased out. It was time for him to turn new soil.

He left it at that. There was a lengthy discussion. He had, in a way, prepared both David Liu and John Hu for his request, and he had talked at length with Blackie about Johnny Wu's work. Of course such a radical change of assignment would require formal action in both Shanghai and New York, but at the end of that day David Treadup felt confident enough to write:

"It is good for a man to become a beginner again, every few years!"

THE CURE-ALL

THE NEW BEGINNING was haunted by memories of an old beginning. Here David and Emily were in the very same two rooms that had been their first married home. They slept in the same ancient iron bed which rattled and squeaked like a Peking cart whenever one even dreamed about motion. Out the window they saw the same arbor with the same charming tangle of climbing roses.

The American Board people at Paoting had generously given the Treadups temporary housing for as long as David would need to buy a small compound for the Association, where the family would make its home for good and where he would have the headquarters for his literacy work; and they had wound up, once again, downstairs from Mesdemoiselles Selden and Demestrie.

Old times! Miss Titty called Em "Hazy" and patted David's cheek. Some things were different: Miss Selden's hair was gray and Miss Demestrie had a lame knee — and the Treadups were five in number, not two. The three boys slept on cots in the "living room." Treadups were all over each other. There was a game called sardines, and they were playing it. No one minded. Paterfamilias was young again. He bellowed, slightly off key, in his cold bath every morning:

> *When you hear dem-a bells go ding, ling, ling,*
> *All join round and sweetly you must sing...*

ON HIS second day in Paoting, Treadup wrote to Johnny Wu in Peking ordering three thousand copies of all four parts of the *People's One Thousand Character Lessons*. The diary: "Might as well be optimistic."

TREADUP knew he would need, in all things, and especially in launching his literacy campaigns in the villages, a Chinese gentleman of impeccable credentials as his partner and agent. An elderly man, to begin with, so all would respect him. Someone who knew the area well. A scholar, perhaps. A Christian. A man of some standing, either of wealth or of position — not one of your rapscallion rice-bowl Christians whom shrewd villagers would instantly recognize as a confidence man. One who was "modern"—who wanted a new China enough to work hard for it. And a man, if possible, with a confident temperament: the sort who would laugh at things that were funny, not only at things that were embarrassing.

He asked everyone and everywhere for such a man, and finally, one day, Dr. Cowley, still holding forth at the northern suburb, grudgingly made a suggestion. Dr. Cowley said he knew a chap named Hsiao, a landholder in a *hsien* to the southeast of Paoting, a man, he said, "of old-fashioned manners but up-to-the-minute thinking," whom he, Cowley, had converted many, many years ago. So long ago, indeed, that one of Hsiao's early adventures as a Christian had been the purchase of his life from some Boxers—at a time when many of his fellow converts were being butchered—by giving up to them his fur-lined coat and American leather shoes. He was in his late fifties, slender and wiry but with the enthusiasm and energy, Cowley said, "of a young billy-goat."

Treadup went to call on this Mr. Hsiao four times. The two men liked each other at once. Impatient as he was to get started, David took his time with this courtly gentleman. Only on the third visit did he broach to Mr. Hsiao his proposal of a new life of hard work and devotion. During the fourth, Mr. Hsiao ceremoniously declared that he would be honored to do what he could to help in this most unorthodox work, teaching peasants to read.

IT WAS not easy to buy land for the new compound. The anti-Christian movement among the radicals had already reached its long arm into the real estate market, where it reinforced the greed that had been there all along. The moment a prospective seller learned that the purchaser was a *mu-shih*, a missionary, the price shot up to the stars. So Treadup went to Mr. Hsiao, who with great discretion found a front man for a front man for an agent of a friend of a friend who knew of someone who wanted to buy some land; and with covers of such depth a purchase was finally made on fair terms—a former temple ground north of the city.

THE EXCITEMENT now in Treadup's letters!

One letter to his parents, on April 23, 1924, tells that New York has asked him for an accurate survey of the plot. He has managed to get his hands on a German transit ("looted from some European store somewhere during some 'revolution'") which he has mounted on a camera tripod, and with this makeshift rig and a couple of Chinese carpenter's plumb bobs and a tape measure, he sallies out, certain that he can lay out the boundaries and get it all down on paper. He soon finds himself surrounded by a swarm of advisers, including neighboring property owners. They are working on the southern side of the property. They have this exchange:

TREADUP "How far does my property extend?"
NEIGHBOR "Into the alley."
TREADUP "But how far?"
SECOND NEIGHBOR "About three English feet. Four feet."
TREADUP "But is there no settled limit?"
THIRD NEIGHBOR "The alley belongs to the abutters."
TREADUP "Halfway out, then?"
FIRST NEIGHBOR "Ay! No! The alley is the only way people have to get through. We have to leave room for the public to pass."

Treadup gathers, after an hour or so of this, that "the proper method, when you want to put up your wall, is to call out the neighbors, name a middleman, move your marker stake back and forth until the protests have subsided to a minimum, and then drive the stake home. That's where the 'official' boundary belongs. . . . "

From a letter to brother Paul, in mid-May:

A carpenter is sawing away on what will be a bookshelf. Two masons, two wall scrapers, three painters, and two paperhangers are all asking for directions on how to do things 'à la Américain!' Every hour on the hour I get down on my knees and pray for patience.

"HE BEHAVES," Emily wrote home,

like a young man who's in love for the first time. In other words, he flaps around like a chicken with its head cut off. Grinning the whole time till you think he's a dementia case. He plans to row on the Fu River, but his shell isn't here yet, so he plays tennis—smashes the ball with all his strength, as if that were the way to get rid of the sins of this world. The awful singing in the morning! I tell you, dear ones, it is a severe trial to live with a happy man.

AT LAST, on a July day, he began.

For weeks he had been hiking into the countryside to get the feel of the villages. He decided to make his start in a group of five villages where the American Board evangelists had, over the years, made some headway.

He and Mr. Hsiao arrived in the first of them on foot. It was a poor village of some twenty-five mud houses, the name of which translated to Second Ma Family Village. They asked around for a Christian farmer whose name Letitia Selden had given David.

They were directed to a field dotted with grave mounds, where the farmer was hoeing along rows of hip-high sorghum. At first the man was suspicious; seeing Mr. Hsiao so well dressed, he must have assumed that some outrageous new tax was about to be levied. But Mr. Hsiao put him at ease: He merely wanted an introduction to the village headman, for, he said, he and his American friend had a great Christian gift to give the village.

Soon they were seated cross-legged on the *k'ang* in the house of a white-haired elder, named, of course, Ma. They were grouped around a low square table on which the women of the house placed hot teapots and riceware cups—the best in the village, no doubt. The village telegraph seemed to be at work, because one by one the senior men of the village drifted in, straight from the fields, and stood by the edge of the *k'ang*, politely listening.

Mr. Hsiao did all the talking. Treadup had primed him. Hospitality floated up into the room on bluish wisps of tobacco smoke, but the villagers' old instincts of caution brought some sharp questions. The presence of a foreigner seemed to be, to these farmers, neither a plus nor a minus; they were used to having missionaries lollygagging around. The only peculiar thing about this one seemed to be that he was so enormous; he groaned trying to sit cross-legged on the reed matting on the hard mud *k'ang*.

By agreement beforehand, Mr. Hsiao did not move fast toward the subject of literacy; he talked around and around it. They left.

MR. HSIAO ascertained a few days later that rumors were flying around that village and all the nearby villages. Two men, one of them hairy, had come to the area to conscript young men and boys to be soldiers; mothers warned their sons to be on the lookout. One of them had captured some souls in his box (taken photographs). They were getting information for a new poll tax; a person must be guarded in speaking to them. They had come to force people to eat religion. They were agents of the government to suppress gambling and opium smoking. How could you believe that they were there to help people, when they asked nothing in return? What fool would work for nothing? Watch out! Trickery!

TREADUP and Mr. Hsiao decided to go slowly: to appear from time to time in the villages, be friendly, not rush things. They began talking after a while about why people in the cities could deceive and cheat country people—they could read. At first they left it at that. The rumors proliferated but died out one by one as the malign predictions were not borne out. Finally one day Mr. Hsiao asked if he and his friend could speak with the villagers at a nearby temple on the next market day. Chief Ma shrugged his shoulders and turned up his hands. That seemed to be permission enough.

SO THEY DID from village to village.

MARKET DAY in Second Ma Family Village.

Mr. Hsiao makes the introduction, but this time Treadup is the main speaker—in Mandarin. He puts on a show. He has brought blind-man posters, but he has brought something else, too, which doesn't seem to have much to do with literacy, at least in an immediate way. It is the battered old Wrestling Gyroscope. He has decided to amaze first and persuade afterward.

Two of the strongest and most unpopular men in the village cannot budge the wheel! Much laughter! The big-nose modulates. He has grown serious. Have these people heard that China is now a Republic?

A few nod yes.

What is a Republic? A Republic is supposed to be governed by the people—the *lao pai hsing*, the "Old Hundred Names." People? Who are the *lao pai hsing*? Is the name Ma not one of the old hundred? Did the people of this village choose the governor of Hopei or the President of China? Did they decide what taxes they should pay? Have *they* decided there should be war all the time, with generals demanding straw and sorghum and piglets? Have *they* chosen to send off their carts and provisions and brothers to be used to kill other Chinese?

There is a heavy silence. Then: "Why do we suffer all these evils? Why don't we have a government chosen by the *lao pai hsing* which serves the *lao pai hsing* instead of feeding them bitterness?" Now he shifts. "How many members of the Ma clan understood why those two men could not push over the wheel?" None. "Do you know why Mr. Hsiao and I understand?" It was because they could read and write. They had studied science.

Then: "How many of you can read and write?"

Two men in the entire village.

"How many would like to be able to read and write?"

No hands.

"Why haven't you learned?"

Answers: "No time." "I have to work in the fields." "We have to eat." "The village has no money, a teacher costs money."

Now the persuasion, in two hours of patient and indirect talking. The gist: A way has been found to teach you how to read and write without taking you away from your farmwork. We will do it in the long winter evenings when it's too dark to work in the fields and when you can't go to market. We will set up evening classes, we will bring the teachers to you—and we won't charge you anything. . . .

At the end of the day Mr. Hsiao and the headman made a kind of pact.

Each put his fists side by side and bowed to the other, to seal some undefined agreement. At least he and Treadup knew they could come back another time.

IT WAS time to send the two older boys off to the mission boarding school at T'ungchow. Philip was fifteen, Absolom twelve. Emily wrote David's brother Paul Treadup:

> Little Abbo, twelve years old! Too tender an age to be packed off! But we have to do it. The boys will be going home to the States to college, and they must be prepared, and everyone says that T'ungchow is a superb school. And all the foreigners do send their tiny ones off — the English way.

The wrench of the boys' departure and the reckless energy of her husband's high spirits once again drove Emily out into the streets.

Letitia Selden had a suggestion. The Congregationalists had taught a flock of so-called Bible women — converts who had become native distributors of tracts, mostly widows or overflow females from poor families — how to support themselves by doing linen tatting of table covers, bedspreads, scarves, and "throws" for export to America. Miss Demestrie had had the supervision of this charity, but her bad knee was making it harder and harder for her to get into the city and back; and Miss Titty asked Emily Treadup if she would like to take on the care of the tatting workers. She said she would.

She found the tatting "factory" — less than a dozen women ruining their eyes in a rented room in a native church compound — a pathetic enterprise. But she listened to the Bible women and began to learn about the life of working people in this northern city. She began to explore. Emboldened by her experiences in Shanghai, she poked into some *hutungs* where a foreign lady had probably never been seen. What she found in those back alleys shocked her even more than the conditions she had seen in Shanghai. The principal manufacture was cotton cloth; the weaving mills were worse, she thought, than Shanghai's filatures. There were also, however, hundreds or perhaps thousands of small piecework shops. Many produced medicines, both Chinese and Western. Emily was horrified by the number of women she saw in this medicine-producing city with trachoma, and children with the hideous white scabs of virulent fungi, and ricksha pullers with volcanic ulcers on their legs.

One day she came home in tears. A crowd of women had followed her through the streets, begging and wailing. She learned from them that they had been hairnet workers, who had used to earn a two-cent copper for each five hairnets they tied (every one with a couple of hundred tiny knots in strands of real human hair), but all the hairnet factories in the city had been shut down. Emily asked the women to direct her to one of the owners. "David! David!" she said. "He sat there in his silk gown and told me that there was nothing *he* could do. He had no control over American fashions. He said very coldly that what had made all those hairnet women hungry, David, was that all the girls in the States have taken to bobbing their hair."

From a letter to her parents in June:

> *Last night there was an appalling fire in the Ching Shang Cotton Mill. It started about midnight, and many of the women and children who worked there were sleeping in the building—they had no other homes —and they were caught in a death trap. The main stairs were either locked or cut off by flames, and the windows were tightly barred—to keep thieves out! There were no emergency exits and no provisions of any kind for fighting fire. The approaches to the factory were so narrow and inaccessible that the fire engines could not be brought onto the scene of disaster. More than three hundred people eventually got out of the building with the help of Boy Scouts and spectators who managed to pry open some of the window bars from the outside. But there were some hundred twenty women and children trapped within who couldn't escape and were consumed by the flames. I ask David, and O Heavenly Father I ask thee: What can I do? What can one woman do to change this world? And then I get even more bitter, and I say to David that there isn't time for him to teach four hundred million blind Chinese to read. And what makes him think that reading is a cure-all? Will reading cure greed or heal the sick or feed the starving? There's so much else—too much!—too much!—my hungry hairnet women, those horrible scabs on children's heads, I can't even think about those charred bodies. . . .*

THERE WAS "much else" in the Treadups' own lives, too, but no matter what hardships came along, or what doubts Emily put in David's way, his mood seemed to feed on adversity, and he went about his work with a blind dash.

The family moved into their new home in the tight little compound. The house was not grand, but there was room for everyone; and David had a study again. Emily found two poorly trained male servants. Just about when the family moved in, the hottest weather came on. For a month the thermometer went each day over 100 degrees. The Congregationalists kindly let the Treadups take ice from their ice house, but in mid-July the supply gave out. There were no electric fans to be found in the city. The three boys came down with a puzzling low fever. Emily had a terrible fright when, making up little Paul's bed one morning, she found a huge scorpion under the covers. The only vegetables in the market were cabbage and a variety of yellow squash. There were no fresh fruits. Both servants fell ill with violent adult mumps which went to their testicles, and Emily had to do all the housework in the heat. David had an attack of dysentery, which, according to his diary, "I dealt with summarily, with a purgative from Calcutta which went through me like canister shot."

ONE DAY a huge crate came. In it was a gift from old Syracuse supporters in the L. C. Smith Typewriter Company. The crate was far too big for a typewriter.

The crate contained, of all things, a motorcycle. Its make was "Indian." It had a streamlined, wire-wheeled sidecar.

Now Treadup and Mr. Hsiao went from village to village by a loud-voiced conveyance never seen in the three thousand years of habitation in those parts. "Chickens and dogs scatter before us. We make more dust than a bandit army. I doubt that there has been more excitement in Hopei since the Grand Canal was opened in the fifth century B.C." The machine made David Treadup—known to all as the *hen ta-ti mu-shih*, the huge missionary—instantly famous throughout the area. He was welcomed wherever he went by a horde of children. Village elders warmed to him, and with Mr. Hsiao's help he felt that he was making rapid progress toward his two goals:

• First, to get each village to take full financial responsibility for the literacy school it would harbor in the fall. This did not seem a heavy burden—just the cost of the textbooks, at two cents apiece; but he had to avoid making this seem like one more miserable tax in a villager's lifelong experience of swindles, extortions, and squeeze.

• Second, to recruit and train a sufficient number of teachers. He called on local officials to second him in this task; and together he and they recruited the corps of teachers from government and mission schools, and from the educated gentry. All of the teachers volunteered, with the best of goodwill, to give their time without pay. Treadup met with them in regional groups to train them in the methods of mass education. His ebullience gave them a lively morale.

But now—just as he began to feel, as he wrote one night, "ready to twist the tiger's tail"—there came two serious interruptions of his work.

SLINGSHOT

FROM A LETTER of August 21 to his Syracuse constituency, thanking them for the Indian:

Inasmuch as we have had 26 inches of rainfall in the last 30 days, I trust you will not find this letter too dry. The average annual rainfall in Hopei is 17 inches. We have had nine inches more than that in one month.

These torrents have put much of our countryside under water. In Paoting, it's estimated that 2,000 rooms of Chinese buildings are down—mud walls simply dissolved. Some of our Christian workers who live next door found themselves surrounded by water rising so rapidly in the yard and rooms that they had to tear down a section of the wall separating their yard from ours and they waded out just before the house collapsed and buried their belongings. They are now digging in the mud and wreckage in the hope of recovering some of their articles. Our front porch is strewn with ill-smelling books, papers, and clothing, recovered and spread out to dry between showers.

It's the old, old story. In the city of Kalgan, northwest of us, a river ran riot thru the city and it is reported that some 3,000 lives were snuffed out in an hour. In the district around Peking, half a million are said to be homeless.

Floods and famine and floods again every few years, and it has doubtless been thus for centuries. When will the hills be planted with forests and proper channels for water be cleared to the sea?

THE HARDSHIPS caused in his villages by the flood made the literacy campaign seem all the more urgent to David, for Emily was right: In his enthusiasm he did think of his work as something of a cure-all. At least he thought that the Chinese nation would not be able to do much about poverty, sickness, flood, and famine until all its Old Hundred Names had reached a level of education that would enable them to deal intelligently with those troubles.

So in October, when the floodwaters had drained away and the lowlands of ruined crops were caked with cracked and curled-up platelets of mud, off he went again and again on his motorcycle, struggling along the rutted roads, often with Mr. Hsiao, often alone.

Sometimes he stayed away for several days. Gridley in Peking had procured for him some good American canvas, and Emily had found sewing women who made a tent on a pattern David designed. With a village chief's permission he would pitch it in a field; he lived frugally, on local vegetables, tinned crackers, and tea. Crowds gathered. Had there ever been such an entertainment? Some villagers came to inspect the canvas, for many farmers were weavers who had small looms in their homes. Villagers watched his every move—even his shaving in the morning. After he squatted to move his bowels a boy would quickly sneak up with a scoop to take the *mu-shih*'s treasure off to the family's night-soil pile.

ONE MORNING at first dawn he was just stretching on his bedroll when he heard curious popping sounds in the distance. He knew of no feast day at this time of year that would call for early-morning firecrackers. He had just stepped out from the flaps of his tent in his pajamas when it seemed that the entire population of the nearby village came running along the cart road, hysterically babbling.

"They gathered around me," David wrote brother Paul,

and at first, as they were all shouting at once, I could not make out what they wanted. I raised my hands for silence, and the headman panted out that soldiers were coming, soldiers were coming! And what did the villagers want? They wanted ME to protect them from the oncoming army! I had heard rumors that the warlords were starting up their fuss again and that General Sun Yueh (a minor Chihli warlord, no kin to the great Sun Yat-sen) might be advancing up the Peking-Hankow railroad, driving out Chang Tso-lin's people. This village wasn't far from the tracks.

Up to that time the talk of fighting hadn't given me the slightest concern. Look at it this way: All of the three big warlords in the region— Wu P'ei-fu in Peking, my friend the Christian General Feng, and Chang Tso-lin up in Manchuria—were open supporters of the Y.M.C.A. —and I mean cash. I had felt completely secure.

But this—being asked to stop an army single-handed! Well, I thought: Little David, get your slingshot out!

In a loud, authoritative voice, Treadup told everyone to go back into the village and stay in their houses—"a command I had reason later to regret exceedingly." Then he strode off across the fields in the direction of the rifle fire, as if he knew just what he was going to do.

In less than a mile he came into a field where he could see, at the far side, the raised causeway of the railway. In the field, huddled behind grave mounds which shielded them from enemy fire, were groups of soldiers. "When this big foreigner walked across the field," David wrote Paul, *the soldiers, a scrappy and dirty lot of young fellows, jumped up from their cover and gathered around me in a crowd and laughed and joked just as though it was a schoolboys' lark. The riflemen on the other side were firing too high as we could hear their bullets well above us whistling in the air. I asked where the men's commanding officer was. They said he was in the next station-town down the line, and they ALL wanted to take me to him! I said an escort of six rifles would be sufficient. You can imagine the argument over which six. Then we set off.*

About three miles to the south the party came to the small headquarters town. Two brigades of soldiers had been stationed there ever since the flood. The water of a canal alongside the town was full of broken furniture, straw from bug-filled beds, and entrails of pigs, chickens, and goats butchered by the troops. The latrines of the town were filled beyond use, and the streets were unspeakably filthy. The commanding officer, a subordinate of Sun Yueh, comfortably stationed in the grounds of a temple, "turned out to be a former officer in Feng's army, a Christian, and a member of the Peking Y.M.C.A.! It was like meeting an old fraternity brother!" Treadup gave the cordial Colonel Ch'i the names of all the villages where he and Mr. Hsiao had arranged to start schools, including the one beside which David had camped the night before. Colonel Ch'i gave his solemn word that he would command the advancing troops to spare each and every one of them from looting.

The colonel said he had some five hundred women and girls under his protection in six of the largest compounds of the town. He asked Treadup to inspect them. "Colonel Ch'i took me to three and we saw some pitiable sights. Some of these girls shrank in terror as soon as they saw uniforms coming into the door. They tried to get under tables or behind one another in the corners of the rooms." The colonel said the town had no funds to feed the girls and wanted Treadup to secure help. Treadup said he would do what he could.

The six soldiers escorted Treadup back to the village from which he had started. During his absence it had been looted from end to end.

The headman, bitterly bemoaning his lot, took me into his house. Boxes, bureaus, trunks — everything had been emptied on the floor and indiscriminately mingled. Ceilings, walls, and floors had been torn up in search for hidden treasure. God's teeth! How I had lost face! Fine protection I had given them! The headman said the looters had gone off with their booty to the east, into a grove of locusts around an old temple.

At last David was able to go back out to his encampment. His motorcycle and his tent were gone.

Back again he went to the headquarters town, to tell Colonel Ch'i what had happened.

HE RETURNED to Paoting exhausted, muddy, and footsore, to find the city in a state of panic. Cool Emily had established their small compound as a refuge, and it was teeming with frightened families carrying loose bundles of possessions. The much larger Presbyterian and Congregationalist compounds were similarly crammed. These noisy relief stations lasted only two days, for at the end of that time the city fell without a shot having been fired, and all the frightened Chinese went home.

The day after that, an Indian motorcycle drove up to the gate of the Y.M.C.A. compound, with Colonel Ch'i riding in the sidecar, wearing Treadup's goggles. The colonel said he had the honor to return T'ao Tu Hsien-sheng's lost equipment. An hour later a mule cart came along, carrying the tent, all of Treadup's other lost gear, and a gift of a lacquered chest (obviously looted). Colonel Ch'i said that the looters of the village had deserted from the army and had gone off along a canal to try to dispose of their goods. He had sent a scouting party after them, had captured them, had cut their heads off, had hung their heads in bamboo cages at his headquarters as an example to his troops, and had returned the stolen goods to the village. The diary:

> Had to swallow hard at idea of Y.M.C.A. man going around beheading people, but didn't think I could say anything when he had just got his face back. I gave him fifty dollars Mex of my own money to "feed the refugee girls down in that town." How glad I was to see my old dust-eating machine!

IN NOVEMBER the teaching began. In spite of flood and war — or perhaps because of them — it was a success beyond David's dreams. He had had to rush up to Peking to buy nearly two thousand more textbooks because the enrollments kept piling in, seemingly without end. He rode from village to village. When he strode into a class, the pupils all put their hands before their mouths to hide their laughter — his huge face was dun-colored with dust except for the pale round circles of white skin where his goggles had been.

At the end of the year news came that Feng Yu-hsiang had pulled off a coup d'état, occupying Peking with his troops and deposing his chieftain Wu P'ei-fu while that super-warlord was off fighting in the north. Feng was bitterly assailed by many Chinese as an arch-traitor; his sobriquet, "the Christian General," gave way to "the Betraying General." But to a David Treadup already sailing on the clouds of his wonderful success, the news seemed very good. "Whatever obloquy he may be suffering, I have no doubt in my own mind as to the man's sincerity and his earnest wish to serve his country." That other quondam Christian Sun Yat-sen had been a disappointment; perhaps this Christian could indeed unify China. Think then what possibilities there would be for God's work in this great field!

BOOK FIVE

⊞

VAST FORCES

MAY 30TH

"IF ONLY I were a bobolink!" David wrote in his diary in March 1925. "I would teach the other birds how to get some verve into their song!"

For he felt, in those early spring days when one village graduation after another was taking place, wholly fulfilled and triumphant. Over the years his science lectures had given him many transient satisfactions, but he had never felt such "verve" as he did now—as he did one morning, for example, in a small hamlet of millet farms on the great northern plain, when a group of newly certified Literate Citizens of the Republic of China crowded around him while he handed out one of the basic readers Johnny Wu's people had been devising. He wrote that looking into the "eyes greedy for books" of those "peasant scholars" gave him "that queer light ache in my chest which I associate with what?—with homesickness?—with thoughts of Emily when we are separated?—with the sweetest memories?"—a sensation, it seemed, akin to the wonderful pain of exultation and self-love he had felt as a boy giving rides to friends in his wherry on the pond at Salt Branch.

EARLY in the spring Dr. Cowley in the mission compound in the northern suburb suddenly erupted with charges, which he very busily circulated among the Paoting missionaries and also shot off through the mails to senior colleagues in Peking and Shanghai, that this Treadup person was

> *getting himself neck deep in a layman's quagmire, low-down secular country business properly belonging to Chinese authorities — temporal work in short that has nothing to do with the bringing in of Christ's Kingdom on earth.*

In his language-study days, David had come to admire this crusty medical evangelist who had braved out so many hardships, and the old man's attack hurt him so much that he made a foolhardy attempt at appeasement. He wrote Cowley a letter in which he pointed out that Johnny Wu's textbooks contained some moral precepts; that a fair number of the teachers he had recruited were Christians who carried on devotional exercises in opening their classes; and that in some villages extra sessions were being set up for religious studies.

Dr. Cowley took Treadup's earnest defense as a confession of guilt, and he came back roaring — now in what seemed to David "a senile rage" — that he was going to "drum all these heathen Bertrand Russellisms and socialisms and Treadupisms out of the mission field."

But in Shanghai David Liu stood behind Treadup. He firmly wrote Dr. Cowley that "the promotion of literacy in itself is one of the biggest steps we can now take towards making possible effective evangelism and Christian nurture in the next few years." This by no means satisfied the old man, who continued to rumble; but it did blunt his threats.

IN MARCH Johnny Wu wrote Treadup that he wanted to "come and take a look at the remarkable work I hear you are doing." The undertaking had indeed had an amazing success. By the time Wu wrote, almost 3,000 "peasant scholars," aged from twelve to sixty, had completed work in all four of the Thousand Character textbooks. More and more farm people were enrolling in future classes.

Johnny Wu's organization, the National People's Education Association, had up to this time been working in the cities, but the surprising wildfire of Treadup's campaign had encouraged Wu to think more actively about the needs of the great peasant population. He had indeed had this in mind from early on. One of the first things he had done, after the formation of the National People's Education Association, had been to send a cable to the United States to Peter Ma, his colleague of those first tentative days of teaching the coolies back in the wartime labor camp in Boulogne, inviting him to join up. Ma seemed especially qualified to plan a peasant program, for he had been studying for a Ph.D. in rural education at Cornell. On his arrival back in China in February, he turned down several attractive offers of safe official jobs in Nanking and Shanghai and did sign up with Wu.

And now the two men came to Paoting, and Treadup took them into "his" villages. David wrote: "What a spree the visit was!" Johnny Wu drank in the possibilities and "his chest got so swelled up with confidence that one thought he would become lighter than air and go floating up into the sky." Wu's electric excitement conveyed itself to all the teachers and scholars who saw it, and a whole month later Treadup was able to write in a letter to Wu that "the universal report is that the wheels in everyone's minds are whirring twice as fast as they did before you came."

Treadup had the even greater joy of learning that the visit had had a long-range effect on Johnny Wu, as well. It had clinched Wu's growing conviction that the most important job of all, in the effort to "make China literate in this generation," would be among the peasants. And furthermore— on the evidence of the work around Paoting—that it might very well be feasible.

Writing to her family about Wu's inspection tour, Emily must have reflected her husband's view:

> *All the light of all our years in China seemed to come to focus during Johnny's visit—I think of a magnifying glass focusing the sun's rays on a bundle of twigs and setting it afire. My David held the glass in his hand!*

BECAUSE of the farmers' labor in the fields, the pace of the actual class-work eased somewhat in the planting time, but David worked no less hard. He and Mr. Hsiao went into new villages, preparing the way for new classes to be formed when the next winter would come. They enlisted and trained new teachers. They revisited the villages where classes had already been held, to try to find ways of keeping the reading and writing alive. "Everywhere I go," Treadup wrote, "I feel that my friend Johnny is looking over my shoulder. I can never forget that the inspiration for all this was and is his." One diary entry expresses his "certainty that old Dr. Cowley is mistaken. If this is not God's work, I cannot imagine what is. I feel humbly close to God in my prayers."

A SERIES of muffled explosions announced the dawn arrival at the compound gate of a coughing automobile. David happened to be at home that morning and he hurried in his bathrobe out to the gate, where he saw an open military-brown Renault with a swooping low hood over its engine and wide glass wings on its windscreen. The driver and a passenger were wearing what looked like gas masks to keep the dust out of their faces. The passenger, removing his, turned out to be a colonel from the staff of Feng Yu-hsiang, the Christian or the Betraying General, depending on one's point of view. David led the colonel into the house, ordered tea from the Number One Boy, and ceremoniously waited for it before asking what he could do for his visitor. The colonel said Marshal Feng (for Feng had promoted himself to what in Chinese terminology corresponded to a field marshalship) wanted to speak with T'ao Tu Hsien-sheng. David asked when. The colonel said right then — he had instructions to return at once to Peking with the missionary in the car. "I decided you don't snub the most powerful man in North China," David later recorded,

> so without even eating breakfast I dressed and put on my dust-tunic and goggles and told Em to expect me when she saw me — if ever. For all I knew he might be going to lop my head off. There seem to be quite a few decapitations these days.

But nothing so drastic waited for Treadup in Peking. Marshal Feng received him in an unadorned room in a large house. The huge bluff man greeted his huge visitor as a beloved old friend: again, the ursine hugs. Feng was dressed in his usual simple uniform with no insignia or decorations. Though in his own house, he wore what appeared to be a battered old round wide-brimmed felt American officer's field hat. His cheeks were shaved but his jowls were not; his closely trimmed beard, unusually heavy for a Chinese, lurked like sinister infolded crow's wings under the broad and jovial face.

"T'ao Tu, my friend," he said in Chinese, "I have been hearing reports of the superb system of teaching you have started around Paoting. I am a great believer in mass education, you saw that I taught my own troops eight hundred characters; but a person of your talent for modern science — I remember your lecture to my men at Langfang! — you must not waste yourself on teaching people to read in a few country villages. Listen! Your assistants can carry on that work. I will gladly offer you five hundred thousand dollars, Mexican exchange, to endow the Paoting program. You and I have more important work to do. I have plans for China — give me six months, eight months — when we have peace — I need your help! Do you recall my classes at Langfang, where I was teaching the men trades? God did not put the Chinese people on this earth to be poor all their lives! . . . "

"He rambled on," David wrote his brother,

> shouting at the top of his voice. He is so sincerely emotional and at the same time so bombastic that it is very hard to resist his torrents, to say nothing of understanding them. It took me nearly an hour to pin down exactly what he was offering me. It appeared that he wanted me to be a kind of 'éminence grise,' a shadow counselor (a 'ta-pi-tzu,' a "big nose," would have to hide behind the coromandel screen in the counsels of power) on education and modernization; he wanted me to start right

away working with his army, and later, when he had unified China, to
make plans for a massive program of rural education. We skirted the
matter of his faith. He seemed a bit slippery. If he is to live out his
ambitions, he needs the students behind him, and I had heard that the
anti-Christian movement had made him a bit cautious about trumpeting
his love for Jesus. Yet he made me get down on my knees with him
and pray for China's poor and for the success of some new long-range
artillery cannons he had bought from the Russians.

At the end Treadup, expressing with elegant Chinese tact the unworthiness he felt in the face of the honor Feng was offering him, said that before making a decision of such importance he would have to correspond with his colleagues in the Y.M.C.A. and consult with his family. The former would take some time, as he would doubtless have to write not only to Shanghai but also to New York. "Not too long!" Feng cried, as if China's future hung on Treadup's prompt decision. Tears came into the burly Marshal's eyes on their parting.

IN "SEARCH" Treadup claims that he had from the first no intention whatsoever of accepting Feng's invitation—or his "bribe" of half a million dollars (Mex)—but his letters to David Liu in Shanghai and Todd in New York, while not pushing for approval, simply reported the proposal in its most modest terms—that Marshal Feng wanted Treadup to "work for his army." He did add that "the Christian movement should give as much assistance as possible to Feng."

There are hints in Treadup's diary that Feng had subtly undermined his elation over the literacy work around Paoting, by suggesting that it was not nearly important enough work for Treadup to be doing. Probably much more significant for David's future were the reminders of Feng's efforts to train his men for trades, and his avowal that God had not put the Chinese on this earth in order to be poor all their lives—the implication being that reading and writing would never in themselves cure poverty. In coming months David was to give much pained thought to that stark conclusion.

Todd from New York, believing from such a distance that anyone called "the Christian General" should be given all possible help, was inclined to support Feng's proposal; but by the time Todd's letter arrived, David Liu had already brusquely vetoed it.

Before Treadup had a chance to visit the Marshal again to decline, all China was shaken by a tragic event in Shanghai. A family venture of the Treadups, a "newspaper" which they called *The Shepherd* and sent to David's supporters and other friends in the States, gave news of it.

"Tackling the Bull by the Horns"
THE SHEPHERD
Paoting   June 1925

When Issued	No Promises	Price: Six Minutes

Editor-in-Chief: David Treadup   Printer's Devil: Philip Treadup
Managing the Editor: Emily Treadup   Proof Reader: Absolom Treadup
Stamp Licker: Paul Treadup

As a "Mass Education Number" of this sheet was fermenting in our editorial brain, an event took place in Shanghai that has set all China aflame. We must try to report it to our constituency. Bear with us if this issue is less light-hearted than the usual baa-ings herein of "sheep."

Your editor was summoned to a conference of "Y" secretaries in Shanghai after the said event, and had an on-the-spot account of it from General Secretary David Y. S. Liu, who played a major role in keeping heads cool.

Here is what happened. During the spring, there was a strike in a Japanese cotton mill. In a fracas a Chinese worker was killed. At his funeral a few days later a band of student activists got in a fight with some Sikhs of the Municipal Police, and a few were arrested. Then they tried what students all over the world try—a street demonstration. It was on May 30. They had banners: "Down With Imperialism," "We Are the Student Brigade," "Innocent Students Are in Jail." They also had dodgers to distribute, and they harangued on street corners.

The police started arresting them on Nanking Road. A large crowd gathered. Traffic was blocked. The Sikhs tried to clear the street, using their batons. The sight of bloody faces infuriated the crowd. It became unruly and surged toward the police station.

A British Police Inspector warned the crowd to draw back or be fired upon. It pressed on. The Briton then gave the fatal command. Some say nine were killed, some say twelve. An equally vague number were badly wounded.

All China caught fire like a dry forest. The very next morning, the Shanghai Chamber of Commerce called a general strike; the Municipal Council retaliated by declaring martial law. The city became like an armed camp, with volunteer militia, marines of several nationalities, and armed police patrolling the streets.

The Shot Heard Round the World at Concord Bridge could not have caused a greater sensation in our country than these shots of folly did in China. By June 2 the students of Paoting were already shouting through the streets, with vitriolic rhetoric and dodgers. There began a campaign of bill posting all over the city, pictures of students killed at Shanghai, cartoons of John Bull and the Samurai, drawings of Sikh policemen with guns in their hands standing over dead students. These latter have been liberally sprinkled with red ink for blood.

There is an explosion of nationalistic feeling. It seems every man, woman,

"THE PAOTING SHEPHERD"
Page 2 (in case you are still with us)

and child is talking about "my country." The outcries are: End business exploitation, cancel extraterritorial rights for foreign "invaders," and stop all Christian "meddling."

All mission work in China is being tried as in a furnace. Christianity is "the foreigner's religion" and "a tool of imperialistic governments." A young man in the next compound, who had been a big help to me in the literacy campaign, came to me the other day with a book by Fosdick I had lent him, saying, "I can't read this stuff anymore. You are trying to denationalize me." I am glad to say that the villagers whom we are teaching have shown no such feelings. They greet me still with signs of great affection. One village chief took me aside to say confidentially that when "they" started killing foreigners, he would hide me behind a false wall he had built to secure his valuables from bandits!

The greatest anger is against the British, and the English missionaries have been called some ugly names. This is too bad. Great Britain has made huge grave errors in China, but many of her Christian missionaries have been heroically self-sacrificing, and have rendered a wonderful service.

Two American missionaries testified in the Shanghai investigation that the shooting had been unnecessary, so we are being treated with the usual Chinese courtesy. But I noticed that of the 20 warships in the Whangpoo, 13 were American!

There is no doubt that there has been a strong Bolshevik influence on the entire movement—for as usual a national paroxism has been dubbed a "movement," this being the May 30th Movement. The anti-Christian impulse has come from Soviet Russian influence on the very nationalistic party of Sun Yat-sen, the Kuomintang as it is called. Much is being said in the business community these days about China going over to bolshevism and allying itself with Russia. If she does, it will only be because she gets more just, friendly, and equitable treatment from the Soviet government than she does from the professedly Christian governments in the West. Russia has given back to China her concessions in the treaty ports. Russia has given up extraterritorial rights. The Chinese feel that the Russians treat them as equals.

Sun Yat-sen, as you may have heard, has just died. It is quite likely that Sun will exert an even greater influence dead than he did alive. Whatever was Christian in him died some time ago, but he stands for an awakening China as no one else has done. People in the south are talking about a young officer who with Russian help developed the Whampoa Military Academy and who wears Dr. Sun's mantle, named Chiang Kai-shek.

Remember the date May 30th, 1925. The "Storm Dragon" has been let loose in China. We shall need all our patience and brotherliness and Christianity to deal with it. China is beginning to find herself. If our calling means anything, we must help.

*   *   *

Next month: MASS EDUCATION!!!!!

IN LATE JUNE, after his return from the meetings David Liu had called in Shanghai, Treadup went to Peking to decline Marshal Feng's invitation. He got a surprise. There was no hug this time. The broad bearded face was a palimpsest: its kindly expression of a "Christian brother" was written on top of barely erased tracings of severity and even hostility. Treadup had agonized over how to refuse Feng's invitation with Chinese-like grace and tact; he could have spared himself the trouble, for Feng gave him no chance to speak at all but launched instead into a baffling harangue, during which he breathed not a word about his earlier invitation to Treadup—nor, for that matter, about what had happened in Shanghai on May 30.

"British journalists," he said, according to Treadup's diary,

> "have suddenly started branding me as pro-Soviet. They say I'm bolshevizing my army. As Britishers they have reason to want to becloud the real issue. I have Japanese, Italian, and Russian military advisers—more Russians, as it happens, because there are more available. Russia has been foremost in willingness to recognize and aid China's attempts to recover her lost nation. We are not interested in criticism by nations that have shown themselves unwilling to do as much. They will call anyone Bolshevik who tries sanely to advance the welfare of the masses. China's faith in evolutionary reform on patterns devised by foreigners is dead. We Chinese must demand the complete and unconditional restoration of national birthrights. When this is assured there will be time enough to talk details of readjustment. We appreciate America's traditional friendship, but right now we are waiting to see whether America, with her relatively small material interests in China, intends to throw her influence toward us or to become the tool of others who want to keep the trade advantages they got by force and by unfair treaties."

A later entry, when Treadup had gone home to Paoting:

> I felt as if it were a case of mistaken identity. He seemed to be shouting to somebody else!—not to his old friend me!—to a member of the United States diplomatic service, maybe. But I know he knew what he was doing. By poking around a little, I found out he had appointed a Chinese educator two weeks ago to the post he had "offered" me. How strange it was to get such a strong whiff—like too much garlic on a breath—of the crafty shiftiness so many Chinese have been accusing him of. The way the May 30th Movement caught on must have made him see that Sun's people have been picking up strength among those masses he talks about. What our lord Jesus needs most, when it comes to "Christian" Chinese leaders, is a good supply of anchors.

THE BOBOLINK'S song went flat. Treadup's Shanghai visit and Marshal Feng's strange outburst worked on his nerves. Some rather daunting difficulties had been turning up in the villages. Because of recent floods, the countryside was suffering from a near famine. In the cold weather villagers had not been able to afford charcoal to heat the temple anterooms or rooms in private houses where classes met. Treadup was having to raise "brazier money" and "scholarship funds" from rich Chinese, because David Liu in Shanghai had been writing him stern letters about how badly he had run over the budget for his experiment, when he had built and equipped his compound.

He was troubled by how hard it was to enlist women in the classes, and to keep them when they did join. He could find no women to teach, and many villagers were opposed to mixed classes of men and women.

Most disturbing of all was the May 30th Movement. "I grind my teeth at being dubbed a running dog of imperialism," he wrote in his diary. "I *love* China! It is my second country!" One night he sat down and drafted a

STATEMENT OF CHINESE AND FOREIGN CHRISTIANS IN PAOTING

We have learned with profound regret of the recent drastic treatment of Chinese by certain of the British and Japanese in Shanghai. We believe that the present crisis is due to deep-seated causes such as:

1. Frequent foreign aggression on Chinese territory.

2. Deep Chinese dissatisfaction with the present continued application of unequal treaties that were forcibly arranged with China as a result of wars. Conditions having greatly changed, treaties should be accordingly revised.

3. The extraterritorial rights of foreigners in China, with no similar reciprocal rights for Chinese in foreign countries, should be discontinued.

"Have become a door-to-door canvasser, just as if I were earning my way through college," the diary reports. We have no way of knowing whether Treadup actually knocked on Dr. Cowley's door with his statement in his hand, but it is clear that the old churl was soon rousing whomever he could to violent opposition to the Treadup paper. The diary reports that Dr. Cowley's cry was: "A citizen cannot give up his rights! How far do you think our cause would have gotten without these rights? They have been God's way of opening up the country to his servants!" Cowley got strong support from the foreign and Chinese Christian businessmen in Paoting, and from a few fundamentalist missionaries in the area. His group began circulating a counterstatement, in the form of a cablegram to Secretary of State Frank B. Kellogg opposing treaty revision and asserting that it was not the unequal treaties that were causing the present troubles but rather "the long-unsettled political conditions in this country aggravated by propaganda of the Moscow Third International."

Once again, as in the days of the Todd tour, Treadup could take satisfaction in a scorecard, but this time his gloating was rueful:

I have harvested 47 signatures. Dr. C. has 12. What a tragedy to be divided in the face of such needs and opportunities! How much longer are some of us going to attempt to make Christianity primarily a system of belief rather than a way of life?

ROWING AGAINST A GALE

ONCE IN THE DEAD of a moonlit night he leaped out of bed and stood like a dim ghost in his pajamas in the middle of the bedroom.

Emily stirred and groaned. "Are you ill, Mr. Treadup?"

David said very loudly, "No! No! I have to find Inventor Wang!"

He had had a dream of a monstrous irrigation pump, as big as a house, made of bamboo poles and *cardboard*, held together by "red ropes which seemed to be alive, they squirmed." From an animal mouth—"like a dog's" —the pump belched out water onto an expanse of parched fields that stretched to the horizon. Waking in a sweat, he had a sharp memory of the man in Shanghai with all his models of crude but ingenious labor-saving devices for the countryside. Wang had come from a village near Tientsin! David suddenly burned with a need to bring him to Paoting.

"Can it wait until morning?" Emily asked.

It had to. "I crawled back in bed," Treadup wrote,

but I didn't sleep another wink. I don't know when I have experienced such a feeling of urgency. This last trip to Johnny Wu has upset me.

THE TRIP to which he referred had been a visit to Wu in Peking a few days before.

We sat in that little cooped-up office in Madame Shen's palatial grounds, and Johnny—there was a sheet of perspiration like a gleam of varnish on that wide plank he has for a forehead, he was so exalted—told me about his new great plan. Johnny is unstoppable. He turns inches into miles and thinks them too short.

Johnny told David that he had decided to conduct an experiment far more ambitious than anything Treadup had even dreamed of — a large-scale rural-education program in one entire administrative district, corresponding to an American county, with its main seat less than fifty miles from Paoting. Wu's colleague Peter Ma was to take charge in Menghsien, a district comprising ten towns and 443 villages, with a total population of seventy thousand families, probably four hundred thousand persons all told.

> *I was bowled over. The audacity of this dream was not just a matter of scale. Johnny wants to do much more than wipe out illiteracy in the 'hsien.' He wants to help that whole district achieve a decent level of literacy, yes, but also of order, of modern agricultural efficiency, of material prosperity, and of social well-being — wants to make it a shining model for the rest of the country. He wants no less than to change China by example.*

What had upset Treadup in Wu's bold plan was the inference from it that universal literacy would only be a beginning. The *whole* of the peasant's life needed reform. Treadup knew he lacked the resources to imitate, even on a very small scale, such a vaulting undertaking. He did not have the skills to help "his" villagers develop better farming methods, more viable social patterns. He could help them to help themselves, of course, by teaching them to read and write. But as to that, what Marshal Feng had said about his wasting his time teaching in a handful of villages had got under his skin. Even Johnny Wu's incandescent faith in him did not seem to help. The sense he had been having lately of his own great worth had suddenly gone flat. One of old man Cowley's favorite epithets to hurl at Treadup had recently been "naive"; it took Johnny Wu's wide vision of China's needs to make David feel the sting of that word.

TREADUP spent almost the entire day after his sleepless night hunting through boxes and boxes of papers for the scrap on which he had written down the name of the village where Inventor Wang lived, and the directions to reach it. He did not find it. He wrote a long letter to his dear friend Mr. Lin at Peikai University in Tientsin, describing Inventor Wang's devices and asking Lin to inquire among his students and among missionaries who covered the countryside, to attempt to discover the man. The diary:

> *Frustrating day. James B. Todd tried, when recruiting me as a volunteer for this field, to teach me BE ORDERLY IN RECORD KEEPING. Always in too much of a hurry! I just throw things in a drawer and run off to the next thing!*

MR. LIN'S answer, which came a few days later, added to David's distress. It barely acknowledged Treadup's request and then launched into what amounted to a nationalistic broadside, with flashes in it of what must have been an old anger. Mr. Lin was sharply critical about the way missionaries had clung to their control of Christian institutions. They had such pride in what they had built, Mr. Lin wrote, that they were afraid to turn it over to Chinese, and what was more, they "loved position and power." And the Chinese "had been taught that it was Christian to give and give."

How sad such a distance from my dear friend, my first and most important Chinese friend, makes me. He used to help me believe — really believe — that I was giving something of value to his country.

IN THE FOLLOWING MONTHS, David was "caught in an undertow." He felt the way he had when he lost his enthusiasm for the lectures, yet they continued to be a smash hit with the audiences. Now, with his confidence in the panacea of literacy undermined, he found his village projects growing faster than ever. The May 30th Movement had swept through the area, but not once in the villages did the fact of Treadup's being a foreigner even suggest itself.

Wu visited Treadup's villages in the spring of 1926, and "with kind words leaping off his tongue," he told David that he was "learning like a child" from what David was doing, particularly from his efforts to follow up with peasants who had completed the course. Wu's praise "made me feel as if I'd been looking at things cross-eyed — maybe they weren't so bad." David became determined to put down his discouragement, redouble his work, and extend it, learning all he could from the pioneering at Menghsien.

The second winter-and-spring of the literacy work was more successful than the first, and by the time the third came around, in the autumn of 1926, he and his growing force of helpers had enlisted all together some twenty thousand students.

EMILY was low. In the fall of 1925, Philip Treadup had applied for a scholarship to Yale for the following year. His father had sentimentally hoped he would go to Syracuse, but the T'ungchow boys seemed to want Yale or Princeton. For Emily, "the sight of that letter going off gave me a frightful pang. He's still my little boy!" During the next summer she had taken Philip to Tientsin and had embarked him on a ship for Tokyo, where he would transfer to the S.S. *President Cleveland,* to sail off into the big world.

She was doing her best to console herself in a new vocation, as a teacher and mother-of-lost-children in the boarding school for seventy orphan girls that the Congregationalists had established in their compound. In the dormitory, which had thirteen rooms, with five or six girls in each, Emily felt, as she wrote home, "nourished to the depths of my soul by the responsiveness of those sweet children. You cannot imagine what extra measure God has given to Chinese children. They are purely and simply angels." Still, she obviously felt, they were not a fair exchange for her own lost angel.

In Paoting the May 30th Movement had stirred up a hostility against foreigners which even beggars had begun to express. Street urchins hung about the gate of the Association compound, and when Absolom and Paul Treadup went out, these ragged Chinese children, not to be listed among the angels, shouted curses at them.

"IT WAS in 1926 or 1927," Treadup wrote in "Search,"

> *that I first began to realize that I was caught up in vast forces — world currents — cataclysms of history — which were to overwhelm the puny efforts of one small person. I felt that I had been on the right track, and that I was making, for what it was worth, a Christian "contribution," but now one tidal wave after another seemed to come along and crush everything in its path. I remember that period as being one in which I felt as if I were rowing into the teeth of a gale.*

China was in chaos. Devastating power struggles were still going on. In the north Wu P'ei-fu had licked his wounds and joined his former enemy Chang Tso-lin, and together they drove Feng out of Peking. As warfare swirled near Paoting, swarms of refugees forgot their antiforeign feelings and crammed the Treadups' and other foreign compounds; some of the local people who had been most vehemently anti-Christian a few months before volunteered to help.

Meanwhile Chiang Kai-shek with the Kuomintang armies in the south had begun a "Nationalist Revolutionary Expedition" to "liberate" China from warlords and foreigners alike. At the turn of the year into 1927 the left-wing Nationalist troops did the unthinkable — seized the British Concession in Hankow. The response of the foreign powers fanned the flames. Britain embarked twenty thousand crack troops from England to defend Shanghai. In that city dark-complected Punjabi troops put on a show of force which was a perfect display of the swank of imperialism, parading through the streets to the strains of bagpipes. Treadup wrote to brother Paul:

> *I got a letter from Hank Burrell in Shanghai the other day in which he said, among other things, "Today I was thrilled to see twelve hundred American Marines march through the city. Their splendid bearing and*

energetic step and fine form filled me with pride and emotion. The band went ahead, and when the bright silk American flag went by it surely looked a lovely sight." I say: Bravado is one thing, and all very well, but those 1,200 are up against 400,000,000 Chinese. This is not just civil war. It is the French Revolution, the industrial revolution, and the Renaissance, all taking place at one and the same time. Most foreigners — even some of our finest Men of God — have a squint in their eyes these days and can't see what's going on right around them.

MEN OF GOD — those who saw clearly and those who did not — were living in bad times. The Y.M.C.A. was faltering. Chiang was less and less able to control the Communist wing of the Kuomintang, and as the southern armies rapidly swept northward, left-wing troops seized or looted Y.M.C.A. buildings in Nanchang, Kienning, Foochow. In Nanchang the troops expressed their contempt for the Christians by stabling their horses in the Association building. In all the cities, the political uncertainty and the surge of antiforeign and anti-Christian agitation were scaring off prosperous supporters of the Y.M.C.A., and fund drives were failing so badly that the Association could no longer pay the salaries of its Chinese secretaries and staffs. David Liu shared with Treadup and others a letter he had written Blackton in New York, in which he said: "A number of our strongest Associations are in life-and-death struggles."

The surge of anti-Christian propaganda was taking its toll all through the mission field. Word came that hundreds of missionaries were evacuating Szechuan, Hunan, and other interior provinces; they had simply given up in discouragement and were going home for good. Many others were choosing not to return to China from furloughs. Old friends of Treadup's were falling in battle. F. Albert Wood, a companion in the lecture work and a colleague in France, had become convinced that the new leader of the southern armies, Chiang Kai-shek, intended to blindfold him, put him against a wall, and execute him with a machine gun; he had been sent home under medical care. During famine relief work in backcountry Roscoe Hersey had come down with a form of encephalitis that was developing a sequel of Parkinson's disease, and *he* was having to go home.

The home picture was not good, either. Letters from brother Paul were telling David that young Americans were staying away from church in droves; the auto, the radio, and the movies were "keeping their minds off the Divine Being." Magazines brought word of growing hostility to missionaries among intellectuals in the States; anthropologists had convinced them that the dismantling of native customs and religions by Western missionaries was bringing about the collapse of moral order in China and elsewhere. Fund raising for missions was getting harder and harder.

TREADUP kept whistling up his spirits. From a letter to Todd:

> *The darker the political situation is, the keener is the realization on the part of thinking people of the urgency and importance of uplifting the masses. We are going great guns. This is one of the strange phenomena of this country that puzzles foreigners who daily read such headlines as WAR, OPIUM, ROBBERY, ect. They cannot understand how constructive forces can be operating while political chaos seems to be the order of the day. But they are, thank God!*

David Treadup could still be seen, many a morning in early 1927, whirling up a funnel of dust across the countryside with the reckless speed of his Indian motorcycle, scattering hens and scavenger dogs and singing so loudly that his voice could be heard by farmers in the fields even over the roar of the engine.

"THE SECOND TIME I DIED"

THE TRAIN kept stopping. He was in a daze of enthusiasm for what he was about to do. "So many delays," he wrote in his diary, never asking himself the reason for them. And: "Train seems to stand in stations forever." And: "Swarms of peddlers selling sugared apples, malt candy, roasted chestnuts to soldiers on troop trains."

Treadup arrived in Nanking on the morning of Friday, March 18. The train was nearly forty hours late. He was serene. One day was like another. He was God's deputy on an errand for China. He had wired ahead to a physics professor at Nanking University, E. K. Johns, whose acquaintance he had made on his lecture tours, asking for a bed. Hiring two rickshas, one for himself and one for his valise, he made his way to the campus. It turned out that the Johnses' house had been crowded the night before—and still was—with a missionary family recently downriver from Szechuan, so Treadup had to be put up in a university dormitory. He didn't mind. "Fine little room," the diary noted. "Solitary prayers, then off to see the scholars."

YEARS LATER, when he wrote "Search," Treadup recalled his trip to Nanking as "one of the most foolhardy boners of my life."

During one of his periodic visits to Peking to consult with Johnny Wu, his dynamic friend had told him that three years' experience in the field had made Wu's literacy people realize that the original bank of characters they were using in their teaching had been selected from literature, rather than from life. Many more words were needed that bore on the humble, everyday doings of ordinary people. "I had in some dim way noticed this myself—I'd begun scribbling lists of words farmers used that were not in the thousand-character text." Wu said that a team of ten men at National Southeastern University, in Nanking, led by the two American-educated scholars, C. H. Chu and Wellington Ts'ao, who had helped draw up the basic thousand-character text used in mass-education teaching, were now back at work, trying to find a true "people's vocabulary." When Treadup learned of this research, his old urge to be at the center of things had taken hold of him, and on an ill-considered prompting he had dashed off to Nanking with his scribbled lists in his pockets, to make the farmers' case for the inclusion of country words.

In the luxury of his generous impulse, two glaring errors:

He had failed to ask Wu's permission to make the trip. "How could I have been so remiss?" he asked himself in "Search."

This was Johnny's show. All those years we had been talking devolution— you don't make grabs for the torch you've handed on—and certainly not for a torch that wasn't yours to begin with. I was just so keen to get in there and help. O how I regret that blind eagerness of mine. Johnny never quite forgave me. Before that we had been brothers; ever afterward we were cousins.

The second negligence—much more dangerous. In his single-mindedness he had simply cropped out of his picture of the real world all the turmoil of recent months. May 30th might as well never have happened. He had totally ignored the fact that missionaries were being evacuated from the interior to save their lives. He had forgotten what he must have known: that Chiang Kai-shek's Nationalist armies were driving northward onto China's midriff. He was, as he later put it, "stupefied by my love of my work."

"THE SCHOLARS" were not at Nanking University, the missionary institution where he was staying, but were at Southeastern University, the government college which had no foreign faculty at all. Professors Chu and Ts'ao welcomed Treadup cordially and assigned a young member of their team to go over with him everything they were doing.

The team was analyzing the vocabularies of accounting books, business letters, public notices, official proclamations, contracts, and various other documents having to do with daily dealings, and their thought was that out of approximately six hundred thousand characters not previously analyzed, they would eventually choose about two hundred for coveted places in the final basic vocabulary for mass education. Treadup spent Friday, Saturday, and Sunday, after church, reviewing the work. He became totally absorbed.

> *Asked God's forgiveness for breaking the Sabbath. Told him I was using his day to hasten the establishment of his Republic on Earth, where no one will be illiterate.*

ON MONDAY afternoon, Treadup began to argue. He and the two leading scholars were sitting around Wellington Ts'ao's desk in a room completely lined with exquisitely compartmented lacquered shelves that seemed to have been made to hold jade carvings—horses so light in their swiftness that they would appear to be carried by doves flying along under their hooves; squat tripod urns incised with lotus leaves for the incense of dreams; camels with their heads thrown back shrieking in protest at the limitlessness of the desert. But no, no. On those black shelves were crammed thousands and thousands of untidy little bundles of paper tied with ribbons—each one a packet of words vying for a place in the sun. A scientific study! Dust everywhere! Treadup in his nasal Mandarin was saying, with a merciless disregard for face, that the scholars' study was too city-oriented, and that two quite different sets of textbooks and readers were really needed, one for city people and the other for peasants. The physical environments and the social and economic needs of the two groups were completely different. Peasants were four-fifths of the population!

There was a rumble of thunder in the distance. To the south? Treadup went right on talking. The two scholars became "fidgety and rather cross."

> *Thought they were riled up with disagreement with what I was saying, so I got peppery. They broke in. Said we were hearing artillery fire. Southern troops approaching. Said I'd better get back over to Nanking University. Everyone expecting frightful looting when the northern troops withdraw. Writing this now in my student room back at the Univ. I had no idea Nanking was in danger. Where have I been? Up in cloud-cuckoo-land is the answer.*

NOW "ANXIOUS to have my feet planted on *terra firma*," he went to Professor Johns's house and asked the good man to tell him what in the world was going on.

Johns was a bald, frail-looking, gentle-mannered professor of applied physics who after twenty-five years in China had become Chinese in every respect, it seemed, except for the pallor of his skin, the lack of acanthic folds in his eyelids, and the sharpness of his small nose, which was pinched by octagonal gold-rimmed spectacles. With sweet patience, he broke off the work he was doing—hiding the family's household goods, against the expected looting—and sat down in his living room with Treadup to serve him tea and tell him all he knew. Shanghai had been taken by the Nationalists a few days before. They were sweeping everything before them. No one expected the northerners to be able to hold out at Nanking. . . . While they were talking, Mrs. Johns came in, a big-boned and strong-voiced lady, and insisted that Mr. Treadup move and stay with them overnight; the dorms would surely be ransacked; he could sleep on the very divan on which he was now sitting. Treadup accepted with pleasure and went for his things.

AT ABOUT ONE O'CLOCK that night, a United States Marine private knocked at the Johnses' gate. Treadup, who in the living room was nearest, went to answer. The Marine said an order had come to evacuate all American women and children to the gunboats in the river at six thirty in the morning. Treadup roused the house. Mrs. Johns, her two children, the Szechuan missionary's wife, and her three quite small ones all rode to the bund in rickshas which David had walked out to round up—for even in the haunch of a night of danger, dozens of half-starved ricksha men could be found slumped on the footrests of their vehicles, dozing, hoping for late fares.

Mrs. Johns carried with her the family's table silver.

ON TUESDAY, Treadup "felt it my duty" to check in at the city Y.M.C.A. building. Nanking's Fraternal Secretary, Appleton Sills, was overjoyed to have such a powerful-looking Association man "drop out of the sky," as he put it. Everyone expected that night to be the bad one. The artillery fire was much closer to the city, and even rifle fusillades could be heard. It was planned to lock the city gates at dusk, but there were doubtless already many fleeing northern troops inside the walls, under little or no control, with weapons still in their hands, and, as always during a retreat, the routed troops were surely going to console themselves for their cowardice by stripping the lost place clean. Would Treadup be willing to join Sills at the Y building? The presence of foreigners—and one of them, especially, so *big*—would protect both the property and the Chinese secretaries, who lived there.

Treadup was delighted to be of use.

That night, however, brought an anticlimax. Because of the locked gates, most of the northern troops had to skirt the city, and those inside the walls retreated, after all, in good order.

WEDNESDAY NIGHT. Sills and Treadup were keeping watch and watch, four hours each, the off-duty man sleeping upstairs in a room with one of the Chinese secretaries. Shortly after three o'clock in the morning, Treadup was on station at an open window of the lobby. Beside him was Y. L. Ch'ien, the Chinese General Secretary. Two younger men who had been helping with refugee work were out at the grillework front gate, which was locked. Bands of Nationalist soldiers began passing. One group, including some officers, stopped and talked with the refugee workers. Suddenly Treadup heard a shout: *"Chi tu chiao! Chi tu chiao!* Christians! Christians!" Then rifle shots. The young men, who had obviously been threatened, unlocked the gates. The soldiers poured in, firing warning rounds into the air.

Treadup hustled Ch'ien off upstairs. A group of soldiers gathered around Treadup, and one, who took the lead, aimed a pistol at the big foreigner's head while others began to reach into his pockets. Treadup slapped off the hands. The man with the pistol put the muzzle against Treadup's forehead and demanded money. Treadup took his passport from his breast pocket and showed it to the talker. The man ignored it and shouted for money. Treadup had on his person two silver dollars and some small change, and he slowly dug the money out and handed it over. The man cursed at the small change and threw it on the floor. He began screaming that he was going to kill this *yang kwei-tzu,* this foreign devil.

> *I sensed that he meant what he was saying. I reached in my fob pocket and pulled out my watch—Em's watch, really, which I gave her for a wedding present, mine's broken and I had borrowed hers for the trip. It is one of my foibles that I need to know what time it is, even when I don't know what to do with my time. The man snatched the watch but was still calling out his threats. He was a madman—a lot of political talk mixed in. The barrel of the pistol was hard against my temple. It was like a wet finger. He was more nervous than I was, the finger trembled. I will tell the truth: I felt absentminded, as if my brains had already been blown out. I was waiting for the wonder embedded in my fear. And then he did pull the trigger—the thing misfired. Just a click. He was furious and began scrabbling to get out the clip to put another in, but the men all ran upstairs and he finally went after them. I had the most delicious feeling of being under a great soft wing lined with down. Or I was at breast. This was the second time I died.*

So he ran upstairs to protect Ch'ien and the other Chinese staff people. Up in the bedroom area the soldiers had already stripped the Chinese staff of their money, rings, watches, and spectacles (seeing this last Treadup quickly slipped his own glasses off and folded them into a shirt pocket).

Sills was nowhere to be seen. The soldiers were now bullying the staff—nudging them with the butts of guns, threatening to shoot them—for being "foreigners' slaves" as Christians. As Treadup stepped forward to try to calm them down, one of them, who appeared to be an officer, began shouting at the Chinese staff men, "Why are you trying to protect foreigners here? What is this foreigner doing here?" And, turning to Treadup: "Get out! Get out!"

At that, realizing that the whole concept of protection had been turned upside down, and seeing the man whose pistol had misfired approaching him again, holding the weapon at aim, so that it seemed he may have reloaded it, Treadup made a decision like that at the waterfall below Kuling when he decided against certain drowning in an attempt to recover Penn Landsdown's body. He slipped out of the room. He was not followed. He ran down to the refectory kitchen, where there were no soldiers. It was still dark.

Treadup had been in the kitchen only a few minutes when Mr. Ch'ien miraculously appeared with Sills, who whispered that he had been hiding in a clothes closet upstairs. The soldiers were still stamping around above. Ch'ien led the two Americans to a side gate of the Y.M.C.A. compound. There the Association mechanic opened the gate and let the three out, then locked it again. Mr. Ch'ien led the other two through back streets to a police station and then courageously went back to his post at the Y.M.C.A.

With Chinese manners the police expressed regrets to Treadup and Sills for the way they had been treated. They took the two men into their squalid barracks at the back of the station and hid them on two k'angs—earthen beds—behind hanging curtains. Some time later a police officer pulled back Treadup's curtain and said that he and his men were themselves loyal to the northerners; the invading troops were from Hunan—the most xenophobic province, Mao Tse-tung's native region, and the base of one branch of the Kuomintang Communist wing—and the police were afraid they themselves would be killed when their station was raided. They were therefore going to dress in civilian clothes and disband to their homes before it got too light. The officer said his men would lend the two Americans some Chinese clothes, so they, too, could get away.

From a letter to Emily:

You should have seen me. What a ludicrous sight. They gave me the biggest stuff they could find, but my wrists dangled and my ankles stuck out over my American leather shoes and a winter wool-lined hat with earflaps perched on top of my head like a split pea pod. O I looked like the scarecrow in 'The Wizard of Oz.' But I just calmly walked along through the streets, as if I were a coolie on my way to work. I was carrying my own clothes in a bundle under my arm. I passed herds of wild soldiers who paid me no mind at all!

Treadup somehow found his way through the unfamiliar city to Professor Johns's house. It was now getting light. Treadup washed up, had a hearty breakfast, and went to chapel with Dr. Johns.

IN MIDMORNING a loyal servant came running to the Johns house to report that one of the other university houses, the Tranters', was being ransacked. Dr. Johns knew that because Mrs. Tranter's elderly mother was infirm and bedridden, Mrs. Tranter had chosen not to be sent off to the gunboats, and the two women were still in their home. At once Johns asked Treadup if he would go with him to see if they could stop the looters and rescue the ladies, and the two set off. Nationalist troops were stationed at the gate of the Tranter house and would not let the two enter. "Dr. Johns was superb," Treadup wrote. "I would have wanted to bluster, but he spoke softly in his pure Kiangsu dialect, and they finally let us in." The Tranters were hysterical. Their house had been ripped apart from top to bottom. All three Tranters had been threatened over and over again. The men had tried to steal the old woman's wedding ring but a swollen knuckle kept it on her finger. From somewhere the men produced a file, and Tranter had had to watch while they sawed away at the ring and got it off.

Seeing that there was nothing to be gained by quarreling with the troops, Dr. Johns persuaded the Tranters to come back to his house. Treadup carried the wasted old lady in his arms like a baby. On the way back the party was accosted by a squad of Nationalists. They searched Treadup's pockets as he stood with the woman in his arms; they soon found he had been robbed already—his glasses were in his inside pocket, pressed against him by his burden. The men took everything Dr. Johns had, including *his* glasses.

Then in his mild and sweet tones Dr. Johns begged the soldier who had taken his watch to give it back to him, as something dear to his heart. The soldier gave it to him. Dr. Johns had it in his hand. Another soldier then snatched it, and Dr. Johns politely began the same speech. Apparently enraged by the gentle man's civility, the second soldier swung his rifle off his shoulder, fired from his hip, and hit Dr. Johns full in the face. Dr. Johns was knocked over backwards by the force of the shot. As the squad ran off, Treadup crouched over the dying man. "It seemed to me that he tried to speak. The face was smashed, but I thought I could *see* an utterance bubbling out from the bloody mass—forgiveness? 'They know not what they do'?"

Mr. and Mrs. Tranter carried the old woman the rest of the way. Treadup carried the dead man.

THAT AFTERNOON the small party in the Johns house, behind locked gates and doors, heard heavy firing with big guns. Late at night there were loud knockings at the gate and shouts in English. It was a detail of Marines, rounding up Americans to take them all out to the naval vessels on the river. The Marines told the group that the bombardment had come from American gunboats, covering the evacuation of the U.S. consulate. The Tranters and Treadup were put aboard the gunboat *Noa*. Treadup persuaded the commanding officer to send him in a gig to one ship after another, to search for Mrs. Johns. He found her on the *Preston*. He told her about the death of her husband.

ON SATURDAY, on board ship, on the way downriver to Shanghai, David wrote Emily. Part of his letter follows:

> We understand that our loyal Christian Chinese—how brave and sacrificial they have been through this whole affair!—buried Dr. Johns in the foreign cemetery yesterday afternoon. As far as we can tell, six foreigners were killed. Miss Gurney (do you remember her from Kuling? the germ lady?) is aboard with us, she has four gunshot wounds, poor thing—and she thought bacteria were going to get her! As we compare stories, we are all sure that the whole ruckus was planned. Officers took part. One bunch of Americans at the university got a long harangue in English by one of them, quoting Lincoln's Gettysburg address. A doctor at the hospital hid in the coal bin all day Thursday. Upstairs the soldiers taunted the Chinese nurses for working for Christians, then stripped some of them naked on a pretense of searching for valuables. Three were violated—poor creatures, they were all pacifists. I have heard of three cases like mine when people were spared by guns' misfiring. Dr. Reolin was kept under guard many hours and it was nip and tuck whether they'd shoot him, till the soldiers began poking around the apiary he kept in his backyard. Well one of them must have thought treasure was hidden in those nice white domes, he tipped one over and the bees swarmed and the men all ran for their lives. I forgot to tell you we saw one dignified Englishman walking placidly along in his formal gray felt Gladstone hat and nothing else but his B.V.D.s. The port doctor had his ring finger cut off so one of them could swipe his ring; he was killed later. At least eight residences were burned to the ground. I am all right Em—physically speaking—I am dizzy at times—bewildered. Our task is going to be harder than ever we thought. How can we help our dear Chinese friends stay sane? How can we stay sane ourselves? A lot of foreigners have begun saying again, "All these people understand is gunboats." I saw with my eyes Dr. Johns go down to death a pure-hearted Christian if there ever was one. See how my hand trembles as I write. I do not dare think about the meaning of these last days and nights.

IN ORDER to reach home in Paoting, Treadup had to go roundabout:

First, by a Japanese ship, the *Narayu Maru,* from Shanghai to Tsingtao, at the throat of Shantung Province. "Sick as on our honeymoon voyage — sea wasn't too rough, at that — a different malady — I am at odds with my Lord God."

Thence, by train northward.

A Commissioner of the Salt Gabelle was on the ship, and his men told him we'd get right thru Tsinan without any trouble on the train. Well we haven't been going right thru as we've been laid off on a siding 4 hours waiting for 5 troop trains to pass us. What is happening to our poor China? There is still hope we can catch the Blue Express out of Tsinan tonight. . . .

THE ELECTION TO STAY

"PRAYER IS not helping me."

He was finding the return to normalcy — his rounds of the villages on the saddle of his Indian — hard to make. "It's as if I had new lenses in my eyes." It was hard now to sustain a passionate belief that the most urgent issue of his days was which handful of country words should make their way into basic literacy texts. David had heard a click at the temple gate of his skull. He had watched a pure man shot in the face five feet away from him. He thought he had actually seen an effort to forgive — or some marvelous but not quite audible afflatus — or perhaps a man's divine soul — leak out from where the mouth had been, in the bubbling blood. He had had to try to make murder seem an aspect of God's wisdom to the man's widow. Even more disturbing, he had felt, as he noted in his diary, "my will crouching in a back room of my brain" as he tried to come to terms not just with the rage in China's ordeal of renovation but with "something dark in the human mind I have not been aware enough of all these years."

HE STRUGGLED for balance. Friends in Shanghai had explanations. They leaned piously to Chiang. They said they had had oracles from former Y men, Christians, now in chairs in the Nationalist government. The Communist wing of Chiang's Nationalist Party had staged the Nanking incident on purpose to discredit Chiang. He would cut this beast's tail. "The leaders of the Kuomintang," Keystone wrote Treadup, "are now determined on a complete break with the left wing or Communist faction, even at the expense of delaying indefinitely the completion of their plans for the unification of this country." In both Shanghai and Nanking, Chiang began executing Communist leaders, scattering them, driving them underground.

David reached for brother Paul. "Sooner or later the Nationalist cause will sweep irresistibly over the whole country," he wrote. And added:

> It is the fault of foreign nations that this Chinese nationalism has such an antiforeign cast, for it is the foreigners who have taught China that the West will listen only to the barking of cannons. I have much sympathy for certain aims in the Communist program, but I cannot forgive what I have seen of their methods, any more than I can forgive Western gunboats. The Communists preach a utopia in some ways not unlike the Kingdom of God we missionaries preach — but they will kill to bring it to pass. I have never believed that human nature is so vile that the only way to bring in a better world would be with whip and gun. Old Dr. Cowley calls me "naive." Am I, Paul? Am I? Have I been wrong all this time? I know in my heart that I (and all my colleagues in this painful field) have brought profound and irreversible changes — for the good! — in China, but I also know that the changes have been far too slow and far from enough. Is the blood of sweet gentle Dr. Johns the price we must pay for faster progress? I shudder to think it.

HERE IS the gatekeeper with a telegram. He has put it on a plate, to hand to the *mu-shih* in style. It is from Austin McDonald, the United States Consul in Peking.

> NATIONALIST ADVANCE RAPID ALL U.S. CITIZENS
> ADVISED EVACUATE PAOTING SOONEST.

Treadup writes Liu in Shanghai:

> There seems to be a consensus that the women and children should leave. Our wives don't like to be hurried away in this fashion: it diminishes them. But Em is packing. Boats are hired to take the party downriver to Tientsin tomorrow. Since as you know we Treadups are overdue for a furlough, Emily is putting things in the trunks so she and the boys could go on ahead to the States if things get worse.
>
> As for the foreign men, I think we agree that we ought to stay by our job. At least until our Chinese friends think we are more of a handicap than an asset. I don't believe that time has come yet.

WORD CAME BACK after a few days that Emily and the two boys had gone to Peitaiho. Absolom and Paul, oblivious of China's upheavals, romped on the sand and galloped on donkeys, whipping their hats up and down like cowboys. Most of Emily's letters to David in those next few weeks have been lost. Did David destroy them? There came a strain between them. David:

> *A telegram from you today, saying that you are engaging passage for Kobe Apr 26th. I am not quite sure from the wire whether I am included in the passage engaged, but you should know that I must stay on here. The Chinese in the villages all feel I should stay on, and I see no excuse for leaving.*

Two days later:

> *I am not sure I would have been in quite such a hurry as you have been to engage passage, as I still believe this flurry will soon pass over. Make your own decision. I will plan to see you off if you go.*
>
> *Be sure and leave out my clothes that you took, especially my best gray suit and the palm beach suits. And if you want anything else from here, let me know.*

Another letter:

> *Why hurry away? Everything here is as peaceful as one could ask, and the opportunity for Christian work is certainly the best it has been in three years. Not a letter from Peking or Tientsin to explain what is the frightful spectacle that is driving us from our homes and work. I have just wired you as follows (with translation of code):*
>
> *UNOOL Is return imperative? Consider with great care.*
> *KUIPL Have concluded not to leave at present.*
> *SNIRN Please cancel passage for*
> *OATRP Mr. D. Treadup.*

Again:

> *I am still in the dark as to what has caused this stampede. I think it's Austin McDonald, the consul. He has been badgering me and everyone else to leave. He is advising Washington to use an iron fist and in preparation for that he wants all Americans out of the interior. Regarding your sailing, you will have to make the decision. I still feel that the family would be safe under the present conditions right here in Paoting. The Five Powers have handed in their note, and that relieves my mind somewhat. If Hoover is substituted for Kellogg, as the papers suggest may happen, we may expect a more enlightened foreign policy by the United States.*

FOR EMILY the summer was heavy. She missed her oldest and dearest, Philip—whose letters from Yale, though mostly cheerful, betrayed (*she* thought, as she wrote in her diary) a "sense of being an alien in his own country." In late June Emily fell sick, with what was diagnosed as sprue. A letter from David to Liu in Shanghai reported that "she has been put on a diet of nothing but strawberries and buttermilk, and is making slow progress."

RUMORS flew around like pigeons with whistles attached to their tailfeathers. That Chiang had retired from public life. That he had married the petal-faced Christian graduate of Wellesley, Soong Mei-ling—daughter of the matron Emily had worked with in the antiopium campaign in Shanghai. New hope for the cause of the cross? But. There was always a but. That the retirement was a sham. That Chiang was back in the field. That he was behind the northward drive. That he was "beheading" the Communist Party. That he had reduced its strength to that number so beloved by the Chinese, for good and for ill: ten thousand. One-fifth of its former strength. So it was said.

· · ·

Out of sight and earshot:

Just before the Nanking incident, the young Hunanese leader Mao Tse-tung published a *Report of an Investigation into the Peasant Movement in Hunan,* in which he argued that the poor peasant was the main force of the revolution, and demanded confiscation of landlords' land; but the thesis was rejected by the Russian-dominated Chinese Communist Party Central Committee. In Russia, Stalin won out over Trotsky, and not long afterward Ch'en Tu-hsiu, the co-founder of the Chinese party (who years before had advocated studying the life of Jesus), was accused of being a Trotskyist and was deposed as party secretary. Mao led an ill-considered peasant uprising in Hunan, was defeated, and fled to a mountain stronghold at Chingkangshan.

IN EARLY AUGUST Treadup sent a cablegram in Y.M.C.A. code to Shanghai and New York:

GYXITRPVUV EHEETLYENK.

Translated, this meant: "Departure Mrs. Treadup and sons postponed indefinitely. Communicate this to home center by cable and letter."

Treadup wrote—perhaps not quite candidly—to Liu, that "after prolonged and very careful consideration of all points involved," he and his wife had decided together that the family should remain in China. It might not be possible for Emily and the boys to come to Paoting in September, when they left Peitaiho, but they could be housed in Peking or Tientsin. When the situation cleared up, they could return to their station. Meanwhile he would go on with his work and now and then visit his family. "It seemed that it was asking too much of Mrs. Treadup to make her take the two boys home and have the responsibility for all three alone for a year." The political situation looked more promising. It might be that before many months they could be a united family in Paoting, returning to America then together when the Association was ready to let them have their furlough.

BUT SHOCKS:

A Chinese saying: "When the lips are gone, the teeth feel the draft." At Paoting the teeth of the north chattered.

The Nationalists surged northward, far faster than anyone had foreseen, in a two-pronged drive. Treadup's old friend General Feng, now an opportunistic Nationalist, approached from Shantung to the southeast. (A bitter disappointment, Feng. Treadup learned that Z. T. Kao of the Association staff had interviewed him. Feng's "religion," if one could give that name to the constant of fanaticism in him, was now based on the "Three People's Principles" of Dr. Sun Yat-sen. "I have dropped my active Christian evangelistic work in my army because I now have under my command large bodies of Mohammedan troops from Kansu.") From the west and southwest, at the same time, came Wu P'ei-fu and Yen Hsi-shan, the warlord of the "model province," Shansi— both now in Chiang's camp.

In the November edition of *The Shepherd*, the lead story was:

WAR AGAIN, OR STILL

Fifteen thousand Northern soldiers in disorderly retreat toward Paoting, breaking into small bands, robbing and looting thru "our" villages as they flee from the advancing Nationalist army. Carts and animals taken by the hundreds from the farmers to move men, food, cannon, ammunition. Bridges blown up and repaired by armored trains. Bombs hurled from airplanes manned by Russians. Panic. Valuables hidden. Many fleeing.

What does it all mean? It means that the "blue-sky white sun" banner is closer to Peking than it has ever been. Does it also mean that literacy is of no use whatsoever? We are not yet prepared to jump to that conclusion. We are carrying on.

Not for long. Chang Tso-lin's northern troops fell back on the environs of Paoting. Treadup was glad that Emily and the children had not yet come home. The local missionaries—all of whom by now had heard Treadup's full account of the horrors of Nanking—decided that they would do well to gather together in, and try to defend, one compound. They settled on the high-walled Congregationalist compound in the south suburb. By cart and by ricksha Treadup carried there a few valuables: his L. C. Smith typewriter; the family silver, such as it was; "a bit of crockery"; his Mount of Olives Bible; a "few sentimental gewgaws."

As it turned out, the pattern of Nanking was reversed: It took three days for the retreating northerners to loot the city, while the Nationalists, following on their heels, were restrained and orderly. The Congregationalist compound was never challenged by the looters. But Treadup's little compound was.

FROM A LETTER to Liu in Shanghai, with a mere carbon to Emily:

The house has been completely wrecked, doors, windows, floors, bath-tub ect. ect. all having been torn out. At the same time, everything I had not carted away has been removed, to use a coarse word, stolen. Everything, that is, except my books. Every one of them is still there — all over the floor, of course. Even the gates of the compound have been carried away. I have had the gate bricked up, but people—civilians, now—are still climbing over the wall, looking for hidden treasure, of which of course there is none left. The future? My own feeling is that perhaps the best thing to do would be to pull down the remains of the house and build a cheap bungalow, putting in an Arcola heating plant and the usual water fixtures, planning an occupation of, say, 15 years. I am inclined to think it would be the cheapest thing to do in view of the damage done. The longer I live, the more I am inclined to advocate a very small compact house for life in China.

HE WAS on his hands and knees with a heavy heart. His papers, like his books, had been scattered all over the floor of his study. He was picking them up and randomly putting them into boxes. Suddenly he stood up, and out from the belly of his misery came a triumphant Onondagan war whoop. He had found the slip of paper with the name of Inventor Wang's village, and the directions to get to it from Tientsin. He slipped it under the cover of his Mount of Olives Bible, to be sure he would not mislay it again.

PEKING fell on June 3, 1928. Two months later the bungalow had been built. Emily and the children were back. Shanghai paid for the new house. New York sent one thousand dollars of U.S. money to cover the Treadups' losses in the looting. Treadup wrote Todd:

> *First. The loss was fairly and squarely ours and not the Y.M.C.A.'s, and we do not feel that the Association was under obligation to assume any responsibility. We were the ones who went into the foreign field "to spend and be spent" in the service. Your gift takes away the satisfaction of our having given something to the Cause of the Master, and I am going to put the money into our work in the villages. I hope the missionary movement will never become so completely organized and institutionalized that it will no longer be possible for one to go out and follow Paul the Apostle in the matter of self-sacrifice.*
> *Second. In my opinion the International Committee was on right lines when you decided to ask their secretaries, who were looted in Changsha, Nanking, here, and elsewhere, not to seek indemnity by appealing to the American government to secure redress. This is not a time in China when a policy of "an eye for an eye" can do anything but harm.*

SOMETHING deeper than the Pauline spirit of sacrifice was operating in David Treadup's psyche. It was expressed in a self-consciously "written" letter he sent to his old counselor and friend, Farrow Blackton:

> *Do you ever get away from the feeling of despair, bewilderment, and hopelessness that has come to you as you have made your way down the crowded streets of a great city in China, like Soochow, or Hangchow, or the native city in Shanghai or Tientsin, or our Paoting, and you have felt the woes of that suffering and patient people settle down on your soul, a burden you are helpless to lift?*
> *Can you ever shake off the sinking of heart that has come as you have suddenly turned aside from the beautiful countryside and paused before the hut of a villager, seeing through the open doorway the dire poverty of the hardworking peasant and his family who in return for their labor do not enjoy even a semblance of the comforts which we of America consider essential to animal life, to say nothing of human life?*
> *The petition "Give us this day our daily bread" is, in the Lord's Prayer, coordinate with "Thy kingdom come, thy will be done." I am at this moment very very low in my mind. I had been so excited about*

teaching all China to read. I think I have to think more about bread. The
bread and wine of the Holy Sacrament—flesh and blood. Bread above
all. The everyday kingdom of flesh.

DANGEROUS GRAYS

ON A BITTER DRY DAY in January 1929, Treadup, wearing a quilted
Chinese coat and a lambswool-lined hat with the earflaps down, boarded an
open gondola railway car with his Indian motorcycle and a small bundle of
spare underclothes and socks. At the Peking station outside the city wall,
he changed trains and went on to Tientsin.

It was late in the day when he arrived there, but he did not pause. He
putted right out of town on his motorcycle, southward, on the road toward
Tsinan. Soon it was dark. His headlight sought, so that he could avoid, the
worst ruts in the sunken dirt road. It was after midnight when he pulled off
into a field, lifted his tent and bedroll from the sidecar of the Indian, pitched
the canvas, and crawled in. "Night so still and cold I felt as if whole weight of
the Cheops pyramid sat up there over me. Hence slept like a mummy."

He was up at five. He boiled water for tea over a can of Sterno, packed,
struck camp, and drove off before the local population had a chance to gather
around and gawk.

The sun was not yet on the shoulder of the morning when he pulled into
a medium-sized village where the first thing he noticed was a house surrounded
by a whitewashed wall made not of mud but of real baked bricks, and
crowned with jagged bits of broken glass. Assuming that this was the house
of the village headman and main landlord, he knocked at its gate.

He asked the woman who answered whether this was the home of the
village chieftain.

She said it was not. The headman lived in the third house down the
village street—a relatively modest structure with a mud wall.

Treadup knew he must clear any errand in the village in advance with
the headman. Though unpretentious outside, the chief's house showed signs
indoors of a fair degree of prosperity: a lacquered chest, brass bowls, new
reed matting. The headman was spending this winter day playing a kind of
chess with a friend. He greeted the foreigner cordially and told him that Wang
the inventor lived in the "big house." The foreigner had permission to visit
him. He would not be the first foreigner to have done so.

Treadup went back and knocked at the gate in the white wall.

Wang was not gambling over a chessboard. He was out in his yard with a crew of men supervising the construction of a large wooden machine; Treadup remembered at once the little model of the tamping machine for road building that Wang had showed him in Shanghai. Wang recognized his caller, and with great good form invited him into the house, directed his wife—the lady who had answered at the gate earlier—to bring tea, and the pair sat down cross-legged on a spacious *k'ang* in a room well lit by the sun through paper-paned windows.

Wang was chubby. He was dressed in the long cotton gown of a man who had no need to work with his hands. Yes, he had prospered. He let out his machines, he said, on a system of rental in kind—in grain, mostly—to which no one objected, because he had helped many of the farmers in the vicinity to grow more crops than ever before. His biggest hit was a device which vastly simplified the drawing up of water from a well, for irrigation; but he had also put many other labor-saving machines to work throughout his entire *hsien*.

"I remembered," Treadup later wrote,

> the burning eyes of this obsessed man when he came to see me in Shanghai. He had wanted me then to help him to help China. And now I saw that he had instead helped himself. Unmarred fingernails! He had three little chins—good eating. I despaired of persuading him to help me to help China.

But that was what Treadup had come to do, and he tried. He reminded Inventor Wang that he had been a coolie once, a down-and-out younger brother; and that he had got his start through the literacy program in France. Now in the region around Paoting, and in the whole district of Menghsien, programs of literacy were catching on. But a farmer had come to Treadup recently saying, "I can read and write all the characters in your books, but my stomach still growls just like my neighbor's who cannot read at all." It was time to broaden the teaching—to help the farmers to acquire better tools, to make better choice of crops, to learn about rotation of crops and better application of manure, to get better seed, and to learn how to control insects and plant and animal diseases. He wanted Inventor Wang to come to Paoting and help the farmers install labor-saving machines—and without charging for the service. It would be Wang's gift to the new China.

Treadup watched Wang as he talked. The roles these two had had in Shanghai were now reversed. It was Treadup now who had a rather wild eye, Wang who was the judicious listener. Through an evident gift for mimicry and a habit of doing favors for a price, Wang had picked up a crude version of the manner of a landlord; but now and then the former coolie peeked through the mask of fat. Treadup did his best to speak to the memories in the mind of that more hidden person, to an idealism that had surely been there. Treadup felt a flicker of anger at the memory of having been called a "dupe" on account of this man and his barrowmen friends. This man a Communist? Not now, not now.

A formal reciprocity would have to be established. And it was now Wang who, as Treadup had done in Shanghai, said, "Give me your address and tell me exactly how to reach you." And, as had been the case in Shanghai, that was that. Treadup left. He did not expect to see Inventor Wang ever again.

TREADUP went to Menghsien, to be tutored himself, and he found the experience discouraging.

There Johnny Wu's people had already mapped out a program far broader than the basic literacy campaign. Its aim was very high: to develop a model *hsien* so enviable that all China would want to copy it. The program was to be threefold. Village People's Schools would carry on the literacy work, and a special farmers' literature would be developed. An effort would be made to raise the farmers' economic level by disseminating modern scientific agricultural methods, adapted to local Chinese conditions. And in a third phase, "modern citizenship training" would help to raise the moral level of the farmers.

What Treadup found disheartening was that the Menghsien experiment really might be called "scientific," while by contrast his own efforts had been, and were bound to stay, intuitive and catch-as-catch-can. Wu had a staff of brilliant mission-schooled and American-educated Chinese rural experts; Treadup had a great deal of willing help, but it was from untrained villagers and country teachers. Some of Wu's experts, including the Peter Ma who had been in France with Wu, were the first Chinese intellectuals ever to "go down to the people," living with the farmers under the very conditions they faced—setting a pattern that, much later, Mao Tse-tung adopted as a basic article of faith and, eventually, as a device for punishment.

Treadup realized on this visit that he worked in "his" villages by hunch and by impulse, seeing one thing after another that needed doing, then frantically trying to do it—like his father in the mornings on the farm in Salt Branch; whereas Johnny Wu's people were gathering hard information that would help them map out the most expeditious and fruitful ways of working.

In a letter about his Menghsien visit, Treadup wrote brother Paul:

The hardest thing to let go of, out here, is the idea that we missionaries have been put here to 'show the Chinese the way.' I am having to stomach the converse. You may remember that I've often said that Wu was my teacher in France. I am going to have to come back and back to Menghsien to learn the Chinese way. I see a future in which, except for occasional flashes of insight that no one else has had, I will always be an "assistant." I will be fifty-one in a few weeks. Physically I feel very young and strong, but I suppose I am on the verge of the great slope. I hope as I meander down it I can accept gracefully the role of a marcher in the second rank.

ALL TOO SOON the time came when Absolom had to apply for entrance to college in the States. With his hearing disability, he had not done nearly so well in school as Philip, but Yale admitted him and furthermore gave him a full scholarship. Although Emily took comfort in knowing that he would have an older brother to watch out for him, she thought of him as her wounded chick and dreaded seeing him fly off. Soon, two of the three would be gone; already, during term time, her nest was bare, because both Absolom and Paul were now away at the T'ungchow boarding school.

As so often had been the case in their lives together, all signs of the strain between David and Emily, which had appeared in his letters of the previous spring, now had vanished. David had had his way. Emily had accepted his judgment with that remarkable deep-pool serenity of hers, into which whatever angers she ever felt seemed always to settle, leaving no trace. Her diary entries, sparse in this period, occasionally noted her missing the boys, but otherwise were radiant. For she had thrown her whole self into the compensatory mothering work at the girls' school. She wrote her younger sister Jane:

How I wish you could have been at our little school yesterday. We had a ball-playing contest. It was an interclass affair, the games played being captain ball and basketball. Excitement ran high when the scores were close. It interests me to see how the girls abandon themselves to the game, not at all caring what happens to their clothes or personal appearance if only they can help make an additional point.

Emily was thrilled by some of the debates the students held during literary exercises on Saturday mornings. The subjects the girls chose showed they were thinking about big problems. Resolved, that the development of China is more dependent on reform measures within the country itself than on more just treatment on the part of foreign nations. Resolved, that the strength of a country is more dependent on the intelligence and good citizenship of the common people than on good officials. How sharply they could speak! This was indeed a "new China." Emily: "It is no longer considered essential that Chinese girls should modestly hang their heads under all circumstances and keep all their thoughts to themselves."

TREADUP took a trip to Peiping (for now that Chiang Kai-shek's government was seated in Nanking, Peking's name had been changed, from "Northern Capital" to "Northern Peace") to get some advice from Johnny Wu on his country work. While he was there he decided to drop in at the Association building to see Thomas Gridley, to catch up on news of all his old friends in the Y.

Sitting in Gridley's office the chatting secretaries heard a slow beat of drums and a mournful blare of trumpets in the street outside—a military procession—a company of soldiers, marching with stiff legs at a strange, formal, funereal pace. Halfway along two men walked with their hands tied behind their backs, one terribly bloodied. "They're going to have their heads cut off," Gridley said—then sharply drew in his breath. He had recognized the uninjured man, who, he said, was a graduate of Columbia and the principal of a school that was introducing the Dalton system of teaching to China— "decent chap, didn't know he was a Red." The other young man was shouting cant phrases over and over: "Throw off the yoke! Down with oppressors!" His guards tried to silence him by jabbing him in one side of the jaw, then the other, with their bayonets, but his bloody mouth kept screaming his defiance and his shibboleths.

"PICTURE of those two men in my mind day and night," Treadup wrote in his diary. And another entry: "Have been thinking about Christian martyrs. Annie Gould and all the others, right here in Paoting."

For some days that memory steeped in his mind. Then he wrote a letter to Todd which was to have a drastic effect on the rest of his life. In part:

> It is time to make some general observations. Bear with me.
>
> The present movement in China is a real people's revolution. It is altogether different from the Revolution of 1911 or any of the subsequent so-called revolutions. Those were waves on an inland lake. This is an oncoming sea tide.
>
> We missionaries are all congratulating ourselves that this is an auspicious time for our Cause. In the Nanking cabinet right now there are ten ministers. Six were educated in American universities—Yale, Columbia, Harvard, Oberlin, California. Seven of them are Christians. Of those seven, two are former Y.M.C.A. secretaries. We very nearly have the government in the palm of our hand!
>
> But remember this: The leaders of the present movement have started something they cannot control. They've unleashed powers which seem thrilling but they have also already gone to heinous excess.

They have stirred desires and aspirations which cannot be satisfied soon, if ever. This means a long period of bitter discontent, striving, and struggle.

Treadup went on here to write of "this epoch of barbaric violence, which an imported Christianity is powerless to tame." The warlord Chang Tso-lin, he wrote, had refused to sign a secret treaty on Manchuria with the Japanese, and the next day a huge bomb blew up his private car on a train and killed him. Treadup then described the Communist terror in Hunan; "I've been told that 20,000 were murdered in cold blood in Changsha alone—probably exaggerated but blood was badly badly shed."

There are grays here, dangerous grays, and most of our Y.M.C.A. people, particularly our Fraternal Secretaries, see nothing but black and white. They think Nanking, being part Christian, is all good, while the anti-Christian Reds are all bad. But James B!—the Communist terror and the slaughter of Reds by Nanking are equally atrocious. The Christians in the cabinet in Nanking seem totally unmindful of the lesson of the church's martyrs; they have blood on their own hands. Our boy's-work secretary in Peiping says that pretend beheadings have become a favorite pastime of Chinese children in their play.

Everyone "on our side" is gloating that the Communists are done with. You must not believe it. They are not yet at work in "my" villages, but several Chinese I have talked with who have come up from the south have told me that a very large majority of the students are still infected by communism of the Bolshevist brand. They are fanatic. Like the early Christians, they are ready to take the sword at the neck for their beliefs.

How should the Y.M.C.A. respond to all this? To me it is very clear. After all the years of our work with the literati and the governing and business classes, who were our sole source of indigenous support, we must face it that the Communists have taught us that we must work—if we really believe in the message of Jesus—for the underprivileged.

Yes, James B. I came out here under the slogan which I think you helped to coin: "Evangelization of the world in this generation." I would suggest that we now need a new one, no less hard to bring to pass: "For Jesus Christ's sake, the abolition of poverty in this generation."

"HUMANIST"

ONE EVENING while Treadup was at supper with Emily, the family's houseboy Li bent over to the master and whispered that there was a peasant on a loaded cart at the gate who was demanding to see him. Li had tried to send the farmer away, the master was eating, come tomorrow, but the man said he had ridden from a long distance and would not be put off.

Treadup went to the gate. The peasant was seated on the bed of a large two-wheeled Peking cart, with a big load, covered with matting, behind him. He said, "I have come." Treadup said, "I see you have come, but what do you want?" After a long pause the man said, "Do you remember a man who came to see you in Shanghai with some models of wooden machines?" Wang! Inventor Wang! He was dressed down to look poor. Treadup had not recognized him. He whooped. Wang jumped down from the cart. Treadup invited his guest to come into the house. Li was outraged at the sight of this peasant seated at the master's dining table, and he set tea before the man looking as if he wished it were steaming donkey urine.

Wang said he would help Treadup in "his" villages on one condition: that Treadup would understand that henceforth the inventor was to live two distinct and different lives, one here, another at home. At home he would be, as usual, Inventor Wang, who manufactured labor-saving machines and rented them out to farmers; here he would be a clever peasant named Sung, who would share with other peasants, at no cost, some good ideas he had had about how to make some machines that would save a great deal of work. For if it ever got back to the farmers to whom Wang was charging rent that in another district he was letting his machines out free, "they would cut me up and feed me to the wild dogs and I would not blame them."

AND SO a new phase of the work began. Wang became Sung for two weeks of each month. Li had to get used to the idea that this uncouth Chinese person lived from time to time in a guest room in the master's house. The peasant Sung, the patron Mr. Hsiao, and the big-nose T'ao Tu Hsien-sheng began to visit villages showing the farmers four devices:

• A waterwheel for drawing up well water. This was Wang/Sung's big item. Its features were a larger rope drum than on the usual waterwheel, so the bucket came up faster, and an automatic bucket spiller, whereas the bucket had formerly had to be dumped by hand. Much friction had been eliminated, so that one instead of two persons could wind it. It irrigated three mou rather than one mou of land, and cost two dollars less than the conventional well wheel.

• A simplified planter. The old-style planters needed the work of three people and a donkey; this one did away with two of the three, and it cost less than the old models.

• An improved harrow, with two sets of clod-breaking teeth, instead of one.

• A more efficient plow, with a guide wheel out front that set the depth of the furrows.

For some reason, even in the villages where Treadup and Mr. Hsiao were well known, the local farmers were suspicious of these devices, shown as full-scale models. Rumors began to circulate, much like those one had heard when they had started their work—that the implements were decoys . . . conscriptions . . . taxes . . . enticements to "eat religion."

"Sung," perhaps not altogether disinterestedly, argued that the suspicion was based on the fact that Treadup was offering to let people copy the machines at no charge; such altruism must be devils' work. But Mr. Hsiao said he knew these people, and the one natural and accepted way to broadcast good ideas was to demonstrate them at the district temple fair, which would soon take place in about a month at a large temple twenty miles from Paoting. The beneficent geomantic influences of the temple would do away with all suspicion.

Mr. Hsiao arranged the necessary permissions. This time Sung set up the waterwheel on an actual well, and he hired three donkeys and three assistants to demonstrate the plow, the harrow, and the planter, on some fallow land he got Treadup to rent adjacent to the temple grounds.

And this time the devices were a sensational success. The farmers, who had brought their best wheat, millet, sorghum, chickens, hogs, and other produce for sale at the fair, actually tried their hands at the waterwheel and the three tools. More than four thousand farmers ground the handle of the waterwheel. Scores of village headmen agreed to let "Sung" and his strange pair of accomplices, the delicate scholar and the enormous foreigner, come to their villages to show their people how to copy the things.

A PERIOD of high heart. Treadup was bursting with ideas. He rushed from village to village putting the ideas to work. It did not matter to him that many of them were borrowed or even stolen from Menghsien. What mattered was that new Chinese energies were being set free, like ten thousand birds from ten thousand cages.

The push for literacy remained at the heart of the work. He formed intervillage alumni associations of the literacy schools and charged them with finding new teachers and starting new schools, and with circulating and using farmers' readers and a periodical that the Menghsien people were publishing, called *The Farmer.*

But he also reached into Y.M.C.A. experience and started new undertakings. The temple grounds where the fair had been held became a kind of headquarters for these new experiments, as well as the seat of one of the largest literacy schools. Here Treadup organized a fly-killing campaign. He promoted the planting of trees. He got villages to cooperate in improving the roads that tied them together. He helped women organize Better Homes Clubs. "Just for a lark" Treadup even gave his beloved old gyro lecture a few times. "Well received. On par with a traveling opera or troupe of tumblers and jugglers!"

O N E D A Y there came a scratchy and puzzling letter from David Liu. The General Secretary for all China reported that he had had "an extremely disturbing communication" from Todd in New York, asking Liu "what has got into our humanist friend Treadup?"

In "Search," reviewing this period, Treadup wrote that his single-minded absorption in the details of his village work must have blinded him to the ominous significance of Todd's code phrase, "our humanist friend."

> *I knew very well that to the hard-line fundamentalists, "secular humanist" was just a goat whisker short of "heathen." Todd was no fundamentalist, but he was saying much more than met my eye. He was saying that if I wanted to substitute the abolition of poverty for evangelization, then I must be more a functionary than a missionary, and a pink one at that.*

Treadup was further misled by the fact that David Liu was not concerned with the real meaning of what Todd had written. Liu was furious because Treadup had written a letter to Todd over his, Liu's, head. He had no interest in the content, only in the insubordination. Treadup had recently had a confidential letter from Burrell in Shanghai telling how difficult Liu had become. He was now "an individualist of the most extreme type, who uses the personal pronoun all the time when talking of Y policy." He had lost the loyalty of the Chinese staff, and, Burrell wrote, John Y. Hu was on the point of resigning. If he left, the Lecture Bureau would surely fall apart. "I know how dear to your heart the lecture work is — thought you should know about this," Burrell wrote.

In his busyness, Treadup had put off trying to do anything about this alarming news; now that he himself was on the mat, it was too late. And in his busyness, he was (he was later to realize) too casual in his response to

David Liu. He simply sent Liu a copy of his letter to Todd, with a longhand note: "Sorry! Didn't mean to cause any short circuits."

HE WAS BUSY. While carrying on work at the temple and making rounds to the villages, he was making periodic trips to Johnny Wu's headquarters in Peiping and to Menghsien to learn as much as he could about improved methods of using bean cakes, roast cottonseed cakes, night soil with added gypsum, and ripened barn dung for manures; about simple controls for wheat smut and rust, and sorghum and millet smut; and simple ways of killing the most common pests—aphis, wheat fly, cutworm, cotton leaf rollers. And he also began to learn from the Menghsien people about real farm income and living expenses, and about farm tenancy, systems of credit, and marketing arrangements, and about the possibility of forming farmers' cooperatives.

"Here," he suddenly wrote in his diary in the midst of his highest good cheer, "I feel as if I had finally walked through the door into reality—and I find I am in a very dark room."

ALL DURING the summer, reports had been trickling in of yet another extensive famine, in the northwest regions of China. Vast areas of the provinces of Shensi, Kansu, and Suiyuan had been suffering from drought for nearly a year. Word now came of a group of forty small children who had been sold to rich landlords for food by their fathers and had been shipped off toward Peiping to be resold. Somehow some American Board missionaries in the interior had managed to have these children ransomed, and they now arrived in Paoting for care. With help from some Chinese Bible women of the American Board mission, Emily took them on at the school. She wrote home:

> They came straggling in. Those who could had walked twenty miles a day for a week. Some of the girls and littlest boys rode in on wheelbarrows. These poor little scarecrows had been living for weeks on a diet of chaff, bean pods, and peanut shells. They are between eight and fifteen.
> Dr. Wells examined them, and then with fears, tears, and palpitations, they were stripped of all their clothes and popped into a real porcelain bathtub and given a bath. For most of them it was their first bath—the people of north Shensi and Kansu believe that water is harmful to them—most men in that area bathe all over twice in their lives—at birth and before getting married—hate washing their feet, hands, or faces, and cutting their hair—more pigtails still in that part of China than anywhere else. So! Quite a lot of terrified squealing! Out they came and we wrapped them in a sheet, weighed them, put on

hospital clothes way too big for them, and tucked them in bed. Why bed in broad daylight? So we could send their clothes to the basement to be steamed!

The next day, when the strange lady (me) said they could put their clothes on and they found them sweet and clean and sterilized with no little itchy creepy creatures in them, and when they were led over to a yard where there were swings and things to play with, and after they were given all they could eat of 'chou' (a millet mush, the main article of diet in this region), cornbread, and vegetables — then they forgot that they had ever been afraid!

TREADUP now received an extremely unpleasant letter from Todd. In part:

Your letter of "observations" is creating some havoc in the International Committee. At your own request, you were put out to pasture after your fine development of the Lecture Department on experimental literacy work under our wing, but reports have come to us that you have spent a large portion of your time on types of work having nothing to do with literacy, work properly under branches of the Chinese National Committee to which you have made no reports, either of plans or of progress.

More serious to some of us is the distinct humanist tone of your letter. One is put in mind of the fact that from the very first, your work in the field has revolved around science. I must put it to you quite firmly that no man can honorably remain in the Y.M.C.A., and the Y.M.C.A. cannot honorably employ any man, who does not have a philosophy of life which has squarely at its center some outside "plus ultra" which we usually call "God," and a deep conviction that that God has been best revealed to man by the life of Jesus Christ.

The International Committee is having to consider whether it can afford to continue your free-lance work in Paoting, or whether it should recommend to the Chinese National Committee that you be returned to the lecture work. . . .

Treadup was aghast. This from Todd, whose evangelistic meetings in China would have been half empty if it had not been for Treadup's lectures! Free-lance! "He has slapped me in the face!" — no mention of turning the other cheek. He shot off a one-sentence letter:

Since you have used the phrase "quite firmly," I must tell you quite firmly that I try every day of my life to be a Christian.

AFTER A FEW DAYS of thought, of prayer, and of talking with Emily, David realized that that had been a foolish and intemperate response, and that if he wanted to continue the village work about which he now cared so much, he would have to rebuild his bridges to both Shanghai and New York. Besides writing long letters to Liu and Todd, describing his work in great detail and giving the best reasons he could for being permitted to continue in it, he asked Johnny Wu, Gridley, Burrell, and Charles Stanton of the American Board Mission in Paoting all to write to both Liu and Todd urging that he be kept on under assignment to the People's Education Movement.

As it turned out, David Liu, for whatever reasons, very much wanted Treadup to stay in Paoting, and he asserted to Todd in no uncertain terms that it was his prerogative as chairman of the Chinese National Committee to assign fraternal secretaries wherever he wished; and besides, Johnny Wu's letter to Todd was wonderfully generous to Treadup, and persuasive about the importance of his work to the Christian cause in China. However, no matter what Liu asserted, the fact remained that New York paid Treadup's salary, the Syracuse backing having faded away over the years, so the issue would have to be settled in the States.

Treadup worked and waited, and at last in mid-July this letter came from Todd:

> *This will report to you the passage by the International Committee of the following motion:*
>
> *Moved, that (1) the International Committee authorizes continuation of Mr. Treadup's salary for a two-year period beyond the end of the current fiscal year; and (2) that inasmuch as Mr. Treadup has been able to give great impetus to the Literacy Movement in North China, the Chinese National Committee's continued assignment of him to this work in the Paoting area be affirmed; but that (3) he and his family being long overdue for furlough, it is further moved that Mr. Treadup be released for furlough for one year, on the usual terms, beginning August 1, 1929.*
>
> *I know this will please you. I want to apologize for the high line I took with you in my last. China's recent turmoil has had us all on the razor's edge. We all look forward to your return to these shores.*

What an outcome! This was an endorsement of sorts—but only two weeks to get ready for furlough: two weeks to try to provide continuity of all that was happening in the villages during a whole year of his absence! To say nothing of only two weeks' time for Emily to pack, and for David to clear everything with Liu in Shanghai, and to arrange passage. David realized how shrewd the deadline was: There was no time for him to fight off this abrupt removal.

MISSPELLED on the passenger list of the S.S. *President Harding* were "Mr. and Mrs. Tredup & 2 sons." Those four were on the high seas when the New York Stock Exchange crashed.

REAPPRAISAL

THE LONG TRAIN snaked through the Rockies. Sitting in the backwards-riding seat of the section he shared with Emily, David looked back now and then out his window and saw what appeared to be an endless caterpillar of Canadian Pacific Railway Pullman cars working around a broad curve, the illusion of infinitude resting in his never being able to see the observation car at the very rear; the great segmented metal worm of progress was forever coming out of some tunnel or emerging from a deep cleft of granite and gneiss beside a white-water torrent.

"I see the track over the grim and majestic mountains, winding through these gorges and threading these tunnels," David wrote in his diary,

> *as standing for my travails. What back-breaking work it must have been to lay down so many ties and pin onto them, spike by spike, all these miles and miles of steel ribbon. Yes. I've been working on the railroad all the live-long day.*

Absolom and Paul, in the section across the car, were quarreling over a card game called Authors. From time to time the train plunged into a tunnel; the car filled with sooty smoke; the boys paused in their arguing, then resumed as soon as the train burst out into the light again.

Emily stood up, crossed the aisle, and murmured to them. They quieted down. Emily sat again.

"I don't like the word humanist," David said.

Emily did not reply; stolid silence was her enigmatic answer.

IT IS still dark. A lodge at Lake Louise, where the family has taken the tickets' privilege of an overnight stay. Treadup, who has not slept well, gets up, dresses himself in stealth, and sneaks out for a lakeside walk. First light reveals through evergreen boughs a glassy surface. Then, as morning seeps across the arch of heaven over the mountains, a magic light works its way under the surface, and David can see, even from the wild path in the woods, clean rocks deep down. After China's rivers this pure water stuns him. His heart quickens—the trapper in his ancestry is alert. He hears a slapping sound. His feet take silent steps on the forest floor; he pushes branches apart. Two beavers are not twenty feet away. One is on watch, the other is felling a stout sapling. Swift, tireless work. Hurry! Cut it up! Swim the branches to the dam! Back again! Chop more! David is reverent. He watches a long time; the beavers never rest. From his diary, that night: "I am so self-absorbed. Brother animal, how does it feel to be me?"

THE TWENTIETH CENTURY LIMITED creeps into Grand Central Terminal. David Treadup and the two sons carry the handbags along what seems a mile of platform; trunks will be delivered later. Emily is wearing a delicate veil, robin's-egg blue, wrapped over a hat of white feathers. All across a continent's span she has obviously been daydreaming about her first encounter with Philip; she has not seen him for two years. It is almost time for the new fall term to begin at New Haven, and she will have to give up Absolom then, too.

Four Treadups pass through the gate to the upper level. There stands Philip. He is wearing a jaunty cloth cap and white buckskin shoes. Emily lifts her arms to raise the veil for a kiss, long anticipated. But Philip, evidently not wanting to be taken for a child, holds back; he takes his cap off and shakes her hand. He shakes hands all round.

"We needn't take a cab," he says. "We have enough soldiers to carry the valises." He is amazed at how Paul has grown. "What a horse!" he says. "Well, Abbo," he says, "off to New Haven, what? Wait and see. It's just swell."

On the Madison Avenue sidewalk, he teams with the brothers, playfully jostling Paul.

"Quit it," Paul says, who thinks he has been unfairly given the heaviest bag.

Philip has scarcely looked at Emily. She has lowered her veil. She says, "What ever has happened to your complexion, Phil? Are you eating what you should?"

"For heaven's sake, Mother!" Philip says.

HERE WAS the encounter David Treadup had been rehearsing in his mind halfway around the globe. Emily had been hearing him grinding his teeth at night. He had tried various approaches on her; she had not allowed him to lean on her, had said, "Whatever you think is wisest, David." Could an angry man pray to an angry God to be freed of his anger, so he could deal coolly with his danger? The hardest thing was to know his own mind. He rose in the elevator at 347 Madison Avenue, his broad forehead as wet as if he had been rowing a scull. Busy, busy James B. Todd had put him off for two days and now kept him waiting in the International Committee anteroom for three-quarters of an hour.

At last. The two huge men sat opposite each other in a sun-lit office. Todd, now sixty-four, was still blond and smooth-faced; such wrinkles as he had were fine, like the tiny cracks in dried enamel. "He had the power if not the glory," Treadup wrote later. Treadup was fifty-one; there were no gray hairs among the brown, and his leathery skin and flaring mustaches "must have made me seem crude and Kiplingesque—a subaltern who had lost his troops in a foolhardy charge—quite out of his depth in this spiffy homeside H.Q. with its mahogany bookcases and broad desk that was too tidy, much too tidy."

"Well, old boy," Todd said. "Welcome home."

Treadup later wrote that he did not like the idea of Todd's being comradely. He wanted a dressing down—harsh words to react against with strong words of his own. Instead he was getting mush. Good trip home? How was the crossing—don't we remember you used to suffer from *mal de mer?* That royal "we"! A winner's picture drawn of an invalid on the high seas; David remembered Todd snorting down the gangway at Hong Kong that time, just having ridden out a typhoon as if it were a tame saddle pony. He decided Todd had never forgiven him for attracting the bigger crowds during their great tour. Suddenly he could not contain himself and burst out with "a line I had intended to keep for much later."

"I don't like the word humanist," he said.

"Oh?" Not ready for that, yet.

"Human, yes. All too. It's that extra syllable. What's that supposed to convey?"

Todd cleared the bassoon throat. "We're having to go through a reappraisal these days, of our entire effort in China. All along the line. You know, David, better than I do, how volatile everything is out there in the field."

From "Search":

So he had me at a disadvantage right off the bat. He was going to be analytical. Havoc of warlords ect., ect. He was too full of love to face me out. The International Committee ect., ect. . . . Soon he actually began to praise me: wonderful pioneering of the lecture program, then on top of that the literacy work. "Your contribution has been unique," he said. Then he added another word. "Idiosyncratic." Spoken as if it were the nicest possible quality in one of his subalterns. I didn't realize it at the time—I was beginning to ease away from my grievance in the radiation of his warmth—but now I've begun to see that he was getting around, in a subtle way, to his scunner against me. I was deviant. I had fractured the Association's norm—or, in other words, got out from under his thumb. Flattered at the time, however, and with a rush of gratitude at being relieved of my painful anger, I barged into his trap.

"Literacy is the cornerstone," Treadup said, "but it isn't the building, by a long shot."

"So that?"

"I found an ingenious man who'd been a coolie in France," Treadup said—and suddenly he was off with a full heart on the story of Inventor Wang and his wooden machines. Todd wanted to know more. Treadup breezed along about things learned at Menghsien. Better seed. Scientific manures. Rotation. "All these things are merely extensions of the lecture program, really. The only difference—acts in fields instead of words on platforms." David Treadup was soon carried away by the full onrush of his sparkling trait of enthusiasm. He was free with his ideas on the ways in which the old methods of the Y were shriveling on the vine. Todd played the part of a fascinated student, and Treadup was all too willing to teach. By the time their talk was over, after an hour, David Treadup had delivered himself into the hands of the reappraisers. Going down in the elevator that day he felt on top of the world. He thought he had dazzled old Todd.

ABSOLOM was to live in a double on the fourth floor of an entryway in Fayerweather Hall, in Berkeley Oval. He and Philip carried his trunk up. Room 403—a living room with a fireplace, and two bedrooms off it. On the bed in the better of the two smaller rooms was a bag of expensive golf clubs. A claim had been staked.

Emily, fighting off tears, was outraged. "A good sport would flip a coin for the bedrooms," she said.

"Abbo will work things out," Philip said in a loud voice for Absolom to hear. "Won't you, kiddo?"

Absolom was pale. He nodded and tried to smile.

David Treadup leaned out the window and looked down at the trees in the paved oval. "Watching the young men in their blazers down there I was filled up with vainglory," he wrote that night. "Was in mind of Absolom Carter. Would he have believed that the bad boy of Enderbury Institute would one day have two sons at Yale College?"

THE THREE remaining Treadups settled in Springfield, Massachusetts, for the year. "I want to distance myself a bit from the muck-a-mucks," David wrote. David's cousin Lloyd Frampton, Jr., the eldest son of David's hosts in New Bedford during his unhappy time away from Syracuse, was a clerk in a clothing store in Springfield, and he had written the Treadups about a modest house in his neighborhood—"self-respecting folks, quite a few foreign-born, Poles and such, nice little high school, our church has a young pastor who is staging *The Mikado* this month—after being stuck off at the ends of the earth you'll find a little corner of real America here." Emily had to adjust to housekeeping; one of the things that was all too real in real America was that you didn't have three obliging servants in your house—a ludicrous notion for a poor family, if you thought about it, in this turmoil after the Wall Street crash. Young Paul celebrated his sixteenth birthday the day the local high school opened; the huge boy was soon a star on the football team. The Framptons kindly took Paul temporarily into their house and loaned their Model A Ford to David and Emily for a fortnight's drive up through New England in early October, so they could see the forests in a blaze of autumn. This was the first time the Treadups had ever had a true vacation together, with no responsibilities of any kind, familial or pastoral. For those few days David's diary was as radiant as the great maples on the Vermont hills. He had won Todd over; he had burned away the awful extra syllable; the three boys' energies were all in gear; his eyes were filled all day with the hot orange of sugar bush, rusty red of oak, yellow of birch, purple of sumac, and limpid blue of God's heaven above. And best of all, Emily by his side. "How good it is to be, all day every day, flank to flank with a peaceable human being! My Emily of the forests!"

LEAVES DRIFTED to the ground—from trees and from illusions. Treadup was summoned to 347 Madison. He took the New York, New Haven, and Hartford. He found his old ally in all his unorthodox undertakings, Farrow Blackton, "remote, like a man suffering from a most unnatural sort of amnesia—inability, that is, to remember favors he had done me. No one has helped me more in the past than he. But this time—well, I got a bit of a chill, as if he were a friendly banker trying to work himself up to foreclose a mortgage on me." Furloughs, "as you well know," Blackton said, were not joy rides. On the average, secretaries on furlough spent three and a half months in study, four and a half in deputation, and the rest, yes, in visiting brethren, going back to the wellsprings of faith, and resting up for work ahead. As to study, he had one suggestion: Kenneth Scott Latourette's recently published *History of Christian Missions in China*. "Then Farrow said a peculiar thing: 'Reading it will give you a chance to reflect on your particular niche in the enterprise.' Was he putting me on guard in some way? That phrase 'reflect on' is one that Chancellor Day used to use in his sermons, in direct connection with the sins he assumed we were all committing daily." As to deputation, the International Committee, discussing his case, had been of the opinion that he should reawaken his original backers, at Syracuse University.

I asked, "Does this mean that the International Committee is cutting me off?" "No no no no," Farrow said, "no, no, no," repeating the word so many times I thought he must have meant the exact opposite. The hairs on the back of my neck began to bristle. I felt like a beast at the mouth of his lair who smells very faintly on the wind a predator.

The very next entry in the diary: "I have always tried to do the right thing."

THROUGH the whole year he did try—always after his own fashion, however, which was sometimes, as he had put it, "deviant." He read Latourette, but he also read John Dewey and Bertrand Russell. There was something surreptitious about the latter part of his reading; even in the privacy of his diary he used only the authors' initials. "Have to know a little better what the other folks are thinking," he wrote. Another time:

Hate to say it, but I find I have a sneaking liking for brother B.R. His mischievousness is attractive, very human. Reminds me of my little sister Grace when she was small. J.D. is all tough beef, B.R. is salt and pepper.

His first money-raising trip to Syracuse was discouraging. Chancellor Day had retired long since, and of course by this time there was no one on the faculty who remembered Treadup. The flavor of the Hill had changed. A huge athletic stadium loomed. Chapel was no longer compulsory. The Y.M.C.A. and Y.W.C.A. had moved downtown. There didn't seem to be a single soul who gave a hang about missions to the heathens.

All these impediments aroused in Treadup a perverse enthusiasm. He took a trip to call on his old acquaintance Elmer Sperry, now nearly seventy and ailing, and begged from him certain gear he said he needed "to steady the feet of some backsliders." The wealthy old man ordered his shops to supply Treadup with whatever he wanted. David set up a workbench in the cellar of the house in Springfield and spent weeks assembling the parts shipped to him by the Sperry people.

In the early spring of 1930 he traveled once more to Syracuse, this time with a spate of crates and trunks. On three successive evenings he delivered "the old faithful gyro spiel" to the Syracuse community, twice at the college and once in the city. "That lecture is a sure shot," he wrote. By the time he finished the last of the series, he had received pledges of annual support for ten years into the future. "A sufficiency until my next furlough, at least," he smugly wrote Blackton.

THE FAMILY was at table in the railroad flat over the Woolworth's five-and-ten in Salt Branch village. Father Treadup was seventy-nine and fuddled. He firmly believed that David was not David but rather his second son, Will, to whom the old man had taken a powerful dislike; he kept barking at David, every time he opened his mouth, to "pipe down" or "drop it, son" or "hang up, that's more than enough from you." David's mother was seventy-six and wonderfully alert. Her eyes seemed huge through her cataract glasses. She was well-informed about China and asked intelligent questions. Dear, mild brother Paul and beaten-down Grace were also there, and so was Emily. Mother Treadup had cooked the meal, and she was constantly jumping up and darting into the tiny kitchen and coming out with new surprises. Sweet potatoes! Baked with marshmallows on top! "I remembered," she said to David.

Suddenly, toward the end of the meal, she turned her big searchlights on David and said, "Son, what's ailing you? You'd better tell your mother about it."

David began to bluster. "What do you mean? I'm fit as a fiddle! How ailing?"

"I just get a bone feeling about you. Don't like the way your voice sounds."

Emily said, "You're right as rain, Mother Treadup. He—"

"You stay out of this," Mother Treadup sharply said.

But Emily finished her sentence. "He's a humanist. Ask him."

"What's wrong with that? That sounds first rate."

"My husband—your son," Emily said, "is too full of love for human creatures."

Father Treadup, with Will still on his mind, gave out a derisory, disbelieving whistle.

"Come off it, Em," David said.

"An excess of love," Emily said, "leads to a spilling over of the sacred into the profane."

"Ah, son," Mother Treadup said, understanding it all, "so generous with rides in that awful rowboat on the Sabbath!"

Recording this conversation in his diary, David commented: "It seemed as if with those magnified eyes Mother could see right through me. What puzzles me is that I had thought I had shed all that worry."

TODD was impressed by the pledges Treadup had garnered at Syracuse— "at a time, my boy, when all eleemosynary institutions are feeling the pinch" —and in giving David his marching orders, now at the end of the furlough, he was so friendly, so ebullient, so Toddish, that David came away feeling that there was indeed nothing to worry about. Good luck with the rural work. Todd did remind Treadup, offhand, that the International Committee had voted him one more year's salary, but the reminder was put in such a way as to give David a distinct impression that there would be a more or less automatic renewal. There was no mention of reappraisal "all along the line." When David left, the handshake between the two huge men was so cordial as to seem like an arm-wrestling match.

Mr. and Mrs. Treadup and Paul sailed from Vancouver on the *Empress of Asia* on May 14, 1930.

INSOMNIAC SOULS

ON THE HIGH JUNE DAY when the Treadups once again threw open the windows of the bungalow in their tight little compound in Paoting, David exclaimed at the pleasure of being back under the immense amethyst sky of North China. The same old noises—China's great changes had not changed the audible China. Roosters celebrating the mounting of hens. The rhythmic hand-drums and melancholy arias of roaming vendors of white cabbage, candied apples, sweet potatoes. The yelping of "wonks"—mangy wild dogs skulking in dangerous packs. Edgy squalls of in-lawed women. Suddenly a flute's questioning murmur. Male laughter, and men loudly clearing their throats to spit, as if such hawking were the war cries of heroes.

The euphoria didn't last long. Treadup spent two frustrating days tinkering with the engine of his Indian motorcycle, which seemed to have come down with asthma. There could be no question here of getting spare parts; he had to file the points of the spark plugs and polish those of the distributor, take down the pistons and rout out the carbon, disassemble the carburetor and give it a good cleaning. For Emily the return seemed not to be as joyous as David would have hoped. She was bereft. Her firstborn, Philip, and her wounded chick, half-deaf Absolom, were on the opposite side of the earth; and even the baby, Paul, was gone—he had taken a summer job in Peitaiho. Her face looked drawn; she complained more than once to David that the ceilings "in this shack of yours" were too low. "I feel like a caryatid," she said.

EVERYTHING had gone slack in the villages.

The Indian charged over the country roads, raising a cone of dust.

Treadup stopped at place after place, and though he was everywhere greeted with great cordiality, and though here and there literacy schools were supposed to be in session, he could see that the life had gone out of the work. On account of Todd's abrupt notice of his furlough, David had not had time, before he left for the States, to make the rounds of all the places where work had been started, to try to make sure that things would be kept going at top speed without him. He realized his managerial error—a really appalling one—in not having developed a strong Chinese deputy, one who could have taken charge in his absence and who would eventually have been able to take over altogether, on the seed-planting principle of missionary devolution. Old Mr. Hsiao, who had been so helpful in getting the literacy work under way, had retired to his home, where he spent his gentlemanly time reading classics from old scrolls. Inventor Wang had stopped coming. One village chieftain told Treadup that a team of agitators for a farmers' union had come through the area—probably Communists—and they had been sharply disapproving of the way the schools were organized. The villagers had not wanted to join a union, the headman said, but they had been frightened by this visitation. In some of the villages, the schools simply stopped meeting. "I am downhearted," Treadup wrote.

I feel as if these people had been going through all those motions, before our furlough, just to please me. Must I start all over again? How can an outsider get them to realize that it is their own future to make?

FROM A LETTER Emily wrote to a church women's group she had met with in Springfield:

After the first busy excitements of being back I experienced what I suppose is a fairly natural reaction—a "post-furlough" depression. This is very strange for me. I am not used to this. At least it was a very level feeling, when after the year away all the contrasts and discouragements of Christian activity in mission work, as well as personal daily living, seemed to pile up on me and possess me.

I felt a first violent shock on the day when a group of Chinese women in a circle of converts here, whom I had considered my friends from beforehand, met to welcome me back. I could not think of one thing this group had in common with any group of women I'd been with at home, except that in both cases we were women, attempting to be Christians in a form of fellowship. Their total situation is so barren and so beautyless. I couldn't help wondering, if I were stripped down to the bare level of existence that is theirs, might I be, in some unexplainable way, better off?

IN LOW SPIRITS neither David nor Emily got much support from the people in the mission compounds. Everyone seemed edgy. Letitia Selden was deeply worried about her yokemate, Miss Demestrie, who, with her creaky knee and a buzzing in her ears, had become extremely cranky—some were whispering that she was having to be shut up in her room quite often. Old Dr. Cowley, who was David's father's age and worse tempered than ever, was triumphant about "the waste of time" of Treadup's literacy program, now proven by what had happened in his absence. Three-quarters deaf, the old man shouted his merciless and baleful judgments at Treadup.

A young man named Christopher Shanks—who had been sent to Paoting by David Liu to organize a Y.M.C.A. in the city—was forever complaining about catarrh in his sinuses, lumbago after tennis, microbes invading what he called his digestive track. People were saying he should be the sunniest person on earth, for he was engaged to be married to a newcomer, Polly Lassiter, a husky-voiced, bouncy, freckled R.N., a graduate of the Cornell nursing school. What more ideal match—a desperate hypochondriac and a trained practitioner of Tender Loving Care? Emily befriended Polly, hoping to have a cheerful friend; but she found this nurse to be, under her jovial surface, "the angriest person I ever knew."

BACK IN MAY, while the Treadups had been on the high seas, Johnny Wu had invited government people and missionaries from all over the country for what he called a Menghsien Literacy Institute—a systematic demonstration of what the Menghsien group had begun to learn about possibilities for China's future. David regretted having missed the Institute, and he now wrote Johnny asking if he might come alone for a few days and "get some practical ideas and store up some energy for my task of starting all over again." Wu was warmly cordial, and in September, as the heat of summer began to ebb, David took a train the few miles southwest to Menghsien.

The place hummed. There were now some two hundred workers in the Menghsien experiment—nearly all city-bred, mostly with college degrees either from universities in the United States or from church colleges in China—a group therefore much influenced by Western culture, conscientiously trying to avoid patronizing the ill-advantaged farm people with whom they were working.

Treadup picked up some new ideas about teaching methods, as well as some techniques for health education, adapted from campaigns David's own Lecture Bureau had first devised. But more important he came away from his visit with two new understandings, neither of which cheered him much.

The first was that the Menghsien group had concluded that in its first spurt of enthusiasm it had tried to do too much too fast. Now the group had set itself a ten-year plan, in three phases: From July 1930 to June 1933, the concentration would be on literacy and education; from July 1933 to June 1936, on agricultural and economic reconstruction; and from July 1936 to June 1940, on village self-government and citizenship training. Ten years! David would be in his sixties at the end of a decade. Did he have the strength and patience to try to match the multifaceted programs of Menghsien, working all alone, for ten long years? And what if ten years, in turn, proved far too short a time?

Secondly, touring Wu's villages, David had his eyes opened to an important reason why change was so hard to bring about. Johnny carefully explained to him the ancient method of built-in social control in such rural areas. It was called the *pao-chia* system. A *chia* consisted of about ten families, with a headman supposedly chosen by the families but usually a creature of the local magistrate; a *pao* was made up of about ten *chia*. Each *pao* was answerable to the district magistrate. Any offense or irregularity of behavior committed by any person within the hundred-family network must be reported to this *hsien* magistrate. Thus from the times of Mongols and Manchus had the rulers held their grip on the countryside; and in this way through the centuries the conservative Confucian mores had been vigilantly maintained. So David had to ask himself another new hard question: Had he—a foreign devil, working alone—the ingenuity, the prestige, the moral force even to put the slightest dent in this pervasive machinery of control?

(From a distance, years later, he would observe that the Communists' double system of control nets—work units and neighborhood units—simply carried on, with doctrinal variations, this ancient method of surveillance.)

TOWARD THE END of October one piece of news did cheer Treadup. He received a telegram from David Liu:

HEARTY GREETINGS PERSONALLY ATTENDED CHIANG KAISHEK'S BAPTISM THIS AFTERNOON OCTOBER 23RD CAUSE FOR THANKS SATISFACTION.

David of course knew that Chiang's wife had long been a Christian, and he had heard that for more than a year various Chinese Christians and American missionaries had been meeting with both Chiangs for Bible study and prayer. David's long-standing and deeply built-in awe of powerful men was stirred by this news, and somewhat later he wrote Todd an enthusiastic letter:

People are ascribing various motives to Chiang for his conversion. Pressure from his wife's family, who hold his purse strings? Courting favor in the West? But the important thing is that in the present state of

affairs in China, he has nothing to gain and everything to lose by be-
coming a Christian. The news of his baptism was received coolly and
without comment in the Chinese press. I'm told that President Chiang
gave as one of the main influences in leading him to seek baptism his
reading of Fosdick's 'Manhood of the Master,' as published in Chinese
here by our Association Press, and he has further asked the Y.M.C.A.
to bring out a new edition, to which he has agreed to write a special
introduction.

Since our work in the China field is so directly influenced by the
political atmosphere, it is reassuring to know that in the newly orga-
nized National Cabinet, in addition to the President, the head of the
Judicial Yuan, the Ministers of Foreign Affairs, of Industry, of Railways,
of Finance, and the Postmaster General are all outspoken Christians,
whose chief contact with Christianity has been through the Y.M.C.A. We
have reason to hope for great days ahead!

THE LETTER Treadup received back from Todd was exceedingly unpleasant. After perfunctory notice of Treadup's reflections on Chiang's conversion,
Todd wrote that he had been reviewing the monthly accounting sheets sent in
from Shanghai, and had come across a disturbing outlay for June—forty-nine
dollars Mex for ten five-gallon drums of gasoline delivered to Paoting from
Standard Oil in Tientsin. "Our budget situation," Todd wrote, "is such that
fifty dollars at a clip for a marginal item like this is rather strong medicine."
David remembered New York's miserly objection, years ago, to the single little
box for magic-lantern slides he had asked for. The worst of it, from David's
point of view, was that Todd then went on to flatter him, saying he had had,
from their talks during David's furlough, "a renewed sense of your unique
combination of devotion and good old-fashioned practical horse sense."

" 'Unique,' " David bitterly wrote in his diary, "equals 'deviant.' "

After long talks with Emily, and some prayer alone, he decided he had
better not try to answer the rebuke. The keys of his typewriter would fly to the
page out of his control! Marginal! How else could a man get from village
to village?

FAR FROM TREADUP'S KEN an inexorable process of history was
grinding away. The Chinese Communist Party was split between a peasant
soviet movement, led by Mao Tse-tung, and a more traditional form of
Marxist urban insurrection, advocated by a Politburo member named Li
Li-san. A Red army led by Mao and others captured Changsha, in Mao's
native Hunan Province, then retired from the city. A second attempt to
capture Changsha was a disaster. David heard vague reports of these battles.

The urban revolt in the coastal cities was also dismally failing, and Moscow, then trying to guide and control the Chinese movement, discredited Li Li-san. Chiang launched the first of a series of major offensives against the Communists. Chiang's people captured Mao's wife and sister in Changsha and executed them.

THE BELL in the tower pealed. In the vesting room of the little chapel in the American Board compound, the groom, Christopher Shanks, in the full rig of a borrowed cutaway, was "green in the gills." The suit was tight under his arms. His head seemed skewered on the sharp corners of his stiff collar. David's diary: "I got the impression that Mr. Shanks's liver had decided to take a vacation on his wedding day." Old man Cowley—who though a doctor was also an ordained minister—was going to tie the knot and was in a foul mood. "Let's get our stumps stirring here," he shouted over the mournful tolling. "What's holding things up?"

What was holding things up was that Polly Lassiter, the bride, had not yet appeared at the chapel entrance. Speculations. Trouble with the veil? A seam had split? The bouquet, promised by the husband of a mission sewing woman, had not yet been delivered?

David Treadup, in his sugar-scoop coat as best man—Chris Shanks having no kin within eight thousand miles—noticed that the groom had gone from green to white; sweat poured from his face. "Young man," Treadup said, "I advise you to sit down in that chair over there and let your head down between your knees. Get some blood back in your temples." Shanks obeyed; his boiled shirt creaked and buckled, and a stud flew across the floor. The Reverend Dr. Cowley, pacing back and forth, cried out, "Tell them to stop that infernal clanging." David went out and laid a hand on the arm of the Chinese boy who was tugging away on the bell pull. Then he stepped around to the chapel entrance, where Emily, who seemed to be Miss Lassiter's only friend and was certainly her only attendant, as matron of honor, was patiently waiting.

"She's half an hour behindhand," David said. "Not the best omen."

"She didn't want my help," Emily said. "I'd better go have a look-see."

Emily walked three hundred yards up a brick path to the house where Polly was living. The door to the nurse's room was closed. Emily knocked.

"Come in." Cheerful sound.

Emily swung the door open and saw the bride sitting in an armchair in a gray dress reading *Northanger Abbey.* The wedding dress was nowhere to be seen.

"My heavens!" Emily said. "You're keeping the whole world waiting!"

"I'm not going through with it," Polly Lassiter said in a calm voice. Her eyes were dry. Her freckled face had its customary radiant look. "He's so . . . so . . . " She gave up on the sentence with a shrug.

Emily was aghast. "My dear, you can't do such a thing at the last moment!"

"I can do it and I am doing it," Polly said.

"Aren't you even going to tell the poor man?"

"I presume you can do that."

"He'll have a heart attack."

"Oh, no, Mrs. Treadup. That is exactly what he will not have."

Emily went back to the chapel. At the vestry door she whispered a summons to David. It fell to David to break the news to Shanks and then to push the unconscious man to the infirmary in a wheelbarrow.

Miss Lassiter was right. Christopher Shanks did not have a heart attack. Indeed, within a day or two he looked better than he had for several months.

DAVID'S DIARY:

The fiasco of these young so-called lovers has made me think deeply about my own good fortune in the connubial line. To think that Em might have married Zeedon, '00! O my dove! Right now I puzzle about the darkness that has settled in you. Dr. Wells says there is nothing to fret about, says her hot spells and chills are part of "that time of life." And of course she misses the brood. But I fear that something deeper has been happening—and if it is happening to her, it is also happening to me. Her soul is insomniac and I seem to hear it sighing and turning over within her. We are so reciprocal in our feelings, she and I, that I am obliged to ask: Is she depressed because of worrying about me—about my work without end in this baffling China field, my work without real hope?

TURNING POINT

ROLAND J. FARKUS, PH. D., had arrived for a three-day stay. Ahead of him had come a letter from David Liu, explaining that Dr. Farkus was carrying out a "field inquiry" for the International Committee in New York.

Dr. Farkus was a short, stout Canadian, with a bald head, rimless glasses attached to his nose by gold nippers, and a perfectly round front decorated by a thick watch chain, upon which, Treadup noticed, Dr. Farkus tugged, as if to get at his timepiece, whenever an answer Treadup was giving to one of his questions began to stretch out beyond a minute or so. At first Treadup gave guarded answers; he was deeply suspicious of this "inquiry." He had a bad feeling that Todd was "trying to get the goods on me."

But the brisk little Canadian soon thawed David out. He was disarmingly candid. The whole missionary enterprise, he said, was at a crossroads. In spite of the Generalissimo's conversion, Christianity itself was under strong Communistic, anti-Christian, and antiforeign attack, and had had to give ground. The number of foreign missionaries had dropped from eight thousand to fewer than six thousand, and it was getting very hard to recruit new Chinese pastors, especially of college and university grade.

At the same time, support for the Y back in North America, Farkus said, was dwindling with the hard times there. David Liu in Shanghai was "hollering for more fraternal secretaries" just at a time when the International Committee was having to tighten its belt.

"Between us," Dr. Farkus said, talking in a low voice, as if to emphasize his trust in Treadup, "Dr. Liu is playing the tyrant in Shanghai, and two of his best men have just slipped in their walking papers—John Hu and Y. Y. Han. Truth is, they can't stand Dr. Liu's high line with them." So Dr. Farkus was having to "take a wee look around the various China stations, try to sort out the sheep from the goats."

At this point Dr. Farkus said some flattering words about "all I've heard about your get-up-and-go up here in Paoting." And then, lowering his voice again, "Young Dr. Shanks here looks like a weak sister. A whiner, what? What's your view of him?"

"You'll have to excuse me," Treadup said. "I can't sit in judgment on a colleague."

"Nicely put! I understand what you're saying," Dr. Farkus said. "Oh, very good. Very good way of answering, Dr. Treadup. I like that!"

"No," Treadup said. "You have me wrong. I don't talk slant. What I'm saying . . . I don't like being asked to be a company spy."

The diary:

O my goodness, what is this talent of mine for diving into boiling water? Is it my "honesty"? I'm afraid I feel it is something uglier. I'm not proud of it, whatever it is. I wasn't surprised to see that watch really come out of the pocket after that. Another engagement. To talk confidentially with "Dr." Shanks about "Dr." Treadup?

David wrote Farrow Blackton later that day, saying that he thought the "Farkus Inquisition" was an unpardonable intrusion into the affairs of the Chinese National Committee. All these years the Association had been proudly talking about its record in devolution—turning over the management of things in China to the Chinese. Then it sends a man out to snoop around and override the judgments of David Liu. No matter how touchy Liu was getting, there was no excuse for this.

The diary again:

> *Not very proud of my letter to Blackie, either. Did I hope it would land, in the course of routine circulation, on that acre of tidy oak in Todd's office?*

"I HAVE to be stabilized by an old friend," Treadup wrote.

So, "as I've done before when bamboozled," he went to Tientsin to see the first Chinese friend he had ever made—Mr. Lin. They met in the presidential office at the university. Mr. Lin was in Chinese clothes; he served Treadup tea in the Chinese way. He had recovered his old bounce. His university was thriving. He was aware and appreciative of the literacy work Treadup had been doing. "I sensed something sad in the ease of his warmth to me—namely, that he had long since ceased needing me." The subject of Christianity never arose; Treadup came away convinced that Lin had moved toward a new inner synthesis, "more social than spiritual." With great energy, and with his familiar flooding emotions, Mr. Lin poured out his excitement about "a new fire that's burning here at my university."

> *This new thing, Mr. Lin said, is different from the explosion of fifteen years ago—Dr. Hu Shih's movement—the Chinese Renaissance. That earlier movement had opened up the Chinese written language and the entire culture, previously reserved for the literati, to the people at large, and it had emphasized practical sciences and a democratic ideal—"just what you were doing with your lectures, my friend." That phase had reached its height, Mr. Lin said, from about 1920 to 1923; then for several years—confusion, warlords.*
>
> *But now—in the last year or so—China's most interesting thinkers, having won this new freedom, were turning their thoughts in an entirely new direction—outside themselves, toward the life and problems of the common people, China's Old Hundred Names. This new tendency, he said, was being called 'Pu Lu Wen Sho,' or the Proletarian Culture Movement.*

The students at Peikai had been aroused during this year, Mr. Lin said, by two new waves within this tide. One called itself the Liberty League. It had been founded a few months before by fifty-one writers and teachers, including the great essayist and story writer, Lu Hsun. A few weeks later, a second organization caught up the students; this one called itself the Federation of Leftist Writers. Mr. Lin gave David the Federation's manifesto, which Treadup later translated into one of his commonplace books. In part:

Art and literature in all ages have taken the joys and sorrows of man as their principal theme. We who are artists and writers of this generation cannot do better than to take as our subject the throbbing heart of the oppressed masses now straining and groaning under its burdens. Let us then join hands and create a proletarian culture movement which shall be our contribution to the cause of freedom in this country.

IMPRESSIONABLE and vulnerable as he was, David took from Mr. Lin and carried back to Paoting just what he had thought he needed—a baggage of refreshment and zest. He happened to encounter old Dr. Cowley a few days later, and he told him about his talks with his Tientsin friend.

"What idiocy and poppycock!" Cowley said. "Your convert, my friend, talks like a Communist. What an easy mark you are!" Telling Emily about this, David was able to discount the curt judgment. He reminded Emily how bleak and hateful old man Cowley had become; the ferocious Christian love with which he had burned so long had made charcoal of him. But in the privacy of his study, that evening, David remembered another time when his enthusiasm had been given a blunt check by a "realist"—after Dr. Elting's itinerative preaching on the country cart, which David had so much admired, when at luncheon that Standard Oil man, Gilbert Olander, had brought David up short by calling Dr. Elting an ass, a numskull, a busybody, and an utterly blind creature. David's remembering that incident is signaled in his diary by a terse entry: "Cowley and Olander—the wet blankets of this world. I suppose I need them."

TREADUP went back to the villages. The first task was to restore the literacy schools. As the weeks and months passed, Treadup was delighted by the alacrity with which the villagers resumed this work. "They want it! They need it!" he wrote after a graduation ceremony that had gone particularly well.

He was on the lookout for a Chinese deputy. At Menghsien he had asked Johnny Wu to give him one of his young college-trained men as an assistant, but Wu had said he was shorthanded as it was, and could not spare anyone. Then Treadup had begun to think that it would be best, anyhow, to try to bring up someone from the villages, so that the moving spirit, after David was out of the picture, would be a native leader, one of the region's own.

In the spring of 1931 David came across a promising young man named Shen Mo-ju. He was the eldest son of a farmer; as a fourteen-year-old boy he had been shanghaied into a warlord's army and had had a leg shattered in a battle. Discharged, he had limped through one of Treadup's literacy schools himself, then had signed on at once as a teacher. His was one village in which the school had thrived all through Treadup's furlough. Shen was, as David wrote, "a person with leadership deep in his eye sockets—he gazes at you with his serene and rather sad eyes and you just want to do anything he asks you to do."

In May David invited Shen to move to the compound in Paoting with his young wife, and to have a grand title: Deputy Director of the Paoting Regional Self-Help Educational and Agricultural Association. Shen accepted, and from then on, as David wrote, "our work stepped up from a canter to a gallop."

TREADUP enlisted three women, Polly Lassiter, Letitia Selden, and, for the first time as a partner in his labors, Emily Treadup, to do health work in the villages. He had learned at Menghsien that there were three principal causes for the devastating death rate in these North China country villages—more than thirty per thousand—and he asked each of these ladies to start a campaign to combat one of the three causes: smallpox; diseases such as dysentery and typhoid, caused by polluted water; and infant deaths, caused especially by something called *tetanus neonatorum,* which came from mid-wives' practice of plastering the cut umbilical cord with mud.

Nurse Lassiter agreed to work part time—for she had ample duties in Paoting—vaccinating against smallpox in the villages. She soon became so excited by her campaign that she petitioned her mission superiors to be temporarily freed for this work full time. David wrote: "She's a firebrand! Lucky Shanks! She would have ground him up and fed him to a cat." First she went to P.U.M.C., the Rockefeller hospital in Peiping, and assured herself of a steady supply of vaccine and sterile cotton. Then she set about training teams of village women who had been outstanding graduates of the literacy schools to administer vaccinations. She equipped each team with sewing needles, cotton balls soaked in Chinese wine for disinfection, tubes of vaccine, and simple report forms on which these Literate Citizens could keep records of names of the villages and of the scores, then hundreds, then thousands of farm people in them who had been vaccinated.

At first Miss Titty was resistant to Treadup's proposal that she work on typhoid and dysentery. Her aching bones. She was no scientist. She didn't know a thing about diseases. Never been sick a day herself. She had lots else to do. Treadup finally realized that the real problem, which she did not seem to want to discuss, was Helen Demestrie. Who would take care of her yokefellow when Miss Titty was out in the villages? David faced this out with her, and Miss Titty recognized that an amah named Sze, whom Miss Demestrie loved and trusted, could stay with her. So out went jaunty Miss Titty with a teaching mission: the bleach she advocated putting in village wells was not foreign deviltry; water for tea and for cooking had not just to be heated, it had to be boiled—you had to see the bubbles; and flies! Flies were dangerous.

Flies must be killed. But the villagers firmly believed that food that flies would not eat must be poisonous. A campaign to kill flies; cash money for every hundred flies brought in to collecting stations! But the villagers believed that the foreigners were going to use these flies to make medicines. Uphill teaching, but Miss Titty kept at it.

David thought long and hard before he asked Emily if she would like to take on the battle against infant mortality. Maybe this work would lift her spirits; on the other hand, might frequent reminders of the death of their own Nancy depress her even more? From the moment he first broached the idea, she was thrilled and aroused by it. She would need careful training. She went off to Menghsien; she spent several weeks at the P.U.M.C. in Peiping. In the end her greatest task was one of education—particularly that of dislodging from the midwives their ancient mud lore, handed down to them from heaven knew what primitive era. By the late summer of 1931, Emily was traveling from village to village, usually by bicycle, attending birthings—"given new life myself," she wrote her sister Jane,

> by all those new lives I have seen brought into being. It is sometimes my privilege to be the one to place the infant in its mother's arms for the first time.

IN AUGUST word came of a calamitous flood of the Yangtze and Hwai rivers. "Just eight or nine months ago," David wrote his mother,

> the Great Famine that had been going on for three years in the northwest came to an end, with estimates of as many as ten million dead. Now this flood. Rich America had great difficulty in relieving the suffering during the Mississippi flood of a few years ago; Americans cannot even imagine what will happen after a disaster like this in poverty-stricken China. One feels that China is floundering around helplessly without a finger being lifted by any other country. The feeling has been growing in China since the Peace Conference in Versailles that she is pretty much alone in the world.

THREE WEEKS later some young officers of the Japanese army in Manchuria fabricated an "incident"—an alleged sabotage of tracks of the South Manchuria railway—which they used as a pretext to seize Mukden and launch an invasion of China north of the Great Wall. Treadup wrote Farrow Blackton:

> The move in Manchuria has stunned us—so unexpected, so unprovoked. A turning point for China—for me and for you and all we've been trying

to do, Blackie. Just when the nation is trying to put all her resources into relieving the unprecedented disaster in the Yangtze Valley—and that tragedy won't be played out through its aftermath of famine and death for months to come—she finds herself face to face with Japanese arms. All over the country there are mass meetings, wearing of black armbands, plans for sending propaganda teams into the rural districts to stir up the illiterate to unite in saving the country. A war psychology is growing— by which I mean an acceptance as fact that the Japanese are a greedy, vulturelike race, bent on exterminating the Chinese, or at least subduing and exploiting the whole of China. Hatred and suspicion is reaching its poison into "my" dreary little villages. I feel as if I had been building a beautiful house out of precariously balanced match sticks, and this wind from Japan will knock it all down.

BOOK SIX

A LIFEWORK

THE CHRISTIAN WISH

TREADUP had never seen the small Paoting church so full. The foreigners were in the rear pews: "I had the uneasy feeling that the flock perceived us as shepherds driving them along."

Here, up front, were the Chinese Christians of the Paoting region, worried about what Jesus would think of the Japanese.

Some twenty foreign missionaries were scattered through the rear pews. Charles Stanton was there, with Dr. Wells, the staunch pair of veterans dressed for the gravity of the Japanese bullying in black serge suits, their faces drawn into hard lines and slicked over from the heat: they were William Bradford and Cotton Mather, to the life. Letitia Selden had Helen Demestrie under her wing in the very back row. Angry old Dr. Cowley was present, off to the left, frowning and sputtering before anything at all had been said. David Treadup sat rammed beside Emily.

David was concerned both for the future of his own work and especially for Emily's state of mind; she had been quickened by her birthing campaign. Treadup's young assistant in the village work, Shen Mo-ju, had started his duties with a fiery will. Treadup hoped the "Deputations" they had been hearing about would not disrupt all that he and the others were doing out in the countryside. Beyond that, as he wrote in his diary, "I had no few misgivings about what sort of un-Christian outcome this meeting might have."

The pastor of the church, Huang Ching, a mild, gentle, pudgy servitor whose spherical head was shaven—a shiny orb upholstered with a radiance of fatty tissue—rose to speak. He was dressed today in a black silk Chinese gown, and in consideration of the secular topic he stood down from the pulpit on the floor level, before the front pew.

There had been a lot of wild talk in the streets, he said. It was not easy for Christians to find a true way to serve their country and make sure the rest of the town believed them patriots. What should they do?

A few days after news came of the Japanese invasion of Manchuria, the Kuomintang, the Nationalist Party, had, as Treadup later wrote, "immediately seized the opportunity to make themselves prominent once more after two years' slump into comparative insignificance in local life." The KMT had put up lurid, ghastly posters throughout the city, picturing the Japanese as apes among men—vile, bloodthirsty, grasping militarists, greedy for the whole of China. Young schoolboys, inflamed by the talk in the streets of the Hun-like Japanese, had gouged out the eyes of the invaders on the posters and had written scurrilous graffiti on them. Then—and this posed the dilemma for the Christians—various organizations in town, including the middle-school students, had organized propaganda bands, "Save-the-Country Deputations," to go out into rural villages to spread the news of the seizure of the lands up north and to warn the ignorant farmers of the danger of imminent violent attack on all China by this enemy. The diary:

> Now in the midst of this hysteria, what part were Christians going to take in loving their country and proving their love? For some unexplained reason, the KMT hadn't sent its letter on the "Deputations" to our Chinese Christian friends. The Christians had, however, felt that they would lose ground in the community if they seemed unpatriotic, and they had written a letter to Charles Stanton of the American Board, asking whether they should send out preaching bands. He had suggested that they invite all their fellow Chinese believers to get together and face the matter frankly; he doubted whether foreigners should be involved. They had answered that although this was certainly a Chinese quandary, they would greatly appreciate our being present for moral support.

Now in the meeting several Chinese responded to Pastor Huang. Typical of one group of speakers was a middle-school teacher, who said, "Many of my students are going out in propaganda bands. I am afraid their message is warlike. Perhaps we should form our own preaching band, to avoid compromise with the Christian ethic of brotherhood." But others were hawkish. A wealthy wholesaler of medicines said, "I have just been in Manchuria, and I think my friends ought to know what is going on there. I have seen, with my own eyes, what the Japanese are doing. They're seizing the main rail centers. They're disrupting Chinese businesses in the area by trickery and violence.

Setting up pathetic puppet committees of Chinese to demand that Manchuria be an independent country. Bribing and arming the *hung hu-tze* ["redbeards," gangs of bandits] to rob trains and plunder villages and cities. It's a dreadful campaign of terror and disorder. Christian love? It would never be able to stop these samurai."

After much discussion, Pastor Huang asked the foreigners present to express themselves. "Though certainly a Chinese matter," he said, "this is primarily a question about Christian conduct, and as Christians we Chinese would like to hear what the missionaries think."

From "Search," years later:

> *I was surprised to find myself on my feet. I delivered myself. I felt glad for a chance to speak, though I had no idea what I was going to say. I heard words coming out: I was not ready to advise for or against any specific line of action, but Christians should now be proving their love for China, not by following all the accepted norms of patriotic demonstration but "in superior ways which would prove them even greater patriots than most others." I felt the sweat tumbling out of my pores, as if my poor body was making an effort to flush out some meaning from this nonsense I was uttering. I must have been overcome by the deep Christian wish that goodness of heart could blunt sharp steel. The madness I had seen in France; the senseless warlord slaughters . . . Whatever might happen, a Christian, I thought, should do his utmost to dissuade others from killing, but as to how — I was, alas, incoherent.*

While he was speaking, Treadup was aware of some kind of commotion behind him. He was so busy framing his sentences in Chinese that he paid little attention to it, beyond having a blurred sense that someone objected to what he was saying. Later he learned that after he had spoken a few sentences, Helen Demestrie had begun to mutter and bounce around in her seat, and Miss Selden, "fearful that Helen would try to make a speech," led her from the hall.

Charles Stanton next said a few words, vague like Treadup's. "I felt comforted by his inarticulateness."

The medicine merchant began shouting: "I warn you against listening to advice to 'find God's way' in all this. Unless we Chinese remember all the grievances of the past against Japan and look facts in the face, we will all find ourselves slaves to the Meiji."

But Pastor Huang calmly suggested that the Paoting Christians send two telegrams: one to the various Christian executive secretaries in Peiping, urging them to unite all the Christian forces in North China in a front to work for a peaceful solution; and one to the National Christian Council in Shanghai petitioning it to cable the League of Nations, urging it to find a speedy and peaceful settlement of the differences between Japan and China.

Then Treadup stood up again—"perhaps to try to make amends, through a concrete proposal, for my previous meandering"—and said, "Should we not send a third cable—to the Christian Council of Japan, expressing faith in our Christian brotherhood there, and urging them to petition their government to withdraw all military forces from the occupied zone?"

All three suggestions were approved.

IN THE CROWD in the street outside the church after the meeting, Dr. Cowley suddenly lurched toward Treadup, shoving Chinese aside to get at him. He was in such a rage that all the sounds he wanted to make seemed to catch in his throat; his Adam's apple trembled as if it were so clogged with bad words that it might explode. "Always knew—you, Treadup!—idiot!—idiot! Those telegrams! What tommyrot! Pussyfooting League of Nations! *Your* suggestion—my gorry—cable to Japs! You have the brains of a six-year-old." And more, with a constant spray of saliva.

Finally Treadup was able to say, "What would you do, Dr. Cowley?"

"Young man," Dr. Cowley said, "I know the Japs. Nothing will stop those people. Except. Except—I don't care—nothing except bullets. *Bullets!*"

"I'd rather find some other way," Treadup said, trying to command his voice to be level. ("Search": "My knees were trembling—anger—or some kind of terror in my heart from the crying out I seemed to be hearing of an Isaiah—or—perhaps?—fear, lurking somewhere just under the surface of my mind, that I may indeed have been a fool?")

"Hah! They'll bury you, my boy. Those Jappies will bury you. Don't invite *me* to your funeral!"

IT TURNED OUT that the Chinese cable office would not accept messages for Japan, so the appeal to the Japanese Christians had to be sent by mail. David reports that he "felt Dr. Cowley's icy spit on my face as I typed the letter."

UNREAL REALITY

IN NOVEMBER 1931, following a widespread custom among missionaries, in anticipation of the Christmas season, Treadup wrote a long "round-robin" letter, addressed to Dear Friends. It told "of a period of great good heart in my work in the spreading of literacy among the Chinese." Pleased with his composition, Treadup splurged and had it printed in a small press in Paoting. The first page had a pretty border of baroque spinach—a Chinese printer's approximation, perhaps, of the *mu-shih*'s description of mistletoe. He shot it off to everyone he knew in both China and the United States.

This is a strange little brochure. It is written for people, among others, from whom Treadup has raised money and perhaps hopes to raise more, but in it he lingers on hardships—endless chilly rides, bicycle wheels skidding in sand. Yet everything is just fine. There is no mention of the "Deputations" of propaganda units ranging the countryside, not a word about KMT pressure or the horns of the Sixth Commandment. One is reminded of Treadup's letters home from New Bedford during the period of the "black hole," when he had flunked out of Syracuse—making out that all's well in a well world. The "reality" of the villages of this letter seems to be a denial of the reality of incipient despair.

Excerpts:

• Picture an old man, hunched over, standing in the doorway of a mud house—wood-framed paper windows on either side of him. You can tell by the way he moves his face, as if there were a dark wind blowing from every direction he faces, that he is totally blind. We are holding the opening ceremonies of a literacy school in the village of Shao T'an. The scholars, farm people in their work clothes, are in the bare courtyard. The old sage says: "Fellow blind people! You have enrolled yourselves in a literacy class. It is to be your blessed privilege within four months to lose your blindness and to see! A marvel!"

• I started out early Saturday morning with Mr. Hsu, one of my new "leaders," heading for Ch'ien Lin, a small walled town nearly forty miles away. The Indian had broken down; we two were on bikes. A good part of the way we had to ride in narrow ruts and watch our front wheels carefully in order to avoid nasty spills. There were several long patches of sand where we had to get off and push, and in those places I was glad the Indian wasn't working.

• Villagers gathered around. They were eager to talk about rumors coming from all points of the compass concerning the poisoning of wells by Chinese hired by the Japanese. All the stories were the same: Groups of two or three traveled about the country with a poison which they threw into village wells. After forty—or seventy—or one hundred—days the water would be poisoned enough to do its dirty work. There were many reports of people made sick from drinking the water and an occasional account of one who had died.

Symptoms differed. In one place, a man drank water from a poisoned well, and his head swelled to twice its normal size. People swore to the truth of deaths but they were never able to say just who it was who died. They have made covers for all the wells, lock them every night, and station constant guards over them.

• A new literacy school. Principal Shih examines the scholars. It is so interesting to see six- and seven-year-old boys outstripping the twenty- and thirty-year-old men in the recognition of characters. Among the students' greatest thrills is some picture taking, for they have never seen a camera. One of the young men asks me how far it is to America. Six thousand miles. The man is thunderstruck and asks: "Have you come all the way on your bicycle?"

• The bicycle ride back from Sze Shu T'an was the hardest trip I have ever taken. The wind was against. It got stronger and stronger. Twice I had to get off and walk for quite a stretch because of the gale. Most of the time I had to lean down over the handlebars and push for all I was worth and then make only a snail's pace. I was all in when I reached home. I was weak all evening. But the next morning I felt fresh as could be, no ill effects of the hard exertion—not even any lameness.

• In Ku Chuan the opening of a mass education class had been scheduled. This ride out was long and strenuous. We were disgusted to find that in spite of the definite appointment, almost the whole village had gone off to a neighboring hamlet to see a traveling *yang ke,* or planting-song show. I left a message for the leaders: I could not make this forty-mile bicycle ride again just for this one class. If they were really in earnest about learning to read, they would have to come up to Ch'ien Lin the next day, Sunday. When the regular meetings there were finished, the opening exercises could be run off. Li and I went away discouraged. Lo and behold!—that whole village showed up the next day, walking the five miles to Ch'ien Lin. The exercises could not be held for them until late afternoon. They walked back to Ku Chuan in the dark.

• It was a terrible bus with no pep whatsoever. In one sandy place it stalled, and all the passengers had to get out and push it through. At the gates of Ch'ien Lin armed militia stopped the bus. The soldiers looked more frightened than the passengers. It came out that there had been a big fire the night before. The burnt-out street had many shops in the bamboo industry, and the heat exploding bamboo poles, large and small, with sounds just like artillery and rifle fire, woke the townspeople with fears in their hearts— bandits had arrived and were ransacking and shooting! Now there was still panic—searching buses—the next morning. There will be a legend, one day, about the bamboo bandits.

IN DUE COURSE a letter came from Blackton in New York that made Treadup furious:

> It is a work of supererogation to teach you anything about writing. Your printed letter is a dandy. It was slightly marred by several typographical errors, but that is a small thing compared with the human interest well presented throughout. You raise a question, however, about the future of documents of this sort. On the one hand, I am anxious that our best writers, among whom without any flattery I put you, should write direct letters to the constituency at home; they make the field vivid to our supporters. On the other hand, you know our budget situation now. Ninety dollars is ninety dollars even in Mex exchange. Furthermore, when a secretary steps outside his own family and personal friends and starts addressing laymen, contributors, and other secretaries, this requires coordination and clearance. 'Verbum sap.'

THE BLUSH

ON ONE of the chilly late days of 1931, David Treadup was at his L. C. Smith typewriter, tapping out a letter to his parents, when Sze, the amah, burst into the house without knocking and shouted a hysterical summons to T'ao Tu Hsien-sheng.

David hurried to the American Board compound. He found Letitia Selden waiting for him at her front door. She ran toward him and clutched at his shirt. He could feel her hand shaking against his chest. "I don't know what to do," she said. "She's never been like this. She's speaking in tongues."

David asked to see her.

Miss Selden led Treadup upstairs. She politely knocked on a door, then entered and beckoned to David to follow.

Helen Demestrie was standing at the foot of her bed. Her hair was snarled. Her eyebeams were like steel rods, holding her fast to some distant fixation. She seemed not to have noticed that two people had come into the room. She was babbling what seemed at first to be nonsense.

"It's Greek," David finally said. "She's reciting something in Greek."

"What is it?"

He listened a long time but, as he wrote later, "felt I was sinking in quicksand." Finally he said to Miss Selden: "My Greek—rusty—I can't say."

He moved slowly toward Miss Demestrie and put a hand gently on her forearm. She sharply drew in her breath and snatched her arm away, as if her flesh had been seared by smoking-hot cooking grease spattering from a pan. She backed against a wall and, glaring directly at David's eyes, she began again to declaim in Greek, now with a frightening vehemence.

The diary:

I felt helpless and useless — this brought back the moment of first seeing the grade sheets posted at Syracuse, with my failures in Latin and Greek up there for everyone to read. I lamely suggested to Miss Selden that Nurse Lassiter might have something to give Helen. I offered to run and get her. As I was leaving Helen Demestrie shot me a triumphant look. She had routed me.

Polly Lassiter took her time getting ready. Boiled a hypodermic needle; fussed up a storm with her little black bag. Must say she was wonderful with the poor raving creature. Cooed and held her hand. No injection needed. Miss Demestrie calmed down. Nurse Lassiter said she thought it would be best if I left, so I did. My miserable Greek! What was she chanting? Rhythmic and noble. Sybilline.

A SUNNY and unseasonably mild afternoon three weeks later. The Treadups had earlier been to divine service in the Congregational chapel, and they had had an ample Sunday noontime dinner. David was stretched out in a Chinese-made copy of a Morris chair; the back had been let down halfway and the footrest extended. He was rather drowsily reading the missionary magazine *The Chinese Recorder*. As he read, he grew more and more restless. For several weeks, now, he had been worrying about Dr. Cowley. The old man's temper had become wild and indiscriminate, directed at whatever object happened to offer itself. He never saw Treadup but he launched some new attack on him; David felt compassion for Dr. Cowley, and now, in his easy chair, he had an impulse to go and make something like a pastoral call on the suffering old fellow. In "Search":

I wonder whether I was driven to that impulse to "help" Dr. Cowley, that afternoon, by my awful need to appease, whenever I feel hostility aimed in my direction.

He rose, put on his shoes, and called out to Emily to tell her where he was going.

"Don't rile him," Emily called back.

The short walk to the American Board compound put David in a good humor. There was a faint smell on the air from somewhere of roasting sweet potatoes. Fleecy small good-weather clouds, cottony wings and harps, dotted the blue heaven. Treadup presumably could be excused for approving of his own merciful love for poor old Cowley.

He walked up the brick path that drew a centerline through the mission compound. Approaching the Selden-Demestrie house, David thought of his first happy days there with his bride. He was just passing the door of that house when it flew open and out came an apparition.

It was Helen Demestrie, naked to the waist, in a long skirt, her flowing hair let down around her shoulders, her eyes flashing, her right hand brandishing a curving, wide-bladed Chinese sword. She was, once again, intoning something in Greek.

She rushed halfway down the path and took her stand, shouting the rhythmic lines, whatever they were, directly at David Treadup.

I felt myself blushing. I could not help looking at her. I could not help seeing something astonishing. Her hair was streaked with gray, her elderly face was hideous in its possession, but her untouched, untouchable torso was that of a much younger woman—unnaturally preserved I suppose by lack, or perhaps just by luck. As she swung the sword the torso moved. In the cold of the day the buds of her bosoms were ruddy and distended. This made her look as if she were (and she may have been, for all I know) in an extreme state of romantic excitation. If she was, it must surely have been a most dangerous kind of desire— the concupiscence of the female praying mantis, who will devour her partner the moment the carnal connection has been made. My flesh crawled.

The material evidence of the danger, flashing in the sunlight, was the heavy sword in her hand. She took a step toward Treadup. His face hot in the cool air, he stood his ground. She was chanting. He was just thinking he would have to take a great risk, be nimble, and dodge around quickly and grasp her from behind and get the sword out of her hand—when he heard footsteps of someone running down the main brick path to his left.

Then he heard Nurse Lassiter shout, "Shame! Shame! Take your eyes off her, you beast! Get away! Go in the house!"

This rebuke did indeed fill me with shame. I dodged off the path to obey Polly's command to go into the house; but the fierce Greek figure swiveled and lunged at me. I broke into a headlong run and got inside and called out for Miss Selden. She must have been napping. I heard Polly Lassiter with wonderful self-command comforting Helen; the Greek recital broke off; I heard the two approaching the front door, and I ducked into a side room. Miss Selden came downstairs in great agitation.

Treadup heard the sword clatter to the floor and the women's footsteps going upstairs. He was wondering what to do; he felt he could not simply retreat with any honor. One woman's steps came down the stairs. He did not think he wanted to see Nurse Lassiter. But it turned out to be Letitia Selden, who looked for him and found him.

She was crying. She took both of Treadup's hands in her hands. "I'm going to need your help, dear boy, dear boy. We have to get her out of this hellhole."

David heard himself saying, "I really thought she wanted to kill me."

"No! No! She would never kill. She hates killing—that's what has taken hold of the poor dear's mind. I think the Japanese have unhinged her, poor soul. The sword was—I don't know—just something in her hand. She idolizes you from a distance, you know. She always has. You are her ideal."

David felt another blush—"a fire under my skin of perplexity and of fear of some mysterious kind of exposure," he later wrote—climb up the back of his neck and spread forward onto his cheeks.

"Did you hear her?" Miss Selden said. "When she is upset she has a frightening memory. She hasn't been near a Greek text for years and years."

I remembered that Dr. Cowley has a fairly complete roster of the Greek authors in two big sets—the original Greek, and English translations. I harbored such a strong memory of my blush that I was determined to track down what Miss Demestrie had been declaiming. The mantis creeping along the branch? My nameless embarrassment, whatever its cause, was strong enough to propel me into Dr. Cowley's lair, where— without explaining the reason—God forfend!—I pleaded with the doctor to lend me his Greeks. After long negotiations he growlingly granted me permission to withdraw one book at a time, for one week at a time—a fine of one Mex dollar for every day overdue! So I started at the top of the alphabet: Aeschylus.

As soon as I began to read, I was startled by the echoes in my mind. I looked on the title page—yes, my friend and ally!—Benjamin Bickley Rogers—translator of this edition, as I gratefully remembered he had been of the dog-eared "trot," published in London, which we students had surreptitiously passed from hand to hand at Syracuse—it got me as far as I ever got in Greek. Thus I had fudged along till I failed. Two things spurred me now, my failed mark on the grade sheet and my blush of the other afternoon—the heat of the latter, drained from my cheeks, simmered in my soul—and I read day and night, shuttling between original and translation. The Aeschylus seemed wrong to me from the start. I did not have to take in every word. Helen Demestrie's passionate contralto had been all too vivid; I could skim and sense whether I was on the right track. 'The Suppliants'—fifty daughters married—no! 'The Seven Against Thebes,' grim, grim. 'Agamemnon.' 'The Libation Bearers.' Nothing there. On the third morning I took the book back, and Dr. Cowley's eyebrows nearly skidded off his forehead. "Does that stuff stick in your craw, young man?" No, I wanted more! Aristophanes next. From the first page, this sounded more like it. I remembered Professor Baistrop exclaiming about the limpid beauty of Aristophanes's language, though the reality of the beauty had bumped dead against my eardrums. 'The Clouds,' 'The Wasps,' 'The Birds,' 'The Frogs.' And then suddenly, late at night, under the cone of light, Emily asleep in the other room, I felt myself prickling with alertness. Yes: here! here! here it was!

MISS SELDEN wanted to get her to the P.U.M.C. She thought she could arrange things to go on Tuesday. She said she preferred not to risk going by train. Would David be an angel and ask Mr. Stanton if they could borrow his Dodge? She could drive; Mr. Stanton knew she was a good driver. Nurse would go. "And of course you must go," she said.

"Do you think that's wise, after—"

"She wouldn't go without you. She counts on you."

Treadup felt the blush reviving inside him, burning in his gullet, as if he had gulped a too-hot liquid. It made its way to his face, this time, in the form of sweat. He tried to say it would be awkward for him to break away; he had commitments to his villages. But his tongue was stuck. He wanted to tell Miss Selden what he had found in Dr. Cowley's books but—from "Search"—

I could not bring myself to speak to her about that play in which the women deny their husbands the joys of the bed until the men stop their war. This Lysistrata—this Demestrie—must have got it in her head that she was going to bring peace on earth by denying to the male world the very thing that men (me? her "ideal"? O God!) would never have dreamed of asking of her. That she was seriously disoriented was proven by her bearing a sword while chanting the pacifist lines. My extreme fear of blushing, of giving myself away somehow, puzzled me at the time, filled me with a guilt that frightened me because it seemed to have no basis in my actions or even in any imaginings that I could recognize. I wonder now if my real fear had less to do directly with Helen Demestrie than that something inexplicable—exactly what, I could never have put a name to—love thine enemies, pacifism, some threat of Christianity to my manliness, somehow mixed up with that half-naked madwoman—that this something, whatever it was, might find its way into Emily's understanding.

He ended by agreeing to accompany the party to the hospital in Peiping. When he told Emily "the surface parts of the story," she said without a moment's hesitation that he must by all means go.

THE PLAN to leave on that next Tuesday changed. Treadup was deeply asleep that very night when some noise disturbed his sleep. When he had wakened enough to hear what noise, he realized it was Miss Selden, outside his window, calling, "David! David!"

From a letter home:

It must have sounded like an elopement, but of course it was not. Miss Demestrie was worse. Miss Titty wanted to leave right away—in the middle of the night. Nurse was with her. Dr. Wells had told Miss Selden she shouldn't wait another minute. But starting quickly is not so simple in China as pushing the garage doors open and sailing out. First we must waken one of our servants to get coffee ready for the party before our start, then send to waken a Stanton servant for car keys and instructions about the car, waken the compound gateman to call the dispensary servant to unlock the lab for distilled water for the battery, then drive with Miss Titty into the city to the Standard Oil Co. for gasoline—that meant waking men up there, too, as there's no such thing as a filling station for the four automobiles in town.

Nurse Lassiter had given Miss Demestrie a shot of morphine, and David had to carry her out to the car. If he blushed doing that, no one could have seen it in the dark. It was three in the morning before they were actually on the road. All along the bumpy way, Treadup felt strong waves of disapproval from Polly, who (he thought) "considered me absolutely disqualified from helping Miss Demestrie because I had looked at her bare torso." Miss Demestrie regained consciousness on the way; she seemed to doze. They reached the hospital at Peiping at about nine.

A CHINESE NEUROPATH named Dr. Ch'en examined Miss Demestrie and diagnosed her ailment as "a late form of dementia praecox." The outlook for her having a future in China, he said, was not good. She would surely come out of this phase of the sickness, but its recurrence within months, or possibly years, was most probable. "It means," Treadup wrote in an urgent note to Emily, "that Miss Demestrie's career in the mission field is ended, and that Miss Selden's must also be uncertain. My heart is heavy for both of them." After a few days, during which it was hoped her condition would improve, Miss Demestrie must go to Shanghai, where a nursing home for neurological patients—the only one of its kind in all China—would undoubtedly admit her until she could be taken aboard a ship for the States.

David explained to Emily that he would have to go along, and indeed that it was up to him to make all preparations. With the help of Center Rush Gridley, he found, at a private clinic for foreigners, a nurse who had had experience with several mental cases, and even with transportation of them to available sanctuaries. She was a Mrs. Conley, a German lady married to a New York Irishman. She was a heavy, jovial, imperturbable woman. Treadup rushed around town. He sent a telegram to arrange for the nursing home in Shanghai. He got travel papers for the four women. He inquired about trains, and found that the railroads were in a state of utter confusion: There had been some kind of Japanese raid near Tientsin, and, beyond the usual panic, there was a wave of patriotic scrambling about on the part of students, who were rushing by the thousands to Nanking to demonstrate for resistance, then rushing back again.

That evening, he wrote another letter to Emily.

In the aft, Henry B suggested a game of tennis. I could think of nothing that would do me more good. I got into some borrowed clothes and I played. Everything was against me, however—sneakers (too small), court (cement), racquet (someone else's), and Henry B who prances around like a leopard. The game would have done a lot more for me if I hadn't lost so badly.

ON FRIDAY MORNING the party was ready to leave: Helen Demestrie, "asleep after Dr. Ch'en gave her an injection of a very strong drug, sodium amytal, which has to be administered intravenously"; Letitia Selden; Mrs. Conley; Nurse Lassiter; Dr. Ch'en; and three Chinese employees of the American Board to carry Miss Demestrie on a stretcher and to take care of trunks and suitcases.

There was a huge crowd at the station. Treadup stood in a long line for tickets. Finally the train pulled in. There was such a crush that Treadup had to get behind Mrs. Conley's broad back and heave and shove her through the door into a car. The bearers were remarkable—held Helen right up over their heads and got her in somehow.

You cannot imagine the unhygienic condition of the car. We were right next to the hot-water station, where dirty attendants handed out hot water for sundry uses to passengers—drinking tea, brushing teeth, washing hands and face ect. The towel used by attendants for washing their own faces was also used for polishing the teacups and pots. Expectorating freely, coughing, nose blowing—all were the order of the day. A family across the aisle with a little baby, not to mention many other children, found it convenient for the baby to use the aisle for duties usually performed more privately.

Helen from time to time roused up from her drugged sleep quite wild, but Dr. Ch'en learned to anticipate this by giving her a shot just as she began to stir.

One expected difficulty during the trip was the crossing of the Yangtze. In Pukow Treadup went to the consulate and arranged for the party to cross over on a Socony launch. No sooner were they on the train on the Nanking side than Treadup remembered he had left his arctic overshoes on the Peiping train.

In Shanghai, the nursing home was expecting Miss Demestrie. The first thing David Treadup did was to go to American Express to tell them about his arctics. Then he went to Thomas Cook and booked passage to the United States for three—the patient, Miss Selden, and Nurse Lassiter—on the *President Wilson,* leaving on January 11. He wrote Emily: "I feel responsible now, and I must stay till they sail. I'm sorry it's so long. Miss Selden especially leans on me."

The next day was Sunday. Treadup went to church with Henry Burrell of the Y, who had kindly put him up. In his letter to Emily:

> *It has been many, many a month since a church service has seemed to be so completely the thing I needed as I did this one. For the first time since we left Paoting I had the opportunity to think with myself. The import of our travels came over me with full force, and I felt like weeping. I almost did several times during the service. I did enjoy the hymns, but it got to me as I sang along and realized how familiar these words were to Helen Demestrie and how far from joyous singing she now was. I realized the tragedy of her state—worse than death in many ways.*
>
> *After church a newspaper friend told Henry Burrell that the chief Chinese delegate at the League of Nations, Alfred Sze, and the foreign minister at Nanking, Wellington Koo, had both resigned. What these two facts might mean seemed to overcome me, and being just in a proper condition for pessimistic suggestions of mind, later at supper table I found my head going around in a whirl that truly made me dizzy.*

Early Monday morning Treadup went to American Express and found his arctics waiting for him. In his diary: "Beautiful China! It is *in extremis,* yet with what delicacy it finds my overshoes for me!"

HENRY BURRELL begged David Treadup to spend as much time as he could at the Lecture Bureau workshop, helping to get things up to snuff. "Going back to old haunts may be a mistake," Treadup wrote. "Things are never as good as they once were."

TREADUP went to see Helen Demestrie every day. Her responses to him varied. She was having lucid periods, during which she held tight to his hand and looked piercingly into his eyes. (No mention of blushing.) Sometimes she was hostile; bridled; muttered in Greek. But Lysistrata seemed to be letting go of her. "Letitia Selden is the one who breaks my heart," David wrote Emily. "It has taken all this to make me realize that Helen was Miss Titty's anchor to windward; now the 'stronger one' is adrift."

AN ENTRY in the diary: "Overnight trip to Nanking. Stirring."
That is all he wrote at the time.

BACK IN SHANGHAI, Treadup resumed his daily visits to Miss Demestrie. One day he called on David Liu, who was at home, in bed, ill with heart trouble, high blood pressure, and some sort of kidney complication. Liu was impatient to be on his feet and back at work. He said he urgently needed to go to the States to fight for money. David protested that he must take time to get his strength back. Liu said, "All right, if you think I should take time, read this." And he handed Treadup a cablegram he had received from Blackton in New York a few days earlier:

> ESTIMATED YMCA DEFICIT OWING TO BUSINESS DEPRESSION
> GOLD TWOHUNDREDFIFTY THOUSAND INEVITABLE MUST
> RESORT IMMEDIATELY SALARY PERSONNEL AND APPROPRIATION
> REDUCTION STOP ADVISE YOU CONFER NATIONAL COMMITTEE
> DETERMINE REDUCTIONS AND LIST MINIMUM TWELVE
> SECRETARIES ORDER PRIORITY POSSIBLE RETURN HOME STOP
> SUGGEST ALSO FURLOUGH COST REDUCTION BY HOLDING SOME
> SECRETARIES HERE POSTPONE OTHERS STOP CABLE
> RECOMMENDATIONS SOONEST

To Emily: "My first thought was: Will I be one of the twelve? But then I thought: If that were a real possibility, he wouldn't be showing me this message."

TREADUP rode out on the lighter to the *President Wilson* with the three women. Helen Demestrie was all too lucid. She knew she would never see China again. She and Letitia Selden wept all the way. Nurse Lassiter, who had never relented toward David, stood apart. At the gangplank Miss Demestrie threw her arms around David and hugged "until I thought she would break my back." In her old familiar gesture, Letitia Selden patted David's cheek. "See you in Tipperary," she said. The diary:

> The trip back up the Whangpoo was a lonely one. I could not have survived my first years in China without Miss Titty's help. It will be a long long way to wherever I see her again.

SAVING THE WORLD

IT WAS on the midnight express to Nanking that Treadup finally wrote an account of the "overnight" in the capital which he had previously failed to record. His handwriting, because he was writing on a moving train, is jagged and scrawly, and this gives the whole affair, as one reads it in the diary, an air of agitation, excitement, worry, and haste.

One afternoon in Shanghai, the shaky scrawl tells us, during the days of anxiety for Helen Demestrie, Hank Burrell called Treadup into his office. He said he had had a call from David Liu, from his bed at home, saying that President Chiang Kai-shek had just telephoned him long-distance from Nanking. The President and his wife wished to invite a group of missionaries from Shanghai and Nanking to confer with them about the present national crisis. Hank wanted Treadup to join the party.

David protested that he was not important enough in the missionary world: the bigwigs had wanted him withdrawn from the field! There were surely others who should take his place.

Burrell said, "David! David! You're a giant! You taught us all how to teach the Chinese." Besides, a missionary from the North should by all means be in the party.

The diary:

> Hank kept at me—kept saying that I am one of the great men of the field—flattery which made me feel cranky and ornery. I don't know how to teach the Chinese. A teacher has to understand his pupils. The more I learn about the Chinese, the less I know.

NINETEEN MISSIONARIES—American, British, and French, fifteen Protestants and four Catholics—took the midnight express to Nanking, in a special sleeping car provided by the President. Appleton Sills, the Nanking Y secretary, had assembled seven Nanking men to join them.

President and Madame Chiang received the guests in their private
bungalow outside the city at five that afternoon.

Spidery words in the diary:

*One had heard of her dazzling beauty. I was truthfully disconcerted by
her graciousness, which had, if I can say it, an icy warmth. She made
me feel that I was the most important nonperson she had ever met. I
noticed a delicate tremor in her hands. He sat straight as a flagpole.
Uniform of very good cloth, immaculately ironed. I was surprised by the
smallness of his shaven head. He may have amassed all his great power
entirely on the strength of his reserve, which is rather terrifying. It
seemed that anyone with that much self-control could easily control
a country.*

At the request of the Chiangs, the group spent the first half hour in
spiritual fellowship, led by Bishop Andrew Selant of the American Methodist
Episcopal Church and by Father Pierre LeFeu, S.J. The service opened and
closed with hymns, for which words were provided on mimeographed sheets
in Chinese, English, and French. "Since we were going in for fellowship,"
Treadup wrote, "I sang the first verse in English, the second in Chinese, and
the third in French—my *parley-vous* being somewhat choppy." The leaders
gave "devotional" addresses, then "several men, but not I, heaven forbid, were
moved to extemporaneous prayer, not always of the briefest sort." Then the
President rose to speak. Hank Burrell later typed up the "substance" of
Chiang's remarks:

*I have asked you, as fellow Christians, to come to Nanking that I might
have your counsel. I appreciate very much your coming.*

*Responsibility for saving the world rests on religion. It is the task
of religion to keep alive the consciences of men and to save mankind
from destruction.*

*This has become increasingly a matter of grave concern. As the
world has gone forward by leaps and bounds in the progress of its
material civilization, it has gone backward in moral and spiritual culture.
Men are neglecting their spiritual lives. In the pathway of such neglect
lie sin, violence, and destruction.*

*Japanese aggression in Manchuria is a manifestation of this sin-
fulness. This becomes more evident day by day as the scope of Japanese
aggression increases.*

*Bolshevism, which set out to destroy all religion, has itself become
a religion. It, however, is a religion not of love but of hate. In Christianity
and bolshevism we have the two most powerful rival religions now at
work in the world. If bolshevism wins, humanity will sink into hell. If
Christianity prevails, the world can yet be saved.*

Japan is wrong in supposing that taking over Manchuria is to her advantage. Imperialism is out of date. It also is opposed to religion. Some have charged Christianity with being a tool of imperialism. True Christianity stands for humanity so cannot be imperialist. Japan is hurting her own interests and is inviting into the Far East the religion of Karl Marx by her present course of aggression in Manchuria.

Various members of the party then spoke, assuring the President of the sympathy and prayers of Christians around the world for the heavy burdens and responsibilities on his shoulders; expressing hope that the Sino-Japanese crisis might be handled so as to secure justice and peace in the Far East, and also, as an Anglican missionary put it, that "the instrumentalities for the pacific handling of international conflicts may be strengthened throughout the world"; and asking how as individuals and as members of their missionary groups they could be most helpful to him and to China in this hour of trouble.

This brought President Chiang to his feet again. His response, David wrote, was "as vague as a river mist." He hoped the League of Nations would be able to do something; on the other hand, the Japanese would not accept decisions of the League. As to what those present could do,

I hope you will help the Christians of China to study the Manchurian question and to understand what is required in maintaining the peace of the world. Christians must show that there is power in their religion which can be brought to bear upon actual problems and difficulties such as we now face.

Shortly after seven the party moved to the city home of President and Madame Chiang, where a banquet was served. At ten fifteen, "after five hours," as Henry Burrell later wrote, "of genuine Christian fellowship and of conference," the party broke up, and the Shanghai group caught the midnight express back.

TREADUP must have been up much of the night in the observation car writing all this, which had happened three weeks earlier, down in his diary. Even when he crawled into his berth he evidently got little sleep, for in a note to Emily the next day he wrote: "Tossed and turned in my lower, thinking about the pain of arranging the end of their calling of those poor distraught women." He may have got a little sleep, however, because the train arrived three hours late.

Appleton Sills, the Nanking fraternal secretary, to whom Treadup had wired ahead, was at the station to meet him. "He was popping like a firecracker," saying: Lucky the train was late. Tied up all morning at the Consulate. Radio messages. Japs attacked Shanghai at dawn. Yes, Treadup, you got out by the skin of your teeth. Bombed the Shanghai railway station. Shambles. Shelling Chapei district. Lucky man, Treadup! Lucky man!

THREE DAYS later David wrote Emily:

> *The inevitable state of panic. All trains from Shanghai are cut off. They say they may have some trains to the north in a day or two—to bring troops down for the defense of Nanking, which everyone expects to be attacked. I'll try to get aboard the first train that leaves.*
>
> *The news from Shanghai is appalling. The railway station and many of the factories along the river have been wrecked by artillery and airplane bombing and incendiary fires. The Japs didn't dare attack the International Settlement and the French Concession. From there, at night, they say you could see the glare of burning buildings in the Chinese city. In the first two days motor cars, carriages, rickshas, and wheelbarrows brought three hundred thousand distraught people from the war area into the International Settlement, most of them with no belongings but the clothes they were wearing. The Y is overwhelmed with refugee work. A huge bazaar and market building being constructed by the Continental Bank, and nearly completed, has been turned over as a camp.*
>
> *Nanking next? I hope I can get out of here and back to you, my Hazy. Sills has just had a phone call from the American consulate, saying that it would be well for women and children to leave, either by the American gunboat anchored in the Yangtze about five miles from Sills's house or by a Butterfield & Swire freight steamer, which can take about forty deck passengers. Margaret Sills is now packing some clothing and bedding in case she and the boys have to leave.*
>
> *The lights went out a few minutes ago. The Chinese newspapers had said that would be a signal for a Japanese air attack. But they have just gone on again.*

DAVID thought a great deal about the session with President Chiang. "We take heart," he wrote Emily, while he was waiting to get away from Nanking,

> *when we know that we have a man of that sort in command of the affairs of China. There is a great hue and cry from super-patriots for resistance "to the last drop of blood." The fact that the League of Nations has not produced any results has given point to the demand for war. But some of us have hope. Henry Burrell was reminding me of the old Chinese tradition for settling quarrels by bringing them to the magis-*

trate at the city gate and threshing them out there in the presence of
one's fellow townspeople. Having taken this contention to the city gate at
Geneva, surely the neighbors can avoid a fistfight.

But a few days later Treadup was writing that every time he felt optimistic he heard old Cowley shouting, "What tommyrot! You have the mind of a six-year-old." He told Emily that he had had a talk one day in Shanghai with the son of Z. T. Tao, the former treasurer of the Shanghai Y.M.C.A. This was the youth who, back in 1912, at the age of fourteen, had tried to rush off to give his life in China's great revolution, only to be caught and brought back by his father. He was now a young man of thirty-three, and he was bitter and cynical. When Treadup told of the hours with Chiang Kai-shek, young Tao exploded.

"Do you know what this gentle Christian is doing to the Communists in Shanghai? It's common knowledge. Do you know about the methods of torture and firing squad he is using? Christian!"

David reported to Emily what young Tao said then:

"The League has committed suicide. The Nine Power Pact and the Peace
Pact—meaningless. The nations don't love peace, they are just some-
what afraid of war. Japan now has all of Manchuria. Next she will take
China proper, and then she will turn on the rest of the world. China has
no choice but to fight. Of course we shall be defeated, but it is better to
die fighting than to give up the struggle. Our fighting may start another
world war, and that is what I should like to see. I know the cost would
be awful, it might be the end of civilization, but then we would all be in
it together. It's the only way we could get help. This episode in Manchuria
has convinced us that China has not a single friend in the world. We are
doomed and we had better die fighting."

IT WAS not yet Nanking's turn, and on January 4, 1932, David Treadup started back north toward Paoting.

DENIAL OF A CHRIST-LIKE PRINCIPLE

DAVID had been away for more than a month. He wrote in his diary:

> *I remember that when you stand on the beach at Peitaiho, on the flat wet sand washed by the incoming waves, the water first rushes up the shallow slope, then drains down under the curl of the next wave, and as the spume of the withdrawal gathers around your ankles there is a very odd sensation: the footing is pulled out from under you. I have that feeling on dry land, here in Paoting, these days. The old underpinnings, which were only sand to begin with, are being sucked away. The threat of these uniformed Japanese is constant: one is tempted to think un-Christian thoughts about their short bow legs, their woodchuck teeth, their ridiculous pointed army hats. Because of their presence there has been a subtle change of atmosphere in the entire missionary enterprise. It pulls the sand out from under our feet. We are all tense. Em is dark again. She says: "What can one foreign woman do?—tend to a handful of tatting women—worry about a few hairnet makers—scrub up a party of starving orphans—ridiculous!—none of it makes the tiniest dent!" Old Cowley is grim as a sparrow hawk; Stanley wears a face ten miles long; young Shanks looks as if he would cry half the time. "My" villagers quarrel and whine. I am coming to a conclusion. Life should be less grim than this. The Chinese have a gift of laughter. It is being whimpered away by my coreligionists. I can't remember a single occasion on which Jesus preached in favor of laughter. Am I going rotten at the core?*

THE YOUNG VILLAGER David had chosen as his assistant, Shen Mo-ju, had done a remarkable job of keeping the literacy schools going during Treadup's absence. The lad had gained so much confidence that the villagers, on the one hand, had begun to grumble that this youth was turning into "a new warlord," and he, on the other hand, now showed some signs of resentment at the return and interference of his superior officer, Treadup.

Besides, patriotic propaganda teams of middle-class, urban-bred students had gone through the villages, planting anger and anxiety in everyone's fields.

In April Treadup went to Menghsien and, making an appeal of urgent need, persuaded Johnny Wu to let him have one hundred red date saplings from the *hsien* nurseries. David and Shen and a team of farmers' sons carried them back to the Paoting area on five Peking carts. Every act in China seemed to need a philosophical-sounding slogan; so as they moved into the district the first of the carts carried a banner reading: "A tree's shade gives peacefulness and long life. Plant one near the village well."

Remembering one kind of success he had had with homesick coolies in France, Treadup went to Peiping in May, and there he bought, in one bazaar after another, scores of Chinese foot-shuttlecocks—chicken feathers in a circlet bound around light metal weights. He distributed these in the villages, setting the requirement that each village select a team of its four best kickers. Soon, even in the busy springtime, there were evening intervillage contests: something entirely new in the experience of the villagers. Village pride began to develop, and Treadup introduced contests of Chinese chess and even essay writing. Through lugubrious Mr. Shanks, he acquired some Y.M.C.A. soccer balls, and June evenings found David Treadup coaching the first of a series of teams that finally constituted a rural league.

In "his" villages Treadup did begin to hear bursts of extremely Chinese laughter—eruptions of astonished pleasure in all these weird forms of big-nose competitiveness.

DAVID persuaded Emily to spend the summer in Peitaiho with young Paul, who was going to work there again as a salesman in the J. M. Dent stationery store. David argued that their son would be going off to Yale in the autumn, and this would be Emily's last chance to be close to a son. The underlying argument, of course, was the one that was on Treadup's mind that spring—life should be more enjoyable than it had begun to seem. Swept along by this conviction, he even promised—sugar on the persuasion—that he would take a month of pure vacation himself, and join them. They rented half a house at East Cliff, sight unseen of course; and in mid-June Emily and Paul left for the seaside.

AT THE BEGINNING of August, Treadup joined his family. "Pure vacation," he had promised Emily; but he had forgotten how to have one. He woke up early every morning and yearned for work of some kind.

He decided to build a wherry—or it would probably be a dory, the latter being the cruder sort of rowboat that he might really be able to design and make. Something to row, in order to get his arms and legs back in shape. He made drawings. He had to take a mule cart to Chinwangtao, and the narrow-gauge railway from there to Shanhaikuan to get the lumber; the family made an expedition of it, in order to see the place where the Great Wall runs into the sea. They climbed onto the wall at the great gate in the city and walked on top of it to the first of the foothills. The diary:

> *Seeing the wall curve up those slopes onto the high mountains beyond made me shiver, picturing the builders at work in antiquity—the cut stone carried up and up there by antlike hordes of slaves—the arrogance and glory of it! Central Kingdom! Contaminating barbarians shall not pass!*

In a lumberyard in the heart of the port David meticulously chose, one by one, some sound cedar planks for his boat, paid the yard owner, and left without so much as a piece of paper to attest the transaction, confident that in three or four days a two-wheeled cart would roll up the road at East Cliff in Peitaiho to deliver what he had bought. And so it did. "China! China!"

He went to work.

EMILY had mended in the soft sea air. There were many friends here, new and old. Picnics at Lighthouse Point and Eagle Rock; paper chases and treasure hunts on donkey back; swims on the great sweep of the beach above Eagle Rock; companionship with husky Paul, who was growing into a copy of his father; hours of solitary reading in a glider on the porch; intimate circles of women around the evening table in the light of kerosene lamps which made faces seem young again; cool nights under a safe canopy, draped like the hangings of an ancient royal bed, of mosquito netting—all these things had gentled her. Not that she had quite achieved her old deep serenity; perhaps that had left her forever with half-deaf Absolom, or perhaps—there are hinting questions in David's diary—she had begun to conjecture that her husband's mission in China was, at its very root, hopeless. But at least she was no longer feeling "level." David celebrated her recovery in his diary: "Cheeks have color again, eyes clear as a fawn's. We've been too hard on ourselves. For years now."

THERE WERE no telephones in Peitaiho.

In the other half of the house lived a maiden named Penelope Dew, about thirty years of age, "plain as an apple pie" (David), but strong and energetic as any one of the sturdy donkeys on which she charged up and down the landscape. She had organized a women's softball league. Her own team were the Bluebirds; they wore dark blue serge bloomers and white middy blouses with bluebirds on the wing appliquéd to the front. Emily, unable to swat a sleeping fly or to catch a pillow tossed in her direction, played as a helpless liability in right field on Miss Dew's unbeatable nine. David watched a game.

> *Penny can't run in a straight line. Hits a hot grounder! She's off to first base! She runs low to the ground, very like a rabbit, with little starts first off to this side, then the other.*

After a morning's work on the dory, a glorious swim, and lunch on the cool porch, one day, Treadup was just dropping off in a nap when he heard a kind of alto braying in the distance—a baby donkey learning how?—which seemed to approach and form itself into his own name, repeated over and over. He arose to see Penny Dew galloping on a donkey up the dirt road to the house. "Treadup! Treadup!" she was shouting, and with her right hand she kept waving her pith helmet at arm's length. She pulled up short at the foot of the stairs to the porch, bounded out of the saddle, and ran up the steps.

She had to take ten deep breaths before she could speak.

"Your friend Dr. Cowley? In Paoting? Shot a Chinese man dead! I just heard it down over at the post office in Rocky Point. That's all they know. Wire came to Bunson. You know Bunson?"

Yes, David Treadup knew Bunson.

"Bad of the doctor," Miss Dew said.

"Bad for us all," David wrote in his diary that evening. And:

> *At a time when the most important task in China is to silence Japanese guns, to use an American gun! What folly! I have long thought the poor old gull was losing his mind.*

A MEETING was called next afternoon by the Rev. Dr. Brady in Rocky Point, on the porch of his house. The Bunsons, the Hugh Murchisons, B. R. Winthrops, Tucklets, Keystones, Henny Henderson and wife, Alice Pond, Penny Dew, and, from Paoting, the Swings and Stantons. More wires had come through, and with help from the Swings and Stantons, who knew some of the background, the following story was pieced together:

Over a period of some months Dr. Cowley's hospital had been robbed of some twenty-five hundred dollars Mexican, in cash, instruments, and drugs. There was a loss almost every night. The old man and his colleague Dr. Wells had tried all kinds of measures to catch the thief, without success. Three nights before, not telling anyone, he had carried out a plan of staying up all night in the hospital, sitting in a straight chair with his fowling piece loaded beside him. Occasionally he made rounds. Sure enough, late at night, he surprised the thief in action. He jumped on him, but old Dr. Cowley was feeble, and the man easily threw him off and ran. Dr. Cowley fired what he said he intended as warning shots, one indoors to summon help, two out in the compound. One of these "warnings" was too well aimed, and it hit the man. He kept on running, climbed the compound wall, and jumped down on the other side. He was found there at the foot of the wall in the morning, dead. He was the janitor in the women's wing of the hospital. As soon as the body was discovered, Dr. Cowley notified the Chinese police, who to his great indignation took him into custody. Eventually they had carried him by train to Peiping and, observing the forms of extraterritorial rights, had turned the culprit over to the American consulate for investigation.

One other extremely unpleasant piece of news had come: The Tang Pu, the radical right element of the Kuomintang, had demanded the immediate trial and execution of Dr. Cowley, for murder. The way the demand was phrased made it clear that if there were to be a trial in a Chinese court, there would most surely be an execution. Reciprocally being shot to death was suggested, rather than the usual decapitation.

What could be done? What should be said?

From the diary, three weeks later:

All I could think of at the time was what I had been arguing all those weeks about the violence of the Japanese—that a tooth for a tooth was Old Testament, Christians could not advocate answering violence with more violence, theft with murder. Their message had to be Jesus's message of peace on earth. What a time for this rash gunfire! Yes, it was murder. . . . Was my thinking colored by the way the old man had been nagging at me for so long, practically calling me a heathen? His temper and his sniping had become quite nasty. Was I, in my innermost self, being vindictive, without knowing it? And were others? Because I noticed that Stanton and Swing were among the strictest in calling for a rebuke.

The discussion on Dr. Brady's porch that afternoon was "full of verbal shot and shell," but it was inconclusive. Finally Miss Alice Pond suggested, and the exhausted discussants at once fell in with her, that what was needed here was a statement addressed to Chinese Christians, letting them know that the missionary community did not believe in shooting anyone, least of all Chinese. Miss Pond, Stanton, and Keystone were asked to draft a statement.

HE BOUGHT some queer native oars from a Chinese fisherman—crude boards for blades at the ends of long sticks. He had painted the dory the day before. It was a beauty. *Ecarg III.* "The paint was *almost* dry. There could be no question that I was in too much of a hurry," Treadup ruefully wrote that night. He hired four carriers, who suspended the dory from shoulder

poles and made their way with it to the beach near Eagle Rock. He had invited
Paul to go out for "a little excursion around Lighthouse Point." It was fairly
calm. They started out. "Had to slog a bit at the oars." Off the boulder-studded
point the wind freshened and David noticed that the seams, which he had
caulked with hemp soaked in tung oil and painted over, were leaking. He
had Paul bail with a wooden scoop he had brought for the purpose, but soon
the water inboard began to gain. They turned back and just made the beach.
"With all my past rowing on rivers and lakes I guess I'm a landlubber,"
David wrote,

> because Henny tells me you have to put a new boat in the water for three
> or four days and let the wood swell up before the seams can be tight.
> Never knew that. Paul thinks me awfully dumb.

TREADUP and his son were just back at the house, the boatbuilder full of
chagrin after this outing, when Alice Pond came cantering up on a donkey
with "the agreed-upon statement." The committee, she said, had decided to
submit it to Chinese- and English-language newspapers in Paoting, Peiping,
and Tientsin. Treadup read it once through—"not as carefully as I should
have"—and said he would sign it. The nub of the matter was a sentence in
which the undersigned declared that they wished to emphasize to Chinese
Christians that "a Christ-like principle was denied by Dr. Cowley's use of
firearms in his effort to defend property from a robber." The statement called
for Dr. Cowley to resign. David handed the paper to Emily. She read it and
said she guessed she wouldn't sign it. Miss Pond asked why not. Mrs. Treadup
said, "I don't know, Alice. I guess I just don't feel like it."

In the end twenty-seven men and women did endorse the statement, and
Dr. Brady sent it off to the chosen newspapers, over a pseudonymous joint
signature: *Veritas (On Behalf of 27 Christian Missionaries of the North
China Field).*

TREADUP recaulked and repainted *Ecarg III* and put her to soak in a
sheltered cove, submerged and held down by rocks in her bilge, for three days.
Then, with a sound and spiffy dory at last, he had barely time—four
days—to work up a complete set of stiff muscles before he had to return to his
Paoting post, leaving Emily and Paul in Peitaiho for two more weeks.

DAVID had wired ahead to Center Rush Gridley, asking if he could spend
a stopover night with him. The grizzled veteran lived in a lovely three-
courtyard house, crammed with enameled chests and glistening vases and

coromandel screens, in a *hutung* far from the Westernized Legation Quarter. Big Treadup had no sooner limped into the presence of big Gridley than his host began to growl at him. "What in thunderation got into you nincompoops down there at the shore? Get sunstroke lolling on the beaches?"

Treadup decided to wait for some meaning to emerge. "Then"—in the diary—

> *all of a sudden—before anything explicit had come forward—it flashed into my mind that Gridley and Cowley were old good friends from early days, almost back to Boxer times. That must be it!*

And it was. Gridley lumbered over to a desk and picked up a sheaf of newspaper clippings and handed them to Treadup. They were from English-language papers in Peiping, Shanghai, Tientsin, and Hankow. Phrases jumped out at Treadup: "cowardly anonymity," "holier than thou!," "toadying to Chinese," "forestalling Chinese criticism by offering up a sacrificial lamb—or a Jacob in place of a lamb," "outrage against tenets of loyalty to one's own," "kicking a man when he's down," "hypocrisy of so-called Christian hanging judges"—and much more.

"My cheeks began to burn," Treadup wrote later. He was trying to think what to say. All he could think of was what had seemed Emily's puzzling and rather sullen refusal to sign the Cowley statement—when his hand turned up, at the bottom of the pile, a different sort of clipping. It was from a magazine, apparently published in the States, called *Fundamentalist Faith*. It was entitled "The Y.M.C.A. in China—A Stench Against Decency."

> We call attention to the absolutely nasty and utterly godless "advertisements" and "picture shows" and "talkies" being put on three times a day in the Y.M.C.A. building, Peiping, China, at 3:00, 5:30, and 9:15 P.M. Sample subjects:
>
> • "Maria Corda in *The Private Life of Helen of Troy.* She lived—and how! Naughty but wise! Nifty but smart. Just a doggone dangerous darling. Take a peep!"
> • *"Don't Tell the Wife*—hotter than hot!"
> • The osculatory picture of a good-looking man and a scantily clad woman is entitled *Ladies Love Brutes,* while a further sentence explains, "A woman's white arms conquer the giant's strength."
>
> Not ten feet from the entrance to the Y.M.C.A. auditorium, where these entertainments suitable only for the red-light district are displayed, stands the foundation stone on which is inscribed in Chinese:
> "Apart from this foundation there is no other; this foundation is Jesus Christ."
> We declare it our increasing conviction that there is no greater waste of Christian money than that which goes into a majority of the Y.M.C.A.s of the world.

Reading this, Treadup confessed to himself in his diary, there trembled in his mind the thought he had been nursing along for some months: Life should have more fun in it. He began to perspire. He did not know whether Gridley had meant for him to see this last clipping. He decided that the safest thing to do would be to ask what had happened to Dr. Cowley, who, when last heard of, had been turned over to the United States Consul General in the capital.

The consulate had sent an investigator down to Paoting, Gridley said, and on the basis of what the man had turned up, the authorities had decided not to bring any charges against Cowley, and they had let him go. Gridley had seen him before he left. "He's a broken man. One thing I must say: He's remarkably forgiving of all you dinged fools down there at the shore."

Before Treadup left for his train the next morning, he was able to work the conversation around to the article in *Fundamentalist Faith*.

"Lucre!" Gridley said. "It's a crying shame. It's what money does to you. New York, you know, has been telling us that their Depression is killing their revenue. We thought we could help, so we rented out the hall to a man named Mayshine Huang. I said at the time, 'A comprador who takes such a first name needs watching.' He made a contract in turn with an outfit called the Continental Amusement Company. It's all legally binding. Our attorneys throw up their hands. There isn't a thing we can do about it."

"I haven't seen a movie in a dog's age," Treadup said.

IN PAOTING the word was out that Dr. Cowley had decided to resign from the hospital and from his mission. Treadup went to call on him. "I was pulled up there against my will as if by a magnet." Dr. Cowley was more courteous to David than he had ever been. He served tea and scones. David could not bring himself to apologize for having signed the statement. Indeed, the statement was never mentioned. Dr. Cowley kept shaking his head. "It was a righteous anger," he said. "I had a patient—a Chinese Christian—carcinoma of the pancreas—pain of the damned—needed morphine. Found the last of our supply had been stolen by that bugger. 'Cain was very wroth.' I slew my brother. There it is, Mr. Treadup. There it is. The mark is on me."

WITH HIS YOUNG ASSISTANT Shen Mo-ju, Treadup began to make plans for an agricultural fair at the grounds of the Seven Dragon Temple, to be held at harvest time.

> *It is my idea to have a 'merry' occasion. These people eat too much bitterness. The article in 'Fundamentalist Faith' scalds me. What is so bad about "take a peep"? Johnny Wu was telling me about the local*

'yang ke'—"planting songs," really little plays, very suggestive, everyone fulfills a dream watching them, even the women and young girls come and laugh openly. We must stage some at the fair.

Treadup and Shen rode helter-skelter from village to village on the motorcycle, making arrangements. Shen said one day he hated the machine— the dust made his eyes fill with gum, he said. He said he would prefer to ride from village to village on a big donkey. "It is me he dislikes, not the dust," Treadup wrote. A few days later Shen was galloping along a country road. His donkey was powerful and willing, but Shen was impatient, and whipped the animal to go even faster. Instead, the mulish side of the ass's temperament took over, and the beast decided it had had enough and on stiffened legs made a sudden stop. Shen flew over the long ears and braying mouth and landed hard on his head. He was knocked unconscious and broke his jaw and lost six teeth. Treadup took him back to Paoting on a Peking cart. Dr. Cowley, saying, "This is my last act of mercy in the China field," operated on Shen's jaw. Even under anesthetic Shen continued to give peremptory orders to his peasant clients. "The worse he does it, the more the poor fellow cares about his work," Treadup wrote.

It was something of a relief that the accident kept Shen out of action during the rest of the planning of the fair.

TREADUP went to the station with Dr. Cowley. All the doctor chose to take with him to the United States were two steamer trunks and a valise. Dr. Cowley was extremely irritable. "I took this as a good sign. He is almost himself. His saintly humility was unnatural." The murderer climbed into a third-class carriage of the train without saying a word of thanks or good-bye to Treadup, and without looking back at the place where he had lived and worked for three decades.

STANTON and Swing were both back from Peitaiho. Charles Stanton was now the senior missionary for the American Board. The very evening of Cowley's departure, he called on Treadup and invited him to move with Emily into Dr. Cowley's house. He said it was clear, in view of economic conditions in the States, that the Board would not be able to send out a replacement for the doctor, even though his leaving was going to cause real hardship at the hospital. The Treadups might as well make use of the fine house the doctor had been living in. Of course Stanton would have to get authorization from Peiping, and eventually from Boston, for this; but he saw no reason why the couple couldn't move right in, on a safe assumption that everyone would see that an occupied house would be better maintained than an empty one.

For his part, Treadup said he, too, would have to submit the question to higher authority—his wife Emily, still at Peitaiho. But he knew how she hated the cramped little bungalow that he had built on a principle of male common sense that left nothing out of account except a woman's feeling of hominess. He was so sure she would want to move that he began packing before she returned.

> *American Board Mission Compound,*
> *Paoting, Hopei,*
> *September 14, 1932.*

Dear Sisters:

This week finds us slightly more settled than a week ago. I finally achieved some curtains for the living room out of some coarse cheap Peking crash and outlined them with orange yarn fringe. The room has four bay windows, and we have kalsomined the walls in light cream, so the room is bright. Dr. Cowley's Shansi chests, with their lovely colors, offset the stern frigidity of David's favorite picture, which he insists on hanging in a prominent place: Moses holding the tablets. The doctor, in his hasty getaway, surely must have left behind by error an embroidered mountain scene done by Hunan artists who excel in that craft. . . .

We have come to feel sorry for testy old Dr. Cowley—to think he shot a man in hot blood—but 'tween me and thee I can't be sorry he's gone. I love his wee hoose.

> *Your devoted,*
> *Em*

THE AGRICULTURAL FAIR

FARMERS arrived from all twelve villages. They came by cart, on donkey back, on foot. They brought their best produce. "Giant turnips"—the diary—"like huge white clouds; muskmelons as big as the moon; Chinese cabbages as hefty as grown children." Pigs, chickens, ducks. Whole families. "I had had no idea there would be so many."

The fair lasted three days. All went home to their villages in the evenings; they arrived back at the Sze-ko Lung Miao temple grounds early each morning, having arisen long before dawn to get there in time. Greater numbers came each day—many from villages outside the zone of David Treadup's past reach.

THE FIRST two mornings there were lectures and demonstrations. Treadup had borrowed several Chinese specialists from Menghsien, to talk to the farmers about the crossing of imported lines of plants and animals with local strains to produce strong and durable hybrids; about green manures and available fertilizers; new methods of well-digging and irrigation; efficient techniques of plowing and cultivation; and systems of rent, sources of credit. Treadup used many of the magician tricks of his lecture program to impress the audiences. Most dramatic were some one-to-one comparisons: a year-old Poland-China hybrid pig from Menghsien alongside a local yearling; two white Leghorn eggs overtipping three local hen's eggs in a vendor's balance scale.

THE AFTERNOONS were given over entirely to pleasure. Besides intervillage contests of shuttlecock kicking and Chinese boxing, Treadup introduced something the villagers had never seen before: tugs of war. Children played Hawk Chasing Sparrow and Beating the Sticks. Bird kites and dragon kites flew in the sky. Costumed clowns staggered around on stilts.

But best of all were the *yang ke*. According to tradition of the region, a poet named Su Tung-p'o (A.D. 1036–1101) became a district magistrate and during his administration wrote *yang ke*, "green-sprout" or planting songs, for farmers to sing while they were planting in rice fields watered by the Black-and-White Dragon Springs, at some distance to the southeast of Paoting. No one could say how these plain narrative gang songs had been transformed into plays for the stage, generally sung in the falsetto voices used by Chinese actors, with instrumental accompaniment. No one knew, either, why the *yang ke* of this region differed so markedly from those of Shanghai, which had become street dances, or of Peiping, where they had become parades of actors on stilts, or of many areas where they were still just simple folk songs. The Communists had already begun to use them as danced political songs— powerful instruments for indoctrination.

In his work in the villages, David had come across a couple of *yang ke* troupes. All the parts were taken by males; until Treadup had come along, the players had all been illiterate and had handed on the texts to young apprentices by memorization.

Treadup had supervised the building of a suitable stage near the front of the temple, where the greatest open space was available.

The diary, later:

The acting in the local 'yang ke' has become very broad and suggestive, so that the most delicate words take on wildly licentious meanings. How they roar! The women, too! How poor old Dr. Cowley would have disapproved! I could not help thinking of the teasing advertisements at the Peking Y.M.C.A. movie theater. I am Mr. Mayshine Treadup! Ah well. These people only have one mean life to live.

MEETING AT THE WATER WELL

Evening, in the Schoolroom

MAN (*enters and sings*) I am Wei Kuei-yan.
Before me the Four Books and the Five Classics.
I cannot study, on every page I read her name.
In my garden at home is a *wu-tung* tree
Waiting for the phoenix to build her nest.
Behind the embroidered screen sit beautiful girls.
How can I pass my examinations? (*Exit.*)

Morning

WOMAN (*enters and sings*) My mother-in-law
    commands me to fetch water.
My shoulder pole is made of boxwood.
In fear I hang a pail on each end of it,
And on my back I carry a well rope twelve feet long.
In sorrow I walk out of the kitchen, out of the gate.
The road leads toward the hill, toward the well.
My husband's name is Chou Yu-tzu, mine is Lan Jui-lien.
He is fifty-three while I am only eighteen.
He is ugly as a carbuncle;
His nose is flat as a monkey's;
His mouth like that of a donkey;
One ear is half rotted away;
He has only one leg, and that one festers;
His short queue smells like sheep wool.
Standing he is like a ghost;
Squatting he is like a millstone.
I climb toward the well.
One step, two steps—lotus steps;
Three steps, four—chrysanthemum steps;

Five, six—the tyrant's lash;
Seven, eight—Pa Wang's whip;
Nine, ten—ten-colored flowers.
Forward nine steps, backward three.
I walk like a pearl-hanging-on-the-rolled-up-screen;
I walk like the spread-of-the-bottle-gourd-vine.
I walk now to the north of the path,
I walk now to the south of the path.
Around the well grow poplars and willows;
Around it stands a white stone railing.

The WOMAN *lets one pail down into the well and draws it up full of water; lets the other down, and draws it up. She thinks of the weight of the water, and rests, and rests. The* MAN *enters and sings:*
I think of the dream I had last night:
I stood on the Blue Bridge and saw a ravishing woman.

He looks in front, he looks behind; he looks to right and left. On the bank an old man of eighty is fishing; below an awkward girl of sixteen is washing clothes. But these are old scenes, last year's scenes. He searches for the scene of his dream. He catches sight of the woman at the well.
Who, who is that?
Her hair is smooth as a cocoon and black as ink,
Braided with red silk threads;
Above each ear she wears a fresh flower,
And a hairpin inlaid with kingfisher feathers.
She is dressed in flowered cloth and a crisp black skirt.
She is the one who was in my dream!

He goes near. He bows. He speaks. She bows in return and asks:
Have you lost your way, young gentleman? Or forgotten
    your home,
Under a spell of the beauty of the grove at the well?

MAN I have not lost my way or forgotten my home.
Beauty has charmed me and made me thirsty.

He asks for a cup of her water. She dips out a ladleful. He pretends to drink, but he stealthily gazes at her lotus feet.

WOMAN Mean-hearted young man—you talk of your
    thirst
And look at my feet!

MAN My thirst is not of the usual kind.

Will you tell me—your family? Your home village?

WOMAN Go away! Go away! Mean-hearted young man;
You have stolen a close look at my feet,
And now you dare ask where my home is!
My mother's home is on the far side of Hua mountain;
My mother-in-law's on the near side.

MAN Will you tell me, young lady,
How old your husband is, and how old you are?

WOMAN My husband, fifty-three; and I, eighteen.

MAN A wife so young and a husband so old!
How you must have suffered, beautiful girl!

WOMAN I do not dislike my husband, though he is old.

The MAN *looks all around and sees no one nearby. He sings:*
Do not be angry, beautiful girl.
May I tell you what is on my heart?

WOMAN Say whatever you want: I take no offense at
    honest talk.

MAN I want to ask you, I want to ask you
To give yourself to me.
Yes or no; do not be angry.

WOMAN Your impertinence makes me angry.
Go ask your sister to give herself to you!

The MAN *asks her to listen to a story.*

WOMAN If it is any good I will listen.

MAN Once long ago Fan Li-hua the Beautiful
Was given in marriage by her bad uncle to Ugly Yang.
On the battlefield she fought a young and handsome
    general;
She fell so desperately in love with him that
She killed her ugly husband and married her beloved.

WOMAN (*aside*) Wicked! A good woman does not
    marry twice.
I am not made of stone. My heart hurts.
What should I think? What should I do?

MAN I am a gentleman's son, from east of the river.

My name is Wei Kuei-yuan.
I will inherit grounds of thousands of mou
And a mansion with ten tens of rooms.
In winter there are furs; in summer, gauze.
If I would smoke, a servant lights my pipe;
If you would drink, a servant brings you hot water.
Why would you not be mine?
Why waste your beauty on a disgusting old man?

WOMAN (*aside*) East of the river! How handsome
    he is!
Though married by my parents to the ugly Chou,
I have fought on the battlefield; I am in love.
(to him) Young sir, I will give myself to you.

MAN   Come with me to the Blue Bridge!
There we will swear our love before Heaven.

The WOMAN *follows him.*

MAN   Here on the Blue Bridge
I, Wei Kuei-yuan, kneel down before Heaven.
I will always love you, beautiful girl.

WOMAN   I, Lan Jui-lien, kneel with my lover . . .
I must go!
My mother-in-law will beat me.

MAN   Wait! Give me a token to remember you by.

WOMAN   I came out to fetch water and brought nothing
    worthwhile.
But take this hairpin.
If you come to the Blue Bridge with this token,
Even though you are a beggar I will not refuse you.

MAN   I must go back to my studies.

WOMAN   Wait! What will you give me to remember
    you by?

MAN   I came out to enjoy the beauty of nature, I have
    nothing.
Ah, let me tear a piece from my blue gown to give you.
If you come to the Blue Bridge with this token,
Even though you are a servant-maid,
I will open my arms to you.

The MAN *leaves.*

WOMAN (*left alone by the well*)
I must carry the two pails of water back.
Have I had a dream?
What is this torn piece of cloth in my hand?

IN A CEREMONY on the third morning Treadup himself awarded prizes. A fine cloisonné vase went to a seventy-three-year-old farmer who had raised a monstrous cabbage weighing thirty-four catties—about forty-five pounds. The most valued prize of all, a Poland-China hybrid piglet, a sow, was awarded to a "demonstration farmer"—a man who had a literacy degree, taught school himself, had introduced Inventor Wang's water-drawing machine and plows and harrows to his village, and had by various means increased the yield of his own land in two years by sixty percent. Treadup called him to the platform, where he received the applause of nearly three hundred of his fellow farmers. He carried the pig under his arm from the platform. Treadup launched into some concluding remarks. The pig became excited, squirmed out of the winner's arms, and ran away out of the temple grounds and across the fields at an astonishingly high speed. Treadup's entire audience dashed off to catch it. "Upstaged by an oinker!" he wrote in a letter to Farrow Blackton in New York, reporting on the fair. "But after a while they drifted back. They'd caught the critter and were willing to hear me out."

FROM THE SAME LETTER to Blackton:

> On the third afternoon there were three special attractions: free small-pox vaccinations; an irrigation demonstration—a beautiful miniature farm some of us had set up in a kind of diorama, with real water ect.; and a flea circus. Yes, a flea circus. It was the biggest hit of the whole fair. I had found it in town one day. About 200 were vaccinated; 275 saw the irrigation exhibit; and nearly 600 saw the fleas. I charged five cash a head—about one-tenth of a cent Gold—for admission, and just about paid for a bunch of the prizes. Lots of men went through two and three times! The sign at the circus entrance said "Adult Education." You see, all the fleas were adults—flealy speaking. They had to be to qualify for the circus. They were truly intellectual fleas, trained by a scholar— a member of the Y.M.C.A.! His little pets jumped into tiny doors and through hoops and around in circles. Wonderful! The fleas are the talk of the whole district. A great boon to my literacy schools, because one couldn't help saying: If a man can teach a flea, what cannot be done with a human—no matter how stupid? Think of this, Blackie, and there will be a song in your heart today. There is hope even for you.

SHANKS' MARES

HYPOCHONDRIAC SHANKS had got wind of the drastic economy drive being forced on the International Committee in New York by the Depression.

Henry Burrell, now the senior fraternal secretary with the National Committee in Shanghai, kept circulating letters and memoranda to all the Y people in China, to keep them informed. Shanghai was putting up a valiant fight to protect the fraternal corps, but to Shanks each blow in that fight struck at his liver, his pancreas, his duodenum, his gall bladder. "I have the most peculiar tight feeling in my upper bowel," Shanks said after one bit of bad news came. "I *wish* old Cowley hadn't shot that bugger. He used to give me something for this—I've forgotten what the wretched stuff was called."

• A copy of a letter arrived from Burrell to Blackton in New York, protesting that whereas the cost of living in every other country where the Association had secretaries was going down, in China it had risen thirty percent since the last adjustment of the salary base, to Gold $1,510 a year; and now New York was asking every secretary to make a voluntary twenty percent "salary contribution."

Our men are not complaining. I find them expressing nothing but sympathy and a great desire to cooperate to the utmost in the difficult ordeal through which we are all passing.

• David Liu had gone to the States to argue against reducing the number of fraternal secretaries in China, but news came in a cablegram that he had suffered a stroke in Washington, right in the office of the Secretary of State, while briefing Secretary Stimson about the situation in China.

• From Blackton in New York to Burrell in Shanghai:

For a week or so it was not possible for us to secure a check through the treasurer's office for any item, including salaries. This was because our banking situation is so precarious and the need for cash so pressing. This is the first time in the history of the International Committee when such a thing has happened. I saw James B. Todd the other day, and he said he had gone through many periods of hard times in his tenure, beginning with the Panic of 1907, but that he had never encountered

anything quite like the present. His statement gave me a fright, because
James B. has always maintained such a high standard of optimism.

"SHANKS gets on my nerves," Treadup wrote in his diary,

> *The source of his ill-being is obvious. He is doing a rotten job. He is*
> *fuddled all the time; he doesn't seem to be able to follow through on*
> *anything he starts. He doesn't like me. I know it's foolish, but this*
> *bothers me, and I try to mollify his hypochondria, and that makes me*
> *angry.*

"I just know they've got me on the list for demobilization," Shanks said
to Treadup one day.
The diary: "Amen."

TREADUP realized that one reason he was able to work with exuberance
through the spring of 1933 was that Emily seemed happier. She took great
pleasure in the big Cowley house—"room to move around and be myself!"
Having lost her sons to the States, she had decided to mother poor Shanks. He
was in the house many evenings, skulking around out of Treadup's sight as
much as possible, whispering to Emily, defining and celebrating his aches
and pains. He brought out a tenderness in her, as if she had found a lost kitten
with the mange; and with such a willing object for this tenderness at hand,
she seemed to recover at least a counterfeit of her old inner peace.

But David, in spite of his flaring energy, was uneasy. From the diary:

> *I feel there has been some slippage. We luxuriate. I even take naps*
> *sometimes! Is it just that we're slowing down with age? What troubles*
> *me is there are two of me—one of me who works with unprecedented*
> *keenness in my villages, the other a homebody with a lackadaisical*
> *streak which distances me from the so-called heathen, the presumed*
> *object of my love. I fear I am settling for less grand dreams than I*
> *once had. And I am more aware of comforts than I used to be. Emily's*
> *adopted baby Shanks can think only of comforts—I caught him blub-*
> *bering last evening with his head on Em's shoulder. But that same*
> *shoulder often cradles my addled bean, too. Em is calm and I want her*
> *to be. I spent all morning supervising the building for her of a new*
> *kitchen stove—a big improvement, it will be, though itself somewhat*
> *crude. It is just built of gray bricks, but with a cast iron top like proper*
> *foreign stoves; and it will have a real oven built in underneath. I'm*
> *rather proud of my design for it.*

ONE SUNDAY Treadup went alone to morning service at Pastor Huang Ching's Chinese church in the city. Pastor Huang preached in his gentle tones on the self-sacrifice of Jesus from the time of his experience in the wilderness until he was nailed to the cross. Again and again he emphasized Jesus's going without anything but the most primitive needs, so that he could better help those who did not have enough in the world. If they were poor, he would be poor. As Pastor Huang went on, Treadup—the only foreigner in the congregation of about two hundred—felt more and more conspicuous. He who lived in the big Cowley house in that compound with the high wall around it. "More than once I felt like sneaking out"—but all the Chinese would have seen him leave. When the sermon was over, Pastor Huang called on Treadup to pronounce the benediction. He tried to do it gracefully.

He was glad to get away from the crowd as soon as he could; but at home he found he had still not escaped, because as he was about to descend to the basement to shake down the coals in the furnace, he met the cook coming in, who "with great flourish and enthusiasm" said, "Wasn't that good this morning!"

Treadup replied, "Perfect," and hustled down to the basement.

"Sometimes I begin to wonder," Treadup wrote that night,

whether I really am a Christian and love my neighbor as myself. But the way out is very hard to find. The standard of living of the Chinese is grades and grades below ours, and we could not begin to subsist on it, our children would starve. Yet they see us as rich, comfortable, luxury-surrounded foreigners who have all we want and can always get more for the asking. Annual salary now $2,240; allowances for children cut off because they're gone; 20% "salary contribution"—very very very tight, it seems to us. Very very very rich, it seems to them. Complex, since we have supposedly come to preach exactly the same Cross as Pastor Huang does.

Another notation, the next night:

Pastor Huang's sermon has made me hypersensitive. Shanks's luxuriating embarrasses me. Once a week he has his cook buy and prepare a goose—makes him save up the down when he plucks the birds, so eventually he, Shanks, will have "a wizard pillow." He has ordered a Victrola from Tientsin. He has an electric fan, like the ones in the hotels, over his bed.

THE NEXT SATURDAY afternoon, Treadup went for a hike with Stanton and Shanks. Spring was arriving; wild flowers were out at the roadsides.

The walk cleared David's head. The superb day began to make him think he wouldn't have to wait for heaven—"I was there already"—when the three men met the compound gatekeeper, Ting, marching calmly along with a paper package under his arm and a shovel over his shoulder, followed by a troupe of merry small boys. Stanton asked him what he was doing, and he replied as casually as if it were nothing, "Oh, burying my nephew Chang's new baby."

Hearing those words, Shanks—just as he had at a crucial moment on his non-wedding day—fainted. Stanton knelt and fanned the white face with his hat. Treadup chafed the cold hands. In time Shanks groaned and opened his eyes on a cruel world.

> *The thought of death—the chirruping boys—Ting's calmness—too much for the poor fellow. We got him back on his feet. We learned afterward that the body in the bundle was that of the third child of some country cousins of Ting's who had lost their first baby from tetanus, the second had been born at the hospital and survived, and the mother had hoped to come to the hospital to have this one, but it was born too soon and met the fate of such a big percentage of newborn babies—mud at the cord!—by quickly developing tetanus. The apparent indifference of the man with the shovel felled Shanks, I guess, but it also made me angry— not at him, but at the abyss that had seemed to open between him and us three, as if his offhand answer had been the rumblings of a devastating earthquake.*

IN APRIL Treadup attended the Second Menghsien Institute. It was a fortnight's gathering—like the first Institute, which Treadup had just missed on his return from furlough three years before—of influential Chinese and foreign missionaries from thirteen of China's provinces, to learn what they could from demonstrations of the sorts of work Johnny Wu and his cohort were doing. Because of his recent visits to Menghsien, Treadup was familiar with most of what was being done, but he found it great fun to see many old friends and to meet new ones. He was chosen as one of the English-language secretaries for the conference, sang in its choir, and served on its Findings Committee. He dined one evening in Johnny Wu's home with several others of Wu's foreign friends.

"What forcibly struck me that night," he wrote Hank Burrell,

> *is the impact this remarkable, fiery personality has had on all of us. I've had a chance, during this conference, to see some lives quite turned around. Edward Robbins, from Shaowu, said something that I've been mulling over ever since. "This," he said, "is Christian Communism. Johnny Wu accomplishes everything the Reds do, but in a Christian*

*manner, in accordance with Christ's teaching that love and sacrifice are
more powerful than authority and rifle fire."*

BY JUNE the issue of "the two worlds" had become: Would it be possible to
get to Peitaiho that summer? The Japanese had seized Shanhaikuan, the port
near Peitaiho where the Great Wall reached the sea—where Treadup had
bought the planks for his dory. This capture had caused great fears among the
Chinese that it was the first move against Tientsin and Peiping and all North
China; among the foreigners, David wrote, "the scandal is that their summer
resort is threatened." Wasn't this shocking? All the same, he yearned to go,
and Emily must. The rail line to Peitaiho and beyond to Shanhaikuan had
been closed. Emily wrote her sister Jane:

> *We have heard that the Hendersons from Tientsin got to Peitaiho on a
> "sand boat," but had to be carried across mud on coolies' backs to get
> aboard, and only canvas protected them over open deck space on which
> they slept. Thank you, I don't go quite that informally! Better boats are
> promised. Mr. Treadup is voluntarily giving up half his vacation—if any
> is possible—to help salvage the morale around here. Due to cuts in
> money from back home, foreign missionaries are leaving China in droves.
> The Chinese are in a terrible state of mind and heart, perfectly sure that
> the foreigners are going to desert them figuratively as well as literally.
> While I gallivant off to the shore a burden falls on David: heat and
> loneliness and mental and spiritual strain in a pretty well impossible
> situation. In those old optimistic lecturing days he never used to take
> any vacations at all, but I'm insisting he take two weeks this summer, if
> we can get to PTH at all.*

In the end, passage became available on a small Japanese steamer
chartered by a Chinese agency; David went along, "to make sure Emily would
be safe." There was an extreme heat wave—106° as they went through
Tientsin by train, which took them only as far as the port at Tangku. It took
some time to settle in their "first-class cabin," for it turned out that the agency
had sold fourteen tickets for the cabin. The children slept two by two in the
bunks, and most of the adults slept, or didn't sleep, on chairs out on deck.
There were sixty on a vessel with accommodations for twenty. It was an
overnight trip. "Mr. Treadup was only a little seasick," Emily reported. The
ship anchored at Peitaiho off West End—the farthest possible point from the
East Cliff house; and the passengers had to be landed on smelly fishing boats.
But finally Emily was at home in a familiar half-house, and David headed
right back for home on the same ship. The diary:

> *Nine-tenths of my life in China seems to be movement with all its
> difficulties. Carts, bicycles, rickshas, trains, shanks' mares, the Indian,*

the swaying decks of teacup ships. I often have dreams of not getting there—wherever, God help me, "there" may be. In my dreams it is a most desirable yet somehow fearful destination. The Garden of Eden?

DAVID to Emily, the night after his return:

Last night I wrote in my diary the phrase "shanks' mares"—meaning, you know, walking—without even thinking of your poor baby Shanks, who misses you unbearably. I wish I were in a position to miss him. He is unbearably on my neck. We eat together; he says, "I can't get anything down if I dine alone." The long, long waits for Mr. Shanks to chew his food—"Chew! Chew! C! H! U!"—and to put down and take up his fork, and to commence again to chew. I hate to say it, but I think he is of the cow family.

He's not all. Most unpleasant conflict between Dr. Ch'en, our best Chinese doctor, and Nurse Alice Connor. She has become overbearing in her zeal to evangelize as she cures; he says her whole trouble is that she is American. She throws quotations from the Bible at him. He remarks that it is useless to quote the Bible because anyone can quote the Bible to prove anything—every passage is capable of more than one interpretation. I'm rather on his side. She's just plain ornery. Shanks the self-healer says, "Her gall bladder works overtime." While arguing ambiguities, she might stop to think that impatience is not patience, cruelty is not kindness, hate is not love, vengefulness is not forgiveness.

Not that Dr. Ch'en is all that easy to live with. He is fervently patriotic and supposedly intelligent. He spends three-quarters of his waking day trying to raise money to buy swords to send to the troops— those great ugly curving broad old swords the Chinese used as far back as the Shang Dynasty, I guess, if that was when the bronze age was— not exactly the thing to stop Japanese cannons and airplanes. Fear is driving everyone mad.

TREADUP was in Peitaiho for the second and third weeks of August. At first the shock of idleness was too much for him, and he had an attack of what seemed to be malaria—fever and chills; then, after "poking down tons of quinine," he had symptoms that seemed to come from the medicine—"dizzy in the knees and wobbly in the stomach." He wrote one day that he hoped he was not turning into Shanks.

Then he wrote:

Shanks and I see each other as a liability, each of us, to the missionary movement. From my point of view, quite apart from his silly nervous-

ness, he is self-indulgent, unloving, and cast in concrete as an American —unable, therefore, even to imagine what it is to be Chinese. I cannot see quite so clearly what it is he thinks is wrong with me as a missionary; and this irritates me, like a case of poison ivy—the real itch of it being a knowledge that, yes, there are real failings, but ones that may always be hidden from me.

TREADUP to Burrell:

I wonder if you've had a chance to read 'Re-Thinking Missions?' No one can claim to be up-to-date about the issues that face the whole cause of Christianity today without having read this report of the Church at work in the world. We expect some of our friends are going to be shocked by it. But we cannot believe that any modern American is afraid of shocks! More and more do I see the handicaps we are working under because of the narrow assumptions with which the work was started here in China by the early missionaries. I do not minimize the courage and the devotion and the sacrifice of their endeavors. They were men and women of their age. I'm afraid that we missionaries of this generation will also be accused of being men of our age and be cursed for the mistakes of judgment which we are making. What delights me about 'Re-Thinking' is that it supports the humble re-thinking I've been trying to do all along. I tell you, Hank, I shouted out loud to Em when I read this bit: "Western Christianity has in the main shifted its stress from the negative to the affirmative side of its message; it is less a religion of fear and more a religion of beneficence. It has passed through and beyond the stage of bitter conflict with the scientific consciousness of the race over details of the mode of creation, the age of the earth, the descent of man, miracle and law, to the stage of maturity in which a free religion and a free science become inseparable and complementary elements in a complete world-view. Whatever its present conception of the future life, there is little disposition to believe that sincere and aspiring seekers after God in other religions are to be damned; it has become less concerned in any land to save men from eternal punishment than from the danger of losing the supreme good." Yes, sir! I have to admit that in recent months my enthusiasm had begun to flag. This book has jogged it up again. I don't feel so alone as I did.

BACK IN PAOTING Treadup found a letter waiting for him that put him to a real test of his commitment. It was from Burrell, and it was not about *Re-Thinking Missions.* Hank wrote that New York had sent a long and "devastating" cable about the financial condition of the International Committee. It was so badly in debt that it was having great difficulty paying interest on loans it had already taken out; accumulated deficits on September 30 were expected to be no less than Foreign $1,569,847.04, and Domestic $840,327.16; it was clear that there would have to be a reduction of at least four fraternal secretaries in the China field. The Chinese National Committee had met in Shanghai, Burrell wrote, and to forestall the cutback had pledged a contribution to New York of Gold $5,000. Imagine it! The Chinese Y.M.C.A. making a contribution to America! But of course that was far from enough. Burrell asked this question:

> *Do you approve that we suggest as an alternative to further staff withdrawals that we all take salaries next year on the basis of dividing what is available among the entire present staff, even though that may make it necessary for many of us to do outside work?*

Shanks came flapping around an hour after Treadup got home and not ten minutes after David had finished reading the letter. Shanks was in an urgent state of foxiness. He had had the same letter, and he had obviously seen his salvation in it. Everyone would share and share alike, and he, Christopher Shanks, would not be demobbed!

"Why don't we send a joint wire to Hank Burrell?" Shanks said. "Would you like me to word it?"

"Hold your horses," Treadup said. "I have to consult with Mrs. Treadup. She might have to go to work to help make ends meet, you know."

"Oh, sir! You know she'd do that for you and me!"

"For me and you. Mr. Shanks, Mrs. Treadup may be a pillow to you. She is my wife."

That evening Treadup wrote Emily in Peitaiho. Two days later her answer came. "We have no choice, do we? We have to do the Christian thing."

WHEN EMILY returned from Peitaiho, Shanks was no longer her damp and apprehensive baby. He raced around trying to deal with his excitement at his so obvious reprieve. He danced in and out of the Treadup house; every noontime seemed to signal the onset of another afternoon of a faun. This depressed Emily. "I'm so bored I could weep," she wrote sister Jane. "I get so sick of my own company and trying to think up something worthwhile to do, when it's so easy just to waste time." She worked up "an orgy of housecleaning" —rifled all cupboards, tore her desk apart, chased every speck of Gobi dust in room corners, washed sweaters and then used the Lux water from them to bathe the dirty compound dog.

> *All the other families here have local servants who go home to their meals. We have three live-in servants (plus Cook Fan's wife), all from*

*different villages and each getting his own meals on our stove, so ever
since I returned there have been three or four different meals being
cooked all day long on our two-hole stove, grand as it may have seemed
when David built it—in addition to endless tubs of hot water for tea,
bathing, washing clothes, scrubbing floors. So you can imagine—no,
you can't, either—the mess of millet porridge bowls and cabbage soup
and teacups and chopsticks adorning the already abominable kitchen.
I'm trying to teach the cook's wife to do all the servants' cooking at one
time. I may have to let the cook go if he doesn't stop screaming at her
and at me.*

SHANKS'S bubble broke just before Christmas. Both he and David Treadup
got identical long letters from Burrell in Shanghai, telling them that "a
thunderbolt" had come from New York. While New York had regarded as
"heroic" the Chinese pledge of $5,000 and had praised the fraternal secretar-
ies' "matchless fellowship in offering to share one another's burdens," the
International Committee's incoming donations had been even worse than
expected, and in the face of "an overwhelming situation," New York had
decided to reduce its entire field staff worldwide to thirty men and to "make
equally severe reductions at home base." The staff in the Far East would have
to be reduced to twelve. This would probably mean cutting China from twenty
men to eight, with four for the rest of the Orient, including Japan, Korea, the
Philippines, and Siam.

Shanks developed cramps in his legs, diarrhea, and athlete's foot. Emily
threw off the blues. Treadup's diary grew laconic:

*When I joined the Y to come out here, I regarded the step as being
equivalent to marriage. It was for life. Dear God, I haven't had time to
make even a proper start in all the things I want to do!*

ON THE LAST DAY of the year, Shanks received the dreaded letter from
Farrow Blackton in New York. Paoting was one of the smallest cities in which
an Association was maintained; it would have to carry on with Chinese
secretaries alone and be supervised from Peiping. Shanks was asked to return
to the States as soon as possible.

All Shanks's symptoms disappeared overnight. The whites of his eyes
became dazzlingly clear. His skin tone pinked up. He began zestfully firing off
letter after letter: complaint that he had not been given notice six months
before; announcement that he intended, upon reaching the States, to "enter
claims against the moral obligation of the International Committee to reim-
burse me for losses due to hurried sale of my furniture and other belongings
of real and/or sentimental value"; assertion that the request that he sail home

within six weeks was "flagrantly unreasonable"; statement that he considered himself entitled to continued participation in the Retirement Fund, the Employed Officers Alliance, and the Insurance Alliance; expectation of placement in a suitable post of Stateside employment; accusation that the reason why he, a fraternal secretary of a regular city branch of the Association, was being demobilized, while Treadup, "engaged in unorthodox tasks," was being kept was that "unlike some other people I failed to keep jawing at the bosses in Shanghai about what a bang-up job I was doing."

Emily, in her diary: "I have never seen Christopher Shanks so happy."

AFTER TWENTY-NINE YEARS

THROUGH THE SPRING and summer of 1934, Treadup went at his work in something like a Calvinist frenzy. He felt a survivor's guilt. Some of the best men in the China field had been demobbed, and he had not.

He had been kept, he said more than once to Emily, not because of his future promise but rather because of his past contributions. If people thought of Treadup at all, he said (as if looking at himself from a great distance), they thought of the lectures—of the vivid way that fellow David Treadup had helped create, in the minds of many thinking Chinese, a readiness to step without cultural shame into the world of machines. He himself had a conviction that what he was doing now was more important for China—"quieter, deeper, more far-reaching"—than that earlier work had been; but he doubted whether anyone else thought so, and sometimes he was stabbed by doubt of it himself.

What he was doing now was far from the main line of Y.M.C.A. work; Christopher Shanks's word "unorthodox" was uncomfortably close to "deviant"—the word Treadup had thought Todd must apply to him. And of course there was the question whether Johnny Wu's native team wasn't doing this work far better than he, a foreigner plugging away in a region alone, ever could. There was nothing for it but to work his head off. "I have to try to earn my keep," he wrote.

HE FELT an urgent need to "lay down concrete footings" in his villages. This was his metaphor for building a foundation for the Chinese to build on—creating a situation in which his own sudden disappearance, if it were to come about, would make no difference at all. But he was far from ready for devolution. What was tricky was that this was not a mode of work that could be ensured by a tight organization of Chinese successors—at least of the sort a single devotee could put together. There were impediments. He was a foreign devil; he was working in a number of villages, each of which had its own local pride and local hierarchy; and cutting across all his efforts in those villages was the resistance of the ancient and conservative *pao-chia* system. His only instruments were personal enthusiasm, the manifest good sense of his proposals, and empirical results: readers became wiser than illiterates, a mou of land became more productive than it had been, pigs and eggs and cabbages grew larger than they used to be.

He knew he was going to have to do one piece of demobilization himself. He would have to replace his principal assistant, Shen Mo-ju, whose early attractive keenness had turned into something rather nasty. His jaw healed, he had become a shouter and a bully. There has always in human history been something dangerous about the rank of colonel—helpless before the commanding general but able and all too willing to stand on the neck of lower echelons. And Treadup knew he had made the awful mistake of dealing with young Shen not as an equal but as a colonel.

There did exist in the villages where David had been working a kind of shadow organization—the network of sponsors, teachers, and "Mass Education Secretaries" he had enlisted, many of whom had great pride in the fruits of their work. David decided that he would ask the most senior and successful of these figures to set themselves up as a Mass Education Council for the region. He would then suggest that they choose a chairman—sure in his bones that if they followed their own wishes this figure would not be Shen Mo-ju. Thus the cruel act of demobilization would not be his doing. He began as he moved about to sound out some of the veterans about the advisability of setting up such a council. He knew he must work slowly and patiently, so as to avoid resistance from the *pao-chia*s, and indeed from these leaders themselves.

THERE WERE encouragements and setbacks:

• In a village called Fan Miao forty children went on strike. In the next village, not three hundred yards away, there had been a literacy school; they had none. They refused in a body to go to the small, old-fashioned local school, where they would have to learn the elementary classics by chanting them out loud. "Youth in revolt," Treadup wrote Burrell (here, he acknowledged to himself in his diary, he was indeed "jawing at the bosses in Shanghai about what a bang-up job he was doing")—"Youth in revolt is common enough in cities but quite unheard of in remote countryside places like Fan Miao." All sorts of turmoil ensued. Village elders cutting up. Such loss of face for the Confucianist village teacher that he jumped in a well; was safely pulled out. Accusations of Communist infiltration. But the children got their school.

• In the village of T'u Ti, a Mass Education Secretary was all set to open three new classes in reading and writing for adults. Four family heads raised a frightful ruckus because one of the classes was for women. They shouted up and down that women gathered in a small temple in the evenings would certainly be molested by ruffians. There were uncouth men in the next village. The women would be raped, one by one. (Treadup: "We all knew it was a cover-up for their objection to women leaving the brazier and cradle.") The other villagers were so intimidated that none of the three classes, not even those for men and boys, could get under way.

• Like a dark weather system moving across the land dropping unseasonable hail, clouds of rumors came across the region, of a Shansi "patriot" who had defected from armies up north and was roaming wild about the countryside with a band of two thousand marauders, robbing and looting even from the poor. This happened just as a new term of literacy schools throughout all the villages was about to begin. The "patriot" was said to be heading for his native province in search of a prosperous place where he could settle down and live off the populace; he was scorching the earth on his way. The peasants were unanimous in their panic. Literacy was the last thing they wanted just then. They dug foolish trenches around their settlements; they mounted impotent night patrols of men armed with scythes. In the end the bandits merely skirted the area. One wounded man was brought to the mission hospital in Paoting; another died on a stretcher just as he reached the hospital gate. The bearers said the death was an accident. The patriot, they said, was not interested in killing farmers; his brigands shot only the knees or feet of those who objected to having the money stolen from them that they had saved over twenty years and hidden behind mud bricks in their *k'angs*.

AFTER this bandit panic had subsided, Treadup wrote in his diary:

> *I try to think I am doing God's work. I'm sure God must have a plan for China, but it seems to me to be, like so much of the Divine, most mysterious. He must have in mind that from all this instability will come — what? What? God knows!*

All this puzzling turbulence had its mundane causes. The Christian Chiang had concluded a so-called Tangku Truce with Japan. Its purpose, his peace-loving avowals notwithstanding, had seemed to be to free his forces to deal with the Communists; its effect, certainly, had been to free the Japanese to extend their hegemony over more and more of North China — partly by terror, by encouraging just such free-lance Chinese bandit forays as this one which had so demoralized Treadup's villages.

Chiang was working out his destiny far to the south. In the early thirties, the peasant-based Communists had established an enclave in southeast Kiangsi Province. In 1931, an All-China Congress of Chinese Soviets had convened at Juichin, in that province, and had elected Mao Tse-tung chairman of the first Chinese soviet government and Chu Teh its military commander. Late in 1931, in May–June and July–October 1932, and again in 1933, Chiang had mounted four vast "extermination campaigns" against the Kiangsi Communists, which they survived by using guerrilla tactics against Chiang's trench and frontal warfare. The urban-based wing of the party in Shanghai had meanwhile been done in by Chiang's goons and Moscow's ideologues. In 1933, Chiang finally changed his Kiangsi tactics and drew a tight blockade around the Central Soviet District. This was now proving effective, and the enclave was shrinking.

All these events were far from David Treadup's consciousness. He heard dim reports, from time to time, of the fighting in the south, and vaguely he was, as he recorded, "pulling for CKS" — since he was a Christian. But mostly Treadup was far too busy in his tiny orbit of the villages to concern himself with history at large.

IN JUNE, Emily went to Peitaiho, where she shared the same East Cliff house with a Baptist couple from Tsinan. David took no vacation at all that summer; he slaved away. "I need to justify myself." He was on the razor's edge of enjoying his misery. The heat was fierce. Summer was a fallow time in the literacy schools. The farmers, exhausted from work in their fields, were not at all sure they wanted a Mass Education Council. Shen Mo-ju was more shrill than ever. But there was a lull in communications from Burrell in Shanghai, and Treadup had begun to believe that his status as a survivor had been confirmed, solidified — when suddenly, on September 3, 1934, the ax fell. Parts of a letter from Blackton in New York:

> Dear old friend David:
>   You are too alert not to have picked up from Burrell and others the painful situation in which we find ourselves here in the International Committee. We have fought from one trench to the other until we were forced to come to terms with the reality of the situation. We have tried to reduce wherever possible and save personnel, but with the necessity of huge new cuts we cannot hope to proceed without touching vital sections of our organism. Among the people whom we are suggesting for adjustment to positions off the China field is yourself, and I can assure

you that it cuts me to the quick to have to bring you this definite word, although I imagine you probably have thought of the possibility of this eventuality long since. I am writing four others besides yourself at this time asking them to come back to the States as soon as possible.

Naturally you will ask what the reasons are for suggesting that you make this adjustment rather than someone else, and you have a right to an answer to that question. We have studied and restudied our whole personnel in China, and we have tried to be fair to the individuals, their families, and also to the work in the field. In your case, the situation lined up in our minds as follows:

1. We are having to think of the survival of as many city branches of the Association as we can. David Liu and John Y. Hu of the Chinese National Committee have assured us over and over again that that survival is directly connected, even now, with the maintenance of fraternal secretaries in supporting positions in those branches. Your literacy work in country villages has been spectacular, as has been everything you have ever put your hand to, but it does not help, alas, in that desperate struggle to survive. The literacy work had its origins with Johnny Wu under the Association, but he has moved away from us. This leaves you, as it were, in limbo.

2. Your present age has also been a factor in the decision. If you were twenty years younger, dear friend, we might pluck you out of your countryside and install you in one of the city branches, replacing someone else. But I think you would be the first to say that it would be hard for you to be sent to Home in this sad game of Parcheesi.

I wish to make it clear to you that certain past allegations, having to do with "Humanism" and matters of emphasis in your religious orientation, have had nothing whatsoever to do with this decision. Todd and others here fully support me in this assertion. There is full appreciation here of your past contributions to the Association and to China. Indeed, it will never be possible to do justice to you in reckoning their value.

That this letter will be tremendously disheartening and disappointing to you I have no doubt, and I wish you to know at once that I am not writing without a full appreciation of the bonds of loyalty to this task in China which through the years have wound about the hearts of yourself and Mrs. Treadup. There is no hard-boiled attitude on the part of anyone here at New York, rather there is the fullest sort of understanding and compassion. We are in a crisis, and we must not close our eyes and ostrichlike hide our heads under the sand. That you are one who is called upon to adjust is in no way a reflection upon you, nor is it a reflection upon anyone who will be asked to take a similar step. We must together mutually sacrifice and try to help each other as much as possible.

I suggest you talk the matter over freely with John Y. Hu and Hank Burrell, allowing them to help you to make whatever adjustments are necessary in the field by way of preparation for a permanent return home. Hank Burrell will provide boat reservations and make transportation arrangements. I earnestly hope for your own sake as well as the sake of the Committee you will make preparations to come immediately.

It has been found helpful in the past under similar circumstances for the secretary to expose himself to friends who may be helpful in finding for him the kind of work in this country he desires, and this may be done at once. Also, you may suggest to us the names of persons in this country, particularly in the Association, secretaries or laymen, who know you best and who would be most helpful in discovering possible openings.

On the other hand, there may be possible openings of one sort or another out there on the field, outside of the Association, which might command your enthusiasm. You will accept this, of course, as a suggestion at long range which may have no meaning whatsoever as far as you are concerned.

In closing, let me assure you of the interest everyone connected with this decision has in the matter or the problem of adjustment which has been forced upon you. I am eager to do everything I can to help. It is our hope that while passing through this vicissitude we shall all find new means of service so the work will be enhanced rather than retarded.

Very cordially yours,
Blackie

FIRST NOTE in the diary:

That it should have come to me in a form letter! Signed in cold blood by my old colleague Blackie! I saw the letter he sent giving notice to that miserable Shanks. Except for the paragraphs of reasons, identical. The same abominable phrases. "From one trench to another." "Touching vital sections of our organism." "Bonds of loyalty wound about the heart(s)." "Ostrichlike hide our heads." Even that frightful Parcheesi metaphor. And O I like "together mutually sacrifice"! This puts me after twenty-nine years on exactly the same grade as that sniveling boy Shanks.

BY THIS TIME Emily was back from Peitaiho, and as soon as he had read the letter, he took it to her. Her response seemed to him, as he commented on it later, ambiguous. She was angry; yet

*there was a little tuck at the corner of her mouth which made me think
she was in some private corner secretly glad. Perhaps she misses the
boys too much. She has lately been calling Paoting "the sticks."*

Without trying to talk it out with her, Treadup "needed a lungful of air"
and went out into the compound to work on his Indian, which had suffered
one of its frequent breakdowns. He began to try with all his strength to free a
machine screw that had seized up solid. Treadup, focusing on its obduracy
twenty-nine years' worth of deflected hopes and accumulated frustration, tried
to force it with a furious paroxysm of strength. The screwdriver slipped from
the slot of the screw head and plunged with raging power between some
spokes and deep into the palm of his left hand. The shaft went almost all the
way through the hand.

Treadup pulled the screwdriver out and dropped it, and without telling
Emily walked to the hospital. There Dr. Wells cleaned the wound and gave
him a tetanus shot. Within hours, according to the diary four days later,

*I'd had reason to know that that was pretty powerful stuff. I came down
with a terrific attack of serum sickness. Well, for two days and nights I
felt as sick and suffered as much as I ever had before. Aches and pains
were at times excruciating. Almost every portion of my body at some
time or other got a dose of the poisoning, from the top of my scalp to the
souls [sic] of my feet. At one time my head felt like one big bee sting,
throbbing from the very center right out through my ears and eyes and
throat. People around here laughed at me, for I did look like a bloated
drunkard with my whole face—eyelids, lips, cheeks—puffed up, and my
eyeballs (what you could see of them) bloodshot and my skin all mottled
red. Now it's Sunday and I'm up and around. I haven't much pep yet,
but I'm coming back to life. My hand (small matter) is healing.*

THIS AFFLICTION gave Treadup time to reflect—and to write short,
blurted entries in his diary, including the ones already cited here. In one
significant note, he wrote that he "almost" admired Shanks's spunk in fighting
for his rights. He supposed he would now lose most of the protection he had
been carrying for his family. He assumed he would automatically be dropped
from the Insurance Alliance and the Retirement Fund; with three sons in
college, he would probably also lose his remaining share in the Educational
Fund, to which he had been contributing for years. Young Shanks "had the
grit to bark at them." "I am beginning to think there was more to that boy than
I had imagined."

Tapping at his old L. C. Smith machine with the first finger of his right
hand, he drafted a very long letter to Farrow Blackton, making a plea for

a reversal of the decision in his case. "Tore it up. Their reasons are too binding. Hopeless."

In some of his entries, his anger seemed to be looping back against himself:

> *If I have a shortcoming, it is that I have been aloof and unapproachable. My Chinese friends have often hinted at this—with sensitive Chinese tact, of course. Strangely enough, my best trait, my enthusiasm, may itself create a distance between me and others—I have too much breeze blowing.*

A single sentence, the only entry all day on the Saturday of that week: "I am praying to conquer my anger."

> Paoting,
> September 8, 1934.

Dear Blackie:

> *It has taken me a few days to digest your letter inviting me to come home and be demobilized.*
>
> *You must not feel pain in doing your duty. Too much solicitude for foreign secretaries makes them soft and flabby. We are stronger men than you think. We don't want to be regarded as those who are 'sent' instead of those who 'go' because they prefer above all other things to go. I feel myself superior in some ways to Robert Morrison, who as you know was the first Protestant missionary on this field, way back—but he was better in one respect than most or all of the present-day Y.M.C.A. secretaries on the foreign field, i.e., he came out without placing primary reliance on a committee or board to keep him here. Since his day the missionary idea has passed into its institutionalized stage, and most of us feel we have a grudge if the committee at home pulls the rug out from under us.*
>
> *In spite of this I tell you frankly, Blackie, that the International Committee owes me nothing. Rather I owe it for twenty-nine years of happy life, for a chance to do for this long a time what I prefer above all other work in the world. I have been paid for nearly three decades to do that which, had I the money, I would have been glad to pay to be allowed to do. Three decades of doing what one prefers above all else to do! How large a percentage of men in this world have such a long lease on happiness?*
>
> *I have talked and prayed with Emily in the days since your letter came, and we have come to one firm conclusion. We will not be coming back to the States. When Todd and you nearly thirty years ago extended to us the call to Association work in China, it was clear to us that this*

was a call, not for a limited period, but for a lifework. Our pledge was as sacred and permanently binding as our marriage vows. We love China, and we belong here. This decision has been harder for Emily than for me, because the three sons she bore are all in America; but she is, anyway, braver than I. We will find a "rice bowl," as the Chinese say. I want to stay at what I am doing, if at all possible, because I think it has a meaning for China's future, and because I do believe it is God's good work.

I will be writing again soon. I hope for all our sakes that the Association comes again onto better days.

Yours in fellowship,
David Treadup

TREADUP apparently could not stop reading Blackton's letter. In an entry on September 15, he wrote:

There is one paragraph which I cannot bring myself to believe for one moment. It's the one in which they deny that my so-called "Humanism" had anything to do with the decision. I believe it had 'everything' to do with it. It shames them that they might be accused of doctrinal rigidity. That passage — "Todd and others fully support me" — just doesn't ring true. I'll put it down right here that I hope I 'am' a humanist, I don't care whether it's with a big H or a small h. It is of the essence of my faith that if I did not love my fellow human beings I could not qualify as a follower of Jesus Christ — that's the very heart of the matter. Beyond that — well, I just don't know what they're talking about.

BARELY RECOVERED from his serum sickness and with a sore and bandaged hand, Treadup took off on a long-scheduled "literacy trip" — a round of graduations in his villages. In his day-by-day account of the trip he wrote sentences that were like steel springs, for he was trying to keep a tight control on his sadness and anxiety. Were these people — about whom, he now found, he cared far more deeply than he had ever realized — going to vanish forever from his life? He found even the annoyances to be an essential part of that for which he felt a premature nostalgia:

Arrived at Li Chia. The teacher away in town on a lawsuit with a relative. He has known for a month that this was to be the day. Gave out 14 certificates without him. Took picture. He will be in a rage that he is not in it, when I send the print. 'Tant pis.'

Each day he started out at dawn. The Indian announced itself from a distance by backfires and by the cone of dust rising in spirals behind it. Each village ceremony, in Ku Chuan, Shao T'an, Ho Chao, Ch'en Ts'un, Ma Ch'iao, in hamlet after hamlet, morning after morning, evening after evening—each had a moment or a story or a personality that "caught me by the neck." "Top of the class was a young humpback—had taken his book with him to the fields." "Druggist Liu, a church member, sixty-three years old, crippled with arthritis, was volunteer teacher." "Took a snap of Teacher Tuan riding his new bike—fell often and took him five trials to get properly started." "Before turning in I read by oil lamp in John 1 about witnessing for the Light—appropriate for this literacy trip!—the blind seeing the light. 'He was not that Light, but he was sent to bear witness of that Light.' " "Thoroughly questioned about many things foreign." "Hard thunder shower. Was not easy in my mind when I contemplated the huge cracks in the wall and the dilapidated condition of the roof of the 'schoolhouse'—a communal village storehouse—where we were sleeping. Might it collapse on me and all my hopes? I might have quieted my fears. Learned in morning the building had been like that for eons. Would likely be for eons more! O China!" "The entire village was assembled at the edge of the settlement at dawn—they had been waiting in the dark for over an hour to welcome me!" "After morning tea, picture taking. So early in the morning it was difficult to find a place where lighting and shadows were suitable. Settled on a farmer's courtyard where the sun was kept off a part of the crowd by a man who climbed on a roof and held up some matting." "Gave out 52 certificates and prizes. Despite protests that it would delay me, they insisted on giving me a lunch of garlic, *kuo mien,* and eggs. Before we had finished a delegation came storming in from the next village wanting to know what had delayed me!" "Young boy bitterly disappointed—he'd passed exams on first three books with excellent grades, but had been sent by his father on errand to another village on the day of the exam on Book Four—no diploma. He tugged at my coat begging me. I had to back up the teacher—no diploma until examined. He called me vile names."

WHEN HE GOT BACK from his trip, Treadup found a letter from Burrell in Shanghai waiting for him. It told him that he would have three months' grace; he would not be wholly "terminated" ("and we are gathered together"—the diary—"to pronounce the last rites over the corpse of Brother Treadup") until the end of the year. Feeling very much alive, he wrote Burrell that he was now planning trips, "at my own expense, if you please," to Menghsien, Peiping, Tientsin, Nanking, and Shanghai to try to find a new base of support.

I want to stay with my villages. I have begun something here, and though I know it will never exactly be "finished," I want to see it farther along. I hope I can find someone who has confidence in me. Have you heard about this New Life Movement of the Generalissimo's? Do you think what I'm doing might fit into its thrust? If you have any ideas, Hank, please oblige!

In the same letter:

I spent yesterday building an arbor for the wild rose and wisteria vines which will cover the walk to the door of this house when you visit us here, Hank. The American Board people say they will keep me on here at a token rental. I built the arbor as a kind of hostage to a stable future for Em and me. Do you want to know something strange? I have never had so much pep as in these last few days. I hammered away like a woodpecker. After that labor I slept so soundly last night that I had no idea that thieves, who must have come over the compound wall, got into our dining room and took away $344 worth of silver—all our wedding silver except a few spoons. But we all know how to use chopsticks, don't we?

E M I L Y seemed to be carrying on almost as if nothing had happened. The day after the thieves broke in, the cook quit. He claimed that his family was in a land lawsuit which would take months or even years to settle; Emily thought the thieves had scared him. "In spite of all the troubles he has caused me for three and a half years," she wrote Jane, "I must admit he's saved me a good deal of trouble, too, and I wish this weren't the moment he chose to leave." The houseboy said he could cook a little, "so we shall see."

It sounds so ridiculous to be so dependent on servants, and yet we are —because every detail of water carrying, emptying, fire tending, vege-table cleaning, not to mention the time it takes to go nearly two miles to town to buy things we can't possibly find or bargain for ourselves—all requires strength and energy out of all proportion. But if we can manage some of the easier details ourselves I guess we shall make out on a reduced standard of living.
   It has turned cold.

In another letter Emily tells about a women's circle meeting at the house. Instead of sewing for the hospital, the group took the afternoon off to play games. They had "quite a wild time" spinning the platter, passing the ring on a string, running a peanut relay race, and playing a game called Three Deep. Emily wrote that the women were

totally unused to such hilarity but most seem to enjoy it, though some are too shy or afraid of doing the wrong thing. One old lady with bound feet fell down twice in her lumbering attempts to be speedy. Another lady prayed out loud for divine assistance in carrying peanuts in a spoon. By the end of the afternoon we were all thawed out. I am so torn.

Sometimes I can't bear the thought that one of my boys might need me close by, back home. But this Mr. Treadup, out here, my hubby and my hub — he has a deep well of determination and grit. I admire him beyond words. So-o-o-o. Play games with the women, Em. Anyway — we had fun on a chilly afternoon! — laughter heals, dear Jane.

THE UNFINISHED TOWER

THE SURGE of energy ebbed. Treadup began having peculiar headaches. His left upper arm began to give him pain, and he worried that the osteomyelitis of his boyhood might be coming back. The wound in his hand, having nearly healed, turned purple and began to ooze. His rounds on the Indian tired him. In the villages there were outbursts of backbiting, jumpiness, and malicious gossip, which Treadup blamed on himself, though objectively he surely should have been able to realize that the incessant rumors of bandits and of advancing Japanese and of KMT troop movements and of roving Communist guerrillas were getting on the nerves of the peasants, who had no clear sense of who was fighting whom or for what earthly reason.

Treadup went to old Dr. Wells for a checkup. With tremorous hands, and peering from behind his pince-nez, the old man tapped over and over again at the great burls of Treadup's knees with a rubber hammer, himself starting a little each time the big athlete gave a reflexive kick, and listening through a stethoscope up and down Treadup's rib cage so long and with such absorption that it was as if an enchanting *Aïda* were being performed in the theater of Treadup's huge chest. When he had finished kneading and poking and squinting, the doctor said in his sad trembling voice, "To me you're a horse, Treadup. I think you'll have to go up to P.U.M.C., if you want to find out a worse truth."

This suggestion suited Treadup. He wanted anyhow to go to Peiping and Tientsin to ask various friends about possible means of support. So in early October — his hand now healed, but his arm very sore and the intermittent headaches continuing — he took off alone. In Peiping he learned that the bed he had counted on was no longer there, for Center Rush Gridley had been demobilized. "This made me deeply sad — that grand old giant!" The doctors bedded him down in a P.U.M.C. ward, between a pale silent missionary attached by a tube to a bottle of clear fluid on a high hook and a Chinese man who groaned night and day at the loss by knife of some particle of his flesh in his nether regions. After three days and four doctors, two sentences were pronounced: an internist named Whitsun thought he had found some kind of systemic poisoning, and a neurologist named Browner thought the big bull was suffering from "a complaint which we usually associate," he said, "with poets and submissive women"—neurasthenia. For the former Whitsun gave Treadup a purgative, several small packets of a powder called emetine; for the latter, Browner suggested exercise, fresh air, a cold bath every morning, a balanced diet, lots of good company—and "no fretting, old boy, it doesn't pay to fret." What about the arm, Treadup asked? Both doctors agreed: a little workout with dumbbells in the morning.

As intended, the emetine made Treadup vomit violently for three days in succession. He felt as if he were crossing an ocean.

WHEN the rough voyage of purgation was over, Treadup assumed that he must have reached a new continent of health. The assumption was itself therapeutic, and in somewhat improved spirits Treadup took a train to Tientsin, to see Lin Fu-chen at Peikai. He wanted to ask his old friend's advice about the possibility of his finding a Chinese, rather than a foreign-missions, financial base for his work in the villages.

He was shocked by Mr. Lin's appearance. Remembering that Mr. Lin was only a couple of years his senior, David saw a suddenly aged man, with a hundred hairs of a long white beard of wisdom on his chin, sipping tea in his presidential office. He asked Mr. Lin if he might be able to suggest some "wealthy gentleman of the old school" before whom Treadup could kowtow and make his appeal, someone like Yen Han-lin, the scholar-official who had so long ago opened the way for Treadup to begin his lecture program.

"My dear Treadup," Mr. Lin bitterly said, "where have you been? Don't you know that all those old literati are now corrupt officials of the Salt Gabelle? Or Japanese errand boys? Yen Han-lin died years ago. His oldest son is a free-lance bandit—he has an enclave down near Tsinan. He's very rich, but I would guess that teaching peasants to read is the last thing he is interested in. Now, if you could teach the farmers to pay taxes promptly to the local bandit-warlord, you'd get backing for that!"

TREADUP traveled to Nanking. He wanted to look into the chance of fitting himself into Chiang Kai-shek's New Life Movement.

The Generalissimo had succeeded in driving the Communists out of their base in Kiangsi Province. In the previous February, in the Kiangsi city of Nanchang, he had made a speech calling for "a movement to achieve a new life." He told his audience that Germany (where, he needn't remind anyone, Hitler had come to power) and Japan (where the military had taken over) were strong because they had adopted a proper style of life. China must "militarize the life of the people of the entire country." He called for a new struggle for order, cleanliness, physical fitness, destruction of pests, punctuality, and abstention from alcohol, opium, and tobacco. The four Confucian ideals— *li, i, lien, ch'ih;* correct behavior, justice, integrity, and honor—must now again be observed. The G-mo promised that New Life would rid the country of poverty, crime, corruption, and dishonesty. The four virtues, after all, had been the secret of success of the ancient kingdoms of Ch'i and Ch'u—as they also were of the strong modern nations. Fascist Italy and militarist Turkey had joined those models in Chiang's harangues; he had added a Blue Shirt Movement as an army adjunct of the New Life Movement.

Treadup's diary:

G-mo, I'm told, has been seeking advice of some missionaries. I hope to make impression on two grounds: (a) principal emphasis has been on urban reforms, and I may be able to sell the idea of an exemplary rural experiment; and (b) the Movement's attack on economic ills ("get rid of beggary") is entirely on basis of molding minds through a reformation of personal habits—e.g., not spitting on the floor will somehow relieve poverty—and perhaps I can sell a deeper exploration along the lines of my present work.

Most encouraging for Treadup was the fact that the Christian G-mo had chosen as the first General Secretary of the New Life Movement a young man named Peter T. P. Jen, who had been a Y.M.C.A. secretary in Mukden before the Japanese occupation of Manchuria. "I ought to be barking up the right tree." In high hopes Treadup called on Peter Jen at an office which David found "as austere as a poem by Milton—looks as if living down to the bone is going to be the cry." The interview brought a sharp letdown.

Too late. It seems that Edward Robbins, the chap from Shaowu whose excitement about Johnny Wu's work at the Second Menghsien Institute so impressed me—he's the one who called the work "Christian Communism"—has got in on the ground floor with just the sort of thing I was going to propose. Robbins's big advantage is that Shaowu is in Kiangsi, which, since the G-mo snatched it back from the un-Christian Communists, he wants to make into a showplace of the New Life.

HIS ARM hurting again—he hadn't brought his dumbbells south with him —Treadup went on to Shanghai. He had no success there, either. But he did have one consolation.

Hank Burrell says I'm well out of the New Life outfit. Says: "Look here, Treads, there's nothing new about the New Life Movement. They want to revive virtues handed down from China's immemorial past. There's a very strong smell of the fascism of Italy, where they're trying to modernize society partly by reviving the ancient spirit of Rome. You mustn't take the Puritanism in New Life for Christian zeal; it's backward looking. You know, in the past we've been the liberalizers: the Y supplied a good deal of the yeast for the present ferment here in China. But—don't quote me when you write Todd—it's the Communists who are putting out the yeast now. If the G-mo's Christianity is any measure, the Christians are falling behind. Very bad. Just my opinion."

Burrell was able to tell Treadup what had been happening to the other Y.M.C.A. men who had been demobilized. Several had gone back to the United States, some to continue working with American branches of the Association, quite a few, oddly enough, to go into the insurance business. Dr. Charles, with whom Treadup had gone so long ago to Soochow to fight the cholera epidemic, and who had later joined the Lecture Bureau, had been demobilized the previous year, and he was now working as a missionary doctor in the Navaho Reservation near Albuquerque, New Mexico. Of those who had chosen to stay in China, one was working for the International Famine Relief Committee, one had taken a position with the salt-tax office, one had joined the Irish Presbyterian Mission, and several were teaching, one at the Shanghai American School, two at Yenching University, two at the College of Chinese Studies in Peiping. "Not one thing that would appeal to me," Treadup wrote.

HE RETURNED to Paoting deeply discouraged. As had happened before, Emily's spirits rose as his declined. He needed a mantle of cheerfulness, and she threw it over him. Her letters now were quite sunny. From one to sister Jane:

On Monday I went into the city and did some shopping. I bought a pair of shoes that would set you laughing if you could see them. Black velvet, lined with felt, with snaps on the sides—they look like the kind of "comfort" slippers that one sees on ancient and infirm grandmothers. However, they are quite stylish, and warm now that cold weather is coming. I also got material for a new dress. I am cutting and sewing it doubling the cloth—also for weather that will soon shiver our bones. My dress will be very snappy, too (I mean it will be fastened by snaps), and when I wear it with the shoes, I hope I will be the only one laughing inside at how funny I look!

I am taking David out for long walks, to buck up his health. (Mine is fine.) I have some favorite objectives. One is a tree, which, according to common belief, was alive before the city was founded, and since the city is 2,000 years old, you can see that the tree is venerable. Of course it's dead, and it's surrounded by a little walled shrine, where people go to worship because they believe a god lives in the tree. They say a foolish man took a branch for firewood, but the pot he cooked in over it melted right away to nothing. Then there's a tomb, said to be of an emperor, to which we walk—a plain mound of dirt, about twenty feet high—you can climb up one side and down the other by a little path. Another sight we like is a "snow-wave" stone. This has been placed on a sort of pedestal in a little pavilion. It gets its name from the fine white wavy lines that run through the stone, which is rather a blackish hue. It is not specially beautiful, no American would look at it twice, but odd rocks are much prized by the Chinese.

TREADUP'S salary had stopped. He and Emily both seemed on dead center; they did not seem to know what to do next. They still paid the servants their wages; the cook bought food; David bought gasoline for his trips to his villages on his Indian. How? Out from her underwear drawer had come the black silk bag bulging with the Mex dollars that Emily had secretly begun to squirrel away just after Nancy's death. The drawer had been like a safe; neither servants nor thieves had ever found the bag.

"She was counting the last few of them out yesterday," Treadup wrote in his diary, "when God looked down and saw two of his sparrows about to fall and decided to do something about us." He and Emily could only think that what happened now had come about through divine intervention. The rescue, Treadup acknowledged much later, had been more mundane. A messenger came from Peiping, saying that Madame Shen, the woman who had been Johnny Wu's first patroness—and who had wept at the first graduation of a literacy class at Chefoo, saying she had never before seen barefoot scholars— urgently invited T'ao Tu Hsien-sheng to wait upon her in Peiping.

Treadup went back on the train with the courier. The old lady received him in one of the formal rooms of her mansion. Seated in a large square ebony chair at the far end of the room, in a court robe embroidered with dragons and storks, she looked a little as Treadup imagined the Empress Dowager must once have looked. She said she had heard of the brilliant work T'ao Tu Hsien-sheng had been doing in the countryside near Paoting. Her friend Wu at Menghsien had told her that T'ao Tu had, as she put it, "reached an honorable parting with his American patrons." She would like to offer her unworthy support, so that the work T'ao Tu had begun could be continued.

Suddenly all circumlocution ended; she hurled a very direct question at Treadup. How much had he been paid per annum?

Two thousand four hundred gold dollars.

Madame Shen cleared her throat. That was more than her miserable little treasury could support, she said. Long pause. But she would be glad to provide the black market equivalent of two thousand dollars gold each year for part of T'ao Tu's support. Would this unworthy sum be of help?

Treadup then did something which, he later wrote, "I couldn't help." He kneeled on the floor and kowtowed thrice to the old lady. Then he stood up and turned two cartwheels—"there was plenty of space"—across the room in front of her.

Madame Shen did not even raise her eyebrows at this performance. She clapped her hands—not applause, it turned out; she was summoning a manservant. One appeared. Soon she had her bailiff, all dressed in black, counting out the whole of Treadup's first year's allowance in Mex dollars. She sent six men with Treadup to Paoting, to make sure bandits on the train would not steal the money.

There was no bank in Paoting that the Treadups could trust, so the entire year's dollars went into the black silk bag, and it went back into the underwear drawer.

THIS PROVIDENTIAL EVENT seemed almost literally to stun the Treadups. Their relief was immense, but it left them logy, dull, and drowsy. Treadup wondered in his diary how Johnny Wu could have heard of his demobilization—for David had been too proud to go begging at Menghsien. He worked it out that Lin Fu-chen in Tientsin must have sent word to Johnny. This meant that at least two Chinese friends really loved him; here was a cause for rejoicing almost as great as Madame Shen's munificence, yet Treadup did not pull himself together to go to Menghsien to thank Wu for nearly three months; and there is no way of knowing whether he ever thanked Mr. Lin.

Through the remainder of 1935, and well into the spring of 1936, Treadup—as he later put it in "Search"—"twiddled my thumbs." The villagers had set up their Mass Education Council, and they had replaced Shen Mo-ju with an older man, a Christian who had been converted by the Paoting Congregationalists; the work went along moderately well. Treadup let himself be caught up in a series of minor projects which he called "garnishing around the edges of the platter."

• Since the Chinese were so fond of tales, sayings, and fables, he decided he would translate and introduce into the literacy syllabus some of the parables of Jesus. He chose The New Patch and the Old Garment, The Hidden Treasure, The Valuable Pearl, The Soils, The Tares, The Pharisee and the Publican, The Good Samaritan, The Laborers, The Lost Sheep, The Lost Coin, The Prodigal Son, The Elder Brother, The Wise and Foolish Builders, The Rash King, The Uncompleted Tower. "Yes! My whole work—an unfinished tower."

• He organized a mass wedding. An elaborate wedding was the greatest source of pride to a Chinese family, and even the poorest peasants would put themselves in debt for years to stage a grand show. Fancy clothing, a chair and bearers for the bride, instrumentalists, a feast—weddings could cost more than a decade's savings, and moneylenders grew fat on wedding loans. Treadup passed the word throughout the district that all couples who wanted a grand wedding could have one in April for only four dollars Mex each—if they didn't mind being married in a herd. The occasion turned out to be a huge success, a holiday for the whole district; twenty-three couples were married on a sunny afternoon. The music, the red-bedecked sedan chairs, the feast of many dishes—every bride blushed, every groom was satisfied.

• Music came back into his life. Not only did he get out his old cornet to work up expressive lips by playing hymns accompanied by Emily on the piano; he formed a choir of thirty of the best singers from all the villages. From the Department of Music at Yenching he got hold of sheet music of hymns translated into Chinese and set to old Chinese folk songs and lute tunes. The chorus, all male, sang falsetto in the style of Chinese operas, but its members also sang in harmony, in the style of American church choirs. They sang, Treadup wrote, "like meadowlarks." Their favorite hymn was *Chen Mei Ke,* "Lord for Thy Revealing Gifts," set to an ancient lute tune:

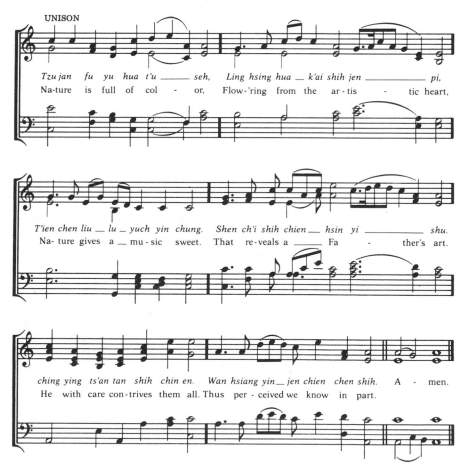

UNISON

Tzu jan fu yu hua t'u _____ seh, Ling hsing hua __ k'ai shih jen _____ pi,
Na-ture is full of col - or, Flow-'ring from the ar-tis - tic heart,

T'ien chen liu __ lu __ yuch yin chung. Shen ch'i shih chien__ hsin yi _____ shu.
Na-ture gives a __ mu-sic sweet. That re-veals a _____ Fa - ther's art.

ching ying ts'an tan shih chin en. Wan hsiang yin__ jen chien chen shih. A - men.
He with care con-trives them all. Thus per-ceived we know in part.

WHILE the Treadups were caught in their backwater eddy—in a strange state, it seemed, of dimmed consciousness—China's larger fate was being speeded up. In October 1934 the Communists under Mao Tse-tung, Chou En-lai, and Chu Teh had broken out of Kiangsi and had begun the astonishing trek that came to be known as the Long March; by July 1935 the force had reached Szechuan Province, in West China, where they were joined by other Communist troops that had been driven by Chiang from Soviet areas north of the Yangtze. The whole force moved on and had adventures worthy of legends. Mao's followers crossed the deep gorge of the Tatu River, in remote West China, crawling over on a bridge of chains anchored at the tops of the rock cliffs on either side of the river's abyss. After a year of forced marches Mao led the wanderers into a barren region of loess land blown down through the centuries from the Gobi Desert.

Chiang Kai-shek, meanwhile, was putting more effort into fighting the Communists than into repelling the Japanese, who were gradually consolidating their de facto control of much of North China. Through an American journalist, Edgar Snow, Mao offered the KMT an end to the civil war and a united front against the Japanese, and Mao wrote two works that were to become basic texts of guerrilla warfare for revolutionary movements for the rest of the century: *On the Tactics of Fighting Japanese Imperialism* and *Strategic Problems in China's Revolutionary War.* Increasingly Chiang's allied forces—particularly the so-called Northeast Army of "Young Marshal" Chang Hsueh-liang, son of the late warlord Chang Tso-lin—urged the Generalissimo to join forces with the Communists to drive out the foreign enemy. Chiang, however, continued to press the fight against the Communists.

IN NOVEMBER, Treadup finally got himself in hand and went to Menghsien to thank Johnny Wu for having persuaded Madame Shen to come to his rescue. "What a lift I always get when I come here!" In a depressed and frightened countryside Treadup found Wu ebullient and optimistic, talking of "a new stage" in the Menghsien work. The experiment had now been going on for seven years; so successful had it proved to be that the central government had taken the idea up, and Wu claimed that there were now some eight hundred rural reconstruction centers scattered through the KMT areas— none so far very effective, Wu said, because they were inadequately staffed and funded. Wu was now excited about the idea of expanding his experiment, which had been focused on a single *hsien,* into a province-wide program, and in spite of the increasing encroachments of the Japanese in Hopei Province, he had begun to make plans with any provincial officials who would listen to him.

WHATEVER stimulus Treadup got from the Menghsien visit seemed to have spent itself pretty quickly. "Getting the habit of napping after lunch," the diary announced. "Setting up a work bench in the back room on the ground floor. Thought I'd build some models for the fun of it—Peking cart, wedding sedan chair, sampan, ect. ect." "Arm not too comfortable." "Believe my stabbing myself with that screwdriver was a case of my old-time 'badness.'" And:

> Em and I been to several American movies in the city, movie house set up by a White Russian fur trader. Some say he's a front for the Japs— softening up the populace. I say, why not enjoy? 'Pasteur' not bad. Last Saturday saw 'White Angel.' Have also managed to see 'David Copperfield,' 'Tale of Two Cities,' 'House of Rothschild,' and a southern mountain feud picture—the first color photography to be shown in these parts. Also a Shirley Temple one, and 'Anna Karenina.'

AT FIVE O'CLOCK in the morning of December 12, 1936, the commander of "Young Marshal" Chang Hseuh-liang's bodyguard, a captain named Sun, roared up in a truck full of soldiers to the gate of a spa in the hot-springs resort of Lintung, ten miles from the northwestern city of Sian, and opened fire. Inside the hotel, which had been cleared of all other guests, Generalissimo Chiang Kai-shek was sleeping; he had come to Sian to order the Northeast Army into action against the Communists. After a brief fight with the Generalissimo's security guards, Captain Sun, soon reinforced by two hundred men of the Northeast Army, broke into the hotel. When they reached the G-mo's bedroom, they found it empty. The window was open. Leading a search party, Sun ran up the snow-covered, rocky hillside behind the hotel. First they found the G-mo's valet, then came on the great man in a hollow hidden by a big rock shivering in the bitter cold, dressed only in a robe over his nightgown, his bare feet cut by his flight up the rough hill. Speaking thickly because he had come away without his false teeth, he said to Sun, "If you are my comrade, shoot me and finish it all." Sun said he would not shoot; he only asked Chiang to lead the country against Japan. Chiang said he would come down if Sun would summon Marshal Chang. Sun said Chang was in Sian, where the Northeast Army was in a state of rebellion; "we came to protect you." The G-mo, greatly relieved, asked for a horse to take him down the hill. Sun said there were no horses around, he would carry the G-mo down on his back; he knelt in front of Chiang. Chiang climbed on the captain's back and rode down the hill.

At the hotel they got in a car and drove off to Sian, where the Young

Marshal held the G-mo captive. Chou En-lai and other Communist leaders came to Sian, and eventually so did numerous KMT officials and Madame Chiang. After much parleying, the captive Generalissimo gave his pledge that he would stop the civil war and join with the Communists in fighting the Japanese, and on Christmas day he was released.

TREADUP'S diary:

> World has heard of dramatic victory symbolized by CKS's release on Christmas day. Everyone around here interprets the whole incident as a proof of Chiang's hold on the nation and of the newly found loyalty of the country to him.

OLD DR. WELLS came down with typhus. Treadup was deeply affected by this simple, kindly old man's illness.

> He is of an age at which a "natural" death might have been expected any day. But now he comes down with this loathsome spotted disease that has been given such low-down names: jail fever, they call it back in Salt Branch, or putrid fever, and here in China it's famine fever. A sickness of the abject and downtrodden. In a way it's missionary fever. Dr. Wells made house calls in the poorest and filthiest slums of the city. If out of charity (in its better sense) you give your heart and time and presence to lousy people, you, too, will be lousy.

On the fifth day of his illness, the doctor died. Emily did all she could for his widow, a frail little woman who would not last long in a world that did not contain her decent husband. And at once the Treadups learned something that shook them. In the Wellses' very first days in Paoting, some time before the Treadups had arrived, they had lost an infant daughter—never mentioned. This was the first the Treadups had ever heard of it. And now Dr. Wells, by his own instructions, was to be buried in a grave alongside the baby's "eternal cradle"—Dr. Wells's words. The funeral was almost unbearable for the Treadups.

> Whenever thoughts of our Nancy cross our minds—and each of us seems to know when the other thinks of her—there is that wall between my beloved Emily and me. My unforgivable absence! We cannot speak to each other about Nancy's grave in Shanghai—the city under the Japanese boot. Will we ever see that tiny headstone again?

A YEARNING FOR HAVOC

ON "DOUBLE FIVE," the fifth day of the fifth month, Chinese calendar, in 1937, the day of the summer festival and Dragon Boat Festival, Treadup, along with the eight American missionaries remaining in Paoting, accepted an invitation to a feast at the headquarters of General Tu Tzu-kwan. This man, who acted as magistrate for a large area around Paoting, was a free-lance commander with vague connections with the Kuomintang; he was immensely popular in the countryside because of his activities as a suppressor of bandits. Several years earlier he had been baptized a Christian, while serving in the army of Treadup's former friend General Feng Yu-hsiang. "His contacts with the church since then," Treadup wrote, "have been spasmodic and superficial, so it is not surprising that he does not know much about what it means to be a Christian." He had discarded a Christian wife and "taken unto himself," as the diary put it, "a modern and handsome young lady as a concubine—the hostess of the banquet and a most attractive one." She had borne the General three daughters and one son, who were all present at the feast.

> *The General is a stout, jovial gentleman who suffers from gout from rich living and has to drug himself to get to sleep at night. He struts about—literally and figuratively—among his guests. He orders his personal attendants around with short commands without a glance at them and always gets immediate and efficient results. He even called on his nine-year-old daughter to bring him a match, strike it, and light a cigarette in his mouth. He took pleasure in reminding us that he was one with us, since he had been baptized a good many years ago. When someone hinted at the fact that he had not been seen at church services within living memory, he replied, "But no one told me when you have them!" I took my courage in hand at that point and said, "We haven't ever sent notices around to any of the church members."*

The General's feast consisted of twenty-five courses, including ducks' tongues, slippery fungus, birds'-nest soup, octopus, and *tsung tzus*, the triangular rice puddings eaten on double five. Afterward the party went out in automobiles to parade before the thousands who were gathered in a great public athletic field by the river. Between aisles of soldiers who held back the commoners, the party was "rushed in our luxury to special places of privilege to watch the performances of these common people (I recognized some from 'my' villages!) who, in the style of past generations and centuries, performed beautiful, skillful, and allegorical feats on stilts or with dragon lanterns or with long cloth festival boats." The women and girls wore artemisia leaves in their hair and hung "tiger" characters on their clothes, to protect them from perils of the season. Whenever the General saw a group at a distance that looked especially promising, he gave a sign to one of his men, and in a moment the soldiers would have a large space cleared right in front of him, and the society or club would run through its stunts for the General. "He looked for all the world like a spoiled child who had a special circus all his own and could call at will for whatever acts he wanted."

COMMENTING on the banquet in a letter to Hank Burrell the next day, Treadup first quoted Charles Stanton of the American Board Mission as having remarked after the feast that it was "disquieting to realize that we were eating exquisitely with one who set his banquets with the accumulated nourishment squeezed from the simple bowls of thousands who live near the starvation level." Treadup went on then to some sharper remarks of his own:

> I have been sad all day, realizing that this General Tu is the KMT's main wheel here. He seems totally unaware of the realities. His China dances on stilts while—as we've read in both Chinese and English newspapers— a Japan to which he shuts his eyes openly plans to build a huge airport not far from here, near a rail junction outside Peiping—quite possibly right in the area of his magistracy. Talk about the ostriches Blackie wrote about! Less than two weeks ago we saw a census report that there are now more than 11,000 Japanese in Tientsin—more than twice as many as six years ago. The Japanese are flooding North China with smuggled articles. We've heard that right on "American Beach," where we often swim in Peitaiho, a small steamer recently beached itself to unload smuggled goods. Everywhere, even in the country markets, are Japanese items for sale. I've seen plenty of them. A Chinese friend said to me, "We can't help ourselves—their goods are being displayed alongside our own—they are cheaper and better—and so what can you expect the poor farmers to do?" He obviously meant equally to criticize his country's neighbor and his own country, China not yet having found ways to meet her own needs without dependence on others. Do you think General Tu would ask such a question? His question is: "Aren't the ducks' tongues delicious?"

IN MID-JUNE Treadup wrote brother Paul that the spring had been so dry that the farmers' crops were being badly burnt out. During a brief downpour the day before he wrote, he and Emily set out pots and buckets and tubs and "practically everything that would hold water except jelly glasses." When the shower had passed, they dumped the water into the house's cistern.

> I don't know whether we even caught a bath's worth. We are almost out of water in the compound except in the bitter wells, and it cost about ten dollars to have one cistern half filled with river water for laundry purposes one day last week. None of us has had a decent tub bath this spring. I heard this week of a deep boring experiment that is being made in North China by some Catholic fathers which may in the course of events make possible a revolution in the water supply of this country. I hope I shan't be dead and gone before it has proven itself.

David told Paul he had had an intestinal upset during part of the previous week. "Except for my arm, I've been as healthy as a brown bear all my life, and I find these little nuisances and 'noyances that I've been having lately very provoking."

EMILY was off in a few days for Peitaiho. Same house; same Baptists in the other half. David hoped to join her for August.

Emily had had the wind taken out of her sails a few days before by the news that Joan Stanton, wife of Charles, was going to have to rush home to the States to take care of her ailing father.

> Em had been counting heavily on Joan's company in the fall. This place is pretty nigh stripped of sensible English-speaking females, what with Titty Selden (and poor Helen Demestrie) gone, and Polly Lassiter with them—may never come back; and Nurse Alice Connor, who is still here, with such a bad mouth. Two or three rather difficult gals remain in the Presbo compound. Some British mesdames in town who wear chokers and gaiters. Sad old Mrs. Wells is going Stateside. In Peitaiho there is a regular garden of ladies, but Em has a bleak autumn to look forward to.

THERE IS a line drawn around Treadup's entry in his diary for July 7, 1937, not because what he did on that day was memorable, but because of the historic event that took place that night. He did not learn about it until the next day.

He had to go to the village of T'u Ti. Because of a downpour after all the drought the roads were swamped, and instead of going by the Indian, he had to ride his bicycle. The man who had come to summon him was able to lead him by detours around the impassable stretches. On the motorcycle on normal roads the trip would have taken forty minutes; that day he biked for six hours. By the time he had dealt with the local crisis it was too late to start back, so he stayed overnight, sleeping in a village inn. To brother Paul:

> *You would have groaned to see me in that filthy hostelry: a carter for my bedmate on a bed consisting of two tables pushed together, a cluttered barnyard outside the open bedroom door, a mule chomping at its grain, the village night guards using the courtyard for headquarters with the usual cursing and laughter at each change of guards through the night. You guessed it: I didn't rest too well—not used to a wooden mattress!*

So much for his day and night. When he got back to the Paoting compound the next afternoon, he found the servants in a panic. It was hard to make out what they were so excited about. They babbled. They wanted to run away to the countryside. Something had come over someone's radio in Chinese about a fight near Peiping between Chinese and Japanese soldiers.

"Dependable news travels here," David wrote Paul a week later,

> *about as slowly as it did back home during the Civil War. You can get a harvest of rumors any time you want, but something to believe—it moves like the inchworm. We get Peiping newspapers from three to six days late. So it has taken nearly a week for me to know that what we have all feared has now started. You probably knew back there from the Syracuse papers the very next morning about the incident at Marco Polo Bridge. Well, the Japanese are making a bold face of it. Having failed to woo the Chinese, they are now going to crush them. I am very low. The Lord's principality of peace has shrunk once again.*

TREADUP had to struggle alone with this new catastrophe. Peitaiho was cut off. Many a day during the three decades of his mission David had been separated from Emily, painfully sometimes for her, sometimes for him; but never had he been unable to rejoin her. "I have had no mail from Em now for two weeks. It is puzzling and upsetting. The last part of the week I finally wired her for news. No answer." The worst of it was that news, when it came, was so unreliable. Treadup recorded in his diary some of the contradictory rumors and bloodthirsty remarks he heard: Peiping captured and occupied by Japanese troops; Tientsin East station reduced to shambles by Chinese bombing; many Japanese planes destroyed and captured by Chinese attack on Tientsin aerodrome. "This situation," a British missionary said, "is getting on my nerves. I dream about it at night—think of the interruption of the missionary work. Did you hear about the street fighting in Peiping and the American Marines that were wounded in it?"—the Britisher gloating a bit at Yank discomfiture. (The report proved false.) Robert Stanton, after hearing a dispatch about the forced landing of a Japanese plane in a storm, with the death of all aboard: "Good! I'm glad to hear it!" The Chinese wife of Dr. Ch'en: "The spirit of the Chinese soldiers is so wonderful. They're not at all afraid of the Japanese and are willing to die resisting them. At Wanping one Chinese soldier in a hand-to-hand encounter cut off one right after another the heads of eight Japanese! That's the bravery they're showing!" At the end of July news came that Tientsin had fallen and that Peikai University had come under heavy bombing and shelling, and had been devastated; no word whether Treadup's old and dear friend Mr. Lin had survived the attack. But worst of all, no news—not a word—from the seashore.

NOW CAME a flood—not of waters but of humanity. By cart, on donkeys, by ricksha, by sedan chair, by bicycle, on ponies, by sampan, and even by camelback, but mostly trudging on foot, the refugees came—men, women, and children, in panic so deep that that most tenacious of Chinese cultural traditions, the need to leave to posterity decent holdings so that one could be revered as an honorable ancestor, even that had been forgotten; all property save a few miserable bundles had been abandoned. The mission compound became a campground. All of Treadup's energies went into setting up and finding supplies for a food kitchen, and arranging to have water carts bring water from the river, and keeping fires going to boil water for drinking, and organizing a first-aid station and hospital tent for the hurt and the sick. One day's entire entry in the diary: "I worked thirty hours today."

ON AUGUST 9 a messenger came to the compound from the U.S. consulate: Word had come from Mrs. Treadup in Peitaiho that she was safe, all was quiet there.

David thereafter wrote her a letter every day, and sent a servant to post it in the city.

ON FRIDAY the thirteenth, as Treadup eventually learned, the Japanese began violent bombing and shelling of Shanghai. The onslaught, then, was going to be a general one, against all of China. Treadup wrote in his diary: "I have been thinking about what Jenser"—the British missionary—"said about the interruption of our work. I, too, have begun to lose sleep over it. When will I be able to get to my villages? Will we ever see 'normal times' again?"

THE DIARY, on the twentieth:

> *All Emily's postals and letters — nineteen of them! — miracle! — got to me at suppertime yesterday. Also a letter from Paul back home! Think of it: full-scale war going on, and the mail gets through. This is China. And so my supper last night was a real feast — lasted two hours.*

Emily's letters gave a bizarre picture — a mixture of crisis and things-as-usual. In one paragraph would be word of a baseball game between the male missionaries and the crew of the American gunboat *Tulsa*, which was anchored offshore; the sailors won, 21-2, and "had such a good time they're coming back to play next Wednesday." In the next paragraph:

> *Scads of troop trains run through Peitaiho Junction down from Shanhaikuan every day. And it seems that every day over the Western Hills — East Heaven, West Heaven, Buddha's Tooth — we see vee after vee of bombing planes going down toward Tientsin: I hope, dear God, not toward Paoting.*
>
> *Renewal of foodstuffs for us in Peitaiho is being handled via an emergency committee cooperating with compradors to get stuff in from Dairen by boat. So far no real difficulty — a brief butter shortage which is now relieved.*

One letter brought the news that Emily had been sneezing and coughing for three weeks. She had thought at first that she was catching cold, but

> *I have had to face it that for the first time in my life I have a bad case of hay fever. The fields are spangled with pinks and buttercups and bachelor's buttons — nature's beauty is my nemesis all of a sudden. Yesterday was rainy, a relief — rained down, up, and sideways all day. But today the west wind is back and I'm stuffy and sneezy again. Why in the world should I suddenly get this infirmity at my age?*

In another letter:

> *Now has come dejecting news. Embassy advices by radio are for everyone to stay put whose business is not urgent or imperative elsewhere. How long, my Davie? Will I be stuck here in cold weather? These houses aren't fit for winter occupancy. Most all of the native shops open for summer trade have packed off. I managed to buy wool stockings, etc., enuf stuff for the first cool weeks.*

ONE MORNING early in September Treadup was wakened by what sounded
to him like a distant roar of airplanes. He jumped out of bed and took a large
American flag he had been keeping ready for this purpose up through a
trapdoor onto the roof and spread it out there. Not five minutes later he heard
the low thumps of bursting bombs; they seemed to be from the direction of
the city and off to the north of the compound. He saw the planes—so high in
the sky the pilots would never have seen his flag.

That evening:

> *Damage in town. Mr. and Mrs. Randolph [he an employe of the British
> trading firm, Jardine Matheson] were killed in rickshas right in front of
> the Hong Kong-Shanghai Bank office—hurrying home—ricksha pullers
> of course also killed. A bomb landed in the Presbo compound, not too
> much damage. They say two or three hundred innocent Chinese nobodies
> were killed in the city. The story in our compound is that where there
> was a crowded refugee camp this morning there is now—NOTHING &
> NOBODY. Empty. Not a single soul of all the refugees is left. Off they've
> gone again, human rockets propelled by blind fear. To where? Back
> home? Farther south? Poor China! Poor China!*

The next day—for the first time in his writings—we see the word
"Japanese" abbreviated:

> *Being angry gives me stomach trouble. Today my bowels gripe at my
> hypocritical countrymen, who made yesterday's death & mayhem pos-
> sible by selling scrap iron and oil to the Japs.*

ON SEPTEMBER 12 David received an urgent letter from Emily, saying
that the officers of the *Tulsa* had been repeatedly urging the American women
in Peitaiho to heed the advice from Washington to get out of the country. The
day before, the *Tulsa*'s captain had convened all the Americans in the resort
and had told them that a U.S. Navy ship was going to make connections down
south with the *President McKinley*, which would be sailing for Manila—
would they go or not? He had been, Emily wrote, "very scornful of our
indecision. He talked to us like swabs." The ladies were of course in a
quandary; they said they couldn't make such a decision without help from
their husbands and without official advice from the U.S. Mission in Peiping.
"What am I supposed to do?" Emily bleakly asked.

The morning after he got the letter David set off for Peiping on a
cart—the rail line had been cut north of the city. The road was clogged with an
opposing current of refugees and Chinese soldiers—the latter shambling

along in disordered flight from an enemy that was said to be approaching three li up the road; but who could trust the rumors? David's cartman had a good strong mule, which shouldered its way pertinaciously forward against the human stream. No enemy. When night fell, David slept on the cart; he was chilled—"I think my gizzard may never thaw out." He reached Peiping the next evening, having seen no sign of advancing Japanese, though there were Japanese guards at the city gates. Fortunately he had brought his passport. "I was hissed at, bowed to, ignored, yammered at in Japanese—I am going to study the language this year!—and finally was waved through."

He went straight to the United States Legation and there learned that that very day there had been a meeting of all the leading missionaries in Peiping, and they had "decided unanimously and emphatically that this was not a time when it was either necessary or fitting to talk about going away. How could they think of abandoning their Chinese Christian friends?" The Minister himself had given his opinion that the advice from Washington was not intended for people in the coastal cities but rather for missionaries in isolated interior places—"devotees" who were unfortunately in the habit of ignoring warnings of this kind anyway. As to the ladies at Peitaiho, the counsel was to get them as soon as possible to Tientsin or Peiping, where, at least for the present, foreigners were not being molested.

PAOTING was captured by the Japanese, according to Treadup, "after a short drumming of artillery fire which killed only innocents." The night after the city's fall he wrote:

Our upbringing is such that we enjoy seeing the underdog put up a good fight. When one has been working with the Chinese for decades for the reconstruction of their country and has seen the miraculous changes that I have seen since 1905, every military success of the Japanese, especially if it is as easy as the one today was, comes as a heart stab. I find myself daily waiting for news that the Chinese have wiped out a Japanese army. I would rejoice at such news.

But I find a restraint on these emotions. I am not the pure pacifist, perhaps not the pure Christian, I once thought I was. I know that the Japanese army is bent on victory. Only frightful destruction of life and property will make that victory possible. I know that the greater the resistance, the greater will be the destruction—the more diabolical will be the means to victory, the more lies will have to be told, the greater hatred will have to be engendered. But I want that dangerous resistance. I find myself yearning for the havoc and bloodshed and lies and hatred—if only the Japanese can be frustrated. Alas, to judge by today, they will not be. China is caving in.

BOOK SEVEN

CAVERN OF

DISAPPOINTMENT

"STUBBORN MISSIONARIES"

TREADUP sat at breakfast on the third morning after the capture of the city. He had cooked some eggs himself. All three of the Treadup servants had left the day before—had joined the hordes of wanderers on the roads. "I could hardly blame them—two have families in Shansi, one in Shantung."

There was a banging at the door of the house. Answering, Treadup found Ting, the compound gateman, standing on the porch with three Japanese in uniform behind him. Ting was in a fury because he had lost face. The Japanese had not honored his command to wait at the gate. Treadup held up his hand to the Japanese, in a stopping gesture, and invited Ting into the house and asked for an explanation of what had happened. This parley gave face back to the gateman. Treadup then returned to the front door and asked one of the three Japanese, who was obviously an officer, what they wanted.

The officer sucked in his breath, bowed, and in fair English apologized for the misunderstanding. Was this Mr. David Treadup?

It was.

All three sucked. All three bowed. The officer apologized again.

What did they want?

Might they come in and talk?

No.

Suck. Bow. Apology. Mr. Treadup was the Y.M.C.A. secretary in Paoting? Yes?

No.

Formal confusion. No?

Used to be. Not now.

The trio were extremely sorry.

Did they have a little list of who everybody was?

Suck.

What did they want?

"I gather," Treadup wrote that day in a letter to Hank Burrell in Shanghai,

that Japanese discourse requires a great deal of hesitation and indirection—a matter of courtesy. I, however, was not feeling courteous, and unfortunately the blunter I got, the slower the cogs moved the wheels in Nipponese heads. But finally I wormed out of them that they wanted to rent the Association building in the city. I was amazed and shocked by the intelligence work they had obviously done in advance of their invasion.

Treadup told Burrell that he explained—clearly and forcefully, he thought —that he had no authority to speak for the Y.M.C.A., because he had been sacked some while back. However, he did know that as a religious and philanthropic institution, interested in education, health, and religious nurture, the Y was neutral as to military sympathies. Thus it would have to take the same attitude toward the Japanese authorities as it always had toward the Chinese. The Association had always refused the Chinese military any use of its building, so it must also refuse the Japanese. Naturally, having been sacked, he could not give a formal reply; but he would be glad to ask the National Committee of the Y.M.C.A. in Shanghai for such a reply.

There was now much sucking of breath. "It was as if the heat of their effrontery had become caught in their teeth." Finally a threat came oozing out. The Japanese army did not want to make a forcible occupation of the building, the officer said; they would much prefer to make a contract to pay rent for use of the building.

Treadup said he could only ask Shanghai for instructions. On account of "certain disturbances," it might take some time for mail to get through.

Paoting, the officer said, was a small and crowded city. Suitable buildings for housing troops were very scarce. Probably the military would be "compelled" to use the Y.M.C.A. building. The branch that wanted the building was aviation. The aviators were highly trained men who would be more careful of the premises than regular army personnel.

Shanghai would have to decide. Now would the gentlemen from Japan please leave the American compound? Or would it be necessary to be in touch with the American consulate to get them out?

The bowing!

Besides, they had interrupted their host's breakfast.

The apologies!

To Burrell:

So they left. I'm afraid I didn't meet too well the test of my Christianity those three men in uniform put me through. You can understand, Hank, that I'm a bit tender about being asked to dicker for the Association from my "limbo," as New York would have it. But for auld lang syne I'd be glad to. Since you have no real choice, what is your decision?

The letter bore a postscript, marked "That evening":

You have less choice than I thought. Our friends have moved into the building. Now what?

THE COMPOUND was full of refugees again, twelve hundred by Treadup's count. He had become, once again, a camp official. On a trip into the city to find bags of millet, he saw a parade of Chinese schoolchildren, with their teachers, carrying rising-sun flags and banners welcoming the Japanese.

Here: one of the lies I was writing about the other night. Their childish faces told the truth behind the lie, and it was bitter—for the faces were blank—showed nothing—and to me that very blankness, so unusual for these expressive children, evidenced their misery, shame, anger that their teachers had let them be coerced into such a humiliating charade.

YOUNG DR. CH'EN at the hospital sent his wife and little daughter away to the south to rejoin her family. He was afraid to have them go off by themselves on such a dangerous journey, but he knew that leaving his job at the hospital would have a bad effect on the morale of the other Chinese doctors and the Chinese nurses. Treadup learned that after many anxious days Dr. Ch'en got a letter from his wife, describing how their train had been bombed, one car wrecked. She and the little girl had been in another car and were unhurt. They had finally reached home safely.

Treadup wrote Emily:

Dr. Ch'en said to me, "I never realized before how much difference being or not being Christian makes. After going through the bombings here—

*and the Japanese coming in—and finding that the Christian doctors
and nurses were the only ones who stayed by, I understand how different Christians are. 'Do unto others...' What strength that rule
gives!"*

*I read in a Peiping paper, which somehow reached here yesterday,
that President Roosevelt had had some harsh words for "stubborn
missionaries" who wouldn't leave the war zones when they were told to.
But these Chinese Christians give us no option. How could we possibly
leave them?*

BY LETTER the Treadups in early October more or less agreed—there was
much agonizing on both sides—that with the cold weather coming on Emily
should move from Peitaiho not to Paoting, where things were still too shaky,
but to the relative security of Tientsin. Without telling her he was going to do
so, David went to get her; he did not want her to have to travel alone. Rail
service from Paoting to Peiping, and from there to Tientsin and the shore, had
been restored, though with many delays along the way.

Stopping over in Tientsin he arranged for Emily to live indefinitely with
a Mrs. Evenrude, the widow of an American businessman. After her husband's
death this lady had chosen to stay on in China, where her standard of
living—a comfortable home in the British Concession, five servants, a carriage and two horses—was much higher than it would have been back in the
States. Although she had never met Mrs. Treadup, she said she welcomed the
prospect of some company in her big house; she offered Emily "a large, sunny
room looking out on an umbrella tree."

Treadup reached the beach early on a Tuesday afternoon and "surprised
Em to tears." He learned that a special car was being arranged for a whole
party of people to travel to Tientsin at the end of the week, so he had "in this
lovely, peaceful place a few days of a Paradise which seemed quite unreal after
Paoting. I can *feel* the joy of thought-free past days in the summers here."

They packed up. Treadup found that his best summer white suit had
turned yellow from alternately growing damp in a closet and then being hung
out to be sunned. "I can be philosophical about chattels when a country
is falling apart." The getaway was "the easiest we have ever had from
Peitaiho. There were not the usual wild crowds of folks hiring baggage carts
and rickshas."

Mrs. Evenrude was waiting up for the Treadups in her house in Tientsin
at four o'clock in the morning.

WHEN TREADUP got back to Paoting, he found that a tactful letter had
arrived from Hank Burrell. Treadup was a brick, Burrell wrote, to offer to

dicker with the Japanese for the return of the Association building, "despite the anomaly of your position as a retiree. You're a good sport, old man." (The diary: "I didn't exactly retire!") One fortunate bit of news, in case David would be willing to go forward with the bothersome business, was that negotiations between the International Committee in New York and the National Committee in Shanghai for transfer of title of the Paoting building to the Chinese had never been completed, so the building was still in fact American-owned.

On a Friday Treadup inspected the Y building. He found several windows broken and a radio receiver smashed.

He then called on the Japanese consul, a Mr. Nakagawa. Mr. N said that anti-Japanese documents had been found in the building, and that since the Y.M.C.A. would therefore not be allowed to resume its activities, the organization might as well let the aviators stay there. Rent would be paid.

Treadup said perhaps Mr. N should reflect upon what he had said. A Japanese military unit had seized American property. The Y.M.C.A. did not choose to rent the building to anyone, and if the aviators did not vacate at once, Treadup would have no choice but to report the matter to the U.S. Legation in Peiping, for instructions from Washington as to whether the U.S. response should be military or diplomatic.

Mr. N repeated his whole rigmarole, as if his prominent ears had not trapped a single word of what I had said. So I repeated my spiel. Deadlock. So Mr. N said the single word, "Sunday."

Treadup returned on Sunday, only to have Mr. N say exactly what he had said on Friday, adding only that the Japanese military had not been able to find any other property as suitable to their purposes as the Y building. Treadup then said the Y.M.C.A. would give the Japanese military authorities three days — until Wednesday — to get out. After that it would be necessary to refer the matter to Washington. Mr. N said, "Ah!" In that case, it would be necessary for Mr. Teddy (as Treadup's letters to Burrell said all the Japanese seemed to think he was named) to speak with the military.

I was sent to a Colonel Harimura — under forty years of age, hair short, a small Hitler's mustache, a sloping posture, beautiful teeth displayed in a fixed smile, the usual green uniform, and a nervous sort of impetuous spirit.

Talking through an interpreter, Colonel H said that the aviators had occupied the building because they had found evidence that anti-Japanese activities had been carried on there.

Treadup said the Japanese military had violated American property.

Colonel H said the aviators had had no way of knowing it was American property.

Treadup said an American flag was on the flagpole at the time, and their aviators had taken it down.

Colonel H said that even in the Japanese army some noncommissioned officers and enlisted men were ignorant, and strangers to foreign affairs.

> Then the needle got stuck on the record again. The Peace Preservation Committee [rubric of the Chinese puppets who were now supposedly running the city] would not allow the Y.M.C.A. to resume its work. Why not rent? Since repetition seemed to be the order of the day, I repeated my (hollow, for all I knew) ultimatum: I would give them three days.

The very next morning another colonel surprised Treadup by calling on him at the compound. He arrived on horseback. This one was named Sasaki. He said he had been in Tientsin for some years and was familiar with the Y.M.C.A. He was a well-formed man—all but his legs, which were severely bowed, as if he and horses were symbiotic; he was friendly, and he spoke good English. He asked if it would be agreeable if the aviators surrendered a few offices for Y.M.C.A. secretaries to use, and then went on occupying the rest of the building. Treadup said it most certainly would not. Colonel S then repeated this request, in much the same words, three or four times. (The diary: "Perhaps the Japanese hope they can bore China to death by means of repetition and so dominate it.") Treadup was adamant.

Then suddenly Colonel S said the Y.M.C.A. could have its building back on November 1.

FROM A LETTER in mid-November to brother Paul:

> I have recently had the coveted opportunity of meeting some Communists. It was not in the dreaded form of bandits or Red troops that I met them. Rather, I had heard they were undertaking rural work of some kind, which might penetrate "my" villages, and I sought them out.
>
> I was astonished that with all the danger from both Japanese and KMT directions, they met me perfectly openly in a small restaurant in the city. There were four of them. Two of the four said they were Christians, one having been intimately identified with the Oxford Group. One of the non-Christians appealed to me especially—the gleam of eye at meeting and parting contained great depth of warmth and feeling—he thanked me for all I had done in the villages. Two had been teachers in a university, one was a graduate student in sociology, and the other was a college graduate working in the area of agronomy.
>
> They told me that with the Japanese occupation of Peiping and

Tientsin, students from the great universities there had been making their way southward. For many the most trying experience had been at the Tientsin railway station, where passengers off the trains from Peiping were subject to be picked out for cross-examination and had to answer "No" with great sincerity to the question whether they were anti-Japanese. If they were lucky enough to get by there, they traveled by foreign steamers to Chefoo, then by bus on to Tsingtao or Tsinan. An outfit called the Peiping-Tientsin Refugee Student Association was distributing them to Nanking, Kaifeng, Sian, Hankow, and Shanghai. Many were joining the Communists. Hundreds are flocking to the Eighth Route Army for military training. Others are enlisting in rural teams like the one I met with.

I was warmly attracted to these new acquaintances—they are earnest, idealistic, unselfish, honest, determined—determined to get something done for others. The two Christians will get it done within the church as far as they can, but it is more important to them, I gathered, to bring economic justice to the poor than it is to stay with the church.

In his diary, that night, Treadup made a confession he had evidently not been able to bring himself to make to his brother:

Since my conversation with my new friends, I have felt something like fear. Two reasons for it: For one thing, I had a sneaking feeling that I had been taken in. They seemed so decent. Yet I have heard such terrible stories of the ruthlessness of the Communists, where it serves their ends. Including executions, and worse. Were they toying with me, those two "Christians"? But the second thing was what really shook me. It had hit me—nothing they said directly—just an obvious inference—and scared me precisely because it had never occurred to me—and should have—long since. The work I've done in the villages has been valuable enough, but I have never touched the roots. There can never be real change without getting at them. I have been scratching the surface. I have been as blind as the illiterates.

EARLY IN DECEMBER Treadup finally took a trip to some of the villages—Li Chia, Shao T'an, Ho Chao, Ch'en Ts'un. He was shocked by two kinds of devastation. There had been a Japanese "punitive expedition" through part of the area; crops had been burned, houses wrecked. And during the Japanese advance numerous dikes had been cut here and there by both sides, and hundreds of mou of land were now caked with dried mud.

That night:

My heart is so heavy. So long kept from my "true" work, I had gone out
with what I thought was a new—if somewhat grim—determination to
go deeper, probe, renew. But no! Dreadful setbacks. Now there was only
the most elemental sort of problem for the villagers: e.g., how to get the
donkey to Paoting to sell it for enough grain to live through a month or
two without starving.

ON THE SAME DAY in December two letters came. One was from Farrow
Blackton in New York congratulating David for his "masterful negotiation" on
behalf of the Paoting Y.M.C.A. and thanking him for having "such a large and
stalwart heart." The other was a round-robin letter from Appleton Sills in
Nanking, who thought that all the world should know in as much detail as
possible about "the appalling, the bestial, the orgiastic, the lust-mad, the
cretinous, the debauched, the bloodthirsty entry of Japanese troops into
Nanking." Sills told, in a long series of hair-raisingly concrete pictures, an
almost unbearable story of murder, rape, looting, arson, drunkenness, and
wanton destruction.

The diary:

I find myself in a peculiar nervous state that I don't know how to
describe—nothing that approaches jitters, not fidgets, certainly not
touchiness—perhaps just plain excitement, accentuated by these two
letters—I am a grand fellow and the Japanese are animals—shocks to
the sense of God's order—to say nothing of uncertainties of comings
and goings, Em's absence, wonderment about future work, the necessity
for unusual decisions, and a slipping hope that the whole world is not
going mad.

LOVE YOUR ENEMIES

"THE DREAM of the literacy that would change China!"

Treadup's bitter line stood alone in the diary. He had made another trip
to some of his villages, near which there was a Japanese encampment. The
next entry:

Could you call homes those empty houses in whose walls yawn great
vacant holes from which doors and windows and even their frames have

*been torn out and burned, along with all the furniture and farm carts
and tools? Ruthless Jap soldiers run in packs like wild dogs, hunting
for women and money and food—and above all for fuel. The invading
soldiery seem to feel the North China cold very keenly. They chop down
cemetery trees. Wardrobes and chests that are heirlooms they smash
into firewood. Bags of grain they take away or feed to their horses.
It is only what soldiers of any country would do, perhaps, and what
victims of war have always had to suffer, since Homer's time. But take
the village of Ku Chuan—now a ghost hamlet of these hollow shells, its
entire population fled as if from a mythic plague—here we had put
seventeen males and nine females all the way through the reading
program; the people had built in the fields six communal wells with
Inventor Wang's improved dumping device; they had introduced hybrid
pigs and white Leghorns; they had planted red date trees; they had—
O, at what cost of hard work!—fabricated at least a glimmer of hope.
All gone—the pigs, the hens, the well buckets—the people—the hope.*

WITHIN the city walls of Paoting, things were relatively stable. Right after
the fall of the city, Charles Stanton, who, Treadup wrote, "has held on to the
purity of his pacifism better than I have—the man just doesn't have an ohm of
anger in him," had gone into the city and, as a friendly neutral, had persuaded
the Chamber of Commerce and other influential Chinese groups to go with
him to the Japanese commandant, with an offer to organize what he called an
Ad Interim Committee of Safety. ("*Id est,*" Treadup wrote, "the Ad Interim
Varsity Squad of Puppets.") Through the touchy days of takeover, this committee managed to hold together a semblance of law and order in the town; rape,
arson, and looting were kept to minimums. Treadup learned that the Chinese
secretaries had taken back the Y.M.C.A. building, but that they were not
allowed by the Japanese to do anything.

AT THE COMPOUND GATE there was now a sign with big black Chinese
characters: "Refuge for Women and Children."

After each Japanese punitive raid in the countryside, usually in retalia-
tion for a guerrilla attack by one of the many roaming bands of Chinese
soldiers, panicky villagers came flocking in: frightened, exhausted women,
with a desperate-looking husband or brother wearily pushing an old wheelbarrow of miserable bedding. "The women fill the compound, because we *have* to
protect them, even in this frigid weather, from the frightful heat that conquest
puts in an invading army's loins—dreadful stories every day of women and
young girls stripped naked and forced by whole squads of Japs—so, the place
being jammed, the husbands and brothers have to be turned away—to go

where?" With comings and goings there was a constant tally in the compound of some sixteen hundred women and children. They slept in the houses, in the chapel, in the hospital corridors, in the schoolrooms, in the laboratories, huddled together, on meager quilted bedding spread over thin straw, on boards laid across desks and benches, or even on the brick floors, in the sharp cold.

I feel almost ashamed even to walk across the yards. The women bow to me.

A good part of my time since lunch this noon has been spent in routing out men who have insisted on jumping over the walls into the compound; there are several vulnerable spots, and though we keep watchmen at the worst places, some men get in anyway. In the daytime they can be led to the gate, but it is a different story at night. So far the largest number I have found is five (tonight, after dark), and the remedy is to put them on duty with the enlarged staff of watchmen. They are delighted. We will kick them out in the morning.

A LETTER from brother Paul told David that on the night of February 8, 1938, their mother had passed away peacefully in her sleep, at the age of eighty-four, in her own bed in the Salt Branch apartment. Paul was worried about sister Grace, who had given her whole self, in the last fifteen years, to taking care of Mother.

It is as if poor Grace has been suddenly and unreasonably fired from a job she had been doing so very well. She's angry and confused. Write her, Davie. She always loved you best.

DAVID felt an overwhelming need to be with his wife. He wrote her that he felt like a traitor leaving the Paoting compound just then, but

I have to check in with our benefactress, Mme Shen, to see whether she feels in present circumstances she can think to go on subsidizing me, when all possibility of rural reconstruction is out the window. And I can also justify my trip by going to see the Protestant War Relief people in Peiping, for I desperately need money for food for my villages. I will steal three or four days in Tientsin.

He spent two whole days getting passes from the United States and Japanese consulates, and from the Japanese military commandant in Paoting — the last of these with the help of Colonel Sasaki, who was now extremely friendly. He was then able to travel to Peiping by train. There is no record of his session with Madame Shen beyond a laconic note in his diary: "Mme S as gracious as her purse is bottomless." She evidently did not advance him cash this time, but assured him of her continued support. He presented his case to the war-relief office and was told that so far only cabled pledges were in hand; the committee was "trying on the Q.T.," the diary noted, "to arrange some bank loans against those pledges. They told me to come back Friday. Perfect. Off to Tientsin."

He found Emily

ragged and thin — reminded me of the way she was in Montclair when I got back from France. Mrs. Evenrude is most generous but makes her generosity felt. I have tried to tell Em how much the refugees and the villagers both need me, but she says she can't help being resentful that for so much of the time we've been in North China she and I (except for occasional short stretches at Peitaiho which have been anything but real vacations) have had to have most of our fun, as far as relaxing play and human relationships outside home and work are concerned, separately. For a time she had to stay at home while I was "out there in civilization," but now she's having a concentrated dose of so-called civilized life while I'm having concentrated work. She doesn't think it's the way things ought to be. She thinks she — not I — should be right there in the compound with the women, and I out in my villages. She's right, of course — as right as Mother, in her different way, always was — but just now I think things are still too dangerous. I've persuaded her to think about Peitaiho for the summer, and then, if things are quiet, back with me in Paoting.

On Friday Treadup turned up at the Protestant War Relief office in Peiping, and to his delight he was at once handed one thousand dollars Mex in bills of various denominations, to be used for relief of the villages near Paoting. He borrowed a money belt from a British missionary named Burgardy, put it on under his clothes, and caught a train for home.

ABOUT AN HOUR south of Peiping, the train stopped at a small town. After a long wait, an attendant came through the cars, telling passengers that guerrillas had broken the line beyond this town, and that the train would have to return to Peiping. Treadup decided to get off and make his way onward to Paoting by whatever means he could find.

As he stood outside the station in the main street, the usual crowd gathered: Such a very big-nose! With such a beautiful suitcase! Presently a not particularly well dressed man pushed forward through the crowd and introduced himself as a Christian. His name was P'eng. He suggested that the best way to travel would be by ricksha. Two rickshas would be best, one for the *mu-shih*, one for his valise; then the pullers could spell each other. Mr. P'eng had a donkey and would be honored to guide the *mu-shih* on his way. It would take two and a half days to reach Paoting; they could spend the first night in a *hsien* town, the second in a large village.

Treadup agreed to this arrangement, and Mr. P'eng magically produced two ricksha pullers at once, who, Treadup guessed, may have been relatives of his.

Off they went. It was windy and cold; by good fortune one of the ricksha pullers had a fur-lined rug in the box under the seat of his vehicle. The little caravan reached the *hsien* town after dark. The city gates were closed. The Christian shouted to the guards within through the crack between the gates; the guards told the party it must go around to one of the other gates in the wall. Mr. P'eng pleaded and finally persuaded the guards to run off to Japanese headquarters to ask for the key to this gate. Finally the gate was opened. Treadup produced his many passes and papers to a Japanese officer. After much discussion the party was admitted to the town. They slept overnight in a Chinese inn.

At dawn they went on. The going was rough, and over one stretch Treadup had to hire two extra men from the country to push the rickshas. When they were about thirty li from Paoting, they were stopped by three armed men.

As Treadup told the story in a letter to Emily:

The leader was a thin, pale, languid man with trembling hands. He ordered the other two to search my Christian friend, P'eng, from head to toe; then they tore up the rickshas, as if they were convinced we had hidden loot in them. They paid little attention to me until the last. Then while two of them puzzled and puzzled over the lock to my suitcase, the head man went over me with evident inexpertness but equally evident determination. In the keen cold he was sweating, and he kept emitting a sound halfway between a groan and a song. He found a few of my own personal dollars in my pants pocket and—with a falsetto cry of triumph— the relief funds amounting to one thousand dollars in the money belt under my clothing. Well, that was that. I could most easily have turned his gun onto this careless thin chap as he went over me. In fact he was so heedless that his nervous hands shoved the pistol in my face several times. I simply pushed it aside—he didn't mind. He laughed once when I did it. We each seemed to know that neither he nor I would kill, but when I told him the money in the belt was for the relief of poor villagers, he became wildly angry, and I thought he might do something foolish. Mr. P'eng was a hero. He used all his wisdom and wiles to try to tease them out of the business. He pretty nearly passed out with grief when he saw them going over me. He went through agony of soul—he suffered. He said he feared that the experience would affect my nerves and upset me, and he said he was covered with shame that compatriots of his would perpetrate this on a foreigner who was trying to help his starving countrymen. I was indeed upset — about the men, because Mr. P'eng had learned that they were opium addicts and had done this because they were slaves to their habit. Their wonderful haul of more than a thousand dollars could only plunge them deeper into their mortification. Of course I also ground my teeth for my villagers — to think of the relief that that amount of money could not now give!

The party reached Paoting the next afternoon. Treadup paid off the ricksha men and in an excess of gratitude gave Mr. P'eng his precious Mount of Olives Bible, which he had had since boyhood. Mr. P'eng could not conceal his disappointment at the nature of this gift.

D A V I D wrote Emily:

I had a terrible dream last night. It was about the death of our poor little Nancy. I was there this time, beside her cradle, and you were the one who had left us. Then it felt as if I was the one in the cradle — my mother was rocking me. O Em, I hate these separations! I wonder if I was right about Peitaiho for you.

O U T C A M E the black silk bag from Emily's underwear drawer. Treadup took out two hundred dollars Mex, and with the help of Ting, the compound gateman, he went shopping for bagged millet in the city. This was no easy task, because the Japanese had commandeered all the grain they could find. "I looked the other way while Ting bribed. He beamed with joy at the discovery that the Japanese are just as bribable as his own nationals." Within two days there was a sizable stack of bags of grain locked in the compound storeroom.

David wrote brother Paul:

Ask your church to take up a collection for us. You'd be amazed how far an American dollar will go here. Did I tell you that I had $25 from Frank Thurlough of my Syracuse class? And we received $4 from the missionary society of a New Hampshire church. These are not absurd gifts. They do their work. Exchange rates now make $1 U.S. equal to $6 Mex (or Chinese currency), and $6 will keep two refugees in this compound for a whole month. You in America can't believe that, I know, but that's because Americans, in spite of Depression and unemployment and all that, don't know what a low standard of living is. We just can't conceive poverty as the Orient knows it. Ten cents Chinese money a day for food (less than 2 cents U.S.) is more than we spend here in the compound *per day per person. That gives not just a starvation diet, but enough rice and green vegetables and beans to nourish people.*

But Treadup's millet was not for the compound; it was for his villages. "Through surreptitious means"—did this mean through the help of some of his literacy volunteers?—Treadup put together a group of eighteen ex-students, who "appeared from nowhere" and somehow had acquired a few pistols, to be an escorting guard for the millet on the way out to the country. It took two whole days to dicker for transportation—two large two-wheeled hauling carts, each with two mules in tandem, for the grain, and two Peking carts with one mule each, to carry the men. Ting, who had handled these negotiations, said they had taken so long not because the cartmen were afraid to go into the country but because they were suspicious. "They know," Ting said, "that we Christians have the defect of being honest." In other words, the bargaining was over "squeeze money."

"THIS IS not an easy life," David wrote in midsummer to Emily, who was back in Peitaiho, which the American authorities considered safe for the time being. David moved from village to village, searching out his former literacy teachers and "Mass Education Secretaries," to set up a network of relief stations. "Two meals of steaming yellow millet porridge each day—not a 'balanced diet,' not even an appetizing one for weeks on end—but it will keep many from starving—for now." He and his old friends among the villagers organized a meager source of income: "Old and young, men and women, boys and girls, squatting on their haunches in courtyards, on doorsteps, in alleyways, on the roads, all alike weaving reed mats of the kind universally used in the homes of North China." Finished mats were loaded on the carts to be sold in Paoting.

Treadup was "living Chinese"—wearing Chinese clothes and himself subsisting on the crudest of diets.

The weather is hot, flies are ubiquitous, and insects that prey on the human body are unavoidable. Physically, nervously, and spiritually I find my energies called upon to the maximum. Eats are not of the best. I try to be doubly careful about contaminated food. Sleep is not long and it's on beds of boards inhabited by fleas who are not on a starvation diet, I can testify. Mosquitoes also. Travel by day is long and tiring.

The people are awake to the fact that the drama is on, and though as yet they don't see clearly what their parts are to be, they are in it. The ground is prepared for the theme of fear, hate, and revenge. All are rising to the call, especially the young people from about twelve years and up. It is awful—appalling in its promise.

ON HIS EARLIER TRIPS into the country, Treadup had not seen a single soldier. This time, when his route took him more than ten or twelve miles from the railroad line, he sometimes encountered two kinds of resisters, often hidden away during the daytime by villagers—mobile units of the Chinese army and Communist guerrillas. Recruits of both kinds seemed to be interchangeable—"former soldiers left behind by retreating armies, bandits, farmers, youths who could not return to their schools or colleges, youngsters eager to 'do their bit.' " They were indistinguishably brave, dedicated, and deeply touching. He saw one group of boys from twelve to sixteen, calling itself "The First Line Youth Corps," marching along in the dust, singing "lusty, martial airs. I remember no songs of World War days that were of such deeply avenging emotion." But, he wrote, "look at their faces, and your heart shakes for these lonely, frightened, hungry, mangy, flea-bitten children who have become separated from their mothers."

ON THE TWELFTH DAY the caravan of carts, loaded with reed mats, was making its way back toward Paoting, when, about fifteen li from the city, it encountered a wave of frightened women and children. Treadup learned from some of them, as more and more came along the road, that a Japanese unit of military police had entered the American Board compound early that morning, had declared the refugee camp "illegal," and had driven the occupants out. None had been molested, but the women had had no way of carrying their bedding and other possessions, so had had to come away just as they were, with the clothes on their backs. And they had no idea where to go.

Treadup turned them around and told them to follow him. Soon he had a troop of more than a thousand women and children walking along behind the carts.

Now came the gateman, Ting, galloping on a donkey. He had come out to find T'ao Tu Hsien-sheng. He was wild. He said that Sze Tan Hsien-sheng (Charles Stanton) and Ch'a No Nai-nai (Nurse Alice Connor) had both been called away to Peiping on separate errands, and the Japanese, apparently knowing through informers that there were no foreigners in the compound, had chosen that time to come and break up the camp. They had not touched the refugee women, but after the campers were all out, they had bound the hands and feet of Ting and the Chinese servants and hospital personnel in the compound (Dr. Ch'en among them), and had ransacked all the buildings.

From a letter to Emily:

I went to the hospital first, because Ting had said that was the worst scene. The unattended patients all hysterical, and things strewn about in hideous disorder. The dispensary was the worst, they'd obviously been looking for drugs — bottles and vials open and broken, pills and powders flung around. And gifts of mercy from faraway countries, tokens of the idea that there might still be such a thing as friendliness on this earth — great boxes of fresh white bandages, cut and folded and rolled by women in Holland, and cartons of towels and hospital clothing from Sweden, and packets of freshly washed old linen and sheets from England — all torn open and scattered indiscriminately in the filth.

Then I went to "our" house. On the whole the losses weren't as major as I'd feared. I tried to figure out approximately, last night, and I think that $250 U.S. would replace everything needing to be replaced. That's plenty, but if the books had been destroyed, or the silver not already stolen — it would have meant a much greater loss. The major losses were pillows, pictures, mirrors, clothing, practically all our dishes, my tools, the boys' toys we had stored in boxes in the attic (skates, BB gun, football, tools, ect.). The oval mirror over your dresser was taken. The best snapshot book of the children has not come to light. I feel as bad over that as any one sentimental loss. O, except they also took my picture of Mother. Now I have really lost her. The Japs showed good taste in stealing all the nicest pictures and leaving the worthless ones, though they did leave my Moses — too gloomy for them, I guess. The sound box from the Victrola is gone, but for some reason they didn't take the sewing machine.

Another new start. I am having to set up the whole refugee shebang again. Then straighten out the house. I am beginning to know how Sisyphus felt.

EMILY wrote sister Jane:

Here I am in our summer resort. The waves measure out the time. There are the usual activities — picnics, paper chases, hikes, donkey rides to Lotus Hills; plenty to do, and you would never know there was a single Japanese in North China, but nevertheless I am having what I call my spinster blues. I was not cut out to be a single woman. David needs me. He has hardly mentioned his mother's passing, he thinks silence equals pluck. I think his mother's death has somehow fixed in his mind the idea that it is too dangerous for a woman to be where he is. I have not been able to raise my spirits very high over that idea. The whole business seems sort of strawish to me after the years I have spent moving here, there, and somewhere else, or he has, with new adjust-

ments to solitude to be made by each of us every few months. It has been worse than ever since my boys abandoned me "to make their fortunes."

TREADUP wasted no time going to the Japanese authorities to protest against their disbanding the refugee camp. He said very little about the pillage. He notified Colonel Sasaki that he was sending a formal protest to the American Legation in Peiping, and that claims for damages would follow.

The consequences of this call were, David wrote in his diary, "electrifying —and most peculiar."

First came a written apology, indited by typewriter in both Japanese characters and English words.

Then came a Colonel Yamamoto—"three-quarters of the Japanese invasion force seem to be colonels"—who "announced, first, that he was to be the liaison with all American missionaries in Paoting, and announced, second, that he was a Christian." His English was nonexistent and his Chinese was poor; he asked for a pad and paper. Since most Japanese and Chinese characters mean the same things, he was able to write, "I pray for the happiness of China and her good people." "I welcomed him warmly," David wrote Emily,

> *and to make a long story short, he came yesterday (Sunday) and preached a little sermon in fervent manner in Pastor Huang's church, by having one of us look up passages in the Bible which he chose. First he would read the Japanese & then he would have Mr. Huang read the Chinese. To save space I merely give the verses—you must look them up, for the more one dwells on them, the more significant they become. The references were as follows: John 3:1-3, Matt. 5:10, Ephesians 4:29. The eeriest, of course, for it cut two ways, was from the Matthew 5:44: "But I say unto you, Love your enemies, bless them that curse you, do good to them that hate you, and pray for them which despitefully use you, and persecute you."*

After these readings, Colonel Yamamoto knelt and prayed in Japanese. Pastor Huang asked Treadup to pray in Chinese. All rose and sang the Doxology. Colonel Yamamoto then took from the pocket of his uniform where he kept his Testament a small hymnal, and he sang, solo, a Japanese hymn.

The diary:

> *What are we to think? The only thing I am sure of, these days, is that life is drenched in polarities. I clean up my ruined house with that man's brotherliness ringing in my ears.*

FROM DAY TO DAY

ONE EVENING Treadup had a conversation with Charles Stanton which, he wrote Emily, was "painful in the extreme."

He challenged Stanton's "stubborn pacifism." He said that what he had seen in recent months had changed his own mind "right down at the basement level." Treadup now could not conceive of himself not using a gun to destroy a mad dog or not using force to restrain a crazy person who was bent on taking the lives of a whole family.

Stanton sharply asked if Treadup thought Colonel Yamamoto was a mad dog.

Treadup said that if you could see in Japanese militarism the negation of everything for which Christianity has always stood, then the analogy of the mad dog would at least be intelligible.

> We went back and forth—ends and means, tooth for tooth, the other cheek, Matthew 5:44, nonresistance, the errors of Emerson Fosdick's emotionalism during the World War—all up and down the scale. Then all of a sudden poor old Charles was looking at me with the tragic eyes of a bloodhound—do you know that bloodhound look? I thought he was going to weep. He said something strange, he said, "O I've tried so hard to be angry!" But that for three months he had been having serious intestinal trouble. Very loose stools and loss of weight—fourteen pounds. Serious trouble with piles. Did I know what nagging pain does to a man? He was going to have to give up. He was going to have to put in for sick leave and go home.

SOMEONE was knocking at the door of the house. It was not yet light. Treadup picked his way to the door among the bodies of sleeping refugee women and children. Ting the gateman was there. He said a tall, thin man had banged on the compound gate, and when he had answered, the man had put this bundle in his hands and had said it was for the big *mu-shih*.

David took the package, which was wrapped in an old newspaper, to his study, lit a lamp, and opened the parcel. It contained eighty dollars Mex in bills, and a note, which said:

I robbed you. I learned that you fed the poor people in Li Chia and Shao T'an. I will return the rest when I can.

STANTON'S collapse troubled Treadup. To lose Stanton would be to lose the last of the American men in the compound. Treadup persuaded Stanton to spend a week with him on a kind of retreat at Wo Fo Szu, the Temple of the Sleeping Buddha, in the Western Hills near Peiping; perhaps the rest would do him good. As it turned out, Treadup himself got the greater benefit from the week's withdrawal from the depressing realities he had been dealing with—an escape into an enchanted zone of timelessness.

The empty, sunlit courts shut the two men away by centuries from the troubles in Paoting and its countryside. They slept in a mossy court where the twisted branches of two towering, crooked pines made stark patterns, by sunlight or by moonlight, that seemed to have been painted by a Chinese master against the high rim of the mountains and the pellucid sky above. The days were hot. In the cool of the evening they strolled on the stone-paved walks of the Emperor Ch'ien Lung's Hunting Park, or visited other old temples nearby. One was the Mountain of Ten Thousand Flowers, a small Taoist temple with weathered red walls among old cedars. Its great treasure was a mummy of an eight-year-old girl. A priest said she had walked into the temple with her grandmother one spring morning two hundred years before. She climbed up on a red-gold table there in the hall and seated herself in the classic attitude of meditation—and never left. "They say she faded imperceptibly," Treadup wrote, "into immortality." The small figure still sat there, her face covered with thick lacquer, an elaborate crude crown on her head. Black characters on scarlet satin banners above her called her the Mother of Ten Thousand Flowers.

In the evenings the two men read aloud to each other, and then talked about, chapters from Alexis Carrel's *Man the Unknown*. As dark came on they would hear the evening chants, high-pitched and in weird cadences, of the black-robed Buddhist priests. At nine o'clock came throbbing rhythms of a huge drum. One evening they slipped into the shadows inside the temple doors and watched a young priest, his face—and the gilded faces of three Buddha figures before him—dimly lit by the glowing of incense sticks and votive candles, as he worshiped the idols with deep rhythms of the drum which poured out from the open temple into the valleys below.

The two men happened to be at the temple on the day and night of the Ghost Festival, at the full moon of the seventh month, when all over China— war or no war—imitation paper money was burned on graves and candles were lighted and set afloat on lakes and rivers, in memory of lonely spirits whose families had died out. Treadup wrote in his diary that he "felt as if under a spell. I imagined the notes of the big bronze temple bell sounding out over the plain, calling to those lonely wandering spirits."

Back in Paoting, Charles Stanton said he felt rested, but in a few days his symptoms returned, more virulently than ever. Treadup reflected in his diary, on his own account, on the days in the Western Hills:

I feel reconnected with China. Somehow in the helter-skelter of life here "at the front," one lapses into what one imagines to be practical ways of thinking—thinking of the kind that gets things done—on its highest plane, the pure thought of Einstein's relativity theory—in my workaday life, the thinking that went into the humble but useful gyroscope. All that swift Western thinking loses track of this other leisurely China that Charles and I have been soaked in. Elements that make our brash Christianity seem infantile. If China the sleeping giant wakens, it will still have these old dreams in the storerooms even of its most practical enterprises.

E M I L Y was back in Paoting. The tone of a letter to Jane in late September was firm—she could hardly be happy in a setting of such confusion and misery, but she was at the side of her husband, and like him she was busy.

No sense dwelling on the disheartening mess in our so-called dwelling. Broken doors and windows, plaster down, paint peeling—acres of dust inches deep.

She wrote that David was taking relief trips into the villages; he had reported in anger that farmers in three of them had been informed that they could not plant sorghum or corn within five hundred meters of the railway lines—so guerrilla bands could not hide there. Charles Stanton had left for the States, his health broken. The robber who had stolen the thousand dollars of relief money from David had in remorse returned almost nine hundred in driblets, week after week. The refugee camp was now reduced to seven hundred inmates. She was busy organizing a primary school, and she was working with her old circle of Chinese Christian women to set up health demonstrations "with spicy dialogue between Mrs. Wise Mother and Mrs. Ignorant Mother."

On a walk outside the compound I saw a flock of our refugee children grubbing in the ground, digging up the small rosettes of green leaves they call "crow's muscle"—a welcome addition to their meager boiled-millet dinners. They were chattering like sparrows. The dingy red trousers of two of them made shifting spots of color on the grass. Suddenly we all looked up. A formation of bombing planes was flying toward the southeast. My heart sank. America says it is sorry, and sends relief—but she lets her private firms sell scrap iron, gasoline, oil, and munitions to keep those bombers flying.

ON THE FIRST ANNIVERSARY of the Japanese occupation of Paoting, a "celebration" was held. All the institutions and organizations in town were commanded to show up for a procession, and they were given banners to carry, expressing (in Chinese characters, of course) the citizens' welcome to the Japanese and their gratitude for all that the occupiers had done for them. Out of a sour curiosity Treadup went to see the parade. It was a sorry, straggling line, pushed from behind, as it were, by a Japanese military band. "Shame and humiliation are the hardest things for the Chinese to bear," Treadup wrote. "They walked like mourners carrying a massive catafalque." But the numbers that turned out were all too impressive. "It's clear that the Japs have a malign grip on this place."

Just as the parade ended, a bomb went off in a motion-picture theater which the Japanese had recently taken over from its former Chinese owners. Credit was claimed by "a group of Chinese who were expressing their dismay that their compatriots were seeking amusement on this day of disgrace in a theater run by the enemy." Fortunately—probably on account of the procession—few customers were in the theater at the time, and only six were injured, none badly. The theater, however, burned down. "It was a dastardly thing to do," David wrote, "but it was surely the most sincere gesture of the celebration."

DAVID had asked Charles Stanton to take some letters to the States for him. From a letter to brother Paul:

> A friend is sailing Stateside, and I shall ask him to carry this with him. Thus I can write frankly. Our posted letters, which go through the Jap censor, have been so self-censored, in order to get them through, that some friends have actually written back, "It is strange how peaceful you are." Do remember the censors when you read the placid and "peaceful" letters which are the only kind that can go by mail. Anti-Japanese articles are neatly snipped out of periodicals from home. It is becoming increasingly difficult to get uncensored news. The only newspapers that dare print neutral news-agencies' items are issued in foreign concessions. Already our one dependence here, the 'Peking and Tientsin Times,' has been banned from the mails, leaving us nothing but Jap-owned sheets. Powerful Japanese radio stations set up such tremendous artificial interference that we can't hear Nationalist Chinese reports. We are feeling more and more isolated.

Cut off in this way, the Treadups knew nothing about the flourishing Communist principality in the caves of Yenan, or about Mao's influential new doctrines, *On the New Stage* and *On the Protracted War.* They had heard, early in the summer, of Hitler's occupation of Austria. And now, in October, the Japanese-owned Chinese-language radio exultantly announced the Munich Pact and Hitler's dismemberment of Czechoslovakia. David's diary: "I half expect this sick earth to fly out of orbit."

FROM EMILY to her sister Jane:

> *We all planned and worked together for the celebration of Christ's Birthday. It was held in the biggest room we have, the chapel. To most of the refugees, it was the first time they had heard the nativity story. The little plays and carols were awkwardly performed but charming. Every group contributed something, from the kindergarten tots to the oldest old ladies' reading class. At the end we went outside, and there at dusk David lit up for the first time a little cedar tree which he had rigged with tiny colored lights. You should have seen the children's faces! If one could only forget their empty, ruined homes out there in the dark of the countryside. One could hardly bear the pain of it. Oh Janey, I feel so homesick for the carol-singing we used to do—going around to the houses, each with its decorated tree in the drawing-room window. Remember?*

TWO DAYS after Christmas there was a bustle in the courtyard one morning. David looked out from his study and saw a group of forty or fifty peasants carrying "a gaily festooned sort of red silk pavilion" high on bamboo poles to the Treadups' door. In it was a large red satin banner. "In China," David later wrote Paul, "we 'say it with banners'—red satin by choice!—with black velvet characters glued on." The characters on this one read, "T'AO TU HSIEN-SHENG—FRIEND OF CHINA." Down one side in smaller characters were the names of all the villages where Treadup had worked.

His diary:

> *Shocked by what must have been the cost of the blooming thing. My feelings were so mixed up! Mostly an overwhelming sense of helplessness. I keep thinking how simplified my work has become. I live and labor now from day to day. I have no time to think about the future of China, but only about how to ease the human sufferings of a few people who are near at hand. When I think about the goals I once had!*

WHO COMFORTETH US

IN THE NEXT two years, Treadup found that it took all his craft and all his nervous energy to work—under, with, around, through, against, and in spite of the Japanese—at this narrow task of alleviating the sufferings of a few Chinese.

ON THE SECOND Sunday in May 1939, he preached a sermon in Chinese at Pastor Huang's church in the city, on this very subject of suffering. The church was packed. Three uniformed Japanese sat in the last pew. One of them was Colonel Yamamoto, the Christian liaison man. The other two were men Treadup had come to recognize as his own private surveillance; they panted around behind his huge bulk, wherever it went, like a couple of faithful spaniels.

Pastor Huang had surprised him with the invitation to preach, and Treadup had asked for two weeks in which to prepare. Never ordained, he had mastered the art of lecturing but not that of sermonizing. "I have not the slightest doubt," he wrote afterward, "that I got much more out of this study than did the congregation." He spent the entire two weeks at his desk.

The typescript of the sermon he ground out in that fortnight, "What Do We Do in Troublous Times?," has not survived, but we know from a letter to brother Paul about it that he chose as his text 2 Corinthians 1:3–4:

> Blessed be God, even the Father of our Lord Jesus Christ, the Father of mercies, and the God of all comfort; who comforteth us in all our tribulation, that we may be able to comfort them which are in any trouble, by the comfort wherewith we ourselves are comforted of God.

Treadup burrowed around in Charles Stanton's library, which that wretched man had "lent" him as he left Paoting in pain and haste. "Fosdick has two grand sermons on the theme, and Weatherhead's *Why Do Men Suffer?* and Stanley Jones's *Christ and Human Suffering* were both helpful." But in the end the substance of his talk came, he wrote Paul,

> *out of the vast cavern of my own disappointment—in myself, in my hopes, in history. You see, I almost preached an anti-sermon. I have*

come to the pessimistic view that in this modern world suffering and tragedy are inevitable. But the saving thing, as I drafted my talk, was this insight of your namesake, Paul the Apostle: The only real comfort comes from comforting others. The Christian God gives us the strength to use difficulty as a trust. Those who come out well in the Beatitudes do not sound to me like Visitors [David's code word for the Japanese]: *the poor in spirit, they that mourn, the meek, the merciful, the peacemakers, they which are persecuted for righteousness' sake. So often people use Christianity as a false escape from hardships and pain: piety as a kind of poultice for their own sores. Here in China one who tries to hold on to his faith moves inevitably toward the Book of Job. I am finding that my only comfort lies in what small comfort I can give to a few who suffer more—much more—than I.*

BORED, Emily went for a walk to the north, toward the Presbyterian compound. Emerging from a grove of trees, she saw a big crowd ahead in an open field. "Thinking to be lifted out of my ennui," she hurried to see what had attracted it.

There had been an execution. The victim lay where he'd fallen forward, shot in the back of the head by the officers of justice (?). Where the executioners had gone I don't know, but the gaping, indifferent crowd was still there. One more bandit had bit the dust. Bandit! That word stands for everything from professional robber-murderers, to desperate starving peasants driven to stealing to feed their loved ones, to Communistic guerrillas. All those poor Chinese just stood there staring. For all I know they may still be there. Thinking what?

Though she was glad to be at David's side, Emily was finding the reality of Paoting under the Japanese to be frustrating and almost as depressing as Tientsin had been for her alone. "I have been blue as Waterman's ink all day," she wrote in one letter. In another: "This free-lance life is Purgatory." Again: "I don't think there's a person on the International Committee of the Y in New York who would send a wife of his to this environment while he was off in villages or away hunting up money or uptown buying millet or—well, just plain absent—four-fifths of the time."

IN THE SPRING of 1939, Treadup was offered three different jobs. One was to teach at Yenching University, in Peiping, in the place of a regular faculty member who was on leave. He was invited to take over the Social and Religious Department of the Rockefeller Institute, also in Peiping. And on the strength of his work in the villages, about which word was spreading, he was offered the directorship of the School of Agronomy of St. Mark's College, formerly of Shanghai, now relocated in Chungking. This last appealed to David: "It would be a grand opportunity to get to the other side of the lines and to work in the atmosphere of the other China." And Emily wanted him to take any of the three jobs; anything for a change. But he recognized "a mulish streak" in himself; he had begun something in "his" villages, and though he did not now see how he could ever "carry it through to Utopia," he feared that he could not face the guilt he would feel if he abandoned his village friends. The offers, however, "gave me a boost—those people must think I'm worth something."

All through that spring he scouted the villages, trying to patch up one misfortune after another. He was often followed by his two Japanese shadows. He invoked again his old complaint—"Treadup on a treadmill"—but this time in a different sense from before: not objecting now to the repetitiveness of his life, but rather to the feeling that he was running hard just to keep from being carried backwards.

TREADUP hired an itinerant troupe of acrobats to entertain the women and children who still camped in the compound. The tumblers had dazzling skills. "They could fly," David wrote,

> and spin and be flung by one another into the tall sky and then land, whether on another's shoulders or on a rickety tower of chairs or on the solid ground, with the lightness of touch of a butterfly's tongue in the heart of a flower. To the amazing daring of their tricks they added noise and patter and laughter—plus suspense—a wizardly show. This particular troupe had the added attractions of a very small boy and an old man who claimed to be 75—and looked it. His antics were so surprising that the crowd had to laugh at the dexterity of such an old codger.

While the show was still at its height, there was a sudden commotion at the back of the crowd: shrieks from some of the women. Treadup ran to see what was wrong. A crazed dog had come into the compound. The three compound dogs were wagging their tails around it as it lunged and snapped and ran howling here and there. Treadup dashed to the toolhouse, next to the gateman's hut, grabbed a hoe, and ran after the dog and with two blows felled it.

The diary:

> My heart hardly even beat fast. When I argued with Charles Stanton about killing a mad dog, I never thought my casual point would be put to the test. But it was—and my choice had to be for the health of the children in the crowd. Luckily, no one was bitten. We don't know

whether one of our dogs may have been nicked. We have been keeping
them chained and are careful to bar all wonks [stray dogs, roving usually
in packs] *from coming in. Only this minute have I begun to perspire; my*
hand trembles. For now I wonder about my relationship to God's sixth
commandment: Put to another test, could I as coldly kill a fellow man?

THAT SUMMER the Treadups decided to have a "real vacation" together at
Peitaiho. Each needed it, and both together needed it. David would take July;
Emily would stay on through August. David eased his conscience over taking
time off with a bleak sentence in his diary: "I cannot single-handed hold the
Japanese in North China at bay."

They took trains to Tientsin, where they planned to stop over for a day to
visit Mrs. Evenrude. At Tientsin East station, they hired rickshas; the pullers
said they could carry passengers only as far as the International Bridge; there
were other rickshas for hire on the other side of the bridge. Assuming that this
was simply some new Japanese regulation, the Treadups proceeded to the
bridge. At the far side there was a checkpoint. A very large number of Chinese
were backed up there, and in another line were a half dozen foreigners.

In a letter to sister Grace a week later, carefully worded to pass the
censors, David wrote:

> *Having been so cut off in Paoting, we had no idea what was going on. In*
> *a nutshell, as we learned later, this was what was up: Ever since their*
> *arrival, the Japanese have found the British and French Concessions in*
> *Tientsin a thorn in their side. They have had no control over what goes*
> *on in them, nor over the Chinese who live there. A few weeks ago a*
> *Chinese bigwig in the North China Provisional Government (Japanese-*
> *supported) was assassinated in one of the movie houses in the British*
> *Concession. Four suspects were arrested by the British police and were*
> *given "protective custody." The Japanese demanded they be turned over*
> *for trial & punishment. The British refused. So now the Japanese have*
> *demanded joint control of the Concessions with the British and French,*
> *and to make their demand stick have blockaded the Concessions — have*
> *strung electrified barbed wire all the way around them. We were caught*
> *at one of the pass points of the blockade.*

Of what happened next, Treadup wrote to Grace only that he and Emily
"got through with no trouble. Our British friends have not been faring so
well — detestable treatment."

The diary tells a different story. The Treadups were kept waiting for
nearly an hour in a broiling sun on a hot city pavement. The checking was
being done in a small shed; they could not see what was going on inside
it. Emily began to look pale. Ahead of them in the line was a British

businessman—a handsome, clubable type, with military mustaches and freckled cheeks; he was in a crisp cream-colored pongee suit. He kept joking to cheer Emily up. It came the Britisher's turn to be checked. Treadup asked the guards if he and his wife could be admitted to the shelter, to get out of the hot sun. The guards let all three in. A Japanese officer told the Englishman to take his clothes off. He indignantly refused. Four guards jumped and held him and a fifth, carefully unbuttoning buttons, removed, one by one, his jacket, tie, shirt, shoes, socks, trousers, and underwear—"until," as David's diary put it,

> there he was, not five feet from Emily's eyes, facing us, as stark as when he came into the world. The Japs handled his privates, made him bend over, probed his anus. I was in a state. As the possibility crossed my mind that they would undress Emily, I saw in my mind's eye the hoe in my hand as it chopped down at the hydrophobic dog. Dear God, my very Christianity, to say nothing of my pacifism, seems to be on trial these days.

But as it turned out, when Treadup handed the guards his passport, they simply waved both man and wife through. Not British.

"THE DAYS at Peitaiho went by so fast," Treadup wrote at the end of the month, "that I don't know what I did with them." He did many things: recommissioned his old rowboat, read *The Yearling*, met with the executive committee of the Peitaiho Christian Service Union, visited friends, went to a Catholic art exhibit, went snipe hunting, rode a bicycle up and down the sandstone roads, taught a Sunday school class of sixth-grade boys, played baseball, went to a musicale ("my rump sore on a very hard seat"), and hiked to Lotus Hills. "The hike was pretty strenuous for Emily, for she found she was quite soft & so she was very tired when we got home." But gradually Emily grew stronger. "We are very close," David wrote. He began to have glimpses, at least, of Emily's former serenity. The salt sea, hot sand, a steady sun, the company of old friends—and complete removal from the agonies of China—were restorative. "We laugh so much here." Late in the month a picnic was rained out. The crowd repaired to the Assembly Hall, where stunts that had been planned were put on. Some British staged a trial of Christopher Columbus for the crime of having discovered America. The prosecutor to one of the witnesses: "Which do you think the better, that the Puritans should land on Plymouth Rock or that Plymouth Rock should land on the Puritans?"

BAD NEWS on arrival back at Paoting—from a ricksha puller. The man who hauled Treadup from the station to the compound told him that during the late afternoon of the day before, the dike had broken on the far side of the river, about a mile south of the city. Treadup realized that this meant the whole area of his villages would very likely be inundated. The effect would be worse than two years before, because now the dikes had been broken not by armies but by rising floodwaters from inland, and because the flood had come so early in the season that nothing in the fields could be saved.

Treadup went into the country on his motorcycle the next day, to the edge of the flooded area. There the villages themselves, which had been built up moundlike over the centuries, several feet above the level of the surrounding fields, were like islands in a huge lake. The expanse spread out before Treadup's eyes for many, many miles, north, west, and south.

He wrote Emily:

The river is still rising, and at a rate that portends a human disaster of proportions which this section of China has not seen for ages. Much worse than 1917. It looks as though water coming this way has been diverted from the Yellow River. If that is so, it means the flood will probably not subside in time for the planting of winter wheat — nothing to eat all this winter and all next spring. All the work for the poor folk in my villages, Em — lost! lost! Will they all die? I feel now almost as if I were Chinese; one trouble follows another; I refuse to bow my head; I struggle to find philosophy to carry me through.

Emily wrote back:

Come and get me as soon as it is safe to travel. I want to be with you.

TWO DIARY ENTRIES:

Aug. 31 All quite speechless over Russian-German Pact, though we were lent an issue of 'Harper's' at the seashore which had an article almost predicting it. Japs mortified. No papers for some days, and radio comes in so garbled with static it's hard to glean much information. So far we Americans seem to be favored nation amongst our immediate environment, both·C & J, which is no credit to us, but comfortable while it lasts. . . .

Sept. 7 And now war in Europe. Mad & foolish humanity! We are on the road to destruction. We cannot measure the pain that is ahead. America thinks she can escape it. Impossible! I understand that American armament makers are selling many times the amount of war material they did only three years ago. America thinks that is her profit. She will find it will help to fill her cup of bitterness.

HAVING ARRANGED all the necessary permissions, David went to Peitaiho for Emily on September 12. She welcomed him with tears. She had missed him, she said, more than ever before. She had gotten hay fever almost the very day after he left. She had been consoling herself for her loneliness by reading *Rebecca*.

Starting from Peitaiho at two in the morning, the Treadups sat up all night in a crowded third-class coach. At Peiping, they learned that there were new breaks in dikes north of Paoting. Partway there, "waters were rushing over the tracks, and we had to crawl along, men standing out on the cow-catcher of the engine to watch the roadbed carefully." Finally, at one stop, they were herded off the train and were poled in Chinese sampans across flooded fields for perhaps a mile, to an improvised wharf. There, on an area covered with straw matting, they were directed to take off their shoes and go aboard one of a dozen bargelike Japanese army motor launches.

Rain fell. On a bamboo frame over the foreigners' launch, the Japanese spread tarpaulins. The barge took off. It was driven by a popping single-cylinder engine. Everyone had to sit Japanese-style on the deck. The wind grew strong; on the wide expanse of water the boat began to rock; the air under the tarps was stuffy. Treadup, thinking himself on a vast ocean, had to lie down.

One of the barges ran aground, probably on a big grave mound. There was a great to-do getting her off. Japanese soldiers splashed around in the water unashamedly naked, pushing and shoving with bamboo poles. The Treadups' barge tugged, and finally the vessel lunged free.

A few miles north of Paoting, the barges stopped, and the passengers transferred across muddy land to another railroad train.

WHEN the waters had drawn back, Treadup was shocked by the swarms of beggars in the city. They were in clusters, each circle of kinfolks sitting around a small pail in which to collect scraps of food from anyone who might be better off. They moaned and whined their miseries, singing time-honored mendicant chants. On one corner Treadup saw a group sitting near a washbasin filled with soup; a little child was on its hands and knees with its mouth down to lap it up, "almost doglike." In another utensil was a small pile of what appeared to be someone's leftovers, which the clan were preparing to divide among themselves. Treadup found it hard to go past these groups without giving them anything.

> *No! I am saving every last penny for my villagers. It is, with me as it is with the beggars, a family matter: this entails a savage inhumanity towards anyone not in the family — rabid patriotism in miniature.*

NEW ORDER

THROUGH that winter Treadup was alternately a beggar himself—before Madame Shen and the various Christian relief agencies in Peiping—and a commuter to the little country of misery of which he was a patriot. In the following spring he had an experience which cast a shadow on all the rest of his life.

IN THE VILLAGE courtyards the usual stocks of grain and fuel had vanished. There were almost no animals. "Plans?" the villagers said. "How can we make plans when we have no donkeys to plow with?" Here and there teams of human beings pulled the plows, making pathetic scratches in the caked mud of the fields, so some meager wheat, at least, could go into the ground; in places, deep foot tracks were visible where plow-haulers and sowers had plodded through still moist mud. In one village where Treadup wanted to feed the children first, he asked that their mothers be gathered so he could dole out what he had. The reply was that the mothers were all in the city begging. Many of the able-bodied men had gone off north to Japanese-dominated Manchukuo, where, they had heard, the squalid life in factories and foundries was far less bad than what they had come to know in the flood district. Treadup found the few men who had stayed behind quarrelsome and savagely selfish; they would eat and let their women and children go hungry. Treadup did not dare carry money into the country; whenever he managed to scrounge some cash in Peiping, he carried it in a money belt to Paoting and at once converted it into barrowloads of peanuts or sweet potatoes or millet—all bought at scandalous prices in the black market.

"Here we live," he wrote brother Paul,

> in stark and deadly anarchy, witnessing the hardest winter among the country people that I have ever seen. Fighting, banditry, kidnapping, robbery, murder, tyranny, starvation. And beyond all that, the oppressive presence of the Japanese. My villagers and I have almost no contact with them, yet they are always somehow there, like a sinister whisper on the air. You never lose your awareness of them. God forgive me for my doubts of his wisdom.

Even in this abysmal time, Treadup's old trait of enthusiasm evidently flickered up now and then. Reaching deep into himself for courage, he scouted around for a few of his former Mass Education Secretaries—"I am amazed at how many of *them* have chosen not to run away"—and with their help he actually set up a number of Relief Schools, as he called them, for both children and adults, scattered through the area. "The curriculum," he wrote, "consists of Coping, Surviving, Making Do, Grubbing Along. Thank heavens our students are Chinese. They are apt pupils in such subjects!"

O N E   D A Y in March Treadup was in the village of Li Chia, helping to set up a Relief School; he was seated cross-legged on the *k'ang* in the home of a young man named Feng, one of his ablest "secretaries." Feng told Treadup that he had been visited the evening before by four men, who said they were members of a Communist team that had been assigned this district "to help the peasants understand the issues of the patriotic anti-Japanese war." The diary that night:

> *Remembering my pleasant (but also, as I recall, slightly puzzling and disturbing) chat with those four bright-eyed young Communists, two years ago, I was at first pleased by this news. But—*

These men, Feng said, had heard about the American *mu-shih*. They told Feng this missionary was spreading American imperialist propaganda in the area through the device of village schools. They had four demands: (1) they must be given time and places to retrain the teachers of the schools in "correct doctrines of the patriotic war"; (2) they must be permitted to introduce their curriculum; (3) there must be no religious teaching; and (4) relations with the American imperialist missionary must be broken off.

"When he told me this," Treadup wrote that night, "I had a prickling sensation—I was ready to pull at my oar."

Feng said he had told the men that under no circumstances could the villagers of the district agree to the fourth demand; that whatever had been good in the entire area in the past several years they owed at least in part to T'ao Tu Hsien-sheng; that the men should talk directly with the American himself.

Treadup—confessing in his diary that night that the demands "made me touchy, irritable, and nervous"—said he would very much like to talk to the men. Feng said he had been so confident that that would be his answer that he had told the team to be on hand at his house the next morning.

The diary, the night before the meeting:

> *I know the twelve villages in "my" area as well as I know the back of my own hand. I love the people in the villages as much as if they were Emily, Philip, Absolom, Paul—and Nancy. The team's assertion to my friend Feng that I've been spreading imperialist propaganda is a LIE,*

as they can learn for themselves by asking any peasant in any of the villages. I am going to go on working for the well-being of the peasants in these villages, whether the team likes it or not. The Communists will not be welcome in the village schools. If it comes to a showdown, they'll find that the villagers will choose me over them. I shall tell them to keep out of the twelve villages, at least for a few months — let it be a separate little province.

AS TO WHAT happened the next day, there is not a word in Treadup's diary. He does not mention the meeting in any of his letters. We can only infer from this astonishing and unnatural silence, and from his behavior in the following weeks, that whatever the Communists said — perhaps some things he had heard himself say — shocked him literally beyond words. He did thereafter continue his work in the villages, and there is no record of further interference by the team. In fact, one sees him trying harder, working longer hours than ever before, cranking up his ardor — but his teeth are gritted, it seems; he is pushing a heavy load. On everything he records from then on, there is a faint but permanent stain, a toxic trace, an imprint of some kind of foreboding.

ONE DAY while David was in the villages, Emily, coming back from a walk, found a cluster of about twenty women at the gate of the compound, begging. Most of them carried little pails for food. They were moaning and crying out with sudden shrieks. Overcome with pity, Emily hurried to the house and, breaking out a bag from David's storeroom, cooked up a large potful of millet gruel. She carried it in her own hands out to the gate. Ting the gateman met her there and asked her what she was doing. She told him she was going to divide the food among the women outside. He urged her not to do it; he said it could only lead to trouble. But she opened the gate and began to measure out shares. She had no sooner put rations in four or five of the buckets than more women, then men as well, appearing from nowhere, began running toward the group at the gate. Emily went on dividing the gruel. When next she looked up, she saw that there must now have been two hundred people there; they were shouting and beginning to push hard. Alarmed at last, she backed through the gate. Ting, asking her to help him, barely was able to heave the gate shut and bolt it. Now there was a sullen roar outside. The gateman ran for a ladder, and he climbed up and looked out. Scrambling down, he said to Mrs. Treadup that there was a mob — a thousand angry beggars out there. He said he was going to go for help. He ran with the ladder to the far end of the compound, climbed and got over the wall, and — as Emily learned later — ran all the way to the city. An hour later two trucks drove up, and squads of Chinese police wielding bamboo poles drove the mob away.

This event was painful enough in itself, but the wording of David's record of it in his diary betrays a new element of strain, as if Emily's foolish action has tended to prove something about his mission that he wishes with all his heart he could deny.

ANOTHER oblique hint of David's shocked state of mind comes in a letter to Paul, in which he stops just short of saying he wants to hear American gunfire with his own ears, right at hand, in North China. "My own opinion," David wrote,

> is that the U.S. is already in this war. I think it would shock some Americans to realize that fact. Emotionally it is clear that the large body of Americans are heart & soul behind the Allies, and actually the Allies are getting much help in the way of vital supplies from our American commercial interests — so much as to improve immeasurably the chances of the U.S. being drawn into this maniacal war. Roosevelt is too much a believer in the rightness of might to stem the tide. From what I can glean here, Americans think only of getting involved in Europe. Believe me, the Japs have another notion. Officially they are more polite to us than to the British, but I can read the stories that eyes tell. Japanese eyes tell me more than I want to know.

THE INCIDENT of the crowd of beggars at the gate had thrown Emily back into a funk. She began to have nightmares. In one, she was running as a beggar herself in a suffocating crowd that was being driven by a pack of wonks to market for sale. She was going to be sold to the Japanese, who splashed around in water naked. She ran and ran from the dogs and then from the naked Japanese in her sleep, and woke up with aching legs.

Then came news that further depressed her. A courier brought a message from the consulate: An order had come down from the State Department, via the legation in Nanking, saying that in view of strained relations between Japan and the United States, all American women without exception must be evacuated from "interior cities" — Paoting's classification, even though it was fairly near Peiping. Would this be a permanent separation? During a fortnight while David tried unsuccessfully to get an exception for her, Emily lay awake at night, wept often in the daytime, and "had a bad case of jitters & fidgets." Finally David made arrangements for her to move to T'ungchow, a suburb of Peiping, about fifteen miles to the east of the city, where the boys had gone to boarding school, and where there was a fairly large community of foreigners — and where he would at least be able to visit her from time to time.

Emily was down on herself. From a letter to Jane:

Since I dissolve all the time anyway, I weep when I think that my leaving makes no hole whatsoever in the Chinese community here. I don't quite know why I am such a flop at crossing the barriers of speech, but what extravert tendencies I have — or used to have — in my own tongue pretty well collapse in practical dealing with the Chinese around me. If only I could have listened to the gateman that day!

THE DIARY:

Oct. 14 A letter today has scared me — from the Japanese National Christian Council about what the Japs call "the New Order in East Asia." The letter stated these aims:

> *"1. To stress the harmony between Christianity and the Japanese national objectives;*
> *"2. To make plain the official purposes for the establishment of a New Order in East Asia and to cooperate in their realization;*
> *"3. To cooperate with all Christians in the occupied areas, seeking to develop understanding of the New Order;*
> *"4. To seek the cooperation of English and American missionaries in Japan and the churches they represent for the rectification of international misunderstandings of Japan, and particularly [this is where I come in — or, rather, don't come in!] to seek to deepen the understanding of the missionaries in China."*

> *Christianity as an instrument of this so-called New Order! The idea revolts me beyond words. It scares me to think that I was the one who had the idea, at that meeting after the Japanese first started all this, of writing to our Japanese brethren asking them to plead with their government to pull out. What frightens me even more is the idea that our faith is as malleable as this frightful letter suggests.*

SUDDENLY there was sunlight in Emily's letters. T'ungchow suited her better than any place she had lived in China. The houses, the trees, the lawns, the hedges, the beds of autumn chrysanthemums, above all the congenial people — the missionary settlement was quite a lot like a New York State village. She was settled "on the commodious third floor of the Timothy house — like us they have sent their progeny off to college in the States." There were many new friends. Miss Huddler, headmistress of the Goodrich Girls' School; Mrs. Door, recovering from an operation; the Spears, Jack and Paulette; the elderly Hendersons, old friends from early days. Then across the way at the American school there were some delightful faculty members, especially Mr. and Mrs. Fergenarder—he a history teacher, she food manager for the school. And Rosalind Door, teaching in her second year—"a girl needing several adjectives, brilliant if not beautiful etc.—we knew her at Peitaiho—remember?" Nurse Alice Connor from Paoting, and another dislocated nurse, Miss Friendly. Almost always there were other new faces, too, people coming and going—parents of students, or tourists who wanted to see a typical missionary setting. "Everyone is so kind to me—they are teaching me how to laugh again!"

In late October David went up for a week, to see for himself. He had a vivid reaction, which must have derived from that session at Li Chia about which he could not bring himself to set down a single word: It was almost as if he welcomed a withdrawal from the harsh mission field he had chosen for himself, taking refuge in comfortable American trivialities. Emily was indeed remarkably restored. Treadup found this T'ungchow world "light-years distant from the bleak universe of my villages." To Paul he wrote how strange yet how bracing it was to visit "this carefree unreality."

> *Every fall the Fergenarders give a picnic for everyone. This year's was last night. The servants dug a big hole in their lawn in which was built a huge bonfire. Over that we toasted buns, roasted meat, fried bacon. Then when it was dark we sat around the fire and sang songs. Eventually we went inside for a meeting of the Pastime Club, an innocuous organization for fun that has been going for thirty years. Anyone may join if willing to go through the absurd ordeal & rites of initiation, and of course everyone does. We all got funny, silly, and raucous. I'd been telling a story all week to anyone I met about the fellow who bought his first suit with two pairs of trousers. "How do you like it?" a friend asked. "Not too much," he said, "it's too hot with two pairs of pants on." When my turn for initiation came I was told to tell a joke "but it must not be about trousers!" I sat down at the piano and strummed and twiddled, and then announced I had played for them the "Refrain from Spitting."*

MARIPOSA

NOT DARING to post such news in the mail, Emily sent a courier to David in Paoting with a letter saying that all the American Board women in

T'ungchow—Mrs. Door and her daughter Rosalind, Paulette Spear, Mrs. Fergenarder, and Nurses Connor and Friendly—had had orders from Boston headquarters to be evacuated back to the States. Mrs. MacDonald and Mrs. Beard from the schools were also going home. The Boston cable had said:

> AUTHORIZING EVACUATION BECAUSE SITUATION REQUIRES
> EXTREME CAUTION BUT NOT YET ALARM. WEAKENING IN
> CONFLICTING GOVERNMENT POSITIONS IMPROBABLE. SPEED
> OF DEVELOPMENTS UNPREDICTABLE. RECOMMEND RESERVE
> PASSAGE RELIEF SHIP MARIPOSA DEPARTING CHINWANGTAO
> NOVEMBER 13.

What should she do?

DAVID sent a telegram to Hank Burrell in Shanghai, reminding him that the Y.M.C.A. had undertaken to pay for the Treadups' homeward voyage, whenever it might be made; saying that consular advice and Stateside decisions of the Congregationalists and others were causing the evacuation of most of the women from North China; that he himself could not see danger looming in the near future; that he would appreciate guidance from New York.

It took four anxious days to get a bleak and all-too-laconic answer:

> BLACKTON ADVISES MRS. TREADUP EVACUATE.

TREADUP went to T'ungchow. He found Emily in bed, with curtains drawn and damp cloths on her forehead. Nurse Connor told him Mrs. Treadup had been felled by a migraine headache while waiting to hear some news from him. Everyone else in T'ungchow seemed to have been seized by a wild energy that looked strangely like elation. Women were crating their flat silver and stuffing their steamer trunks and supervising servants in closing up their houses. Men were talking about God's will and making plans for bachelor quarters in some of the houses. Emily mended quickly after his arrival, but David wrote in his diary that he felt the onset of

> *something like a migraine of my own. It's a pounding of my temple bells.*
> *Is it pique and wounded vanity that makes me think the unthinkable—*
> *that Emily's accession to New York's wishes has a tinge of alacrity to it?*
> *I see no reason for all the excitement. Down my way the Japanese have*
> *been scrupulously polite during recent weeks. I suppose it is always the*
> *case that people on the spot have much less sense of danger than people*

who are thousands of miles away with headlines dancing in their
eyes — or even than people in a zone of quarantine like this unreal New
England village of T'ungchow. I cannot bear the idea of a permanent
separation. Except for Nancy's death, this is the hardest thing that has
happened to us since we were married. But what's to do? I can't leave. I
don't want to leave. No men are leaving.

On October 30, with less than two weeks till the sailing, David went to
Peiping to make a reservation on the *Mariposa* and to get permission
from American and Japanese authorities for Emily to return with him to
Paoting to pack up the family belongings — all but his clothes and books — for
her departure.

TREADUP sent a cablegram to Farrow Blackton at the Y.M.C.A. International Committee in New York, asking him to arrange for Emily to live in a
small apartment or rented rooms in the village of Thornhill, New York, about
thirty miles north of New York City. The Treadups' old China Y friends, the
Keystones, had retired there, and though they were now quite old, they would
be company for Emily; and besides, and more important, she would be near
but not right on top of two of her sons, Philip and Paul, who worked and lived
in the city. Absolom had gone off to Maine, where he was living in an old
house, alone, working at odd jobs; if he tired of that existence, he could move
down and live with his mother.

THE TREADUPS went to Peiping with all of Emily's luggage. The heavy
pieces — two trunks and seven wooden boxes (into one of which, at the last
minute, David had placed all his diaries up until the current year, so, whatever
might happen in China, his memories would be safe, God granting the
Mariposa a safe crossing of the waters) — all these they consigned to a
shipment of evacuee baggage that was to go to Chinwangtao by rail under
United States Marine guard. Then, with the Fergenarders, Mrs. Door, and the
Spears, they had what David called, in his diary, "a two-day bat." There were
errands to do, but mostly they had fun. Emily seemed transformed. She was
warm, sweet, and calm. Some of the quiet of earlier years had come back into
the deeps of her eyes. David was "both enchanted and in mourning." They
went to the exquisite park of the Pei Hai — North Lake — for a picnic lunch.
They went to see *Pinocchio* and "laughed like the children the film was
designed to entertain — and right afterwards felt so sad we wondered how we
could ever have laughed."
Then they went together to T'ungchow to wait for the day of departure.

ON THE EVENING of November 11, there was a gala send-off party for the evacuees. The evening began with a much postponed musicale at the North China American School. The star of the evening was Rosalind Door, who taught piano, among other things. The Treadups and Spears

> blew ourselves to a basket of flowers for her and had them taken up at the proper time. Of course she gave the audience the obligatory smile and bow, but up until breakfasttime this morning she had not yet read the card on the basket nor had she brought the flowers home with her. They rested all night on the floor of the recreation hall at the school. She is as disappointing as she is fascinating.

After the concert the adults went to the Ladies' House in the American Board compound, where Nurse Connor and Mrs. Fergenarder put on a spread for twenty-three guests at a long table which stretched from the inner end of the dining hall through an archway into the living room. Everyone was dressed up—long dresses, stiff shirts, bow ties; David wore his old, slightly greenish sugar-scoop coat, which, forewarned of this grand affair, he had brought from Paoting. Mrs. Door was the *kwei k'e*—guest of highest rank—and sat at one end of the table. After tomato juice cocktails came the faintly Chinese main course—rolls of thinly sliced beef enclosing delicious shredded onions and carrots, fried *pi ch'i* cakes, mashed potatoes, twisted rolls; fruit salad; and homemade fig-and-walnut ice cream, cookies, and coffee.

> Then were we 'je nao' [a Chinese expression meaning "raucous"—literally "hot-noisy"]! We split up into evacuees and residuees. Each group was instructed to put on a stunt to illustrate what they thought the others would be doing after the evacuation. The evacuees performed first: a skit of a meal at young Nancy Runner's house—she practically the only female who was to stay—all the gents vying to sit next to Nancy, arguing with her for dates, ect. ect. We residuees put on a scene at the Chinwangtao dock at departure time. The climax was Jim F. entering with Rosalind Door's swanky fur jacket on just in time to catch the boat, to the relief of frantic Mrs. Door (yours truly).

Next Rosalind Door, Nancy Runner, and Nurse Friendly were initiated into the Pastime Club. Miss Friendly did a sketch of reporting to the Westboro, Massachusetts, sewing circle her impressions of a missionary compound. Rosalind repeated "Twinkle, twinkle, little star" backward at great speed with surprisingly few errors. And Miss Runner spoke a poem in four languages, French, German, Chinese, and finally English:

I know my heart,
I know my mind,
But my noblest part
Sticks out behind.

THE EVACUEES planned to leave Peiping on November 12, but the ship was delayed by a day. David and Emily had "one of the happiest-unhappiest days of our life together." In the morning the Y secretary in the city, Franklin Prout, delighted them with a cablegram from Blackie:

MRS. TREADUP ARRANGEMENTS SUGGESTED BEING CARRIED OUT.

As a going-away present Prout generously loaned the Treadups his Ford car for the day. They drove out for noonday dinner with Professor and Mrs. Randolph Tinker at the beautiful campus of Yenching University, outside the city, and then went to the Summer Palace, two or three miles away.

We spent two hours in this dreamlike place, climbing to heights, rejoic-
ing in the distant Western Hills and the lovely lake below us, and
strolling through the palace buildings in this huge garden. We voyaged
through our past years as we talked on the deck of one of the strangest
craft on the waters of this earth, the great stone ship at the edge of the
lake. This place made us proud of China and glad to have been so much
a part of China. At four we started back. I never felt so close to Emily.
Dear woman! Reckless in her sadness at leaving, she let me drive with
an arm around her through the fall countryside — browns & yellows &
greens of many shades — a bright sun bringing out all the splendor of
China's red-gold-green-blue buildings as they cast their long purple
shadows on the land.

AT FIVE O'CLOCK in the morning on Thursday, November 14, 1940, David Treadup handed his wife into a car of the special train for *Mariposa* evacuees. Treadup's diary suggests that their emotion had all been spent on the previous day and during their last night together — "endless wakeful whispering"; it was too early in the morning, as they said good-bye, for anything like grand feeling. Emily's one outburst came with a moment of bitterness that she could not say a proper good-bye to any of her Chinese friends. Then, bleakly: "Darling, do you think I *have* any Chinese friends?" Mostly there were anxious exchanges: Had she remembered her wristwatch on the night table? Would he cable Blackie to have someone meet her in Chicago and help her change trains there? And then — a high-pitched whistle, and the rude chuffs and hissing, which ever since boyhood had thrilled the nerves of David Treadup, of a locomotive's first strenuous efforts of removal.

TREADUP, unable to face the Paoting house alone just yet, went back to T'ungchow to spend a fortnight with the other husbands who had been left behind. On his last night there, December 1, he was invited with Jack Spear, Mac MacDonald, Richard Beard, young Huebsch, and one or two others to a buffet supper at Jim Fergenarder's house with the hope that later in the evening they could get the "Treasure Island" program on the radio.

> *Just before eight thirty Jim tried to tune in. There was a lot of static and scratching. Just as we were about to give up, in came the voice of the "Treasure Island" announcer as clear as if he were right in the room with us. We stayed with him for the next half hour in anticipation of the Sunday evening "Mail-Bag," hoping there might be some word about the 'Mariposa.' Finally the announcer said he was giving the program over to a Rev. someone or other. And what did he do but introduce in person Mrs. Frank Door and her daughter Rosalind! That was the first spine-tingler — hearing those familiar voices all the way from the USA with messages to all of us. Mrs. Door read Polly Fergenarder's letter about having landed on good old Stateside soil at noon on Saturday, their plan at first to try to talk over the air, and then the decision she and others had taken to go on by train that night. I was sure from that that Emily would have gone on, too. Then a letter to 'Mr. Treadup.' It excited me so that I actually missed details of the message — had to get the help of the rest of the crowd to recall them afterward — but I did get it that dear son Philip had crossed the country to meet his mother, and they were going on by the northern route that morning, and loving words she didn't mind having the whole world tuned in on. In San Francisco it was around five or five thirty in the morning, so I knew that Em and her firstborn were well on their way across the continent, probably soon to wake up to a desert sun in Nevada.*

TREADUP returned to Paoting the next day. In his frequent letters to Emily over the next weeks he reported that he was "picking up after you in this house where you left things that couldn't be taken or weren't worth taking"; he was "homesick for the first time since I came to China more than 35 years ago"; he had "been in a restless mood all week"; he hadn't got around to going out to the villages yet, and that was "bad for my morale." A week before Christmas a package of presents, jointly mailed from New York on October 4 by Philip and Paul, arrived. "I didn't enjoy opening it. I took my two pieces out and put the rest of the things back in the carton again. There wouldn't be any point in sending them back over the ocean." Christmas day alone was "very hard. I got my cornet out to try to cheer up, but of course I had no lip."

EARLY in January 1941 David wrote Emily:

I have climbed all the way up a steep decision. Of course I have cleared it with Mme Shen, and after some thought she wept openly before me and declared my decision had made her happier than she had been for a long time, and that of course she would continue our support. I have also gone down to Menghsien and discussed it with Johnny Wu, who is enthusiastic. I am going to move out to one of the villages. I haven't decided which one, yet, for of course I'll have to talk it over with the people out there. I have decided that I cannot live "above" the friends I am trying to help. It will not be easy. I must learn to be poor. I hope to learn now, at last, what it truly means to be Chinese.

CUP OF BITTERNESS

AFTER much conferring and thought, Treadup moved to the village of Ma Ch'iao—a place that had four advantages, from his point of view. It was a village of medium size. It was more or less at the geographic center of the area where he had worked. One entire family had departed, so there was an empty house for him to use. And one of his best Mass Education Secretaries, a man named Mi, had chosen to stay on there through thick and thin.

The physical move was less strenuous than the psychological one. Treadup packed all the family belongings and most of his books in large tin-lined wooden boxes, which he bound with nailed-down metal strapping; he locked the boxes in the compound's storage room. In Paoting he bought cold-weather Chinese clothes—long-sleeved jackets and voluminous trousers padded with cotton quilting, a fur hat with earflaps, felt-lined cloth shoes. On moving day he was able to pile everything he took with him—bedding, toilet articles, spare Chinese-style clothes, a few books—onto a large flat-bedded wheelbarrow, which, with the stubborn pride of his newly chosen role, he himself pushed over the rough roads into the country. "Glad to say," he wrote the next day, "I'm as fit as a cougar—uh, maybe an elderly cougar—few stiff muscles—bit weary—but the old Syracuse Navy slogger still can stay the four miles of the course, only this was more like thirteen."

That next day he walked off his stiffness, hiking back to the Paoting compound to get his motorcycle, which he would need for circuits of the villages. He had thought it best to notify the Japanese authorities that he was moving, since they would make it their business to find out anyway; he explained forthrightly exactly what the nature of his work would be, so far as he could guess at it. His most difficult negotiation with Colonel Sasaki was over arranging to have a drum of gasoline for the Indian sent out to Ma Ch'iao.

MA CH'IAO'S twenty-three "gates," or courtyards, stood along two parallel lanes and contained the stayers-on of thirty-four families of four clans, Ma, Ch'in, Han, and T'ung. The courtyards all faced south, to pocket as much sunlight as possible. They had low mud walls; near each gate was an odorous walled compartment where the treasure of the family's night soil was heaped. The courtyards were bare, for until the flood pigs and fowl had roamed there. Six months before, the population had been more than two hundred; now so many of the men had gone off that there were only 127 mouths left. Some of the men had been shanghaied—literally kidnapped —by night raiding parties of Kuomintang units off to the southwest; some had joined Communist guerrilla bands; some had gone off as bandits; and some had drifted north to Manchukuo, looking for work. The women now outnumbered the men, two to one, and the remaining men tended to be elderly or infirm.

Treadup's new home had belonged to a T'ung family. Like all the village houses, it had three rooms. The door from the courtyard led into a small central room which contained the cook stove and storage space. "Upper" and "lower" bedrooms were to left and right, each having a mud-brick k'ang and a large window with translucent coarse white paper glued to its frames.

The T'ungs, who had had so little hope for Ma Ch'iao's future that they had all fled from it, had obviously done their best, while still there, to appease the spirits and powers that they believed ruled their lives. A picture of the kitchen god was on a shelf over the stove, and nearby was the carved wooden frame of their ancestor shrine, from which they had taken with them the individual wooden tablets to particular forebears. In a futile effort to bring more male offspring, the upper bedroom door had a picture beside it of the child god, riding a unicorn and carrying a baby boy. On the empty chests, which the fleeing family had left behind, were squares of red paper with wishful characters: "Get Money and Receive Precious Things," "Ten Thousand Ounces of Gold." On either lintel of the courtyard gate were pasted colored pictures of Ch'ing Ch'ung and Yu Hsi, warriors of darkness and light, who would—it was hoped—keep thieves away. A mud hut in the courtyard, about the size of a doghouse, was a shrine to the potent animal spirits: the fox, the snake, the weasel, the badger. And even the deserted pigsty bore luck notices on red paper, "Fat Swine Are In Here."

But the reality was barren. The larder was empty; there were no pigs or precious things; there was not even any human excrement in the manure box. The T'ungs had run away.

NORTH CHINA'S postal service, still so amazingly efficient between cities and along rail lines, did not reach into humble villages where bandits and Communists might roam, and it was a long time before Treadup's friend and helper from Ma Ch'iao, Mi Tu-ch'uan, having errands in Paoting, stopped by at the American Board compound on his way home and picked up letters from Emily.

The first of her letters expressed concern, bordering on alarm, at David's idea of moving to a village. She begged him, long after the die was cast, to reconsider. She seemed less worried by the physical danger he would face than by—what was it?—he could not quite be sure what she was trying to say. Was she worried that he was losing his mind?

> You have been under a strain for so long—the demobilization—money problems—the Visitors—my leaving. Do be careful, David. Wouldn't it be best to remove yourself to T'ungchow, where there is still a small community of people who speak your language and share your values?

Her own news seemed good. David got a sense of her great relief at being back in America. She liked Thornhill—a quiet small town of just over two thousand. She lived on the second floor of a snug house on Poplar Road, with some "congenial young folks named Hurd; he the village comptroller, she a teacher in the high school, lovely alto voice, solos at the Congregational church." The Keystones had been hospitable. The librarian of the small village library had moved to another town, and Emily was thinking of taking on that job—three or four days a week—it would give her something to think about. Philip had been an angel. "He is strong-hearted like you. He has watched out for me ever since I put foot on the dock out west." He had a serious sweetheart; Emily was not sure she liked the girl—"a mother has very particular ideas about the kind of woman her son should marry." Paul was doing quite well in the city, working in "some kind of grain factoring office—a trifle too much interested in money, there's something hard about our youngest. All the same, he has charm enough for ten men. Well, maybe he'll support us in our old age." She had had word from Absolom, who sounded a bit sour on life, in Maine; he was coming down to see her in the spring.

The last letter Treadup opened told him his father had died.

The next morning he had a toothache.

MI TU-CH'UAN was the eldest son of the former village chief, who had deserted his family, gone off to Manchukuo "to earn money for their support," and never been heard from since. At fifteen this son had lost his left arm, which had had to be amputated after a flatbed cart had overturned in a rutted road and fallen on him. Sturdy, yet spared from heavy farmwork, he had become a crop watcher—on guard to prevent brigands and ne'er-do-wells from other villages from stealing produce from the fields. On perpetual night duty, he had had so much time to think that he had become a rude philosopher. He had learned to read and write in the first of the literacy schools, and since then he had been village teacher, scribe, treasurer, and, despite his youth (he was now twenty-three), its sage. He had a broad, open face with an unusually large mouth which made his speech seem fierce and portentous. He laughed easily and often in these times of perpetual gloom, and sometimes therefore seemed out of touch with reality. Thus there was, as the diary put it, "something slightly idiotic about him," but he was so eager to please, so energetic, and so cheerful that, for want of his father, he had become the most influential person in the village. He had welcomed Treadup's residence in Ma Ch'iao with unaffected and touching warmth and had at once become his valued colleague. Treadup, for his part, remembered the disastrous colonelship of Shen Mo-ju, and he realized from his first day in Ma Ch'iao that despite all the time he had previously spent visiting the villages he had never remotely approached the inner truths of Chinese rural life. So from the very first he was determined to learn all he could from young Mi, and to deal with him as an equal.

THE DIARY:

> The central question is this: Must we limit ourselves to coping frantically with one crisis after another—flood, brigand raids, KMT levies and kidnappings, Communist "re-education," Japanese punitive expeditions, heaven knows how many other curses and scourges? Must we simply bow our heads and try to get through "seven lean years"? Or are there any ways to think of a bigger picture, a longer future—a less oppressive rural life? I have been trying to approach this question, first of all, with humility, reasoning from a most modest case. I reside in this microcosm. It may yield, perhaps indirectly, macro-conclusions. I work on the theory that small, exemplary solutions may eventually be proliferated.

ACCORDING to village lore, Ma Ch'iao must have been at least four centuries old—the sizes and numbers of the grave mounds which dotted the fields told this. The place had once been prosperous. Forty years before, there had been ten big horses in Ma Ch'iao; since the flood there had been only two thin donkeys. Of the 326 mou the villagers now tilled, more than two-thirds were owned by absentee landlords. The average area worked by the families was only eight mou, less than two acres. The villagers gave several reasons for the impoverishment of the place: bad luck in childbirth, too many females; greed of the landlords; depredations of warlords and bandits; KMT and Japanese taxation; natural disasters; but worst of all, and underlying all the troubles, a ruined *feng-shui.*

Feng-shui (literally, "wind-water") was the ancient form of geomancy which held that all things, and especially graves, must be placed with careful thought to the configuration of the landscape—to whether ever present dragons might be offended by a lack of harmony in watercourses, alluvial formations, and the structures thrown up by man. The *feng-shui* of Ma Ch'iao, Mi said, had been ruined by a huge burying ground to the northeast, bought and built three or four decades ago by a rich merchant of Chinese medicines from Paoting. It was a square ground, occupying thirty-eight mou (far more than any Ma Ch'iao farmer tilled), and it was surrounded by willow trees—the local dragon had been deeply disturbed. By way of proof of this, Mi told Treadup that the day after a young girl had been buried there, two men in Ma Ch'iao had stabbed each other to death in a quarrel over a trifle.

> *Superstition! I am astounded and depressed by how ridden these people are by omens, charms, signs. Even Mi, the most intelligent man in the village, schedules every important act of his life by a ridiculous almanac called 'The Yellow Calendar.' He pointed out to me that this book stated that this year's annual waters were controlled by three dragons who would release great spates—and look! had there not been that terrible flood? The calendar lists propitious days for offering sacrifices, marrying and burying, taking baths, cutting fingernails, erecting beams, making wine and contracts, submitting to acupuncture. Mi says people are most careful to plow, spread night soil, plant, weed, and harvest on the days decreed in the 'Yellow Calendar'—no matter, apparently, whether the weather is favorable. Mi said his maternal aunt had been cured of a hard lump in her belly by swallowing the page in the book on which were printed the magical curative characters of a sage named Chiang T'ien-hsi. The village put in one of Inventor Wang's efficient self-dumping well buckets, but Mi says no one will use it because his father told*

everyone that that well has been spoiled by being too close to, and to the southwest of, a nearby T'ung family grave mound.

DAVID wrote Emily that she should not worry about him.

I am not only 'compos mentis,' I am thriving. Of course I have some doubts and tribulations. Will I ever be accepted? On one level these people like and trust me; somewhere under the surface, alas, there abides the conviction that I am a barbarian. Something defiant in me, since I can't help being a 'mao-tzu' [hairy one] anyway, causes me to grow a mustache at this time. It is getting as splendiferous as the one I grew back in Kuling days. How in love you and I were that summer, Em! Apart from a pesky toothache I have been having, my sorest tribulations—I can count them—eight thousand—are to be found in each mile that separates me and thee, my Kuling belle. But please don't fret: I'm not letting myself go. I shave my chin every day. You ask a reasonable question: What do I think I am doing? I am trying to know China. At last. In a way, my interest in a larger future has been revived by this experience—you know that I had become rather discouraged, had caught myself thinking only on a narrow, day-by-day catch-as-catch-can basis. Against a future time—for I am positive that the Visitors will not be here forever—I want to be one American who knows rural China. In that day I could be useful. I am making a beginning. I learn so much every day. I feel 'alive' to these people, Emily.

The diary:

Realized after I had sealed the letter that I hadn't even mentioned Father's passing. I guess I've been too busy to take it in. I know that just now I need his courage of that day at the ice pond, more than I ever have needed it.

ON A MARKET DAY in the nearby village of Li Chia, Treadup saw at a distance a young man who looked familiar, but for a time he could not place him. Too late—on the way back to Ma Ch'iao in his Indian, with Mi in the sidecar—he remembered where he had seen the fellow. He was one of the four Communists he had met in his first talk with the young team members, more than two years earlier.

The very next day he returned to Li Chia and went to Feng's house. It being the dead of winter, Feng was not in the fields; he was at a friend's house, his wife said, making some village plans. Treadup followed her directions, and found Feng gambling with three other men. Everyone was embarrassed. Treadup took Feng aside and, saying nothing about the gambling, told him he wanted to meet with one or more members of the Communist team that had been in Li Chia some time before. At first Feng said that would not be possible. He had no idea how to reach them. Treadup was patient. He did not say he had seen one of them the day before, for that would have caused Feng to lose face. He simply explained that he was now curious to know just what the Communists were advocating to villagers in the district; he wanted to get acquainted with some of them; he was not interested in getting them in trouble. Finally Feng said he would "do some investigating." Could T'ao Tu Hsien-sheng come back three days later?

TREADUP could not. His toothache suddenly became much worse; one whole side of his face was swollen.

He boarded his motorcycle, rode to Paoting, changed to Western clothes, drove on to Peking, and went straight to the Peking Union Medical College dental clinic. His regular dentist, Dr. Curtis, was jammed up with appointments, so he resorted to a Dr. Yang, who took one look in his mouth and told him to come back the next day.

He decided to spend the night in T'ungchow. The bachelor quarters in the Fergenarders' house took him in. The men were impressed by his mustaches. The next morning Jack Spear came down to breakfast with a big black mustache painted on his face; he blew out one cheek to match Treadup's swelling. "See what I can do in one day?" he said. One tip of the painted mustache curled downward, the other end upward. He called this "the Mona Lisa effect."

That afternoon Treadup spent two hours in Dr. Yang's chair. "His technique," David wrote Emily,

> is the roughest that I have ever admitted into my mouth, he let me know I am a foreigner, I just hope the results will be worth it. He lanced the infection. I have to go back tomorrow and Wednesday for follow-ups.
>
> Earlier this evening I attended a concert of Nancy Runner's 'a cappella' choir. Twelve people, all but one Chinese, singing Bach ect., mighty 'espressivo' (although every note was 'sforzato,' accented to the skies, their larynxes a bit squeezed, as if enthusiasm had them by the throat). Ultra-refined. Hard work had gone into it. But I must admit I began to pick the thing to pieces when we got back to Jim's house. Then the fellows landed on me for being critical—saying hoity-toity criticism was the missionaries' greatest fault. My point I thought was obvious— that it's a shame to ram our Western sounds down Chinese necks. The men really bristled at me, and I began to wonder whether their sharpness with me had anything to do with Johann Sebastian Bach—whether it

wasn't something altogether different — whether they didn't think my going down to live in a village was, shall we say, "out of bounds" for One Of Us. For a few minutes I felt like a regular flea. Then the fellows got Christian again — tolerated me, tried not to scratch the bites.

After two more "fierce sessions" in Dr. Yang's office, Treadup was dismissed to go home. The swelling had subsided, and what pain now remained was Yang-induced. He stopped overnight in Paoting on the way back. The diary (this he did not write to Emily):

All three compound dogs killed. Our own people shot them in the head. Dr. Ch'en's version: With the foreigners all gone, no one was taking care of them; seemed the merciful thing to put them out of their misery. But Ting the gateman confided the truth to me. He said Communist guerrillas had ordered everyone in the whole area to kill their dogs, so that when the guerrillas stalked about on night raids, no barking would betray them.

BACK in the villages, Treadup went straight to Feng and asked him to arrange for him to see the Communist team. Feng said they had been offended by his not showing up the last time; they hadn't believed the toothache story. They said they would not talk to him. They wanted the villagers to ask him to leave.

"It seems," he wrote that night, not referring directly to his last devastating talk with the Communist team, but evidently reacting partly to it,

that if you are rude, Communists, too, can lose face. But it's worse than that. I can't work with these people — or rather, they won't work with me; I remain, to them, a 'mu-shih,' and that settles it. I can't work against them, either — that would be to support the KMT, and the KMT is too discredited among the villagers. Was it Blackie who wrote that I'm 'in limbo'?"

And the next day, a deeply discouraged line:

I begin to see the force of Em's advice that I remove myself to T'ungchow and mix with my own kind.

WE HAVE no way of knowing what sort of recovery from this low mood Treadup might have been able to make, given time, for three days later — on December 8, 1941 — at six o'clock in the morning, just as he was finishing his breakfast of millet gruel, a hard-boiled egg, and tea, he heard loud quarreling at the head of the village street. He went out to see what was going on. There he found Colonel Yamamoto, the Japanese Christian liaison with the missionaries of the area, and Treadup's own two Japanese shadows, surrounded by a dozen village men, all of whom were shouting at once.

Treadup approached the group. Colonel Yamamoto made friendly signals to him. Treadup raised his hands to quiet the villagers. One of the shadows could translate from Japanese to mangled Chinese for Colonel Yamamoto, but not without long discussions as to nuances of meaning. Through this interminable process of decoding came the following approximate essences:

YAMAMOTO *"You will have to come with me."*
TREADUP *"Why?"*
YAMAMOTO *"Didn't you hear, on the radio?"*
TREADUP *"There are no radios in Ma Ch'iao."*
YAMAMOTO *"Japan and the United States are at war."*
TREADUP *"What!"*
YAMAMOTO *"The Japanese have sunk the American fleet. Very sorry, all Americans are being taken into detention. You must get your things and come with me."*

The villagers were wild. They offered to disarm and kill the Japanese on the spot. Treadup said that would do no good. Other Japanese would come and take him away, and the village would be horribly punished. There was nothing for him to do but obey.

Treadup learned through the decoding shadow that his detention might be for a long period; he should fill up one trunk with things he would want. Treadup went back to his house and packed Western clothing for warm and for cold weather; a Bible; writing materials; toilet articles; a mess kit and canteen; all the diaries he had not sent home with Emily.

Villagers carried the trunk to Colonel Yamamoto's truck. The farewells that followed, there in the street, were "like good cloth being torn."

Colonel Yamamoto drove Treadup into the city of Paoting.

The diary:

God must be a poet. His rhymes, though, leave something to be desired. I am under detention, along with the handful of Americans remaining in Paoting, in, of all places, the Y.M.C.A. building.

BOOK EIGHT

田

ENTERING

THE CENTURY

IN THRALL

THE FIRST DAYS had the rough texture of surprise. Captivity was a mystery, and in its thrall Treadup did not have the energy even to think about the meaning of his new state of life.

THERE WAS plenty of room. Nineteen men of six nationalities were housed in the gymnasium. Two women, Dominican tertiary nuns recently arrived from Shensi with wilted starched wimples and dusty white habits, had the privacy of an office room. These were the only "enemies" rounded up, in or near Paoting. The boards of the gym floor, on which the men slept supperless the first night, reeked of tung oil. There was no heat. Treadup ached. "My bones were like rusty scrap iron." No less than twenty military police had been assigned to guard the foreigners; the duty men coughed and nattered all night.

Captors began padding around in stockinged feet at five o'clock on the morning of Tuesday, the ninth. They carried kerosene lanterns to cut the darkness. They fed their guests a breakfast of millet mush and pickled turnips, and green tea. They dragged in palliasses — big cotton bags stuffed with straw — for their guests thenceforth to sleep on.

After dawn a superior officer entered with a blinding smile — five chromium teeth glittered in his jaws. With the help of an arrogant Formosan interpreter, Japanese to Chinese, the officer announced that the American fleet had been turned turtle at anchor at Hawaii. He spoke as if this were a matter of course. Most of the businessmen did not understand Chinese; Treadup translated into English, which two Britishers, naturally, and two Belgians, a Dutchman, and a Swede readily grasped. The Dutchman received the details with unseemly relish.

The officer had a desk carried into the gym, and seated at it he began to interrogate his guests, one by one.

A SQUAD of ten men went with Treadup to the Congregationalist compound. This was called an inspection. The commanding officer wanted to know who the few remaining Chinese in the compound were — the gateman, the gardener, three ministers, four doctors, a dozen nurses, charwomen, cooks, launderers, coolies, all according to their callings and functions. A consular secretary listed buildings and their uses. Treadup's only written reaction to all this was: "Their attention to exact details is breathtaking." Two men with a bucket of foul-smelling paste and a big brush affixed large paper seals, with death warnings and dire red chops on them, to all doors except those of the hospital. Round-the-clock guards were stationed at the compound gate. At this, Ting the gateman retired to his k'ang, ill, evidently felled by a massive and irreversible loss of face. Two men of the troop took Treadup back to the Y.

THE JAPANESE, Treadup noted later, seemed to have been transformed by the success at Pearl Harbor. They walked straight, looked one right in the eye, sucked in less apologetic breath before speaking. They were polite. "They had stopped being caricatures of themselves," David wrote in "Search," "and had turned into real people."

ON THE TENTH all the foreign guests were summoned to the headquarters of the military police. They were carried there in a truck which backfired through the streets, alarming the populace with sounds of yet another war. Guards stood on the running boards.

The officer with metal teeth turned out to be the commander of the MPs. His name was Matsuyama. He was very friendly. He made a speech, complete with graceful gestures of the arms — he seemed to be conducting the sweet

music of war. He said pleasantly that the Japanese had a duty to protect all
the peoples of Asia against the perfidy of the British and Americans. A great
ship named the *Prince of Wales* had been sunk near Singapore (one of his
hands sank to the bottom of the sea). The American air force in Manila had
been destroyed on the ground; Japanese had landed (a hand beached itself on
the Philippines). The guests, he said—giving the impression that a new
measure of indulgence would follow each such Japanese triumph—were now
free to return to their homes. The homeless Catholic ladies could either remain
at the Y.M.C.A. or lodge with others. All door seals would be removed.

Colonel Matsuyama handed out to each guest a lengthy and intricate
declaration form, with instructions to list all property at the person's home
and place of business, giving the exact nature, size or quantity, and value of
every item; and to return the filled form by the following Wednesday. Next he
waved in the air a list of thirteen regulations governing foreigners in Paoting.
These, he announced with agreeable flashes of chromium, were lenient. He
read them. It was stipulated that every person must procure an identification
card. Movement would be restricted. Special passes could be obtained in
exceptional circumstances. All cash money would have to be surrendered. The
diary: "Found it hard to concentrate on mundane matters."

The foreign guests were now dismissed to go home. On foot. It was a
long walk to the American Board compound—especially for the nuns, whom
Treadup had invited to inhabit the quarters of Letitia Selden and Helen
Demestrie. The strong nuns carried their own sparse baggage.

THEY WERE "free" but not free. Captivity, Treadup soon found, could have
relative degrees. He and the nuns were no longer confined in the Y, but
Japanese guards still manned the compound gates day and night; three
guards took turns at the door of the Cowley house, where Treadup was living;
and three kept track of the nuns. (Too close track, those ladies quite calmly
confided to Treadup after the first night. Treadup gathered that the guards,
who had obtained ladders from somewhere, were vigilant at the bedroom
panes perhaps to see whether there were weapons concealed beneath all those
yards of white drapery. "These women have tough fiber," Treadup wrote. "No
hysteria.") The foreigners' movement was indeed restricted. One had to obtain
permits to go to the gate to obtain permits to go to town to obtain permits to
do anything whatsoever.

In all dealings the Japanese were scrupulously polite—even, the sisters
reported, while peeping, for beyond the glass they had encouragingly kept
smiling and nodding. But they were, it seemed to Treadup, active to a fault.
"Like mosquitoes. Always buzzing at your ear and endeavoring to land on
skin." He obediently tried to draw up the required inventories, but he was
interrupted again and again for what were called "routine inspections." An

architect came to survey the buildings. A doctor came to look at the hospital. An army cook came to examine the kitchens. Treadup concluded that the Japanese wanted to use the compound to quarter troops.

The young lieutenant in charge of the gate guards was especially friendly. Named Koniishi, he said he had lived twelve years in California, though his accent and grammar suggested that the stay, if there had been one, had been much shorter. He remained at Treadup's shoulder all day. He knocked at the door in the evening, wanting to play parlor games. Treadup found a Crokinole set that had belonged to the boys; the pair made up rules as they went along. "I had a nice time," Treadup wrote.

> It was my first chance to unwind into my living self. I had a companion in bewilderment. Under the layers of Greater East Asia Co-Prosperity Sphere nonsense lay a homesick and scared human being.

THE NEXT MORNING Koniishi came with a summons for Treadup to appear at military police headquarters in town. In a frigid, barren office, Treadup was submitted to a fierce questioning, by metal jaws himself, about his work in the villages. Matsuyama put his questions courteously, but a Korean interpreter into Chinese, feeling the power of his necessity, snarled in the style he evidently imagined suitable for the New Order in East Asia. It seemed to be suspected that Mr. Teddy had ties to guerrillas. Many of the questions were obviously based on items Koniishi had reported from the conversation over Crokinole the previous evening. So much for soft feelings for a homesick and scared human being. At one point, Matsuyama called in a medic to take Treadup's blood pressure, to see if he was lying.

The diary: "Was having difficulty hearing, especially on the right side. Is it that I can't believe my ears half the time?"

AT THE COMPOUND the nuns told Treadup that they had had permits to go to Paoting to buy some dry goods they needed. In the street they had encountered the Dutchman, their fellow captive the other night at the Y, being trundled along by two Japanese at his elbows. He was in tip-top spirits. He said he had heard on the radio that New York had been bombed by two unmarked planes.

MEAGER NOTES in the diary:

On Wednesday, the seventeenth, Treadup dutifully handed in his inventory. He did not, however, dutifully hand in all his cash. The stocking containing the Mexican silver dollars of Madame Shen remained in the drawer.

On Thursday Treadup went to the hospital and asked Dr. Ch'en to look in his ears. The doctor removed from his right ear "enough wax to polish a ballroom floor."

ON FRIDAY MORNING Koniishi brought a chit notifying "Mr Trodop" that he was expected at the military police office at one thirty in the afternoon. The sisters received the same notice, and it turned out that all foreigners had been summoned.

> First sign that new changes were in store for us: Good-mannered, chromium-toothed Matsuyama has vanished. New Colonel Nomura presides. His style is exclamatory. He shouts, the message passing through the nasty Korean interpreter's mouth just as loudly, that there are new regulations. No foreigners may stay in Paoting. The Imperial Government has impounded all "enemy" property here. Foreigners must now remove themselves, either to the Legation Quarter of Peking or to the British or French Concessions of Tientsin. Japanese military will provide necessary communications with those cities for persons wishing to make arrangements. No time to think. I grasp at idea of Mrs. Evenrude, with whom Emily stayed in Tientsin. I know that when women were evacuated from North China, she refused to leave, Tientsin being her "only home." Send telegram.

A reply came that very afternoon. ("These Js are mechanical toys—wind 'em up and they *move*.") It turned out that Mrs. Evenrude was overjoyed at the prospect of having a man in the house.

TREADUP'S departure could be prompt. All the movable family belongings were already in the eight tin-lined boxes he had packed before moving to Ma Ch'iao. He hired a cartman to carry the boxes to the railroad station. The Catholic sisters, who were going to take asylum with some Maryknoll nuns in Peking, went with him, in rickshas; so did Lieutenant Koniishi, who had been sheepish ever since the interrogation he had caused. It turned out that Koniishi was to be his guard all the way to Tientsin. Treadup was feeling a little stout: Madame Shen's dollars were in a money belt around his waist.

The Japanese put their guests in a second-class car. For the first time in eleven days, Treadup sat still. Thought ensued. On its heels came a terrible crash.

I remember that I began by wondering what I was getting into. Barely knew Mrs. Evenrude. Recalled Em's complaints about how Mrs. E made her generosity felt. Then—suddenly—sensation of dizziness—I was visited by the most terrible comprehension. All these days I had been too busy, or too confused, to see it. I was leaving my vineyard. Would I ever come back? I might never again see roses bloom on the arbor I built to celebrate my love for my wife and sons. Worse than that, far worse than that. The bottom had dropped out from under my useful life. My entire life for Christ had been utterly wasted. Lectures!—where had they led? The villages!—hollow shells. Everything I had done had been swallowed up into absurdity. A future? How long would the Visitors be here? How long would I be, in effect, a prisoner of war? All the news of the war fronts we had been getting was bad. I thought: I am sixty-three years old—finished before my time.

WHAT IS MAN?

BY THE TIME Treadup reached Tientsin, he had a headache which seemed to peak and throb at the very top of his skull. "It was as if my loftiest thoughts had turned out to be painful."

At the Tientsin East railway station, military police took this bleak and worn-out Treadup into a side room and asked him for his papers. He surrendered them. Three MPs held a long discussion. They went away. Half an hour later they returned. Through an interpreter into Chinese, they told Treadup that his intercity pass was invalid. It had been tampered with.

Treadup, feeling great heat at the top of his head, demanded to see it. Koniishi stood to one side, not helping at all. The men showed Treadup his pass. Sure enough, it had first been made out with Peking as the destination, and then the characters for Peking had been crossed out and Tientsin substituted. The MPs argued that Mr. Teddy may have done this himself.

Treadup shouted at Koniishi to speak up. Koniishi shrugged; said he knew nothing.

Then, for the first time in his memory, Treadup became wildly angry. He shouted that all Japanese were madmen. As if that were not enough, they were stupid madmen. They were idiotic victims of their own bumbling. They were so used to treating people like dogs that they had become worse than dogs themselves. Treadup's roar was impressive, and the interpreter was too frightened to tell the Japanese what the man was saying. This was a new frustration: the anger was not reaching its goal. Treadup's shouts grew even more abusive. He was nearly twice as big as the Japanese soldiers, and as he railed at them, he leaned over toward them with his fists clenched, and they retreated, running away out of the room on short legs like—like what? He could not think what. A picture was at the edge of his mind, but he could not quite summon it.

Ten minutes later they returned to the examination room and said Treadup could proceed to the British Concession.

In "Search":

I trembled in the ricksha all the way to Davenport Road. I was deeply humiliated by my un-Christian behavior. My head hurt. I was puzzled and scared by my loss of control. At one turning I laughed out loud. The laughter frightened me, because it seemed so irrational. I was afraid my headache was turning my brain toward hysterics. It took much time and great distance for me to realize that I had had a wonderful moment of feeling triumphant in the midst of my thorough defeat—for it had been at that moment that the picture which had hovered just off the periphery of my imagination at the station flickered into and out of my mind. A cruel image. A covey of fat little quail chicks running along the ground. That was what they had looked like, scurrying out of the room. In other words I had begun to uncover something that had been hidden from me all my life because it seemed that Jesus would not have approved:—namely, that shouting produced results, that hot anger ripened fruit faster than sunlight could.

MRS. EVENRUDE'S welcome left much to be desired. "You have come at a bad time," she said. "I have an ulcer on my leg. Just like a miserable Chinese beggar."

She pulled up her long skirt and showed Treadup a bandage on her left leg with an ugly greenish stain on it. She turned and showed it to Koniishi. He sucked in air and bowed at her leg.

She said to Treadup, "This infidel is charming," and she asked Koniishi if he wanted a cup of tea. He evidently had decided to pretend he did not understand English. She said, in Chinese, "*Ch'a! Ch'a! Ch'a!*" He made as if to understand and bowed. So they sat in the living room with curtains drawn and drank tea in a silence that was heaped up against the false language barrier. Treadup fumed. Mrs. Evenrude bobbed her chin up and down and smiled to Koniishi; in delicate mimicry he bobbed and grinned at her. At last they got rid of him.

An hour later two Peking carts pulled in at Mrs. Evenrude's gate, with all of Treadup's boxes. "What *is* this?" Mrs. Evenrude asked. "Have you come for life?"

There was a pounding at the top of Treadup's head. "They would have taken my things," he said, "if I had left them."

"This is not a godown," Mrs. Evenrude said. She peckishly told her Number One Boy and her coolie to put the boxes in an empty room in the servants' quarters.

Treadup was to stay in the room Emily had used, looking out on the now leafless umbrella tree. He fell onto the bed, shoes and all. When he woke it was dark. He felt worse than ever.

OVER a frugal supper, Mrs. Evenrude grew talkative. "My husband, Simon Evenrude," she said, "was a curious man. Of course, you have never been married to a lawyer, so you wouldn't know. Everything had to be precise. We lived by question and answer. My life, Mr. Treadup, was one long cross-examination. He's dead and gone now, but I'm in the habit. If you want to know anything in this house, you have to come at me with sharp questions. I won't volunteer anything. You'll just have to keep after me."

To try to oblige her, though he did not have his heart in the work, Treadup asked some questions. Gloria Evenrude, he learned, had grown up in the Berkshire hills of Massachusetts, daughter of a schoolteacher. She had had a Methodist education at Wellesley, "but to tell the truth I could never get so much as a peep out of Jehovah in answer to a prayer — when I really *needed* something — I plumb gave up."

She and her husband had gone to Tientsin Union Church because it was expected, "but to tell the truth, Mr. Treadup, you people are so long-winded. Boredom knocks the faith out of a person."

How did she pass her time?

"Oh, I do the usual committee work. I putter. Fuss."

How had she met her husband?

He had hung out a shingle in Pittsfield. "He was around. You know."

Why China, then?

"Simon had a classmate who went into B.A.T." — British-American Tobacco Company — "and he just wrote Simon and said, 'Why don't you come out here? It's a good life. Tientsin Club. The Racecourse. Summers at the beach.' So we came."

Treadup's head hurt. He was running out of questions. *Had* it been a good life?

Well, yes and no.

Mrs. Evenrude looked expectantly at Treadup. She obviously was waiting for a follow-up question to her cryptic answer.

But Treadup said, "I have a headache."

This announcement transformed Mrs. Evenrude. Her voice, which had been sharp and combative, grew soft and kind. She said Dr. Cunningham had promised to come in to dress her ulcer the next morning. He lived just three houses along. She could send her coolie Liu over and ask him to come right away.

No, Treadup said. He thought he would go to bed and see whether he could sleep it off.

Mrs. Evenrude came around the table to feel his forehead. Her hand was cool, with a feathery touch trembling from concern. "No temp," she said. "Thank heavens."

THE HEADACHE was worse.

"It keeps knocking. Right at the very crown."

"Let's have a look-see," the chubby little doctor said. He had merry eyes. Treadup was not in a mood to meet them for long. A milk-white hand popped a thermometer in Treadup's mouth. Standing beside huge Treadup's chair, Dr. Cunningham could barely lean over to see the top of his head. "Look here, old chap," he said. "You've a great ruddy boil there."

He started Treadup on hot compresses. "I'll send over a book to read," he said. "Passes the time when you're balancing a hot bag on your bean."

He kept his promise. Half an hour later a servant came with a leather-bound book. It was the Thomas Shelton translation of *Don Quixote de la Mancha.*

BEFORE supper on Christmas Eve Mrs. Evenrude decorated a Christmas tree with shiny baubles she had made herself, and she clipped to the branches little tin candleholders into which she stuck pretty three-inch candles with twisted flutings of wax of different colors. Then she set up, across from the piano in her living room, a crèche, its Mary and Joseph and manger and Christ child and wise men and shepherds and sheep all made of papier-mâché. She told Treadup she had ordered these figures from the Chinese craftsmen who made those remarkably lifelike figures and objects that the Chinese liked to burn at the graves of the newly deceased to keep the dead company on the other side. "They did not want to make sheep. They said sheep were foul—no one would want *them* in the spirit world. I went to some trouble to tell them the story of the Nativity, but when I said that the child's mother was a virgin, they turned away from me. None of them ever looked at me again. They thought I had the evil eye. Foreign-devil lies! They tripled their price. Look what they *did* with the Virgin Mary. You'd think she was a White Russian prostitute." Mrs. Evenrude cocked her head to one side. "I like her that way. It deepens the mystery, don't you think?"

At midnight Mrs. Evenrude, dressed in a red flannel peignoir, got Treadup up out of bed, and the pair—she leaning on his arm and limping, he in his pajamas holding a damp facecloth on top of his head—went downstairs to light the candles. "It was breathtakingly dangerous," Treadup wrote Emily.

We sang "O Little Town of Bethlehem," our every exhalation blowing the tiny flames toward the dry needles. It is a wonder that I am alive to write this letter.

Early Christmas morning Dr. Cunningham dropped in. Mrs. Evenrude's leg was bad, and Treadup had already written in his diary: "Head more sore! More heat!" The doctor said he wanted to take the two to St. John's Hospital to make some blood tests. Mrs. Evenrude crankily ordered her carriage, and soon the angry lady, silent Treadup, and the bubbling little doctor were riding through the Tientsin streets behind the clopping of a chestnut mare.

"Are you enjoying the book I sent you?" the doctor asked Treadup.

"You chose it because it's about me, didn't you?"

"My dear fellow, you must cheer up. I think you have this pestilence on your noddle because the dem thing's so full of darkness."

The pair reached home in late afternoon.

The noon Christmas dinner was switched to evening. Pain did not curb Treadup's appetite. He wrote:

Delicious!—capons, roast potatoes, rutabaga, peach pickles, hot biscuits, jelly, fruit cup, salad, steamed puddings w hard sauce, nuts, coffee. The old girl outdid herself. Thought about what the doc said and tried to laugh—at him—with him—he is such a madcap. But I have no gaiety in me. None.

THE DIARY: "Boxing Day. Boil alarming. Nursing it all along, and reading." Dr. Cunningham came in three times during the day.

He is very kind, bounces around like a sprite. But I am not up to it. My spirits in a sharp decline all afternoon. The work of my mission has been a waste. I am nothing.

In the night he wrote:

Waked up in a bad sweat. O Lord God, what have I done to anger you? I remember that when Mr. Lin was in desperation, that time when I took him to Peitaiho, we read the Book of Job together. Job had far worse than I: 'many' sore boils from the sole of his foot unto the place where I have mine.

The next morning, these words—not exactly words of comfort—copied from that book:

"I will not refrain my mouth; I will speak in the anguish of my spirit; I will complain in the bitterness of my soul. . . . My soul chooseth strangling, and death rather than my life. I loathe it; I would not live alway: let me alone; for my days are vanity. What is man, that thou shouldest magnify him? and that thou shouldest set thine heart upon him? And that thou shouldest visit him every morning, and try him every moment? How long wilt thou not depart from me, nor let me alone till I swallow down my spittle? I have sinned; what shall I do unto thee, O thou preserver of men? why hast thou set me as a mark against thee, so that I am a burden to myself? And why dost thou not pardon my transgression, and take away mine iniquity? for now shall I sleep in the dust; and thou shalt seek me in the morning, but I shall not be."

YET HE WAS. In the morning Dr. Cunningham brought him two more books: volumes of essays by Montaigne and Emerson.

"You have American books?" Treadup asked.

"I have Montaigne in French if you prefer. When you have a mite more pepper in you, Treadup, you must come and see my library."

The diary:

Nursed head most of day, read. Toward evening boil opened with copious discharge and relief! The relief was such that I thought of the day of my conversion—not that the main load is off my shoulders this time: the load of the end of everything. That misery is far sorer than a mere boil. But the physical relief is sweet. The poison—what is it? hatred of those who destroy?—is draining out of me.

Another entry:

Tonight I read, side by side, Montaigne's and Emerson's essays on friendship. In all my years in China I have never had an English friend. Have I had any friends? Mr. Lin—used to be a friend. (I tried to find him the other day: was told he had left for free China in November.) Johnny Wu a friend?—no—he teacher, I pupil. Em? Yes! Em, my one dear friend. I am so lonely. I think I might try having an English friend. I like this little doctor. He is different.

ON THE TWENTY-NINTH, eight inches of snow fell. This much snow was rare for Tientsin. A wind came down off the Gobi Desert and piled and sculpted dynamic banks and eddies ribbed with ripples, as if the snow-drifts themselves were dunes of desert sand. The white-trimmed pine trees in Mrs. Evenrude's garden seemed to leap into classical painted scrolls. Treadup looked up from his book. "Why does such ravishing beauty make me so sad?"

The next day his sadness was edged with disgust—but in his passive state he was for some reason unable to push his blues over the edge into anger. A squad of Japanese soldiers bluffed their way past the coolie at the gate of Mrs. Evenrude's compound, brazenly tramped to the back of the enclosure, and with axes lopped off branches of the pine trees and took them away, apparently to use them in some sort of festive decorations for their triumphant New Year. They befouled the beautiful drifts with their indiscriminate footprints and left the trees disheveled and undressed to their hips. Mrs. Evenrude was in a state.

The following night, New Year's Eve, as Mrs. Evenrude and Treadup sat silently reading before a coal fire in the grate in her living room, there was a sudden roar of motorcycles, a pounding at the gate. Mrs. Evenrude sent a servant to investigate. Soon five Japanese in uniform burst into the living room. One announced in bad English that he was the consul general of Tientsin City. They were all drunk. "We pay social call," the consul cheerily said. "We go along Davenpole Road, every home we pay social call. How do you *do*? Are you Happy New Yeel, Mrs. Evellude?" He was not too drunk to know exactly where he was.

Mrs. Evenrude's rage of the previous day, which she had nurtured and treasured ever since, now suddenly vanished into thin air. Her strong will had turned gracious. She rose and gave her hand to the consul to be kissed. Then she rang for Number One Boy and sent for some port wine and seven glasses. "We had a little party," Treadup wrote Emily, in a letter that somehow reached Thornhill six months later (China! China!).

The most awful New Year celebration I ever witnessed. Mrs. E kept looking to me to entertain her friends, but I was Mr. Wet Blanket. I never heard so much giggling in my life as from those five. Mrs. Evenrude invited them for breakfast the next morning. They came! She served them waffles.

TREADUP'S boil dried up; Mrs. Evenrude's ulcer got worse. Dr. Cunningham was in the house every day. David learned how to change Mrs. Evenrude's dressings. Each time the doctor came, he sat down to chat awhile.

He has beehives in his compound. Today he got down on his hands and knees and did a dance of the kind worker bees do in summertime to alert their colleagues where to go for pollen. So earnest in his gyrations and

waggings of his head and shoulders, his little hands pitter-patting on the
carpet — I think I would have known exactly where to look: over in the
Russian park. He knows something about everything. He has lectured
me on Persian rites of Zarathustra, animal prows of Viking ships, Italian
landscape in the poems of Horace — on shoes and ships and sealing wax,
and cabbages and kings. He makes me talk. He draws science out of me,
as if drawing blood out of me with a pipette. "My God, Treadup,"
he said. "Stir your stumps. You're a dead thing, the way you are.
Stand up, man!"

In another note, Treadup wrote that it was strange to be living in "a lay atmosphere." Boredom with sermons had driven the faith out of Mrs. Evenrude, and Phinneas Cunningham was an agnostic. "I pray alone," Treadup wrote.

One day Dr. Cunningham told Treadup how he had happened to come to China as a non-missionary doctor. His father, he said, was a friend of Disraeli; he had helped persuade Disraeli to give the vote to workingmen in the Reform Act of 1867. This elder Cunningham had nine children, the last born when he was very old. He started out a zealous Christian and raised his first five children in the Anglican church. But after he read *The Origin of Species* he became just as zealously apostate, and refused to baptize his younger children. One of the first batch of the faithful, Phinneas's older sister Elizabeth, went to China as a missionary, with the China Inland Mission. Fifteen years later Phinneas, youngest of the faithless second batch, having studied medicine, grew restless and, "with nothing better to do," traveled to China, where his older sister got him a job with a government university; and he eventually took up practice of his own in Tientsin. He said he never wasted his time in church. "Hocus-pocus, pray for a crocus! Bah!"

A Sunday finally came when Dr. Cunningham invited Treadup for tea at his home. The house was "about to tumble down from the weight of the books in it." On all the walls, piled on desks and tables, scattered on the floor. Treadup remembered complimenting Yen Han-lin on "the fragrance of learning" in his calligraphy room; here, "I breathed the rank smell of this man's intelligence — such a small head, to contain so many tomes!"

After they had talked awhile, Treadup volunteered to help out at St. John's Hospital. He said he did not know what he could do, but he had come to the conclusion that he had better do something.

"Good man!" the little doctor said. "We'll start you out on bedpans. That'll shake you out. That'll cure you of the dims."

A FILLED ROUTINE

A NEW LIFE began. On the day he was to start his volunteer work, Treadup took Mrs. Evenrude to the hospital in her carriage. Her leg was still suppurating, and Dr. Cunningham wanted to keep her under his eye. The doctor had a tailor waiting to measure Treadup for whites to wear at work. Miraculously a suit was ready in an hour. "Thou behemoth," the doctor said, "thy force is in the navel of thy belly, thy tail moveth like a cedar, the sinews of thy stones are wrapped together, and thy bones are as strong as brass, and furthermore, thou great beast, it took three bolts of our best cotton cloth to cover thy belly and thy bum."

It turned out that this mischievous medical gnome had meant it about the bedpans. "I think I never knew before," Treadup wrote at the end of the day,

> what it means to be a missionary. I humbled my flesh today for the relief and easing of sufferers. The small Chinese nurses need my strength to lift women, as well as men, up for the pan. One of the heathens I serviced was Madame Evenrude. She was decently covered with a sheet the whole time, but she swore at me like a sailor. We know each other now.

And so life became a filled routine: work at the hospital in the morning, reading in the afternoon, a brisk walk three times around the Recreation Ground (he had a pass) late in the day, and reading again in the evening. The doctor loaned Treadup *David Copperfield*. Then *Tristram Shandy, Dead Souls, Moby Dick*. Then one day he said, "It's time for you to stop being an adolescent and become a man. I mean, it's time for you to read some poetry." He put into his hands the poems of John Donne and *The Tempest*. "The advantage for you of Donne," Dr. Cunningham said, "is that he was a preacher who knew that a soul is connected to a body." Then of course *The Tempest* would disconnect things again.

MRS. EVENRUDE'S leg cleared up. To celebrate Chinese New Year, which fell on February 14 that year, she put on a dinner for Treadup, Cunningham, and three purple-cheeked Englishmen from the business community. She served delicately glazed Peking duck—except that it was chicken. That was all her cook could buy in the black market. After dinner everyone played rummy. "I could hear my mother's voice," Treadup wrote. "*Cards,* son? Next thing we know, you'll be making *wagers.*"

THE JAPANESE had imposed a guard on the hospital. The MPs—and in general all Japanese officials and military personnel—were being correct in their behavior. Dr. Cunningham had developed a code for use in front of them. Pearl Harbor was when "the sun came up." The Japanese were all named Jonathan. The Chinese police in the puppet government were "blackies." The guards' demeanor at the hospital was variable, because the Japanese had a policy of changing commanding officers every ten days or so, presumably to forestall fraternizing of any kind. One Jonathan-boss asked to have the men of his guard vaccinated. Treadup assisted. The men were terrified. Treadup held their arms in his vise grip while little Cunningham scratched the skin. Each victim laughed hard when it was over.

IN MID-MARCH all the foreigners in Tientsin were summoned to a meeting. It was held in Gordon Hall, in Victoria Park. This building was named for Charles ("Chinese") Gordon, who had laid out the original British Concession, had then gone on to fight the Taipings and later had become the martyr of Khartoum. Treadup had been in the building often during his Tientsin duty days. He had written to brother Paul in a letter in 1906: "It is a kind of castle out of Sir Walter Scott—a romantic materialization of the British imperial dream—Gothic windows, crenelated battlements, crocketed finials." With a Japanese officer in a newly pressed uniform pacing back and forth under its proud British proscenium, as David wrote after this meeting, "the moment carried masonry and wood and human presence about as far as they could go toward the ridiculous."

The doubly captive audience was treated to a long lecture on the reasons for the war. "We had heard that gramophone record played often," Treadup wrote that night,

> but what was dampening was the news he gave us—all bad. I had thought I was getting my morale back, but the future looks black. This Jonathan rubbed it in. Singapore had fallen. The "gleat Amelican Genelal Douglas MacAuthle" had been humbled on the Bataan Peninsula south of Manila. The liner 'Normandie' had been set fire to in New York harbor and had rolled over on its side. There had been big ships sunk in the Java Sea. Everywhere, to believe this officer, the might of America and

Britain availed naught. As he spoke on and on, I found myself suffering a terrible and very strange attack of homesickness. Why strange? Because: The home I yearned for with all my sick heart was Ma Ch'iao. My villages! I had a deep, deep nostalgia for a sense of worth.

HE WENT on feeling worthless until April 15, when a new amazement occurred. A batch of mail arrived from the United States. "In wartime! This is China for you!" Four very old and very soiled and crumpled letters from Emily, showing obvious signs of having been steamed open. They were not cheering. Emily's alarm at all the news of the war and her fears for David in the long period of his silence—these were oppressive. He had no way of knowing whether the letters he had written had reached her, whether her anxiety had been relieved in the two months since the last of these of hers. Half a world's distance now seemed cosmic.

One piece of news she gave him: James B. Todd had died. The diary:

How sad I am about the difficult old warrior, after all. I thought him thick-skinned, and I resented his never liking my lecture program. Many grievances. Yet there was a grandeur about him, just the same. His vision never wavered. He was greedy for souls. I mourn him, truly. Yet as I write this I have another thought: What fun Phinneas Cunningham would have poked at old Todd! I can just hear him: "What a whale! What an everlasting whale!"

After that, no more letters came from Emily.

AS MRS. EVENRUDE recovered all her strength, she became worse and worse tempered. "She holds bedpans against me," Treadup wrote.

Figuratively, I mean, of course. When it comes to bodily functions, I think she is a little touched. She will never forgive me, she says, for— as she puts it—having intruded with my miserable receptacle on her "most secret relationship with Father Time." Everyone's true clock, she says, is in his entrails. "You sneaked in there and tried to read my bowel clock!"

She punished Treadup by making him feel he was becoming a nuisance. She had a hundred complaints. He used up enough bed linen for an army; he ate like a hairy mastodon; when he cleared his throat it sounded like two ships colliding; reading at night in the still chilly evenings, he used more coal than the Kailan Mining Administration could mine.

One day she ordered him to remove his "boxes of trash" from the room in the servants' quarters. She needed the space, she said, for "contingencies."

Phinneas Cunningham, to whom nothing was ever a ruffle, said he would find storage for the boxes at the hospital.

It took Treadup six days to get permission from the military police to make the move. Since the goods were going to a hospital, the Jonathans insisted upon opening the boxes and inspecting the contents. A day was arranged. The MPs tore off the metal strapping and threw things everywhere. Treadup repacked. But the carters Treadup had hired for that day did not show up. The MPs said the deal was off.

Treadup then had to go through the entire process of getting permission all over again, even including the inspection. The metal strapping of the boxes had to be stripped off once more, the contents all dumped out, the boxes repacked and restrapped.

Both times Mrs. Evenrude gave tea to the Jonathans but would not let Treadup have any.

At last the boxes were gone. But that was not the end of Mrs. Evenrude's vexations.

YET SHE COULD be tender. One day some coolies came to unload coal and wood, a supply for the next autumn. When they were finished unloading, she herded the coolies into her broad pantry and gave them a party. There must have been twenty of them. She fed them tea and cinnamon toast and scones with marmalade. They were filthy, poor, half-starved men, covered with coal dust. They wolfed this outlandish foreign-devil food in fearful yet ecstatic silence. Mrs. Evenrude hovered about, with pools of love in her eyes.

Her own household was not eating too well. Prices in the city were soaring. A picul of rice cost $250 in the rocky official currency. A half catty of brown sugar cost $3.20, a catty of pork $4.50. Decent food was hard to find. All the eggs and fresh vegetables in Cathay were going down Japanese necks. All this made what happened one afternoon a week after the coolie party especially moving.

There was rapping at the compound gate. Chou, the Number One Boy, came to Mrs. Evenrude and reported in the pidgin English he insisted on using, "Three piece no-good man, Missee. I tell them go way chop-chop?" Mrs. Evenrude asked what sort of men—Japanese or Chinese? "Chinee man. No good." Mrs. Evenrude told Chou to admit them to the back courtyard. He went away shaking his head.

Treadup went with Mrs. Evenrude to the platform by the kitchen, overlooking the back courtyard. There they found a delegation from the pack of coal coolies of the previous week. These men had brought from the country a live hen, a string of garlic, some huge radishes, and a basket of eggs. Treadup, turning to Mrs. Evenrude, saw that there were tears streaming down her cheeks. "Treadup, you brute," she angrily shouted, "get yourself down there and accept those gifts for me."

IN APPEASEMENT, on a Sunday morning, Treadup asked Mrs. Evenrude if she would like to go to Union Church with him. He thought she didn't have enough to do.

She refused. "Ten years ago," she said, "when I was trying to decide what to give up for Lent, I suddenly thought, 'I'll give up church.' I did, and I've never been back. It was a great blessing to be free of it. It will take more than you, Treadup, to get me back in that bad habit again."

Treadup went alone. The diary that night:

Shocked by the stupidity of the sermon. Reverend Planson—has had Union Church pulpit for decades—has lived well, I would say. English vicar type. Elegant Oxford tongue pushed around by a mule's brain. Rotund, shining pate with natural tonsure round sides and back. Spectacular red nose. His text St. Matthew 26:39: "O my Father, if it be possible, let this cup pass from me." It is just before Judas betrays Jesus in the garden at Gethsemane. Reverend Planson got all ensnared in the question of the nature of the wine in the cup. Spent twenty minutes of flawless grammar on it. Came to the suggestion that there was 'sake' in the cup. This must have been his idea of a subtle attack on our oppressors. Were the Japs going to kiss us in the garden? Was there, I wondered, a jug of wine in Reverend Planson's nose? Shocked is not too strong a word. I find myself deeply troubled tonight by the echoes of his cant, his pomposity, his complacency, his distance from all reality. O my poor villages! Prayer sticks in my throat like phlegm.

IN MAY came Mrs. Evenrude's seventieth birthday. She was furious all day.

ONE AFTERNOON while Treadup was out for his walk in the Recreation Ground, a Japanese in military uniform—"but without officer's tabs, or any sign of rank, I noticed when I got home"—arrived saying, in rudimentary English, that he had been ordered to make an inspection of the house. Mrs. Evenrude must have been wearing her disguise as a charming woman—which, Treadup noted, she almost always managed to have on when Japanese showed up. She received the man with cordial acquiescence. She guided him, like a chatelaine, from room to room. She opened all the closet doors. She pointed out the views from the windows.

The man demanded quarters for the night. He designated Mrs. Evenrude's guest room as his choice. She sent for Number One Boy to put the best linen on the bed.

The man ate a big British dinner—made delighted sucking noises over the boiled cabbage. He drank half a bottle of port. (The diary: "I got the creeps thinking of Reverend Planson's fillings of the cup of woe.") After dinner, it being rather warm, the man took off his tunic and his boots, undid his belt and fly, and "made himself at home in his underwear." Mrs. Evenrude kept up a front, chatting with him—or, rather, at him—as if he were draped in admiral's braid. The man stumbled upstairs quite drunk shortly after ten.

The next morning Treadup decided to stay home from the hospital. The man was still snoring at eleven o'clock. Treadup then went to the military police. A party of four MPs returned to the house with him. They got the man out of bed and took him away.

No explanation was forthcoming. The diary, two weeks later: "I must have been to the MPs ten times to ask about our overnighter. All they will ever say: 'So sorry, investigation not finish.' "

It never was finished. The mystery was never solved. From time to time Mrs. Evenrude would sigh and say, "Wasn't that a lovely chap who dropped in on us? So much better manners the Japanese have than the Chinese."

THE DIARY:

> *I guess I love this cranky old woman, but I don't know how long I can stand the life with her. If it were not for Phinneas, and his books, and my telling myself that the patients at the hospital suffer more than I, I don't know what I would do. I am so worried about Em worrying about me. O Em, I am so lonely! I am such a failure!*

A LESSON IN COMBAT

TIENTSIN'S heat was coming on like a panting wonk—a mangy, wild, bad-breathed, scavenging Chinese dog of a summer. "Something," Treadup wrote,

> *is happening to the Jonathans. Something is happening to Mrs. E. Something is happening to me. God—if, by any chance, you have washed*

your ears lately and can hear my crude yawp amongst all the hideous noise up here in North China—please help us all. Are you listening?

TREADUP had long since graduated from bedpans. He was now, without bearing the title, the chief administrative officer of the hospital, in charge of personnel, laundry, cockroaches, kitchens, floor-mopping, scouring the black market for food for the patients—all the odds and ends of basic existence under occupation. The work did not make him cheerful.

On Monday, June 15, 1942, at seven thirty in the morning, this huge factotum and his tiny friend the chief medical officer arrived at the hospital together on foot. The hospital gateman, greatly exercised, told them that the third floor was swarming with "yellow jackets." The two men ran up.

In the O.R. the Jonathans were systematically pulling out the surgical instruments and wrapping them in newspaper bundles and stowing them away in wooden boxes which they had brought with them. They absolutely cleaned out the instruments, even Ob and Gyn. Phinneas began to howl. The senior J claimed in atrocious English that he was an M.D., and he produced a piece of paper—orders from a very high altitude, somewhere way up around the Emperor's forehead. I have never seen my dear Phinneas so crushed; in that instant the cricket lost his song.

The yellow jackets started in on boxed apparatus, cystoscopes and such, and packed the boxes away, even empty ones. They rifled small drawers, taking used gloves, rubber tubing, scrub brushes. They left the dressings untouched, and for some reason they did not pack the supply of surgical needles. Dr. Cunningham protested every item in little broken yelps. The Jonathans worked stolidly, ignoring him. Everything from the operating room walked out—tables, furniture, bottles. They overlooked one small instrument table, which they had heaped with other loot, and a few odds and ends were left in the autoclave, still hot from the morning sterilization.

All the Japanese trooped out with their loads. They seemed to be leaving. Treadup steered poor Dr. Cunningham to his office on the second floor.

Soon came the self-styled M.D. with a demand to be led to the drug stockroom. The Japanese cleaned out everything there except six pounds of ether, a drum of leper oil, and ten gallons of alcohol. The X-ray room was locked. "Give key," said the M.D. In the X-ray room the M.D. asked Cunningham so many foolish questions that the Englishman finally turned to Treadup and said, "This man is not a doctor. I cannot stomach any more of this." He left.

The non-doctor ordered Treadup to have the X-ray machine disassembled; he would come back for it with a truck later in the day.

Where were the hypodermics? Treadup led him to the closet.

They packed all the hypes, needles, thermometers; a case of laundry soap;
I.V. tubes; our three precious copper sterilizers. All this time the false M.D.
was trying his English out on me. He said: "I think you are very sorry."
I said, "I am much more than sorry." But when I asked him his name,
he suddenly forgot his English and couldn't understand my question.

Next, the wards. The non-doctor ordered his men to clear off the
dressing carts and medicine trays.

I called a halt to that. I said, "We have twenty-one patients here who
have to be cared for until we can arrange for them to go home. We need
this stuff." He said, "How long patient stay?" I said, "If they stay
only twenty-four hours, they will get the best care we can give them."
I began un-Christianly to shove the little bugger. He said, "Understand!
Understand!" and ordered the things put back.

A Chinese doctor named Han came into the ward. Non-doctor demanded
his stethoscope. Dr. Han took it off from around his neck and handed it over.
Treadup said ("my voice was climbing the registers"), "That does not
belong to the hospital. That belongs to Dr. Han."
"How many hospital have?"
"There are five doctors in the hospital. Each owns one."
"You keep two. I take three." The doctor reached Han's stethoscope back,
baring his teeth in a samurai grin. "Divide. Spirit of Meiji," he said.
"You go back to Tokyo and get an order personally signed by Mr. Meiji.
Then we give you three stethoscopes."
Treadup moved a few steps toward the doctor.
"Understand! Understand!"

PHINNEAS CUNNINGHAM disassembled the X-ray machine himself with
tender loving care. "You know, Treads," he said at one point, "I brought
this tube up from Shanghai sixteen years ago with it in my lap all the way."
Dr. Cunningham laid out the parts in meticulous order on the X-ray room
floor, so he could explain how the machine should be reassembled. He had to
tear out part of a wall to free the developing tank.
It was nine at night and nearly dark when the Japanese sent their truck.
This time the M.D. did not even come; he sent a noncom and ten Chinese
coolies. There was no one to whom to explain the complicated reassembly.
The Chinese coolies—"out of a well of wisdom which neither Phinneas
nor I could plumb"—destroyed the X-ray machine. They slid and thumped the
heavy parts down the hospital's concrete stairs, severely chipping the edges of
the steps and crumpling the metal of the apparatus. Whatever was sensitive
in the machine they treated roughest. They dropped some parts from waist

level onto the pavement beside the truck. With a coolie chant they swung the box containing the precious tube three times and hurled it up onto the truck.

> *That's that. Sixteen years of merciful work have come from that machine; it has paid for itself in compassion. If a machine could have a heart, it would have had one. It will take no more pictures. Ever. No one will be able to put those damaged parts together. At first Phinneas was saddened by the destruction of such a beautiful device, but later he laughed and said, "Those poor coolie geezers gave us a lesson in combat, what? Instinct!"*

IT WAS OBVIOUS that the Japanese planned to appropriate the hospital building. Without telling Mrs. Evenrude, who had grown extremely touchy, Treadup hired a cartman and moved his boxes back into the room in Mrs. Evenrude's servant quarters. They made the move under cover of darkness, and Treadup paid the cartman and his helper extra to be very quiet as they worked. He also gave Mrs. Evenrude's Number One Boy, Chou, a big tip, and Chou happily assured Treadup: "No talkee, no talkee." Treadup's gloomy comment:

> *Is this my old badness? It is the first dishonest thing I can remember doing in all my years in China. I suppose there is no real harm. She never goes down into the servants' courtyard; she will never know. But of course I know. What else could I have done? Phinneas said I must do it.*

TREADUP was showing signs of self-doubt. He started a new commonplace book, in which he entered passages from books Cunningham was lending him, with sketchy but telling comments. An early entry:

> *Herman Melville — keen sense of good and evil — yet merciless toward missionaries — does he speak of men like angry Dr. Elting, grim old soul harvester? Or poor Cowley, the murderer? Or me, cheater of a helpless old woman? 'Typee,' ch. xxvi: "May not the unworthiness or incapacity of those who assume apostolic functions upon the remote islands of the sea more easily escape detection by the world at large than if it were displayed in the heart of a city?"*

JAPANESE SOLDIERS had begun to loot foreign homes. Word got around that Arthur Elmslee, long the Tientsin branch manager of the Hong Kong–Shanghai Bank, had bribed the Japanese to allow foreigners in the city to store their most lootable valuables in safe deposit boxes in the bank building, even though the premises had been taken over by the Japanese. Dr. Cunningham told Mrs. Evenrude about the subterfuge. She flew into a rage at Treadup for having withheld this information from her. "But I just learned it from Phinneas myself, this very day, exactly when you did," he protested. This defense did him no good. She was convinced he had known for some time. He went with her to the bank in her carriage. She deposited some necklaces, most of her flat silver, and some cheap bric-a-brac she called "my heirlooms." She remained implacably furious at David.

> *Simon Evenrude must have had a black tongue. She learned some curse words from him that I have never heard before. It is hard to listen to filth in a woman's mouth — harder to think I may be the filth she says I am. I thought I was warding it all off, when she said, "I know that you brought your miserable trash back to my storage room, you sly b — st — d." Chou must have spent my tip and told her. She has caught me. I am still blushing, two hours later. The filth is on my hands. I have a pain in my old place in my left upper arm.*

The next night Treadup wrote:

> *Mrs. E has broken down with headaches and sleepnessness. She took to her bed when we got back from the bank yesterday. Hide nor hair of her since. My arm pesky.*

THE JAPANESE gave notice that they wanted the hospital building on August 1. On July 20, eight Chinese Christian pastors were admitted, who had been tortured by Japanese military police. The men had suffered frightful burns, inflicted by lit cigarettes, some on the soles of their feet, some on their private parts. One had lost all his fingernails. The Japanese were convinced that these men had contact with Chinese Communists. In David's commonplace book, entered that night:

> *I could not reach them with my sympathy. I doubt if anyone could. 'Ecclesiastes' 4:1: So I returned, and considered all the oppressions that are done under the sun: and behold the tears of such as were oppressed, and they had no comforter; and on the side of their oppressors there was power; but they had no comforter.*

IN MID-AUGUST the Japanese took over the hospital and quartered a battalion of men there.

Treadup's diary:

> *Phinny is amazing. He bounced up from the floor after the Jonathans stole everything, and now he says, "Cheer up, my bucko! They're des-*

perate." News has trickled through, ever since the spring, that the Js have not been having things all their way — big battle off New Guinea, battle in the Coral Sea, American foothold in the Solomon Islands ect. ect. But closer to home: There are many flat-bottomed motorized boats newly gathered in the river along the Bund. And now these troops stationed on us. Phinny says this means there must be a guerrilla suppression afoot upriver. The Nips are being harassed, he says. I kneel and pray for my friends around Paoting. O dear villagers, have strength!

But Dr. Cunningham was wild about the Japanese presence in the hospital building, and he could not face going into it. He sent Treadup each day to check on what was happening.

The place was a shambles. Furniture had been broken up and burned. The old Pierce Arrow the hospital had used for an ambulance had been dragged out in the street and stripped. Locks on doorjambs had been broken. Windows had been smashed. Dr. Han, who lived on the fourth floor, had been threatened; a bayonet had been plunged through a panel of his bedroom door.

Worst of all — at first, Treadup could not bear even to tell Dr. Cunningham about this — the hospital library, the doctor's pride and joy, had been taken over as a bunkroom, and the books had been dumped out in refuse piles with wet garbage; scavenging Chinese children were carrying them off to sell for paper. Among them were priceless works on Chinese medicine, some of them ancient. Treadup went straight to the Tientsin Commandant's headquarters to complain; and he went to the Chinese puppet police to ask them to keep an eye out for books with the hospital chop on their end papers and to return any they found.

General Yamamura, Deputy Commandant for the Tientsin District, came in person to the hospital, rebuked the commander of the bivouacked battalion for the desecration of the library, and asked Treadup for a written report and an accounting of everything taken from the hospital from the time of the original raid. At the end he half-bowed stiffly and said, "Very sorry."

The diary: "Could it be that books still have some meaning in this violent world?"

David and Phinneas together spent three evenings totting up the hospital's losses, and David then took to the Deputy Commandant's office a claim for U.S.$68,633.

There was never any acknowledgment.

Aug. 23. Hot, clear day. Was working in Lib clearing up and sorting books piled in corners. Some have actually been returned by the blackie police. While I was shelving books, J officer in negligee accosted me, asking in quasi-English what right I had there & saying it was useless to clear up & put books on shelves as they would only be thrown out again. Obviously offended that we had put the Deputy Commandant on his neck. I was very polite, I bowed when he bowed, I said I was sorry when he said he was sorry. I then added that I would knock the teeth out of any person I found taking the books off the shelves. I thought Phinny would suffer a hernia laughing when I told him this. He said, "Treads, you are alive after all." I notice books have not been moved since. One's being bulky has its advantages. Many books however still missing.

TIME OF OUTRAGE

THE HOUSE on Davenport Road was dark day and night. On its south and west sides, Mrs. Evenrude had had the usual straw matting put up on bamboo scaffolding to ward off the summer sun's rays. She kept the shutters closed on the other sides. Even in what little gloaming light was left in the house she squinted, as if dazzled. It was hard to tell in the unchanging dimness what time of day or night it was. It always seemed, in any case, to be the right time for outrage.

TREADUP was wakened by the sounds of footsteps on the ground floor of the house. He switched on a light and looked at his bedside clock: it was one thirty in the morning. Yes, there were sounds of hard shoes on wood floors. He went downstairs and found two Japanese soldiers wandering around. They had *sake* on their breath. They spoke no English. Treadup went to the front door and pointed their way out. They pointed instead at the hall stairs. They were too drunk to be afraid of the big foreigner. They started up the steps.

In her bedroom, meanwhile, Mrs. Evenrude had wakened. She heard the hobnail shoes on the stairs. She took a dinner bell she kept by her bed out onto the sleeping porch and began to ring it hard.

The men ran.

In the morning Number One Boy Chou told Mrs. Evenrude that her one remaining carriage horse had been stolen. The diary: "She has taken to her bed again. She keeps a damp cloth over her eyes. I seem to have wrenched my arm—painful."

A JAPANESE OFFICER and a squad of men came to the house with a document authorizing an inspection. The paper had impressive red and blue official chops all over it. It seemed a bona fide order. The men went into every room of the house. When they entered her bedroom, Mrs. Evenrude took her damp cloth off her eyes and looked at them, then put it back again without saying anything.

> *The b — st — ds (Mrs. E's word, I never thought I would use it) made off with my little gyroscope. The one I have had ever since Salt Branch. Mama sent it to me, all the way to China. It made Teacher Chuan's eyes sparkle and that was what gave me the courage to go on with my lecture idea.*

DR. CUNNINGHAM said he thought Treadup was quite possibly suffering a recurrence of the osteomyelitis of his youth. There would of course be no way now to make tests at the hospital. He suggested a period of bed rest. If it got worse, Treadup might have to go to Peking to have it checked. Dr. Cunningham lugged some heavy books to Mrs. Evenrude's house: Kant, Locke, Spinoza. Later, Nietzsche.

> *How strange. It was my teacher Maud Chase who brought me books when my arm was bad in my seventeenth year. Now Phinny. "You are preparing yourself," Phinny says, "to enter the twentieth century." I thought I'd entered it forty-two years ago!*

In early September Dr. Cunningham brought Marx, Weber, Freud. In the evenings the two friends talked about what Treadup had read.

> *His eyes are still mischievous, wit cascades off that little pink tongue. But I know something Phinny will not admit even to himself. He is every bit as blue as I am.*

IT WAS three o'clock in the afternoon of an Indian summer day in late September. Fan in hand, Mrs. Evenrude was in a cool valley between headaches. She walked like a sentry from room to room. Treadup was reading *The Interpretation of Dreams* in the parlor: Dr. Cunningham had said he could sit up for two hours each afternoon. David had just come to Freud's assertion that some dream content is always supplied by images registered on the mind by the previous day's events. He lowered the book to think about this. Since he had started this book, he had been trying to retain his dreams, often lighting a light as he wakened from them, and making immediate notes. He began testing a dream from the night before.

Mrs. Evenrude was strutting about dressed up as a Chinese dowager lady. She had a pig's snout. She shrieked.

At the edge of his rumination Treadup heard the front door screen slam. He felt a thrill like an electric shock. The shriek had been real—not in the remembered dream. He ran to the front door.

A completely naked Japanese man was squatting on the grass near the pine trees and defecating. Mrs. Evenrude was running toward him crying out, "Shame! Shame!" The man half rose. He staggered—drunk. She poked him in the ribs with her long fingers. She began cursing him. The man smirked and dodged in a provocative dance. Mrs. Evenrude slashed with her fingernails, the man's skin was in danger. (Treadup's diary, later: "Could it be that the Jonathan was showing signs of sentiment for a seventy-year-old dowager lady?") Mrs. Evenrude began screaming for Chou! Liu! Treadup! When all three appeared the man ducked into the pine trees, snatched up his clothes, and ran for the compound gate, which hung open.

Mrs. Evenrude held tight to her tantrum all day long. She ordered Chou to have Liu make a barbed-wire fence around the grass plot in front of the house. Treadup tried to tell her this was a foolish project; he was rewarded with a blistering stream of abuse. Bars on the gate: open for no one. Get a mason to put broken glass in mortar on top of the wall all the way around. Have Liu keep a big cudgel handy. Go and buy two big wonks. Damn you, Treadup, don't you have any firearms?

She was still swearing and shouting orders from her bed at two o'clock in the morning.

TREADUP was down for breakfast the next morning in his dressing gown. Mrs. Evenrude, in her red winter peignoir, was still rattling and rumbling. Her hair was uncombed.

There came sounds of a fuss at the gate. Mrs. Evenrude rose and went herself, on very fast little steps, to see what it was. Treadup followed, asking her to calm herself.

At the gate Chou said there was a "number two topside boy"—meaning a middle-rank Japanese officer ("boy presumably because he was not white")— outside, wanting to come in. Mrs. Evenrude ordered Chou to open the gate six inches. There stood an officer with a bar and two stars on his collar. He said in English that he had an order to inspect. He reached a piece of paper forward. Mrs. Evenrude snatched it and tore it in four pieces and threw them in the officer's face. She screamed vile slanders on his ancestry and on "your scum of an emperor." The officer blanched. He forcibly pushed the gate wider, stepped forward, and slapped Mrs. Evenrude hard on the cheek.

Treadup stepped into the gate, his fists up. The officer drew a revolver. The diary:

> *A picture flashed in my mind of Dr. Azariah Dudley Morton, on the morning before my conversion. The famous pistol episode. I had a moment's fantasy, to the music of Mrs. Evenrude's gasping for breath, of baring my heart and advancing on the officer, offering Christ's love and mine — especially sweet, given to an enemy. But it did not take long for prudence to get the better of me. I knew that if I moved another inch he would shoot. What would Jesus Christ have thought of that?*

Treadup then raised flat hands in a pacifying gesture. He explained to the officer what had happened the previous afternoon. He said the lady was upset. He also said that to slap a lady was an inexcusable offense, particularly for a military man. He would have to report the incident to the officer's superior. The man recovered himself. He put the gun away. He almost bowed. He quickly walked off.

MRS. EVENRUDE vanished. Two hours later Treadup, who was worried about her, went hunting for her. He found her in her dressing room, packing a trunk. "I have to get out of here," she said.
"Where will you go?"
She went on folding dresses into the drawers of the trunk.
"You offended his precious emperor," Treadup said.
She began to weep.

THAT EVENING Treadup wrote a letter to the Deputy Commandant of the Tientsin District, with whom he felt he had made something like a humane contact over the books missing from the hospital library. He gave an account of the slapping, and entered a formal complaint. He marked on the letter that he was sending a copy to the United States Secretary of State, in Washington, D.C., U.S.A. — though he gave no clue as to how the letter would reach America. He sent Chou with the letter the first thing in the morning.
Chou had not been back twenty minutes when the Deputy Commandant himself and four people from his staff appeared at Mrs. Evenrude's gate, to investigate. The Japanese refused to enter the compound; they stood in the street. They asked Treadup and Mrs. Evenrude many questions. What division was the man from? Did he have an O or an X under his insignia of rank? Mrs. Evenrude thought an O, but she could not be sure. Treadup had not noticed.
The next morning an officer with two interpreters came to write down all the details of the slapping incident. They, too, stood at the gate, refusing

to enter. They asked many questions about the cause of the slapping. Neither Mrs. Evenrude nor Treadup mentioned anything about the emperor.

"I think they are excited," David wrote, "because there is a question here of a possible breach of manners. That would matter almost more than life or death."

The day after that, nothing having been heard from the Deputy Commandant, Treadup wrote a letter about the slapping, at Mrs. Evenrude's request, to the military police. He sent it by Chou. No answer came.

As days of silence came marching along, Mrs. Evenrude became more and more furious. She kept rearranging things in her trunk. Finally she sent Treadup in person to the Deputy Commandant's headquarters. Having spent so much time in bed, Treadup felt weak. The Deputy Commandant, not surprisingly, could not be seen just then. Treadup left word that an apology was expected.

None came.

The diary:

Mrs. E has broken down again. She lies there with the damp cloth over her eyes. I hear her mumbling. Phinny has given her a dose of salts and a good talking to, but nothing stirs her.

THE DAYS groaned and became weeks, the weeks were insomniac and became months, autumn got the shakes and became winter. Nothing really changed. There was nothing to do but read and talk. Once in a while one could write a letter demanding an apology or claiming a reimbursement, but the letter would never be answered. Mrs. Evenrude did not live in her house; she haunted it. Treadup's arm neither improved nor worsened. Phinny brought books. The Jonathans were tense, polite, and outrageous. This could go on forever. In January Treadup wrote:

This has been the worst winter of my life. Even if I thought the mail would get through I wouldn't dare write to Emily, because I would only frighten her more than ever. I miss her as though I had had the better part of me amputated—I have eerie shadow sensations in the stump where she was cut away from me, as if that part of me, which she was, were still there. No more letters have come from her.

THE MELANCHOLY WEIGHT of Joseph Conrad exactly suited Treadup's nerve tone. He came as close as he could, in those chilled days, to delight, when he came across the Eldorado Exploring Expedition in *Heart of Darkness*, and recognized, "as if they stood right in the jungle of this room with me," some of the businessmen of Tientsin—Olander of Standard Oil, Skinner of B.A.T., Elmslee of Hong Kong–Shanghai Bank: men who swaggered through life cutting down "natives," men who were, as Conrad caught them, "reckless without hardihood, greedy without audacity, and cruel without courage."

"And now I have it in my mind," Treadup wrote,

> *that precisely what is lacking in my life is any touch with the "natives." Three Chinese servants in this house do not a country make. My mission was to the Chinese. I am in jail with a crazy old broken American woman. Oh how I miss the laughter, the fortitude, the yearning for a better life, even the quarrels and the grubbing and the pettiness and the cosmic sense of futility, of my dear villagers! Try as I will to give the Jonathans the benefit of the doubt—victors in war have always been beasts—I cannot forgive them for having taken me away from China itself. From even a clear memory of Teacher Chuan, of my lost A Ch'u, of that crusty self-taught Inventor Wang. Mr. Lin! Johnny Wu! That fine young one-armed Mi in Ma Ch'iao. David Liu, for that matter, even when he had become so difficult. With all their faults there is a sweetness in the Chinese nature for which I have a craving, and a need, as if I had a debilitating nutritive deficiency.*

TREADUP and Dr. Cunningham had a pointless quarrel with the Japanese about coal. The hospital's bins had been filled with enough coal to heat the building through the winter, but now Japanese officers, quartered elsewhere, were helping themselves to basketfuls from the hospital supply and carting them off to warm themselves. Phinneas Cunningham clung to the stubborn belief, in the face of all reports, that Britain and America would defeat Japan in a few months, that the hospital would soon be returned to its rightful proprietors, and that "realistically," therefore, the present coal was *his*. The Jonathans were purloining *his* coal. The two men made the rounds of all authorities. "It is like playing blindman's buff," David wrote. "You are spun around, blindfolded, then you grope to try to catch hold of someone." The whole thing ended when a certain Captain Tsuzumi, Department of Supplies, Tientsin District, pointed out that the coal in the hospital bins was running low, and that since it was Mr. Cuddingman's coal, it would be up to Mr. Cuddingman to buy more coal to get through the rest of the winter.

THE RUMOR pigeons began to fly again. *Something* was going to happen. Enemy foreigners were all going to be put in a prison. Or perhaps they were going to be killed.

BY FEBRUARY everyone seemed to be staying in bed most of the time. Even Phinneas Cunningham. Treadup was afraid Mrs. Evenrude was going mad. She had long conversations with people who were not in her dark rooms. The Japanese raided houses at their pleasure. They came knocking on Mrs. Evenrude's gate, asking for "English food" and girls. They stole the shrubs from her garden, saying "Thank you, thank you, very sorry," and beaming with smiles. Weak Treadup wore out his legs going back and forth, with his arm in a sling, to the military police with protests, claims, and bills of particulars. He killed a rat in his bathroom.

ON MARCH 8, 1943, at 3:15 in the afternoon, a polite young man with a German accent from the Swiss consulate called on Mrs. Evenrude. He told her and David Treadup that he was mediating for the Japanese Consul General, and he had an order for all "Japanese enemy aliens" in Tientsin. They were to prepare themselves for removal on March 13 and 14 to a Civilian Assembly Center ("—euphemism, we fear," the young Swiss delicately said, "for concentration camp, you must be prepared for an indefinite stay") at Yin Hsien, in southern Hopei Province. Heavy baggage, which might consist, for each person, of a bed, bedding, and not more than two small trunks or foot lockers, should be ready for collection at the Recreation Ground, on Recreation Road, on Thursday, the eleventh. Eating utensils, metal mess kit if possible, must be taken. All American and British subjects should be prepared to depart, with only such hand luggage as they themselves could carry, on Saturday, March 13.

Mrs. Evenrude swam up out of her murk. "I am all packed," she firmly said.

BOOK NINE

⊞

THE KNOTS
UNDONE

A SMELL OF SMOKE

HERE CAME David Treadup, doing coolie work.

The Japanese consular police were herding some three hundred fifty foreigners into the area of the Recreation Ground usually set aside in clement seasons for clay tennis courts. Treadup, wearing a fur hat and a black overcoat with a velvet collar, was trundling a contraption he had put together: a "knock-down" wheelbarrow, two bamboo poles supporting a V-shaped platform, the forward point of which ran along on a sturdy wheel purloined from the tea-service cart in Mrs. Evenrude's parlor.

On this rig rode his valises and those of Phinneas Cunningham. A vehicle of this sort was needed, because both men's bags were crammed to bursting with books. The best advice held that the stay might be long. "Shakespeare," Phinneas had said, "has more utility in the long run than extra underwear." (A supply of underwear and other haberdashery—and, among the miscellany, David's cornet—had gone forward with the men's clothes in their trunks.)

"I had pain in my arm but did not feel it, if such can be," Treadup later wrote. He felt "a false lift"—false, because it had no motor but curiosity. Any

change was better than no change. The dreadful monotony of his useless-
ness had at least been interrupted. He was worried about Mrs. Evenrude,
who for some reason had been put down for a second transport of internees;
he did not know whether she was strong enough to manage alone in her
house for even a few days. But he had the consoling company of Dr.
Cunningham, who marched along beside him looking like a hunchback—the
little doctor was carrying a haversack, which bent his frail figure cruelly
forward, for the kitbag, too, was full of books. The doctor kept pointing
out to Treadup the bright side of every disastrous moment of this mass
humiliation.

The Japanese consular authorities had set up areas for registration and
for baggage search on the porch of the nearby pavilion—a small building of
an architectural style which was wildly incongruous in the light of this day,
for its bulbed and spiked roof conjured images of the proud palaces of the
great days of the British Empire in India. At this very second, Japanese
noncoms were scornfully flinging out onto the examination tables illegally
held currency which they had discovered under the false bottom in a suitcase
of Arthur Elmslee of the Hong Kong-Shanghai Bank. He was clearing his
throat with a great roar, as if the hard lump of the humbling of the Union
Jack were lodged somewhere just under his epiglottis.

When Treadup's and Cunningham's turn came, a bit later, the Japanese
laughed to see the little traveling library, but they made no difficulty about it.

THE WOMEN and older men were anxious about the expected ordeal of
carrying their bags on the long foot march—more than half a mile—to the
railroad station, but at the last minute the Japanese authorities, better than
their word for once, turned up with two large lorries, on which they built
mounds of the heaviest bags. Treadup paid for the foresight he had invested in
his barrow by having to push it with its load all the way.

The procession of three hundred fifty British and American Tientsiners
out from the "Rec," along to the rim of the French Concession, down to the
Bund, across the International Bridge and to the railroad station presented a
sight for thousands of Chinese lining the way—and for Japanese cameramen,
busy turning the cranks of their cameras to provide the home front with some
cheerful entertainment. The diary:

> They liked my funny little cart, and one of them stuck his lens right in
> my face. I puffed out my cheeks and made cross-eyes. If a picture of the
> Imbecile Enemy was what they wanted, I would give it to them.

AT THE RAILROAD station, a Japanese officer shouted through a mega-
phone that a train would soon be ready. It turned out that there was a wait
of nearly two hours.

When I saw how many women there were, and indeed how very many children, some of them quite small, I felt a flash of helpless rage at Todd and Blackie and the other people in New York for having been so dogmatic about Emily's evacuation—and at myself for having accepted their advice. I wanted her now standing beside me. Then I thought: Would I want to put her through all this? Then I thought: Yes. Being the woman she is, she would be happier here—'knowing.' By this time I was so raw and my arm was so sore that I nearly bit poor Phinny's head off when he asked me some inconsequential question.

Finally the whole crowd was loaded, bags and all, onto just two Chinese third-class coaches, with merciless unpadded wooden benches. Treadup left his wheelbarrow on the station platform. Not everyone could find a seat; Treadup sat on his bags. The train crept across the countryside at what seemed to Treadup about ten miles per hour. There was nothing to eat or drink, save what picnics people had brought for themselves. After dark, no one but children slept.

In the middle of the night, at the rail center of Tsinan, all were obliged to change trains. Women needed help with their bags. Children, wakened, screamed with fear and hunger. The new train finally moved. Treadup felt feverish.

Late in the afternoon of the second day, the exhausted company arrived at the Yin Hsien station. Buses and trucks were waiting for the internees. They rode out of the city and through its suburbs into the country, and they were offloaded on a terraced hillside, planted with willows, between a river and a compound wall.

I was listless, tired, downhearted, in pain, but that wall roused me. My buttocks prickled at the sight of it. It was as if I were in an old wooden house and waked up from a deep sleep smelling smoke. This was the usual eight-foot gray brick mission-compound wall, familiar to me as an often seen boundary of refuge for foreigners, setting the limits of a peaceful sanctuary from the Chinese universe roundabout—except that now there was a difference: guard turrets had been erected at the corners of the wall. This was no refuge. This was a prison.

ON EDGE

THE FIRST sensations, within the wall, were not so alarming—merely of bone chill and brain dampness.

The Tientsin troop was led in and lined up on an athletic ground next to a brick church with a corrugated tin roof. There the Japanese camp authorities held an interminable roll call; there were two or three more names than people, the usual mix-ups, endless palavers in Japanese at a high pitch. Treadup and Cunningham stayed tight, side by side.

This place, they knew and could see, was a former missionary compound, in which there had evidently been a large college or middle school, a hospital, a church, and several Western-style residences; now all was drab and befouled. Most of the passageways were cluttered with all sorts of furniture and trash thrown out from the buildings, presumably by uncaring bivouacs of Japanese troops and, later, by quartermasters in hasty preparations to receive these internees.

At last the group was marched to Building No. 24. The men were placed in dank basement classrooms from which everything had been removed except some reed mats to sleep on—not enough to go around. Each chose his floor space and piled his luggage beside it. Then the Tientsiners, having been directed to carry along their own eating utensils, were escorted to Kitchen No. 1, where they formed in long lines to wait for food.

Half an hour later Phinny and I had drawn close enough to the servers to see something important: there was not a single Chinese in the compound. We were being helped by folks, as we soon learned, from Tsingtao. They had been in the camp about a week. Merchants, bankers, lawyers, doctors, musicians, missionaries, former soldiers—people just like us Tientsiners—were manning the kitchen and serving lines. There would henceforth be no servantry in our lives. My first thought: Dirty work I don't mind. But this is verily the end of the end of my mission to the people of China. Cut off. Cut off. I remember the time, long long years ago, when I first arrived in Tientsin, and I thought—in the way we thought, back in those days—this is war, and I am a Christian soldier, a General for Jesus, and I must have courage. Now? I'm down to the root of it. Yes, I must have courage. Now I am really to live an army life, with a mess kit in my paw, waiting in line. A prisoner of war of a sort—not quite the kind of hero for Christ I envisioned when I was that boy so wet behind the ears.

The famished travelers were given a hot, watery brew, in which bits of Chinese cabbage, field carrots, and leeks could be seen to float, and plentiful bread that had been baked, as the servers said, right in the compound.

I bedded down in my clothes on the chilly floor. How unforgiving that concrete was! I hardly slept at all. I thought and thought about Emily. I am safe, Em. My body is safe. But it is hollow, null, and void. I tried to pray. I made several efforts. I would start my silent habitual line of address to the Almighty, only to have the feeling that there was no ear up there. There had always, all my life since I came to know God, seemed to be two of us when I prayed. We were together. But now it seemed as if I, like old Mrs. Evenrude, was mumbling to myself in an empty room. It was the sensation of talking on the telephone and realizing that the line has gone dead. This frightened me.

HIS BODY was not quite so hollow as he thought: In the morning, after a breakfast of bread and tea, he had the urge to go to the toilet. He asked directions. Walking from Kitchen No. 1 to the nearest latrine for men, he got a sense of the choked scope of his new universe.

The compound was large—more than five acres, Treadup guessed—but it was nonetheless a prison. To the right of the main gate stood the church, and beside it the athletic field where the group had been assembled for roll call the evening before, and again that morning just after dawn. Running southward were two straight alleys, on both sides of which stretched about a dozen rows of long, narrow, one-storied buildings—evidently former student dormitories. They reminded Treadup of the rows of stables at the Tientsin Racecourse. Beyond these dorms, to the south, were two large classroom buildings, and farther yet, strictly out of bounds to the campers, were spacious courtyards with several substantial brick houses formerly occupied by missionaries, now sheltering the Japanese camp authorities in fine style. To the west, in a swerve of the enclosure, stood a large hospital building, with tennis courts and a basketball court beside it.

The men's W.C. to which Treadup had been directed was on the way back to Building 24, where the Tientsiners had spent the previous night. There was a long line waiting.

In the diary, from this time onward, Treadup more and more addresses Emily, as if he were writing to her. Now:

Em, I cannot describe the horror of that latrine, when finally I could enter it. The Japanese had taken out the Chinese-style squatting toilets and put in some flush ones—but Lord! only 23 for hundreds of people. I had to stand in line nearly half an hour. And then—Gehenna! The conveniences have pull-chains for flushing from wooden tanks overhead, but there is no water supply, and the cesspools below had all backed up, so the toilets were all full and flooded. Human leavings were awash on the floor. Perhaps Dante or Virgil could have described the stench—this was surely the stink of the vilest ring of hell. I suppose the closest bond one can form with his fellow man comes from walking in his excrement— the most equalizing stuff on earth: that of the genius smells as bad as that of the idiot, the emperor's perhaps worse than the beggar's. But it isn't stuff that makes one love his brother man. Except at sea I have always thought I had a strong stomach—here I added vomit to the mess. Even Phinny, my indomitable Dr. Pangloss, cannot, for once, see anything good about this. After his visit to the latrine this morning he came to me and announced that we will all die within a month. I don't mind if we do.

TREADUP went back to the basement room in Building 24 and lay down on the concrete, with his rolled-up overcoat as a pillow. He did not try to read. "Against my shut eyelids, Em, I could see strange shifting patterns of lights— like those I saw when I went under ether, all those years ago when my arm was operated on." It seemed to him that his essence, his selfhood, had been condensed into some sort of hot liquid which was now being siphoned out of his head and torso and into his throbbing arm. "I tried prayer, but again I seemed to be talking into a wind. The fragments were torn from my mouth and blown away. I was afraid."

He had no idea how long this went on.

The next thing he was aware of was Phinneas Cunningham's pink face peering into his. It was a matter of course that the doctor would have bounced back from the mood of the death sentence he had so grimly pro-nounced earlier; but Treadup winced. That rosy face was too bright for his infirm eyes.

"Rise and shine, old sport!" Cunningham said with a robustness which grated on Treadup's ears. "You are needed."

Treadup sat up. "I'm dizzy," he said.

"Look here, Treads. You can't funk now."

"My arm," Treadup said.

"Yes, yes," Cunningham said. But, he went on, the arm would simply have to wait a week or two, or perhaps even longer. The hospital was a shambles. He, Cunningham, was going to be in charge of getting it back on its feet. The commandant of the Jonathans, he said, had ordered certain commit-tees to be set up, to manage the various operations of the camp. There would be three to five internees on each. Phinny had been given the chairmanship of Medical Affairs. And, he said, "I suggested you for Number One on Engi-neering and Repairs. It was unanimous, Treadsy-boy. Old Olander of Standard Oil backed you up—said you're a brick—been to one of your lectures—'a practical noggin,' he said—said you're soft on the Chinks but after all there are none of them in here, are there? It was unanimous, Treadsy-boy. Come on! Ally-oop! On your feet!"

"I'm not up to it."

"Look here, Treadup . . . "

"God himself damn you! Leave me alone."

THE DIARY, two days later:

> *Em, I loathe this person, David Treadup. He is not I. He is a stranger.*
> *Imagine using a curseword against my dearest friend—next to you.*
> *I have never used such language in my life before: blasphemy: learned*
> *it from terrible Mrs. Evenrude. I have bit my tongue ever since. I just*
> *lie here. My arm is hot. Phinneas makes me go to meals. Can't eat any-*
> *thing but a little bread. Thank heavens I am constipated—don't have to*
> *face the River Styx. When will our beds come? I can't sleep on this*
> *bedrock.*

EARLY the fourth morning Treadup saw a sight which shook him at least partway out of his lethargy. On his way to Kitchen No. 1 from the basement room, he passed near one of the men's latrines. In the open area in front of it, he saw a number of men in black trousers rolled up above their knees, bare to the waist in the March air, working with shovels and buckets in a trench half filled with a foul-smelling ordure. They were clearing the drains and cesspools for the latrine.

> *Catholics, Em! I have always thought Papists to be self-indulgent and*
> *high-living, with their Benedictine liquors and feasts of suckling pig.*
> *How wrong that mythology must have been. Have I been a bigot? These*
> *people were so stolid and vigorous, and so insouciant, roaring at each*
> *other in what I took to be Dutch and Belgian and laughing like sailors on*
> *some sort of drunken wading party on a shore-leave beach—but they*
> *were slopping about in that glaucous, scummy soup of urine and feces—*
> *talk about your Augean stables! My word, how I admired them! I honor*
> *those Romanists. They put the rest of us to shame.*

THE BEDS and trunks came. The Tientsiners were assigned permanent quarters. Married couples and families were housed in the rows of ten-by-twelve rooms in the long, low dormitory buildings. Bachelors and spinsters were placed in former classrooms in the large buildings.

Treadup and Dr. Cunningham now lived with nine other men in a room on the second floor of Building 23. Treadup felt pent up. "There is not space in this pigsty for me to expand my rib cage enough to fill my lungs with air." He had calculated that he had thirty-six square feet of floor area for his bed and his gear. This gave roughly three feet by four at the foot of the bed for what he called his "parlor." The Jonathans had provided a bookcaselike cupboard of open shelves, floor to ceiling, nailed against the wall beside each person's slot.

Even when the boys were with us, you and I always had privacy and quiet, Em, and since you pulled out I have been alone. This confinement is very trying. I am having sordid quarrels. My loneliness in prayer scares me. My arm makes me furious. Everyone seems to take the attitude that because I am big I take up too much room.

B E S I D E S Treadup and Dr. Cunningham, the room held:

• A potbellied retired sergeant of the U.S. Fifteenth Infantry Regiment in Tientsin, a bully by nature and training; he had lived a shady life in the French Concession there, some said as a middleman in sales of smuggled curios.

• An Englishman with startling mustaches like porcupine quills, a grand personage high up in Kailan Mining, owner in Tientsin of the great racehorse Kettledrum, which had won the Tientsin Champion Stakes five straight years.

• An American derelict, formerly a Socony engineer, whose "better years," he told everyone, had been in the Bahrein oil fields in the Persian Gulf, now a lank, gaunt sausage of a man suffering agonizing cramps and sweats in forced withdrawal from his beloved *paikar,* the fiery Chinese liquor.

• A muscular American Negro dance instructor from the Voytenko Dancing School in Tientsin.

• A Eurasian, half Belgian and half Chinese, a salesman of cameras in a Tientsin store, who looked and acted like a ravishingly beautiful woman.

• A Pentecostal missionary, a bachelor with rattling dry bones under leathery dry skin, a kindly but rather repugnant man, with little dark velvety bags like bat bellies under his eyes, who groaned and babbled hair-raising fragments of sermons in his sleep—bringing loud roars for silence from the sergeant and the dancer.

• An English executive of Whiteaway Laidlaw, the largest department store in the British Concession, a sensible, direct, practical, unemotional man, an observer of rules and a mediator in all storms in the room.

• The former chief steward of the posh Tientsin Club, who still wore the black coat, double-breasted gray waistcoat, and striped trousers of his Club uniform, all of which he somehow kept impeccably clean, a straight-backed figure, honorable and correct, yet also mischievous, a fountain of laughter, a man, as David soon wrote, "too good to be true."

• A mean little Australian errand runner for the Customs Service, with a fake limp, who told a new lie every day about imaginary past glories—as the pilot of a smuggling plane, as a photographer of nude women, as a big-time Shanghai gambler—reduced now to a finicky, sneaky, sniveling complainer, scornful of Americans whatever their station but embarrassingly obsequious to upper-class Englishmen.

ON THE MORNING of March 25, word got around that a new transport of internees from Peking was to arrive. The Tientsin kitchen was given responsibility for preparing their evening meal. In the afternoon Dr. Cunningham made Treadup get up out of bed to help him at the hospital, which was almost ready to take its first patients. Late in the day Treadup found himself among the onlookers as the exhausted Peking people straggled in at the main gate.

> *Em, they were tired, but they looked like people from a real world. I realized that in only a few days my hold on the pride and dignity of a free man had given way. I had the mentality of a prison inmate. I was dead wrong in thinking I would want you to go through all this with me.*

Three days later the second Tientsin contingent came in, and again Treadup stood by the doctor's side to watch the arrival. This time both kept an anxious eye out for Mrs. Evenrude. There she was!—being carried in a "fireman's chair" by two priests. She had her arms around their shoulders, and she was nodding and laughing as if this were the nicest outing she had been on in years.

At seven that evening, Dr. Cunningham had her in a bed in the first ward in the hospital to be opened, one for women.

THE DIARY:

> *What I cannot stand is waiting in line to go to the toilet. The latrines are orderly and clean now; the cesspools, though dangerously close (Phinny says) to the water wells, are working; buckets of waste water are kept at the facilities to flush them with. It's not the mess; it's the humiliation. My bowels are tied up. I wait half an hour for my turn and then can't do anything. This hasn't happened to me in four decades in China.*

TREADUP lay abed much of the day.

One morning Dr. Cunningham said, "I can't treat your arm until the hospital is straightened out. You will be helping yourself if you help me. Get up, now."

I felt very angry at first, Em, but I held my tongue this time, and in the end I was grateful to him. He put me to work on the horrendous pile of debris beside the hospital. Everything had been ripped out by the Jonathans, presumably when they were stationing troops here. Phinny was in a hurry, because inmates were scrounging all sorts of things for their rooms from the junk piles outdoors, and he didn't want to lose any possible medical gear that way. You would be astonished at what useful things we turned up. Much scientific apparatus — the equipment of the physics and chemistry labs thrown out on the ground without regard for value. Phinny and his staff are adapting all sorts of salvage for medical purposes.

The work tired Treadup, and that afternoon he collapsed onto his bed again. He wrote in his diary awhile. Then his mind drifted. Suddenly someone was shaking his shoulder.

"Get out of bed, you damnable malingerer," a voice was saying ("in that sort of English accent, Emily, that seems to have been brought on by the swallowing of a wet piece of flannel cloth—do you remember old Bishop Francis at the Centennial in Shanghai—Lord Frawncis, we used to call him?"). This was the voice of the high-toned Mr. Ramsdel, bereft now of his Kettledrum. Red in the face. Beside him, the Customs Service wharf rat, Drubbins—"pale as a fish filet," Treadup later wrote. This mismatched pair had somehow quickly teamed up to make everyone else in the room miserable, with their constant carping and complaints.

"It's a bloody shime, big bloke loik you," Drubbins said.

Treadup sat up. He felt a surge of anger. "I worked all morning," he said. "I have been excused from assignments because I have an infected arm." His own words enraged him even more—they sounded like the last thing he intended: an appeal for sympathy.

"And I have the runs," said the rat. "The blighters didn't excuse *me*."

"And I a toothache," said Mr. Racehorse. "You lie here scribbling."

Drubbins thrust his face so close to Treadup's that David could smell his breath—"air from an abandoned cellar." "You're a bloody nuisance," Drubbins said. "Going to take you up with the Jappies, I am. You've shoved your bloody bed four bloody inches into my particular premises."

I'm on edge. Everyone's on edge. This matter of inches is everything. I scrambled out of bed to check the chalk marks on the floor, and my bed was in fact an inch or so in Drubbins's area. Being in the wrong threw me quite out of kilter, and I began raving at the two persecutors.

THAT AFTERNOON Dr. Cunningham opened a men's ward, and his first admitted patient was David Treadup.

OUT OF TOUCH

HE CAME up from ether seeming to be on a deck chair on a very rough day. A basin was providentially in place, just in time. A beautiful face swam into focus for a few seconds, then faded. Later it was there again. He felt less seasick.

At an indefinite time he heard a woman's voice, "That's better, Mr. Treadup."

He saw that it was a nun. He groaned. He had counted on Em.

TWO DAYS LATER he was able to read, and even to write a little. There was a gauze drain in the wound in his left arm. He still had a lot of pain. The nun, Sister Catherine, bathed his forehead with a cool damp cloth. Every few hours Dr. Cunningham came to change the dressing and to chat, and in the evenings he came back and talked for a long time. He had brought David a book on the Epicureans and Stoics.

My little friend Dr. Rubber Ball comes bouncing in here and tells me to get that dark cloud off my forehead. You make me irritable, I say. Look at these ancients, he says, their 'ataraxia'—tranquillity—tranquillity, Treads! —two, three centuries before your Jesus Christ and his agony on the cross. When he says this, I feel an icicle in my heart. I am puzzled by this sudden fear. I am not used to fear.

Another entry:

Avoidance of pain. O how I would like to achieve it. Phinny says I will, at least in my arm, in a few days. He says these sulfa drugs that the Jonathans let him have (perhaps the very ones commandeered from his hospital in Tientsin!) are better than faith, when it comes to healing sore arms. But it is the pain in my self, which the drugs can't touch, that frightens me. I had thought Epicurus was more joyous than he turns out to be. Those were very cool nerves he had. No raptures. Anchored under a lee shore out of the wind. It doesn't seem enough to me. Both these schools taught different sorts of resignation; I want and need more than that. I read late last evening, till the print blurred. Realized this morning I forgot even to try to pray last night.

"THE ONLY THING that kept my head above water in those days of my utter raggedness," Treadup wrote in "Search,"

> was Phinneas Cunningham's elation. He seemed to dart about on free air like a chimney swift. His joy lay in improvisation. He and his colleagues imagined a hospital and then materialized it out of match sticks, and pieces of cellophane from cigarette packages, and cold-cream jars, and hatpins, and battered mess kits. The Jonathans provided some equipment later on, but at first everything had to be dealt up by ingenuity. Phinny told me that for a successful mastoid operation on a child from Tsingtao, Flanner, the chief surgeon from P.U.M.C., had to boil up a carpenter's hammer, use a retractor made from a Meccano set, and make sutures with a woman's sewing kit.

Yet there are numerous notes during the days of his recuperation which suggest that Dr. Cunningham, with his repeated jibes at Treadup's faith, his railing at the "high tone" of missionaries in the camp, his mockery of Christian cant, was causing Treadup increasing pain and fear. "I wish I were back to Ma Ch'iao!" he wrote once. "I am at my wits' end."

SISTER CATHERINE sat beside his bed each afternoon. She prayed a great deal. Treadup lay and peeked at her over his book as she ran beads through her fingers, her lips silently moving. It was hard to tell her age; the wimple shaded her face; he thought she might be ten years younger than he. Her eyebrows were black smudges on her paper skin. She had amazing physical strength for a woman of her age, and one so willowy and fine-boned. Her touch was as cooling as menthol. She pursed her lips at Dr. Cunningham's heresies. She answered questions openly but asked none.

She had been born, she said, in Milwaukee, in a large German-American family; she was the third of eleven children. Her father drank and beat her mother, who died—"she was ready for a vacation"—bearing the eleventh child. Four of the six daughters became nuns "in order to get away." Sister Catherine had been in China for thirty-two years, all of them spent in the far interior, in Shensi Province. Yet now she did not seem in the least dislocated; she acted at home in the internment camp.

Treadup wrote "to" Em, a month later, that with her so far away when he was in the hospital, Sister Catherine had been the dearest and safest woman on earth to be with, for she was capable of such a hovering closeness that one could almost hear her rapid heartbeat, yet at the same time she kept herself at such a distance that "looking at her was like gazing at a mountain vista on a high-sky day with a cool north wind." Probably, he wrote, the miles of this distance lay in the ever true keeping of her oath of chastity. But she did not seem, like some of the nuns, de-sexed. Pure, yes. The love she gave a male hospital patient held more in it than the word "charity" could contain.

One afternoon he was reading about Epicurus. He was feeling low. Here was a passage in which Epicurus urged a man to be honest, prudent, and fair toward others—not in order to be a good man, but simply in order to escape the censure of society and thus avoid one kind of pain. Suddenly tears started into David's eyes. At once Sister Catherine was up out of her chair and had put a hand on his arm. "What is it, Mr. Treadup?" she asked.

"I don't *know,*" he said. Then he said, "Will you forgive me?"

"What for?"

"I don't *know.*"

"Yes, my son," she said. "I forgive you."

He began to sob. She took his shoulders in her arms and held his head against her breast.

IN "SEARCH":

> *I see now that I should have taken that emotional break as a warning— or as advance notice—of the far deeper plunge that was to come in a few days. My convalescence was misleading; I guess I was in an unusually vulnerable state. I must not have realized how angry I was at God the Father for having snatched my mission, and therefore, as it seemed, the meaning of all my past life, away from me.*

WHEN Dr. Cunningham discharged Treadup from the hospital, he arranged with the Housing Committee to have the big man transferred, because of his infirmity, to a room in one of the long, low dormitory buildings, where he would have only two roommates and less hullabaloo than in his former quarters. David did not like this transfer. He confessed to Emily in his diary that being separated from Phinneas frightened him.

> *I was humiliated, being so big and looking so strong, to have to stand by and watch two slight fellows carry my bed and baggage over from Building 23. They certainly didn't like it. They cut some very black looks at me.*

Treadup's new roommates began at once to quarrel with him. Having been just two in the ten-by-twelve room, they had been quite comfortable.

Now they had a jostling, nonworking giant and all his gear to contend with.

One of the men was a sporty bachelor, Cyril Watkins, Tientsin agent for the Jardine Matheson trading company. As everyone else became more and more seedy, he wore silk shirts, handmade in Hong Kong with his initials on them, and Liberty silk neckties with paisley patterns. He had posted on the door a set of fourteen rules of the room: "Beds made before breakfast. No clothes left lying about. Knock before entering . . . "

The other roommate was a Rumanian, Ion Titu Corbuc, who, Phinneas told David, had had a reputation in Tientsin as a tout at the Racecourse. It had not taken him long to find a new life as a scrounger: he had built a short wooden ladder, which by day he kept hidden under his bed and by night leaned against the compound wall, in order to bargain over it with Chinese farmers for eggs, peanuts, malt candy, sugar, honey, tobacco, and matches, which he sold to his fellow inmates. In this "over-the-wall" commerce he was in frantic competition with a group of Catholic fathers, who had early commandeered, for night use, the mounds of earth the Japanese had raised against the inside of the wall for sharpshooters when the camp had been a Japanese military bivouac. The monks had become kings of the black market, partly because of their excellent command of both spoken and written Chinese. As a trader, Corbuc was unctuous, smiling, agreeable; as a roommate, he was contemptuous, whining, short-tempered, and often vicious. Cunningham thought he may have bought his occupancy in the room from a corrupt member of the Housing Committee.

Dr. Cunningham had asked the Employment Committee to give Treadup four days of convalescence before assigning him to a task. His roommates here, as in the former room, were infuriated by the inactivity of this hulk, and they criticized him for everything he did or did not do: for growling when his arm hurt, for reading and writing in bed, for staying in his pajamas when the Japanese dawn roll call required everyone to go to the doorway of his room.

TREADUP was assigned to be a kettle and pot washer in the Tientsin kitchen, No. 2.

This turned out to be hard work, especially at first, while he was still weak. The bulk cooking was done in vast, shallow, round-bottomed iron cauldrons, four feet in diameter, in which soups and stews were made. This meant that Treadup contended, over and over again, for hours at a stretch, with crusted gravies and fatty mucilages and blackened residues. The wooden covers of the great kettles were particularly hard to clean. There was, as well, an endless oncoming rush of spoons and ladles and smaller utensils in which the kitchen staff cooked black-market eggs for the internees. The soap supplied by the Japanese was itself greasy; his scouring brushes soon lost their stiffness.

The Tientsin kitchen served about five hundred fifty mouths; Kitchen No. 1, Tsingtao, served seven hundred fifty; Kitchen No. 3, Peking, about four hundred fifty. Each meal's serving took about an hour and a half; but each meal's mess took a kettle washer at least three hours to clean up. Treadup worked two meals a day. Grim in his thoughts, his vision still turned mostly inward on himself, he was only dimly aware of the long lines waiting for their turns at the dripping ladles at the great kettles. He sealed himself off from the hubbub of kitchen workers around him.

NOW CAME what Treadup later called "the precipitating incidents." Objectively, these happenings were not nearly so shocking as had been many things he had seen and experienced in the field; their significance, their force for precipitation, lay in his overreaction to them.

• A wiper working at Treadup's side was Irrenius P. Cashman, a Presbyterian missionary who was known throughout China as one of the finest leaders of the Christian movement. He was used to sitting on managing boards, and he had been "surprised" at being assigned to the lowly kitchen cleanup squad. But, he said, dropping out one of his famous "saws," "You are never quite safe from being surprised until you are dead." As Treadup gradually became more aware of the people around him, he found himself growing annoyed by Renny Cashman's habit of passing judgment on his fellow man. One of the assistant cooks, a Baptist missionary raised on a South Carolina farm, had a sweet, yielding nature. "Poor fellow," said Cashman, "he always chooses to be the anvil rather than the hammer." ("Mr. Cashman is too ignorant of physical science and the farrier's trade to know that in the long run the anvil always breaks the hammer, not the other way around.") A cockney steamfitter who had worked for the Tientsin Municipal Council kept forgetting to do things he had been asked to do. "Putting Off is the main sheet in that sinner's Gospel," Cashman said. It got back to Treadup that Cashman had said of him, "Treadup is a good man, but his mind is dark with thunderstorms."

Dark indeed it grew one day when he overheard Irrenius Cashman complaining about the helpings he was being given on the chow line. "These people have me doing donkey work," he was saying to the woman with the ladle, his voice rasping with anger. "You might at least feed me enough for me to bear my burden."

The kitchen supervisor, a Briton named Slawter, former executive of the coastwise traders Butterfield & Swire, stepped quickly forward and made the most of the fact that this time our friend had categorized himself—as a donkey. He said, "We're all asses here, Mr. Cashman. Kindly refrain from being a silly ass."

At that Irrenius Cashman exploded.

Serpents, toads, and spiders came out of his mouth, Em. I have never heard such vile speech. Not that he cursed or blasphemed. It was just sheer moral arrogance and contempt, with overtones of an overindulged only child denied its sweets. Slawter shouted in a brusque voice, "Stop your braying, Mr. Cashman." Well! The very idea! That really got the donkey heehawing. I wish I could say it was funny. It made me very much afraid—as so much seems to do, these days. I had always been in awe of Irrenius P. Cashman's reputation as a man of dignity, compassion, and humility—"God's truest man in the field," everyone always said. What is happening to us—to me?

• Here was Miller, the potbellied ex-soldier from the room in Building 23, in charge of the supply-collection detail inside the compound gate. Treadup was taking his assigned turn, as all the men did in rotation, at this hard labor. Yes, Miller was a bully—born to it, and from having sergeanted for so long. His tongue was white hot. There were no such things as adjectives and adverbs in his lexicon—only modifiers standing for excrement, urine, private parts, the rectum, women's breasts and buttocks, and a range of shocking sexual practices far beyond Treadup's ken. But it had gradually come to David that under his hectoring, Miller was astonishingly tender to the weak and the sick. He blustered at, but filled in for, goldbrickers. Roar he might, but he obviously heard and understood the faintest whisper of pain from anyone else.

Supplies were brought into the compound on Chinese carts and wheelbarrows—at first with Chinese muleteers and barrowmen; but the Jonathans, having become suspicious of secret communications with the outside world through the carters, had ordered the Chinese bringing the supplies not to step inside the gate. From then on campers had had to lead the mules or push the wheelbarrows to the supplies depot, several hundred yards away near the south wall. Chinese mules had their own ideas about appropriate language from a driver, and their responses to strangers, especially strangers who had never had mules as friends, were not always cordial. The wheelbarrows were worse—they were wide and their loads were high, and balancing them on their huge single wheels was not easy. Some of the loads had to be carried on Chinese coolie poles. Here were businessmen, whose habitual exertions had been cricket, tennis, and golf, and missionaries, who had not done much more than kneel to pray, all doing the work of louse-bitten Chinese wharf coolies. And here was Miller, in charge, hurling obscenities like a Georgia chain-gang boss.

One morning everything had gone wrong for Treadup. He had cut himself shaving. At breakfast, climbing over a bench at a table, he had spilled his bowl of bread-mush. After twenty-five minutes on the latrine line, he had failed to perform again. He reported five minutes late for the supply-collection detail, and Miller had put his mouth against David's ear and filled it with decibels and filth. Treadup's lot, then, was a mule cart piled high with leeks. He tugged sharply and angrily at the bridle. The mule threw its head back and brayed. Treadup yanked the head down. The mule reared and then kicked, banging at the cart with its hind hocks and losing its balance in the traces, pulling the cart over on its side and spilling the leeks on the ground. Miller charged at Treadup like a bull, growling unthinkable curses at him. "Get out!" he said. "Get out. You're dismissed. Get out. Go to bed, you ——— overgrown baby." He drove Treadup away and gathered a squad to right the cart.

"He must have sensed," Treadup wrote,

> *how exhausted and beaten I was. He was rough but merciful. I felt the kindness in his sound and fury. Miller has never been saved, but there is perverse brotherly love behind that hateful bullying front. I say perverse: he may be kind for scummy reasons, for all I know. But I think St. Pete will not hesitate at the pearly gates when Miller shows up. I can't bring myself to speak to him. He frightens me. Not his foul mouth. No. What frightens me are his faith, hope, and charity. They terrify me. Faith? I don't know what I mean, but it's there, in something, and it's more enviable to me even than his amazing carnal knowledge. Forgive me, Em, but you and I seem to have missed out on a few things. That idea, too, frightens me.*

• Two ancient Belgian Dominican friars, with white beards and faces like old manuscripts, had been assigned to do nothing all day but swat flies at Kitchen No. 2. One of them was unspeakably dirty; he had, as Irrenius Cashman said, "a bad habit"—his long black gown was caked with mud on the skirts and greasy droppings on the lap; his beard was as unkempt as a bluejay's nest. The other, Father Julius, by contrast, was spotless and constantly preened himself like a cat: even while he banged his flyswatter all about, he combed his long, wavy, cobweb-fine beard with the other hand. He said he was ninety-one years old. He had arrived in China the year Treadup was born. He had served out most of his mission in Peking, and there he had taken up the study of ancient Chinese bronzes. The other friars said he was a world-famous scholar, and he talked to Treadup, between whacks, with his eyes transported by the exquisite vision of memory, about ritual vessels of the Shang, Chou, and early Han dynasties. He described to the huge American, as Treadup scrubbed the cooking cauldrons, the ancient casting of these artifacts by the still-used lost-wax method—"old, *old* things, my boy, going back to sixteen centuries before the birth of Our Lord Jesus Christ, sir." Father Julius had been one of those to decipher the ideographs with which some of the objects were decorated.

> *I lie in bed thinking about him, Em, and get the horrors. Here he is, at ninety-one, this distinguished scholar with a mind as hard and bright as bronze itself, and what is his destiny?—to kill flies. He is, in a narrow field, a great man. And this is what he has come to: flap, flap, flap. Ever more flies keep coming, as if he were actually multiplying them with his blows. Futility! I actually wept, thinking of him last night, Godforsaken as he is. As we all are.*

• Drubbins had organized a brothel. Miller, the ex-soldier, told Treadup about it. Three White Russian women from Tsingtao, he said, and a half-Chinese, half-French wife of a no-good American ex-sailor. He told Treadup the number of the room—one of the small rooms in the dormitory rows.

> *I was drawn to it, walked past it often, Em. I promise you it was not that I wanted to enter. I wanted to condemn, to blame, to stare it out of existence. Then one afternoon, in broad daylight, I saw little Frances Player, the daughter of those Presbyterians who used to be in Tsinan—remember?—the girl's about seventeen—go right in that door. I checked later to see whether I had mistaken the room number. I had not. What did I do about it? Nothing. Nothing—except to stop passing that way.*

• A foolish Dutch priest, a stout, pink man, was caught by a camp guard bargaining with two Chinese farmers over the wall in broad daylight. The Japanese commandant charged the Discipline Committee with dealing him a severe punishment. Guards collared the Chinese farmers and kicked them and beat them with bamboo rods; the whole camp could hear their screams. The Committee staged a trial of the priest. The sentence: He must stand on a mound by the wall every night for a week. In other words, they were sentencing him to deal "over the wall" by night rather than by day.

Later, in the dining hall, Treadup heard roars of laughter from a table of friars. The "condemned" man was regaling some who had not been there with the story of his hour at the bar of justice.

> *Phinny guffawed when I told him about it. But Em, this disturbed me, horrified me. Not just the cynicism of it. The beatings, almost to death, of those poor Chinese. This winking at the regulations by our supposed court. You know I have always believed in the rule of law. The floor of values I've stood on all my life is unsteady, as if there were a mild but constant earthquake going on. Yes and No are topsy-turvy.*

• Treadup went to Sunday service. Oh, no! There in the pulpit was Reverend Planson, from Union Church, in Tientsin. He had not failed to bring his purple cassock, his white silk surplice, and his leaden clichés and commonplaces with him in his internment baggage. "Probably the worst sermon I ever heard." The text was Romans 10:12: "For there is no difference between the Jew and the Greek: for the same Lord over all is rich unto all that call upon him." Planson seemed to be suggesting that in the Yin Hsien camp there was no real difference between the British and the American, they were God's children, even Belgian and Dutch Catholics might conceivably be God's children; yet he managed to suggest, in easily decipherable code, that Americans were colonials, lacked education, were muddled in their thinking, used bad grammar, and were materialists; even their missionaries were materialists.

> *This idiotic sermon cheapened everything. I will not be able to go to church when Planson is to be in the pulpit. I may not be able to go to church at all, for I am so fearful in the pews. I cannot wait for the service to be over, so I can go outside and breathe.*

• Physically stronger, he had become voraciously hungry. It was an unhealthy hunger, a survivor's hunger, something like that he had felt after the drowning of Penn Landsdown in the mountain stream near Kuling, so many years before. Only the memory of Irrenius Cashman's outburst kept him from whining at how little he was served at meals. Even when a server made some allowance for his huge frame and gave him an extra dollop, it never seemed to be enough. The bread, baked at a common bakery for all the kitchens, was fresh and usually tasted good, and he could eat as much of it as he wanted, but "bread melts away to nothing in the mouth," he wrote.

He was on the evening shift. One of the wipers was ill, and the pot washing seemed to last forever. Most people had left.

> *Something got into me. I suddenly tingled with what I must have thought was canniness. My heart began to pound. I told Spencer Dodd, who was wiping, to run along, I'd be glad to finish up. He's a young sprig, and he has taken a fancy to a plump Tsingtao girl, Molly Someone, so he was glad to run off. I was alone. All the cooks had called it a night. The meat had been delivered for dinner the next day, and of course I knew where it was hung. I carried a stack of pans into the kitchen, quickly slipped a knife from the rack at the cutting tables, dodged into the cool-room, and hacked off a beautiful slab of lean pork from a whole side on a hook there. I put it under my shirt, I felt against my chest the cool strength it would give me within, when I ate it. I was crazy, Em. I hadn't thought how I would cook it, or how I would hide it from my roommates. But O I was happy!*

"Not you, Treadup!"

Treadup wrote that he nearly fainted. It was Slawter, the supervisor. He must have ducked back in to the kitchen for something he had forgotten.

"I'll have to report you to the Discipline Committee, old man. I wouldn't have thought it!"

TREADUP'S case came before the Discipline Committee two mornings later. Now he experienced firsthand what the Dutch priest had gone through—except that the outcome was very different. The proceedings were exceedingly British. "The only things lacking," Treadup wrote, when he had achieved some distance from the event, in "Search," "were wigs on the judges and barristers." The presiding officer was the former head of the Legation Quarter police force in Peking, a large, portly man, now jovial, now stern. Treadup recorded in his diary that he wanted to say to the Committee: "You let the priest off the other day. He was venal. I was only hungry." But "something—was it a rag of pride I still wore?—something held my mouth shut." The Committee sentenced Treadup to two perambulations of the compound wearing around his neck a sign:

I AM A THIEF

On this awful walk Treadup encountered Miller, the ex-soldier, who clapped him on the shoulder and congratulated him for having been a bad boy. Corbuc, the Rumanian scoundrel in his room, looked at him later with pity, so badly had he bungled his theft. At night, unable to pray, he felt a fearful punitive trembling settle in his empty belly.

THE CRISIS, when it arrived, took him by surprise. Though he came, later on, to give it great importance, referring to it as his "counterconversion," we lack a full, coherent narrative of it, perhaps because he was never sure how deep the change in him actually ran. The first note, the morning after, is brief:

Up all night. Torn to pieces. I was alone in the room, Corbuc out smuggling, Watkins visiting his British friends in Building 24, a drinking party as usual. I am in quicksand.

Then, a blank day, and then, two days afterward:

I turned in, three nights ago, thinking myself very tired, but I could not sleep. I got up and began pacing. Bare feet, cold. The strangest feeling. Others seemed to be in the room with me. I was not dreaming. I suppose my imagination was overworked, by the stress of recent days, and by my inability to pray. Phinny was there in my mind, Irrenius Cashman was there, Miller the ex-sergeant, Reverend Planson, the pink-faced smuggling priest, and, perhaps, at the very edge of my perceptions, Sister Catherine. I felt very angry, I argued with the night air. Horrible Planson began speaking to God—and to my surprise his tongue was smooth— seeming to offer me words to address to God: "Thou art the God of my strength: why hast thou cast me off? why go I mourning . . . ?" Miller's curses burned my ears, and Renny Cashman's arrogance made me furious. Then—were they whispers I heard from Sister Catherine?— or were they from a great distance?—from you, Emily, far away? "My beloved is like a roe or a young hart: behold, he standeth behind our wall, he looketh forth at the windows, shewing himself through the lattice. My beloved spake, and said unto me, Rise up, my love, my fair one, and come away." I saw the pink-faced priest laughing; I laughed, too. I felt bitterness toward Phinny; he had cut into my arm. I don't know how long I walked back and forth. I remember that I threw myself to my knees beside my bed, the way I used to when I was small, and I may have said "Jesus friend of little children." Whatever I said, the line was dead. No one was listening. There was the most awful void. Then nasty Cashman said, "Your prayer should be, 'Let the day perish wherein I was born, and the night in which it was said, There is a man child conceived.'" At some time in the night, after more, much more, of my confusion, they left me. I was exhausted. I fell onto the bed and slept soundly.

Nothing, here, about the consequences of the experience, devastating though they were to be for him. He does not speculate—he never will— whether he imagined those presences with him in the room, or was suffering some sort of psychic accident. Several days pass before he can write:

I am calm. I am out of touch with God. It may be that I realized that night—that I now think—that there is no God. On that point I am not sure. I still feel capable of amazement; I walked out this morning and was dazzled by the shimmering line of dew, touched by the new sun, along the upper edge of the wall that holds me imprisoned. I feel as if my hands and feet had been tied for a long time, and that the knots have suddenly been undone. This has been an eerie experience. I don't think I am going to be quite so afraid any more. If there is a God, I must be a disappointment to him.

THE INNER FRAME

HE FELT no raptures, but he began to notice some spring in his legs. The colors of the day had gained intensity. He ate his food slowly, savoring the tastes. He was not so tired at work as he had been. He was still susceptible to fear, but now the fear, when it came, responded to real dangers, real concerns, and it was edged with the old familiar expectation of surprise, which he had first experienced as a boy, watching the dog Tub give birth to her pups. Fear was no longer dominant. He was open to minor pleasures. Memories of major ones, long asleep in him, rushed forward.

IN "SEARCH," a few weeks later, as his loss of the bulk of his faith hardened in him, he wrote:

> What was happening now was altogether different from the period after my conversion at Syracuse. This was a much calmer aftermath, though colder. I felt, all along, this time, a deep sense of loss—a loss of years of habits of thought, a loss of God's wings over me in the nest, a loss indeed of some kind of narrowness, tightness, which had made life easy for me, without my even knowing it. Yet the gain was palpable, too: Now, right away, I had access to a range of feelings that seemed to me greater than what I had known before. Nonsense and folly, my own and others', were more visible than before. I still wanted to be good in the eyes of others, but the whole idea of sin had found its proportions. Living at close quarters with Miller, the bullying ex-sergeant, and Irrenius Cashman, the supposedly sainted missionary, each with his astonishing contradictions folded into him; and with Sister Catherine, and with the shabby Corbuc and rodent Drubbins, and with Flanders the Tientsin Club steward, "too good to be true," and Phinny, and Ramsdel the pompous Kailan Mining executive—stripped down, all of them, to their most primitive conditions of value—living so intimately together, in such raw states of hunger and need—it seemed to me I was seeing some human constants at work which made the idea of being cleansed of sin by Jesus Christ illusory. One could believe in illusion and take strength from it, and I suppose I had, for all those years, but the moment illusion

is seen for what it is—whoosh! its beauty and support are gone. The outcome was bleak for me. It would take a new order of courage to live without this support. Yet the possibility of courage had itself taken on a new meaning, somewhat painful, but challenging, because there was no hand but mine, now, on the tiller.

TREADUP was on his way back to his room after the noon shift of pot washing. The day was so brilliant that he felt himself embedded in a universal sapphire. The compound was livable. Cleanup squads had got rid of all the rubble and debris that had made the camp so unsightly at first, and the English gardening mania had begun to tell a cheery story in a large plot alongside the hospital.

As Treadup walked past one of the two water-boiling sheds that had been set up to provide water both for drinking and for showers—this one was called "Waterloo" and the other was "Dew Drop Inn"—he found Flanders, the club steward, manning the pump which raised water to the holding tank for the boilers. This pump, and others like it around the camp for various water uses, had to be serviced all day long by turns of strong men. "Chief" Flanders, forever tidy in the eye of his club clientele, was in his immaculate black jacket and striped pants. Flanders had always been slightly condescending to Treadup, who had not been "clubable" when he had lived in Tientsin, but now, when Treadup, in the good mood of this bright day, called out a greeting, Flanders stopped pumping, straightened himself, responded with the slight bow of respect he usually reserved for clubmen, and then with an involuntary groan stretched his arms over his head.

"Your back's sore," Treadup said.

"The pump handle's frightfully awkward," Flanders said.

"I see that," Treadup said. "The fulcrum is much too low."

Treadup, "finding myself excited by the problem," examined the pump, then went straight to the plumbing shed of the Committee on Engineering and Repairs. He knew the man on duty, an engineer from the Tientsin Municipal Council, and he persuaded him to let him have the parts and the tools necessary to see if he could heighten the hand pump Flanders was working on.

Hacksaw, threader, wrench, and muscle—two hours. Flanders had left. Treadup pumped hard to make up for the lost time. He could work standing up straight.

THE DIARY:

When I wrote the other day about a new, wider range of feeling, I did not take note of something at which I marvel: I mourn the great loss I have suffered, it is bitter and impoverishing, there is a huge hollow place, yet at the same time I am joyous and feel free. I am waking up from a sleep. Phinny kept at me all that time about "entering the twentieth century." Perhaps I have begun to do so. That thought gives me some strength. Part of my joy, I think, comes from my sense that in spite of this void in my spirit, I can look back on my mission in the China field without shame or guilt. It was not all error and mummery. I really think I gave what I could give with a whole heart. And this: Old Todd was onto something, after all, with what I thought was his so offensive charge of "humanism." This experience I have gone through here must have been brewing in me for a long time.

IT WAS May, and the weather was fine. The food preparers worked outdoors, at a long table outside the kitchen. One afternoon Treadup, taking a breather from washing pots, stepped out into the soft air. The workers there were chatting. Treadup heard a familiar, somewhat metallic voice. Mrs. Evenrude! The seventy-odd-year-old woman, who had not done a stroke of domestic work for three-fourths of her life, was peeling turnips. He watched her, without stepping forward, for a long time. She was chatting away like a catbird. Her face was strong and clear. She was doing this menial work with great dignity and amazing deftness and rapidity. When Treadup finally intruded, she threw down her knife and the turnip she was working on and flung her arms around his neck. Treadup had a sudden vivid memory of another unexpected embrace, from long ago, when old Dr. Elting, on the porch of the Astor House in Tientsin, had taken raw young Treadup to his breast, and astonishing tears had come to David's eyes. Now, rather, David's impulse— equally astonishing to him—was to laugh. Stiffening, perhaps sensing this, Mrs. Evenrude drew back and presented Treadup to her co-workers, formally, as if she were serving high tea on Davenport Road.

HE TALKED one evening with Sister Catherine, and, for the first time, looking in her eyes, he saw the deep pools of her loneliness. He touched her with something he perhaps carelessly said, and she suddenly opened out to him with a shocking candor. She was frightened. She had stopped menstruating. She said she had endured all sorts of troubles in China; others had always praised her calmness, her equanimity. But here, in this crowded camp, she was cut off, alone, and now, as she so strangely put it, considering her vows, "barren."

Sister Catherine's loneliness reached like a pickpocket into his. Soon she was in full possession of his starved love for Emily. She drew from him many pictures of Em: the maiden with nut-brown hair in the Y.W. canteen at

Syracuse; the seasick bride riding up the China Sea; the pale being beyond the terrible wall she had built around herself, after the loss of Nancy; the cynosure of four thousand men on His Majesty's Transport *Tyndareus*. On and on. The nun, having with her disciplined charity put aside her own distress, listened to his, saying nothing.

Emily! As he tried to tell Sister Catherine about Emily's serenity, he suddenly found it hard to describe; it had subtly changed, it baffled him, it became an enigma. He was faced with wondering what Em would think of him now. Would he seem a stranger to her? Would she accept him as he now was? Was he, puzzling over something he had seen so often in her, at a distance from her that was not just geographic? "I was disturbed by these thoughts, and they made me dishonest," he wrote. "I did not tell Sister Catherine a word about my apostasy." And then, a perplexing line: "I didn't want to hurt her feelings."

EUSTACE HOCKING, former chief engineer for Kailan Mining and now head of the camp Committee on Engineering and Repairs, asked Treadup if he could find spare time to raise the level of the handles of all the other water pumps around the compound. The committee assigned Treadup a helper. He called their undertaking the Great Yin Hsien Civilian Assembly Center Rainmakers' Spine-Straightening Company Limited. He pieced the work out, between pots and pans, over a two-week span.

Then on a Monday morning Phinny Cunningham asked David if he had seen that day's posting of the week's assignments by the camp Employment Committee. Treadup went right to the notice board and found that he had been transferred from kitchen work to Engineering and Repairs.

Now came a burst of energy which was—on a somewhat lower scale of grandeur—like the one he had had after his first lecture tour in the spring of 1911. He felt, in fact, easily three decades younger than he had a month before. His arm was all healed. He ran three times around the perimeter before breakfast each morning. His mission now was modest. Its slogan: Modernize the Yin Hsien Camp in This Generation!

His ingenuity opened out like a morning glory. First of all, he rearranged the carpenters' and fitters' shop to make it more efficient; he trained the men to think of their tools as precious extensions of themselves, to be cared for as tenderly as their own limbs and extremities. (He even pointed out, as a measurement of value, the sense Sergeant Miller gave to the word "tool." "I could never have uttered such a thing a month ago, and even now I felt a little thrill of shame. My fellows encouraged me by laughing.") Cannibalizing materials already in the compound, he designed and supervised the refashioning of the camp's hot-water boilers. Phinny importuned him to rebuild some of the hospital's facilities. He headed a team that did over the

Tsingtao kitchen *while it was being used.* Every day brought a score of break-downs, collapses, accidents.

In June he succeeded Eustace Hocking as chief of the Committee on Engineering and Repairs. Dr. Cunningham said he had "engineered" the replacement. Hocking was in fact happy to step down into an easier job. The diary:

> *I must confess I wanted it. Hocking is a friendly fellow, but he is muddled in his thinking and cannot take things in sequence. I'm going to make things hum.*

TREADUP played third base for Tientsin. In the fine weather there was a softball game every evening. There were kitchen teams, city teams, corporate teams—B.A.T., Kailan, Standard Oil.

> *I hit one over the wall for a four-bagger last night. I don't think I've had so much fun since those games at the summer conference at Silver Bay, when I was how old?—fourteen? We have an arrangement with the Jonathans for one of their guards to shag for us when somebody knocks one "out of the park"—obviously we can't chase balls outside the compound. It's a long peg from third to first, and I manage to get the ball over there. I've booted a few, but so has everybody else. The big surprise is the Catholic team. Their left fielder is a bishop. The best player in the whole camp is their pitcher, we call him Father Windy. He talks constantly while he is pitching—to himself, to the batter, to the umpire, to the crowd in the stands. Which, by the way, is always a big one. Half the camp turns out to root for a team. Even the British come out to be amused by the chaps playing rounders. The nuns and priests all come to watch. Two young nuns act as cheerleaders. "Rome! Rome! Rome! Rickety-rah!"*

TREADUP wrote: "My 'I' has moved into my eye." By that he apparently meant: Now he was aware of the world. He wrote in another note that he realized how "shut in" he had been for so long.

One use of his eye (and ear): He began going—as he had not done at first—to the entertainments that were put on in the church building each week. The Pekingers were particularly active in staging these evenings. A young pianist and conductor from the capital, Peter Plumb, gave some recitals on a grand piano which the Japanese had, after much importuning by the internees, shipped to the camp from Peking. Plumb organized, rehearsed, and presented an orchestra and chorus in performances of Stainer's *Crucifixion* and *The Daughter of Jairus,* Mendelssohn's *Hear My Prayer,* and parts of Handel's *Messiah* and a Bach oratorio.

After hearing the Bach, Treadup wrote:

What a superb sense of order, struggling against almost uncontrollable inventiveness! The composer must have thought he had a special relationship with his God, who said to him, "Tame your wild imagination so that ordinary human beings can hear what you're saying!" How I envy that, in my spiritual deprivation. If I were a genius, perhaps I would need a God so much that I would still have one.

The Tientsin entertainments tended to be more popular "and frankly," Treadup wrote, "more fun." A company put on *The Pirates of Penzance.* Treadup played his cornet in the orchestra. ("I started tooting again about three weeks ago. Corbuc the Rumanian runs howling from the room when I practice. My poor fat lip could manage Sullivan; never could have done the Bach.") Groups got up satirical skits. A squad of hearty British men, dressed up as chorus girls, staged an all-male *Folies Bergères.* And, finally and inevitably, David Treadup went to work in the engineering shop, and in early July, to full houses on two successive evenings, "trotted out Good Old Gyro." The lecture was a great hit. He had trained Miller, the ex-sergeant, to be his assistant, and Miller turned out to be very funny. "Is there a clown hiding in every retired sergeant?—there's a certain kind of humor, after all, which has cruelty at its core." Treadup himself "felt on the wing up there. Of course it was that dear old spiel—automatic, by now." He was obliged to realize that he was becoming a Camp Personality.

THE DIARY:

Em, I am at home here in a community, with as much sense of belonging as I have ever had—more, even, I think, than in Salt Branch—far more than in Ma Ch'iao (alas that that should be so). The citizens here have, through a remarkable effort of cooperation, mastered all the basic services that we need, using no labor but our very own. We even have some refinements, now: a laundry, a sewing room, a shoe repair shop, a watch-repairing service. We have a library—the heart of its collection, it goes without saying, being the load of books from Phinny's Tientsin house that he and I lugged here. The Peking American School and the Tientsin Grammar School are going strong, and there are evening courses for adults, with language study predominating—the preference being for Chinese—but with about 25 other courses, too: Greek classical drama, a history of the industrial revolution, ect. A resourceful lady has started something called the White Elephant Exchange, where people can trade things that are useless to themselves for things that are useless to others. Theatricals, concerts, puppet shows, shadow pictures, skits, and sports contests keep us busy. The church is full all day Sunday—three or

four early Catholic masses, which I have visited out of curiosity, the
music is splendid, especially for the pontifical masses; then an Anglican
service at eleven; the "free" Protestant denominations in a Union Service
in the afternoon; and hymn sings in the evenings — the last not nearly as
popular as an outdoor Sunday-twilight show put on by a Dutch priest,
which consists of skits, jokes, and community singing, all to a great deal
of laughter. It would be a full life if you were here.

Even in his diary, while addressing Em and writing about church
services, he could not bring himself to tell her about his alienation from
Christ.

ON THE EVENING of July 7, 1943, David Treadup drew his ration for
supper and walked into the dining hall, craning his neck to find a place to sit.
He saw Phinny waving to him, beckoning from across the way. David went to
him. He had saved a place. David found Mrs. Evenrude also at the table. With
Sister Catherine. ("Had no idea they knew each other.") And more: Miller,
somehow excused for the evening from kitchen work; "Chief" Flanders of the
Tientsin Club; his two roommates, Cyril Watkins and Ion Corbuc; Eustace
Hocking; Boggs, the Pentecostal missionary from the first room (where
Phinny still lived). "I was suspicious. What *was* this little caucus?" The
people at the table sat in silence, watching Treadup wolf his food. He wiped
his chin. Suddenly there was a circle of waiters and table clearers around the
table, and one of them was holding a cake with a single candle burning on it.
The circle broke into a comical *a cappella* version of "Happy Birthday." The
whole dining hall clapped, cheered, and shrilly whistled.

I had completely forgotten it was my birthday. Completely. Away from
you, Em, I must have an inexorable need to lose track of time — which is
elusive in my head, anyway, as you know. Sixty-five years old. Can you
believe it? I must say, I feel forty-five right now. I was so touched by the
warmth of all the folks. How did this celebration come about, anyway?
Phinny told me later that Mrs. Evenrude had remembered the date, got
the bakery to do up the cake. Goodness, she asked me my birthdate one
day months ago, in her most crotchety period. I went to bed early, in
order to lie there and think back over the years. I hardly slept at all.

THE NEXT MORNING he arose at five o'clock, went to the camp library,
and at a desk there wrote at the top of the first page of a new quarto notebook
with marbleized cardboard covers, one of several he had brought from Tientsin
to use for diaries, these words:

SEARCH

Ever since I arrived at this place, and for some time before this spiritual experience I have recently had, I have noticed that my memory has been unusually active. In captivity, nostalgia for the wild grows strong. Perhaps my separation from Jesus Christ has obliged me to try to remember what it meant to be close to him. Perhaps my separation from my wife has forced me to rely, for the special sort of warmth she gave me, upon reminiscence. I think of my boyhood often. Each day I bank interest on my debt to Absolom Carter. Kind women are with me day and night—my mother, Maud Chase, Mrs. Farleigh, Mrs. Kupfer, Letitia Selden, Madame Shen; they all hover about me and keep me from being lonely. Especially, and always, Mrs. David Treadup of dearest recollection.

These memories come to me spontaneously, helter-skelter, to meet a moment's need for comfort or comparison. Each recall has had a transient value; together, the mass has not cohered in any way. Because of my apostasy, if that is what it is, I have now determined that I will try to make a systematic search, through the tangled nets of my memories, for whatever meaning I can find there—a search, I presume, for the inner frame upon which the house of me stands.

And so he began the work which we have seen so often quoted from in these pages. It became his habit to rise early every morning, before the sun, and well before roll call, and to go to the library, where he could be alone, and to write for an hour or so. His diary entries, which he made in the evenings, become less voluminous; quite often days passed without any notation at all.

"A PARADOX has ruled my life," he wrote in a passage toward the end of "Search." "It is this: The busier I am, the more time I have to do things." In conformity with this rule, Treadup now took on, in addition to his ever increasing engineering work and his writing, the functions of warden for his dormitory block.

The wardenships had developed as a convenience, to make the daily roll calls less onerous. At each roll call, the Japanese required every inmate to stand at his or her room door to be seen and counted. At first the morning roll calls had been at ten o'clock, but as this interfered with morning chores the time was changed to seven thirty. It was the warden's duty to get everyone up on time, but not too soon, to show a face when the consular police and guards would come by. Treadup had the physique and force of character to get even the laziest slugabeds out—some, to be sure, in nightgowns or pajamas, some men with shaving lather on their jowls muttering about the tyranny of "that blockhead," meaning Treadup, the head of their block. So good did Treadup's record become that soon the guards began to take his word for the attendance of Block 17, without having to see each face.

How thankful certain sleepers were! "I must confess I got a little drunk on their gratitude."

The pleasure of this intoxication led Treadup to make yet more of his wardenship. Each internee received, each month, a small amount of "comfort money" in North Chinese currency, provided by the American and British governments and delivered to the camp by Swiss consular couriers. There was a camp canteen, supplied by the Jonathans and run by the former manager of the Whiteaway Laidlaw department store in Tientsin. The campers could spend their money at the canteen to buy eggs, fresh fruit, honey, and a few delicacies, such as ginger, spices, and dried fruit, as well as such things as soap and cigarettes. The long lines of waiting customers were a great nuisance, and Treadup offered to be the buyer for his block. Each morning at roll call he would take orders, and later in the day he would buy for everyone; he kept charge accounts. Other wardens took up the practice, and soon the lines at the canteen were much shorter.

Treadup then extended the service yet again, offering to act as middleman with the black market. At first he approached Corbuc for help, but the shady Rumanian was after much bigger fish than a few sweet-toothed campers. Corbuc told Treadup to go to the Catholics for retail goods. Treadup asked Sister Catherine to "recommend an honest trader," and she put him in touch with a Belgian Passionist missionary, Father LeGrange. Soon Treadup— and the two assistants he had enlisted to stand in line and run errands— were supplying the residents of Block 17 with sugar, honey, jam, sourballs, and even *paikar*, a powerful Chinese grain liquor. "What would Mama have thought!"

> There's a gold fringe on my pleasure in this work: It is said to be getting dangerous. Why does that delight me so? The Jonathans are punishing the offenders they catch. Why? Because they smell money, they want the business for themselves. But they would never suspect Mr. Teddy! He is so conscientious!

IN ORDER to monitor each internee's general health, Dr. Cunningham had early instituted a universal monthly weigh-in of every person. Weighing Treadup in his rotated turn, not long after the birthday party, Phinny found that David had gained eight pounds, but he said that on account of the earlier osteomyelitis he wanted David to come in for a full checkup. A few days later Phinny went over him from sole to crown; took blood and stool and urine into his little lab. The next day in the dining hall, Phinny: "Treads, you have been lying to us about your age. You are a young lion."

ONE OF the few entries of more than two or three lines in the diary during this period:

The weather is fiercely hot. Both men and women have reduced their clothing to a minimum. Besides the heat, economy has forced this on us, as we know we cannot replenish clothing supplies while in camp. The exigencies and conditions of camp life have shattered all the common and conventional patterns of occidental apparel, and the results have been extremes of vanity and variety in camp costumes—highly picturesque and often daring. Since we men have been reduced to the level of Chinese farmers and coolies, we go, as they do, with our bare backs to the sun, and some wear nothing but underwear briefs. I have joined the brown race. The women wear the most abbreviated "sports suits," cut to modern bathing suit patterns, and sometimes even more spare. Female beauty (and, alas, ugliness) is being evidenced, in some cases flaunted. Some of the missionary women, who have been most strict in their speech in the past, have suddenly become startlingly immodest in their dress. Is one supposed to look away, or not?

IN LATE JULY two rumors sneaked around the camp: that all the Catholics would soon be leaving; and that there might be a repatriation of American citizens. In August—the sad miracle of confirmation of one of the rumors. It seemed that the Apostolic Delegate in Peking from the neutral Vatican had somehow convinced the Japanese that the priests and nuns were not their enemies. So they were to be allowed to return to Peking and to missionary work.

On the day of their departure, as the Catholics were assembled on the athletic field to be loaded with their baggage into trucks, all the rest of the inmates gathered around the field and at the gate. Like others, Treadup rushed around saying good-bye to friends—to Father Windy, to the outfielding bishop, to Father LeGrange. He found Sister Catherine, busy supervising the loading onto a truck of some nuns' luggage. He spoke her name.

"Ah, Mr. Treadup," she said, quickly turning to him. "I need Mrs. Treadup's address. I don't know why I hadn't thought of it sooner. I will try to get a message to her through Rome—to tell her what a fine man her husband is."

"Cool and distant," Treadup later wrote.

I told myself she was keeping strong emotions under check; now I have moments of wondering whether there was any feeling at all. "What a fine man." Drily said. She seemed a teacher or a nursemaid—after all that I had invested in our friendship.

Treadup ran to the nearby library for a piece of paper and a pencil. By the time he got back, Sister Catherine had been loaded into a truck and non-Catholics had been pushed back by the guards to the edge of the field. He waved toward the nuns' truck that she was in, but everyone was waving and shouting, and he could not tell whether she saw him.

THE FOLLOWING PASSAGE appears, strangely, not in "Search" but in the diary:

I think I can write about this at last. About the team of Communists sitting comfortably on the 'k'ang' in farmer Feng's house in Li Chia village, confronting me. I have never been really at ease, seated on a flat plane with my legs crossed under me. Those young men were trying to make me sweat, anyway. They were hammering away at the theme of my complicity with businessmen in the rape of China. They were too sophisticated to use such phrases as "running dog," but it was clear that they were convinced that all missionaries were tools of nations and corporations, which, with their insatiable cupidity, systematically exploited the poor of the world.

I argued that there were missionaries and missionaries, and I did break into a sweat.

They cited, very bitterly, three cases in which missionaries in the northwest, in Shensi, had informed to the authorities on Communists and had caused their arrests and deaths.

I lost my head. Instead of pointing out to them the missionaries' opposition to such "imperialistic" things as Boxer indemnities and extraterritorial rights, I began shouting about the Communist slaughter of innocents in Hunan. Our session was becoming ugly. Those young men and I had both reached each other's tender places. They gave me an oral thrashing I have never gotten over.

I had a chat today with Gilbert Olander, the crusty Standard Oil man from Tientsin. He gave me reason to remember—was it my first year in China?—his calling the old missionary Dr. Elting an ass, a numskull, and a busybody who hadn't "the faintest idea what the Chinks are all about." As a missionary I myself felt light-years from Olander then—and always have—until today. I certainly never felt I was a running dog for him in China! I can admit now that I disliked and feared him and his kind. But today he congratulated me on my work in Engineering and Repairs, and he actually said, "We should have let you missionaries run the place. You fellows get things done." Of course what he grudgingly admired was strictly a matter of efficiency—energy, really—nothing more. But what a turnabout!

SOLID NEWS came, on the twenty-third day of August, 1943, right from the Jonathans' mouths, that the Americans in this camp would all be repatriated within a fortnight. The last page of "Search":

With these few lines I shall stop work on this document. It will remain, like everything else in my life, incomplete. I had intended to read what I have written, to peruse it over and over again, paying close attention to what could be seen between the lines, and then pen some grand conclusions. "My mission to Cathay, brothers and sisters, was . . . " Now there will not be time. There may not have been the possibility. For what lies between the lines is doubtless gossamer, which would be torn by removal. My self.

BOOK TEN

TIME
TO LEAVE

ACCEPT AND ENJOY

HE WALKED out the gate. He expected a wild surge of elation—he was going to Emily!—but instead he felt—what—*ataraxia?* A serene emptiness? Or possibly nothing? Or nothing, anyway, but surprise at how little he felt?

He and nearly three hundred others were at the top of a terraced slope. At the foot of the hill the little river wound its slow way northward, reflecting the blue of a champion sky. The terraces were covered with grass freshened by recent rains. Tall willow trees, growing on the different levels of the bank, mingled their feathers in a yellowy canopy overhead. Dappled early sunshine played on the flanks of the black-and-white cows of the camp dairy, which were grazing on the green steps of the hill.

Notes written later in a shaky hand on the train:

Father had Holsteins. Black and white, too, but much bigger than those runty cattle. That hit me: my memory put me in the barn, my nostrils and ears were full of the sugary smell and the quick thunked plashes of warm milk squirted into the pail. Yes, there on the embankment outside the compound I had a small-boy feeling. Chores were over. Only now, aged sixty-five, do I realize how sweet the chores had always been. Inside the barn, inside the compound wall, I had been free—busy, orderly, useful. Released, I felt at loose ends. A great deal had happened to me in Yin Hsien camp, and now all I could feel was a paradox: the loss of the freedom of confinement.

On the camp road, at the top of the ravine and next to the gray wall, were several motor lorries, onto which the repatriates, Treadup among them, were loading their hand luggage. The Japanese, perhaps glad to be rid of three hundred, were allowing a certain looseness. Boys and girls and some bold adults, who were staying in the camp, sat atop the wall, with their legs outside; other adults were standing at various places within, where the ground rose high enough for them to look out. Inside, the camp orchestra was playing good-bye tunes, and those on the wall alternately sang and showered the repatriates with farewells. Mrs. Evenrude was inside; she had decided to stay; China was her "only home." Treadup was careful not to look up toward the wall, for fear of seeing Phinny.

A DIARY NOTE on the southward trip:

Hsuchow, delay of several hours. Rumors of line broken by Chinese guerrillas. Picnic food supplied by Jonathans at Yin Hsien, supposed to last whole trip, already running out. Long chat with Swiss diplomatist who is neutral observer of exodus. Fresh-faced 26-year-old, sprightly, perfect English, this is an adventure for him. We had a charming conversation about Rousseau—sweltering RR car, wooden benches, the Social Contract—thank you, Phinny, for my late learning! Pleasured away a terrible afternoon.

IN THE INNER COURT of a dormitory at St. John's University, in Shanghai, where the repatriates were being housed, an inspection of luggage was to take place. Trunks had been shipped ahead.

The repatriates were ordered to find their baggage and stand by it, waiting for the examiners. This examination turned out to be different from any Treadup had experienced in North China, and it made him realize that the Yin Hsien regime had been a relatively benign one. From where he stood by his trunk, he could see the contemptuous Japanese examiners—from Customs and the gendarmerie—unfolding and shaking out each garment from a trunk, and heedlessly dropping it onto a pile on the ground; and then he saw excitement, resentment, gesturing, shouting, on the part of outraged Americans, as the inspectors seized articles which they ruled, quite by whim, it seemed, as forbidden, and threw them into large baskets and carried them away. It looked like official plunder.

Then Treadup saw something that made him gasp. A book was thrown into one of the contraband baskets. His back diaries and "Search" were in his trunk. In total disregard of orders of the day, he darted out through the unguarded gate of the courtyard, ran to the university administration building, and found the young Swiss consular representative in the office he had taken over.

> *Begged the boy to come posthaste and "commandeer" my various notebooks. He demurred. Said he hadn't license to interfere in Japanese procedures, so long as they conformed in a general way to the Geneva Convention. I suddenly heard myself saying, "Then you will have a suicide on your hands, Monsieur Ramminet." He gave me a long, queer look. He must have seen smoke in the pupils of my eyes. Emily and my sons were very far away in my mind. My life seemed to be in my "Search"—intrinsically worthless scribbling, perhaps, but at the moment, at least, I was overwhelmed by a conviction that I couldn't live without some tangible effort, even if unsuccessful, to comprehend the past. I think it may have been Jean Jacques Rousseau who saved my writings. Young Ramminet and I had made a kind of social contract with each other—came to an unspoken understanding about what is valuable on earth, what is worth sacrificing something for—in our talk on the train.*

Ramminet slowly rose to his feet. He walked deliberately to a closet in one corner of the office, picked up a canvas bag, at the mouth of which were a hasp and a padlock; and he said, "Show me the way." Ramminet would not run. He said, "If you would cheat a Chinese, you must cover your action with a loud flurry. To cheat a Japanese, you must be calm as a stone. It is not easy to cheat either one. Mr. Treadup, you are too agitated. Try to be calm."

They walked slowly into the courtyard and to Treadup's trunk. Treadup opened it. His hands were shaking. He rummaged for the notebooks. He straightened and handed them to Ramminet, who dropped them in the bag and locked it.

A Japanese gendarme was suddenly there—yes, calm as a stone. He asked in excellent Chinese what the two men were doing.

Ramminet said he had confiscated some Swiss property.

The gendarme demanded that Ramminet give him the bag.

Ramminet said it was a diplomatic pouch.

The Japanese said it would have to be examined.

Ramminet reached in a pocket and drew out a paper. Treadup could tell it was a Japanese document, because it had simplified Japanese kana characters, clues to pronunciation, alongside its Chinese ideographs. Ramminet asked the gendarme to look at it. The gendarme took the paper, and Treadup saw the blood drain from his cheeks—this was "a physical picture of a loss of face." He handed the document back to Ramminet and without another word walked away.

Ramminet said to Treadup, "I shall return your papers to you on the ship."

Treadup was so confused that he said, "What ship?"

Ramminet said, "The ship that will take you to heaven. If you had killed yourself, you would have gone to hell. Seventh circle."

Sept. 19 Sunday. Early breakfast, inspection of hand luggage. I was so complacent, now, as to be truly calm. Was I wood or stone? Seeing I had two straight razors, they stole my better one (my ticket to the Seventh Circle, had I made that voyage—today that idea seems to have been quite insane—not my idea at all—yet at the time it was all too real). Roll call. Then in buses to the Customs House on the Bund. Another examination.

AS AN ELDERLY MAN, Treadup was given a choice berth in a first-class cabin on D Deck—A Deck being the lowest steerage deck, E Deck being the highest. The ship was called *Teia Maru*—S.S. "Asian Empire"; she was the former *Aramis* of the French shipping company Messageries Maritimes, captured by the Japanese, it was said, in Saigon. She was a gray creature with seven huge white crosses painted on each of her flanks. She had been rerigged to carry twice her normal capacity of passengers, so that fifteen hundred repatriates could be accommodated, from camps around Shanghai as well as North China, and also, as it was to turn out, from Hong Kong, the Philippines, and elsewhere.

For two passengers our cabin would have been luxurious, with a window instead of a round porthole, beds with "Simmons" mattresses, wide and most comfortable, four commodious wardrobes, two with full-length mirrors, and a good lavatory with sitz-bath. But two other men have been assigned to the cabin, and they have to sleep on the floor on straw mattresses similar to those provided for the wooden bunks built into all the public rooms of the ship. In the big lounge on E Deck, 240 young and middle-aged women sleep on such bunks—we call that saloon the Sardine Tin. To our astonishment, the ship is filthy: the Japanese are usually so finicky.

ON SEPTEMBER 20, 1943, the *Teia Maru* was eased by tugs away from her wharf in the Pootung district of Shanghai, and she steamed slowly downriver. The diary:

For all these days I have been empty. I have been waiting for some emotion—any emotion—to surface. When I left Yin Hsien, nothing. No release, no joy that I would be rejoining Emily. Even when I talked, yesterday, and thought I meant what I said, about suicide, I felt nothing —no fear, no sadness, nothing. Some transient alarm, yes, over the thought of being separated from my "Search" and my diaries. But even that implied a consciousness of my emptiness—a sense that only written words could give my flesh and blood meaning. Such fear as I had—not even strong itself—was that I would never again feel anything 'real.'

This morning, on the Whangpoo River, as the ship nosed toward the unknown, my eye carelessly brushed across a certain wharf, and I was startled by a vivid picture of the day in 1905 when I walked down a gangplank, just there, and first set foot in a place that did not seem to me to be China at all. And suddenly, in wave after wave, I crashed into knowing that I was sailing away from all that has been life and breath to me for nearly four decades. I wrote, a moment ago, "toward the unknown." Certainly not toward a place I can think of as home. What new start can a man of my age make? I said out loud, "Good-bye, Johnny Wu!"—meaning: Good-bye, Phinny; good-bye, Mr. Lin; good-bye David Liu, Christian General, dear A Ch'u, and all the others; good-bye to everyone and everything. Then I began thinking of my beloved villagers, and I had to rush to my cabin or make a fool of myself in public.

A CHANGE of air, waterscapes, a landfall—green mountains against the sea and a sense of the miracles of diversity in the terrains of this earth. Each surprise of arrival helped mitigate, minim by minim, the enormous pain of having taken leave of a lifetime. Stanley Bay, off Hong Kong. A new party of repatriates aboard, among them a number of Filipinos with merry children. Sunday, September 26: San Fernando, a hundred fifty miles north of Manila—the great lizard spine of Luzon looming to the east. Fifty tons of anomalous sugar aboard. And 130 repatriates who had been interned at Manila—"reunions with many North China missionaries, who were caught here on their way home to the States in '41." Another ocean ride. "Strange: the wind blows, but I have not once been queasy on this trip." Saigon, one more small group of repatriates, mostly gaunt, tendinous missionaries from the interior of Indo-China. Lush fruits and vegetables thrown in heaps on one of the decks—no room in the holds, which were full of repatriates' trunks. Down the Mekong River from Saigon, under a sky with watercolored cotton clouds put to the torch by the setting sun, around the bends of a crooked channel between spreads of mangrove as far as a top-deck eye could see. "What an imagination behind such wonders! My disbelief is being tested." An anchorage in the straits forty miles off Singapore, an oil tanker alongside to refuel the *Teia Maru*. Then a surprising run to the southeast—the Straits of Malacca said to be mined—around the southern tip of Sumatra: volcanoes, the torn cone of Krakatoa.

> *Tonight Ramminet, a fellow named Murchison, and I took our steamer blankets to the top deck and spent the night in deck chairs there stargazing. Murchison some kind of business fellow, captured in Manila, had traveled around these seas, at home in all the heavens. He pointed out the major stars. The Southern Cross is high, up 25° or more, and Scorpio is almost at the zenith. We watched the constellations revolve around the South Pole. I began to feel my proportions. Some of those pinpricks of light started traveling in this direction millions of years ago, and the light would have traveled—I could hear my lecture-hall voice saying this in my spiel "Phenomena of Light"—would have traveled more than 63,000 times the distance between the sun and the earth in every single one of those years. What of my puny 10,000-mile lecture tours? My burnt-out instant—sixty-five years?*

AS THEY STEAMED up the Sumatran coast, a Lutheran missionary named Halze died. He had suffered a stroke just after the heavy baggage inspection in Shanghai; it was said that he had blown up, fatally as it proved, because the official Jonathans had stolen a silver cup that he had won in his youth for outstanding scholarship at the University of Wisconsin. Treadup was surprised to learn that the dead man had been six or seven years younger than he. Someone said the man had died of an extreme case of repatriation sickness.

> *Didn't know him but for some reason was drawn to his funeral. It was on C Deck aft, at five in the morning. A Reverend Tarpenson conducted the service. Ramminet was there. About fifty people attended. The engines had been stopped and the vessel slowed, not to a full halt but to a calm drift through the dark gray-blue waters of the hour before dawn. The body was wrapped in canvas, weighted, and lowered over the rail at the very stern. There is a somber beauty in burial at sea: "We commit thee to the deep." I wondered afterward what had made me want to see this stranger's remains thrown overboard. Then I recalled that at the*

service Ramminet gave me a very curious and sharp look; and I made a connection—realized that I have been trying to penetrate (perhaps he has, too) the mystery of my threat to him of suicide. I did not feel— I have not felt—I do not feel the least bit suicidal. Like everyone else, I have had the symptoms of repatriation sickness. I am sad. I am truly sad to leave so much that is unfinished behind. I have found I can feel a sea-deep and "real" sadness, and I can only say that this ability to feel such strong emotion leads me to want life, not an end to life. I cannot wait to be with Emily again. I have even more distant thoughts. I want to go back to China.

ON THE TEN-DAY VOYAGE across the Indian Ocean, Treadup, apparently turning toward vigor of mind, toward ever more intense thoughts of Emily, showed signs of becoming conscious of his body. He noted in his diary that everyone talked all day about food. "The dietary," Treadup wrote, "is such that all the men and many of the women with robust appetites leave the table hungry three times a day." At breakfast passengers were served, among other things, "a small portion of rice porridge to which some liquid representing milk and some substance representing sugar have already been added." There were skimpy helpings of meat and vegetables at night.

On the ninth day came a frightful shock. Members of the crew were set to shoveling the fruits and vegetables that had been stored on the open deck overboard. They had all begun to rot. The passengers could have been eating more all along.

Our outrage is tempered by the conviction that these people are losing the war. They are demoralized and hopelessly inexpert—so striking in a race from which we have come to expect the utmost in spotlessness and efficiency. The crew are disabled men and young boys. They have a filthy ship. They do not care. They are on a voyage toward futility.

FRIDAY, October 15. At a long wharf in Goa, the Portuguese enclave on the west coast of India, under a green headland crowned by an ancient stone fort, huge electric cranes, like gigantic herons fishing at the water's edge, reached down into the holds and drew up nets bulging with trunks.

Saturday afternoon: land leave for passengers. On the foreshore there was an intricate network of narrow-gauge railroad tracks, many of them rusty with disuse and overgrown with thick, unweedy grass—"felt good to the soles of our feet, which had been treading only the corridors of a ship for weeks."

Treadup and Ramminet took a walk on this turf together. They were allowed by Indian guards as far as a curious stone structure, a kind of shrine, at the foot of the headland, which they specially asked to visit. Over the arched doorway of this small building stood a life-sized statue, in the robes of a papal nuncio, of Francis Xavier, the sixteenth-century Jesuit missionary who opened up Japan to Christ, died on his way to China, and was buried back here in Goa. Ramminet—"a somewhat backslid Catholic," as Treadup put it—talked with fervor about Francis Xavier's strange, powerful mix of mysticism and horse sense.

Suddenly I found myself, under the stern gaze of the saint, blurting out to this Swiss boy my loss of confidence in God. He blushed as I spoke, as if my confession amounted to some sort of accusation against him. This is the first person to whom I have unburdened myself. I never even told Phinny. It was a great relief. I have felt as if I had been maintaining myself in disguise, all this recent time, as still a devout Christian missionary. His tactful response—silence—helped me to master the intensity of my catharsis.

The two men turned back toward the wharf, and there, beyond, inching inside the breakwater, was a white ship with huge black letters on her side: GRIPSHOLM SVERGE DIPLOMAT. The liner was warped slowly in to the wharf forward of the *Teia Maru*. Her decks swarmed with Japanese, who were being repatriated from the United States in exchange for the Americans from the Far East. A flag—big red dot on a white field—broke from the *Teia Maru's* superstructure, and the passengers on the *Gripsholm* gave out a pealing, high-pitched cheer. At this, Treadup suddenly found himself in tears, which he tried to hide from Ramminet. "My joy couldn't have been for the Jonathans' patriotism," he wrote later. "I think it was for the great beauty of the white ship. It was going to carry me to Emily."

ON TUESDAY, October 19, exactly one month after Treadup had boarded the *Teia Maru* in Shanghai, he marched in a semicircular line of passengers from a gangplank at the bow of the Japanese ship to one at the stern of the Swede; while in a similar but wider loop in the other direction, the Japanese repatriates simultaneously walked from the bow of the *Gripsholm* around to the stern of the *Teia Maru*. On the deck of the Swedish ship, while the passengers waited for the just-vacated cabins to be cleaned, Treadup was served, as everyone was, a glass of ice water, which he had not sipped for years; and he was given, as everyone was, a box of chocolates. Delightful! But it was only a few hours later, when he had been assigned to a luxurious four-bunk first-class cabin with three gray-haired men—a Baptist from the island of Hainan, a Catholic father, and a well-known Presbyterian missionary, linguist, and explorer from the borders of Tibet—and when these four had gone together in response to a bell to the dining saloon, and there in a buffet line had been allowed to heap all sorts of delicacies on their plates, taking just as much as they wanted—only then did David Treadup feel the surge he had expected from the beginning, way back at Yin Hsien's gate, the flood of exultation and gratitude for the sense of ease, of material well-being, of open choice, of being trusted—the sense, at last, of being a man released from long captivity.

NOW CAME a delay of two days, while the giant cranes and the Indian porters labored at a mutual transfer of luggage and mercies. From the *Teia* to the *Gripsholm* went innumerable casks, clearly marked with red crosses, said to contain a mixture of fish and soy beans, for distribution to Japanese in the United States. Two sorts of Red Cross packages went the other way: boxes about twice the size of suitcases, marked "Medical Supplies for One Hundred Adults for One Month—Details Below"; and smaller cartons containing "comfort packages" for American prisoners and internees held by the Japanese. "I thought: One of those boxes is for Mrs. Evenrude."

During the two days the passengers of the two ships were allowed to mix freely ashore. The diary:

> On the evening of Oct. 19, my Presbyterian explorer roommate and I accosted a substantial-looking Japanese man and had a long talk with him. He was from Los Angeles, where he had been in the importing and wholesale business for 31 years. He was thoroughly Americanized. He had been a member of the Los Angeles Chamber of Commerce and president of the Japanese Chamber of Commerce, and had been interested in promoting many Japanese cultural activities—Kabuki and No drama, and so on. On Dec. 7, '41, he was arrested and held for some days, first in the city jail and later in the county prison, where he lived on jailbird rations. After fierce interrogation he was interned in a concentration camp in Montana, under civilians, and was later transferred to Arkansas, in a camp under Army control, where the regime was strict and harsh. He had been summoned back to Japan—by whom he didn't say. His business had been destroyed, the years wiped out. What could be waiting for him in Japan, save defeat and ignominy? Upon parting we exchanged cordial handshakes and mutual good wishes.
>
> The next evening I talked for a few minutes with six Japanese girls, perhaps 15 to 18, who had come over near the 'Gripsholm' to say goodbye to their favorite Swedish dining-room steward. We talked while they giggled and hopped from foot to foot, waiting for him to appear. They were of a typical American-schoolgirl type—talkative and somewhat

frivolous, modishly dressed as pert California girls. None of them knew either spoken or written Japanese. Their parents were still interned, and they were going to live with grandparents in Tokyo. They were critical of the inferior accommodations on the 'Teia.' All said they couldn't wait to get back to America. Enemy aliens! These conversations have made me think that in China I must have got a false picture of the Japanese: the images of them must have come to me distorted, the lines of sight somehow bent—refracted through the medium of war. It is hard to think of them as Jonathans anymore, after talking with these young women.

AS SHE had been first to arrive, the *Teia* was first to leave. She went out on the twenty-first. "Most spontaneous were the gestures of farewell, and the waving of hundreds of handkerchiefs from the decks of both boats." The *Gripsholm* sailed the next morning.

NOW ON the benign sea came "a moment of utter astonishment." Mail Call. At the time assigned to P-through-T, David Treadup called at the Purser's Office, expecting—from long habit of such expectation—nothing. He was handed a packet of eight letters, seven from Emily and one from brother Paul.

I could hardly breathe as I made my way through the corridors to my cabin. I threw myself on my berth and read and read and read. I went over those pages many times, till the words had burned their way into my memory. Five of the letters had been written in July and August, after Em had been notified by the State Department of the repatriation, and had been given an address to which to write. One letter had been written back in October 1942, and of course not mailed back then. There was, Em wrote, a huge stack of unmailed letters waiting for me at home. Home? O such a difficult hour. These letters were from a stranger.

Em "seemed to be writing from the moon." Perhaps she was bitter, though she would not say so. She did say she had lived with fear for David so long that her hair was pure white. She wrapped up her news in tight sentences, each of which contained explosives. Young Philip, now thirty-four years old, was married and had two children, the first of whom was named David Treadup. The second, a girl, bore the dangerous name Nancy. Phil was a teacher at a private school for girls. Absolom, who was thirty-one, was still in Maine. He had a drinking problem—no further details given. Paul, still factoring in New York City, was "the Croesus of the family." He had just bought an Oldsmobile "with a Hydromatic—it shifts gears for itself—whatever that means." He sent his mother two hundred dollars every month. He was very big and "as handsome as his absent father" and had six or seven girl friends. Em was still working at the village library. "I have a wide acquaintance among people who owe money for overdue books."

Brother Paul wrote with excessive economy:

> As you can imagine, Davie, these have been hard hard years for your wife. She holds on very bravely. Do not be distressed by her appearance when you see her.

ON NOVEMBER 3 the *Gripsholm* tied up at a dock in Port Elizabeth, South Africa, and on the morning of November 15, exactly two months after Treadup left Yin Hsien, the ship made the harbor of Rio de Janeiro. After the ship put out from Rio toward the north and home, David found a cablegram slipped under his cabin door. He tore it open. It was signed EM.

BROTHER PAUL PASSED AWAY SUDDENLY TODAY HEART LOVE

David wrote that the word "heart" in the message "mercifully threw its weight in two directions—Paul's finished him, Em's love filled hers. Without the latter, I would be a man overboard." A later note: "I had wanted so to talk with Paulie. He would have understood"—would have been, this must have meant, the one person in the family to whom David could have trusted word of the withering of his belief.

THEY WOULD be crossing the equator soon. The air was warm. The waters had traded whales for flying fish.

One morning the passengers saw a supine rainbow. They looked down on it from B Deck. It seemed to lie flat on the water, stretching from just off the side of the ship in an elongated horseshoe shape clear to the western horizon. All of it except the rosy top point seemed to be on the water. It was not in the sky at all, and it was not so much an arc as a narrow ellipse. The ends of it seemed to bend in toward each other, as in a hand magnet.

Murchison—"what an extraordinary businessman, he seems to know about all natural things"—told Treadup and Ramminet that what they were seeing was a secondary rainbow; the primary one was overhead, but dimmer. He said the one on the water had the purple inside.

> I had forgotten—I had used this in my section on prisms in my lecture "Phenomena of Light"—that primary rainbows always have purple on the outside of the arch. This morning's fanciful quirk of nature gave me pause, as I remembered my conviction, delivering my lectures, that God

had made all scientific laws under the firmament. What can I think now? How did this perverse casting of the spectrum down upon the sea come to be? Is the universe mindless? I asked Murchison what he thought. "My God, Treadup," he said. "We have enough to worry about. Why don't you just accept and enjoy?" A practical man's advice. I must try to heed it.

TREADUP could not sleep. He got up at about three o'clock to see an almost full moon in the west, washing the cold sky and sea with silver. He rose again about four and watched the pilot climb a rope ladder up the hip of the ship. By six o'clock in the morning of December 2, 1943, the ship was anchored off the quarantine station on Staten Island. All passengers were called on deck, where they formed a mob and milled about for an hour. No one was examined. The yellow Q flag came down from the mast and the doctor went over the side: The ship's doctors must have satisfied him, no plague on board.

Passing the Statue of Liberty I remembered the eager young man, still at Syracuse, who had come to New York to be judged for his calling, his appointment put off, who then came to Bedloe's Island and climbed up in the statue and savored his romance with the idea of going across the ocean to bring succor to "your poor, your tired, your huddled masses." My boyish dream!

By the time breakfast was over, the ship was easing into a dock on the Jersey side, just across from the lower tip of Manhattan. Baggage went off in the morning, to be sorted and stacked by initials in the Customs House. No hope, word came, of getting off the ship until the next day.

AFTER lunch the next day Treadup found a note under his cabin door: "They will not let me on the dock. Am at Prince George Hotel. God has brought you home to me. Emily."

THERE WERE four examiners: three F.B.I. men and a Navy ensign. They were at a desk in the purser's cabin. The questioning was dry—utmost courtesy with the slightest push of authority behind it. All the usual: age, birthplace, names of family, length of residence in China, places visited in the Orient, occupation, education, skills, language capabilities.

Then we came to the part that was like pressing the hot jelly out of the gauze bag of boiled fruit—judgment on political and military situation in North China. The ensign said he was particularly interested in this last, and he asked me to have lunch with him. I told him politics and military affairs were out of my line. We had a puzzling talk.

They were not through with him. The investigation resumed after lunch. He had struck fire with his answer to the question, Had he ever encountered Communists in the villages where he worked? The men wanted every shred of conversation repeated. One finally asked, "Mr. Treadup, do you disapprove of America's war effort?"

Treadup said, "I disapprove of war."

This statement had to be carefully and extensively parsed, as if its four words contained, cleverly ambushed in them, many relative clauses and adverbial phrases and modifiers and qualifiers. I was reminded of diagramming complex sentences for Absolom Carter at Enderbury Institute. But I had only spoken, and meant, four words.

The senior F.B.I. man abruptly said, "Thank you, Mr. Treadup. You are free to go ashore."

I felt a hostility. I wanted to explain. But the line of people waiting to be examined was long. He waved me off.

A RAIN OF LOVE

HIS HEART "going like a cannonade," Treadup stepped to the reception desk and asked for the room number of Mrs. David Treadup. He had left his trunk on the dock and had taken a taxi to the Prince George.

The clerk said, "Ah. There is a message."

He disappeared around a partition; he was gone "for five years." Then he returned and said, "They have asked that we ring the room. We have done so. The young man will come down."

David sat in a chair in the lobby. At last a thin man with a balding head, dressed in a tweed jacket and gray flannel trousers, walked toward him, rising and falling a little too jauntily with each step, "as if he were riding a camel." David saw a flashing picture in his mind of the time when this son, Philip the

Yale man, had met them at Grand Central and had kept his loving parents at arm's length, giving them manly handshakes; and the father now reached out his hand in something like self-defense. But Irrenius Cashman had been right—"you are never quite safe from being surprised until you are dead"— for Phil opened his arms and threw himself forward into one more never-to-be-forgotten embrace: old Elting on the Astor porch; Mrs. Evenrude outside the camp kitchen; and now, Philip Treadup, responsible oldest son, "in a hug that I immediately understood as a warning, given with love, that I must hold myself together for my meeting with his mother, my wife." Philip at once put the warning into words.

"Mother's had a hard time," he said.

"Let's go be with her."

"She's afraid you'll be shocked."

"Let's risk that."

E X C E P T for laconic entries, usually only a few lines acknowledging movement or sharp change of some kind, David Treadup's diary falls nearly silent with his disembarkation from the *Gripsholm*, and remains so for several months. Perhaps he could not bring himself to write down honest words that might wound someone who happened to peek into the notebooks. For his reunion with Emily, from his point of view, we have to rely on a passage from a lengthy "Addendum to Search," which he wrote four years later. There is a merciful distance from the event in the account.

> *My first thought was that we had blundered into the wrong room. One problem for me, as I walked into Room 344 that morning and saw Em for the first time, was that I had somehow never had an opportunity, up until then, to think of myself as an old man. One possible signal of that reality, my sixty-fifth birthday party, in the camp at Yin Hsien, had come at a time when I was enjoying a burst of newly discovered vitality. There was only one candle on the cake. I was in health, I was useful. The clock and the calendar aren't necessarily reliable measurers of time. Here, before me, begging me with her eyes not to look at her, was an old woman. This was the reunion in Montclair, after France, raised to the 'n'th power of difficulty. What made it terribly hard was her being so afraid of my looking at her. Of course I embraced her—partly, perhaps, to get her out of my field of vision—no! I loved her, I had promised myself an ecstasy—and I found myself holding a creature so fragile and so nervy that there came into my head something Murchison had said on the ship: that a hummingbird's heart beats six hundred times a minute. My mind brimmed over with memories of my Emily; I was grateful for her existence; I wept with joy. She was the first to speak.*

"Thank God! Thank God, at last! Oh, David, let us pray." And she sank to her knees. And here, at once, I was put to a test which I had no choice but to fail. Within a minute of our being rejoined, I was dishonest with Emily Treadup. I knelt. I knew she expected me to be the one to utter the prayer, in a firm voice. I cannot remember a word of what I said. But I do remember that I knew as I spoke that I would never be able to tell my wife, whom I had never deceived before, what had happened to my beliefs in Yin Hsien. It would fell her. And I also remember that I thought: Poor Philip, how embarrassed he must be.

Mrs. Treadup, who has become, if anything, more religious than she was previously, kneels beside a desk chair, steadying herself with one hand on the lyre back of the chair; Mr. David Treadup, who has lost on the trailside *x* part of his faith, kneels facing one wall, leaning his forehead against the plaster, as if he would totter without that support, mouthing a prayer as falsely as a Pharisee; Mr. Philip Treadup doing what?—looking out the window, so as not to witness this mawkish travesty? Whereupon, rupturing the prayer, the room's door buzzer sounds, and without waiting for an answer, in bursts Mr. Paul Treadup, the youngest, the entrepreneur, who cannot be blamed for his surprise at seeing two elderly people scrambling to their feet. Paul, like his father, is huge. He is noisy and impatient. He wants to organize things: picking up the trunk at the dock, getting the folks out to Thornhill, where they belong.

PHILIP wrote his brother Absolom, in Maine, a letter about their father's return:

When I saw him there in the lobby, I couldn't believe my eyes. I guess I'd forgotten what a giant he is. He looked forty years old. His hair is still brown, and he has great big soldier mustaches. He embarrassed me by grabbing me. He almost broke my back. I tried to tell him how emaciated Mom had grown, but he cut me off, so we went up. It was heartbreaking, Abbo. The looks on their faces. You could tell he was trying not to look horrified, it certainly showed, and she was trying to look attractive. I thought, my God, he looks like one of her sons, like one of us. Believe it or not, those two got down on their knees and prayed. I think that was Father's idea. There were tears in his eyes. I didn't want to listen. Right in the middle of it, in barged Paul. He looked his part— in a brand new double-breasted pinstripe suit. He started pushing Mom and Dad around. I want you to know, Abbo, that Mom did very well in all this. Frail as she is, she had great dignity. In a way, Father was right in thanking God in his prayer for the survival of her beauty. It's an interior thing—right there inside the shell of her. As for him, I'm not ready to

judge. He seems to have been living an unreal life for so long that he is
not really one of us. He seemed right out of that book we had in Paoting,
was it called 'Heroes of Myths and Legends,' or something like that? By
Charles Lamb, was it?—in that Godwin's Juvenile Library that Father
kept for us in his study. He's bigger than life, but it's in a child's book. I
just hope this animal doesn't crush what's left of poor Mother.

D A V I D moved into the tiny apartment in the Hurd home—the second floor
of a wooden house built in the 1920s, having a bedroom, fortunately with a
double bed, a small sunny parlor, and a cramped kitchenette. The adjustment
must have been harder for Emily than for David; he was used to the stifling
quarters of Yin Hsien. In letters to his surviving sister, Grace, and to Absolom,
Treadup wrote that the Keystones, whose having settled in Thornhill was a
main reason for the choice of the village when Emily had returned to the
States, were both dead. To Grace:

Almost all the old Y friends I have been telling you about all these
years seem to have departed this mortal coil: J. B. Todd, Blackie
Blackton, Albert Wood, Frank Bulmer Wolf, Henny Henderson, Center
Rush Gridley—all gone. Roscoe Hersey is still alive, but very ill with
Parkinson's, I hear. They say Hank Burrell from Shanghai is in the New
York office. And I have heard that my dear Letitia Selden is still with
us, out in Ohio. To tell the truth, I feel lonely.

In a letter to Absolom:

Your mother has the radio on a lot of the time. I guess that when she
was alone, it—and her perky canary, Oswald, have you made Oswald's
acquaintance?—were her only company. I can't get used to being
bombarded by news. In the internment camp we heard nothing, and it
was our greatest blessing, I can tell you. Our concerns were with the
day-to-day needs of living with each other, things over which we our-
selves had control, for the most part. And we didn't have to go to bed
every night thinking about how many people were burned alive in a fire
raid on Yokohama, or how many died or lost their homes in a massive
B-17 attack on Stuttgart. I am shaken by the changes in values in
America since I was last here. I think perhaps all the killing all over the
world has loosened everyone's fastenings. Everything seems to be speeded
up. The greed on the home front is what shocks me. Grab grab grab. . . .

Again to Grace:

Confidentially, I am terribly worried about Emily. Her blood pressure is
extremely high—210 over 90 some of the time. She is taking medication

for it, but the pills seem to disagree with her. She hardly eats any-
thing. She seems listless—not the Emily I knew. Her only pleasure—
and she still rises to it every afternoon—is going to the library. I
gather she is wonderful with children, matching books exactly to
their young personalities. Except for an allowance from son Paul, her
minuscule salary is all we have to live on; she frets about groceries,
about my being hungry—I got used to that in camp! Ecarg, did I do
this to her, by sending her home? I need to find some work. I'm jumpy.
It is bad, my being underfoot for Em all the time in this little box
we live in.

APPARENTLY David never told Emily about his crisis of belief at Yin
Hsien. On the programs for Sunday services at the Thornhill Congregational Church, his name shows up, early in 1944, on the Music Committee.
Was he practicing on a cornet in that tiny parlor, in the afternoons, while
Emily was at the library? He was evidently going to church. Could he
deceive Emily for long? We can only guess at the price they both paid for
his deception.

COULD HE lecture to church groups about China? The Gyroscope and Its
Applications? What would he do for a shop, to build his apparatus? How
much would churches be able to pay? Twenty dollars a night?

One day a letter came from Hank Burrell, who cordially invited him to
come to New York, to visit the Y.M.C.A. International Committee headquarters
at 347 Madison Avenue. Hank wrote: "I have some good news for you."

The Hurds, downstairs, let David use their telephone. He called Burrell.
He accepted Hank's invitation, and they set a day in the following week for
the visit. Perhaps hoping for a clue to the good news, Treadup said he needed
advice about getting a job—"You know me, I need something to burn the old
excess calories." Burrell said he was sure they could figure out something. For
instance, some of the Association retirees were selling insurance. Hank was
very friendly.

Treadup went into the city. The diary did record this trip:

Was nervous and touchy. After all, the Y had dumped me. Riding up in
elevator was tempted to turn around and go down without getting off.
Alighted, however. What a surprise. All the new young men gathered
around. Hank made me sit in the board room and talk to them for an
hour. David Treadup—renowned veteran of the China field! Why, those
youngsters bowled me over with their veneration. Of course I didn't tell
them 'everything.' I think part of what created the atmosphere was

Hank's nostalgia for adventures of yore. Biggest kick yet to come, though. Hank took me back to his office and teased me for a long time, talking about opportunities, none of which appealed to me. Insurance. Encyclopaedias. Fuller brushes, seriously! Ringing doorbells—no sir, not for me. Then—bang!—he said the International Committee was mindful of my great contributions in China, the Lecture Bureau, literacy campaigns, all such, and that they had voted, two weeks before, in spite of my demobilization (or because of it? did they feel some twinges of remorse at last? did the Y have a heart after all? or did it just happen to have some cash?) to award me a pension. They were doing this for all surviving demobs. Two hundred a month for life. Bolt out of the blue! I wondered: Was I obliged to tell him I am no longer sure I believe in God? I decided to hold my tongue. This thing restored my faith at least in my fellow man. With this, Em's library stipend, and the "allowance" son Paul gives us, we two can manage, now.

SCRAPPY NOTES in his diary suggest that Treadup was finding it hard to accept the idea that he was in retirement. The calories were banked up in the big stove of his body. His strength was a liability. The diary: "Enthusiasm without an object—combustion engine without wheels." He patronized his wife's library and spent every morning with a book; in the afternoons he went for long but aimless walks. In a chance meeting with a local high-school teacher, he hit upon the idea of teaching a machine-shop class; the principal, when David took it to him, said it would not be possible to appoint Mr. Treadup as a teacher because he did not have the requisite professional credits. This rebuff appealed to Treadup's stubbornness. He called on members of the school board with a proposal for a machine shop, to be "taught" by an accredited teacher of something else, who might or might not know about mechanics, with David Treadup as a "custodian"—in plain English, a janitor—who might, while "cleaning up," give the students pointers. It took months to negotiate this ridiculous ruse. When the village taxpayers' association objected to the cost of the shop, Treadup scrounged all the necessary equipment, gratis, from a local garage, from a Chrysler dealer, and from a plumbing contractor. Beginning in September 1944, he began teaching twenty senior boys, three times a week, some rudiments of mechanical engineering. The diary: "Motorize the Village of Thornhill in This Generation!"

ABSOLOM would not leave Maine to come and visit his father, so Treadup decided, during the Easter break, 1945, to take a bus to Maine to see him. David later wrote Grace a letter about the trip:

He lives in an ancient farmhouse, full of dry rot and odors that seem to have been trapped indoors since the early nineteenth century. I guess he had tidied up some in my honor, but the mess! — I had to hold my tongue, not to shout at him as if he were an eight-year-old who hadn't made his bed. This young fellow with a Yale degree works a few weeks at a time — till he is fired, I guess, for not showing up — at odd jobs: sweeping out, clearing trash, delivering, helping out on lobster boats. The fenders of his old Pontiac are all bashed in. I did have to shout at him, to make myself heard. He loves his deafness. It seems that his only friend in this world is his deafness. I took him to Saco, to a medical-equipment place, and fitted him out with an up-to-date hearing aid which seemed to be just right for him, it was costly, and we took it home, but he showed up the next day without it — said it "spooked" him. He never touched a drop of spirits in my presence, but he was obviously on the edge of being tipsy all the time.

On the second day of the visit, Treadup took a long walk to try to decide what he should do. He had, the evening before, skirted close to the question of psychiatric help, but Absolom had flown into a rage. "*You*'re the one who needs a shrink! Look what you've done to Mom! Phil wrote me what you've done to Mom." Holding tight to his patience, then, Treadup suggested — "with what a qualm!" — that his son seek help from the local pastor. "Jesus Christ!" Absolom had shouted. "Just what I need. *You* to save my soul!" Then would he at least come to Thornhill to talk with his mother? Absolom did not hear that question. Bristling: "What was that?" Treadup spoke the question loudly. "What? What?" Then the same question a third time, very loudly. At that, Absolom, saying nothing, had got up and had left the room, slamming the door.

"As I walked on the country road, grinding bones in my mind about Absolom," Treadup wrote his sister,

I was suddenly overwhelmed by feeling. It was as if a thunderstorm had broken and I was being drenched by the quality of mercy. This had nothing to do with Abbo, directly anyway. What was soaking me, through and through, all of a sudden, was my love for Emily. It came on first as a rush of gratitude. Then I realized that all through the time in China when I was alone, after she had gone off on the 'Mariposa,' she had steadied me, even from a distance — insofar as I was steady at all — the corrective balance in her — no wonder the gyro has been my most beloved talisman all these years. My diary, all that time, was nothing but a letter to her. This downpour of feeling was important to me, because it was clean like the rain it resembled. When we are together in that little apartment in Thornhill, I am distracted by her frailty, it gets in the way

of distinct memory. Grace, if I have been of any use in this world, if I
have helped poor China in the smallest degree — if I can turn things
around and give Abbo any courage — it will have been thanks in large
degree to what Em has taught me about love.

Things had not been turned around by the time Treadup left Maine.
Absolom would not give an answer, yes or no, about visiting his mother.

E D W A R D   R.   M U R R O W ' S voice on the radio was confident. The taut spiral
was winding down. The Allies had broken the huge German counterattack in
the Ardennes, the last desperate convulsion of the Wehrmacht. The Russians
had captured ruined Warsaw and were moving on Berlin from east and south.
Douglas MacArthur had bravely waded ashore to face the cameras on Leyte;
the Marines' flag was aloft at Iwo Jima. Notes in the diary record the steady
turn of Treadup's mind toward a return to China. How Emily's fragility
figured in this swerve of mind we can only guess. "Thinking about villages."
"Have written Burrell." "Wonder about possibilities of government service —
my age a concern?" "Was thinking today about those boxes fastened with
straps in the servants' quarters of Mrs. Evenrude's house. When she is freed,
will they still be there?" "Where is Johnny Wu? Believe he went to Chungking
or environs." "Making vocabulary cards — need to juice up my memory of the
language."

T R A V E L I N G again by bus, Treadup went in April on a westward loop to
visit two women. He made brief notes of the trip in his diary.
     In Salt Branch he found sister Grace

shrunken — almost a hunchback. Arthritis of the spine. Has come
through her suffering to something like cheerfulness. Chewed over
old times. Town rather nice — has managed to remain a backwater,
majestic maples. Shock for me: Walked to pond, found site of old
icehouse, and beside it on the bank of the pond came on rotted-out
skeleton of someone's old rowboat. Knew it couldn't possibly be 'Ecarg,'
but was suddenly overcome by memories of days of innocence. Boy
again. The sound of the ripples against the wood at the cutwater —
bliss! Then, walking back, felt stiff joints, felt sadness of downward
slope. The unfairness: this whole visit permeated by this unfairness.
Dearest brother Paul gone, no chance to say good-bye. That dry-rotted
shape reached into me for something young. I want to make good use of
the time I have left.

Letitia Selden was living in Monrovia, Ohio, to be near the state hospital for the insane where Helen Demestrie was a patient. She insisted that her David sleep on the sofa in her two-room apartment. Already in her mid-eighties, Miss Titty had a vigorous, broad-hipped stride and a full voice to express clear thoughts. She had no car, she walked every morning to an A & P and carried her bundles home, and walked to the hospital every afternoon. She was, it seemed, indomitable. But to Treadup's dismay, she was deeply negative about China and the Chinese. She said he would be a fool to go back. "Believe she cannot forgive China for what she thinks it did, as if on purpose, to poor Helen." She did not suggest that Treadup visit Helen—"I didn't know whether I should ask." Slowly David began to see that Miss Titty was negative about everything, that she was suspicious of everyone, that she nursed a lurking anger at the whole world. She began to criticize David for little things he had done, or not done, many years ago in Paoting.

It's as if her personality had turned over inside her while she was sleeping one night, and when she waked up the sweet and giving woman of the past had vanished, and a rather nasty scold had taken her place.

Treadup, who had hoped to be warmed by Miss Titty's familiar old-aunty touch, and to talk about possibilities for a return to China, went home, instead, chilled and—"Cassandra got to one part of me, for she was so clear and incisive in her pessimism"—even doubtful about the wisdom of trying to return, doubtful about the possibility of going back to anything like the best of the past: "folly of trying to recapture the joy of rowing my wherry under the summer sun."

But something alive and stubborn was working in him, and before he arrived back in Thornhill, he was already making new notes: "Best chance, Free China?" "Must investigate Quakers."

THE BLOW was delivered with the assistance of the merciless postal service. Apparently no one on the Thornhill Free Library Board had the fiber or the pity to deliver the message face to face.

Treadup saw Emily tear open the envelope. She spread the letter out with the flat of her hand. She pushed her spectacles up on the ridge of her nose. She began to read.

Then David saw the paper begin to shake. He took it from her. *We are grateful for your long and faithful service to the Thornhill Free Library . . . a younger candidate . . . as of June 1, 1945 . . .*

David tried to find something comforting to say. Emily shook her head. Her mouth moved, as if she were chewing. No sound emerged. Her eyes strove to give messages, she was learning that she was mute. She never spoke another word.

OF EMILY'S swift, speechless decline and death we know nearly nothing. It is as if her silence silenced David; after all his years of faithful recording, it seemed he now could not face blank pages. The coroner's certificate gives pneumonia as the cause of death; that was presumably a secondary, if final, cause. The funeral was held at the Thornhill Congregational Church on August 29, 1945; Pastor Nemoh Mendell presided. In the entire time after the arrival of the letter from the library, there are but three entries in the diary. The first:

> *July 14. Absolom finally came down to see his mother. Too late. Her inability to speak not therapeutic for a deaf person. He blames me. He left angry today.*

The second condenses into a pair of lines his weeks of pain:

> *Aug. 23. Held her hand all day. Her fingers so icy. She says a great deal with her eyes.*

The third entry might be thought callous—he has realized that he may before long be free to go to China by himself; it may also be read, perhaps, as a desperate reach for some hold on "the best of the past," in which Emily, of course, had had an enormous share. The entry was terse.

> *Wrote the Quakers today. They may not be interested in a godless man.*

A LIFE WORTH LIVING

HE DESCENDS the gangway from the S.S. *Cameron Merchant*, carrying two suitcases as lightly as if they were empty.

This is—or is it?—the very same Shanghai wharf onto which he first set foot four decades ago: the landing stage, back then, of puzzled letdown and disappointment. Was *this* China? These wharves have been the scene of all the returns—from the European trip to gather equipment for his lecture program in 1910, from France in 1919, from his difficult furlough in 1930; a setting, each time, of the strong emotions of a renewed impulse, a sense that the clock has been wound up again.

How much more intense than ever his feelings this time! A regenerative force—echoing, perhaps, in memory of Emily, the years of her stabilizing

influence on him—must have been at work in him in recent months to restore
his enthusiasm, for it gives a remarkably youthful look to a face we see in one
of a set of photographs of notable arrivals taken by the Shanghai *Evening
Post*. It bears hard marks of the past: crow's-feet around the eyes, frown
channels between the eyebrows, parallel writings across the forehead, the
weathered, leathery wrinkles of a gold miner or offshore fisherman, incised
and enhanced in his case, however, not only by sun and wind but also by
indoor storms: of thought, pain, laughter, remorse, doubt, mourning, stubborn optimism.

The optimism, he will write later in his "Addendum," is a little out of
hand. The diary:

> *This time I have half a billion U.S. dollars behind me! When I think of
> my first budget proposal for the Lecture Bureau—I was going to change
> China—$275,000—and Todd thought it outrageous.*

THERE IS scant record of what happened to David Treadup right after
Emily's death. The oldest son, Philip, seems to have been, as always, almost
painfully considerate and self-sacrificing; it was he, apparently, who made
funeral arrangements, and who kept after his father to make sure that he was
eating well and exercising. (David wrote: "The boy is too solicitous. There is
something sheepish about him. Was I like that at his age?") Philip brought the
grandchildren to visit often, to cheer up their granddad. Emily had been
cremated and buried in the Thornhill cemetery; Philip planted a dogwood at
the head of the grave.

Paul had put up money for the funeral and for his father's comfort, and
then had kept a distance.

Absolom had had the greatest benefit, of the three sons, of what so often
happens to a man when his mother dies—he became more like her. He wrote
his father a touching letter of apology for "my inability to understand you,"
and he seems to have made, for some months at least, a real effort to pull
himself together.

IN THE ENTRIES Treadup made in his diary during this period, we
find repeated hints that in direct ratio as he mastered the very first stages
of his grief at losing Emily, there was quickly confirmed in him a passionate
desire to go back to China, to find the meaning, beyond what he had been
able so far to puzzle out in "Search," of all his years of his mission, at Emily's
side, in the China field. One bald entry: "Was our life together in China
worth living?"

Even before Emily's decline, he had begun shopping around for a way to
go back. The Quakers, while they had with characteristic charity given David

Treadup the benefit of doubt of his doubt, had not had anything to offer in the China field that would have made good use of him. The consular service had no slot for a man of his age.

Then suddenly—less than a month after Emily died—something came along that bowled him over with "its potential for good." Hank Burrell wrote that the United Nations Relief and Rehabilitation Administration, which had been established two years before, was desperately hunting for qualified staff for its enormous undertaking in China. Notice is taken in his diary, then, of numerous trips to United Nations headquarters in New York, but he writes little of what happened there. In the end, the UNRRA officials, whose recruitments of staff for China had been dredging up from various countries a polyglot catch of able and not so able people, were apparently so glad to find someone who spoke fluent Chinese and had had years of experience precisely with Chinese people of the sort who would need relief and rehabilitation, that they could easily overlook his advanced age. A physical examination proved him a marvel of preservation. They hired him.

They hired him, to his amazement, at a high level of staff responsibility, designating him, on the somewhat flimsy basis, evidently, of his years of lecturing to the Chinese about technical matters, as manager for the Shanghai headquarters of rehabilitation in the area of transportation. He was later to realize, with some chagrin, when he was transferred out of this post, that his being entrusted with such a station was evidence not of the richness of his gifts but of the poverty of UNRRA's staffing. The transportation program was ambitious. It called for provision to China of substantial numbers of landing craft, tugs, barges, lighters, cranes, dredges, repair shops, aids to navigation; locomotives, freight cars, rails, ties, bridge materials; earth-moving machinery, road-building equipment, and trucks.

The overall program for China dizzied Treadup with the grandeur of its magnanimity. He writes to impress his sister Grace: "This is a global generosity that makes the whole missionary enterprise from 1807 on look like a poor little Sunday school picnic by comparison." He wrote her that the UNRRA undertaking for China was to be the largest devoted to any country in the world, and was in fact to be "the largest program of free aid to any land in the history of the world." The agency had budgeted U.S.$562,500,000 for supplies alone for China. This was the half billion "behind" the exuberant Treadup.

So it was that as he disembarked in Shanghai, in November 1945, from one of the first three vessels to carry UNRRA supplies to China, he was in need of the kind of balance Emily used to give him. "Think of it!" he writes his sister.

A man who has just been teaching a dozen high-school students how to thread pipe and connect up light switches is now to take a hand at spiffing up an entire nation.

HE WAS skirting a delusion of grandeur. The quarters to which he was assigned — an apartment all to himself, complete with paid manservant, in the modern, skyscraping Broadway Mansions, looking across Soochow Creek down over the magnificence of old Shanghai's Bund and Settlement — fed the delusion. Perhaps he saw some glimmer of the danger of his euphoria, for the first thing he did, after he had dropped his bags off at his apartment, was to humble himself. He went on foot to the old Christian burying ground and stood for a long time looking at the tiny headstone on which was carved:

NANCY KEAN TREADUP
1911–1912

"Poor little innocent," he wrote in his diary that night.

If we had life to do over again, if we could rewind the reel and start the camera running again, would the pictures come out just the same, would we make the same mistakes?

While he was at the cemetery, he looked for, but could not find, A Ch'u's grave; this frustration left him feeling confused. He thought he had lost his way walking back through the Settlement, until he suddenly found himself standing stock-still in front of the building at 29 Quinsan Gardens, where he had founded the Lecture Bureau and built its shop. Then by choice he walked past the Yates Road house, and then past the cramped little house near the Racecourse where the family had lived after the break in France.

The diary:

Emily. No, it does no good to set your name down on paper. I left you when Nancy was sick. I still feel it. The rest of my life will be an apology to you. I have so much to thank you for. I miss you. I need you. I make you a promise: I will try every day to listen to your voice, your consoling, corrective, wise, loving voice.

THE BOSS is Belgian. In time the staff will call him the Gourd, for he is narrow at the shoulders and huge at the belt. He sits glaring at Treadup through glasses with peculiar blue rims. His voice is deep with the authority of a dispenser of budgets; he speaks English with an accent that is Oxford-by-way-of-Ghent.

At this their first meeting, at nine o'clock the morning after his arrival, David Treadup is enormously excited. He cannot wait to put his share of half a billion dollars to work. The atmosphere of the office is expansive — the Y.M.C.A. was never as grand as this. The suite, on a low floor of the Broadway

Mansions, is furnished in a style appropriate for philanthropic chats with Chinese officials: Upon a figured Tientsin carpet are arranged heavy rectangular overstuffed chairs, covered with gray muslin, and dispersed among these chairs are low tables, with glowingly varnished sandalwood tops, holding teapots and cups and ashtrays.

The Gourd is fitted snugly into one of the chairs, and he quickly brings Treadup down from his dreamy mare's tails in the sky. David soon sees, in fact, that "Monsieur Barrat has the great advantage, as a bureaucrat, of being able to detect at once the worst feature of every outcome."

There are, already, very bad features. The S.S. *Cameron Merchant*, "as Treadup well knows," says Barrat, is tied up at a Yangtsepoo wharf; two other ships are anchored in the roadstead, waiting for dock space. All three ships are loaded with goods for the relief of debilitated China. But CNRRA—the Chinese National Relief and Rehabilitation Administration, which has been set up with offices in Shanghai to manage the distribution and utilization of UNRRA materials, and to guard jealously the sovereignty of a divided China— CNRRA has made absolutely no plans for the handling of the cargoes of these three vessels.

As M. Barrat's briefing spreads its net of gloom, Treadup begins to feel the ache in his chest that he associates with the loss of Emily. M. Barrat, with his fierce little eyeballs pasted on the other side of the blue-rimmed circlets of glass, speaks of China's miseries: floods, epidemics, famines; then war. People driven from their homes. Transportation disrupted—"your basket, Mister Sreadup" (The Director seems to believe the name is Threadup). In Free China, paralysis. Inflation. Corruption.

The bureaucrat's voice has gone deeper and deeper, in its melancholy plunge, until it seems to come from the floor of the sea. He is not done with the bad. The end of hostilities brought chaos. China and UNRRA were faced with the staggering task of providing assistance to a population and area greater than those of all liberated Europe.

Enough! Enough! . . . But no, not enough.

One of the ships on the roadstead, the *Liberty Manassas,* has matériel for transportation. Look at the manifest. They have sent thirty tons of rails. Railroad ties are not scheduled in the next four ships. They will not come for at least three months. This is Threadup's basket. The *Liberty Manassas* will dock when the *Cameron Merchant* clears; who knows when that will be?

A N D   S O he went to work. He must find godowns for storage of road-building machinery. The rails would have to be left in the open; they would have to be carried to their resting place, if and when he found one, by teams of coolies, length by length, for there were no other means of transporting them. He must find out from CNRRA where the most urgent railroad repairs were to be, and plan for eventual shipping of the rails—after the ties had come, of course.

He had six young assistants, two of them Chinese. Everyone was confused. There was a constant rush of activity, yet nothing ever seemed to get done.

His CNRRA counterpart, a man named Hsing, was infuriated that Treadup had "interfered" in the matter of godowns and storage space for the rails. No matter that CNRRA had made no arrangements; everything beyond the landing derrick was a Chinese prerogative.

David became muddled. It was hard to get up in the morning. He was stabbed, over and over, especially when Hsing attacked him, by the "lost-love" feeling. He began to attribute his inefficiency to his state of mourning.

I have feelings like those when I thought I was infatuated with Miss Tenant in sophomore year at Syracuse. She would promise to join me for a Glee Club concert, or Mandolin Club, or some such, and then — without notice — not appear. Now my 'real' love, Emily, is doing this to me. It is most distracting.

HE STRUGGLED for equilibrium. "Wish I had my singles scull. Rowing would help. If I could get the ache out of my legs, I would be able to think better." He bought a bicycle and rode for miles every morning before breakfast. "Thought of Phinny today. Wish I had time to read." "I need Chinese friends. All I get is Hsing's vituperation." He began a hunt, and finally he traced John Y. Hu, the last head of the Lecture Bureau. Hu, now a vice-mayor of the city, was delighted to hear from him and invited him to his home.

At first I thought, "I have found heaven at last." Hu's wife, who went to Wellesley, is a gentle, delicate woman of, I would say, fifty-five; she made me feel like a long-lost uncle. Her praise of Emily dissolved me. She fed me a banquet of ten dishes, each of which carried in its distinctive flavor a code of reminders — of past feasts, of friendships of other years, of great hopes and shared dreams and wild ambitions for China. But gradually, it seemed to me, the atmosphere chilled. John Hu never liked me. He was in the awkward position of being my successor as the Bureau chief, and I am sure he resented my constant "foreign" pressure to get standards back up to snuff. For my part, I always thought there was some flaw in him: mental laziness, coupled with a devastating vanity which presented the laziness to the world as a virtue, as some kind of philosophical repose. Thus his laziness became a rebuke to my Western "push." I wound up this evening with a very faint bad smell in my nostrils:

Hu appears now to be much richer than he was when he worked for the Y. Wonder how he got that way, during the years of China's pain.

BY JULY, Shanghai was clogged. Docks were crowded with huge earth-movers, road-graders, road-finishers—"vast heaps of rusting steel"—"'Sreadup's basket'"—because China lacked trained operators to run them, the fuel to drive them was too costly, and no one thought roads could be built in China with these great machines as cheaply and well as they could by old-fashioned coolie labor: hordes of the poor crushing rock with hammers, toting baskets, tamping down the dirt, raking out the asphalt by hand. White flour lay in warehouses for months until it could be sold to the rich, who were used to it, so the proceeds could be used to buy rice and millet suitable for the starving poor. With some items, such as raw cotton, it cost five times as much as the cotton was worth to ship it to mills for processing. In any case, CNRRA was broke—the government was spending most of its hopelessly inflated money fighting Communists—and could not pay for lighters, tugs, cranes, and trucks to unload ships. Warehouse owners refused to take cargoes because their past storage bills were unpaid. Stevedores declined contracts until their arrearages on invoices were settled.

The Gourd was in an ecstasy of bureaucratic pessimism. He called a meeting of his senior staff, which whipped off a message, signed by every senior officer, to UNRRA headquarters in New York, demanding an embargo of Shanghai, a complete shutdown of shipments, until the Chinese authorities cleared its glut.

The meeting then turned to a discussion of staff matters. UNRRA's Shanghai staff was now enormous—1,400 people—and the Broadway Mansions hummed with dissatisfactions, envies, power plays, back stabbings. At the end of the meeting, M. Barrat, who apparently lacked the courage to demote people face to face, read off a long "memorandum of reorganization," through which David Treadup learned, among many other things, that he had been relieved of his Transportation job—evidently Shanghai's choking up was somehow his fault—and had been transferred to Food, at a level two notches lower.

All I can say is, Huzzah! Was not cut out to do the impossible. Now stuck with the improbable—a challenge, at least. And food: better. I never felt a real calling to a mission in earth-movers.

BUT it is not better.

We see him now climbing the stone steps from the river to the city of Changsha. The Food people in Shanghai have been delighted to have

Treadup aboard—a Chinese-speaking person who has actually had experience of famine-relief work in China—and they send him at once to survey the UNRRA–CNRRA operation in the famine district of Hunan Province.

It is August. The river is low. There are many steps to ascend to reach the throbbing life of the city. Bicycling in Shanghai has strengthened Treadup's legs, and he takes the rises like a youth. Changsha has always excited him. He remembers his sense of the vitality of the Hunanese when he arrived for his first lecture here. He recalls his howls of agonized exhilaration, scattering the servants like frightened chicks, as he let himself down into a cold bath at his Yale-in-China digs each morning of the first literacy campaign, which was opening up such a delirious sense of possibility. Even the memory of the bombing here—"the first time I died"—has become, from such a distance, thrilling.

But this time, as he makes his way through the crowded streets, he senses that the Hunanese vigor has been sapped. Faces are drawn. Beggars abound. The pace of street movement drags. . . .

HIS INVESTIGATION drags. Within a week he has concluded that the UNRRA staff people are well meaning but incompetent. Only two out of seventeen assigned to the province can speak Chinese. All are exhausted, more by frustration than by hard work. The Chinese authorities seem to regard them as hostile intruders. The seat of the trouble, it seems, is the Ministry of Food.

It takes Treadup three days to make an exploratory appointment with a middle-level personage at the Ministry of Food. Cordial reception. Good manners. Charming jokes. UNRRA much appreciated. Not a single nugget of hard information.

It takes Treadup a month, poking around the markets and warehouses, bribing informants, badgering the Ministry, calling on people who worked, years ago, on the literacy campaign, and generally making such a nuisance of himself that he is questioned three times by agents of the Generalissimo's blue-shirts, to find out the staggering truth of the matter:

What was more natural than that UNRRA, which has budgeted U.S. $133,488,000 to provide food to hungry China, should have turned, through CNRRA, to the Chinese government's Ministry of Food for assistance in distributing its beneficence? But what Treadup learns is that the name "Ministry of Food" is misleading, for the agency has one task only: the procurement of food for the Nationalist armies. And what is happening is that right in the famine area of Hunan the Ministry of Food is buying up local grain supplies, scarce as they are, with printed money, and taking them off for the well-fed army, while UNRRA food is being openly sold on the market—to provide revenue for the Ministry of Food to buy local food. There has been a delicate issue about what prices should be charged for the UNRRA grain and rice: If they are sold at the market price—high, now, because of the famine— they cannot be bought by those whom UNRRA regards as "appropriate consumers," the poor and the hungry; if they are sold far below the market price, the temptation for speculators to buy them and then resell them at the market price becomes irresistible. Tens of thousands die of starvation. Besides all this, grain is stolen from warehouses and put on sale; officials bribe each other for shares of illicit profits; a cartel of merchants has a channel into the Ministry of Food; inflation has put the UNRRA food at any price far out of the reach of the hungry.

Treadup returns to Shanghai in a rage. The famine scar burns. His handwriting in the diary is spidery. He rants at the Gourd. Word gets back to him that he is showing Bad Form. He persists.

"My anger," he wrote later in "Addendum,"

ran very deep in me, because this experience made me wonder about all the years of patient work I thought I had done in the China field: my lectures, the literacy drives, my trying to understand what it means to be Chinese and poor in my villages. What good had any of it done? What was left of it all? Greed. Corruption. Thievery. Cruelty to the starving poor. I felt that Monsieur Barrat was telling me—as he kept saying, "Don't be so excitable, Sreadup, these are very old things, the world still turns on its axis, the sun comes up every morning"—really telling me that I had misdirected my whole life. That I had wasted all my years. That Emily had wasted all her years. This is enough to make a person very angry.

THE HOT ENERGY generated by anger burns the linings out of a man's brakes. Treadup's bulk, hurtling along from hour to hour with such intensity of rancorous enthusiasm, was impressive, even to his superiors. He got permission to go to Nanking, which after the defeat of the Japanese had become the capital, to try to smoke out the CNRRA people there.

Treadup learned that Appleton Sills, the former Y secretary with whom David had muddled through the dangerous 1927 crisis in Nanking, was back in the capital, working as a civilian with the American truce teams set up after General Marshall's mediation between Chiang Kai-shek and the Communists. He gave Treadup a bed and an ear into which to pour fury. "Sills is philosophical," Treadup wrote. "Chinese civilization, he says, is three thousand years old. One mustn't try to change it in ten days' time."

It took Treadup ten days to find out that CNRRA was helpless. It simply did not have the money to distribute UNRRA supplies.

Why not? By alternately roaring and cooing Treadup finally arranged an

interview with an assistant to Madame Chiang's brother-in-law, H. H. Kung—
the once-upon-a-time Y.M.C.A. secretary who was now Minister of Finance
and incidentally one of the richest men in China. The assistant told Mr.
Treadup not to worry. "We have mobilized our resources!" The government
had recently budgeted 432 billion Chinese dollars for relief and rehabilitation, he said; this (printed) money would soon make itself felt all up and
down the line.

Back at CNRRA some days later, Treadup found out that not one cent of
this large sum had been allocated to CNRRA. The government's "relief and
rehabilitation fund" had been appropriated by the Executive Yuan to various
established Ministries for urgently needed repair and maintenance projects,
which were designed to improve their respective capacities to produce revenue
for the war against the Communists.

Back in Shanghai, Treadup wrote a terse report to his superiors in Food,
with a copy to M. Barrat:

> *Government service to CNRRA is all of the lip. The whole idea of
> national relief of the distress of the individual victims of war is utterly
> foreign to those in power. The Executive Yuan, the Ministry of Finance,
> the Central Bank of China—none of them has given the slightest evi-
> dence that they care a fig for their populace as individuals. When the
> Central Bank lends money to CNRRA, it holds large amounts of food in
> warehouses as collateral for the loans—the point of which was suppos-
> edly to distribute the food! The only aim of this government is to
> maintain itself in power.*

Barrat summoned Treadup. He sat in one of the overstuffed chairs in the
conference room, rattling Treadup's memo in his hand.

"My dear Sreadup," he said. "One doesn't put hotheaded and intemperate opinions like these down on paper. Don't you realize that some Chinese
secretarial person down the line—you know, one of our smiling friends?—
right here in our office—one of these loyal and hardworking people—is
certain to feed this document back to Nanking? Oh, they will love it, Sreadup!
It just goes to prove what those interfering foreigners are like."

Now the anger curled back on the angry man himself. Treadup's response
to Barrat's rebuke: docility. In "Addendum":

> *Had I learned nothing in all these years? I was just as meek as I was
> when Chancellor Day dressed me down for my pranks at Syracuse—just
> as skulking as I was about the letter I wrote to the 'North China Daily
> News' on the Y's role in the boycott. What is this terrible need I have for
> obedience—need to do "the right thing"? Why can't I shed myself of it?
> I used to think I was obeying God's will. I no longer have that dodge—
> of Christian acceptance—Christian meekness—the other cheek. I no*

longer have the help — the rationalization — of prayer. I talk with Emily, a kind of prayer, I try to listen to Emily's voice, but — well, it fades, it fades, we are on a long-distance line. I tell myself that I have taken on too much for one man in this life. It is not China I have wanted to change "in ten days," but human nature. Maybe Barrat is right. Old traits are constant; the axle grinds along; the sun will come up as usual tomorrow morning. But — damnable certainty — no matter what the sunrise looks like, I will start another day unsatisfied, incomplete, unfulfilled, because if I cannot help being obedient to "the authorities," neither can I help being obedient to my mulish and unchanging and hopeful self.

All through the following months, David worked hard at whatever was assigned to him, and hated both the work and this stubborn self of his.

BY THE SUMMER of 1947, as all hopes of peace between Chiang and the Communists dwindled away, it was clear that UNRRA had about run its course of usefulness, such as it had had. On paper, the agency could make some claims. It had "shipped" two hundred thousand tons of grain and rice inland; had repatriated twenty-thousand-odd Overseas Chinese to homes in Malaya, Indo-China, Burma, and elsewhere in southeast Asia, and repatriated eighteen hundred European refugees, mostly Jews, who had been stranded in China; had provided relief during epidemics of cholera, smallpox, and plague; had helped close a great gap in the Yellow River's banks and restored China's Sorrow to its prewar channel; had helped rebuild roads and railroads; and had provided seed, tools, fertilizer, pesticides, livestock, and expertise to agricultural areas in so-called Free China. Treadup knew the underside of these accomplishments — knew what had happened to the "shipped" food; knew that as fast as roads and railways were repaired, the Communists disrupted them again; knew the costs in inflation and corruption. Billions of Chinese dollars had been budgeted in 1946; the next year, trillions. The government's nerves were raw. On a visit to Shanghai, Appleton Sills told David that in July the Generalissimo and Madame Chiang had received a group of Chinese Christians, representatives of the National Christian Council, at their house in Nanking, and Madame Chiang had insisted that the government's first duty was to fight the Communists ("Jesus Christ did not appease Satan," she said), and the G-mo had "scolded them like schoolboys and dismissed them." UNRRA was in serious conflict with Nanking over the United Nations' right and duty to provide relief and rehabilitation to Communist areas; more and more, it appeared that UNRRA was being used to support one side against the other.

The diary: "People are saying we'll last until about November. Will I never have a chance to see my villages again?"

HERO

THERE IS a first time for many things. Treadup has gone to a cocktail party.

It is taking place in the Astor Hotel, on the Bund, in the very same high-ceilinged main salon in which Treadup had his decisive conversation with the old veteran Joshua Bagnall more than four decades earlier ("You know that water runs downhill, don't you?"), under the very same wooden-bladed fans winding the years on their slow-moving spools. What seem to be the very same Chinese "boys" in black trousers and starched white coats shuffle in black cloth shoes from group to group, carrying, this time, trays of glasses that contain iced enchantments—amber, white, plum-colored, sparkling. From one of these trays David Treadup casually takes something, he has no idea what, in his big fist.

The party is for Senator Franklin P. Royster of Georgia, who has come to China on an "informational tour, so I'll know how to vote when these clever Chinee fellas start passing the hat for cash money round Washington, D.C." Someone has tinkled on a glass with a spoon, and he has just said this. His eyes do a buck-and-wing. He did not mean that about begging. He is being playful. He is feeling generous toward China. At the moment of his speaking, China is falling apart. A frightful civil war is exacting the most efficient kind of population control—that of the slaughter of large numbers. In the cities of so-called Free China, people have to carry suitcases full of inflated cash to buy the simplest goods. UNRRA is panting exhausted toward the finish line. The American effort to mediate between Chiang and the Communists, with all its paraphernalia of truce-team jeeps and high-level parleys, has long since proved a dismal failure. In the face of this history the senator beams like a seraph leaning against the heavenly throne and speaks of "a shining future for this great country. I have been amazed by the energy of this city. With God's help we will lift Shanghai up and up until it's just like Atlanta, Georgia."

The little hot wind of the speech dies down. The guests mingle. Treadup, sipping at he knows not what, is himself borne along, to his surprise, on the high energy of Shanghai. He finds himself talking with a young man. This person has an outdoorsman's skin and a heavy look of sincerity. He is the only person at the reception who is wearing a Chinese padded cotton jacket. He is intelligent. How did this begin? He is asking Treadup questions about "his" villages near Paoting.

How did he know about them?

An incomplete answer: He is, he says, the son of a missionary; the name is McIntosh. Treadup would not have known the family; they were stationed in Chengtu, far inland. The young man seems to need to say at once that he is agnostic—"too much church when I was a boy."

What does he do?

Works for C.I.C.

How is that again?

Indusco, he says. Gung Ho. Chinese Industrial Cooperatives. He is only in Shanghai for a few days, to pick up some "gear." He wonders whether Mr. Treadup could wangle a mimeograph machine out of UNRRA for him.

Treadup promises, without a moment's hesitation, to do so, then suffers a sudden swoop of suspicion. Is this why McIntosh introduced himself?

No, the young man says. He wants to hear every detail of the literacy campaigns. "I know all about you," he says.

MCINTOSH called Treadup the next morning and asked him to have lunch. The Chinese restaurant was cheap and noisy. McIntosh shouted his admiration for the older man, and Treadup began to feel a lift of artificial vitality, something like that with which the beverage at the reception for Senator Royster had surprised him last evening. McIntosh said that Treadup's rural work in the district near Paoting could be called famous among the younger workers for C.I.C. "You're a hero, you know," McIntosh said. Because here, for once, was a foreigner who had "gone down to the people" and at least tried to experience what it was like to be one of them. "This is what we try to do in Indusco—you showed us the way."

Treadup searched the young man's eyes for any little shifts of dis-ingenuousness. It had been so long since anyone had praised him that he felt rushes of both gratitude and caution. What did the boy want?

COLIN MCINTOSH was strong, in the sense that he was enthusiastic and energetic. He was chunky, muscular. "We went for a walk, he walks like a two-cylinder engine with a heavy flywheel." During the walk he gave Treadup a brief sketch of his life, the main feature of which seemed to be his "finding" himself. He had been sent to the States at fifteen to go to a private school; he had then attended Antioch College, where, in accordance with the policy of the place, he had gone through alternating terms of study and what he called "life-situation work periods"—he had learned the plastering trade in Cleveland, worked in apple orchards in Oregon, crewed on a fishing dragger out of

Nantucket. When he had become eligible for military draft, he had become a conscientious objector, lying to the various draft authorities about religious convictions he no longer held. "I was and am against killing, that's *basic,* so I wasn't really being dishonest." He did alternative service as a firewatcher in Maine. After the war he heard about the industrial cooperatives in China and "came out here because I thought I could contribute." Was he trying, in his way, to carry his father's work forward? "I never knew my father," he said. "He was always off somewhere. Mother was forever holding him up to me as the perfect servant of God, but the little I saw of him, he seemed an everyday sort of person—mediocre."

Noting these things, Treadup wrote:

> *I'm a bit leery of his fastening himself on me. Still, there's something about him—something naive and eager—that makes me think back to my own early ignorant days in Tientsin.*

McIntosh didn't seem to want anything except the mimeograph machine. Treadup had forgotten that easy promise, but he kept it. There was so much mismanagement in the UNRRA offices that he was able, with a little twinge in his diary of wondering whether this was one more example of "my badness," simply to fill out a slip in triplicate, and lo!—a brand-new machine was boxed and delivered to the Chinese Industrial Cooperatives, in care of Colin McIntosh, Esq., 27 Carpenter Road, Local.

THE HERO WORSHIP did not abate with the delivery of that box. McIntosh really did seem to think that David Treadup was a great man. The admiration modulated into solicitation and became, at a certain point, hard-edged. The diary:

> *He begs me—he says he hasn't the authority to invite me, so he begs me—to come to work for the industrial cooperatives. No money. No security. Mere subsistence, and frugal at that. But the C.I.C. would be, he says, my "natural habitat," among the Chinese poor helping them to help themselves. With an accuracy which startles me, he says I am unfit for the UNRRA post, he says my being with UNRRA is "bizarre," he calls it a "deviation" in my life, he says I am a teacher (he even knew about the science lectures, he had somehow heard about the day I preached to General Feng's soldiers), he says I would be "purged of this Broadway Mansions poison" and would be living "on the Chinese level."*

THEN suddenly young McIntosh stopped calling. Treadup notes this in his diary, and there are hints that the sudden silence has put him slightly off balance. He sends a Chinese messenger boy from UNRRA with a note to McIntosh at 27 Carpenter Road; the messenger reports that the addressee has left town.

> *Frustrating. I had just begun to take half seriously the idea of going with C.I.C. This boy had made it sound my sort of thing. I do so long to be back in touch with "real" Chinese people. Can't remember whether McIntosh said it first or I said it first, but anyway the thought emerged that eventually I could take the co-ops right to "my" villages. Now I don't know how to reach these people. Can't simply go to Kiangsi Province and expect to find them.*

TEN DAYS passed. A note came to his office: "Lunch Tong Sung Restaurant, 12 o'c? CM."

Treadup went. McIntosh was looking very pleased with himself. Without even greeting Treadup, he said, "Look, I have a letter for you from Rewi."

Treadup read it. It was an invitation from Rewi Alley, the New Zealander who had founded the C.I.C., to go into Kiangsi and join the movement. It spoke of "everyone's knowledge of the work you did in the countryside in Hopei Province," and of "my own belief that you would give our younger workers valuable insights in how best to inspire, and be inspired by, their Chinese colleagues."

McIntosh said the reason he had left town so abruptly was because he had

> *realized the only way to get me to take this thing seriously was to "make it official." He had undertaken two five-day journeys in order to "recruit" me. Flattering.*

David Treadup was recruitable. It took him two weeks to disconnect himself from UNRRA.

THEY WENT together to Kanchow, in Kiangsi. Of what happened in the next three months, Treadup left almost no record. His diary dwindled to intermittent short notes—exclamations and blunt comments. The life was hard, but he evidently thrived. He slept on an earthen *k'ang* in a small house in Kanchow, sharing quarters with Chinese co-op staff people, McIntosh among them. He wore Western clothes. His diet was, as one note made clear, "basic." He became reacquainted with rats, bugs, and fleas. He was occasionally in danger. But he was "back in real China." "In my element." "After UNRRA frustrations, this is *it*." "Learning—preparing." "Fired up every day and walloped by nightfall."

One of the things he soon learned was that Colin McIntosh had led him into a mare's nest of difficulties. The co-ops had from the beginning had a somewhat orphaned status with the Nationalist government, and in the last three or four years the KMT had made life particularly hard for them. Rewi Alley, the founder and driving force of the movement, had by now given up on the Nanking government and was in the process of shifting his own fiery energies to the far northwest, to a region near, but not yet in, the expanding Communist enclave. The cooperative movement in the KMT areas was dying out, save for a few islands, like this in Kiangsi, where it had sputtered along under dedicated local leadership. It was in this part of southern Kiangsi that the Communists had established their earliest rural soviets, before Chiang's punitive campaigns had driven them off on the Long March, and the people in the countryside had become accustomed to co-ops. We find references in Treadup's diaries to surviving co-ops making soap, candles, cigarettes, towels, glass, and leather goods. His energies went into developing a machine shop, a repair depot, and a small foundry—the last of which apparently never got off the ground.

The staff people were subject to constant harassment by KMT agents. One note tells of something that happened before Treadup arrived: a staff man had been taken off in broad daylight and buried alive. Treadup himself was told more than once to leave the area, and once "rcd. threat would have legs broken if not out by next week." Treadup ignored the threat, and it was not carried out.

THERE ARE several brief notes on Colin McIntosh, who at Kanchow seems to have been a constant presence, but an increasingly prickly one. "CM riding me about my Chinese—struggling with dialect." "CM laughs at my manner with my co-op people: says I'm pokey." Treadup began to suspect that McIntosh was finding a discrepancy between the legend of David Treadup, which he had cherished, and the mere man, close at hand. Treadup had an uneasy feeling that McIntosh had decided that the "hero" was, after all, rather like his father—"an everyday sort of person—mediocre."

One day Treadup and McIntosh were working with a new co-op which had been formed to shape and bake k'angs—the enormous glazed clay jars which were used to store grain or water or whatever. They were in a village courtyard, out in the sun, "warmed by it," David wrote later in "Addendum,"

> and by the full blaze of our optimism. My motor was purring. In fact, it was going much too fast, for I was explaining the mechanics of a cooperative venture without having put across to the group the virtue of an alliance in work which would reach outside the circles of family and clan to village, 'hsien,' even mother China, for the profit and good of all.

The group was growing confused and restive. McIntosh started laughing —a nasty bark. "Mr. Treadup," he said then, in English, "when you get carried away, there's a bad sound in your voice. It's the missionary whine. I know it so well from my dad. It's as if you were so carried away by some preacher when you were young that you swallowed what he was saying whole, and it got caught in your neck. A strange sound—not your natural voice. I wish you'd slow down, or something—try to be yourself."

The young man was getting more impertinent every day. But I thought about what he said, and I realized he was right. I began to listen for this "bad sound," when I got excited, and I thought I heard it—a faint echo, I do believe, of the evangelistic tones of Jock Terrum, the Scottish rugby player who was so important to my conversion. I hadn't thought consciously of him for half a century, but there he was, sitting all that time in my Adam's apple. I think the sound comes when—whether I know it or not—I want to hypnotize people, the way he did.

AS THE WEEKS pass, there are more and more hints that Treadup is impatient to move north to his villages around Paoting, with the aim of establishing co-ops there, if they do not already exist. In late October: "2 shops now self-sufficient," "winding down," "people unhappy abt my announcement my withdrawal," "excited," "must admit I'll be relieved to get away from my young admirer, who thinks less and less of me," and

Farewell "feast," if you could call it that, at Tang Su restaurant. Could not avoid slight inebriation—McIntosh had warned me toasts absolutely obligatory.

On November 3, 1947, he left.

JUBILEE

TREADUP went "back" by way of Tientsin. On the way he began writing more at length again in his diary.

He looked up Phinneas Cunningham. In the face of a mountain of difficulties, Phinny had reopened his hospital; he was buying, begging, borrowing, stealing, and making with his own hands all the sorts of things the Japanese had taken away from the place. He had chivvied some equipment from UNRRA. He had brought his books back from Yin Hsien and was rebuilding his library. "He is a little older," Treadup wrote,

> so, like everyone who ages, he is not exactly the same as he was when he was younger—he is more so. The cheerfulness has hardened, even in these few years, into a fiery and somewhat painful crackling of good humor. The energy is confirmed into a boisterous laughing anger in a body which doesn't move quite so fast as before.

They talked. "You undermined my faith," Treadup said.

"But not your character," Cunningham said, with an ironic leer.

Then Treadup told his friend what had happened to his belief. During all this time, the only other person he had made his confession to was the young Swiss consul, Ramminet. Here was a dear friend to tell, at last.

For once, Phinny curbed his sharp tongue. "Does it feel better, to travel light?"

"No. Days are much more difficult. The fact is, I don't know what to think about anything."

"Ah. Welcome!"

"What has kept you going, Phinny?"

He stood up, walked to the window, and looked out into the street. "Disgust," he said.

"Come on!"

"Books," he then said.

"Phinny! I remember your telling me about riding all the way from Shanghai with that X-ray tube on your lap. Books?"

"That's where the record is," he said.

"Not enough for me. I need people."

"You know, then, what to think about people? Me, for instance?"

MRS. EVENRUDE had died in the camp—"withered on the vine right after you left," Dr. Cunningham said. Treadup went to her house, now occupied by a Chinese banker. The owner was not at home. With a small bribe Treadup persuaded a servant to let him look in the room in the servants' wing where his strapped boxes had been left behind. No sign of them, but

> I thought I recognized the socks the servant was wearing. So be it. In recent months I have become far removed from the concept of property, beyond bare necessities. I feel unencumbered.

HE WENT to the Peikai campus and found his oldest Chinese friend, Mr. Lin, living in honored retirement in a house on the university grounds.

Strange convolution: I used to worry about "losing" this my one convert. I did not tell him I had lost myself. We talked, anyway, about China, about the future. He thinks the Communists will win, and he welcomes that outcome. I told him how the young Communists in the villages had stung me, how cruel they had been. "The powers were cruel to China," he rather sharply said. But we parted loving each other. Before I left, we turned away from the future and stirred up some memories. He kindly (if awfully concisely) said I had helped China. He is such a pure man that even those spare words are a treasure to me.

HE RODE on a Peking cart from Paoting to Ma Ch'iao.

As I approached on the slightly raised, rutted causeway, thrown about on the hard platform of the cart, I experienced a sharp letdown. It was hard to believe that it had been nearly six years since I had been snatched out of "my" villages by the Japanese, and I suppose that in my almost constant yearning for a return, in all that time, I must have idealized the setting, softened it into some sort of nostalgic dream of yellowy willow trees over trig curving roofs, and smoke drifting up to a cloisonné sky. But here it was, on a November day, squalid, muddy, gray, mean, chilly, and a little frightening.

But then: The cart had for some distance been announcing itself to the village by the loud squealing of its ungreased axle, and as it now reached the mouth of the village street, children ran out, stood stock-still for a few moments, taking in the picture—scrawny mule, bulky two-wheeled cart, Chinese cartman in padded cotton clothes, huge *yang kwei-tzu* wearing a fur hat with turned-down flaps; seeing which, terrorized, they all turned and fled to their respective courtyards. Very soon afterward women popped out at the various gates, took a long look, and then, as if in response to a shared telegraphy, suddenly turned and ran together out the street toward the fields, "for all the world as if they were fleeing hearth and home forever." But soon they came back, leading their men, and in a few minutes the entire population of the village was assembled around the cart, and everyone was shouting at once their welcome to their old friend. "I tell you. The jubilee had come. I was home."

HE KNEW, from experience, that he must move slowly. This was not easy to do. Perhaps he was feeling his age. He visited, again and again, all his old haunts: T'u Ti, Li Chia, Ku Chuan, Shao T'an, Ho Chao, Ch'en Ts'un, every hamlet, every cluster of mud houses on the familiar rounds. The Indian had long since disappeared—taken away, someone told him, by the Japanese. He traveled now either on foot or on the back of a hired mule. Everywhere he was welcomed warmly, almost as a long lost clansman. This was deeply moving. He was trusted. So he began, carefully, to talk about co-ops.

He had decided that the first co-ops should be organized to build Inventor Wang's labor-saving devices: the well-lift, the harrow, the controlled plow, and others. He wanted to set up a merchandising cooperative to distribute these products, not only in his villages but throughout the district. He hoped that later the co-ops would branch out to other needed items, and to some of the staples that had been produced in Kiangsi, such as soap, candles, cloth shoes, and leather goods.

By the spring of 1948, he was, he noted, "as rushed as a squirrel when the acorns have fallen." Besides struggling to establish the co-ops, to which the villagers rallied not without resistance and skepticism, he found himself caught up in an effort to rebuild his network of literacy schools. He was pushed to the latter work by the villagers themselves, some of whom had been students in them a decade earlier.

AS MONTHS passed and season gave way to season, the going got harder and harder. The co-ops thrived in the cold months, while the fields rested under a green blanket of winter wheat, but in summer, when both men and women worked their own plots all the lit hours, it was almost impossible to summon leftover energy for cooperative work. The products had to be sold at the cheapest possible prices, and raw materials—particularly wood and nails —were expensive and hard to find. The provincial government was suspicious of the co-ops, as a radical experiment dangerous to the set ways of doing things, and it harassed Treadup with nuisance regulations and impromptu taxes; and what financial success the co-ops did have attracted the usual buzzards of corruption. The countryside was unsettled. Civil war was raging, it seemed, in all directions; panics like those of the warlord period occasionally broke out, and sometimes the villagers were swept into sudden waves of refugees—gone today, back day after tomorrow, exhausted and still frightened.

And for David,

I don't know exactly what the trouble is, but I am not as fulfilled as I think I used to be, before the war. Is it just that my old bones are tired? Perhaps it is that I saw so much that we had built collapse into trash

when the war began—so that I am constantly aware of the acute vulner-
ability and evanescence of "progress." Or, as I suspect, it may be that
I was sustained in some blind but effective way, back then, by my faith
in Jesus Christ, my belief that prayer really would make trouble go away,
my confidence that I could help others to be more godly persons; whereas
now, when doubts of my "mission" crop up, they take hold, and they
propagate, like dandelions.

Nevertheless, his stubborn side kept him going.

I T   W A S not a surprise to Treadup when, early in February 1949, a Communist team came in to take over the district of the villages. For months,
he had heard reports of the victories of the People's Liberation Army over
KMT troops, moving closer and closer from the direction of Manchuria—
victories achieved even though the Nationalists had had support from the
United States, particularly in the transport northward of their armies. Treadup
had seen copies of two Mao works, *The Present Situation* and *Our Tasks,*
disseminated from Yenan, laying out confident plans for a general offensive
against the Nationalists, and news had been coming in of the inexorable
success of the offensive. The diary:

> *Doing time with UNRRA taught me: Free China, with its weariness and*
> *corruption, has become a political vacuum. This other element rushes in*
> *to fill it.*

Tientsin had fallen to the People's Liberation Army on January 14, and two
weeks later Peking had surrendered without a fight. And a week after
that, Communist military units and political cadres came into Paoting and
its environs.

What *was* a surprise—and it was a nasty one, at first—was that among
the cadres of the takeover team were two of the four who had so harshly and
cruelly criticized Treadup, sitting cross-legged in a *k'ang* in Feng's house in
Ma Ch'iao, back in 1941, in that session which had been so traumatic that it
took years for Treadup to write a single word about it.

A further surprise: The new arrivals, and in particular the two young
men he had met before, were most friendly to him. That pair seemed to have
total amnesia on their previous session with the big American. They wanted
him to stay. The C.I.C. were invaluable. Treadup's work in literacy and
agricultural improvements was well-known. He was recognized and honored
as a friend of the Chinese people.

Accordingly, the work went on—now, apparently, more smoothly than
ever. Diary notes tell of the cadres' helping with the acquisition of raw
materials; of relief from taxes and other harassments; and of an abrupt end
to all "squeeze."

ON OCTOBER 1, 1949, there was a celebration in Ma Hsien, the district town, to which everyone from all the villages went. The Chinese People's Republic was being proclaimed on that day in Peking. The team leaders urgently invited Treadup to attend. All over the town radio loudspeakers announced that Mao Tse-tung had been elected Chairman, that in accordance with Mao's vision in *The People's Democratic Dictatorship*, a People's Political Consultative Conference was to be convened. In a temple ground there were long speeches, punctuated by firecrackers. The crowds in the streets seemed dazed by the good fortune the radio kept telling them had fallen to their lot. Many groups danced in *yang ke*, political "planting dances." Vendors chanted praise of their candied apples, malt sticks, peanuts, hot roasted sweet potatoes. Jackdaws darted among kites in the sky, as if even birds were getting news of change. Speaker followed speaker; each had lungs packed tight with words. The crowds passively listened until sodden with oratory. The foreigner Treadup was asked to utter a few sentences about industrial cooperatives.

> *There was no room left in their ears. But I felt at home on the platform, I felt I was one of them. I had a good time all day! Several old friends from my villages spoke to me, and without exception they said they had enjoyed the 'yang ke' at my agricultural fair more than the ones they were now being trained to perform.*

TREADUP himself seems to have forgotten all about the criticism session of 1941. The diary:

> *Have been impressed by the discipline and self-control of the team. They have displayed none of the legendary cruelty of the Party that was responsible for the Hunan massacres, ect. Under the impression that I am still a 'mu-shih,' they assure me that they mean to guarantee the freedom of religion. They have a clear purpose which was unquestionably mine in my villages, before the war: to raise the farmers' standard of living. They do all they can to enable and encourage our work. So far they have not been vindictive even against the landlords.*

Later entries are less euphoric. He notes that the U.S.S.R., Great Britain, the Netherlands, Norway, Sweden, Finland, and Switzerland have recognized the People's Republic; that the United States, on the other hand, has withdrawn its diplomatic people from China—some were said to have gone with Chiang Kai-shek to Formosa; that Mao announced, to a meeting of the new People's Political Consultative Conference, that China's foreign policy would "lean to one side"; and that that leaning had taken Mao out of China for the first time in his life, to Moscow.

ABSTRACT MAN

OF WHAT happened on November 23, 1949, and during the following weeks, we must rely on "Addendum," for, as Treadup notes in that document, "They took pencil and paper away from me—they might better have cut off my right hand."

This later account begins on the morning of the twenty-third; he was working with a new co-op for the manufacture of wooden plow handles, beams, and moldboards, in what had been a storage shed in the village of Shao T'an.

> *I remember distinctly that I was bending over showing the members how to shape the beam with a drawshave, how to work carefully down along the grain and never against it, when I became conscious, at the outer edge of my field of vision, of a pair of legs in the particular kind of gray padded cotton cloth the cadres all seem to wear. I went on with my instruction until I was finished. There was no effort to interrupt me. When I looked up, I saw one of my two old "criticism" friends, backed up by four PLA [People's Liberation Army] soldiers. The team leader called me aside—presumably so I would not lose face before the members of the cooperative—and said, quietly, that I was under arrest. I asked what for. He said he was not at liberty to reveal that to me. He suggested that I dismiss the class and come peaceably with him. Seeing no use whatsoever in doing anything else, I obeyed him.*

The cadre and the soldiers had come in a light truck. Treadup was seated on a wooden bench between two soldiers in the tarpaulin-covered rear of the truck, shut away from the cab; consequently he did not know where he was taken—he later deduced he was in Ma Hsien. He was placed in a room furnished with a cot, a bucket, and a stool. There was a high window, through which he could see nothing but the thin light of wintering skies.

HE LIVED alone in that room for two months, not knowing the charges against him, deprived of writing materials and of books. He walked constantly back and forth, like a creature in a zoo, to keep up his strength. "My only companions were figures in memories; I visited them day and night." He scratched a calendar on the wall with a chopstick, and marked off the days with successive chopsticks which were brought him each day with his meals. The food was decent, if frugal, Chinese fare—vegetables, steamed bread, tea, sometimes a little chicken or fish. A wordless barber came and shaved him with a straight razor once a week. ("If they had had execution in mind, it would only have taken a flick of his wrist.") The universe of fleeing moments was compressed into his rectangle of sky; sometimes at night he watched stars on their journeys across the little frame. "I thought of the immense heavens that night on the top deck of the *Teia Maru*, with Ramminet and Murchison—the sense of the void grinding inexorably around the poles—that same enormous wheel of the nights and days was turning and turning all this time, while I knew nothing about anything, in my little box of a room." He slept surprisingly well.

He had three guards, in rotation, all of whom were extremely friendly. One of them was from T'u Ti, one of Treadup's villages, and he spoke warmly of past times in which he clearly remembered T'ao-tu Hsien-sheng; as a boy of twelve he had been at Treadup's agricultural fair. He chatted amiably with the door open.

No one questioned Treadup. No one would tell him why he was being held. He asked his guards again and again to get someone to come and tell him what he had done to deserve being buried alive in this way. One of them, one day, shrugged and said merely, "Tiger hunt."

ON THE MORNING of January 23, 1950 ("according to the wall calendar"), shortly after the silent barber performed his rites with his dangerous implement, a cadre, a young man of about twenty-five, came to Treadup's holding-room and told him to follow him. Treadup asked where he was being taken. To People's Court, the cadre said. "After so long in my dark room, the bright light outdoors pressed the sights of the town hard against my retinas." The cadre led him into a temple courtyard, where a large crowd of people was assembled.

On the platform before one of the former shrines, a young man was making a fierce speech, at a shout, winding his argument around and around with his active arms. The cadre led Treadup up onto the platform and ordered him to kneel facing the crowd.

Now, in a series of chants by the speaker, and for the first time, I heard—or half heard—I had been packed into a small silent space for weeks, and now I was in this hubbub, shocked and astonished— everything was a blur—I thought I was hearing this man list the accu-

sations against me. The charges, if I could trust my ears, were so copious that I could not possibly have been worthy of them. Did I hear the speaker cry out, with the most sincere conviction, that I was an agent of American capitalism? At once, as if all the evidence had been presented, he asked the crowd, "Is he guilty?" With heartfelt unanimity, they affirmed my guilt. Now I thought I was back in my cell, having a bad dream. The speaker. "He is an American spy. Guilty? Yes, in a thousand voices. He had tried to subvert the state. Yes! He had planned to assassinate the leaders of the Ma Hsien team. Oh, Yes! He had hidden a machine gun in a cavity built into his 'k'ang.' Yes!

At this point, Treadup writes, he became convinced that the decent, kindly young Communists who had so impressed him and so honored him in the first months after their arrival had for some reason all gone stark raving mad. "Or was I still in my box, was *I* mad? Was all this a chimera?" He was, at any rate, furious. In a very loud voice he called out to the speaker: "Those are all lies."

The crowd let out a sigh of what seemed to Treadup a gaseous kind of applause: "Aaaah!"

The speaker, however, was pleased. This was apparently just what he had wanted. He appeared to believe that his victim had by his outburst hopelessly lost face. He said, "You tell the truth, then. Were you a *mu-shih* in the following places: Paoting, also the villages of Ma Ch'iao, Ch'en Ts'un, Shao T'an, Li Chia, Ho Chao, Ku Chuan, T'u Ti?"

Treadup could not deny that he had been.

At this the speaker took off with a long harangue on Christianity — supernatural riddles to confuse simple minds, a device of the upper classes to make the oppressed think that their miseries would be eased in another world, and so to be able to keep on exploiting them — and it came clearly, if belatedly, to David Treadup that his crime was that of being an abstraction.

At once I was faced with this: Why not tell them I had lost the best part of my faith? They were barking up the wrong tree. They could not object to the freethinker I thought I had become. But no. I instantly decided I could not do that — any more than I could have told Emily of my change of heart and mind. The man who was on trial here was that other man who was me in the past. I could not turn my back on him. I must defend myself in him. And anyhow, I had to face it that whatever I might say would be useless. A defense against such magnificently fraudulent charges would itself take on the taint of fraud. But of course I couldn't help myself. I had to try to fight.

TREADUP (*again loudly, this time not to his accuser but to the crowd*) "Some of you know me. Tell this man. I taught you to read and write."

ACCUSER (*as if in answer to what had just been said*) "Jesus did not understand the laws of dialectics. Love can only function in a classless society. Where there are classes, a tiger can only love a tiger—it eats all others. Jesus tried to build a bridge directly from a slave society to the Kingdom of God. His revolution failed. It had to. He did not take into account the necessary steps of social development. What do you say to that?"

It was extremely difficult to deal with this kind of talk. I couldn't parry his gospel with the one I had abandoned. Whatever I might say, it would be delivering a punch to a pillow full of feathers.

TREADUP "I say that you find me guilty first, and then put me on trial afterward."
ACCUSER "You think it is enough that Lin Fu-chen recently called you 'a good man.' " ("*I was shocked at how much these people knew. How could he have known this? Mr. Lin and I had had a private conversation.*") "You think it was enough to 'do good' in the villages I have named. But what you did weakened the people's resistance to the landlords. You confused class distinctions. You did not work according to the dialectics of Ma K'e Sze."
TREADUP "I have studied Marx. Your own people have been telling me until recently that my work in the villages was in accordance with his and your principles. Why this turnaround? I have been trying for weeks to find out why you arrested me."

I could see by a flicker in the eyes of my un-friend that I had scored at least a minor point. He must have sat in on discussions of my work with the local team. But my little success, if it was one, passed unnoticed where it counted, with The People. For my accuser now began to call on men and women from "my" villages to testify against me. This was the cruelest mockery of all. As I saw it, the poor villagers had been fed bushels of lies to vomit out on me.

The first to testify was one-armed Mi Tu-ch'uan, the splendid young man who, being left behind in the village because of his infirmity, had become the local wise man and, in his early twenties, the village elder, and who had worked so closely and affectionately with Treadup. He could not bring himself to look at the accused as he told of having dug out the *mu-shih*'s *k'ang* after he had been taken away by the Japanese, and having found hidden, in a hole alongside its oven, an American-manufactured military rifle—an M1. (*"Their falsehoods were made of cement—convincing details. My old fowling piece, with which I used to hunt snipe, and which I kept wrapped in rags in a cavity in the k'ang to keep it clean!"*) A man whom Treadup had never seen before said that the accused had extorted grain from the farmers and had delivered it to an American corporation based in Paoting—"a landlord to landlords."

Fighting for my sanity, I worked it out that this last charge must have arisen from some kind of misunderstanding of my transactions, buying grain for my starving villagers with the relief money I'd raised in Peking, back before the war. But then at once I realized I had let myself be drawn into a zone of plausibility which was very dangerous to my reason. I bit my lip to keep myself from saying anything.

As if to reinforce this plausibility, one witness after another acknowledged that the Chinese Industrial Cooperatives were above blame, and granted that Treadup had done "some good things." But the word "exploit" was the catchword in refrain.

It was a long entertainment, lasting most of the day, in the tradition of Peking opera. My knees were in great pain.

When at last the show appeared to be boring even the Accuser, he called on the crowd once more to acclaim, *viva voce,* the guilt of the prisoner.
Was he an enemy of the people?

In the roar I now heard, I thought I could distinguish different tones — of the gullible, of those who hated the abstraction I represented, of those who knew some history and would never forgive the foreign powers for their part in it, but also of some who were too shrewd and wise to have been taken in by the charade of the day, and — oh, yes, I could hear them — of those who loved me. They all pronounced the same word: Yes!

The Party Secretary of the district delivered the sentence, which had obviously been written out before the trial began: Despite the guilt proven before the People's Court, despite the crimes against the Chinese people of the prisoner, despite his conspiracy with the American government to oppress the Chinese people, and because of his mixed record, which included certain mitigating evidence of attempts to "do good," this man would not be returned to prison, where some might think he belonged for the rest of his life, but instead would be expelled forever from the People's Republic of China.

H E W A S given thirty days in which to arrange transportation. The team leaders in the area of the villages were now just as cordial to him as they had been when they first arrived. They returned his diaries, which they had "borrowed" — and of course, this was where they had found some of the material they had used against him in the trial, such as Mr. Lin's praise of him. Many villagers came to call, and perfectly openly said that Mi Tu-ch'uan and the other village witnesses had of course not meant what they had testified that day. Of course he would understand that all those things had all been "necessary."

Their attitude toward the fiasco of the trial fascinated me. Many of those people truly liked me, perhaps even loved me; I really believe so. They seemed to accept that in a time of change—change that was giving them hopes far more opulent than those I had been able to offer them—certain celebratory rituals would be necessary. In a way, my trial was like one of the political planting songs they dance to. The pleasing emotion they feel while dancing has no relationship to "facts" or "reality" or "truth." It never occurred to them that they were committing a crime of violence against me, because, as they saw it, the ritual itself simply asked an abstract figure to atone for real crimes committed against them for a long time by much larger outside forces, as vague but also as threatening to them as fox spirits, of which the abstract man is asked to be a miniature representation. After the trial, I was no longer abstract. I was the man they knew and liked, and they resumed their former relationship with me, not knowing that my heart was broken.

A SOLEMN CHARGE

JUNE 4, 1950, Thornhill, N.Y.

On one of the many buzzer buttons he had himself rigged within reach of the various places in the apartment where he might come to rest, he tapped, in Morse code, the three dots, three dashes, and three dots by which mariners radio to nearby vessels their cry for help in extremity: SOS, Save Our Ship.

Unknown waves before me roll,
Hiding treacherous rock and shoal . . .

Downstairs, in the Hurds' rooms, the rasping sounds of the buzzer, which Treadup had installed in the kitchen, made Gertrude Hurd, who was ironing clothes and listening to the radio, jump so that she dropped the iron with a clatter to the floor. She pulled its plug and raced upstairs. Mr. Treadup was slumped over in a chair in the sun window, with a notebook in his lap.

THE NOTEBOOK has scrawled on its cover: ADDENDUM TO SEARCH. Philip Treadup would later come on these recent entries, among many others—all presumably written here in the Hurds' house, at this very window, in the months since his father's return from China:

• *Coming home from China, I went aloft in an airplane for the first time in my life. The Chinese took me to Canton by train and slipped me out to the lip of the New Territories of Hong Kong, where, at the very border, they simply dumped this enemy of the people to fend for himself. I still had some money saved up from UNRRA, and casting it to the winds, I rose into the air on the back of Pegasus. My lecture on aviation was written longhand on the folds of my brain—the dynamics of the parallelogram of forces on the curved upper edge of the wing—the ratio of thrust to mass—the torque of the propeller—all theoretical. But this, this was real, this rising spiral up out of the bowl of Hong Kong into a blue blue of elation—my heart was amazingly strong in its response to such magic. Pegasus leapt to Hanoi, Rangoon, Calcutta, Karachi, Cairo, Paris, Shannon, Gander, Presque Isle, and New York. The sights I saw! The driest and the wettest parts of the earth; snowy peaks and desert sand; jungles and barrens; and castles of clouds worth a century of dreams. I was out of touch with the mystery I used to call God, but I trembled more than once in awe at the inventiveness of whatever forces, blind or intelligent, had shaped all that I saw. Of course it would be son Philip to meet me on the ground at New York. I was on 'terra firma,' but I was not home. I collapsed in Customs.*

• *In my imagination, my sons stand around me. Philip is pallid. He does the right thing, every time. Gentle with his children. I can imagine his pupils dropping off to sleep in the classroom. Abbo, how I love that impassioned boy! Who, I guess, hates me. Unable to hear, he sees everything—too clearly. And Paul? What, in his upbringing, made him such a materialist?*

• *My lost love. I sit in this sunny window, in this little room, looking out on a horse chestnut tree, its shamelessly erotic blossoms giving their lust to the bright light of a June day, and I remember. O Emily, I remember everything. I remember the evening at Syracuse, long before I could be sure of you, when I took you to vespers at Park Church, down in the city, and afterward I "tried to say some kind words." I don't remember what they were. They must have been awkward, and, to be sure, they fell far short of the feeling behind them. What I remember now is that as you responded—kindly, too, but of course without the steady knowledge that I already had—you tilted your head. We were near a street lamp. Your eyes glistened, almost as though you were crying. What I saw, as clearly as if the summer light of this sensuous moment of this day of my old age had been showering down all around us then, was your mysterious calm. Sometimes over the years your serenity frightened me, because it was so deep, I could not sound it to its bottom. But I, an old man, am a young man looking now into your eyes under the streetlight on the sidewalk outside Park Church, and I see that you have the calm of someone to whom it has been given to know how to love. What I saw then is what I have worshiped all my life. Christ was my metaphor. You were my reality. You had the secret of peace on earth, and goodwill.*

• All America is suffering from the "lost love" pain. China. There is much talk about why we "lost" China—as if we ever "had" China. The loss I feel, coming back this time, is in the stable values of our society. We no longer seem to hold to the simple Emersonian law that good deeds will be rewarded and mean deeds will reap retribution. In fact, the doers of mean deeds appear to have frightened the country so much that they have been, virtually speaking, put in charge. Senator McCarthy: Look!—he's driving out "the China hands," so many of whom are sons of missionaries. Why? Ironically, because they loved, and understood, the China we have "lost." So here's a paradox: The Communists hound me, a neo-missionary, out of China, and the American tiger-hunters hound the "mishkids" out of the State Department—me because I am un-Chinese, and them because they are un-American. It is not the object of love America has lost, so much as the capacity for it.

GERTRUDE HURD used Mr. Treadup's telephone to call an ambulance. She then called Dr. McCandless; her husband, at his job in Ossining; Philip's wife at the school; and Paul's secretary at his office in New York. Then she looked at the clock: nine fifty-five.

It seemed to take forever for the ambulance to arrive. Mr. Treadup was breathing as if he were snoring; all she could get by way of pulse was a fluttering like that of a moth trying to get out a window.

The ambulance came. The two attendants were calm as checkout clerks at a supermarket. One of them put an oxygen breather, attached to a small portable tank, to Treadup's nose and mouth, while the other unfolded a stretcher. It was all the two men could do to lift the huge ruin and carry the bulk of it aslant down the narrow stairs.

Gertrude Hurd rode with Mr. Treadup to the hospital in the ambulance. She told Philip the next day, "Everything was done that could be done. I was a wreck. I wanted to climb right into a hospital bed myself. I love your father. He surprises you every moment with the sweetness that's hidden under that power he has. Do I have to say 'had'?"

PHILIP, who had farther to come than Paul, arrived first, at about five in the afternoon. Dr. McCandless told him that the outlook was unclear; Philip's father's history of previous minor cardiac disturbances was not encouraging. Dr. McCandless spent the entire night in the room with his patient; when Philip considerately asked, during the evening, if the doctor shouldn't go home and get some rest, McCandless said, "With most patients, I certainly would." Philip sat the night out in the visitors' room at the end of the hall. Big Paul arrived at about ten o'clock, demanded to see his father, found some things at once to complain about, in the sick man's presence, to Dr. McCandless, and then began blustering at the nurse's desk about putting the old man in a better room. One nurse finally asked him if he wanted her to call four orderlies to remove him from the hospital. He told Phil he liked it that she knew she would have needed four.

At about ten thirty, while all this was going on, David Treadup had a second heart attack.

IN THE MORNING, Dr. McCandless, himself ashen, stubbled, and drawn, said to the sons that the second attack probably would have been fatal had their father not been in the hospital, where immediate emergency measures could be taken. Paul said he had two important appointments in the city, and left. Philip spent the day in the room. His father was weak and exhausted. In the afternoon, he seemed to regain strength. When Gertrude Hurd came in the room, he took her hand and said he was sorry to have "put her through the wringer." She kissed his hand and cried. Later he joked with Philip about Paul. "The Treadups have one mule in every generation," he said, allying himself with Paul.

Things seemed to be going well, and Philip and Dr. McCandless both went home for a night's sleep.

When they returned the next morning, the sixth, they found him weaker, though no further attack had been observed. Paul showed up. The two sons decided to send a telegram to Absolom — he had no phone. Late in the afternoon, an answer was delivered:

HEY POP HANG IN THERE COMING TOMORROW.

Paul took the telegram in to their father. He understood it and spoke pleasure with his eyes.

DAVID TREADUP'S big heart had nothing left but a whisper on the morning of the seventh. Dr. McCandless said there was such serious damage from the second attack that there was little hope for the heart to function normally again. Paul met Absolom at Grand Central and took him out to the hospital; they arrived in midafternoon. Their father was drowsy from his medication, but he opened his eyes, recognized Absolom, and said puzzling words, which, as Philip later wrote in a long letter to his Aunt Grace, the three boys finally figured out to have been an effort to get out an exultant shout from a childhood game: "Ally-ally in, home free!"

Soon after, he lost consciousness. He roused a few times after that, murmured, and floated back into the dark.

At a few minutes before six that evening—no one remembered later exactly what time it happened—the torn muscle of life stopped the faithful work it had done for almost seventy-two years.

PHILIP, as he had done after his mother's death, arranged everything. The body was cremated and buried in an urn beside the other urn. The graveside ceremony was private—children and grandchildren, Pastor Mendell of the Thornhill Congregational Church. The Y.M.C.A. issued a memorial letter to its current and demobilized secretaries. A small notice, written by Philip and paid for by Paul, appeared in *The New York Times*. It described the deceased, in abrupt summation, as "longtime Y.M.C.A. secretary in Shanghai, China. Revered father of," and so forth.

THE THREE BOYS were present for the reading of the will, a week later. There was, of course, very little for David Treadup to have left his sons but memory and advice. But indited on a separate sheet at the end of the document were these words, in phrasing which their father must have considered worthy of an attorney, dashed off in the bold longhand of the diaries:

> I, David Treadup, being at this writing of sound body and mind, do solemnly charge my sons and heirs to take the necessary action with all dispatch, whenever it may be possible, in order to remove my ashes, and those of my wife, Emily Kean Treadup, from their resting place in American soil, and to transport them and reinter them close adjacent to the grave of Nancy Kean Treadup in the Christian Burying Ground, Shanghai, China.

FOR NEARLY a quarter of a century, there was a far greater distance between China and America than the physical miles of half the globe's girdle. It was not until the early 1970s, not until after Richard Nixon's trip to China to begin the process of normalization of Sino-American relations, that dutiful

Philip, by then himself past sixty, began to apply for permission to go to China. His first efforts were through the Chinese Embassy in Ottawa, for the Canadians had long had cordial relations with the Chinese; but he never could get past a certain functionary whose name seemed to be T'an, whose English was faulty, and whose outlook was negative. Later, Philip made efforts to see someone—anyone—on the Chinese delegation to the United Nations; but the name Treadup seemed to carry no weight, and he was never encouraged to present his case. He tried to make use of his father's having served with UNRRA, to open the way to the Chinese delegation. He tried to find a link through journalists who had served in China in early days. He besieged the Y.M.C.A. offices for help, which they seemed reluctant to give, until he realized he was a nuisance. He wrote more than once to Huang Hua, the chief of the Chinese U.N. delegation, who was said to have gone to a missionary school when he was young. Philip even sent a cable to Chou En-lai, who, he had learned, had been taught by missionaries in the middle school founded by Philip's father's friend, Mr. Lin Fu-chen. For nine years, from 1972 until 1981, nothing did any good.

In the mid-seventies, hoping that it might help, Philip had joined a Connecticut branch of the U.S.-Chinese Peoples' Friendship Association. He did this in spite of his inimical feelings toward the country where he had been born. His "report letters" to his brothers give a picture of a man with a rather conventional American attitude toward Communism; perhaps, as well, this "sheepish" son felt that Communist China had dealt unfairly with the father who had loomed so large over him. Nevertheless, he attended discussion groups of the Friendship Association, holding his tongue. He watched long Chinese moving pictures. He took his small grandchildren to picnics on the shores of Long Island Sound, where they flew Chinese kites.

In 1981, at last, through this organization, he saw a glimmer of light. The Association was planning to sponsor a tour of China, for Connecticut friends of China. Philip applied and was accepted. He borrowed money from brother Paul, bought his tickets, and in September 1981, with one suitcase and a padlocked black wooden box which he carried onto the plane with him, he took off with Pan Am from New York to fly over the North Pole to Tokyo, whence he flew in a Chinese National Airlines plane to Beijing.

It was doubtless in character for this frail, pallid, bald, haggard, stubborn, unimaginative, and doggedly faithful man, now seventy-two years old, not to have explored in advance with the Chinese the real purpose of his trip.

AT THE BEIJING AIRPORT, the friends of China from Connecticut quickly developed hostile feelings toward one of their party.

This Philip Treadup, who had tended to be standoffish with the others in the band of Sinophiles—he had kept his nose in a book (not about China, a seatmate had noticed) on the planes — suddenly turned out to be fierce and voluble. He had seemed so bland. And now, at the exciting time of their long-anticipated arrival in the country to which they felt so well disposed, he held up the entire group in Customs for three hours while he mulishly negotiated, through an interpreter, about the strange box he was carrying. He told its story with hot eyes. He obviously had a need to demonstrate that he was not one to be outtalked by Communist bureaucrats. The Customs men, seeing no documentary authorization, announced to him that they would have to confiscate the box. Mr. Treadup said that in that case, they would have to hold him, too; he was not going to let himself be parted from the remains of his father and mother. This filial passion could not but appeal to Chinese officials. They called in their superior officer. He, in turn, felt it necessary to consult with his superior. That man, too, had a superior. Telephone lines hummed up and down the trellis of responsibility. After two hours, an American from the office of the United States representative in Beijing, not at all happy about having had his dinner hour interrupted, arrived to mediate.

Fortunately Philip had a document from the Francis Shaughnessy Funeral Parlor, of Thornhill, N.Y., U.S.A., concerning the contents of the box, and Francis Shaughnessy, a very old man and a mortician of style, had taken the trouble to affix to the document a nosegay of red ribbon, which was fastened in place by a blob of reddish sealing wax imprinted while molten with the handsome logo of the Parlor. This document, carefully translated, and eventually photographed, seemed — along with the ferocious sincerity of this elderly man, who kept saying that his father had loved great China more than he loved his own natal land — to help carry the day. Then, just when all seemed to have been settled, a message came down the line to the Customs men. The box would have to be opened and searched. Mr. Treadup objected to this impiety in the most forceful terms. The Customs men, their careers on the line, insisted with faces of steel.

Trembling, Mr. Treadup unlocked the box. Within, two urns. It took some time to break their seals. Off lids. A gray dust. The senior Customs official sent a courier running off for a pair of chopsticks. Delicately, when they had been produced, and while Mr. Treadup fumed, the top man stirred one of the chopsticks in the first urn, to be sure nothing was hidden there; the other chopstick in the other urn.

Finally, subject to certain regulatory stipulations, Mr. Treadup was authorized to carry the box on his travels. The urns were resealed with gummed paper.

By this time, China's friends from the Nutmeg State were so frazzled by outrage that their whole trip would be colored by bickering amongst themselves, and, indeed, all along the way they would even be heard complaining often, and quite sharply, to their Chinese hosts — about hotel accommodations, hurried schedules, food, delays, lack of freedom to talk with "ordinary"

Chinese, rain, propaganda, bad coffee, the length of Peking operas, ambiguous translation, no provision of drinks before dinner, prices of the bits of jade in Friendship Hotel gift shops. . . .

FROM A LETTER from Philip to Paul:

I almost wish I'd listened to you. You kept telling me this was a foolhardy errand. Just an old man's whim. But I still think we had to respect his wish. What burns me is that no one has ever heard of him. He might just as well never have existed. In fact one of the officials at the airport gave me a long lecture about missionaries. I finally said, "Look, you are offending me, you know that I am the son of one." He stopped after that. My own feelings about being back here are weird. Of course up to now my main reaction has been irritation. But certain noises — smells — just the sound of the people talking. I wish I could go to Peitaiho and see the beaches again. Tiger Rocks. I'm tired. When that man began poking in Mom's ashes, I thought I might lose control.

PHILIP looked at the sights of this China and tried to imagine that he was using his father's eyes. He could see nothing good. His hostility extended beyond the Communists, whom he blamed for forgetting the name Treadup, to dynasties of the past. How absurd to have built a ship of stone and have set it "afloat" on glassy illusion on the blue lake of the Summer Palace, Beijing. What ridiculous pomp, for an emperor to memorialize himself by building a vast army of terra cotta soldiers to guard his tomb, at Xian. Really, to give to a pavilion a ludicrous name like "Lotus in the Breeze at the Crooked Courtyard"! — as these people had done at West Lake, Hangzhou.

It was all a wait. At long last, on September 24, Philip Treadup found himself on the famous Bund of imperial romance, on the Whangpoo, at Shanghai.

PHILIP TREADUP had obtained from the Y.M.C.A. in New York the names of Chinese who had been secretaries of the Association in Shanghai of his father's day; he had also obtained a map, drawn by the Shanghai Municipal Council in 1934, which showed four cemeteries — none explicitly named on that map as the "Christian Burying Ground." The young man, Shu, whom the Chinese Friendship Association had provided as a guide for the tour, and whom the Connecticut friends called "The Shoe," was obviously bored by the endless routine of sightseeing to which he had been condemned, it seemed, for life, and the novelty and challenge of the quest of this difficult Treadup person appealed to him. He undertook to help. He did make it clear, of course, that if they succeeded in finding Mr. Treadup's late sister's grave, Mr. Treadup couldn't just dig—he would have to get permission from the proper authorities to bury the urns he had brought from America.

On the party's third day in the city, young Mr. Shu knocked at Mr. Treadup's hotel door. He proudly said that through acquaintances whose parents had been members of the old China Democratic League, which before the Revolution had been the third largest party in China, after the Communists and the Kuomintang, he had found a son of Han Ye-yuan, who had apparently been Mr. Treadup's father's successor in a post for the Y.M.C.A. He would be glad to take Mr. Treadup to see him in the evening.

Philip to Paul:

We took a taxi. A dismal part of the city. We got out and walked along a dark alleyway. Row houses, like tenements. Second floor. Two rooms for a family of four, one light bulb, maybe twenty watts, hanging down from the ceiling. Depressing. Mr. Han astonished me. He remembered me! He is exactly my age. Our whole family had been in their house. I hadn't the faintest recollection of it. All he remembers about Father is that he was so big. He seemed very suspicious of The Shoe. Also, slightly upset by the box. I take it with me wherever I go, I'm not going to lose it after all this effort. He looked at the map, said he'd take me tomorrow, Sunday, to look for the right cemetery, if the Friendship Association people give permission. Though he said he didn't know just what a foreign cemetery looked like. Didn't remember any open place in Shanghai with stone slabs or shafts, such as I described. At first he didn't want to talk about the past. But then he told me what he had gone through in the Cultural Revolution. It seems everyone is opening up on this subject now. They kept him in a cellar for a while. They made him work as a bricklayer. He talks offhand about this, but says his heart is not good. We start at nine tomorrow morning.

AFTER breakfast Mr. Treadup and The Shoe took another taxi, picked up Mr. Han, and drove out to what was shown on the map as Bubbling Wells Road. The map was clear. A right turn. Then a left onto a curving street. And there. That was where the first graveyard should have been. Instead, there was a large, boxlike, concrete apartment house, "as bleak as a prison." They drove around and around. The cemetery was nowhere to be found.

All four cemeteries had disappeared.

WITH THE HELP of Mr. Han, who had turned out to be a most friendly person, Philip Treadup obtained an interview with Liu Banli, Deputy Mayor of Shanghai. They sat in muslin-covered overstuffed chairs with a low-lying table between them, which held covered cups, a jar of tea leaves, and a thermos of hot water. Deputy Mayor Liu, who spoke good English, poured tea with his own hands, and he offered Philip a cigarette, but Philip did not smoke.

Philip told what he had come to Shanghai to do. He had the wooden box with him.

The Deputy Mayor expressed himself as deeply touched by Mr. Treadup's respect for the wishes of his father. He believed he may have heard of the lectures offered "before liberation" by the Y.M.C.A. They were, perhaps, rather famous.

Deputy Mayor Liu then said that all the foreign graves in Shanghai had been plowed up in the fifties and sixties. Indeed, he said, this was not just a question of foreign graves. Old Chinese graves had been plowed up all over China, to the great consternation of the descendants of the dead.

"In the countryside, we needed the land for crops. Here, we needed the real estate for buildings for our people."

Philip, to Paul:

All that effort for nothing. Wasn't it just like Father to get up some wild goose chase like this? I tell you, Paul, that box weighed a ton going back to the hotel.

BUT LATER Philip's anger was turned in another direction. He did not give up. He applied for permission to leave the tour and take his box to Paoting. "I made this decision on my own, without consulting you," Philip wrote,

because I knew you would agree that somewhere there — if I could find the old compound — would be an appropriate place for the ashes. And how could I have consulted, anyway? I suppose I could have telephoned. But I went ahead.

But Mr. Treadup's going to Paoting, the Friendship people said, would be quite impossible. There were no hotels for foreigners in Paoting. The Friendship people were sorry. And they were firm.

I argued and argued. It's just hopeless here. Back home, if you want to go somewhere, you just buy a ticket and go. I got so mad I said, O.K., I'll take the damn box home to the States, just fly me out of here. But no, they said I was a member of the tour, all arrangements had been made for me to go with the tour, I must stay with the tour. So now we go to Canton, to see sights I have no taste for. Oh, Paul, Father would have been so humiliated. I certainly am. I'm beyond anger now. Think of it, his wanting so much to come back to China, even dead.

PHILIP TREADUP carried the box with him to Canton, where he stayed in the hotel the whole time. To Hong Kong. And back to the United States. He commissioned the Francis Shaughnessy Funeral Parlor to bury the urns, once more, in the little cemetery in Thornhill, New York, in the circle of dappled shade thrown by the now quite large dogwood tree.

NOTES

Some of the traits and experiences of the central character of this fictional biography, David Treadup, were suggested by some of those of six actual missionaries to China, Fletcher H. Brockman, G. Herbert Cole, Lewis L. Gilbert, Roscoe M. Hersey, Sr., Hugh W. Hubbard, and C. H. Robertson; but Treadup is "like" no one of them.

If it be thought that the name Treadup, with its hint of a striving for ascension, is somewhat pat for a missionary, here are the surnames of some real missionaries who went to China: Bible, Cross, Service, Whitechurch, Upchurch, Innocent. There was one named Boxer. One named Dudgeon.

Throughout the book, all characters are fictional except recognizable historical figures, who bear their own names, and a few persons who enter the story for reasons that I trust will be evident to the reader, such as Roscoe M. Hersey, Sr., Henry R. Luce, Sr., and a few others. China hands will recognize some characters as having been suggested by actual persons of some historical consequence (such as Chang Po-ling and Y. C. James Yen); these figures, however, play fictional roles here, so their names, like their selves, have been changed.

In preparing to write the book, I found invaluable background material in the files of the Y.M.C.A. Historical Library (YHL), formerly in New York City, now in Rosemont, Illinois; the files of the American Board of Commissioners for Foreign Missions, in the Houghton Library, Harvard (HL/ABCFM); and documents in the Day Missions Library, Yale Divinity School (DML); and I received assistance from the archives of the International Institute of Rural Reconstruction (IIRR), New York City.

I must acknowledge, with gratitude, most valuable encouragement and guidance, from the inception of this work, from John K. Fairbank; a careful and generous reading of the manuscript, and many crucial emendations, from Knight Biggerstaff; helpful criticisms and suggestions from Jonathan Spence; and much appreciated leads from James C. Thomson, James T. C. Liu, Valentine H. Rabe, and others. None of these scholars can be held responsible, obviously, for the fiction I have spun out of this piece of the past. Y. C. James Yen gave me generously of his time. I am most grateful to Judith Jones for her sensitive and always wise editorial suggestions. For help in the uncovering of background materials I must also thank Ellen Sowchek, formerly Librarian, and Margaret Byrne, formerly Assistant Librarian, of the Y.M.C.A. Historical Library; Martha Smalley, Archivist of the Yale Divinity School Library; Nancy Anderson, Librarian, Wolcott Civic Free Library, Wolcott, N.Y.; Diane Perushak, Curator, Wason Collection, Olin Library, Cornell University; and Mrs. Ping-shen Chin,

International Institute of Rural Reconstruction. My thanks also, for various kinds of assistance, courtesy, and/or permissions, to Mary Jane Alexander, Erin Endean, Grace M. Frost, Rev. Chandler W. Gilbert, Mrs. Josephine Gilbert, William L. Holland, Ward N. Hubbard, Rev. William N. Lovell, Dorothy Galt MacArthur, Emma Rose Hubbard Martin, Thomas C. Mendenhall, Carl and Shelley Mydans, D. R. Robertson, R. C. Robertson, Ashmead Seabury, James E. Sheridan, Rev. David M. Stowe, and Gladys Hubbard Swift.

The most important primary sources, among many others in the libraries I have mentioned, were:

Papers of Roscoe Monroe Hersey, Sr., and Grace Baird Hersey, in possession of the author's family, and in YHL; papers of Fletcher S. Brockman, G. Herbert Cole, Clarence Hovey Robertson, in YHL; papers of Hugh W. Hubbard, in HL/ABCFM and IIRR; letters of Lewis C. Gilbert and Lois G. Gilbert, in DML; and letters and reports of Y. C. James Yen, in YHL and IIRR.

Other primary sources:

Ruth A. Brack, "Weihsien, Shantung Province, China, Dec. 8, 1941–June 5, 1942," typescript; Howard S. Galt, "The Internment Camp at Wei Hsien, Shantung, March–Sept. 1943," ms.; Howard S. Galt, "A Journey of Repatriation, Wei Hsien to New York, Sept., Oct., Nov., Dec. 1943," ms.; A. W. March, "Diary of a Prisoner of War Under Japan, Dec. 8, 1941 to Sept. 19, 1942," ms.; all in DML.

Charles Wishart Hayford, "Rural Reconstruction in China: Y. C. James Yen and the Mass Education Movement" (Ph.D. dissertation, Harvard, June 1973), mimeographed, in IIRR.

Among the many secondary sources consulted, I am especially indebted to the following:

Pat Barr, *To China with Love* (London: Secker & Warburg, 1972).

Fletcher S. Brockman, *I Discover the Orient* (New York: Harper, 1935).

John K. Fairbank, ed., *The Missionary Enterprise in China and America* (Cambridge, Mass.: Harvard Univ. Press, 1974); in particular, essays by M. Searle Bates, James A. Field, Shirley S. Garrett, William R. Hutchinson, Stuart Creighton Miller, Clifton J. Phillips, Valentine H. Rabe, Arthur Schlesinger, Jr., Philip West.

Grace M. Frost, *Red Creek Once Upon a Time* (Red Creek, N.Y.: privately printed, 1978).

W. Freeman Galpin, *Syracuse University* (Syracuse: Syracuse Univ. Press, 1952).

Sidney D. Gamble, *Ting Hsien: A North China Rural Community* (New York: Institute of Pacific Relations, 1954).

Shirley S. Garrett, *Social Reformers in Urban China: The Chinese Y.M.C.A., 1895–1926* (Cambridge, Mass.: Harvard Univ. Press, 1970).

Kenneth Scott Latourette, *World Service: A History of the Foreign Work and World Service of the Young Men's Christian Association of the United States and Canada* (New York: Association Press, 1957).

Basil Mathews, *John R. Mott* (New York: Harper, 1934).

Timothy Richard, *Conversion by the Million* (Shanghai: Christian Literature Society, 1907).

Laurence Salisbury, "Chinese Coolies and the War," *Saturday Evening Post*, Oct. 25, 1919; also anon., "Young Men's Christian Association with the Chinese Labor Corps in France" (Y.M.C.A. pamphlet, Paris, 1919); William Howard Taft et al., eds., *Service with Fighting Men: An Account of the Work of the American Y.M.C.A. in the World War* (New York: Association Press, 1922).

James E. Sheridan, *Chinese Warlord: The Career of Feng Yu-hsiang* (Palo Alto: Stanford Univ. Press, 1966).

Paul A. Varg, *Missionaries, Chinese, and Diplomats: The American Protestant Missionary Movement in China, 1890–1952* (Princeton: Princeton Univ. Press, 1958).

The Vision of a Short Life: A Memorial of Warren Bartlett Seabury, by his father (Cambridge, Mass.: privately printed, The Riverside Press, 1909).

PAGE

5 *Resistance to something:* Henry Adams, *The Education of Henry Adams: An Autobiography* (Boston: Houghton Mifflin, 1918), p. 7.

16 *The God that holds:* Clarence H. Faust and Thomas H. Johnson, eds., *Jonathan Edwards: Representative Selections* (New York: Hill and Wang, Inc., 1962), p. 164.

44 *While holding firmly:* Galpin, *Syracuse*, Vol. II, 37.

46 *is to be a Christian:* ibid., 458.

51 *We do not wish:* ibid., 321.

54-5 *Be unselfish, Quicken a man's:* Helen Campbell and Katherine Westendorf, *The Heart of It*, extracts from Horatio W. Dresser, *The Power of Silence* and *The Perfect Whole* (Boston: Geo. H. Ellis, 1897), pp. 14, 65.

67 *O powerful goodness:* Leonard W. Labaree, Ralph Ketcham, Helen C. Boatfield, Helene H. Fineman, eds., *The Autobiography of Benjamin Franklin* (New Haven: Yale Univ. Press, 1952), p. 153.

84 *This is a council:* Report of the First Student International Convention of the Student Volunteer Movement for Foreign Missions (Boston: T. O. Metcalf, 1891); Varg, *Missionaries*, p. 60.

85 *"An essential principle:* Mathews, *Mott*, p. 57. John Foster, the advocate of decisiveness, was a failure. The Baptist church to which he ministered dismissed him because he could not attract and hold a congregation.

89 *In visiting the sea ports:* John Pinkerton, *Modern Geography* (London: T. Cadell & W. Davies; T. N. Longman & O. Rees, 1803), p. 337.
    Ten Buddhist nuns: Varg, *Missionaries*, p. 109.

91 *filled with clocks:* Isaac Taylor Headland, *China's New Day: A Study of the Events That Have Led to Its Coming* (West Medford, Mass.: Central Committee on the United Study of Missions, 1912), p. 9.

96 *This moral mummy:* Charles Henry Fowler, *Missionary Addresses* (Cincinnati: Jennings and Graham, 1906) pp. 32–3; Varg, *Missionaries*, p. 113.

97 *She is not desired:* Helen Barrett Montgomery, *Western Women in Eastern Lands: An Outline Study of Fifty Years of Women's Work in Foreign Missions* (New York: Macmillan, 1911), p. 48; Varg, *Missionaries*, p. 117.

125 *THE WALE:* slightly adapted from Seabury, *Vision,* p. 96; used by permission.

145 *"with bodies of brass:* Barr, *To China,* pp. 15ff.

147 Quotations from conference are from *China Centenary Mission Conference Records* (Shanghai, 1907), passim.

160 *Duty to parents:* F. W. Baller, trans., *The Sacred Edict,* 4th ed., revised (Shanghai: China Inland Mission and Presbyterian Mission Press, 1917); translation slightly altered.

163 *We started out:* Account suggested by Seabury, *Vision;* used by permission of Seabury family.

250 *"concoctions,":* Barr, *To China,* pp. 86–7.

288 *Without exception:* Pearl Buck, "Chinese War Lords," *Saturday Evening Post,* Apr. 22, 1933, p. 77.

289 *the rifles and field guns:* Chien Yu-wen, *Hsi-pei tung-nan feng* [Winds from the Northwest and Southeast] (Shanghai, 1935), pp. 44–5; Sheridan, *Warlord,* p. 30.

293 *When we fight:* Sheridan, *Warlord,* p. 76.

310 *"The only possible medium:* Hu Shih, *The Chinese Renaissance* (Chicago: Univ. of Chicago Press, 1934), p. 50.

331 *The intellectuals:* adapted from J. C. Keyte, *In China Now* (London: United Council for Missionary Education, 1923), pp. 45–6.

358 *evidence was found:* On Mao's putative involvement in the Changsha literacy campaign, see Li Jui, *Mao Tse-tung t'ung-chih ti ch'u-ch'i ko-ming huo-tung* (*Comrade Mao Tse-tung's early revolutionary activities*) (Peking, 1957), pp. 166–8, 181–2, cited in Hayford, "Rural Reconstruction," pp. 50–1.

476 "Meeting at the Water Well": adapted from "The Meeting at the Blue Bridge," Sidney D. Gamble, *Ting Hsien: A North China Rural Community* (New York: Institute of Pacific Relations, 1954), pp. 350ff; used by permission.

487 *"Western Christianity:* Commission of Appraisal, William Ernest Hocking, Chmn., *Re-Thinking Missions: A Laymen's Inquiry* (New York: Harper, 1932), p. 19.

507 *Chien Mei Ke:* Chinese words by Ernest Y. L. Yang, (Peiping: Yenching University Department of Music, 1931).

550 *One day while David:* The incident of the beggars at the gate was suggested by an unfinished and unpublished ms. sketch by Thornton Wilder provided to the author for this use by Gilbert Harrison, author of Wilder's biography, *The Enthusiast.*

INDEX OF
CHINESE NAMES

Except at the very end of this book, I have used the system of English spelling of Chinese names of persons and places appropriate to the time span of most of the story — namely, that known as the Wade-Giles system. At the end, the more modern pinyin *spellings are used.*

John Hersey was born in Tientsin, China, in 1914 and lived there until 1925, when his family returned to the United States. He studied at Yale and Cambridge, served for a time as Sinclair Lewis's secretary, and then worked several years as a journalist. Since 1947 he has devoted his time mainly to fiction. He has won the Pulitzer Prize, taught for two decades at Yale, and is a member of the American Academy of Arts and Letters. He has revisited China three times. He is married and has five children. He lives in Key West, Florida, and Vineyard Haven, Massachusetts.

A NOTE ON THE TYPE

The text of this book was set in a digitized version of Aster, a
type face designed by Francesco Simoncini (born 1912 in Bologna,
Italy) for Ludwig and Mayer, the German type foundry. Starting
out with the basic old-face letter forms that can be traced back to
Francesco Griffo in 1495, Simoncini emphasized the diagonal
stress by the simple device of extending diagonals to the full
height of the letter forms and squaring off. By modifying the
weights of the individual letters to combat this stress,
he has produced a type of rare balance and vigor.
Introduced in 1958, Aster has steadily grown in popularity.

Composed by
Superior Printing Company,
Champaign, Illinois.

Printed and bound by
The Haddon Craftsmen, Inc.,
Scranton, Pennsylvania.

Designed by
Iris Weinstein.

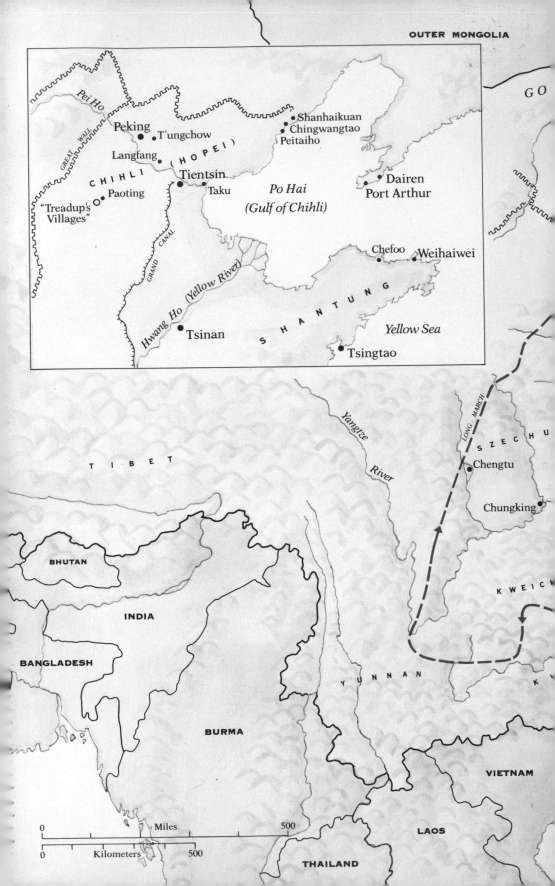

OUTER MONGOLIA

GO

Pei Ho

GREAT WALL

Shanhaikuan
Chingwangtao
Peitaiho

Peking
T'ungchow

CHIHLI (HOPEI)

Langfang

Tientsin

Taku

Paoting

"Treadup's Villages"

Po Hai
(Gulf of Chihli)

Dairen
Port Arthur

GRAND CANAL

Hwang Ho (Yellow River)

Chefoo   Weihaiwei

S H A N T U N G

Yellow Sea

Tsinan

Tsingtao

TIBET

Yangtze River

LONG MARCH

SZECHU

Chengtu

Chungking

BHUTAN

KWEICH

INDIA

BANGLADESH

KWEIC

YUNNAN

BURMA

VIETNAM

LAOS

THAILAND

0   Miles   500

0   Kilometers   500